A CONTINGENCY APPROACH
TO MANAGEMENT: READINGS

McGraw-Hill Series in Management

KEITH DAVIS • CONSULTING EDITOR

Hicks and **Gullett:** Modern Business Management: A Systems and Environmental Approach

Johnson, Kast, and **Rosenzweig:** The Theory and Management of Systems

Kast and **Rosenzweig:** Organization and Management: A Systems Approach

Knudson, Woodworth, and **Bell:** Management: An Experiential Approach

Koontz: Toward a Unified Theory of Management

Koontz and **O'Donnell:** Essentials of Management

Koontz and **O'Donnell:** Management: A Book of Readings

Koontz and **O'Donnell:** Principles of Management: An Analysis of Managerial Functions

Levin, McLaughlin, Lamone, and **Kottas:** Production/Operations Management: Contemporary Policy for Managing Operating Systems

Luthans: Contemporary Readings in Organizational Behavior

Luthans: Organizational Behavior

McNichols: Policy Making and Executive Action

Maier: Problem-solving Discussions and Conferences: Leadership Methods and Skills

Margulies and **Raia:** Organizational Development: Values, Process, and Technology

Mayer: Production and Operations Management

Miles: Theories of Management: Implications for Organizational Behavior and Development

Mundel: A Conceptual Framework for the Management Sciences

Newstrom, Reif, and Monczka: A Contingency Approach to Management: Readings

Petit: The Moral Crisis in Management

Petrof, Carusone, and **McDavid:** Small Business Management: Concepts and Techniques for Improving Decisions

Pigors and **Pigors:** Case Method in Human Relations

Porter, Lawler, and **Hackman:** Behavior in Organizations

Prasow and **Peters:** Arbitration and Collective Bargaining: Conflict Resolution in Labor Relations

Ready: The Administrator's Job

Reddin: Managerial Effectiveness

Richman and **Copen:** International Management and Economic Development

Sartain and **Baker:** The Supervisor and His Job

Schrieber, Johnson, Meier, Fischer, and **Newell:** Cases in Manufacturing Management

Shore: Operations Management

Shull, Delbecq, and **Cummings:** Organizational Decision Making

Steiner: Managerial Long-range Planning

Sutermeister: People and Productivity

Tannenbaum, Weschler, and **Massarik:** Leadership and Organization

Vance: Industrial Administration

A CONTINGENCY APPROACH TO MANAGEMENT: READINGS

John W. Newstrom, Ph. D.
William E. Reif, Ph. D.

Department of Management
College of Business Administration
Arizona State University

Robert M. Monczka, Ph. D.

Visiting Associate Professor of Management
Michigan State University

McGraw-Hill Book Company

New York   St. Louis   San Francisco   Düsseldorf   Johannesburg   Kuala Lumpur
London   Mexico   Montreal   New Delhi   Panama   Paris   São Paulo   Singapore
Sydney   Tokyo   Toronto

A CONTINGENCY APPROACH TO MANAGEMENT: READINGS

1234567890KPKP7987654

Library of Congress Cataloging in Publication Data

Newstrom, John W   comp.
    A contingency approach to management

    (McGraw-Hill series in management)
        1.   Management—Addresses, essays, lectures.
I.   Reif, William E., joint comp.   II.   Monczka,
Robert M., joint comp.   III.   Title.
HD31.N488   658.4'008   74-9913
ISBN 0-07-046415-4

This book was set in Times Roman by Black Dot, Inc. The editors were Thomas H. Kothman and Michael Weber; the designer was Pencils Portfolio, Inc.; the production supervisor was Judi Frey. The drawings were done by Eric G. Hieber Associates Inc. Kingsport Press, Inc., was printer and binder.

To Diane, Nan, and Shirley

Contents

Preface

The field of management is currently experiencing dramatic changes. This in itself is not particularly new since management, in terms of both its concepts and their application, has always been characterized as developing and dynamic. What is new is the direction and extent of change that is forming an integrative, highly adaptive approach to management known as *contingency theory*.

During the twentieth century the study and practice of management has undergone evolutionary, if not revolutionary, changes in its theoretical constructs, techniques, methods, and tools. Fundamental changes can best be illustrated by the various taxonomies or classification systems that have been developed to characterize the emerging schools of thought, such as classical-neoclassical-behavioral, or process-quantitative-behavioral-systems, or process–empirical–human behavior–social system–decision theory-mathematical. Other writers, primarily concerned with the structural properties of organizations, refer to organizational designs as mechanistic (bureaucratic) and organic.

Each of the schools of thought has made a significant contribution to our understanding of organizations and their management. At the same time, the various disciplines and their unique approaches to the study of management have raised more questions than they have provided answers, generated confusion on the part of practitioners, and generally led to what Harold Koontz referred to over a decade ago as the "management theory jungle." Instead of producing a unified body of knowledge that would more closely meet the prerequisites of a science than an art, these specialized approaches have resulted in more divergence than integration. The common failing of all schools of thought is their continual devotion to codifying a set of principles of management that can be applied universally to all organizations and in all managerial situations. Unfortunately, the results of the universalist approach are generally disappointing.

Another shortcoming of the present body of management knowledge is the lack of attention given to application and the subsequent dearth of meaningful attempts to bridge the widening gap between theory and practice. One of the factors contributing to this situation is that practical experience, a valuable input when building models of organizations, has not been given sufficient emphasis. The realities of managing highly complex, multidimensional systems have often been ignored in the theorist's concern for designing internally consistent models, or abstractions, of organizations.

The challenge then is twofold: to develop a theory of management that is capable of providing convergence among the several schools of thought and between theory and practice. It is proposed that both challenges can be met by the *contingency approach* to management. The contingency approach can best be described as a logical extension of open-systems theory. It takes a decidedly ecological approach and views organizations as complex systems of interdependent parts operating within the context of an environmental suprasystem. Contingency theory is concerned not with just identifying the key variables and relationships that comprise different systems but with *understanding* the multitude of roles and *defining* the patterns of relationships (interactions) that contribute to the organization's ability to achieve its objectives efficiently and effectively.

Emphasis is placed on diagnosis, or situational analysis, so that given an understanding of the organization and its operating environment, management can design the structure and management and operating systems that will be most nearly optimal for any given situation. What constitutes "right" decisions will no longer be based upon fundamental truths, or universal principles, but will be contingent upon the specific conditions and circumstances within which the decision is made and will be implemented. Contrary to the other management schools, the contingency approach does not assume it can provide ready answers to most situations; rather, it provides the conceptual framework and accompanying techniques, methods, and diagnostic tools that management can use to understand the situation, identify the factors (contingencies) affecting the decision, develop and analyze alternatives, and select the course of action that will best meet the requirements of the organization and its various interest groups.

Contingency theory recognizes that managing a hospital or a university is not the same as managing an industrial firm, and that even within the same organization the techniques and methods employed will necessarily be different depending upon variables such as functional area (e.g., production, marketing, finance and accounting, research and development) technology, degree of structure, organizational level, characteristics of the workers and management, and many others. Furthermore, similar organizations operating in dissimilar environments may need to practice management differentially because of differences in the competitive, cultural, economic, political, social, and legal climates.

The contingency approach to management is also an attempt to unify theory and practice. It takes the position that theory acquires value only to the extent that it is successful in application and that theory must be adaptable to the needs and realities of the practitioner. It acknowledges that there are few universal principles that apply equally well in all situations. Instead, it emphasizes the conceptual framework, thought processes, and diagnostic and analytical skills that will enable managers to set objectives and develop the most appropriate means for achieving those objectives within the given situation. The contingency approach does not view theory as an end in itself but as a means of support for the manager who is responsible for achieving organizational objectives.

The purpose of this book of readings is to provide the student and practitioner of management with an understanding of contingency theory and its application. In doing so, it does not discard the more traditional approaches to management. Quite the opposite, it uses the knowledge and insights acquired from the process, behavioral, quantitative, and systems schools as the foundation upon which to build a greater understanding of management and how it can be applied contingently.

The book is divided into four parts. Part One traces the evolution of management thought and introduces contingency theory as the logical means for extending and integrating present knowledge of the structure, process, and dynamics of organizations. Part Two applies contingency theory to the design of organizations and task structure. It supports an open-systems approach to understanding the external and internal considerations that are primarily responsible for shaping the structure of organizations. Part Three focuses on the managerial process. Primary consideration is given to the functions of planning, decision making, directing (motivation, leadership, and communications), and controlling. Part Four addresses the vital issues of organizational conflict and change. It applies contingency theory to the critical tasks of resolving conflict and managing change in a manner consistent with managerial efforts to achieve organizational objectives.

This book is designed to be used along with a basic text in an undergraduate principles of management course.* It also can be used effectively in an introductory graduate course in management or to give added depth and a strong diagnostic emphasis to case courses in management and business policies. It is intended that the book can be used by those who are interested in adding a new, modern dimension to principles of management courses and by practitioners who are interested in taking a contingency approach to the practice of management.

The readings were carefully selected on the basis of (1) individual quality, in terms of support for and clear presentation of contingency views; (2) readability, so that the book would be appropriate for students who have little previous background or experience in management; (3) recency of publication, so that the readings book truly can be an up-to-date supplement to the basic text; and (4) contribution of the article to the overall theme of the book to ensure both continuity and comprehensive coverage of all important aspects of contingency theory.

A readings book by its very nature requires the cooperation and support of many people. We would like to express our sincere appreciation to the authors whose articles were selected for their contributions to the development of

*A chapter-by-chapter correlation chart for some of the most widely used textbooks in the field follows this preface.

contingency management theory. They are, collectively, primarily responsible for the quality of this book. Each of these authors and his original publisher are identified at the beginning of each reading. We would like to thank our colleague Dr. Keith Davis, Professor of Management at Arizona State University, for his early encouragement, continued support, and helpful advice in this undertaking.

John W. Newstrom
William E. Reif
Robert M. Monczka

CROSS-REFERENCE TABLE

(For relating this readings book to selected management textbooks)

Section of Newstrom, Reif, and Monczka	Kast and Rosenzweig, *Organization and Management: A Systems Approach* (2nd ed.), McGraw-Hill	Chapters In: Koontz and O'Donnell, *Principles of Management: An Analysis of Managerial Functions* (5th ed.), McGraw-Hill	Dale, *Management: Theory and Practice* (3d ed.), McGraw-Hill
Introduction	1–5, 19	1–5	1–7
Organizational Design	6–9	12–14, 16–20	8–9
Job Design		15	10
Planning	17	6,7,8,10,11	13
Decision Making	14, 15, 16	9	20, 24–26
Motivation	10	26	15
Leadership	13	25,28	16
Communication	12	27	
Controlling	18	29–32	17
Conflict Resolution	11		
Management of Change	22, 23	24	12,27

Section of Newstrom, Reif, and Monczka	Hicks, The Management of Organizations: A Systems and Human Resources Approach (2d ed.), McGraw-Hill	Miner, The Management Process: Theory, Research, and Practice, Macmillan	Longenecker, Principles of Management and Organizational Behavior (2d ed.), Merrill	Donnelly, Gibson, Ivancevich Fundamentals of Management, BPI
Introduction	1,2,24,26	1–3	1,2	1–3
Organizational Design	5,6,17,25	7	8–10,12	5,11
Job Design		8		
Planning	4,16	4,5	4–6	4
Decision Making	29	6	7,11	13–18
Motivation	23	14	24–26	6
Leadership	3,7,8,18–20	10	20–23	8
Communication	31	11	21	
Controlling	21,22	12	22	10
Conflict Resolution	9,10,11	13		
Management of Change	32	9	13,27	12

Section of Newstrom, Reif, and Monczka	Newman, Summer, Warren, *The Process of Management: Concepts, Behavior, and Practice* (3d ed.), Prentice-Hall	McFarland, *Management: Principles and Practices* (3d ed.), Macmillan	Hellriegel and Slocum, *Management: A Contingency Approach,* Addison-Wesley	Sisk, *Principles of Management: A Systems Approach to the Management Process,* South-Western
Introduction	1	1–3	1–3	1,2
Organizational Design	2,3,4,5,6	14–17	4,5	10–13
Job Design	10			
Planning	16–19	6–9	8	4–7
Decision Making	11–15	4,5	6,7,13	9,14
Motivation	24–27	10,11	9	22,23
Leadership	8	21	10,11	18
Communication	20,21,23	12	12	16
Controlling	22	22		17
Conflict Resolution	7,9		14	
Management of Change	28		15,16	15,20

Part One

Introduction

The contingency theory of management has been acclaimed as the path out of the management-theory jungle, and concomitantly as the approach most likely to succeed in integrating the various contributions to management theory into a unified body of knowledge. It also has been cited as the approach most capable of narrowing the gap between theory and practice. The purpose of this introductory section is to explore the rationale behind these assertions and to provide the reader with a basic understanding of contingency theory and its relationship to the more traditional process, behavioral, quantitative, and systems schools of thought.

Luthans discusses the traditional approaches to management and shows how present trends in the quantitative, behavioral, and systems approaches are emerging into a contingency theory of management. He defines the contingency approach as a midrange concept that falls somewhere between "simplistic, specific principles" and "complex, vague notions" and emphasizes the need to develop a theory that can facilitate improved practice. He also discusses several contingency models in the areas of organizational design, leadership, personnel management, operations research, and behavior modification that could serve as prototypes of a contingency theory for management as a whole.

The Shetty article provides a framework for understanding how different types of organizations may be appropriate for varying combinations of variables that are characteristic of the firm's internal and external environment. He identifies four sets of variables, or forces, that management should consider in designing an organization. They are forces in the environment, forces in the manager, forces in the task, and forces in the subordinates. He concludes that most organizations are formed through an evolutionary process of change rather than by conscious design and argues for a contingency approach that will provide an adequate framework for a rational approach to developing organizations.

Carlisle questions the value of generalized theories of management to a manager in his unique organizational setting. As an alternative, he proposes a situational approach that will serve as a guide for applying management techniques. He identifies four dimensions of situationality, all variables of the internal environment, that provide the basis of his contingency approach: (1) *repetition* of the task or operation performed, (2) the *scale* or size of the project, (3) *technology,* or the scientific and technical complexity of the project, and (4) the extent and nature of *authority* provided the supervisor and work group. Carlisle also presents a strong argument for developing a method for measuring the dimensions so that organizations can be more meaningfully diagnosed.

Reading 1

The Contingency Theory of Management: A Path Out of the Jungle

Fred Luthans

Over a decade ago Harold Koontz wrote about the existing management theory jungle in which he identified six different theoretical schools of thought.[1] Although Koontz wrote the article to defend the process approach, his efforts have turned out to be a losing battle. The traditional management process has failed to unify management theory.

Today a jungle of management theories still exists, but there are some clearly identifiable paths that seem to be leading out of the jungle. The purpose of this article is to identify the paths and trace them through the jungle and beyond. The figure accompanying this article can be used as a guide to the discussion; it shows that the path leading up to the current jungle was the process approach. Other names applied to this path were classical, traditional, universal, operational, and functional.

The starting point for this process approach can be traced to the work of Henri Fayol. In 1916, he identified the universal functions of management as planning, organizing, commanding, coordinating, and controlling. He also described some universal principles of management such as unity of command and equal authority and responsibility. Unfortunately, Fayol's work on the functions and principles of management did not become part of the mainstream of management theory in this country until the 1950s. Since that time, there have been many other process theorists, but they have not added much to Fayol's original conception of management theory.[2]

Much of the terminology has been changed; for example, Fayol's commanding is now known as directing or leading. Also the meanings of Fayol's functions have become broader; for example, planning now incorporates communication, motivation, and leadership. The principles have also changed in terminology and number. Yet, despite these changes, the universality assumption is still made, and the process approach as a theoretical base for management remains basically the same as that given by Fayol over fifty years ago.

The process approach has undoubtedly had some unjustifiable criticism over the years. However, it is also true that it was not strong enough to weather the storm of protest in recent years. This approach became overgrown and

"The Contingency Theory of Management: A path out of the jungle," Fred Luthans, *Business Horizons*, June 1973, pp. 67–72. Reprinted with permission.
[1]The six schools identified by Koontz were the management process, empirical, human behavior, social system, decision theory, and mathematical schools. Harold Koontz, *Academy of Management Journal* (December 1961), pp. 174–88.
[2]Probably the most widely recognized standard bearers of the process approach in modern times are Harold Koontz and Cyril O'Donnell, authors of *Principles of Management* (New York: McGraw-Hill Book Company, 1972). The book, which came out in 1955, is in its fifth edition.

entangled by other theoretical approaches. By 1960 the process path had been completely overrun, and two separate paths emerged in opposite directions. These new paths became known as the quantitative and behavioral approaches to management.

THE NEW PATHS
Quantitative Approach

The quantitative approach has its roots in the scientific management movement that actually predates the process approach. However, as a major thrust in management theory, the quantitative approach really got under way about 1960. This new approach made a clean break from the traditional process orientation of management.

During the 1960s the quantitative approach was characterized by the techniques of operations research. Various mathematical models were developed to solve decisional problems. However, it soon became apparent that, although OR techniques were effective tools for management decision making, this approach fell short of providing a theoretical base for management as a whole.

Starting in about 1970, the quantitative approach turned away from emphasis on narrow operations research techniques toward a broader perspective of management science. The management science approach incorporates quantitative decision techniques and model building as in the OR approach, but it also incorporates computerized information systems and operations management. This latter emphasis in the quantitative approach marked the return toward a more broadly based management theory.

Behavioral Approach

At about the same time the quantitative approach broke off from the process base, the behavioral approach struck out on its own. At first the behavioral path was characterized by human relations. Simplistic assumptions were made about human beings, and equally simplistic solutions to behavioral problems were offered. The human relations movement in the 1960s searched for ways to improve morale, which was assumed would lead to increases in productivity. This approach certainly did no harm, but it also produced few, if any, results.

Around 1970, about the same time the quantitative approach moved from emphasis on narrow operations research to a broad management science perspective, the behavioral approach had a parallel development. This path veered toward a more broadly based organizational behavior approach, and now relies heavily on the behavioral sciences and makes more complex assumptions. More direct attention is devoted to organization theory and organization development. Organizational behavior is the result of the interaction between the human being and the formal organization.

New Directions in Management Theory

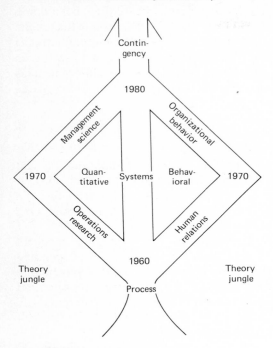

Systems Approach

While the quantitative and behavioral approaches were going their separate ways, a new trend appeared—the systems approach. During the 1960s to the present, it took up where the process approach left off in unifying management theory.

As a specific, theoretical approach, systems can be traced back to the natural and physical sciences nearly a quarter of a century ago. The application to management has been more recent. The systems approach—physical, biological, or managerial—stresses the interrelatedness and interdependency of the parts to the whole. Systems has served as a magnet to attract the quantitative and behavioral approaches to management.

At the present time, both the management science and organizational behavior detours are heading back toward the main path of systems. In management science, the new emphasis on computer applications and operations management techniques are systems based. The same holds true for organizational behavior. The formal organization is viewed as a system consisting of structure, processes, and technology, and the human being is conceived of as a system containing a biological-physiological structure, psychological processes, and a personality.[3]

[3]Fred Luthans, *Organizational Behavior* (New York: McGraw-Hill Book Company, 1973).

Whether systems will actually unify the quantitative and behavioral approaches to management only time will tell. To date, the quantitative, behavioral, and systems approaches are clear but distinctly separate paths through the jungle. However, as indicated by the figure, both the behavioral and quantitative paths are headed toward the systems path. If the three approaches do come together in the next ten years, then the results may be something entirely different. This something that is different from the sum of the parts is referred to in the figure as the contingency theory of management.

CONTINGENCY THEORY

The beginning of a path called contingency or sometimes situational is just starting to emerge.[4] The figure indicates that by 1980 this path may be the one that leads management out of the existing jungle of theories. The pressure leading to a contingency theory has largely come from people who are actually practicing management.

For the past fifteen years, scholars, consultants, and practicing managers have attempted to apply either quantitative or behavioral approaches, depending on their orientation, to all situations. The performance results of this universalist assumption were generally disappointing. Certain quantitative approaches worked in some situations with some types of problems but not in others. The same was true for behavioral approaches. For example, job enrichment seemed to work well with skilled technicians but not unskilled machine operators.[5]

Two of the difficulties encountered in practice were that the quantitative people could not overcome behavioral problems and the behavioral people could not overcome operations problems adaptable to quantitative solutions. In the 1970s it is becoming more and more apparent that neither the quantitative nor behavioral approaches have all the answers for all situations.

Many of today's management theorists believe that a systems-based theory can solve the quantitative/behavioral dilemma. The December 1972 issue of the *Academy of Management Journal* was entirely devoted to general systems theory (GST) applied to management. The authors weighed the pros and cons of whether GST can unify management. The majority concluded that the systems approach is appealing and has a great deal of future potential, but is as yet incomplete. The open, as opposed to closed, systems view is able to cope better with the increased complexity and environmental influence facing today's managers. Systems concepts such as entropy (a system will become disorganized over time) and equifinality (a system can reach the same final state from different paths of development) are quite applicable to the present managerial situation.

---

[4]For example see Robert J. Mockler, "Situational Theory of Management," *Harvard Business Review* (May–June 1971), pp. 146–55, and Fremont E. Kast and James E. Rosenzweig, *Contingency Views of Organization and Management* (Chicago: Science Research Associates, Inc., 1973).

[5]William E. Reif and Fred Luthans, "Does Job Enrichment Really Pay Off?" *California Management Review* (Fall 1972), pp. 30–37.

Despite the advances made in general systems development and the trend for both the quantitative and behavioral approaches to move toward a systems base, a contingency path seems better suited to lead management out of the present theory jungle. Kast and Rosenzweig, who are closely associated with the systems approach, support this view, at least for the present. They call for a contingency approach, a mid-range concept that falls somewhere between "simplistic, specific principles" and "complex, vague notions."

The contingency approach "recognizes the complexity involved in managing modern organizations but uses patterns of relationships and/or configurations of subsystems in order to facilitate improved practice."[6] Important breakthroughs in various subsystems of management (organization design, leadership, behavior change, and operations) have already demonstrated the value of the contingency approach.

CURRENT CONTINGENCY APPROACHES

Pigors and Myers have been associated with a situational approach to personnel management for the past twenty-five years. However, the work of Joan Woodward in the 1950s marks the beginning of a situational approach to organization and to management in general. She clearly showed in the British companies studied that organization structure and human relationships were largely a function of the existing technological situation. Armed with this and supporting follow-up evidence, some organizational theorists such as Lawrence and Lorsch began to call for contingency models of organizational structure.[7]

Organization Designs

The contingency approach to organization design starts with the premise that there is no single design that is the best for all situations. The classical approach was to say that a bureaucratic design would lead to maximum efficiency under any circumstances. The neoclassical theorists pushed decentralization for all conditions. It is inferred that even the modern free-form systems and matrix designs have universal applicability. In practice, the classical, neoclassical, or modern structural designs did not hold up under all situations.

For example, bureaucracy was not able to cope with a highly dynamic situation; decentralization did not work well in a highly cybernated situation; and the free-form, matrix designs were not adaptable to a situation demanding

---

[6]Fremont E. Kast and James E. Rosenzweig, "General Systems Theory: Applications for Organization and Management," *Academy of Management Journal* (December 1972), p. 463.

[7]Joan Woodward, *Industrial Organization* (London: Oxford University Press, 1965). Follow-up evidence from William L. Zwerman, *New Perspectives on Organization Theory* (Westport, Conn.: Greenwood Publishing Corporation, 1970). For examples of support for contingency models see Paul R. Lawrence and Jay W. Lorsch, "Differentiation and Integration in Complex Organizations," *Administrative Science Quarterly* (June 1967), pp. 1–47, and, more recently, Y. K. Shetty and Howard M. Carlisle, "A Contingency Model of Organization Design," *California Management Review* (Fall 1972), pp. 38–45.

cutbacks and stability. Even Warren Bennis, who has been a leading advocate of discarding classical, bureaucratically organized structures and replacing them with modern free-form, behaviorally oriented structures, has recently retrenched. Ironically, because of his actual experience as a practitioner, he now admits that bureaucratic structures may be appropriate in certain situations.[8]

The contingency designs are conditional in nature. The bureaucracy may work best in a stable situation and the free form in a dynamic situation. Technology, economic and social conditions, and human resources are some of the variables that must be considered in a contingent organization design.

Model of Leadership

More has probably been written about leadership than any other single topic. Although all this attention has been devoted to it, for years research was not able to come up with any concrete results. Most often the leader and his traits were examined. Recently, the work of Fred Fiedler, who emphasizes the importance that the situation has in leadership effectiveness, has produced a significant breakthrough. Based on years of empirical research, Fiedler was able to develop a contingency model of leadership effectiveness.

In simple terms, the model states that a task-directed leader is most effective in moderately favorable and moderately unfavorable situations.[9] Of special interest, however, is his ability to classify situations according to the three dimensions of position power, acceptance by subordinates, and task definition. This type of classification is the necessary goal of any contingency approach.

Model of Behavioral Change

Although not generally recognized in a managerial context, the contingency approach has been widely applied to behavioral change in mental health and education. Based on the principles of operant conditioning, this approach assumes that behavior depends on its consequences. Therefore, to change a person's behavior, he must be able to perceive a contingent relationship between his behavior and the consequence of that behavior. This contingent relationship, once established, will affect the frequency of subsequent behavior.

The author is currently directing a major field research program that is using this contingency concept. The approach is called Organizational Behavior Modification (O. B. Mod.). It can be used to train industrial supervisors through a process method of instruction to be contingency managers of their workers. Preliminary results of this program are very encouraging.[10] The study has demonstrated that when first-line supervisors apply O.B. Mod. techniques to their subordinates,

---

[8]Warren Bennis, "Who Sank the Yellow Submarine?" *Psychology Today* (November 1972), pp. 112–20.

[9] Fred Fiedler, A Theory of Leadership Effectiveness (New York: McGraw-Hill Book Company, 1967).

[10]Fred Luthans, Robert Ottemann, and David Lyman are currently in the process of writing the study in monograph form. Published results may be available in late 1973 or 1974.

desirable job behaviors leading to improved performance can be accelerated through the use of reinforcement and undesirable behaviors can be decelerated through the use of punishment.

However, the key to the success of the approach depends upon the worker's ability to perceive the contingency that if he behaves a certain way, then his behavior will result in a certain consequence. The if-then contingency pattern used in O.B. Mod. is similar to the contingency approaches used in organizational design and leadership style.

Approaches in the Quantitative Area

Although the examples so far are primarily drawn from organizational behavior, the quantitative areas have also begun to use contingency approaches. Operations research itself is actually based on a situational premise. The starting point in developing any OR model is to account for the situational givens. However, as OR was applied through the years this premise was often abused. Questionable initial assumptions which were often totally divorced from reality were cranked into OR models. However, in recent years with the development of a broader management science approach, more attention is being given to situational factors. Recent books in the management science area have begun to use a situational framework. For example, Stanley Young states that:

> We must know under what conditions it is advisable to move from Linear Programming to rule of thumb and then back to Linear Programming. There is an over-concern with single decision rule, and we must learn how to use different combinations of rules under a variety of operating conditions.[11]

This article suggests that a contingency approach may be the path out of the existing theoretical jungle in management. The process path was split by the behavioral and quantitative paths. However, neither of these approaches by itself seems capable of leading management out of the jungle. Currently, the systems path seems to be drawing them together toward a unified theoretical development, but by the time the juncture is reached in the future, something may emerge which differs from the sum of the parts. This outcome is predicted to be the contingency theory of management.

The successful contingency approaches in the behavioral and quantitative areas which are beginning to surface are evidence of the potential that a contingency theory may have for leading management out of the theory jungle. The overall goal of a contingency theory of management would be to match quantitative, behavioral, and systems approaches with appropriate situational factors.

[11]Stanley D. Young, "Organization as a Total System," in Fred Luthans, ed., *Contemporary Readings in Organizational Behavior* (New York: McGraw-Hill Book Company, 1972), p. 109. For other examples see David W. Miller, and Martin K. Starr, *Executive Decisions and Operations Research* (Englewood Cliffs, N.J.: Prentice-Hall, 1970) and Thomas R. Prince, *Information Systems for Management Planning and Control* (Homewood, Ill. Richard D. Irwin, Inc. 1970).

Although this goal would be difficult to reach, the contingency theory could serve as an effective framework for development. Fiedler's work proves that it is possible. His contingency model could serve as a prototype. The challenge for the future is to develop a contingency theory for management as a whole.

Reading 2

Is There a Best Way to Organize a Business Enterprise?

Y. K. Shetty

For many years an attempt to define an optimum organization structure has resulted in diverse approaches. In recent years, however, there has developed a new direction in the area of organization design. The research evidence seems to suggest that there is no "one best" way to organize, as it was once postulated. The design is conditional. It must be tailor-made for the firm. An appropriate design to one technological-market condition may not be suitable to another. What type of design is more suitable in a particular setting depends on the internal and external environment of that particular organization.

The earliest attempt to explain the phenomena of organization was made by writers and practitioners who have come to be known as classicalists.[1] The classical organization is characterized by a pyramid consisting of positions which are ordered into a hierarchical system of superior and subordinates. Each function has well-defined activities and responsibilities, demanding specialized competence and authority. The organization has complex mechanisms, rules, regulations and procedures. Human action within this framework is explained mechanistically by the obligations of position in a hierarchy. Ultimate control of the organization rests at the top of the hierarchy. Reliability of behavior is maintained by directives, by rules and regulations, and by standard operating procedures which prescribe the exact manner in which duties are to be performed. In short, the organization is a machine; the manager is the engineer who can draw on a body of principles to design the structure most suited to his ends—most rational instrument for implementing objectives and policies.

For quite some time the principles of classical organization largely based on bureaucracy have met with widespread acceptance among practitioners. However, in recent years the approach is coming under constant attack. The most insistent criticism leveled against classical organization theory comes from exponents of behavioral sciences. They claim that classical theory is too

"Is There a Best Way to Organize a Business Enterprise?" Y. K. Shetty, *S.A.M. Advanced Management Journal*, April 1973, pp. 47–52. Reprinted with permission.

mechanistic and thus ignores major aspects of human nature. The rational model has been attacked as an abstraction that overlooks dynamic human behavior, in particular, the non-rational elements in human conduct and their implications for practicing managers. Some of the critics even go the extreme of claiming that the theory is incompatible with human nature. As an alternative to classical approach, behavioralists have suggested certain modifications in the structure.

The behavioral organization theorists[2] argue that organizational effectiveness is achieved by arranging matters so that people feel that they count, that they belong, and that work can be made more meaningful. They do not necessarily reject the classical principles, but they feel that there goes more into an organization design than rules and regulations and strict rationality.

For example, people, one of the major inputs in any organization, are all human beings, yet everyone is unique to some extent from the next one. Everything man does cannot necessarily be explained rationally. There is a certain amount of subjectivity to an individual's actions; that is, his actions are based on his personal value system. Behavioralists, particularly the earlier ones, do not necessarily prescribe any one form of organization structure but believe it can be improved by modifying it according to the informal structure by less narrow specialization, by less emphasis on hierarchy, by permitting more participation in decision-making on the part of the lower ranks, and by more democratic attitude on the part of the managers.

In recent years some writers have suggested a new type of organization structure known as the organic-structure—a structure in which there is a minimum of formal division of duties. In this structure, hierarchy will be deemphasized: people will be differentiated not vertically, according to rank and role, but flexibly and functionally according to skill and professional training. According to this view, organizations will be made up of temporary task forces in which membership will shift as needs and problems change. Warren Bennis[3] argues that bureaucracy—that is, the classical structure—is too rigid to be serviceable in the time of rapid technological change and that it will, therefore, eventually disappear, to be replaced by the task-force type of the organization of the future.

THE DESIGN PROBLEM

If the organizer follows the classical principles, the resulting structure will necessarily be characterized by a hierarchy, a division of labor, and a series of rather precisely defined jobs and relationships. This is closer to the functional type of organization. On the other hand, the earlier behavioral scientists do not necessarily prescribe any one form of organization but believe the classical structure can be amended and improved by taking into account the human element. In recent years some theorists have suggested an "organic" type of structure, which deemphasizes specialization and authority and concentrates on problem solving. This comes closer to project organization.

Thus, organization models can be portrayed on a scale running between mechanistic at the one end and organic on the other. Organic organizations are characterized by less formalized definitions of jobs, by more stress on flexibility and adaptability and by communication networks involving more consultation than command. Mechanistic organizations are more rigidly specialized functionally and, in general, define the opposite pole from an organic continuum. In between this continuum there are various types of patterns which an organization can display. In other words, the range of patterns may fall anywhere on the scale's continuum. On the one extreme the organization is highly mechanical in structure and at the other extreme it is highly organic.

The relevant practical question is what factors or forces should a company consider in deciding how to design an organization? These are of particular importance:

Forces in the Managers

The designing of an organization at any instance will be influenced greatly by the many forces operating within the managers' own personality. They will, of course, perceive their organization problems in a unique way on the basis of their background, knowledge and experience. Their initial decisions will be in terms of what industry the organization will enter, how it will compete, where it will be located, the kind of organization it will be, who will be the top managers and who will directly influence the organization structure. All these decisions have to be made in the context of the relationship between the environment and the managerial philosophy of the entrepreneurs involved.

Alfred Chandler[4] has clearly shown the relationship between the strategy a business adopts, consciously or otherwise, and the structure of its organization. He cites different kinds of organization structure will be necessary for coping effectively with different strategies. The choice of corporate purpose and the design and administration of organizational process for accomplishing purposes are by no means impersonal procedures, unaffected by the characteristics of managers.

How strongly the manager feels that individuals should have freedom and autonomy in their own sphere of work will have an important influence in organizational design. Douglas McGregor[5] identified the bedrock assumptions about human nature which support markedly different approaches to organization and management—the theory "X" and "Y." The organization structure emerging from the managerial value system implied by the view that man is inherently lazy and pursues goals contrary to the interests of the company will not be the same as that which will emerge from the obverse image of the human nature. The implicitly held management value system manifests itself in contrasting organizational designs.

The manner in which work is organized, decision-making authority is distributed, span of control, shape of the organization, etc. all depend upon the underlying value system of managers. Theory "X" value system might predominantly lead to an organization closer to mechanistic structure, which will emphasize high specialization, close control, centralized decision-making etc. Theory "Y" value system might predominantly lead to less job specialization, wide span of control, flatter organization structure, and decentralized decision-making, etc.

Forces in the Task

The task element in an organization situation is the central point of concern in any type of organization design and analysis. The nature of the task will have important influence on how the organization is designed. Significant empirical literature is emerging relating technology to various organizational variables. Joan Woodward, Charles Perrow,[6] and several others consider technology to be a major determinant of organization structure. In her study, Joan Woodward reveals some interesting insights into the relationship between technology and organization structure. She found that successful organizations in industries with different production methods were characterized by different organization structures. Successful firms in industries with a unit or job shop technology had wider spans of control and fewer hierarchical levels than did successful firms with continuous process technologies. According to her study, the companies at ends of the scale of technical complexity (unit production and continuous process production) were more likely to be characterized by organic systems than firms in the middle range of the scale.

One of the elements of technology which is also related to the organization pattern is the nature of workflow. The amount of discretion given to subordinates seems to vary according to the type of specialization—where the activities of one individual or department are closely dependent on other individuals or departments —is characterized by more lateral relationship in order to obtain effective coordination between specialized groups. At the same time, under this type of specialization the subordinates have a "vested interest" in their own typical point of view or approach to problems and are unable to see the impact of their actions on others. Only the personnel at the top would have the interest of the total organization and, thus, be able to see the overall picture and integrate the efforts of the different parts in order to achieve the overall organizational goals.

Under parallel specialization—where work-flow is organized so as to minimize the amount of coordination—employees see themselves as responsible for a total process, something with an observable output, and are able to see the total efforts rather than a part. Under this system natural teamwork develops as each man sees that his contribution is needed to complete the total work. For these reasons, under parallel specialization, a more organic type of organization may be appropriate, but the interdependent specialization may call for a less organic type of structure and less and less delegation of authority to the lower levels.

The size of an organization, especially in terms of the number of people employed and units produced, influences the kinds of coordination, direction and control, reporting systems and, hence the organization structure. Where an organization is small, interaction is confined to a relatively small group, communication is simpler, less information is required for decision-making and there is less need for formal organization aspects.

Forces in the Environment

The environment in which an organization as a whole functions—its product and supply markets, the field of relevant technical knowledge, its political and socio-cultural environments—has a strong influence on the organization structure. Studies of Lawrence and Lorsch, Burns and Stalker, Emery and Trist, and Galbraith[7] suggest that the most effective pattern of organization is the one which enables an organization to adjust to the requirements of its environment. It is argued that the pattern of these environmental requirements over time, particularly with respect to their variability, may be such as to create different levels of uncertainty with which the organization has to cope through its structural arrangements. These different environments will tend to require different structural accommodation.

Lawrence and Lorsch[8] found that organizations operating effectively in different environments had different patterns of differentiation, and had developed different organizational mechanisms to achieve their differentiation and the integration required in their environment. They have found from their research of ten firms in three distinct industrial environments, that the environments of uncertainty and rapid rates of market and technological change, place different requirements on the organizational design than do stable conditions. According to their study organizations with less formal structure and widely shared influence are best able to cope with uncertain and heterogeneous environments. Conversely, organizations with rigid structure will be effective in more stable environments.

According to Burns and Stalker,[9] in the science-based industries such as electronics where innovation is a constant demand, the organic type of organization is made appropriate. Lacking a frozen structure, an organic organization grows around the point of innovating success. Studies of communication reinforce the point that the optimal conditions for innovation are the lack of hierarchy; whereas an organization, not primarily concerned with technological innovation, but preoccupied with production problems, requires a mechanistic type of structure, where coordination is facilitated.[10]

On the whole, considerable research has indicated that organizations with a low degree of formal structure could more profitably cope with changing environments than those which have a higher degree of formal structure.

Forces in the Subordinates

Some research evidence seems to suggest that a major contribution to organizational effectiveness will derive from adapting the structure to accommodate more adequately the psychological needs of organizational members. Argyris, Herzberg[11] and others have drawn attention to the conflict which is likely to prevail between a traditional definition of formal organization structure and the needs of psychologically mature individuals. Herzberg has developed a two-factor theory of employee motivation which suggests specific structural adaptation to provide the "job enrichment" through which to enhance motivation and performance. Therefore, before designing organization structure, it is necessary to consider a number of forces affecting the subordinates' behavior and performance. The subordinates' desire for independence, skill and motivation for assuming responsibility, need for a sense of achievement, etc. will greatly influence the organization structure.

Research suggests that, compared to unskilled workers, skilled workers and professional personnel are more involved in their job and are more anxious for an opportunity to have a high degree of autonomy on the job and an opportunity to participate in making decisions relating to it.[12] Studies consistently show that scientists as well as professional employees want autonomy and job freedom. They prefer not to be commanded in the same way as other employees in an organization.

There is also research evidence to suggest that some workers have positive attitudes toward work, who can be called "motivation seekers," while others, who seem relatively unaffected by the same conditions, can be called "maintenance seekers." Perhaps the significant difference is that maintenance reaches a state of relative fulfillment at the primary needs level, whereas motivation seekers continue to be motivated by the need for a higher level of social security.[13] This implies that certain forces in the subordinates will have substantial influence in designing an organization structure.

The above is a brief analysis of selected elements which would indicate how they might influence a company's actions in designing an organization. This analysis scarcely exhausts all the elements in these forces. Looking at the selected few, however, one can begin to understand which types of design might lead to organizational effectiveness. The strength of each of them will, of course, vary from instance to instance, but the management which is sensitive to them can better assess the problems which face it and determine which mode of organization pattern is most appropriate for it.

Most organizations are formed through evolutionary processes than by conscious design. At certain stages design or redesign takes place, but this is merely a codification of modification of the results of the evolution. An adequate framework for developing organizational theory should make it possible to increase the role of a conscious design process in the development of an organization. Hopefully, the suggested model would provide such a framework.

REFERENCES

1   The more important contributors to classical organization theory are: Henri Fayol, Frederick Taylor, Luther Gulick, James Mooney and Lyndall Urwick.

2 The contributions of behavioral scientists come from many sources. The more important among them are: Elton Mayo, F. J. Rothlisberger, Kurt Lewin, Mary Parker Follet, Chester Barnard, Chris Argyris, Rensis Likert, and Douglas McGregor.

3 Warren Bennis, "Organizational Developments and the Fate of Bureaucracy," *Industrial Management Review*, Spring 1966, p. 52.

4 Alfred D. Chandler, *Strategy and Structure*, (Cambridge, Mass. M. I. T. Press, 1962).

5 Douglas McGregor, *The Human Side of Enterprise*, (New York: McGraw-Hill, 1960).

6 Joan Woodward, *Industrial Organization: Theory and Practice*, (Fair Lawn, N.J. Oxford University Press, 1965): Charles Perrow, "A Framework for the Comparative Analysis of Organizations," *American Sociological Review*, April 1967, pp. 194–208.

7 Paul R. Lawrence and Jay W. Lorsch, *Organization and Environment*, (Boston: Harvard Business School, 1967): T. Burns and G. M. Stalker, *The Management of Innovation*, (London: Tavistock, 1961): F. E. Emery and E. L. Trist, "The Causal Texture of Organizational Environment," *Human Relations*, February 1965, pp. 21–32: J. W. Lorsch and Paul R. Lawrence, *Studies in Organization Design*, (Homewood, Ill. Richard D. Irwin, 1970), pp. 113–139.

8 Paul R. Lawrence and J. W. Lorsch, *op. cit.*

9 T. Burns and G. M. Stalker, *op. cit.*

10 J. W. Lorsch and Paul R. Lawrence, *Studies in Organization Design*, *op. cit.* pp. 113–139.

11 Chris Argyris, *Integrating the Individual and the Organization*, (New York: Wiley, 1964): Frederick Herzberg, *Work and Nature of Man* (New York: The World Publishing Company, 1966).

12 Howard Vollmer, *Employment Rights and the Employment Relationship*, (Berkeley: University of California Press, 1960).

13 M. Scott Myers, "Who are Your Motivated Workers?" *Harvard Business Review*, (January-February, 1964), pp. 73–88.

Reading 3

Measuring the Situational Nature of Management

Howard M. Carlisle

Many writers in recent years have noted the lack of a general theory of management and have been alarmed at the numerous conflicting concepts which exist in the "management theory jungle."[1] Various attempts have been made to develop principles of management which have universal application and which are universally accepted. However, little agreement exists to date regarding the scope, principles, or areas of emphasis composing this amorphous field of study.

As the universalist movement gained strength, it also attracted a large number of highly vocal critics. The critics have not been, and are not now, necessarily attempting to undermine the contribution of the universalists, but they are concerned with the theoretical uniformity demanded at this stage of the development of a general theory and with the direction in which universalists are pursuing future developments.

Many feel, as I do, that a continued search for universally applicable principles of management will probably slow the development of a general theory. Concern instead should be with the differences in management—differences which make each situation a new challenge in terms of managerial decision making and executive action. I will explore the internal environment of organizations with the aim of categorizing several of the significant physical dimensions which tend to create the dynamic uniqueness of each decision-making situation.

HISTORY AND CRITICISM
History of Universalist Philosophy

Before pursuing this "law of the situation" in more detail, I will briefly review the universalist viewpoint and the primary objections to it. This is necessarily sketchy because of the extensive literature on this subject and is, therefore, presented not with the aim of providing new insight, but of clearly identifying the ideologies and concepts of the various groups involved so that semantic confusion can be avoided. This semantic confusion is one of the major ingredients of the under-brush in the jungle concept popularized by Harold Koontz.

Henry Fayol, is of course, considered the father of the movement with his fourteen "principles of management" which comprised a partial list of "acknowledged truths regarded as proven on which the manager could rely."[2] Fayol, however, expressed caution, noting that "there is nothing rigid or absolute in management affairs" and that "principles are flexible and capable of adaptation to every need."[3]

Many others followed in a similar vein. In 1939 Mooney and Reiley outlined certain principles common to all forms of organization. Alvin Brown in 1945 elaborated ninety-six principles of organization. Urwick, Gulick (and in major texts published since the mid-1950's), Koontz and Cyril O'Donnell, and George R. Terry have furthered the doctrine of the universalists. In the Koontz and O'Donnell text, principles of management are defined as "fundamental truths of general validity which have value in predicting the results of managerial action."[4] The reference to general validity is aimed not just at the businessman, but at all managers in all types of organizations, both private and public. Furthermore, "anything significant that is said about the functions of one manager applies to all managers" involving "all executives in all occupations.[5]

Three Areas of Criticism

Criticisms of the universalists, ignoring those who reject the whole process approach, can be grouped into three categories which tend to be overlapping and somewhat redundant, but are useful for my purpose in this article.

- The principles are criticized as so general and abstract that they are of limited value to the manager or to the student. Herbert Simon in 1945 referred to them as "little more than ambiguous and mutually contradictory proverbs."[6] Ernest Dale states that "a principle so broad as to cover all types of situations is necessarily so broad as to tell us little we did not know before."[7]
- The principles are challenged in terms of their usefulness from a "universal" standpoint. Each manager in his day-to-day activities faces situations which have variables different in magnitude or basic nature from situations other managers are facing or the same manager has faced previously. The manager's main concern, therefore, becomes one of identifying and reacting to the modified or new variables in the situation, not the similarities. Under these circumstances, absolutes tend to vanish when each situation or decision is unique in some respects from all previous situations or decisions faced by the manager.
- The third criticism, which is my primary concern in this paper, relates to the emphasis which is placed on the universal aspects of the principles. The emphasis on universals tends to disguise the primary difficulty which is the application of these principles in dynamic business environments. Terry notes that "knowledge of a principle is helpful, but one must know when it applies and how to apply it."[8] It is this "when" and "how" that have been too often neglected. As Joan Woodward concluded from her studies, "In Taylor's work, as in that of all the adherents of the classical school of thought, the process of adaptation is more important than the rules themselves."[9] Too often management researchers have shrugged off the problem of application by stating that it "remains the manager's job to use his judgment in determining when to apply a certain principle," rather than attempting to identify and causally relate environmental differences.[10]

EMPHASIS ON PRINCIPLES

Implicit in these criticisms is a challenge of the emphasis on "principles" rather than "techniques." As noted previously, principles are considered as "fundamental truths of general validity" and encompass under Fayol's interpretation such formal organization concepts as unity of command and specialization in division of work. A technique is considered as a device or method to achieve a purpose. Techniques include budgets, network, analysis, financial ratios, and systems or methods of this sort which are purposely varied depending on the situation.

At this stage in the development of management knowledge, management principles, in attempting to bridge the similarities among varying situations, must of necessity be vague and general and, therefore, are of limited predictive value.

The application of techniques is a much more meaningful problem for the typical manager. His problem is to apply these techniques in an environment which is extremely dynamic and which has not been adequately dissected and causally interrelated for his analysis and utilization. The better a manager understands how ecological variables affect a given situation, the easier it will be for him to successfully react to the situation. For both principles and techniques alike, the primary concern for the manager becomes the conditions for their use.

CLASSIFYING THE VARIABLES

Previous Attempts at Identifying Situationality

In some respects this approach has already been advanced by researchers but only on a limited front. In production management conditions have been identified which dictate different types of plant layout; in managerial accounting certain conditions call for flexible budgets and others for fixed budgets. In relation to the use of authority, we normally distinguish between situations which call for autocratic authority from those where participative management is more desirable. Yet, over-all, little has been done to classify and weigh the variables which are of primary significance in management situations. As William Gomberg states, we need "to develop a number of functional types of management which describe the different behaviors that arise under different sets of circumstances," and to establish "a series of categories . . . with the accent on differences rather than sameness."[11]

One of the first efforts to classify the variables in management situations was made by Chester Barnard in his classic, *The Functions of the Executive.* He identified five factors[12] as being important:

- The place where the work is done.
- The time at which the work is done.
- The persons with whom work is done.
- The things upon which work is done.
- The method or process by which work is done.

In a similar vein, William G. Scott lists five basic parts of any system of organizational theory: the individual, formal organization, informal organization, status and role patterns, and the physical setting in which the job is performed.[13] Edward H. Litchfield, in his informative article on a general theory of administration, notes that there are at least four dimensions of the administrative process: the administrative process itself, the individual performing the process, the total enterprise within which the individual performs the process, and the ecology within which the individual and the enterprise function.[14]

One of the most comprehensive lists of "strategic" factors in any situation is outlined by William B. Wolf in his management readings book. He notes twenty-two variables as follows: charter, location, physical facilities, size, ownership and control, labor force, history of organizations, competing organizations, leadership, labor market, economics of markets for supplies, public image of the organization, technology, formal organizational structure, status systems, cliques and interpersonal interactions, communications systems, finances, formal systems of controls, supervisors, job design, and strategic policies[15]

Another approach was taken by Preston LeBreton in his book on general administration; he describes management as consisting of the processes of planning and implementation and sets up seventeen dimensions to help "understand the nature of the variation occuring in the . . . processes."[16] He further attempts to measure the intensity of these dimensions by establishing scales on a continuum, varying in terminology, but ranging from low to high in each instance.

Richard N. Farmer and Barry M. Richman in their studies on comparative management have established certain variables external to the firm. They have identified these constraints as educational, sociological-cultural, legal-political, and economic. They have also attempted to provide more precision and understanding by quantifying these variables. As they note,

> Mere identification of the external factors determining managerial effectiveness is useful; but to know more exactly which of these is most important, and by how much, would be still a better guide for analysis and policy decisions[17]

ADEQUATE BASIS STILL NEEDED

While all of these approaches provide some insight and have moved further down the path to a general theory of management, an adequate theoretical foundation is still needed. Primarily our needs at this time are for better tools for measurement and analysis, a comprehensive, uniform means of classifying and integrating existing knowledge, and more precise terminology. Once these are obtained, they will serve as a basis for establishing criteria and developing understanding necessary to identify and assess the variables responsible for situationality.

Existing Dimensions of Situationality

In reflecting on my industrial experience, examining research studies, and reviewing the writings of many of the authors previously mentioned, I have concluded that there are several existing dimensions which are important to operations managers in "sizing up" or measuring the administrative complexity or demands of the internal environment of a firm. For the operations manager there exist overriding factors in each situation, requiring his evaluation, which are critical in terms of the methods, concepts, and techniques he uses in pursuing a course of action. Since these dimensions are the major guideposts of operations managers, they will logically serve as the beginning of an analytical approach which could significantly contribute to the building of a general theory as it relates to operations management.

Before getting to these dimensions, the three widely accepted and well-recognized variables in operations management decision making should be enumerated. These are: the schedule or time for the project; the resources or dollars made available for the project; and the performance or results anticipated. Every major decision a manager makes is a trade-off involving these three variables. Developed in recent years, PERT and PERT/Cost, earned value systems, and performance budgeting concepts are good examples of the use of these three dimensions in planning, control, and management reporting systems. Since there exist effective means of measurement and control of these dimensions, I will not discuss them further.

THE FOUR DIMENSIONS

Proposed New Dimensions

Of the many variables of the internal environment of the production-oriented firm, I have selected four for analysis because they are currently viewed by managers, at least implicitly, as common causes of administrative complexity. These have not been subjected to the same degree of formal recognition or measurement as the decision-making variables; thus, their utilization by managers and researchers has been hampered. These dimensions of situationality in operational activities are as follows:

- The repetition dimension.
- The scale dimension.
- The technological dimension.
- The authority (or control) dimension.

The repetition dimension is a measure of the frequency or number of times that a specific operation or project has been performed by the firm or work group. Such knowledge is highly important to the manager as it determines the management systems, methods, and techniques which are to be applied. Thus, if the situation involves a series of tasks which the work group has repeated many times, it dictates such decisions as a product plant layout, standard cost system, relatively broad span of control at the first-line supervisor level, and flow control from a production control standpoint.

If the work is a "one-of-a-kind" project which involves tasks unfamiliar to the group, the manager must rule out standard cost systems, product layout, and these other approaches; he must consider in their place such systems as PERT for planning and control, project costing, and project organization. In the past industrial operations have been categorized on the basis of "continuous production" or "intermittent production," but a repetition dimension with appropriate scales of measurement (ranging from simple to highly complex) could be formally developed. Such a dimension would be a much more exact and scientific device to evaluate this important characteristic of production operations. The assumption used to develop the scale is that the more a task is performed, the simpler it becomes.

The scale dimension is a measure of the size of the project. Small projects of short duration obviously do not demand the sophistication in terms of formal measurement, reporting, or control systems that are necessary for a $20-billion, 10-year project aimed at placing a man on the moon. When firms are small, interaction is confined to a relatively small group, communication is simpler, less information is required for decision making, and the need for formal aspects of organization (job descriptions, procedures, etc.) are much less and much more simple. Coordination becomes a relatively minor task rather than one of predominant significance.

Virtually every major management decision the administrator makes is affected by this dimension. Communication networks, reporting systems, operating procedures, cost systems, formal organization, staffing, and many other systems, techniques, and processes are dictated in type and degree by the intensity of this dimension.

The technological dimension is a measure of the scientific and technical complexity of a project. Highly scientific projects create entirely different problems in terms of communication, planning, organization, staffing, directing, and financial control than do projects involving more simplified, readily understandable activities. Because of the rapid advance in knowledge and the increased specialization in each technical discipline, semantics alone creates an almost insurmountable barrier. When one serves in an integrating capacity or holds a position involving contacts primarily with other functional groups, knowledge and understanding are greatly hampered by the complexities of scientific data and jargon.

Aerospace projects are a good example. Because of the technical complexity and scale of these projects, conventional planning and control techniques have not been adequate, and new systems such as PERT have had to be developed. As a result of this same technological complexity, the project management form of organization was established, and many other management innovations have taken place. Research and development activities in all firms are generally treated differently from an administrative standpoint because of their scientific nature. The assumption behind the technology scale is that the more the product produced or service provided is inherently involved in scientific or "state of the art" technology, the more complex is the project or activity to administer.

The authority dimension is a measurement of the extent and nature of the authority provided the supervisor and work group. The control over a project is dependent upon such factors as the amount of authority delegated to the project leader and the number of groups and organizations which must participate in decision making. Thus, the administration of a project is greatly affected depending on whether the supervisor is owner of a sole proprietorship, reporting to an executive committee, subject to a domineering boss, operating under a government contract which requires the concurrence of the government in all major decisions, or a member of an executive committee or special task force.

Very rarely does a manager's authority reach between 90 and 100 or the extreme of the scale of this dimension, as there are always both formal and informal checks and balances in the organization which prevent a manager from exerting a free hand. The sheer number and nature of individual concurrences required in decision making is one of the major variables in a situation. It determines both the nature of the decisions a manager makes and how he makes them. It affects the whole course of a project in terms of organization, group behavior, response time in taking corrective action, complexity of coordination, and other such factors. It is also one of the most difficult dimensions for the student to appreciate and evaluate in the classroom.

MEASURING DIMENSIONS

Feasibility of Establishing Numerical Scales

Since these dimensions are intended as measures of the complexity of certain aspects of the internal environment of a firm, their real value will only come through numerical expression. If they are not capable of reliable and valid numerical expression, they too become only vague guides of limited usefulness. On the other hand, if effective measures of intensity can be developed, they will be useful predictive tools as well as valuable analytical devices to compare and evaluate situations.

Is it feasible to assume that scales can be developed? Since the dimensions all deal with primarily physical attributes of firms, experience would tend to substantiate that such scales are attainable. The learning curve is an excellent example of a repetition scale that is useful in predicting direct labor costs. Other repetition measures should likewise be developed as guides to the utilization of other management resources and techniques.

The scale dimension is one obviously admirably suited to measurement. The size of an organization or operation has rarely been quantitatively related to management methods or techniques, although Graicunas did establish a geometric relationship between complexity of span of management and number of subordinates (a scale relationship).

Technology was substantiated as a major causal factor in the nature of formal organization in the South Essex, England, industry studies chronicled by Joan Woodward. As she notes from the study, "Different technologies imposed different kinds of demands on individuals and organizations, and these demands had to be met through an appropriate structure."[18] As a follow-up to the original study, a method was developed to numerically express a number of the technical parameters.[19] One of the most significant conclusions of her study is that there is a critical need to further refine these methods of quantification. She states, "Techniques have to be found to describe systematically, and evaluate quantitatively, complex and intricate manufacturing situations,"[20] an aim which is consistent with the establishment of a technological dimension as proposed in this paper.

The authority dimension, which is different in nature from the other three, nevertheless contains features which can be numerically expressed. One of the key factors in this dimension is the number of individuals or groups which must be involved in the decision-making process, which is obviously quantifiable. The other aspect is the extent of authority held by these various groups and leaders. This is somewhat more nebulous but still measurable in terms of types and degree of authority. Thus, each of the four dimensions have features which are subject to measurement, although they must await further refinement and research before they can become valuable guides for managers.

HIGH RATINGS
Dimensions Are Measures of Administrative Complexity

These scales are to be interpreted as measures of administrative complexity. A high rating on the repetition scale would represent new operations and activities involving challenging problems in terms of planning and control; a low rating would represent a more routine production situation. A high-scale dimension would represent extremely large projects with the accompanying difficulty of coordination, organization, and control. A high rating on the technological dimension would represent complex engineering or scientific activities difficult to comprehend, manage, and control. A high rating on the authority dimension would indicate a large number of groups involved representing complexity in terms of reaching decisions and implementing them on a timely basis.

Validation of this composite complexity is represented by our major aerospace programs. These massive engineering projects deserve their reputation as one of the most difficult management challenges which exists today in relation to managing operations, as a result of the high repetition, scale, technological, and authority dimension ratings. It would also appear that the authority dimension plus the scale dimension is the primary contributing factor for the more than fifteen months required to develop an annual budget in the federal government, versus the probable less than one-day span required for some small business proprietors.

PROS AND CONS
Advantages and Limitations of the Dimension Approach

There are four primary advantages to the establishment and quantification of internal dimensions of industrial firms:

- The dimensions provide valuable analytical tools to identify and classify the internal environment of a firm and explain the relationship between this environment and management practices and techniques. They are not merely descriptive tools but predictive ones.

- They should provide guidelines to the utilization of various techniques, systems, and methods in management. This should result in improved managerial efficiency.
- They will help structure the theory and terminology of management, at least as they relate to industrial operations.
- They will serve as a basis for identification and analysis of other variables critical in managerial situations. This, in turn, will help crystallize management theory.

These advantages accrue to current managers as well as the researcher. They will also be a boon to the teacher. One of the drawbacks of management courses is that they seem to the student to be too vague and lacking in specifics. This more concrete structuring of theory and knowledge would help overcome this. With refined dimensions the first step in case analysis would involve evaluating the situation in the case in terms of these dimensions. This would point out the alternative systems and techniques to be applied and would also be instrumental in arriving at a recommended course of action.

The limitations of this dimension approach relate to the feasibility of developing valid and reliable instruments. Unless they attain these features, they could be misleading and potentially more harmful than valuable. Also the dimensions are directed at the internal physical setting of a firm, whereas many of the most critical factors are human factors or external environmental factors. However, the proposed dimensions are not intended to be comprehensive. These dimensions were selected as a starting point because as physical attributes they are more stable, concrete, and measurable.

A third limitation is that the critical factor in practice is the interdependence of the variables which would be hard to assess even if valid individual scales were developed. This is true in many respects. Because a project or product does not involve scientific methodology (low on the technology scale), it cannot be concluded that the project lacks complexity. Other variables could offset this, and at least until a more complete classification of variables is established, the evaluation of only a few variables must be undertaken with extreme caution. However, the isolation of even a few variables will provide some structure in what has been a very confused and neglected aspect of management.

EVALUATING VARIABLES
Conclusion

Management theory and practice have experienced giant forward strides in recent years, but we still lack a well-structured general theory of management. Much of the approach, at least by the traditional school, has been to attempt to develop general principles of management which relate to all managers in their individual settings. Because of the broad scope of activities and operations which these principles must cover, they are of necessity very general in nature. Furthermore, the basic problem for a manager in the typical dynamic environment is to perceive the changes which are occurring so that he can modify his approach based on the revised demands of the situation.

Over the years, a very large bag of tools has been developed for the manager, including cost systems and concepts, operations research methods, techniques of supervision, and other aids encompassing every process or activity in which the manager is engaged. The basic problem for the manager is to properly evaluate environment variables affecting the current situation so that he can properly apply the required techniques.

The proposed dimensions of repetition, scale, technology, and authority are an attempt to identify, classify, and quantify some of the important internal physical attributes of a situation. These scales are measures of administrative complexity and should serve as guides to the application of management techniques and concepts. They are attempts to get away from the generalizations and semantic vagueness which typify much of management analysis today. Even though obvious limitations exist to the current status of this approach, it proposes the direction in which lies the potential unfolding of a general theory of management.

REFERENCES

1   Harold Koontz, "The Management Theory Jungle," *Journal of the Academy of Management,* IV:3 (Dec. 1961), 174–188.
2   Henri Fayol, *General and Industrial Management* (English trans.; London: Sir Isaac Pitman & Sons Ltd., 1949), p. 42.
3   *Ibid.,* p. 19.
4   Harold Koontz and Cyril O'Donnell, *Principles of Management* (4th ed.; New York: McGraw-Hill Book Company, 1968), p. 1.
5   *Ibid.,* p. 54.
6   Herbert A. Simon, *Administrative Behavior* (New York: Macmillan Company, 1945), p. 240.
7   Ernest Dale, "Some Foundations of Organization Theory," *California Management Review,* II:I (Fall 1959), 84.
8   George R. Terry, *Principles of Management* (5th ed.; Homewood, Ill.: Richard D. Irwin, Inc., 1968), p. 18.
9   Joan Woodward, *Industrial Organization: Theory and Practice* (London: Oxford University Press, 1965), p. 247.
10 Herbert G. Hicks, *The Management of Organizations* (New York: McGraw-Hill Book Company, 1967), p. 364.
11 William Gomberg, "An Inquiry into the American System of Industrial Management," Dalton E. McFarland, ed., *Current Issues and Emerging Concepts in Management* (New York: Houghton Mifflin Company, 1966), II, 81.

12 Chester I. Barnard, *The Functions of the Executive* (Cambridge: Harvard University Press, 1938), pp. 128–129.
13 William G. Scott, "Organization Theory: An Overview and an Appraisal," in *Current Issues and Emerging Concepts in Management,* II, 162–163.
14 Edward H. Litchfield, "Notes on a General Theory of Administration," *Administrative Science Quarterly,* June 1965, p. 23.
15 William B. Wolf, ed., *Management Readings Toward a General Theory* (Belmont, Calif.: Wadsworth Publishing Company, 1964), p. 325.
16 Preston LeBreton, *General Administration: Planning and Implementation* (New York: Holt, Rinehart and Winston, 1965), p. 18.
17 Richard N. Farmer and Barry M. Richman, *Comparative Management and Economic Progress* (Homewood, Ill.: Richard D. Irwin, Inc., 1965), p. 325.
18 Woodward, p. vi.
19 *Ibid.,* pp. 268–274.
20 *Ibid.,* pp. 247–248.

Part Two

Organizational Structure

Organizational Design

This section provides a broad, macro view of organizations and management. It is primarily concerned with classifying the external and internal variables that help shape organizational structures and management systems. The focus of attention is on creating internally consistent (efficient) organizational designs that are capable of functioning effectively within the context of given environmental constraints.

The contingency approach to organizational design is based on the premise that there is no one design that is best for all conditions. It assumes that the structure and processes of organizations are products of many forces or pressures and that organizational design evolves through a series of complex and dynamic interactions among those forces. In the long run, the successful organization is the one that is capable of understanding the forces that are instrumental to its effectiveness and making sound managerial and operating decisions that are consistent with situational needs.

Contingency theory helps to explain why different organizational designs are consonant with specific combinations of forces and their interactions. Weber's bureaucratic system, for example, may work best in stable situations where a premium is placed on hierarchical structure, authority relationships, and programmed approaches to decision making. On the other hand, a more behaviorally oriented, organic model may be more effective in dynamic situations where success is contingent upon temporary, and in some cases informal, relationships, nonroutine decision-making processes, and a high degree of responsiveness to change in technology and conditions in the environment.

Ross and Murdick provide a good review of the classical, behavioral, and organic approaches to organizational structure and show how the essential characteristics of each provide a good foundation for the emerging contingency model. They discuss four variables or contingencies that should be considered in designing an organizational structure: the manager, the work, the environment, and the individual contributors or subordinates. They propose that no one model of organization is universally appropriate and that the right structure is a function of the interaction among the four variables, each of which must be considered in light of the others and against the productivity requirements of the organization.

Lorsch and Lawrence, in a classic article, present a highly integrative, comprehensive, and empirically based contingency model of organizational design. Their model states that differences in departmental specialization—in the terms of degree of departmental structure and members' orientation toward time, others, and the environment—are dependent primarily upon three characteristics of the environment: (1) the certainty of information at a given time, (2) the rate of change in the environment, and (3) the time range of the task performed. They suggest that functional departments within the organization (production, sales, and research) have different, specialized orientations and, therefore, must be structured differently in order to facilitate the productivity of each and the organization as a whole. They also propose that the greater the differences in orientation between departments (organizational differentiation), the more difficult it will be to achieve the high degree of coordination (integration) necessary for organizational effectiveness.

Newman states in his article that corporate strategy and management structure are highly interdependent and that both are influenced by the technological environment within which strategy is developed. In support of his argument he discusses four sets of variables that need to be considered in developing a coherent management design. They are: (1) organizational features, (2) forms of plans, (3) elements in leadership style, and (4) features of the control process. He introduces technology as the intervening variable and relates appropriate management structure to the type of technology, with particular emphasis on the way a technology deals with change. The article also provides a good transition to other sections of this book dealing with the management processes of planning, decision making, leadership, and control.

The Kubicek articles take an organizational-audit approach to designing the most effective structure for a given situation. In Part 1, he describes in detail the analytical process that is involved in fitting the organization to its internal and external environments, paying particular attention to the capacity and expectations of the organization, its technical and social systems, and the economic, social, political, technological, and competitive trends that may affect its ability to perform efficiently. In Part 2 he provides contingency guidelines for designing an "ideal" organization.

Galbraith presents a case study of how one company went from a functional to a pure matrix organizational design in order to conform more nearly to changing organizational requirements. He discusses within a contingency framework the six factors that help to determine choices among types of organizational designs. They are diversity of product line, the rate of change of the product line, interdependencies among subunits, level of technology, presence of economies of scale, and organization size.

Reading 4

People, Productivity, and Organizational Structure

Joel E. Ross
Robert G. Murdick

Of all the current concerns of business and government, the most far-reaching is productivity, chiefly because it is so linked to foreign competition, and, related to that, because the declining rate of increase in productivity is a primary cause of monetary problems and inflation. If improved work output from both professional and production workers is the answer, threats certainly won't get it, and neither will exhortations. But organizational and management restructure might.

To quote chairman Gerstenberg of General Motors, "Better productivity results from better management." Another automotive executive, Chrysler's Eugene Cafiero, puts it more forcefully: "We've got to stop bossing and start managing." The 3M chief executive, Harry Heltzer, adds, "You can't press the button any harder and make the automated equipment run any faster. In a rising cost spiral you've just got to find ways of pressing it more intelligently." Among those more intelligent ways of pressing the button are innovative forms of organization and methods of managing.

By and large, managers have overlooked or underemphasized two major sources of increased productivity. The first is the salaried side of the company, that broad area known as white collar and middle management. One company that examined it was Hercules Incorporated, the chemical giant. It reached the conclusion that those groups are overcompensated in relation to their attributable productivity gains to a greater extent than hourly workers. Other companies and studies have found that in general those groups are growing relative to direct labor; they exceed 60 percent in many cases. Moreover, few of them work to any standard of performance or under any productivity measurement system, and it is widely estimated that they seldom top 50 percent of their potential.

A possibility of immediate improvement here lies in stimulating and helping lower and middle managers to do a better job. They are often so bogged down in procedures, paperwork, red tape, and other trappings of organization structure that they have little time left for the more productive jobs of planning, organizing, and communicating. Their jobs are so narrowly defined and supervision is so close that motivation is killed.

The second source of increased productivity is the organization structure, the framework that facilitates organizational dynamics and guides company operations. Most managers are handling their physical and financial assets acceptably but are overlooking their human resources. A careful analysis of the

"People, Productivity, and Organizational Structure," Joel E. Ross and Robert G. Murdick, *Personnel*, September–October 1973, pp. 9–18. Reprinted with permission from the publisher. © 1973 by AMACOM, a division of American Management Associations.

costs of the human resources would very likely lead to better management and organization of these resources. In general, payrolls are running in the neighborhood of eight times earnings, so it is obvious that an increase of, say, 5 percent in productivity (through improved turnover, better organization, and so on) would have a really significant impact. Surely, such potential gains make trying new approaches to organization worhwhile. Let's see where our choices lie in this area.

The Classical Organization Structure

The classical or bureaucratic, hierarchical organization continues to be the most common corporate structure. It is easily understood; it is traditional; and it works reasonably well. This traditional structure provides the foundation on which modern adaptations are constructed. The basic tenets of the classical structure are specialization of work (departments), span of management (nobody supervises over six subordinates), unity of command (nobody reports to more than one boss), and chain of command (authority delegation). The manager determines work activities to get the job done, writes job descriptions, and organizes people into groups and assigns them to superiors. He then establishes objectives and deadlines and determines standards of performance. Operations are controlled through a reporting system. The whole structure takes on the shape of a pyramid.

How do we arrive at a bureaucratic, pyramidal structure? The answer lies in an understanding of how a company grows and develops. In the beginning communication is simple and effective because activities and communications channels are few in number, but as operations grow in size and communications become more complex, proper coordination and direction demand written directives and procedures. Communication is between offices, not people. More growth means more complexity, and that calls for more policies, procedures, and further formalization. In time the proliferation of systems, procedures, and regulations demands greater departmentation and more staff people to coordinate operations. But a characteristic of the pyramidal structure is the rather tight hold the man at the top has on the reins of authority.

Criticizing the systems, formality, and controls of the bureaucracy is getting to be a profitable vocation—witness *Parkinson's Law, The Peter Principle,* and *Up the Organization.* Some of the charges leveled at the classical structure are these:

- It is too mechanistic and ignores major facets of human nature.
- It is too structured to adapt to change.
- Its formal directives and procedures hinder communication.
- It inhibits innovation.
- It pays the job and not the man.
- It relies on coercion to maintain control.
- Its job-defensive behavior encourages make-work.
- Its goals are incompatible with those of its members.
- It is simply out of date with the needs of the Seventies.

Many of those criticisms have a basis in truth, but except in small organizations, the classical structure appears to be the easiest way to cope effectively with complexity. Bureaucracy, with all of its "evils," is an organizational requirement when we go beyond the face-to-face stage of communication. The major arguments in favor of the classical approach are these:

- It has overwhelming acceptance by practicing businessmen.
- It works.
- It is easily understood and applied.
- It isn't set in concrete—it can accommodate modifications such as the behavioral or organic ones when the need arises.

Recent business events point to the value of classical methods. In the late Sixties, LTV Corp., Litton Industries, Gulf & Western, and other conglomerates were having a field day with free-form management, which was characterized by loose controls and a high degree of decentralization of authority. For a while, it appeared that doing without some of the old standbys such as performance standards and controls was having some success, but now tight controls are back in favor. Two outstanding conglomerates, IT&T and TRW, never fell for the free-form management idea: both retained the fundamentals of planning and control, maintained strict reporting procedures that required substantial involvement on the part of division managers, and insisted on accurate projections, but they did establish an environment of reporting informality that made the best advice in the company accessible to everyone. In short, they used the old-time, proven methods with the necessary adaptation for human involvement to make them work.

Despite the criticisms frequently leveled at it, this structure will probably be around for a long time to come. Not long ago, a survey of the Fellows of the Academy of Management, a group of distinguished senior management professors, attempted to forecast the shape of the organization of the future. The result was a 75 percent probability prediction that the dominant organizational structure in 1985 will still be the classical pyramid.

The Behavioral Model of Organization

The most persistent criticism of the classical organization structure comes from the behavioral scientists. Their basic quarrel with this structure is that it is too mechanistic and therefore tends to overlook human nature and the needs of people. Some maintain that organizational trappings such as structure, procedures, and controls actually violate human wants and inhibit productivity; others contend that the pyramidal structure, although perhaps suitable for a stable environment, is unable to accommodate the change that is characteristic of modern organizations.

In the behavioral model an attempt is made to overcome some of the mechanistic-structural objections to the classical organization. The model assumes the objective of economic productivity output as given, but it adds a new dimension—employee satisfaction. This satisfaction, which presumably leads to greater productivity, is a function not so much of structure as of individual perception and personal value systems. Harlan Cleveland, who has had a distinguished career in business, government, and higher education, expresses the view of the behaviorists fairly well when he decrees, "The pyramid structure of less than a generation ago must be replaced by 'horizontal systems' in which control is loose, power diffused, and centers of decision widespread."

Essentially, the idea is that the pyramid should be modified to provide:

- A more democratic attitude on the part of managers.
- More participation in major decisions at lower levels.
- Decentralization of decision making as far as possible.
- Less emphasis on hierarchy and authority delegation.
- Less narrow specialization of work tasks.

Most managers react to the behavioral model in one of four ways—with skepticism, with a pretense of acceptance but an actual intention to manipulate people and decisions, with general agreement but confusion about how to implement the model, or with an enthusiastic desire to adopt the model as a modern way to motivate people in the company. Among those who seem to be genuinely committed is Chrysler's Cafiero; he has said, "Let responsibility extend down to its lowest practical level and give authority to go along with it. The lowest level in a lot of cases is the guy right on the line."

At Chrysler, assembly workers in selected plants are authorized to reject substandard parts, work sitting instead of standing, and paint their machines any color they wish. Other companies that have acted to involve workers and let them participate in decisions about their work and to reduce the specialized and monotonous nature of the job include AT&T, where selected typists can now research, compose, and sign their own letters without supervision. Another is Motorola, where female hourly workers who formerly performed very specialized tasks (for example, wiring or soldering) on a walkie-talkie assembly line now assemble the entire product and approve its final checkout.

There is a lot of talk and speculation about the behavioral approach to improving organizational productivity, but its application is still limited and experimental. Companies that have tried to modify their organizational approach in that way are few and most have done so on a trial basis, but its acceptance should accelerate because it makes good economic sense and because it looks as if the workforce, including lower and middle management, will demand it.

The Organic Model of Organization

Also behavioral in nature, the organic approach to organizational design goes one step further in that it addresses itself to the fundamentals of structure and specialization of tasks. Warren Bennis, its foremost proponent, argues that the traditional structure is too rigid to adapt to the frequent changes brought about by modern technology, and to accommodate those changes, organizations should be made up of temporary task forces.

He summarizes his proposal this way:

> First of all, the key word will be temporary. Organizations will become adaptive, rapidly changing temporary systems. Second, they will be organized around problems-to-be-solved. Third, these problems will be solved by groups of relative strangers who represent a diverse set of professional skills. Fourth, given the requirements of coordinating the various projects, articulating points or "linking pin" personnel will be necessary who can speak the diverse languages of research and who can relay and mediate between the various project groups. Fifth, the groups will be conducted on organic rather than on mechanical lines; they will emerge and adapt to the problems, and leadership and influence will fall to those who seem most able to solve the problems, rather than according to the programmed role expectations. People will be differentiated, not according to rank or roles, but according to skills and training. . . . Though no catchy phrase comes to mind, it might be called an organicadaptive structure.

Generally speaking, the organic approach to organization and productivity has had only moderate acceptance, although its use is spreading. In many ways it overcomes the familiar objections to bureaucracy by allowing more freedom of action and less narrow specialization.

Emerging Concepts: The Team Approach

How can the essential characteristics of the organic model—described as temporary, flexible, and accommodating to change—be achieved within the traditional pyramidal structure? The answer is the team approach, which has several versions. The one called project management is widely used; matrix management and venture teams management are evolving.

The team, or plural, approach to problem solution and management is nothing new—committees and other coordinative devices have been with us for centuries. The modern team approach, however, was popularized by the Navy's Special Projects Office use of PERT in the Polaris program and is finding increased use in nondefense applications. Indeed, some form of team organization promises to be the major innovation in dealing with complexity and change during the coming decades.

Now let's turn to the various versions of the team approach.

Project Management   Assume that you have a plan that requires the coordination of two or more functional departments, such as accounting, marketing, finance, or engineering. The plan may involve the development and design of a new product, deeper market penetration of an existing product, cost reduction, acquisition of or merger with an outside company, management development, new financing, construction and location of a new plant, or even overhaul of the entire company. How do you organize to accomplish the job?

The first inclination is to form a task force or committee, the device that comes to mind when one department has difficulty in handling a problem alone and where the organization structure is admittedly unable to deal with change. The drawback is that the committee is rarely given the power to make decisions and implement plans of action, and, in fact, that type of body, with its diffused power and lack of specific individual responsibility, is not appropriate for decision making.

Another solution might be to assign responsibilities for the various parts of the task to an operating manager of one of the functional departments, but here the problem is that serious top management involvement is necessary to resolve conflicts and to assure that all steps are coordinated and taken. Therefore, this tack is bound to be disruptive.

A third approach might be to establish a project manager with complete, undiluted authority for all aspects of the project. That is the organizational device being used more and more in aerospace as well as a variety of other industries, and we'll become better acquainted with it as we move away from process production systems into unit production and service output. The central idea is to assign one individual, the project manager, the responsibility for planning, work scheduling, budgeting, and controlling. His job is to ensure that the task or the project is completed within the established standards of time, cost and technical specifications.

Matrix Management   Matrix organization gets its name from the fact that a number of project managers exercise planning, scheduling, and cost control over people who have been assigned to their projects, while the functional managers exert line control, in terms of technical direction, training, compensation, and the like, over the same workers. Thus, there is shared responsibility for the worker, and he must please two bosses.

Two excellent examples of this kind of management in operation can be found at Honeywell and Texas Instruments. When General Electric decided to quit the computer business, Honeywell acquired the pieces. It set up 20 managerial task forces, made up of about 200 people from both its own staff and GE's to integrate manufacturing, marketing, engineering, field services, personnel, software, and the inventory of actual product lines. Honeywell's chairman called it a textbook exercise in how to merge painlessly.

In the case of Texas Instruments, matrix management is a way of life, and has been carried to a high degree of sophistication. Broad company objectives are broken down into a series of strategies and methods for achieving them, and those strategies, in turn, are translated into several hundred tactical action programs (TAPS). Each TAP has a project management system.

By contrast, it should be mentioned, in the line project management organization each employee has only one home—the project to which he is assigned or an auxiliary service group. Usually, a number of projects are active at the same time but in different stages of their life cycles. As new projects build up, people are transferred from the projects that are approaching their ends. The project manager has complete responsibility for resources of money and men and con- tracts for auxiliary services, such as centralized testing in an R&D organization.

Venture Teams   "The greatest challenge facing most corporations today is the development and marketing of new products or services that will produce a profit in the face of increased risks of failure," says a manager in a leading marketing research firm. The venture team is a recent organizational innovation designed to meet the demand for a breakthrough in product marketing.

The venture team is somewhat like the project matrix management team in that its personnel resources are obtained from the functional departments. Other similarities include organizational separation, the team of multidisciplinary per- sonnel, and the goal-directed effort toward the achievement of a single result— here, product development and introduction. The venture team also may have a flexible life span, with a completion time loosely defined by broad time and financial goals. To be successful, members of venture teams have to be generally well accepted by others in the organization, because the interaction of the venture manager with those in other segments is considerable.

For companies that are committed to growth and for those whose success depends on the marketing of existing products and the development of new ones, the venture team approach offers a promising alternative to the operations traditionally found in marketing departments.

Emerging Concepts: The Contingency Model

Thus far we have examined the classical, pyramidal form of organization structure, modifications of it, and a number of related approaches, behavioral and organic. Unfortunately, however, even taken together all of these concepts fail to come up with a workable systems approach to organization. The contingency model, which attempts to do so, represents the latest thinking and research in this area. (Howard M. Carlisle, of the University of Utah, explains it in detail in *Situational Management: A Contingency Approach to Leadership,* to be published in October by AMACOM, a division of American Management Associations.)

The contingency model seeks to answer the question of what factors, forces, or variables—contingencies—should be considered in deciding how to design an organization structure. The most important are these:

The Manager   Corporate personality, strategy, policies, and plans reflect the personal, social, and ideological goals of the top-management group, frequent- ly of the top man himself. It follows that top management is the most important variable in shaping the company's organization structure. Organizations per se don't have objectives; people have them, and through them, they set organizational goals. Their value systems and their philosophy of management combine to act as the shaping force in organizational design. For example, how do the managers view individual freedom to make decisions, as opposed to normal authority channels within the company? What is their attitude about leadership? How do they see the interaction between the company and its external environment?

The Work   Since accomplishment of tasks to achieve organizational goals is the primary reason for organizing, a fundamental determinant of structure is the nature of the tasks. The work determines factors such as span of control, authority delegation, and the extent to which an organic, as opposed to a bureaucratic, structure is adopted. And a growing body of research evidence relates technology to organization design—different technologies seem to have different "management content." At the risk of oversimplification, we can probably conclude that in low-technology, stable, continuous-process industries, there is less need for adaptive organizations.

The Environment   The elements that set the climate of a company are social, political, economic, and technological, as well as those related to product and supply markets. The environment is therefore complex, and the more a company interacts with it, the greater its impact on the organization design.

The greatest environmental interaction probably occurs in the context of hard-headed market considerations, such as the availability of resources and capital, the products or services the company sells, and the competition anticipated. Other market considerations are the changing demand for the company's output and the technological or other factors that may change both demand and production methods. It isn't difficult to see why a stable environment, such as that of the steel industry, would demand a different pattern of design and behavior than would an environment of uncertainty and flux, such as that of the computer industry.

The Individual Contributors   Because an organization structure is nothing without people to man it, the human element is an essential factor. We now have a growing and perhaps conclusive body of evidence that increased productivity and other desirable results can be achieved by adapting the structure to accommodate the needs of organizational members. That is not academic clap-trap, but practical business sense.

Building an Adaptive Organization

What does all this suggest and what practical use has it? It suggests that the right structure is a function of the interaction of the variables, each of which must be balanced against the effect of the others and against the desired output of the organization. In practice, no one style of organization design is universally appropriate; perhaps, however, there is a universal truth in the observation of Joseph C. Wilson, of Xerox, that the greatest strength of a company is the spirit of innovation and adaptation to change. To check the presence of that spirit and the "adaptability quotient," here are some questions:

- Do you blame most of your productivity problems on labor?
- Have you identified the output and costs of the nonhourly workforce, including white collar and lower and middle management? If so, are those groups working to a standard and can you identify changes in their productivity?
- Do you know what a 5 percent increase in productivity of each category of worker would do for profits?
- Do you have a program for identifying the value of your human resources and the costs associated with them in much the same way as other assets?
- Do you have a true management of human resources program, not just a personnel department that maintains records?
- Do your people cling to old ways of working after they have been confronted with new situations?
- Are the older managers living in the past and passing their thinking along to the younger men?
- Is your reputation one of safety, security, and "a nice place to work"?
- Has management developed a low criticism tolerance?
- Does company esprit depend upon one or more outdated "rites"?
- Does your entire operation depend on tight controls?
- As you see it, is line-staff conflict nonexistent and staff specialists are doing their job properly?
- Have you reviewed the company situation to see whether some form of team organization would work?
- Are you willing to delegate and let subordinates make mistakes?
- Have you reviewed the relationship between these determinants of organizational design—managers, work, environment, individual contributors—to see whether you have a mix that fits your structure?

The focus of all this probing of the organizational structure is, obviously, human resource management. Here we come full circle, back to concern with productivity, because that is determined to a large extent by employees' reaction to the company's "socio-work" environment, and it, in turn, is determined to a large extent by company structure—the organization of work and people.

Reading 5
Organizing for Product Innovation
Jay W. Lorsch
Paul R. Lawrence

• How can we get our research people to be more responsive to the needs of the market?
• What can we do to get our salesmen more involved in selling new products and seeking new applications?
• Why are our production people so conservative when it comes to introducing new products?
• How can we get sales, research, and production people to pull in the same direction on product development?

Questions such as these have become of increasing concern to executives in companies operating in the many industries characterized by rapid technological and market change, in which new and improved products are the key to corporate success. Several years ago we were all concerned with obtaining effective research organizations. It was generally believed that if a climate could be developed in which talented scientists and engineers could work creatively, we would be assured of a constant flow of product improvements and new products. As companies have become successful in developing more effective research organizations, however, it has become increasingly apparent that creative, innovative researchers are not enough by themselves. What is needed, as the questions above indicate, is an organization which provides collaboration between scientific innovators and sales and production specialists, so that:

The skills of the innovators can be directed at market needs and technological problems.
Sales and production specialists can be actively involved in the commercialization of ideas developed in the laboratory.
And, as a result, ideas can be transferred smoothly from laboratory prototype to commercial reality.

HOW COMPANIES INNOVATE

We can begin our discussion of the problems of organizing for innovation by briefly examining the essential functions of any organization. Basically, an organization, whether it be the product division of a diversified chemical company or a corner drug store, provides a means by which more than one person can work together to perform a task that one individual could not perform alone. This

"Organizing for Product Innovation," Jay W. Lorsch and Paul R. Lawrence, *Harvard Business Review*, January–February 1965, pp. 109–122. ©1965 by the President and Fellows of Harvard College: all rights reserved. Reprinted with permission.

means each individual or unit of the larger organization will be performing some specialized portion of the organization's task.

The first function of an organization, then, is to divide the total task into specialized pieces. The organization's second function is to provide a means by which units working on different parts of the total task may coordinate their activities to come out with a unified effort. While these processes of specialization and coordination are essential in any organization, they are particularly crucial for companies competing in developing new products.

Perhaps the best way to understand the specialization and coordination required in the innovation process is to describe the steps involved in developing products in the two plastics companies we studied. These were prominent companies in their industry, chosen to show similarities and contrasts in their organizational approach to product innovation. To protect their identity, we shall refer to them as the "Rhody" and "Crown" companies. It should be stressed that the two companies sold their products for industrial applications and there was, therefore, a constant demand not only for major new products but also for a flow of modifications in properties and processes that could improve the performance of old products and yield new applications for them. In our description of the innovation process we will be referring to the steps required for both types of innovation.

Required Collaboration

Exhibit I provides a schematic representation of the innovation process as the executives in the two organizations think it should be in order to obtain effective innovation. As we have already indicated, there are three major groups of specialists in each organization. Sales, production, and research specialists are each coping with a different sector of the organization's environment, and each should have a different portion of the total skills and knowledge required to discover a product idea and convert it into a tangible product:

- The sales department in dealing with the market environment should be in a position to extract information about market trends and customer needs.
- The research department in dealing with the scientific environment should be able to provide data about the technical and scientific feasibility of any new product development.
- The production department should have a store of knowledge about the limits of plant processes from the production environment.

Information from the sales department about customer needs and from production about processing limits has to be passed on to the research unit so that this information can be assimilated with the scientific feasibility of developing or modifying a product. Within the limits set by the needs of the customer and the capacities of the production process, the research units are then required to come

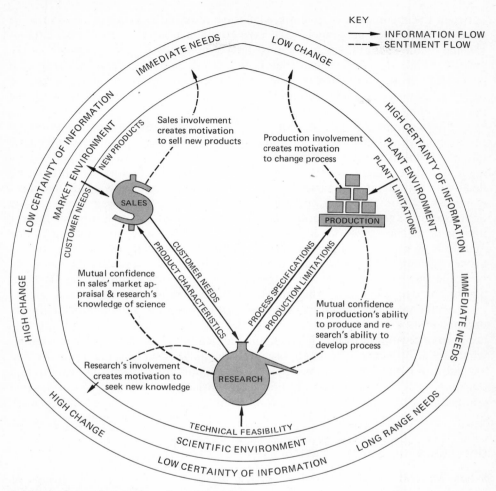

Exhibit I Scientific transfer process: the ideal.

up with a new development. If they succeed, it is then necessary to transfer information back to the sales department about product characteristics and to the production department about process specifications. With this information sales should be in a position to make and implement market plans, and production should have the data for planning and executing its task of manufacturing the product.

In short, product innovation requires close coordination between research and sales, on the one hand, and between research and production, on the other. This coordination is necessary not only to provide the two-way flow of technical information described earlier, but also to develop mutual trust and confidence between the members of the units which are required to collaborate in product development. Sales personnel must have confidence in research's knowledge of science, while research scientists must have confidence in sales' appraisal of the market. Similarly, there must be mutual confidence between research and production about production's ability to operate the process efficiently according to specifications and about research's capacity to develop a process that can be operated efficiently.

Product innovation, then, requires close collaboration between the sales and research units and the production and research units if the specialists involved are effectively to bring their separate skills to bear on a successful product development. However, the complexity and uncertainty of the factors which must be dealt with (at least in companies developing a multiplicity of new products) make it necessary for this coordination to take place at the *lower* levels of the organization. Executives in both Rhody and Crown indicate that it is difficult for managers at the upper levels of the organization to keep in touch with the multitude of rapidly changing factors which must be considered in the day-to-day process of developing many new products. Only the specialists on the firing line have the detailed knowledge of markets and technologies to make the frequent day-to-day decisions which the innovation process requires.

So far we have presented only a description of what *should* happen in both organizations if innovation is to be successfully accomplished. But our interests are in investigating not only what should happen but also, and more importantly, what *actually* happens in each organization as a result of the processes of specialization and coordination required for product innovation. We want to find out in what ways the groups of specialists working on diverse tasks in the two companies are different in their ways of thinking, in the ground rules they work by, and in terms of the organizational structures in which they work.

DIMENSIONS OF SPECIALIZATION

When we undertook our study, we decided to find out first how groups of specialists actually were differentiated. We expected the differences to be related to the problems of obtaining coordination between units. Exhibit II presents our findings about the dimensions along which the departments were different. Departmental differences are classified in terms of four main dimensions: *(a)* degree of departmental structure, *(b)* members' orientation toward time, *(c)* members' orientation toward others, and *(d)* members' orientation toward the environment.

Each of the differences between departments is seen to be a function of the characteristics of the environmental sector (market, science, or plant) with which a unit is coping in performing its task. Groups, such as production units, which have a very certain environment (as measured by the certainty of information at a given time, the rate of change in the environment, and the time range of the task) are highly structured. Because they are working with a highly stable environment,

Differences in departmental organization structures are important. One department may have very tight rules and procedures, very close spans of supervisory control, many levels in the departmental hierarchy, and frequent and very specific reviews of departmental and individual performance. Such a department is high structured. In another department just the opposite situation may occur. There may be fewer rules and regulations, very infrequent reviews of a general nature, broader spans of control, and fewer levels in the departmental hierarchy. Most departments, of course, fall in between these two extremes of the continuum.

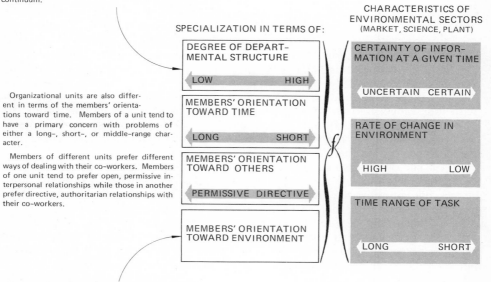

Organizational units are also different in terms of the members' orientations toward time. Members of a unit tend to have a primary concern with problems of either a long-, short-, or middle-range character.

Members of different units prefer different ways of dealing with their co-workers. Members of one unit tend to prefer open, permissive interpersonal relationships while those in another prefer directive, authoritarian relationships with their co-workers.

SPECIALIZATION IN TERMS OF:

DEGREE OF DEPARTMENTAL STRUCTURE
LOW — HIGH

MEMBERS' ORIENTATION TOWARD TIME
LONG — SHORT

MEMBERS' ORIENTATION TOWARD OTHERS
PERMISSIVE — DIRECTIVE

MEMBERS' ORIENTATION TOWARD ENVIRONMENT

CHARACTERISTICS OF ENVIRONMENTAL SECTORS (MARKET, SCIENCE, PLANT)

CERTAINTY OF INFORMATION AT A GIVEN TIME
UNCERTAIN — CERTAIN

RATE OF CHANGE IN ENVIRONMENT
HIGH — LOW

TIME RANGE OF TASK
LONG — SHORT

Each department's members have different orientations toward the environment. They are primarily concerned with the specific environmental sector with which they are coping. Scientists can be expected to be more concerned with the development of new technical knowledge, while salesmen are primarily concerned with the customer and the activities of the competition. Production specialists are most concerned with processing problems, material costs, and so forth.

Exhibit II Relation between departmental specialization and environment.

they tend to develop explicit routines and highly programmed ways of operating, adopt a directive interpersonal style, and also find a short-range time orientation useful for the performance of their task.

On the other hand, units, such as research, which are coping with less certain environments tend to be less structured, are characterized by a more permissive interpersonal orientation, and have a longer time orientation. These characteristics are consistent with an uncertain, nonroutine task, since effective performance of such a task requires opportunity for open consultation among colleagues in seeking solutions to problems and freedom to consider and attempt different courses of action.

Principal Patterns

How do the differences in orientation and structure characterize the departments in Rhody and Crown? Exhibit III summarizes our findings on this question. The data presented here are representative of the *general* pattern which exists in both organizations; some minor variations between the two organizations are not depicted. We see that:

• Members of each department tend primarily to be oriented toward the sector of the environment with which their task involves them. Research people tend to be more oriented toward discovering new scientific knowledge, while sales people are more concerned with customer problems and market conditions, and production personnel indicate a primary concern with production costs and processing problems.

• In time orientation, the research scientists tend to be more concerned with long-range matters which will not have an impact on company profits for several years in the future. Sales and production specialists are primarily concerned with the more immediate problems which affect the company's performance within the current year.

• The interpersonal orientations of the members of the units in both companies are also different. Research and sales personnel tend to prefer more permissive interpersonal relationships, while production specialists indicate a preference for a more directive manner of working with their colleagues.

• As for the degree of departmental structure, the research units have the lowest amount and the production units have the highest. The sales units, which seem to be performing a task of medium certainty, have a structure which falls between the extremes represented by research and production.

What we find in both companies, then, are units which are quite different from each other both in terms of members' orientations and the structure in which the members work. These differences in ways of thinking about the job and in

	Departmental structure	Orientation toward time	Orientation toward others	Orientation toward environment
Research	Low	Long	Permissive	Science
Sales	Medium	Short	Permissive	Market
Production	High	Short	Directive	Plant

Exhibit III Patterns of specialization.

ground rules and operating procedures mean that each of these groups tends to view the task of innovation somewhat differently.

Impact on Ability

While we next want to examine the influence of these differences on the process of obtaining coordination, we should first emphasize a point which too often has been overlooked: The differences have a *positive* effect on the ability of each individual unit to perform its particular task. The common orientations and ground rules within a unit and a departmental structure which facilitate task performance direct the efforts of people in the unit to their segment of the organizational task and enhance their ability to carry out their mission. Because the units are performing different tasks, we have to expect that they will develop different departmental structures and that their members will be oriented differently. If attempts were made to standardize the structures of all units and to have all members of the organization oriented in the same direction, we would lose the benefits of specialization.

The two companies in our study recognize this fact to differing degrees. At Rhody the differences along the four dimensions tend to be greater than at Crown. Each department at Rhody not only has a structure conducive to the performance of its task, but also tends to be more highly concerned with a single task dimension or with a particular period of time than does the same unit at Crown. While in both organizations the specialization of units enables them to address their separate tasks, the units at Rhody, by virtue of their higher degree of specialization, often seem to be better able to perform their individual tasks.

ORGANIZATIONAL PARADOX

While specialized orientations and structures facilitate a unit's task performance, we would expect the patterns to be closely related to the problems of coordination in both firms. Because members of a given department hold common attitudes about what is important in their work and about dealing with each other, they are able to work effectively with each other. But to the extent that the ground rules and orientations held by members of one department are different from those held by members of another, we would expect the departments to have increased difficulty achieving the high degree of coordination required for effective innovation.

The data we collected through a questionnaire about the effectiveness of coordination between departments at Rhody and Crown confirm this expectation. When two units are similar in departmental structure and in the orientations of their members, we find that they have few problems in obtaining effective collaboration *with each other.* But when units tend to be on opposite poles along the four dimensions, we find that there are more problems in integrating their efforts. Within each organization there is clear evidence that the greater the differences in orientation and structure between any pair of units, the greater the problems of obtaining effective coordination.

Although this relationship holds within each company, we find an interesting paradox when the two organizations are compared. As already indicated, there is a higher degree of specialization and differentiation at Rhody than at Crown. Pairs of units which are required to collaborate at Rhody tend to be less similar than the comparable pairs of units at Crown. Since units at Crown are more similar, this *should* mean that Crown encounters fewer problems of coordination. However, this does *not* turn out to be the case. Rhody appears to be achieving better integration than Crown, even though it also has a higher degree of differentiation. In short, within each organization there is a relationship between the effectiveness of coordination and the degree of differentiation, but the organization which has the highest degree of specialization also has the most effective collaboration.

The significance of this paradox grows if we recall that specialization is a two-sided coin. Specialization is useful because it is necessary for the performance of individual departments; on the other hand, it can have negative consequences in that it is at the root of the problems of achieving the coordination required for innovation. At Rhody we have a situation in which one organization is able to have its cake (in the form of specialization) and to eat it too (in the form of coordination).

Contrasting Methods

Does the explanation reside in the methods used by the two organizations to facilitate coordination between units? We believe it does.

Attempts at devising methods to improve coordination between the specialized departments involved in product innovation are certainly not novel. New-product departments, or coordinating departments with other appelations, have been established in many organizations with the primary function of coordinating the activities of research, sales, and production specialists in the development of new products. Similarly, many firms have appointed liaison individuals who are responsible for linking two or more groups of functional specialists. Another frequent device has been to develop shortterm project teams with representatives from the several functional departments to work on a new product. Finally, many companies have relied on permanent cross-functional coordinating teams to deal with the continuing problems of innovation around a given group of products.

Both Rhody and Crown have developed the same types of devices:

1 In each company there is a coordinating department which has the primary task of coordinating or integrating the innovation activities of the research, production, and sales units.

2 Each company is making use of permanent cross-functional coordinating committees which have representatives from each of the basic departments and the coordinating department. The primary function of these committees is to serve as a setting in which coordination can take place.

Since both organizations are utilizing the same devices to achieve coordination, it is pertinent to ask whether there are differences in the functioning and effectiveness of these devices. The answer provided by our investigation is an emphatic *yes*.

We now turn to an examination of these differences, looking first at the coordinating departments, then at the committees.

COORDINATING DEPARTMENTS

In addition to seeking teamwork among research, production, and sales, the coordinating departments at Rhody and Crown perform certain other tasks. At Crown the department is also involved in market planning and the coordination of sales efforts. At Rhody the coordinating department is also involved in technical service and market-development activities. As might be expected, both departments have developed orientations and structural characteristics somewhat different from those of the other units in the companies.

Key to Coordination

While various similarities exist between the two coordinating groups, there is also, as our measurements reveal, a major distinction:

• At Rhody the coordinating department falls in a middle position on each of the four dimensions we have considered. That is, if we compare the department's degree of structure and its members' orientations with those of the sales, production, and research departments, it always has an intermediate value, never an extreme one. For instance, members of the coordinating department have a balanced orientation along the time dimension. They are equally concerned with the short-range problems of sales and production and the long-range matters with which research wrestles. Similarly, coordinating personnel have a balanced concern with production, scientific, and market environments. The degree of departmental structure and the interpersonal orientation of coordinating members also fall between the extremes of the other departments.

• At Crown the coordinating department is in the middle along the structure and interpersonal dimensions but tends to be highly oriented toward short-range time concerns and toward the market environment. Personnel indicate a high concern with immediate sales problems, and less concern with longer-range matters or with research or production environments. On both the time and the environment dimensions, therefore, the coordinating department is not intermediate between the departments it is supposed to be linking.

The foregoing difference, which is shown schematically in Exhibit IV, appears to be related to differences in the effectiveness of the two units. Our questionnaires and interviews indicate that the coordinating department at Rhody is generally perceived by members of that organization to be doing an effective job of linking the basic departments. On the other hand, the coordinating department at Crown is not perceived to be as effective as most members of the Crown organization think it should be.

Observations by Executives

The reactions of executives in the two companies pretty well explain for us why the intermediate position of the Rhody coordinating department is associated with effective coordination, while the imbalance in certain orientations of the Crown unit inhibits its performance. The following are a few typical comments from Rhody managers:

> "The most important thing is that we have the coordinating department with its contacts with the customers and its technically trained people who are in contact with research. They are the kingpins. They have a good feel for research's ability, and they know the needs of the market. They will work back and forth with research and the other units."

> "Generally speaking, the feeling of close cooperation between the coordinating unit and sales is echoed in the field. The top salesmen all get along well with the coordinating guys. You take a good coordinating fellow and a good salesman and that makes a powerful team. In our business the boys upstairs in the coordinating unit are top notch. They know what the lab can do, and they know the salesman's problems."

But at Crown the comments of executives have a different tone.

> "My biggest criticism of our situation is that the coordinating department isn't a good enough mechanism to link the research activities to the customer. We need a better marketing strategy on certain products and some long-term plans. The lack of planning in the coordinating department is deplorable. One of our troubles is that the coordinating people are so tied up in day-to-day detail that they can't look to the future. They are still concerned with 1964 materials when they should be concerned with 1965 markets."

> "Our problem is we can't clearly define the technical problems the customer is having. Theoretically the coordinating men should be able to handle this for research because they know the customer best. But they are so involved in present business that it takes all their time. They have a budget they have to live up to, and the best way to make money is to sell existing products. They know that selling existing products is more profitable than selling new products, so they keep on selling existing products to live up to the expectations of the budget."

In other words, we have a marked difference in reaction. What managers at Rhody are stressing is that the coordinating unit in their organization is effective because it has a familiarity with the problems, orientations, and ways of operating of the basic units it connects. At Crown the primary complaints about that organization's less-effective coordinating unit are that its members tend to be too oriented toward immediate sales matters.

A AT CROWN COMPANY

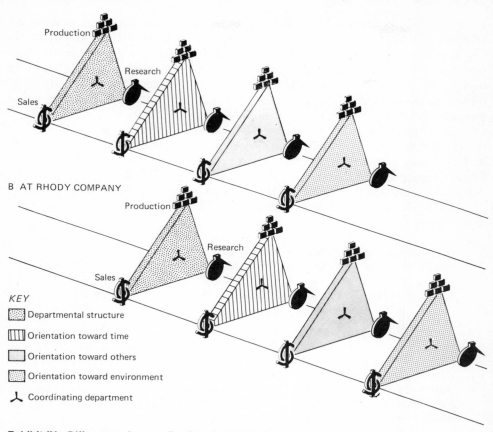

B AT RHODY COMPANY

KEY

▓ Departmental structure

▥ Orientation toward time

▢ Orientation toward others

▒ Orientation toward environment

⅄ Coordinating department

Exhibit IV   Differences in coordinating departments.

The situation in these two organizations seems to indicate that for a coordinating department to be effective in linking the several specialized departments, it must be intermediate between any two along each of the several dimensions of orientation and structure. When a coordinating department is in this position, its members have more in common with members of the other units. Coordinating personnel tend to think and act in ways which are more understandable and agreeable to members of the other departments—and this facilitates collaboration. If members of the coordinating department have orientations and ground rules which are more suited to one specialized unit, as is the situation at Crown, their ways of thinking will necessarily be different from the other departments—and this situation will impair their effectiveness as coordinators.

CROSS-FUNCTIONAL GROUPS

Even in an organization like Rhody, where the coordinating unit is doing an effective job of facilitating cooperation between the specialized units, certain disagreements between the various specialist units seem to be inevitable. Management's problem is to provide a setting in which attempts at resolving these disagreements can be made effectively. Both organizations in this study have turned to permanent cross-functional coordinating committees as devices for providing a setting in which to work at achieving coordination between units.

In investigating the functioning of these committees in the two organizations, we again want to obtain an assessment of their effectiveness as well as some understanding of the factors which might be related to their performance. If we listen to some of the comments made by members of both organizations, the differences between the devices in the two companies become apparent.

At the Rhody company, managers make comments such as these about the cross-functional teams:

"Our problems get thrashed out in committee. We work them over until everybody agrees this is the best effort you can make. We may decide this isn't good enough; then we may decide to ask for more people, more plant, and so forth. We all sometimes have to take a modification and be realistic and say this is the best we can do."

"I may want us to do some work on a particular new product. The coordinating guy may say, 'Let's get the customer to change his process instead.' A research guy may say we need both. It is the way we do it that becomes argumentative and rightfully so. These things take several meetings to work out, but we are never really stalemated. We have decided in our committee that we won't stalemate. There is more than one way to our ends. If I don't agree with the others, then I abdicate my position—sometimes gracefully and sometimes not.

"We had a disagreement about releasing confidential information to a customer and had quite a discussion about it. This was only the second time we had gotten so formal as to have a vote. I was outvoted three to one, but that afternoon I was the one who had to call the customer and give him the information as we had decided."

"Since we have had these committees, we are working more closely with other groups. It is really working out. In the past, production was reluctant to give us information, and they wanted to keep the prerogative of making process changes. Since this committee has been operating, there has been a greater exchange of information . . . ."

At Crown the executives speak differently about their experiences with cross-functional committees:

"Unfortunately, the committees are not decision-making groups as much as I would like. Generally there is a reporting session. We don't have time going over all these things to make some of the decisions which need to be made. I would like to see more hashing out of the problems and making of decisions. Of course we do make decisions every day between us."

"If I want something very badly and I am confronted by a roadblock, I go to top management to get the decision made. If the research managers are willing to go ahead, there is no problem. If there is a conflict, then I would go to their boss."

"I think these meetings only intensify the arguments. I haven't learned much that I didn't know already before I got to the meeting. It used to be that we had some knock-em down, drag-out fights, but then we would get things settled. But this doesn't take place anymore, so there isn't any place for us to resolve our difficulties."

These and similar comments indicate that members of the Rhody organization find the cross-functional committees an important aid in achieving collaboration, while members of the Crown organization do not. They also indicate, as do our observations of meetings of these committees in both organizations, that there are at least two important differences between the functioning of these committees in the two organizations. Before going into these contrasts, however, we must first point to an important distinction in the organizational structures of the two companies.

The Crown organization tends to have a higher degree of structure (tighter spans of control, more specific rules and procedures, and so forth) in *all* its parts than does the Rhody organization. One important aspect of this difference is that the level at which decisions about product innovation are supposed to be made is much lower in the organizational hierarchy at Rhody than at Crown.

Decision Authority

The significance of this distinction becomes apparent if we turn to look at the teams at Rhody. In this organization team members are in most cases first-line supervisors who (being right down at the working level) have the detailed market and technical knowledge required to make decisions. They are the only persons who attend the meetings, and they usually have the formal authority to make decisions.

Our observation of meetings at Rhody, along with comments made by company executives, indicate that there are ground rules or norms operating in cross-functional committees which sanction the open confrontation of disagreement between members. Members of the committees tend to recognize their differences and seek ways of resolving them within the constraints of the situation with which they are dealing. This working through of disagreements often takes a great deal of emotional and intellectual effort, but members of the committees at Rhody tend to persevere until some resolution is reached. After decisions are made, the members of the committees are highly committed to them. As we learned from one executive, even though a member is not in initial agreement with the decision taken, he is expected to—and he does—carry out the actions worked out in the meetings.

In contrast with the situation at Rhody, we find at Crown (as we would expect from the greater degree of structure throughout this company) that members of the committees are at a higher level than their counterparts at Rhody, but even these managers often do not have the authority to make decisions. Furthermore, because they are at a higher level, they usually do not have either the technical or market knowledge required to make the detailed decisions necessary to develop products.

As a consequence of this situation, members of the Crown committees often bring both their superiors and their subordinates to the meetings with them—the superiors in order to provide someone who has the authority to make decisions, the subordinates so that someone is present who has the detailed technical and market knowledge to draw on for decisions. Bringing in all these participants results in meetings two or three times as large as those at Rhody.

Resolving Conflict

Our observations of meetings at Crown and the comments of executives indicate that there are other shortcomings in the Crown committees. The norms of behavior in these groups sanction withdrawal from disagreement and conflict. Whenever there is a disagreement, the members tend to avoid discussing the matter, hoping it will magically go away. If this doesn't place the problem out of sight, they find another avenue of avoidance by passing it on to their superiors. As a consequence, many decisions which should be made at Crown seem to get dropped. They are not picked up again until they have festered for so long that somebody *has* to deal with them—and it is often too late by that time.

There will always be disagreements between members of departments which have highly different orientations and concerns. The problem facing members of coordinating committees is to learn to fight together constructively so that they can resolve these differences. At Rhody members of the cross-functional teams have developed this ability. They work at resolving conflict at their own level. They do not withdraw from disputes, nor do they try to smooth over their differences or arrive at some easy compromise. Rather, they seem willing to argue the issues involved until some understanding is reached about the optimal solution in a given situation.

In essence, the committees at Rhody have developed the ability to confront their differences openly and search persistently for solutions which will provide effective collaboration. At Crown, on the other hand, the committees avoid fights and forfeit the opportunity to achieve the coordination required for innovation.

CONCLUSION

The foregoing comparisons seem to provide an answer to the paradox of the Rhody organization achieving both greater specialization and more effective coordination than the Crown company does. The effective coordinating unit and cross-functional coordinating committees allow members at Rhody to concentrate on their specialties and still achieve a unity of effort. Sales, research, and production specialists are each able to address their separate departmental tasks and work in a climate which is conducive to good performance. At the same time, the men in the coordinating department, who have a balanced orientation toward the concerns of the three departments of specialists, help the three units to achieve a unity of effort. The cross-functional committees also provide a means by which the specialist groups and the coordinators can work through their differences and arrive at the best common approach.

At Crown, in spite of the fact that the specialist departments are more similar in orientation and structure than are the units at Rhody, there is more difficulty in obtaining unity of effort between them. Since the coordinators are overly concerned with short-term matters and sales problems, they do not effectively perform their function of linking the three groups of specialists. The cross-functional committees do not contribute much to coordination between these departments, either. They do not provide a setting in which problems can be solved, since authority to make decisions often resides in the higher levels of the organization and since norms have developed within the committees which encourage members to avoid conflict and pass it on to their superiors.

But what about the results the two companies have achieved in the market place? We have been asserting that both a high degree of specialization and effective coordination are important in achieving product innovation in this situation, but we have not presented any evidence that Rhody, with its greater specialization and more effective coordination, is in fact doing a better job of product innovation than is Crown. The following figures do show that the Rhody organization *is* achieving a higher level of innovation than Crown:

- At Rhody, new products developed in the last five years have accounted for 59% of sales.
- At Crown, the figure is only 20%, or just about one-third of Rhody's.

Part of this difference may have been due to some variation in market and technical factors confronting the two organizations. However, since these two organizations have been operating in the same industry and have been confronted by similar market conditions and technical problems, and because of the different levels of coordination and specialization achieved in each company, it seems safe to conclude that there is indeed a relationship between innovation performance and the internal organizational factors we have been discussing.

Management Challenge

While this discussion has been based on an examination of two organizations in the plastics industry, there is no question that the requirements for specialization and coordination are just as urgent in other industries confronted with the need for product innovation. It seems safe to generalize that, whatever the field or function, managers interested in improving their record with new products must recognize two essential organizational ingredients of success:

   1 Specialists who are clearly oriented toward their individual tasks and who work in organizational structures which are conducive to task performance.
   2 Effective means of coordination which permit specialists with diverse knowledge and orientations to work together. (There will be disagreements and conflicts among these specialists, but the organization must provide a means to resolve the conflicts in such a way that the full energy of research, sales, and production people can be brought to bear on innovation.)

   Our discussion has focused on two devices to achieve this coordination—*coordinating departments* whose members have a balanced point of view enabling them to work effectively among the several specialist groups, and *cross-functional coordinating committees* in which members have learned to confront their differences and fight over them constructively so they can reach an optimal resolution. But other means of coordination are also available. The challenge confronting managers responsible for organizing for innovations is to work at developing means of coordination which permit effective specialization *and* effective coordination. This is the combination that is needed to produce the constant flow of innovations necessary for corporate growth in changing markets.

Reading 6
Strategy and Management Structure
William H. Newman

The matching of strategy and management design presents a challenging opportunity to scholars of management. It calls for skill in building a viable, integrated system; it draws upon insights on many facets of management; and it plunges us into a highly dynamic set of relationships. Both synthesis and refinement of theory are involved.
   Moreover, as A. D. Chandler demonstrates in his classic study, *Strategy and Structure,* keeping managerial arrangements in tune with strategy plays a vital role in enterprise survival and growth.[2] The accelerating pace of change in economic, technological, political, and social forces will lead companies to adjust their strategies more often in the future than has been typical in the past. And with each

"Strategy and Management Structure," William H. Newman, *Journal of Business Policy,* Winter 1971–1972, pp. 56–66. Reprinted with permission from Mercury House Business Publications Ltd., London.

shift in strategy the appropriateness of existing management design should be examined anew. Consequently, the issues we explore in this paper hold practical as well as theoretical significance.

Our discussion is divided into four parts: (1) strategy is defined; (2) the concept of a coherent management design is set forth, with particular attention to those features most likely to be affected by strategy; (3) then an analytical approach for matching strategy and management design is examined; and (4) implications for heterogeneous as well as homogeneous enterprises are identified.

Scope of Master Strategy

Strategy, as the term is used in this paper, sets the basic purposes of an enterprise in terms of the services it will render to society and the way it will create these services. More specifically, master strategy involves (a) picking particular product market niches that are propitious in view of society's needs and the company's resources, (b) selecting the underlying technologies and the ways of attracting inputs, (c) combining the various niches and resource bases to obtain synergistic effects, (d) expressing these plans in terms of targets, and (e) setting up sequences and timing of steps toward these objectives that reflect company capabilities and external conditions.

Obviously, the formulation of strategy calls for diagnostic skills and keen judgment. A great deal of analysis and theorizing remains to be done on this frontier. It is an area of study in itself. The present paper, however, focuses on another task of central management—the interrelation between master strategy and management design.[3] Here we assume that strategy does get formulated and periodically revised. Such strategy will become effective only when it is linked to a mutually supporting management design.

Integrated Management Design

Discussions of "strategy and structure" often focus on organization structure only. If the match between strategy and management design is to be fully effective, however, more than organization must be harmonized. The nature of the planning process, the leadership style and the form and location of control mechanisms are also intimately involved. This more inclusive view of management arrangements—planning, organizing, leading and controlling—we call management design.

Management designs differ. Every university is, and should be, managed in ways that are different from those used to manage the bus system that brings students to its doors. Likewise, within the university, the managerial design best suited to research laboratories is inappropriate to the cafeteria. To be sure, several common processes—organizing, planning, leading and controlling—are essential for each of these units, but as we adapt various concepts to the unique needs of each venture refinement is vital. Management sophistication is revealed in this adapting and refining of the design.

Need for Coherent Management Design

In each particular situation the phases of management should be synergistic. That is, organization structure should facilitate control, control should generate useful data for planning, planning should be conducted in a way that assists in leading, and so forth. These mutually supporting effects are a vital feature of a good management design. Yet in practice a surprising number of instances arise where just the opposite pull occurs. Tensions mount instead of reinforcements.

A striking lack of synergy arose when one of the nation's leading railroads undertook a sweeping decentralization. According to the plan, regional managers were to replace a highly centralized headquarters as the focus for operating decisions, and these regional managers were given significantly increased authority. Unfortunately the control mechanisms did not change with the organization design. Detailed reports continued to flow to the vice-presidents at headquarters, and these men continued their previous practice of stepping into trouble spots and issuing orders. Confusion resulted. The fact that legal and technological reasons prevented regional managers from making their own plans regarding prices, train schedules, new equipment, wage rates, and other important matters merely aggravated the situation. So the actual planning mechanism did not line up with the announced organization. It soon became obvious that the total management design had not been thought through.

The chief executive of a computer company, to cite another example, decided that participative leadership would stimulate the engineers and other technical people in his firm. He arranged for all managers and vice-presidents to first-line supervisors to have T-group training so that everyone would understand the new leadership style. The results were not entirely happy. Competition forced the president himself to make several key decisions, specifications had to be frozen, pressure was placed on production people to meet tough deadlines, and budgetary-control limits were stipulated by headquarters. This top-down planning was a well-established pattern within the company. But to many managers who had just got the message about participative leadership, the former planning procedures suddenly became oppressive. Their morale was hurt rather than helped because their expectations, which had been raised by the leadership training, were soon undermined by use of the old planning mechanisms. Here again we see that a change in one phase of management was not matched by necessary adjustments in other phases.

Prominent Features of a Management Design

Recognition of need for a coherent management design raises a question of what is embraced in such a design. What features do we need to consider?

It is not very helpful to suggest that elements in the management design for a particular situation can be selected from the many concepts covered in management literature, even though this statement is true. Such guidance is too broad. In order to narrow the focus a bit, let us concentrate on those managerial arrangements most likely to be affected by choice of strategy. In other words, which features probably will need adjustment when we fit a structure to new requirements?

Analysis of a wide variety of management designs points to the elements listed in the accompanying tables as distinguishing features. In any single design only a few of these features will dominate, and others may be insignificant. In addition, for unusual circumstances a feature not listed here may be critical. Nevertheless careful consideration of the features listed will enable us to comprehend and to deal with the management designs of most enterprises.

1 Distinguishing Organizational Features. Organization is widely acknowledged as a prime vehicle for adapting a management design to new needs. In fact organization often is overemphasized. Some managers make a change in their formal organization and then assume everything else will fall in place. To be fully effective, however, several compatible changes in formal organization are frequently necessary. These changes must be incorporated into informal behaviour, and supporting adjustments must be made in other facets of management.

Key personnel, the last feature listed in Table 1, warrants special emphasis. It is always involved in a change in management design, and it may be as vital to the success of a change as any other feature. Men capable of functioning in new jobs should be carefully selected and should be given time to learn new patterns of behaviour.

2 Distinguishing Forms of Plans. The need to think carefully about forms of plans is illustrated sharply in any international airline. Preparation of tickets in Vienna that will be understood in Nairobi and Seattle, that can be reissued in Baghdad and cancelled in Tahiti, and that provide the basis for allocating the fare collected among a dozen different airlines, requires an impressive use of standing operating procedures. Nor can equipment maintenance be left to local ingenuity. On the other hand, company-wide policies relating to sales promotion and pay-rates for baggage handlers must be cast in broad terms or shunned entirely. Then if the airline enters the local hotel business in several countries, the appropriateness of world-wide policies and procedures must be examined anew. For each subject, either too little or too much planning can lead to great confusion.

Questions about the kinds of plans suitable for a specific situation typically centre around the topics listed in Table 2. Planning, in contrast to organizing, often receives scant attention during the preparation of a management design. This disregard of planning arises from two confusions. First, the substance of specific plans may be so engrossing that little thought is given to the more basic issue of the form in which guidance will be most useful. Second, the process of arriving at a decision is confused with the mechanisms introduced to guide decision-making activities throughout the enterprise. When shaping a management design, we are primarily concerned with these mechanisms (standing plans, project planning,

Table 1 Organizational Features That Are Likely to Vary With a Change in Strategy

Centralization versus
decentralization
Degree of division of labour
Size of self-sufficient operating
units
Mechanisms for coordination
Nature and location of staff
Management information system
Characteristics of key personnel

Table 2 Planning Features That Are Likely to Vary With a Change in Strategy

Use of standing plans
 Comprehensiveness of coverage
 Specificity
Use of single-use plans
 Comprehensiveness of coverage
 Specificity
Planning horizon
Intermediate versus final objectives
"How" versus results

intermediate objectives, and the like) because they help pull the entire managerial effort into a coherent thrust.*

3 Distinguishing Elements in Leadership Style. The leadership features listed in Table 3 are aspects of leading that should be adjusted to fit the total management design.† Many guides to good leadership practice that emerge from behavioural research apply to virtually all settings, and so they are not included in this particular list.

Leadership style is intimately tied to the temperament and beliefs of each manager. Consequently this style is more difficult to change than, say, departmentation or control reports. Nevertheless, all of us can modify our behaviour to some degree, especially when the environment in which we work reinforces our new behaviour. If a manager cannot provide the kind of leadership needed in a given situation, replacing him is an alternative. So even though leadership style is not easy to change, it should be included in the total process of matching management design to strategy.

4 Distinguishing Features of the Control Process. The design of controls all too often lags behind shifts in other aspects of management. The railroad reorganization mentioned earlier revealed a failure to revise controls so that they

---

*Good decisions on specific problems are vital, of course. But the elements of decision-making are similar in all sorts of situations, whereas the forms of plans and the organizational assignment of planning tasks differ widely. Consequently it is the latter arrangements that deserve prime attention when we prepare a management design.

†R. J. House in "Leader Behavior and Subordinate Satisfaction and Performance: A Motivational Theory of Leadership," *Admin. Sci. Quart.*, forthcoming, shows that the character of work has a significant bearing on the impact of various leadership styles. He cites several studies where role ambiguity, reflecting routine versus non-routine work, is an important variable in the kind of leadership action that is effective. J. J. Morse and J. W. Lorsch also stress the effect of the nature of work on leadership in "Beyond Theory Y," *Harv. Bus. Rev.* (May 1960). The influence of technology is at least implicit in W. Hill, "The Validation and Extension of Fiedler's Theory of Leadership Effectiveness," *Acad. Management J.* (Mar. 1969).

Table 3 Leadership Features That Are Likely to Vary with Changes in Strategy

Participation in planning
Permissiveness
Closeness of supervision
Sharing of information
Emphasis on on-the-job satisfactions

Table 4 Control Features That Are Likely to Vary with Changes in Strategy

Performance criteria emphasized
Location of control points
Frequency of checks
Who initiates corrective action
Stress on reliability versus learning
Punitive versus reward motivation

would reinforce major moves in related areas. Over-reliance on short-run, quantitative measurements shows a similar tendency to pay too little attention to control structure. Yet controls can provide the synergy we seek in an effective management design.

The features of control most likely to need adjustment when changes are made in other phases of management are listed in Table 4. Closely associated with changes in these features should be a refinement of the management information system, which has already been listed under organization. Although the preparation of a total management design rarely starts with control, no plan is complete until provision is made for control.

Weaving the various features of organizing, planning, leading and controlling that have been singled out in this section into a coherent management design calls for great skill. Each enterprise needs its own unique system. Fortunately, synergistic benefits are usually possible if we are ingenious enough to make reinforcing combinations, such as those suggested under "Nature of Technology" in Table 5. A company's design is effective, however, only when it fits neatly with the company strategy, as pointed out in the next section.

Influence of Strategy on Design

The idea of a management design is a useful concept because it turns our focus from analytical refinements to reinforcing integration. The preceding section identified an array of variable features that should be considered in building such an integrated design, and indicated how some combinations of these features tend to be destructive whereas other combinations promote coherence. We can now tackle the tougher task—relating management design and company strategy.

Technology: The Intervening Variable. The best bridge between strategy and design is "technology." Here we use technology in a very broad sense to include all sorts of methods for converting resource inputs into products and service the consumers. The inputs can be labour, knowledge and capital as well as raw materials.[5] Thus an insurance company has its technology for converting money, ideas, and labour into insurance service just as an oil company has its technology for converting crude oil and other resources into petroleum products.

Table 5   Typical Features of Management Structures for Three Types of Technology

Features that distinguish management structures	Nature of technology		
	Stable	**Regulated flexibility**	**Adaptive**
Organizing			
Centralization versus decentralization	Centralized	Mostly centralized	Decentralized
Degree of division of labour	Narrow specialization	Specialized or crafts	Scope may vary
Size of self-sufficient operating units	Large	Medium	Small, if equipment permits
Mechanisms for coordination	Built-in, programmed	Separate planning unit	Face-to-face, within unit
Nature and location of staff	Narrow functions; headquarters	Narrow functions; headquarters and operating unit	Generalists at headquarters; specialists in operating units
Management information system	Heavy upward flow	Flow to headquarters and to operating unit	Flow mostly to, and within, operating unit
Characteristics of key personnel	Strong operators	Functional experts in line and staff	Analytical, adaptive
Planning			
Use of standing plans			
Comprehensiveness of coverage	Broad coverage	All main areas covered	Mostly "local," self-imposed
Specificity	Detail specified	Detail in interlocking activities	Main points only
Use of single-use plans			
Comprehensiveness of coverage	Fully planned	Fully planned	Main steps covered
Specificity	Detail specified	Schedules and specs. detailed	Adjusted to feedback
Planning horizon	Weekly to quarterly	Weekly to annually	Monthly to three years or more
Intermediate versus final objectives	Intermediate goals sharp	Intermediate goals sharp	Emphasis on objectives
"How" versus results	"How" is specified	Results at each step specified	End results stressed
Leading			
Participation in planning	Very limited	Restricted to own tasks	High participation
Permissiveness	Stick to instructions	Variation in own tasks only	High permissiveness, if results OK

Table 5 (Continued)

Features that distinguish management structures	Nature of technology		
	Stable	Regulated flexibility	Adaptive
Closeness of supervision	Follow operations closely	Output and quality closely watched	General supervision
Sharing of information	Circumspect	Job information shared	Full project information shared
Emphasis on on-the-job satisfactions	Limited scope	Craftsmanship and professionalism encouraged	Opportunity for involvement
Controlling Performance criteria emphasized	Efficiency, dependability	Quality, punctuality, efficiency	Results, within resource limits
Location of control points	Within process; intermediate stages	Focus on each processing unit	Overall "milestones"
Frequency of checks	Frequent	Frequent	Infrequent
Who initiates corrective action	Often central managers	"Production control" and other staff	Men in operating unit
Stress on reliability versus learning	Reliability stressed	Reliability stressed	Learning stressed
Punitive versus reward motivation	Few mistakes tolerated	Few mistakes tolerated	High reward for success

By extending our thinking from strategy to the technology necessary to execute that strategy, we move to *work to be done.* Once we comprehend the work to be done—both managerial and operating work—we are on familiar ground. Most of our management concepts relate directly to getting work done, and so preparing a management design to fit a particular kind of work falls within the recognized "state of the art."

The use of technology as an intervening variable produces the arrangement shown in Figure 1. To maintain perspective and to highlight key influences, strategy should focus on only a few basic ideas. Its formulation is by necessity in broad terms. We cannot jump directly from strategy to management design because we have not yet classified the array of actions that will be necessary to execute the strategy. Thinking of technology helps us to elaborate the work implications of the strategy and thereby provides us with the inputs for shaping a management design.

Types of Technology   Technology, especially in the broad sense in which we are using the term here, deals with all sorts of situations and methods. For purposes of relating technology to management, however, we can concentrate on

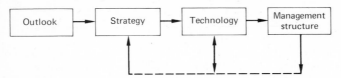

Figure 1 Outlook to design

only a few characteristics of the technology. For instance, the way a technology deals with change is very significant for our purpose.

In a company with a given strategy and technology, the need for change will fall somewhere along a continuum of infrequent to frequent. Similarly, the kinds of changes the company typically faces will fall somewhere along another continuum ranging from brand new, unprecedented problems to familiar, precedented problems; in the case of the familiar problems, the company will have a well-established pattern for resolving them.

Using these two characteristics of a firm's technology, we can set up the matrix shown in Figure 2. Of course, many technologies will fit around the middle of one or both dimensions, but by thinking about technologies toward the ends of the scales we arrive at three well-known types of businesses.

Enterprises confronted with unfamiliar problems rather infrequently are basically *stable.* Paper mills and other firms processing large volumes of raw materials fall into this category. When the need for change moves from infrequent to frequent, and the problems remain precedented, we encounter businesses that display *regulated flexibility.* Job shops—used by management writers since Frederick Taylor to illustrate management concepts—fit this category. But when the need for change is frequent and the problems are unprecedented, as often occurs in the aerospace industry, we face a sharply different situation. Here technology requires an *adaptive* structure.

These three technology types—stable, regulated flexibility, and adaptive— are found in many lines of endeavour. In the health field there are retirement homes, hospitals, and medical research labs. In government, offices for Social Security (old-age pensions), for unemployment compensation, and for the training of hard-core unemployed illustrate the types. In the service industries examples are telephone operations, newspaper publications, and management consulting.

In contrast to the first three types, the fourth division in the change matrix does not point to a clear type of technology or management design. Unprecedented problems that arise only infrequently are handled by some temporary arrangement. This *ad hoc* setup does not exist long enough to modify the underlying structure.

From Technology to Management Design.   An intriguing aspect of the three technology types just identified is that each leads to a well-known management design. The usual relationships between technology and design are shown in Table 5. For each of the distinguishing features of a management design, discussed

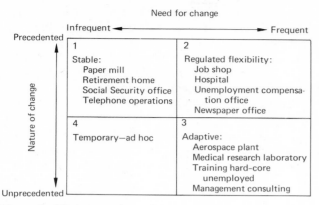

Figure 2 Change matrix.

earlier in this paper, we can see the typical response to a stable technology, a regulated-flexibility technology, and an adaptive technology.

The primary features of each design remain substantially the same even though the companies come from different industries. For instance, when the work situation is stable—as it usually is in a paper mill, retirement home, Social Security office, and telephone exchange—then planning tends to be comprehensive and detailed, intermediate goals are sharply defined, decision-making is centralized and central staff is strong. In addition we find limited participation and close supervision. Controls are focused on dependability and efficiency, checks are made frequently and few mistakes are tolerated. These and other management features indicated in Table 5 enable an executive working in a stable situation to convert resource inputs into the maximum output of consumer services.

Actually, in our modern world regulated flexibility is much more common than the stable technology just described. A job shop, hospital, unemployment compensation office, and newspaper all face a continuing procession of new situations, most of which can be handled by well-developed techniques for resolving such problems. For this kind of technology the typical management design introduces flexibility by the use of craftsmen and professionals, by separate scheduling units, by careful programming of workloads, by close control of work passing from one stage to the next, by prompt information on the status of work at each stage, and so on. The kind of flexibility needed is anticipated, and provisions for dealing with it are built into the system. Each person understands the limits of his discretion, and other conditions are fully planned and controlled so that reliability of the total system is not lost.

Adaptive technology calls for quite a different management design. The research laboratory, consulting firm, and hard-core unemployed training project all face unprecedented problems frequently. Here operating units become smaller, greater reliance is placed on face-to-face contacts, authority is decentralized, planning tends to focus on objectives and broad programs, leaders use participation and expect high personal involvement, control checks are less frequent and concern results rather than methods. These and other features listed in Table 5 are often called "organic," or sometimes "democratic."

This adaptive type of situation is what many human relations advocates dream about. It provides ample opportunity for employee participation and self-actualization. However, the fact that only a small portion of all work involves frequent, unprecedented problems explains why a lot of human relations training has failed to find practical application.

Of course, no company will fit exactly into any one of the technology-management design types we have described. But the examples do suggest how thoughtful analysis of technology provides a basis for designing a suitable structure.[6]

Related Influences on Design.   Although the analysis of technology in terms of the frequency and uniqueness of the problems it faces is a fruitful first step, we should not overlook other influences. For instance, technology will also be affected by complexity and the need for speed. When several interrelated variables affect the work, as in building a communications satellite, more thorough planning and control will be necessary. The need for speedy action usually has an opposite effect. Here the urgency to get prompt action reduces the opportunity for thorough planning and control; quick results now may have a higher value than somewhat improved results a month later.

Size and uncertainty should also be taken into account. A larger volume of work will support the expense of more division of labour, mechanization, and specialized staff, and greater size complicates communication and coordination. For both these reasons an increase in size tends to add to the planning and control.

Uncertainty permeates many activities. Because of an unknown environment or unpredictable responses to our own actions, we are confronted with uncertainty. If time permits we may try to reduce this uncertainty by further tests and experiments, and this will probably add staff to our organization and reduce the permissiveness in the structure. On the other hand, if such attempts to reduce uncertainty are impractical we may hire men with the best intuitive judgement we can find, get rid of our staff, and decentralize authority to the experts. This latter response to uncertainty, which is favoured by the managers of some conglomerates, creates a simple, lean management design.

Management design, then, must be developed in light of a variety of influences. However, the added dimensions just cited still fit into our basic proposal of moving first from strategy to character of work, and then from work to management design.

Compound Design With a Company

Thus far we have discussed the management design for a whole company. We have assumed that one technology and one design predominates, and for a single-function company this holds true. Most enterprises, however, are more complex. Within the corporate scope quite different activities may take place. So if we are correct in urging that management design reflect technology, the concepts should be applied to parts of a complex company as well as to the whole.

Diverse Technologies of Departments.   Consider the Greenfield Company, which has a strategy of performing the complete job of providing new, low-cost housing, from land acquisition to planting shrubbery in the play yard. Separate departments deal with architecture, real estate and finance, component manufacturer and building. The architects are the planners who conceive of types of construction, space utilization, layouts, and specifications that will create good housing at low cost; their work ranges from the highly unique and creative to the painstaking preparation of specifications for actual construction. The real estate and finance people spend a lot of their time negotiating with government agencies and other outsiders; their problems are technical and often unique. In contrast, manufacture of components (standard wall-sections, bathroom and kitchen modules, and the like) is standardized, routinized, and mechanized as much as possible. Actual building construction, necessarily, is "job order" in character, and requires the synchronization of various craftsmen.

In this one company, two of the major departments, architecture and real estate and finance, come close to the adaptive type described in the preceding section. The building department clearly displays regulated flexibility, and the component manufacturing department is moving as close to the stable type as volume permits.

A university is as heterogeneous as the Greenfield Company. Although the suitability of the same technique for teaching biology, logic, and fine arts is debatable, everyone will agree that managing a controller's office and the buildings and grounds department is in a different category. Other enterprises may not have as much diversity as the Greenfield Company or a university, but mixed activities are very common.

This diversity has serious implications for management design. Many executives who have had successful careers in one type of design believe their style of managing should be extended to all parts of the company. We often find that the managerial practices that are well suited to the dominant department of a company are automatically applied throughout. Such consistency in managerial methods does have benefits, but the astute manager will at least consider the possibility of using different administrative styles for diverse departments.

Composite Design.   Generally, when a department is both large and important to the strategy of the company it should be managed with a design suited to its own activity. This means that companies embracing diverse technologies should use several different managerial styles. The justification for this mixture of managerial styles lies, of course, in the improved performance of the respective departments.

Such diversity has its costs:

   1 *Cooperation between departments becomes increasingly difficult.* Voluntary cooperation between groups with different values, time orientations and willingness to take risks is inevitably strained.[7] Divergent management designs add to this "cultural barrier." Because the departments are so different, we may even separate them geographically—remove research laboratories from the plants, separate mills designed for long production runs from those for short runs, and so on. When management designs of departments differ sharply, special liaison staff or other formal means for coordination is often needed. Having deliberately accentuated the difference between departments, we then add a "diplomatic corps" to serve as a communication link between them.
   2 *Company-wide services drop in value.* With a composite design, the rotation of key personnel is impeded, budgeting is complicated, training programs fit only parts of the company, capital allocation procedures have to be tailored to different inputs and criteria. In other words, synergy arising from pooled services and reinforcing features of a management design is lacking for the company as a whole.
   3 *The task of central managers is complicated.* Understanding the subtleties of the several management designs and personally adjusting one's leadership style to each calls for unusual skill and sophistication. Most managers, often unconsciously, favour departments whose management design they find congenial.

   Blended Designs.   Because of the drawbacks of a composite design, and because dissimilar departments may be too small to support their own distinct management structure, we often try to blend two or more systems. Some types of designs are compatible. For instance, both the stable and the regulated-flexibility designs used as examples earlier call for a high degree of central planning, strong staff, limited permissiveness, and control at intermediate points. The chief difference lies in frequent adjustment by one system to variations in client requirements; nevertheless, these adjustments normally occur within anticipated limits and often follow rules. Consequently a combined arrangement that accommodates both technologies (for example, the component manufacturer and building construction in the Greenfield Company) can be devised. The blended design is not just what each department would do for its own purposes, but the modification can be tolerated.
   Another common arrangement is to build one strong structure and then recognize that exceptions must be made for some segments of the total operation. For instance, accounting usually gets special treatment in a research laboratory, just as members of the advertising group are accepted as "oddballs" in a manufacturing firm. If the people in the exception spots have enough missionary zeal for their specialty to withstand the normal pressure to conform with the majority, the mismatch can function reasonably well.*
   The fact that many companies need a composite, or blended, management design does not detract from the major theme of this paper. Coherence in each management design is vital whether the design be simple or complex. The

springboard for shaping each design is the character of the work to be managed; the character of the work, in turn, is a function of the company strategy. Diversity of work and the resulting complexity of designs only multiply the components that we have to take into account. The combined result, of course, is a whole mosaic of planning instruments, organizational relationships, leadership influences, and control mechanisms.[8]

A final check, after arranging the many parts, involves going back to the master strategy of the enterprise, identifying the elements that are keys to success, and then asking whether the management design promises to emphasize these elements. In thinking through the necessary refinements of a design we are always in danger of losing perspective on the major mission.

Summary

1   The interaction of two areas of management thought—master strategy and management design—offers an unusual opportunity for fruitful synthesis.

2   The "strategy and structure" approach to this synthesis should be expanded. More than organization structure is involved. Adjustments in planning, leading, and controlling, as well as organizing, are often needed to execute a new strategy; and the integration of these subprocesses into a total *management design* is vital.

3   Of course, a particular change in strategy will affect some facets of management more than others. Several facets likely to need adjustments are listed in Tables 1 to 4. Note that controllabe variables are identified within each of the subprocesses of management.

4   Matching management design and strategy directly is difficult. A useful bridge is to focus on "technology" as the intervening variable. Here "technology" is used broadly to embrace the conversion of all sorts of resources—human and financial as well as physical—into services and goods for consumers. Fortunately, we can relate technology both to *strategy* and to *manageable* tasks.

5   One characteristic of a technology is its accommodation to changes. A matrix based on frequency of changes and their novelty helps us understand three common types of technologies: stable, regulated flexibility, and adaptive. Figure 2 gives both business and non-business examples of each type. And for each type we can identify likely features of an appropriate management design. For instance:

Stable technology fits well with detailed planning, intermediate goals, centralization, close supervision, tight control.

Regulated flexibility fits well with separate planning and scheduling staff, controlled information flows, circumscribed decentralization, limited use of participative, and permissive leadership.

Adaptive technology fits well with planning by objective, decentralization, high personal involvement, control focused on results.
(For further elaboration see Table 5.)

6   A corollary of the proposition that management design should be varied so that it is *(a)* integrated within its parts, and *(b)* matched to specific company

strategy is that no single management design is ideal for all circumstances. We cannot say, for example, that management by objectives, decentralization, participative management, or tight control are desirable in all situations. Company strategy is one of the important factors determining what managerial arrangement is optimal.

7   Turning from a total company to its constituent parts, if the preferred technologies of various departments *within* the company differ sharply, their optimal management structure will also differ. Central management is then confronted with a dilemma of either having a mismatch of technology and management design in some departments or coordinating diverse management designs.

While much refinement and amplification remains to be done, the foregoing approach to synthesizing diverse management concepts has exciting possibilities: it provides a vehicle for putting content into a "total systems" treatment of management; it helps reconcile conflicting research findings and experience about particular managerial techniques; and it suggests some very practical guidance for managers who wish to implement changes in their company strategy.

REFERENCES

1   This paper has been adapted from a concluding chapter in W. H. Newman, C. E. Summer, and E. K. Warren, *The Process of Management*, 3rd ed. (Englewood Cliffs, N.J.: Prentice-Hall, 1972). Explanations of concepts treated tersely in this paper—such as strategy, planning, organizing, leading, and controlling—will be found in that source.

2   A. D. Chandler, *Strategy and Structure* (Cambridge: MIT Press, 1962).

3   For recent discussions of strategy formulation, see H. I. Ansoff, *Corporate Strategy* (New York: McGraw, 1965); R. L. Katz, *Cases and Concepts in Corporate Strategy* (Englewood Cliffs, N.J.: Prentice-Hall, 1970): E. P. Learned et al., *Business Policy: Text and Cases* (Homewood, Ill.: Irwin, 1969), text portions; and W. H. Newman and J. P. Logan, *Strategy, Policy, and Central Management* (Cincinnati: Southwestern, 1971).

4   See R. J. Mockler, "Situational Theory of Management," *Harv. Bus. Rev.* (May 1971), for references to literature stressing need to adjust management to specific situations.

5   For an expansion of this concept of technology see C[harles] Perrow, "A Framework for the Comparative Analysis of Organizations," *Amer. Sociological Rev.* (Apr. 1967). Other writers have explored the relation between technology and structure, but they have concentrated on the narrower concept of physical conversion of materials. See T[om] Burns and G. M. Stalker, *The Management of Innovation,* 2d ed. (London: Tavistock, 1966); J[oan] Woodward, *Industrial Organization* (London: Oxford University Press, 1965); D. H. Hickson, D. S. Pugh, and D. C. Pheysey, "Operations Technology and Organization Structure: An Empirical Appraisal," *Admin. Sci. Quart.* (Sept. 1969).

6   For a more generalized discussion of the impact of technology and goals on organization, see C[harles] Perrow *Organizational Analysis: A Sociological View* (Belmont, Cal.: Wadsworth Publishing, 1970), Chaps. 3 and 5.

7   See P. R. Lawrence and J. W. Lorsch, *Organization and Environment* (Boston: Harvard

Graduate School of Business Administration, 1967), for an insightful study of coordination difficulties between dissimilar activities.

8 Interrelationships between planning, organizing, leading, and controlling are examined explicitly in Chapters 15, 21, and 27 of W. H. Newman, C. E. Summer, and E. K. Warren, *The Process of Management,* 3rd ed. (Englewood Cliffs, N.J.: Prentice-Hall, 1972).

Reading 7

Organization Planning: What It Is and How to Do It Part 1—The Organizational Audit

Thomas Kubicek

Organization planning is not a new development. What *is* new is the much greater concern with it today; a concern which is almost universal.[1]

Professor Glueck, writing in *The Australian Manager,* estimated that on the average large American companies reorganize at least once every two years and the larger they are, the more frequently they are likely to reorganize.[2]

Until the last few years, long-range planning in Canada was rather scarce.[3] This situation would seem to be changing, however, judging from the reports in various news media that reorganizations have contributed the lion's share of the total income of Canadian management consultants.

WHY THE CURRENT INTEREST IN ORGANIZATION PLANNING?

Many writers[4] have eloquently portrayed for us the emerging trends, pregnant with new threats and opportunities, that have been generated inevitably by what Marshall McLuhan calls the "technological determinism" of our changing times.

"Organization Planning: What It Is and How to Do It (Part 1—The Organizational Audit)," Thomas Kubicek, *Cost and Management,* January–February 1972, pp. 33–41. Reprinted with permission.
    [1]Out of the top 100 U.S. corporations, 66 have announced in their annual reviews that they have recently reorganized according to D. Ronald Daniel of McKinsey & Company in the November/December 1966 issue of *Harvard Business Review.*
    [2]William F. Glueck, "The Achieving Organization," *The Australian Manager,* August 1968. See also quotation from Daniel in A. Toffler's *Future Shock* (New York: Random House, 1970), p. 116.
    [3]A survey conducted in the mid-sixties by the University of Western Ontario's School of Business Administration revealed a definite lack of future planning in Canadian corporations, according to *The Business Quarterly,* Summer 1966, pp. 54–62.
    [4]Among others, Kahn and Wiener in *The Year 2,000;* Peter Drucker in his *Age of Discontinuity;* and J. K. Galbraith in *The New Industrial State.*

Out of the incredible array of new trends and pressures, however, let us consider with L. Greiner only the following observations on our society today:

—computer technology has narrowed the decision span
—mass communication has heightened public awareness of consumer products
—new management knowledge and techniques have come into being
—technological discoveries have multiplied
—new world markets have opened up
—social drives for equality have intensified
—governmental demands and regulations have increased.[5]

All these observations suggest a permanent change in our private, as well as our organizational, life. If change, to paraphrase Warren Bennis, has become a permanent and accelerating factor in our lives, then adaptability to change becomes increasingly the most important single determinant of survival.[6]

Since human organizations do not adapt automatically to change, it was inevitable that they would develop a sensing and coping mechanism in formalized organizational planning that would monitor environmental changes while initiating the continued adaptation of the structure to these changes.

Although some managers continue to have reservations about planning, few doubt that this mechanism facilitates the formulation of multiple objectives, and that these objectives focus on the maximum use of available resources by exploiting opportunities in such a way as to reconcile all the conflicting short- and long-range goals of stakeholders. Since intelligent organizational planning ensures success along a predetermined course and under conditions of constant change, there is much greater (executive) interest in planning today.

SCOPE AND NATURE OF ORGANIZATIONAL PLANNING

Not very long ago, "organizational planning" was limited primarily to the manipulation of one particular department, and even that was often only at the lower organizational level. Today the target is all organizational levels, including the top managers themselves.

Although a basic distinction has always been made between the organizational planning approach and the organizational development school, there are a number of similarities between the two and people often use the terms interchangeably. There is a difference, however, not only in their primary aims but also in their strategies and timing, and the two should not be confused.

Organization planning is a strategy with a basically shorter-range time horizon. It strives to achieve effective organization by intelligently balancing the

[5]Larry E. Greiner, "Patterns of Organization Change," *Harvard Business Review,* May/June 1967, p. 120.
[6]Warren Bennis, "Democracy is Inevitable," in *Changing Organizations* (New York: McGraw-Hill, 1966), p. 17.

expectations of an enterprise, including both its internal and external environments, within the framework of rational organizational principles.

Organizational development is a continuous and longer-range effort to remove the organizational and interpersonal barriers which impede organizational and individual performance. Therefore, its primary concern is for the growth of people who, when properly developed, will themselves tend to modify the organization structure in such a way as to permit improved performance.

This paper is strictly concerned with organization planning and will be limited to the function of reorganization.

THE REASONS BEHIND IT

Organizational planning implies that, since we are thinking of changing the organizational structure, something must now be wrong with the present structure or soon will be. Why do organizations go wrong and how important are their structures for efficient and effective functioning?

According to Harvey Sherman, the Director of the Organization and Procedures Department of the Port of New York Authority, the key reasons for poor organizational performance are the following.[7]

1   Inertia or social lag (programs, key people or other conditions have changed but organization has not kept up).

2   Failure to recognize that there is an organization problem. (This might be due either to the fact that the company is getting acceptable results despite poor organization, or that a problem is perceived that is regarded as other than organizational.)

3   Over-emphasis on organization structure (preoccupation with the mechanics rather than the dynamics of organization results in moving boxes around with no relationship to basic problems).

4   Copying the other fellow's chart.

5   Unwillingness by top executives to make a needed organizational change because it will hurt a loyal long-service subordinate.

6   Organizational action taken by top executives to solve a personality problem without adequate regard for other consequences of such decisions.

7   Inadequacies in organization theory (organization principles frequently contradict each other and organization theory has not told us under what conditions each applies).

Greiner modestly reduced the manifestations of organizational decay to only three broad categories of dysfunctional managerial behavior:

1   Orientation towards the past rather than the future.

2   Insistence on organizational ritual rather than concern with challenges.

[7]Harvey Sherman, *It All Depends: A Pragmatic Approach to Organization,* (Alabama: Univ. of Alabama Press, 1966), pp. 27–28.

3 Departmental allegiances rather than loyalty to overall company objectives.

Applicable as all these factors may be, they are only symptoms of a more important underlying cause, i.e., the speedy obsolescence of organizational structures today due to increasing socio-economic and technological complexity under conditions of rapid environmental change. To this root cause, only flexibility and adaptability are the antidote.

WHO SHOULD DO IT?

There seems to be little agreement about who should be responsible for initiating, implementing and maintaining an effective organization.

Some managers believe that this is the prerogative and prime responsibility of each department manager. Others hold that in our modern organizations a separate organization planning department is not only better qualified to do this delicate job, but would also serve as an agent of permanent change. Some companies may prefer to appoint outside task forces or consultants, while others would prefer inside task forces and outside consultants.

Further difficulty and confusion arise when organization planning is not clearly defined. The content and scope of the job vary from company to company, and books and articles on organization planning are not much help in defining the task. Some discuss only single-event type reorganization, while others seem to imply a continuous planning function.

Greiner had such a single-event type reorganization in mind when he recommended that top management initiate and implement changes for reorganization. To be successful, he believes, the implementation must be done in gradual stages so that the redistribution of power takes place easily with the active participation of all management levels.[8]

The diversity of approaches to organization planning and the lack of consensus about who should be responsible for it are clearly apparent in a survey conducted among the 770 largest corporations in the United States (see table).[9] Although only six categories have been shown in the table, a further variety existed within each category with differences in the scope and nature of planning being indicated by a variety of titles.

In spite of this lack of consensus about the who, how and what of organization planning, most surveys reveal a number of similarities. In fact, there is a good indication that those companies which have introduced organization planning departments have developed a better understanding of the activities necessary to manage change. Professor Glueck, who conducted a survey among

[8]*Op. cit.*, pp. 119–128.
[9]Joseph K. Bailey, "Organization Planning: Whose Responsibility?" *Academy of Management Journal*, June 1964, pp. 95–108.

Category	Approach being used	Number of companies using approach
1	Special department for organizational matters	61
2	Responsibility for organizational matters assigned to an already existing department	98
3	Responsibility for organizational matters reserved for "top management"	182
4	Responsibility for organizational matters assigned to a specific individual or group	90
5	Responsibility for organizational matters shared by "top management" and "divisional and/or departmental management"	153
6	Responsibility for organizational matters delegated to "divisional and/or departmental management"	55
		639*

*The actual response to the survey was 82.99% (639 out of 770).

58 American companies, summarized the prime goals of their organizational departments as follows:[10]

1 Achieving efficient use of resources.
2 Adapting to internal and external changes so that the department is organized to achieve *current,* not past goals.
3 Preventing excessive or poorly planned organization change.
4 Managing conflict within the firm so that minimum amounts of organizational resources are expended on internal contests.

Organizational changes which the various agents (organizational planning departments, task forces, etc.) are attempting to bring about may range anywhere from minor structural modifications to a complete reorganization and reorientation. While sometimes only commonsense adjustments are called for, often drastic changes and sophisticated strategies are necessary.

Since few companies will escape such drastic changes unscathed, correct timing is very important. Many companies have learned the hard way that it is not easy to judge the best time to act. Mr. Ralph Cordiner "testifies that he launched his basic reorganization of General Electric Company only when he felt confident

[10]*Op. cit.*

of three years of high business activity because, in his opinion, the company could not have absorbed all the internal re-adjustments during a period of declining volume and profits."[11]

In spite of the risk involved, however, organizational change is inevitable in our modern world. Since it is inevitable, how do we plan for it successfully?

ACTIVITIES INVOLVED IN ORGANIZATION PLANNING

What steps and priorities must organization planners follow when faced with a reorganization?

Since the environment and objectives of each organization are different, there can be no uniform solutions to organization problems. However, a certain uniformity in the approach to reorganization may be desirable and even essential to success.

The approach in this paper will include the following steps:

I   Organizational audit: analyzing "what is"
II Designing the structure and implementing the "good fit."

I Organizational Audit: Analyzing "What Is"

Every organization should periodically review its structure to ascertain the most effective method of satisfying the needs of every stakeholder.

To this end, the planner must first determine *where he is* before any improvement takes place.

While the purpose of the following model (Exhibit 1) is to help us better visualize the key variables which must be properly balanced if the organization structure is to resemble a "good fit," it may also serve as a guide to indicate those key areas which must be examined if we are to determine the whats, whens and hows of "what is."

In accordance with our model, three dimensions of organization will have to be examined if we want to determine properly where we are now and where we should be going in the future. These dimensions are:

a   The enterprise: its capacity and expectations
b   The individual: his potential and expectations
c   The environment: its constraints and challenges.

a   The Enterprise: Its Capacity and Expectations

i   The Purpose of the Enterprise

Not too long ago, companies were able to remain for years in the same trade. They were proud of their matured expertise in their particular line of business. Today, this is neither possible nor desirable.

[11]William H. Newman, "Shaping the Master Strategy of Your Firm," *California Management Review*, Spring 1967, p. 86.

Exhibit 1 The key variables to be considered for a "good fit" in designing organization structure.

A good example of the need for changing organizational purpose is provided by the world-wide Singer Company of New York. From its original role as a sewing machine and vacuum cleaner manufacturer, it has been reorganized into five divisions including consumer products, defence and space systems, office equipment, education and training, and industrial products. It is now "entering its second century with a strength greater than ever."[12]

Many other examples might be cited. The Bell Telephone Company of Canada has changed from a "telephone" company to a "communications" specialist, thus becoming Bell Canada. The Canadian Pacific Railway Company has changed from a "railway" to a "transportation" organization and become Canadian Pacific, and so on.

Thus, any company whose main concern is to remain viable and successful must continually determine "who are we and what is our mission?" It must not hesitate to *drop its traditional line* if an objective appraisal of environmental trends indicates that this is necessary.

The following questions will be useful in determining the strengths and weaknesses inherent in our present business purposes:[13]

1 What business are we in?
- what is our product? our service?
- are we doing the right thing?
- are we neglecting export opportunities?
- what business should we be in?
2 Who is our customer?
- are we aiming our products at wrong customers?

---

[12]See the report on Singer's success in *The Monetary Times,* March 1970; also *Dun's Review,* January 1969, p. 28

[13]This section is based on ideas formulated by P. F. Drucker, *Managing for Results* (New York: Harper and Row Publishers, 1964).

3   Who is our competitor?
• how competent is he?
4   What are our weaknesses?
• are we assigning resources to "managerial egos"?
• are we allocating high priority resources to "yesterday's breadwinners"?
• are we marketing products consumers do not want?
5   What are the most urgent tasks for the next five years?
• what results are desired?
• what decisions must be made and in which areas?
6   Are the purposes of our organization known to all our employees so that
they might relate their roles in the enterprise to the advancement of such
purposes?

ii   Organizational Objectives

While only top management must determine the purpose of the enterprise,
organizational objectives must be set for every area in which performance
directly and vitally affects the survival and well-being of the enterprise. For it is
company objectives that help to establish management priorities and identify key
departments and activities. If such key activities are not properly determined,
managerial efforts and company resources are easily dissipated. To avoid such a
disaster, one of Europe's major chemical manufacturers, the Solvay Company, is
using the following four-fold approach:[14]

1.   Objectives relating to the nature of the business, i.e.:

—grand design   To be the leading company in a particular business
—mission   i.e., "communications" or "transportation," etc.
—short-range plan   Open a new branch in Quebec City
—long-range plan   Five-year targets in volume, earnings, share of markets, etc.

2.   Objectives based on "Key Result Areas":[15]

—profitability
—market standing
—innovation
—productivity
—physical and   i.e., "We want a 15% return on total funds invested."
financial resources   (Similar statements would have to be made in all the
—manager performance   other seven "key result areas.")
and development
—worker performance
and attitude
—public responsibility

3.   Objectives based on internal constraints and challenges, i.e.:

—capitalize on company-owned technical potential (continue research and development as a key activity)

[14]R. W. Knoepfel, "Establishing Corporate Objectives at Solvay," *Long-Range Planning,* June
1970, p. 14.
[15]Based on Drucker, *The Practice of Management* (New York: Harper and Row, 1954), pp.
62–84.

—avoid style businesses with seasonal obsolescence
4.   Objectives based on external constraints and challenges, i.e.:
—reputation
—capitalize on the fact that younger people are better educated, availability of more leisure time.

Organizational objectives represent not only ends towards which all organizational actions at all levels should be directed, but they also represent standards against which all expected preformances should be measured. They, therefore, should be realistic targets. They must also be concrete, contained within a definite time dimension, and future-oriented. All in all, they must be operational.

What is operational today, however, may not be operational tomorrow. A rapidly changing environment can cause even the best operational objectives to lose their relevance. Constant periodic reviews are therefore necessary. For this purpose, the following questions may be helpful:

1   Have organizational objectives been written out?
2   Are they consistent with the purpose of the business?
3   Have they been stated in terms of results (dollars, units, time periods)?
4   Do employees understand the company objectives? Policies? Programs?
5   Has it been clearly defined what (why and when?) each segment of the enterprise should do to achieve its objectives?
6   Have the company objectives been integrated vertically, horizontally, and laterally within a perfectly harmonized hierarchy?
7   What data do managers study before establishing objectives?
   •   are departmental objectives merely an extension of past operations?
   •   are they developed in relation to long-range company goals?
   •   are they developed with proper regard to resources, facilities, and time available?
8   Are comparisons of the "actual" with "projected" results made periodically (monthly-quarterly)?
   •   are reviews of forecasts possible?
9   Are problems being anticipated before they become critical?
   •   is the philosophy "we will cross the bridge when we come to it" often used?
   •   are immediate remedial actions taken as soon as the need may arise?
10   If strategic objectives cannot be reached satisfactorily, is this because of:
   •   insufficient personnel?
   •   lack of trained personnel?
   •   insufficient capital?
   •   other reasons?
11   Are performance reviews "results-oriented" and are they related to company (departmental) objectives?

- are they "trait-oriented"?
- are there any performance appraisals at all?

iii The Capacity of the Enterprise for Effective Action

In relation to its purpose and objectives, how well does the enterprise grasp its opportunities, handle its threats, and solve its problems? Does the company philosophy systematically focus on opportunities and is its strategy based on organizational strength? What constraints in the various functional areas make this difficult? The following questions should help in examining strengths and weaknesses in the key functional areas of the enterprise.

Corporate Philosophy and Strategy

1 Have our structure and strategy been developed around the style and philosophy of our chief executive?
2 Is the commitment to purpose and objectives "real" or merely "lip service"?
3 Are expectations of all stakeholders well-monitored and the satisfaction of their needs included in our corporate strategy?
4 Is the central focus of our corporate strategies on maximizing opportunities through systematic use of available resources?
5 Does this approach permit us to develop an organizational climate in which people are allowed to grow?
6 Are both economic and social needs considered in the company policies? Are they well-balanced?

Financial Capacity

1 How does our R.O.I. compare with the industry's average?
2 Will cash generated from operations in the next five years be sufficient to meet our fixed and operating capital requirements?

Marketing Capacity

1 Are our corporate strategies flexible enough to fit the changing market?
2 Is our share of the market increasing or decreasing?
3 Are we selling in all markets available?
4 Are we highly dependent on just a few customers?
5 Are all of our customers equally profitable?
6 Do we have an incidence of costly seasonal inactivity?
7 Who will be our future customers?
- what kind of service must they have?
- what channels of distribution will they need?
8 How well do we compare with our competitors in their development of: new products, new markets, new strategies, new services?

Production Capacity

1   Are our plant operations as efficient as those of our competitors, or do we have any problems in this area because of
- plant location?
- lack of skilled labor?
- obsolete equipment and production processes?
- inefficient quality control?
- other reasons?

2   What products will we be selling in the future?

3   What facilities and what degree of automation will be needed?

4   How many and what kinds of people will be needed?

5   Are our resources of raw materials guaranteed for the next five (ten) years?

Information Systems' Capacity

1   Has it been recognized throughout the organization that the fullness and timeliness of relevant information is one of the key prerequisites of effective organization structure?

2   Has information become an end rather than a means to an end?

3   Do we know what information is needed?
- in what form? where? when?

4   Is our information system adequate?
- useful for planning (with complete financial and nonfinancial data)?
- useful for control (coming in the shortest way and in the most complete manner, thus avoiding bottlenecks)?

5   Do we know where our profits come from?
- which departments? which products? which areas?

6   How much communication is allowed to affect interfunctional activities?

iv   The Capacity of the Structure for a "Good Fit"

Depending on the different philosophies of various schools of thought, there are a number of ways to approach the analysis of the organizational structure. The perennial question is "which one to choose?" A typical weakness of the various approaches is that none, except the classical theory, would suit all situations. In organizational analysis, we need a technique which is simple and has as much general application as possible. Drucker's "three-way analysis" may well be suitable. This consist of: an activities analysis, a decision analysis, and a relations analysis.[16]

To explore these three areas, the following questions might prove a useful guide.

[16]*Ibid.*, pp. 193–201.

Activities Analysis

1   What work, related to purpose, must be performed?
2   Does the structure permit work not related to the purpose?
3   Do managers have enough time for planning and reviewing?
4   Do we know in which areas we under-perform and why?
5   Who is accountable for results?
6   Of our managers, who is expendable and who is indispensable and why?
7   Are our managers permitted to function in a style in which they feel comfortable?
8   Is there a lack of integration of organizational activities? Why?

Decision Analysis

1   Has everyone been given sufficient information and authority to enable him to discharge his responsibilities?
- does the whole firm (the department) depend on one man?
- who in the organization (department) can replace him?
- is decision-making located at lowest possible levels?

2   What kind of decisions would be needed to achieve our purpose most efficiently?
- where in the organization should such decisions be made?

4   Which are the main profit centres and which are the important cost centres?
- what contributions must they make?

Relations Analysis

1   What contributions to the organizational purpose must every manager make?
- with whom is he to work?
- on what contributions from other managers must he rely?
- are there any functional barriers to the proper integration of major organizational units?

2   What is the relationship of organizational members to staff specialists?
- is there duplication of effort?
- is there duplication of resources?
- are some functional departments like "islands," with the communication bridges to others missing?

3   Are there many auxiliary positions, e.g., assistants, coordinators, etc.?
4   Are relationships between divisional managers and head office consistent with the system design?
5   Does everyone know who his immediate boss is?
6   Does the whole system depend on:
- command? negotiation?

Finally, a few questions may indicate the degree to which the integration of the various sections within the whole occurs:

1 Does the organizational structure reflect the structure of the objectives and are activities, decisions, and relationships assigned around the work flow?
2 Is the conceptual organization in harmony with the actual organizational processes?
3 Which organizational principles are being constantly violated?
4 What type of structure do we need?
• how many levels?
• how wide the span of control?

b The Individual: His Potential and Expectations

i What Are the Employees Like?

1 What is their age profile?
• is there an imbalance?
2 What special skills have they?
3 If the individual is not contributing fully to the organization, is it because:
• people are placed in wrong organizational units?
• a proper organizational climate is missing?
4 Are employees committed to company objectives?
• is there widespread apathy?
5 What special skills will we need for the success of future operations?
• how many people are needed and when?
• how many people are presently capable of new responsibilities?
• do we have enough managers able to manage change?
• how many new managers will be needed in the next five years?
6 What can be done to bridge the gap between what we need and what we have?

ii The Organization's Expectations of the Employees

1 Are there written statements of objectives and have they been communicated to and understood by the employees?
2 Are all responsibilities and authority clearly defined in writing?
3 Have all individuals been delegated sufficient authority to enable them to carry out their assigned responsibilities?
4 Does the organizational climate enhance, or deter, job satisfaction?
• what is the company philosophy about its individual and social responsibilities?
• are there many incidents of conflict between individual expectations and managerial philosophy?

5   Are awareness and understanding of human relationship problems actively encouraged throughout the organization?

6   Do personnel policies stimulate (or inhibit) the best performance on the job?

- are there any growth incentives?
- are there ample opportunities for advancement and promotion?
- what is the rate of turnover? where? how much absenteeism is there?

7   Is there a systematic and logical wage and salary plan?

8   Are existing resources always considered in staffing?

- Have sound methods for recruiting, selecting and training been developed and used?

9   Is there a general policy that managers take an active interest in the development of their subordinates?

- what help, advice, and training facilities are available?

10   Has training been integrated with the enterprise's long-range goals through a systematic evaluation of data about the organization and its success or failure in achieving organizational objectives?

iii   The Employees' Expectations of the Organization

1   Has the control function been designed to guarantee effective achievement of organizational goals, or to make sure people are doing what they are told to do?

2   Are performance and progress measured through established standards of quality, time, utility, cost, etc.?

3   Is it company policy to analyze deviations from standards as close to the point of performance as possible to encourage immediate corrective action?

4   Are all managers accountable for results?

5   Are candidates for management positions identified early in their careers, or only when they are needed to fill a vacant position?

6   Is there a noticeable preference for conformists who often can offer only immediate abilities despite their willingness to "follow the rules"?

7   Have suggestions for improvement been encouraged from employees?

- what is the incidence of suggestions generated? suggestions used?

c   The Environment: Its Constraints and Expectations

The analysis here should consider not only present and potential strengths and weaknesses in the internal environment, but also trends in the external environment that could affect the development of the company.

Exhibits 2 and 3 outline some of these considerations in the internal and external environments.

COMPLETING THE ORGANIZATIONAL AUDIT

The final stage in the organizational audit will be to analyze the answers to all these questions. This is a two-step procedure.

Exhibit 2   Fitting the Organization to the Internal Environment

Technical systems

1 *Marketing Subsystems*
   a) The nature of our products;
   b) innovative ability (in products, in service);
   c) promotional strategies;
   d) research and intelligence system;
   e) adequacy of customer service;
   f) delivery performance.

2 *Production Subsystem*
   a) The kind (old-new) and location of plant;
   b) productivity and output;
   c) methods and processes;
   d) patents and R & D;
   e) quality and cost levels;
   f) level of performance;
   g) useful life and existing products and plant.

3 *Financial Subsystem*
   a) Financial position;
   b) evidence of profitability: return on investment and cash-flow generated by profits;
   c) bank credit;
   d) potential for obtaining outside funds;
   e) need and capacity for growth;
   f) fully-owned, or a subsidiary?

4 *Management Process (Planning, Controlling, etc.) Subsystem*
   a) Objectives and plans (short and long-range);
   b) individual and organizational information systems: financial, non-financial, past and future;
   c) network of procedures, policies, strategies;
   d) methods of measuring performance;
   e) standards for measuring results.

Social systems

1 *Climate for Human Resources Utilization*
   a) Practices and policies in selecting, hiring, training and retirement;
   b) leadership styles: enforcing direction, or enlisting cooperation;
   c) people assumptions and management philosophy;
   d) environment for accomplishing change;
   e) degree of mobility;
   f) rewards from work: intrinsic-extrinsic;
   g) methods of performance appraisal and promotion;
   h) group norms and work processes;
   i) managerial tensions and status anxiety;
   j) management-labor relations;
   k) codes of ethics;
   l) pressure group systems and sources of power;
   m) patterns of supervisory behavior.

2 *Inventory for Skills and Attitudes*
   i. Brought from external environment:
   a) age, education, skills, experience;
   b) culturally learned behavior: attitudes, needs, expectations, values, achievement orientation, language.
   ii. Developed by the organization:
   a) skills: technical, inter-personal and work-team effectiveness;
   b) attitudes: sense of achievement, role perception, adaptability to change, orientation towards technological advance and innovation.

Exhibit 3   Fitting the Organization to the External Environment

1   *Economic Trends*
   a) Availability of investment capital: present-future;
   b) return on investment: steady, declining;
   c) price levels-deferred price increases;
   d) rising labor costs;
   e) rising taxes;
   f) desirable level of productivity vs. the limits to potential markets;
   g) credit system: monetary and fiscal policies;
   h) degree of market freedom:
   i) labor force: skilled-unskilled;
   j) unions: their expectations and needs;
   k) changes in income groups;
   l) changes in spending habits.

2   *Social Trends—Sociological Changes*
   a) Population growth and changes: age, education, more older people, fewer children, trend to urban centres, suburbia;
   b) consumer expectations: cost, quality, kind;
   c) consumerism: caveat emptor, credat emptor;
   d) education: quality, availability, free access;
   e) changing philosophy of life: leisure, life employment, achievement, dependence;
   f) role of religion: weakening, potential;
   g) changing family life:
   h) changes in social values: protestant ethics, social ethics, civil disobedience, permissiveness, prevalence of irresponsibility;
   i) unions: labor-management peace, militarism, violence;
   j) public resentment of pollution;
   k) ethnic factors and culture.

3   *Political Trends—The Role of Government*
   a) Political democracy—representative government;
   b) legal climate: legally enforceable contracts;
   c) taxes: favorable-unfavorable;
   d) government expectations and needs;
   e) government controls and regulations;
   f) other regulatory bodies;
   g) government stability and instability;
   h) degree of civil disobedience;
   i) impact of political ideologies;
   j) likelihood of political shifts: revolution, separatism;
   k) security of investment;
   l) legality vs. legitimacy.

4   *Technological Trends—New Knowledge*
   a) Increased R & D and new knowledge;
   b) scientific and technical information;
   c) rate of technical innovation in processes, products;
   d) rate of obsolescence of products, processes, machinery, skills, knowledge;
   e) degree of use of technical talent;
   f) automation;
   g) need for synthetic materials.

5   *The Market and Its Competitive Trends*
   a) The market: size, composition, location, trends: who is our customer?
   b) share of market: ours? competitors'? competition: Canadian? foreign? who IS our competitor?
   c) new competitive strategies;
   d) new end uses for company's products;
   e) availability of information on foreign markets, foreign labor and transportation costs;
   f) competence of competition;
   g) goodwill and community standing.

First, the information is analyzed strictly from the viewpoint of the company's functional adequacy in each particular micro-area: i.e., Should the emerging trends point out that an exceptional opportunity exists for marketing an entirely new type of product, does the company have the proper mix of knowledge and facilities to produce it? Does it have the right distribution channels to market it? Are there sufficient funds to finance it?

Secondly, the effective overall potential of the firm to achieve objectives in the area of its newly-planned purpose must be clearly determined: i.e., Are the emerging opportunities in the external environment consistent with the overall corporate purpose and are the goals being derived from this purpose?

If a serious gap results from the matching of the firm's strengths and weaknesses with the environmental threats and opportunities, and the various alternative strategies (and technologies) with the alternative goals (and results), then ways and means must be sought to bridge this gap. Only when a reasonable harmony between the alternative solutions and acceptable goals is achieved, may the designing of the "good fit" of the organization structure begin. This will be described in the second part of this article to be published in the next issue of this journal.

Reading 8

Organization Planning:
What It Is and How to Do It
Part 2—Designing the "Good Fit"

Thomas Kubicek

The first part of this article outlined an approach to the organizational audit, culminating in an analysis of the firm's strengths and weaknesses in relation to the environmental opportunities and threats. This analysis should be approached from two viewpoints:

1 The firm's functional capacity to take advantage of an emerging opportunity in the environment.
2 The effective overall potential of the firm to achieve objectives in the area of its planned purpose.

Ways and means must be found to bridge any serious gaps resulting from a matching of the firm's strengths and weaknesses with the environmental threats and opportunities, and the various alternative strategies (and technologies) with the alternative goals (and results). Only when a reasonable harmony between the alternative solutions and acceptable goals is achieved, may the designing of the "good fit" of the organization structure begin (see Exhibit 1).

"Organization Planning: What It Is and How to Do It (Part 2—Designing the "Good Fit")," Thomas Kubicek, *Cost and Management*, March–April, 1972, pp. 33–42.

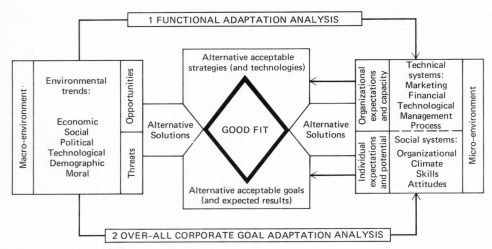

Exhibit 1 Analysis of the results of the organizational audit.

II Designing the Ideal Structure and Implementing the "Good Fit"

During this process it will be necessary to identify opportunities and threats existing in the external and internal environment. The mere recognition of opportunities is not enough, however; expected results must be balanced with appropriate and available means. After determining which of the old objectives must be rejected, we must re-allocate company resources to those new strategies, tasks and technologies that will optimize the attainment of new goals.

The redeployment of resources from old to new priorities will require a redistribution of power and a changing of the communication channels. Exhibit 2 shows how the strategy of changing the focus from old opportunities (which are becoming sterile) to new goals (necessary for survival) results in a changed emphasis (new power centres) that will substantially affect the structure of the whole enterprise. For effective organization must always reflect the structure of new objectives.

a What Determines the Most Effective Organization Structure?

Although, according to Dale,[1] the actual design of the "ideal" is not as difficult as the implementation, it is still necessary to utilize the best thinking of theoreticians and the sound experience of practitioners. Thus, we should ask ourselves: "What is it that determines different kinds of organizational structures in the light of existing modern organization theory and practice?" What guidelines exist, and how will they help the practitioner do a good job?

Among other classifications in organization theory, three broad approaches

---

[1]Ernest Dale, *The Great Organizers* (New York: McGraw-Hill Book Co. Inc., 1960), p. 137.

are usually mentioned in connection with designing an ideal structure:

1   classical, or traditional approach
2   neo-classical, or participative approach
3   socio-technical systems approach.

Although none of them should be applied uncritically, they all have something to contribute.

The simplest and most often used is the classical approach. It is strictly organization-oriented. It emphasizes structuring the organization around the task on a man-to-man relationship in accordance with organizational principles which may be universally applied. Although today this school represents a range of slightly differing theories rather than one rigidly defined theory, proponents of the other two schools often criticize its principles as "obvious and unscientific over-simplifications." Despite the undeniable advances in management theory, however, it cannot be said that anyone has yet produced a substitute as workable or as satisfactory to the needs of the practical manager.

The participative approach, which is a man-oriented extension of the classical model, is equally simple in its application. An often-quoted example is Likert's integrated organization based on the overlapping group structure. Its principles are as follows:[2]

a   Principle of supportive relationships (subordinate must see the situation as contributing to his sense of personal worth),
b   The use of group decision-making and group supervision,
c   The use of high performance goals and aspirations (which provide a high integration of organizational and personal goals).

While this method ensures three-way communication, it also permits each supervisor to influence his boss. By making the goals of individuals within the organization compatible, it strengthens the bonds of organization. However, Likert's approach (and that of other human relationists) also suffers from over-simplification, i.e.:

•   Greater morale is not necessarily followed by greater productivity.
•   The cost of time spent on committees often outweighs the benefits of participation.
•   Participation may not always give rise to the best decisions.
•   The tyranny of the group often replaces that of the autocracy.
•   Participative style does not work equally well with all people and in all situations.
•   In some situations the "get-tough" management policy is the best answer to increased productivity.

[2]For a detailed outline of this theory, see R. Likert, *New Patterns of Management* (Toronto: McGraw-Hill Book Co. Inc., 1961).

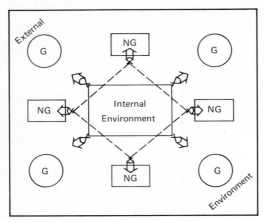

G   Yesterday's goals

NG   New–future goals

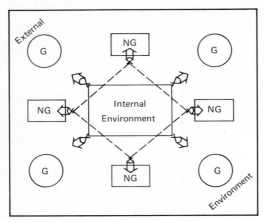 Vectors of power (new and old)

– – – –   New structure

————   Old structure

Note: The Internal Environment which exists within the
boundaries of the enterprise's structure represents qualitative,
rather than quantitative factors.

Exhibit 2   The effect of changed goals
(and strategy) on structure.

Recent behaviorist research has already generated enough proof that the problems of organizational life run much deeper than some of the prescriptions of the human relationists would imply. There is a difference between forced participation and true participation. A change in values is needed before a true participation would evolve naturally from the attitudes of managers. For this reason, the modern systems approach emphasizes changing people first, rather than structures. This school, like the traditional one, is also based on universally applicable principles.

That there are fundamental truths which are universally applicable was first challenged by Chester Barnard as early as 1938.[3] He postulated that the important situational variables that determine the actual outcome of managerial decisions are:

- the place where the work is done
- the time at which the work is done
- the persons with whom work is done
- the things upon which work is done
- the method or process by which work is done.

[3]Chester Barnard, *The Functions of the Executive* (Cambridge, Mass.: Harvard University Press, 1938), pp. 128–129.

Following Barnard's example, many authors defined their own versions of situational variables in a complex socio-technical environment. In fact, this approach encompasses so many definitions and such a vast territory that it may mean different things to different people. While the classical and participative approaches suffer from over-simplified assumptions about the nature of human beings and their environment, the systems approach suffers because it is too complex to be easily understood and used by practical managers.

For example, to mention only the few recent studies which came out with situational variables, Joan Woodward maintained that the technology and system of production are directly related to the organizational structure. Accordingly, if we knew what specific technical change is planned, we could easily predict what the requirements of the organizational structure would be. We could also assess the appropriateness of the existing organizational structure and its ability to achieve objectives in its particular technological field.[4]

Woodward's concept of the socio-technical system (somewhat modified) and the size of the firm (as a key factor in place of technology) was introduced by Professor David Hickson and his colleagues. They concluded that, although the organization of both small and large firms is affected by technology, the organizational structure of the larger firm is "buffered from technology itself" by specialist departments and standard procedures. Consequently, at the head office level of larger organizations, the hierarchical structure is similar and the management principles have a general application.[5]

Closely related to Woodward's "technology" and Hickson's "size" were the "organic" and "mechanistic" organization patterns introduced by T. Burns and G. M. Stalker. In stable industries, effective organizations were those patterned on a so-called "mechanistic model" which is performance (routine) oriented with a vertical command-type hierarchy. In dynamic industries, on the other hand, effective organizations were the problem-solving oriented "organic systems." These are characterized by loose job descriptions and methods, and by procedures continually being redefined by both the vertical and horizontal interactions of all participants in the common task. Vertical command is replaced by lateral consultation. In such complex situations, the solutions to organizational problems cannot be delegated to a number of specialists with a clearly defined hierarchy as is done in the "mechanistic model" under stable conditions.[6]

In their empirical study of ten organizations (plastics, consumer foods and standardized containers), Lawrence and Lorsch focused on the key problem of this school: "How do we tailor the organization to its complex environment and

---

[4]For more details of Joan Woodward's research, refer to her *Management of Technology* (London: HMSO, 1958), or to its expanded version under the title of *Industrial Organization* (London: Oxford University Press, 1965).

[5]For details of the findings of the Birmingham research conducted by Derek Pugh, David Hickson, C. R. Hinings and C. Turner, see "Dimensions of Organizational Structure," *Administrative Science Quarterly*, June 1968, pp. 65–105.

[6]The influence of technical change on organization structure is well presented in a classical treatise by T. Burns and G. M. Stalker, *The Management of Innovation* (London: Tavistock, 1961).

the complex needs of its members?" Instead of attempting to find the best way to organize, they sought a conceptual framework which would have less chance of missing important factors when analyzing the structural design of organizations than other, simpler approaches have.[7] Central to their model are the environmental requirements for differentiation and integration.[8]

Since each departmental unit is working in its own unique environment; (marketing, scientific, techno-economic, manufacturing), it develops its own particular structural pattern determined by its tasks and its members' predispositions. Consequently, for effective functioning, a particular pattern of differentiation and integration among various units is a must. If we want to design an organizational structure which will fit the environment and its members' needs, the following two rules should be observed:

a   Group those units which have similar orientation and tasks. They will reinforce each other's need for differentiation.
b   Group those units which require low differentiation and tight integration. In this way the co-ordinating task of the manager will be simplified.

How do we ensure the necessary integration of intergroup efforts? Lawrence and Lorsch mention two ways:

a   by the use of the basic integrative mechanism—management hierarchy where low differentiation exists.
b   by special integrative mechanisms—cross-functional teams, integrative departments, etc.—where more differentiation and tighter integration are required.

While the preceding theories differ considerably in their approach, there is no basic contradiction in their findings. In fact, each tends to reinforce the other.

Although many important advances have been made, an adequate conceptual framework is still missing. One useful generalization is "The Law of the Situation" (a term first used by Mary Parker Follett) or the "socio-technical system." It introduces a number of variables into a complex environment, inter-related in many complex ways. Its biggest weakness is that the onus is on the manager to properly diagnose the environmental variables before he applies the proper techniques. While such a vast territory may daunt the sensitive organizational planner, it would also reinforce his desire for a ready-made guide to help

[7]P. R. Lawrence and J. W. Lorsch, *Organization and Environment: Managing Differentiation and Integration* (Boston: Division of Research, Harvard Graduate School of Business Administration, 1967).

[8]*Differentiation:* defined as "the difference in cognitive and emotional orientation among managers in different functional departments, and the difference in formal structure among these departments." *Integration:* defined as "the quality of collaboration that exists among departments that are required by the environment to achieve unity of effort." *Ibid.*

answer his perennial question: "What determines the most effective organizational structure in my particular and pressing situation?"

Another group of systems-oriented people had found at least a partial answer to this question in the matrix organization which, some claim, is the first step towards industrial humanism. Today a number of American companies, such as American Cyanamid, Caterpillar Tractor and National Cash Register, are experimenting with this form of organization which originally developed from Taylor's "Functional Foremanship." In Canada, too, some companies are involved with the matrix structure, notably Northern Electric's former Advance Devices Center (ADC) in Ottawa, now the independent Micro Systems International.

Is matrix the answer to an organizational planner's prayer for a most effective structure?

Some say that if you "spell out, in writing, in advance, every possible detail of a matrix project," that is, if you determine "who does what, when and for whom," it will work. But if agreement is only verbal, "the matrix just won't work," says Peter Duffy, the manager of program methodology at Sylvania's Electronic Systems group. On the other hand, Prudential's Dustin stresses that the difference between success and failure with the matrix lies in the equilibrium of power between the project co-ordinators and the functional specialists. Where the technical aspect was a key variable (as in defence industries), the matrix system worked. But many have concurred that "Things are very different when it has to turn in a profit."[9]

Obviously the matrix structure is not the answer to our problem either. Except for the need to diagnose carefully the environmental variables and to recognize that each situation, being unique, dictates a different strategy and action, no common steps or priorities have been identified. Failing such operational integration of recent findings, the practitioner is still forced time and again to reach back to the traditional organizational principles as the only readily available guide to solving everyday problems.

b The Process of Developing a "Good Fit"

Having defined an organizational purpose which will open doors to new and challenging opportunities and permit the setting up of objectives directed toward the improvement of present and future performance, management must now define the results which must be obtained when the goals have been reached.

When this has been done, such information must be communicated to all organizational levels for as wide an acceptance as possible. One cannot expect the new organization to perform well unless every member knows what is expected and when and why. A company newsletter is often used to spell out the corporate

[9]Based on information in John Pernham's "Matrix Management: A tough game to play," *Dun's Review*, August 1970, pp. 31–34.

objectives and the reasons behind them. Whether such means will be sufficient to ensure the self-motivated commitment of employees to organizational goals remains a critically important question, however, and one which management must answer for itself before proceeding.

Once the objectives have become known and accepted as desirable, the following three routine steps will produce the "IDEAL" design:

- Specify clearly all activities necessary to achieve the required results;
- Group these activities around the technologies involved in related major organizational functions (i.e., production, sales, finance, engineering, R&D);
- Integrate all functions into a basic system and draw up an "ideal" organization chart.

Ernest Dale, an ardent critic of traditional principles, found that during the process of building the "ideal," successful companies often used the traditional organizational principles as guides. He lists nine principles against which (at the time of his survey) companies were screening their "ideal" designs.[10] If we take into consideration correspondingly applicable situational modifications derived from recent behavioral knowledge, such principles can still be regarded as useful guides for coping with modern organizational problems. Consequently, it is possible to validate the "Good Fit" of the "Ideal" against the classical principles modified when necessary by newer findings under either the participative, or the systems, caption (Exhibit 3).

Different alternatives always complicate the situation since they suggest either a structural or a strategic modification, or both. By carefully weighing the alternatives against each other, either the integration of both, or the one which is most appropriate to the situation and the goal, should be adopted. However, if the resulting construct is still seriously at odds with the thus modified organizational principles, its justification should be further re-examined. Where weaknesses cannot be eliminated, the design should be seriously reconsidered. When no weaknesses exist, we have a "Good Fit,"[11]

c The Process of Implementing the "Good Fit"

The reorganization process, especially in larger companies, is a massive task. Successful implementation therefore takes some time. Since all organizations differ from each other, the process of implementation will not be uniform either. Its nature will depend on the particular situation, on the one hand, and on the strategy of the planner, on the other.

For example, Greiner's model of reorganization[12] depicts a process which is triggered by an outside "stimulus" at the top of the power structure where it

---

[10]*Op. cit.*

[11]For an interesting discussion of this process, see D. R. Daniel's article "Reorganizing for Results" in the November/December 1966 issue of *Harvard Business Review,* pp. 96–104.

[12]Larry E. Greiner, "Patterns of Organization Change," *Harvard Business Review,* May/June 1967, p. 124.

Exhibit 3   A Guide to Designing an "Ideal" Organization

Principles on which traditional organizations have been built	Classical approach to an "ideal" organization	Behavioral approach to an "ideal" organization	Systems approach to an "ideal" organization
1 Effectiveness:	Measure effectiveness of each function by comparing its contribution to company revenue. The effectiveness of personnel resources and physical facilities could be measured by the "input-to-output" ratio (i.e., effectiveness in use of resources has increased if there is an increase in units produced without a corresponding increase in man-hours worked). Where applicable, consider also social costs vs. social revenue. (In general, effectiveness means doing the right things.)	Behavioral scientists have a different interpretation of effectiveness. Provision must be made for effective integration of personal growth goals with organizational growth goals. According to Likert, this could be facilitated by providing opportunity to participate in the decision-making process (i.e., introduce Management by Objectives).	Since effectiveness is measured in terms of attainment of overall goals of the total system, the effectiveness of any subsystem is measured by its contribution to the overall objectives. The overall goals, however, may still be measured in terms of input/output, R.O.I., or other means. Since systems are based on group performance, individual performance can be judged only within the group (does he facilitate, or slow down the work of others?). Effectiveness results from cooperation rather than competition among the functional subsystems. This ensures better integration and coordination of all information flows and thereby an effective use of all resources (i.e., more effective use of time and elimination of repetitive functions result in higher productivity).

Exhibit 3 (continued)

Principles on which traditional organizations have been built	Classical approach to an "ideal" organization	Behavioral approach to an "ideal" organization	Systems approach to an "ideal" organization
2 Efficiency:	Determine to what degree a company fulfils its economic objectives (i.e., speed, accuracy, quality and cost). Since there are no uniform standards for measurement, the interpretation of this principle varies with different people (at different organizational levels) and results in a somewhat vague criterion. (Efficiency means doing things right. It is a mechanical process.)	To a behavioral scientist, efficiency means a number of things: i.e., degree of satisfaction achieved in different structures; degree of creativity of various work-groups; degree of adaptability to change. An ideal organization should have a built-in provision to facilitate the achievement of such individual, group and organizational objectives. In fact there is more emphasis on productivity than efficiency. (Efficiency is considered as a human process.)	The whole purpose of the systems approach is to increase efficiency which is based on the idea of "one best way" that would integrate all parts. Every dollar spent is intended to contribute to the ultimate objectives of the total system. Thus organizations must be built up from an analysis of information needs and communication networks since efficiency depends on the accuracy of information available. Great efficiency results from pre-programmed solutions at the operational level. The non-programmed tasks are attended to by the planning level. Each subsystem is designed to do a particular task and when the task is completed, the subsystem is disbanded.

(The inefficiency of the traditional structure often results from the fact that inertia allows organization units to become a permanent fixture.) |

work into the smallest number of dissimilar functions. Resulting units or departments should be established as separate entities whose nature and number are determined by their relative contribution to the purpose of the enterprise. Basic criteria are: economic (scale) and technical efficiency. Departmentation by product, territory, customer, process, function is widely used. The resulting structure is the sub-grouping of individuals around specialization which permits control and coordination. (This must be done cautiously to prevent each department running its own affairs for its own benefits.)

social need of the individual for membership in a cohesive group. Also an intrinsic motivation built into the task (i.e., job enrichment, bottom-up management, junior boards) should be considered. A goal-oriented relationship between the superior and subordinate could be an answer to this problem. A structure which permits participation in decision-making may alleviate the inherent weaknesses of the traditional model which often results in centres of power and jealously guarded personal empires. (Best structure is variable of the work to be done and the people who do it.)

While the systems approach ignores traditional lines of division, it emphasizes grouping of such activities as the coordination of a more efficient decision-making process with a minimum time spent on communication. Accordingly, the whole system is divided into subsystems and sub-subsystems. These replace such traditional organizational formations as regions, divisions, departments. Instead of the conventional line, line and staff and functional kind of structure, the system consists of three levels with clearly delineated functions:

1 top level: non-programmed decision making,
2 middle level: (computer) programmed decision making,
3 lower level: physical production and distribution processes.

While at the operating level a matrix shape may be more appropriate, the overall form still may be pyramidal. Individual specialized activities are integrated at the managerial level by the planning council. At the operational level they represent a pool of resources which, together with other facilities, are allocated by the planning council (through its operations and resources allocation committees) to specific programs.

Exhibit 3 (continued)

Principles on which traditional organizations have been built	Classical approach to an "ideal" organization	Behavioral approach to an "ideal" organization	Systems approach to an "ideal" organization
4 Functional Definition with Authority and Responsibility:	Develop efficient operating procedures by defining the content of each job in such a way that: **a** duties are clearly stated **b** the work of each man is confined to the performance of a single leading function **c** set dividing line between departments at the point where work changes hands **d** organization structure should define job requirements.	Since most men are motivated by challenge (making their own day-to-day operating decisions), meaningless routine tasks suppress the real capabilities of employees. Poor performance will result from too detailed a routinization. According to Simon, it is not possible to determine the behavior in the organization "in advance and once and for all by a detailed blueprint and schedule." For results let people make more decisions about their work, provide for a meaningful job enrichment (Herzberg), and create a climate which will facilitate an effective interpersonal and intergroup relationship. While the classical approach results in jobs which are "a means of subsistence," it emphasizes jobs as "satisfying experience."	This task commences with the definition of goals and sub-goals and it ends with the description of men, machines and materials which will produce the desired goals. As in the classical approach, all duties must be clearly defined and written up in a manual. Job descriptions are broader in scope at the operating level. They are less clear at the planning level. However, the work should be confined to the performance of a single leading function. Contrary to the classical approach, operating problems are discussed with all other units. With their consensus, new solutions become operational. Environmental boundaries both external and internal must also be clearly defined. Providing autonomous tasks for each team may facilitate the development of leadership since each team is responsible for its own planning, organizing and controlling. Thus, each group must have all the authority needed to carry out responsibilities. Before delegating authority, a requirement for information and communication must be determined. A lack of information may limit discretionary authority. If decisions are made at positions where the communication burden is minimized, the speed and

5 The Chain of Command:

Provide for simplicity and unbroken chain of command. Effect coordination through the principle of "unity of command." Both could be facilitated by a chain of superiors from the highest to the lowest rank. This determines the authority responsibility, power and communication. Functions should be arranged hierarchically (scalar principle). (This principle is responsible for the pyramidal shape of the classical structure which is known to achieve economies of scale and company-wide coordination.) Such an environment is considered by some as "regimented," which may produce a conflict between the official (scalar) and expert authorities.

The pyramidal shape facilitates management's orientation towards paternalistic-subjective behavior. Its inherent weakness is the conflict between the need to motivate individuals and the built-in pressure on them. Other conflicts derive from the superior authority of hierarchy vs. the authority based on expertise. Likert's solution to this problem is to link work groups together in a democratic work environment through individuals who hold overlapping membership in different groups (linking pin). Some object that such arrangements are slow and wasteful oversimplification of the organizational reality (Dubin). The following questions should be considered: **a)** How much participation is healthy and desirable? **b)** Is cooperation the sole factor needed to optimize a business situation? **c)** How can men identify their individual contribution when they are members of a group?

Fundamentally a system is built around an information centre with the authority to direct problems to appropriate units. Thus the function of authority within such organizations is to ratify the operational procedures that various teams have agreed to. The focus is on developing relationships that will maximize cooperation. The appropriate pattern of organization is contingent on the work to be done, the particular needs of the people involved, and the particular situation (Lorsch). While the pyramidal shape still exists, many designs (flat, tall, matrix) are possible. Companies which need coordination may switch from functional hierarchy to project management. In such systems the specialist would be reporting to his functional superior as well as to the project itself. (This process may result in a lack of coordination between projects and costly duplication of effort.) Hierarchical relationships are still required, but in systems their form is much different. The concept of equifinality negates the necessity of formal chain of command. To achieve a desired coordination of all functional areas, managers must have the authority to cut across departmental boundaries. The authority based on knowledge prevails. Decisions are made by groups rather than individuals.

ease of decision-making are increased. Each organization must be designed as a unique system.

Exhibit 3 (continued)

Principles on which traditional organizations have been built	Classical approach to an "ideal" organization	Behavioral approach to an "ideal" organization	Systems approach to an "ideal" organization
6 Channels of Contact:	To overcome difficulties which may arise from the principle of "unity of command," it is often necessary to provide other channels of contact (by-passing the formal chain) (i.e., Fayol's "gang plank").	Provide for upward, downward and lateral communication whose quality and speed are essential for effective function-ing of organizations. Since group behavior is the framework for all social systems, personal and organizational achievement may be facilitated by the ac-commodation of both structured and unstructured dynamic net-works i.e., "systems of overlays" (Pfiffner and Sherwood), "link-ing pins" (Likert), and various types of participation work teams. Communication is always improved where per-suasion replaces command.	Classical organization insists on communication following channels and decisions being made by those who have formal authority. In practice, however, informal power systems are often superimposed on the formal structure to expedite decision-making. The systems approach considers organization a communication network in which managers are at the central channels of contact. A minimum effort is to be spent on communication. One way to achieve this is to put people closer together. Another way is to create a number of subsystems which constantly interact internally and externally, with suppliers, customers, and creditors, etc. Such interaction of various subsystems is necessary for organizational survival. If all parts of a network do not interact, there is no system, merely a collection of parts.

7 Balance:

Balance the key organizational units by an equal distribution of their relative power. Make sure that the advantages of decentralization are not outweighed by increased costs and decreased profits. A good balance between centralized control and decentralized flexibility is always desirable. Easier coordination may result if the advantages and disadvantages of departmentalization can be balanced (i.e., by process type departmentalization and customer, or product departmentalization).

The basic assumption of behaviorists is that at the lowest levels the problem-solving process is spontaneous. Therefore, the organization balance should be built around the concept of decentralization. This arrangement will give managers and employees initiative and hence a keener interest and pride in their work.

Since balance represents the total systems concept, the management control system should embrace all aspects of company operations. Only total systems can ensure that all parts are in balance. Since any change in one area will generate change in another area, each system needs a self-regulating tendency (homeo-stasis). When environmental change is excessive, the organization adjusts to it and moves to restore equilibrium. The organization itself will undergo a systematic change in the process. Further, the long-term planning process helps the systems designer to integrate all sub-goals into a harmonious whole. Power equalization is effected by the breakdown of organizational goals into specific units responsible for specific tasks, thus eliminating concentration of power at the top. In matrix structure equilibrium exists among groups and within groups, thus avoiding the creation of empires within the system.

Exhibit 3 (continued)

Principles on which traditional organizations have been built	Classical approach to an "ideal" organization	Behavioral approach to an "ideal" organization	Systems approach to an "ideal" organization
8 Control:	This principle introduces a number of monitoring activities which are focused on identifying deviations from standards and finding errors. Some of the sub-measures according to Dale are: **a** comparison (to standards) **b** information (objective evidence) **c** integrity of command (control is not command) **d** uniformity (corresponding to structure) **e** exception principle (exception from standards) **f** utility (timely reports vs. history) **g** avoidance of red tape (abuses of bureaucratic formalism).	Traditionally this principle deals with a "negative" con-straining form of control. The behavioral approach asks: Is double checking absolutely necessary? It holds that a built-in potential for "self-control" facilitates the growth of both the individual and the organiza-tion. Scott Meyers coined a phrase "Every Employee a Manager" meaning that, should planning and control be turned back to the task, the result would be a proprietory attitude of employees with an increased satisfaction and productivity.	Control subsystems serve the operating system to achieve greater flexibility and effectiveness. The automatic corrections are facilitated by a built-in feedback mechanism. Exceptions from standards are specified in terms of cost, perform-ance or stability. They are measured at different points and stages of the process. All controls are evaluated on a cost/benefit basis. When a large deviation occurs, a defensive mechanism is immediately set in motion. Total systems control is a mechanistic system. It ignores behavioral systems and is based on information flows. Its functions are to **1)** predict, **2)** compare predicted with actual and, **3)** produce the deviation from actual and predicted results. Essentially it consists of two subsystems of control: **a)** a system of pre-programmed solutions for problems in marketing, production, finance, and **b)** a central control sys-tem (planning system) which deals with unpredictable operating and en-vironmental problems. Each control system must report deviations quickly and its design must be consistent with the objec-

tives of the larger system. It must be preventive, rather than punitive. The automatic feedback must guarantee a reduced time lag between input-output range.

Perpetuation depends on the system's ability to adjust to environmental trends. It provides for continuity and adaptation which is facilitated by the concept of entropy. It facilitates a continuous monitoring of political, social, technological environments and customer expectations. While the classical model emphasizes stability without change, the systems approach perpetuates through a control mechanism which permits continuous self-renewal of the organization. It is therefore designed to monitor both environmental inputs for new product development and internal demands by the system for developing human resources. Potential for promotion, age, and normal path of succession for the use of the planning system is indicated by a human resources inventory schedule.

9. Perpetuation:

Provide a hierarchy of positions for increasing scope of responsibility and authority. These should be related to each other in such a way that replacements for each higher position are always either readily available or in training.

The success and survival of every modern organization depend on the creation of a self-renewing system which will be capable of adjustment to the socio-techno-economic changes. One of the critical questions here is: How can we build into our organization a continuous and effective program for developing human resources? To be able to do so, the new value system must recognize both social and economic values. Such an environment should then promote both individual and organizational growth.

provokes a reaction and then continues through five more phased "stimulus—reaction patterns" down to the level of acceptance of the new practices.

Basically, once top management has finally decided to reorganize, it must create an environment in which the redistribution of power will be possible. The key problem in this process is the people, i.e., how to minimize personal rivalry, how to minimize the fear of change, how to prevent status anxiety, how to make people want to co-operate.

In most organizations, the major reorganization is accomplished by an outsider. However, the outsider should be no more than a catalyst or consultant in the actual work of planning and implementing the individual changes. A similar catalyst-consultant role would be appropriate for the organizational planning departments where these have been created. Their job is to study, analyze and recommend—to sell, not to tell. No such single department can be assigned the authority to alter the direction of the business and effect basic changes at different organizational levels. This is the job of the task force, or several task forces, which are selected from various departments within the organization. This was done in the recent reorganization of Northern Electric, and also of Air Canada.

Since 1968 was the most profitable year in the history of Air Canada, it came as a surprise when, shortly after this news was announced, the airline's brand-new chairman, Yves Pratte, called on McKinsey and Co., Management Consultants, for help. In January 1970, following the McKinsey Report, Pratte announced a radical reorganization to be effective as of May 1. To this end, he immediately formed two task forces and gave them exactly three months to come up with a new company. The model they had to work with was a company with "no less than 20 vice-presidents, tightly controlled regional operations, stepped-up promotional and publicity programs, a computerized personnel administration, a strategic development plan, reorganized operational plans, revised marketing approach and revamped customer service organization."[13]

The main reason for this radical change was that, in spite of its "technically superior performance record," Air Canada was found grossly lacking in customer service, marketing strategy and planning necessary to keep the company viable in the "difficult years which lie ahead for the whole airline industry." As it was, with its "unique Canadian blend of bureaucratic indifference, coupled with a superior attitude" which relied solely on its proven operational competence, the airline was not equipped to face new emerging socio-economic trends.

Since it takes some time for the top management to become convinced that the present structure is dysfunctional, time is always a crucial element in the implementation of organizational change. Although Air Canada planned its change to take effect over a three-month period, actual implementation extended to well over a year. But the time period varies from company to company, depending on the seriousness of the environmental pressure, the flexibility desired, and the "surgery" needed. Invariably it may extend from one to three

[13]See "Air Canada Discovers People," *Monetary Times,* June 1970, pp. 32–35, and elsewhere in the Montreal daily press.

years, by which time it may be necessary in some cases to start planning further reorganization.

The implementation usually proceeds through the following sequence of activities:

1　Identify the difference between WHAT IS and the IDEAL.

2　Prepare manpower inventory to determine who does what, who reports to whom, who has authority and how much.

3　Review the potential use of the present staff in the IDEAL, i.e., prepare a list of all suitable candidates and their special skills, experience, aptitudes, and potential.

4　Ascertain what personal problems with respect to vested interests would be involved in implementing the IDEAL.

5　Determine the problem areas and further revise the design. Ascertain whether the necessary approval for the revised design will be forthcoming from all superiors and subordinates.

6　Step-by-step (under short-term experimental conditions) put the revised version to work. Then evaluate results and make further recommendations.

7　Prepare an itemized schedule of all changes that are being recommended under the final reorganization plan and effect the change to introduce the "GOOD FIT."

And where will we go from here?

Once fully implemented, our ideal structure which has been properly "fitted" to all key variables would become a blueprint for potential success. Such a structure would ensure the enterprise the best possible service in each of its chosen fields. However, as soon as new environmental realities begin to temper the present opportunities, and new forces begin to interfere with effective leadership, the process of organizational renewal starts again; for the pattern of modern organizational life is one of constant re-appraisal of strength in relation to emerging threats and opportunities.

Today, only flexible organizations which are highly sensitive to changing conditions can survive in a society where change has become an everyday reality. Since the modern slogan is "keep adapting, or die," the process of reorganization is never finished.

CONCLUSION

A constant feedback monitoring the macro- and micro-environment is one of the key prerequisites for organizational success. To this end, a sensing instrument is needed which permits the development of a meaningful and intelligent strategy, on the one hand, and immediate corrective actions on the other.

Many agree that the "ideally fitted" organization structure is the answer to this problem. Such a structure is usually a result of a successful reorganization. However, the success of a reorganization does not depend solely on the soundness of the "ideally fitted design." A complementary, and equally important, concomittant is the ability and willingness of both the top management and their subordinates to alter their behavior in accordance with the objectives of the new structure.

Whether this can be done or not will depend on the determination and sincerity of top management. In the case of Air Canada, Chairman Pratte made it quite clear that this is an important battle and a rather serious situation when he said: "If any of my vice-presidents falls down on the job, out he goes. If Air Canada does not succeed, out I go."

One of the most difficult tasks for top management which intends to forge ahead with a total reorganization is the creation of an environment which will generate the necessary enthusiasm and promote the willingness of all organization members to work hard towards achieving their common goal. Unless the top management is completely sold on the project, this environment will never be created. Without such an environment, the needed co-operation will not arise. Without such co-operation, the whole project will be doomed.

Reading 9
Matrix Organization Designs: How to Combine Functional and Project Forms
Jay R. Galbraith

Each era of management evolves new forms of organization as new problems are encountered. Earlier generations of managers invented the centralized functional form, the line-staff form, and the decentralized product division structure as a response to increasing size and complexity of tasks. The current generation of management has developed two new forms as a response to high technology. The first is the free-form conglomerate; the other is the matrix organization, which was developed primarily in the aerospace industry.

The matrix organization grows out of the organizational choice between project and functional forms, although it is not limited to those bases of the authority structure.[1] Research in the behavioral sciences now permits a detailing of the choices among the alternate intermediate forms between the project and functional extremes. Detailing such a choice is necessary since many businessmen see their organizations facing situations in the 1970's that are similar to those faced by the aerospace firms in the 1960's. As a result, a great many unanswered questions arise concerning the use of the matrix organization. For example, what

"Matrix Organization Designs: How to Combine Functional and Project Forms," Jay R. Galbraith, *Business Horizons*, February 1971, pp. 29–40.
[1]See John F. Mee, "Matrix Organization," *Business Horizons* (Summer, 1964), p. 70.

are the various kinds of matrix designs, what is the difference between the designs, how do they work, and how do I choose a design that is appropriate for my organization?

The problem of designing organizations arises from the choices available among alternative bases of the authority structure. The most common alternatives are to group together activities which bear on a common product, common customer, common geographic area, common business function (marketing, engineering, manufacturing, and so on), or common process (forging, stamping, machining, and so on). Each of these bases has various costs and economies associated with it. For example, the functional structure facilitates the acquisition of specialized inputs. It permits the hiring of an electromechanical and an electronics engineer rather than two electrical engineers. It minimizes the number necessary by pooling specialized resources and time sharing them across products or projects. It provides career paths for specialists. Therefore, the organization can hire, utilize, and retain specialists.

These capabilities are necessary if the organization is going to develop high technology products. However, the tasks that the organization must perform require varying amounts of the specialized resources applied in varying sequences. The problem of simultaneously completing all tasks on time, with appropriate quality and while fully utilizing all specialist resources, is all but impossible in the functional structure. It requires either fantastic amounts of information or long lead times for task completion.

The product or project form of organization has exactly the opposite set of benefits and costs. It facilitates coordination among specialties to achieve on-time completion and to meet budget targets. It allows a quick reaction capability to tackle problems that develop in one specialty, thereby reducing the impact on other specialties. However, if the organization has two projects, each requiring one half-time electronics engineer and one half-time electromechanical engineer, the pure project organization must either hire two electrical engineers—and reduce specialization—or hire four engineers (two electronics and two electromechanical)—and incur duplication costs. In addition, no one is responsible for long-run technical development of the specialties. Thus, each form of organization has its own set of advantages and disadvantages. A similar analysis could be applied to geographically or client-based structures.

The problem is that when one basis of organization is chosen, the benefits of the others are surrendered. If the functional structure is adopted, the technologies are developed but the projects fall behind schedule. If the project organization is chosen, there is better cost and schedule performance but the technologies are not developed as well. In the past, managers made a judgment as to whether technical development or schedule completion was more important and chose the appropriate form.

However, in the 1960's with a space race and missile gap, the aerospace firms were faced with a situation where both technical performance and coordination were important. The result was the matrix design, which attempts to achieve the benefits of both forms. However, the matrix carries some costs of its own. A study of the development of a matrix design is contained in the history of The Standard Products Co., a hypothetical company that has changed its form of organization from a functional structure to a matrix.

A COMPANY CHANGES FORMS

The Standard Products Co. has competed effectively for a number of years by offering a varied line of products that were sold to other organizations. Standard produced and sold its products through a functional organization like the one represented in Figure 1. A moderate number of changes in the product line and production processes were made each year. Therefore, a major management problem was to coordinate the flow of work from engineering through marketing. The coordination was achieved through several integrating mechanisms:

> *Rules and procedures* One of the ways to constrain behavior in order to achieve an integrated pattern is to specify rules and procedures. If all personnel follow the rules, the resultant behavior is integrated without having to maintain on-going communication. Rules are used for the most predictable and repetitive activities.
> *Planning processes* For less repetitive activities, Standard does not specify the procedure to be used but specifies a goal or target to be achieved, and lets the individual choose the procedure appropriate to the goal. Therefore, processes are undertaken to elaborate schedules and budgets. The usefulness of plans and rules is that they reduce the need for on-going communication between specialized subunits.
> *Hierarchical referral* When situations are encountered for which there are no rules or when problems cause the goals to be exceeded, these situations are referred upward in the hierarchy for resolution. This is the standard management-by-exception principle. This resolves the nonroutine and unpredictable events that all organizations encounter.
> *Direct contact* In order to prevent top executives from becoming overloaded with problems, as many problems as possible are resolved by the affected managers at low levels by informal contacts. These remove small problems from the upward referral process.
> *Liaison departments* In some cases, where there is a large volume of contacts between two departments, a liaison department evolves to handle the transactions. This typically occurs between engineering and manufacturing in order to handle engineering changes and design problems.[2]

The Standard Products Co. utilized these mechanisms to integrate the functionally organized specialties. They were effective in the sense that Standard could respond to changes in the market with new products on a timely basis, the new products were completed on schedule and within budget, and the executives had sufficient time to devote to long-range planning.

[2]For a more detailed explanation, see Jay R. Galbraith, *Organization Design* (Reading, Mass.: Addison-Wesley Publishing Co., Inc., 1971).

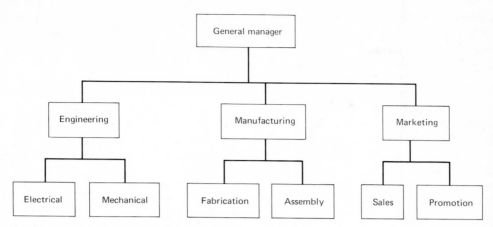

Figure 1   Standard's functional organization.

Matrix Begins Evolution

A few years ago, a significant change occurred in the market for one of Standard's major product lines. A competitor came out with a new design utilizing an entirely new raw material. The initial success caused Standard to react by developing one of their own incorporating the new material. They hired some specialists in the area and began their normal new product introduction activities. However, this time the product began to fall behind schedule, and it appeared that the product would arrive on the market at a time later than planned. In response, the general manager called a meeting to analyze the situation.

Task Force   After a briefing, it was obvious to the general manager and the directors of the three functions what was happening. Standard's lack of experience with the new material had caused them to underestimate the number and kinds of problems. The uncertainty led to a deterioration in usefulness of plans and schedules. The problems affected all functions, which meant that informal contacts and liaison processes were cumbersome; therefore, the majority of the problems were referred upward. This led to overloads on the directors of the functions and the general manager, which in turn added to the delays. Thus, the new situation required more decision making and more information processing than the current organization could provide.

The directors of engineering and manufacturing suggested that the cause of the problem was an overly ambitious schedule. More time should have been allowed for the new product; if realistic schedules were set, the current coordination processes would be adequate. They proposed that the schedules be adjusted by adding three to six months to the current due dates, which would allow more time to make the necessary decisions.

The director of marketing objected, reporting that the company would lose a good percentage of the market if the introduction was delayed. A number of big customers were waiting for Standard's version of the new product, and a delay would cost the company some of these customers. The general manager agreed with the marketing director. He proposed that they should not change the schedule to fit their current coordination processes, but that they should introduce some new coordination mechanisms to meet the scheduled due dates.

The group agreed with the general manager's position and began to search for alternative solutions. One of the solution requirements suggested was to reduce the distance between the sources of information and the points of decision. At this point the manufacturing director cautioned them about decentralizing decisions. He reminded them of previous experiences when decisions were made at low levels of the engineering organization. The data the decision makers had were current but they were also local in scope; severe problems in the manufacturing process resulted. When these decisions were centralized, the global perspective prevented these problems from developing. Therefore, they had to increase decision-making power at lower levels without losing the inputs of all affected units. The alternative that met both requirements was a group with representation from all the major departments to enter into joint decisions.

The group was appointed and named the "new product task force." It was to last as long as cross-functional problems occurred on the new product introduction. The group was to meet and solve joint problems within the budget limits set by the general manager and the directors; problems requiring more budget went to the top management group. The purpose was to make as many decisions as possible at low levels with the people most knowledgeable. This should reduce the delays and yet ensure that all the information inputs were considered.

The task force consisted of nine people; three, one from each function, were full-time and the others were part-time. They met at least every other day to discuss and resolve joint problems. Several difficulties caused them to shift membership. First, the engineering representatives were too high in the organization and, therefore, not knowledgeable about the technical alternatives and consequences. They were replaced with lower level people. The opposite occurred with respect to the manufacturing representatives. Quite often they did not have either information or the authority to commit the production organization to joint decisions made by the task force. They were replaced by higher level people. Eventually, the group had both the information and the authority to make good group decisions. The result was effective coordination: coordination = f(authority $\times$ information).

Creation of the task force was the correct solution. Decision delays were reduced, and collective action was achieved by the joint decisions. The product arrived on time, and the task force members returned to their regular duties.

Teams   No sooner had the product been introduced than salesmen began to bring back stories about new competitors. One was introducing a second-generation design based on improvements in the raw material. Since the customers were excited by its potential and the technical people thought it was feasible, Standard started a second-generation redesign across all its product lines. This time, they set up the task force structure in advance and committed themselves to an ambitious schedule.

Again the general manager became concerned. This time the product was not falling behind schedule, but in order to meet target dates the top management was drawn into day-to-day decisions on a continual basis. This was leaving very little time to think about the third-generation product line. Already Standard had to respond twice to changes initiated by others. It was time for a thorough strategy formulation. Indeed, the more rapid the change in technology and markets, the greater the amount of strategic decision making that is necessary. However, these are the same changes that pull top management into day-to-day decisions. The general manager again called a meeting to discuss and resolve the problem.

The solution requirements to the problem were the same as before. They had to find a way to push a greater number of decisions down to lower levels. At the same time, they had to guarantee that all interdependent subunits would be considered in the decision so that coordination would be maintained. The result was a more extensive use of joint decision making and shared responsibility.

The joint decision making was to take place through a team structure. The teams consisted of representatives of all functions and were formed around major product lines. There were two levels of teams, one at lower levels and another at the middle-management level. Each level had defined discretionary limits; problems that the lower level could not solve were referred to the middle-level team. If the middle level could not solve the problem, it went to top management. A greater number of day-to-day operating problems were thereby solved at lower levels of the hierarchy, freeing top management for long-range decisions.

The teams, unlike the task force, were permanent. New products were regarded as a fact of life, and the teams met on a continual basis to solve recurring interfunctional problems. Task forces were still used to solve temporary problems. In fact, all the coordination mechanisms of rules, plans, upward referral, direct contact, liaison men, and task forces were used, in addition to the teams.

Product Managers   The team structure achieved interfunctional coordination and permitted top management to step out of day-to-day decision making. However, the teams were not uniformly effective. Standard's strategy required the addition of highly skilled, highly educated technical people to continue to innovate and compete in the high technology industry. Sometimes these specialists would dominate a team because of their superior technical knowledge. That is, the team could not distinguish between providing technical information and supplying managerial judgment after all the facts were identified. In addition, the specialists' personalities were different from the personalities of the other team members, which made the problem of conflict resolution much more difficult.[3]

Reports of these problems began to reach the general manager, who realized

[3]See Paul R. Lawrence and Jay Lorsch, "Differentiation and Integration in Complex Organizations," *Administrative Science Quarterly* (June, 1967).

that a great number of decisions of consequence were being made at lower and middle levels of management. He also knew that they should be made with a general manager's perspective. This depends on having the necessary information and a reasonable balance of power among the joint decision makers. Now the technical people were upsetting the power balance because others could not challenge them on technical matters. As a result, the general manager chose three technically qualified men and made them product managers in charge of the three major product lines.[4] They were to act as chairmen of the product team meetings and generally facilitate the interfunctional decision making.

Since these men had no formal authority, they had to resort to their technical competence and their interpersonal skills in order to be effective. The fact that they reported to the general manager gave them some additional power. These men were successful in bringing the global, general manager perspective lower in the organization to improve the joint decision-making process.

The need for this role was necessitated by the increasing differences in attitudes and goals among the technical, production, and marketing team participants. These differences are necessary for successful subtask performance but interfere with team collaboration. The product manager allows collaboration without reducing these necessary differences. The cost is the additional overhead for the product management salaries.

Product Management Departments   Standard Products was now successfully following a strategy of new product innovation and introduction. It was leading the industry in changes in technology and products. As the number of new products increased, so did the amount of decision making around product considerations. The frequent needs for tradeoffs across engineering, production, and marketing lines increased the influence of the product managers. It was not that the functional managers lost influence; rather, it was the increase in decisions relating to products.

The increase in the influence of the product managers was revealed in several ways. First, their salaries became substantial. Second, they began to have a greater voice in the budgeting process, starting with approval of functional budgets relating to their products. The next change was an accumulation of staff around the products, which became product departments with considerable influence.

At Standard this came about with the increase in new product introductions. A lack of information developed concerning product costs and revenues for addition, deletion, modification, and pricing decisions. The general manager instituted a new information system that reported costs and revenues by product as well as by function. This gave product managers the need for a staff and a basis for more effective interfunctional collaboration.

---

[4]Paul R. Lawrence and Jay Lorsch, "New Management Job: the Integration," *Harvard Business Review* (November–December, 1967).

In establishing the product departments, the general manager resisted requests from the product managers to reorganize around product divisions. While he agreed with their analysis that better coordination was needed across functions and for more effective product decision making, he was unwilling to take the chance that this move might reduce specialization in the technical areas or perhaps lose the economies of scale in production. He felt that a modification of the information system to report on a product and a functional basis along with a product staff group would provide the means for more coordination. He still needed the effective technical group to drive the innovative process. The general manager also maintained a climate where collaboration across product lines and functions was encouraged and rewarded.

The Matrix Completed

By now Standard Products was a high technology company; its products were undergoing constant change. The uncertainty brought about by the new technology and the new products required an enormous amount of decision making to plan-replan all the schedules, budgets, designs, and so on. As a result, the number of decisions and the number of consequential decisions made at low levels increased considerably. This brought on two concerns for the general manager and top management.

The first was the old concern for the quality of decisions made at low levels of the organization. The product managers helped solve this at middle and top levels, but their influence did not reach low into the organization where a considerable number of decisions were made jointly. They were not always made in the best interest of the firm as a whole. The product managers again recommended a move to product divisions to give these low-level decisions the proper product orientation.

The director of engineering objected, using the second problem to back up his objection. He said the move to product divisions would reduce the influence of the technical people at a time when they were having morale and turnover problems with these employees. The increase in joint decisions at low levels meant that these technical people were spending a lot of time in meetings. Their technical input was not always needed, and they preferred to work on technical problems, not product problems. Their dissatisfaction would only be aggravated by a change to product divisions.

The top management group recognized both of these problems. They needed more product orientation at low levels, and they needed to improve the morale of the technical people whose inputs were needed for product innovations. Their solution involved the creation of a new role—that of subproduct manager.[5] The subproduct manager would be chosen from the functional organization and would represent the product line within the function. He would report to both the

---

[5]Jay Lorsch, "Matrix Organization and Technical Innovations" in Jay Galbraith, ed., *Matrix Organizations: Organization Design for High Technology* (Cambridge, Mass.: The M.I.T. Press, 1971).

functional manager and the product manager, thereby creating a dual authority structure. The addition of a reporting relation on the product side increases the amount of product influence at lower levels.

The addition of the subproduct manager was intended to solve the morale problem also. Because he would participate in the product team meetings, the technical people did not need to be present. The subproduct manager would participate on the teams but would call on the technical experts within his department as they were needed. This permitted the functional department to be represented by the subproduct manager, and the technical people to concentrate on strictly technical matters.

Standard Products has now moved to a pure matrix organization as indicated in Figure 2. The pure matrix organization is distinguished from the previous crossfunctional forms by two features. *First,* the pure matrix has a dual authority relationship somewhere in the organization. *Second,* there is a power balance between the product management and functional sides. While equal power is an unachievable razor's edge, a reasonable balance can be obtained through enforced collaboration on budgets, salaries, dual information and reporting systems, and dual authority relations. Such a balance is required because the problems that the organization faces are uncertain and must be solved on their own merits—not on any predetermined power structure.

Thus over a period of time, the Standard Products Co. has changed from a functional organization to a pure matrix organization using dual authority relationships, product management departments, product teams at several levels, and temporary task forces. These additional decision-making mechanisms were

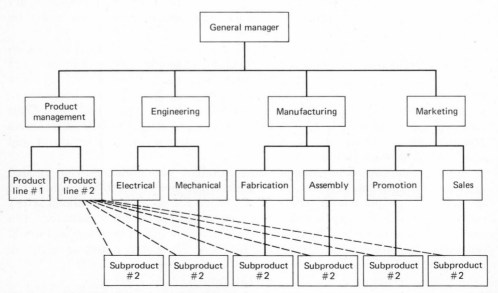

Figure 2   Standard's pure matrix organization.

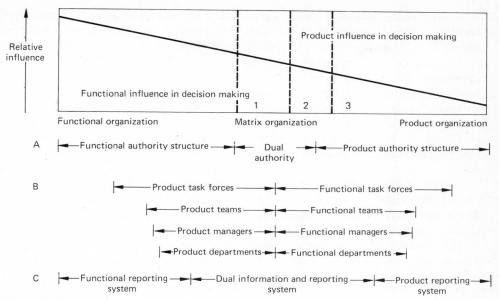

Figure 3   The range of alternatives.

added to cope with the change in products and technologies. The changes caused a good deal of uncertainty concerning resource allocations, budgets, and schedules. In the process of task execution, more was learned about the problem causing a need for rescheduling and rebudgeting. This required the processing of information and the making of decisions.

In order to increase its capacity to make product relevant decisions, Standard lowered the level at which decisions were made. Coordination was achieved by making joint decisions across functions. Product managers and subproduct managers were added to bring a general manager's perspective to bear on the joint decision-making processes. In addition, the information and reporting system was changed in order to provide reports by function and by product. Combined, these measures allowed Standard to achieve the high levels of technical sophistication necessary to innovate products and simultaneously to get these products to the market quickly to maintain competitive position.

HOW DO I CHOOSE A DESIGN?

Not all organizations need a pure matrix organization with a dual authority relationship. Many, however, can benefit from some cross-functional forms to relieve top decision makers from day-to-day operations. If this is so, how does one choose the degree to which his organization should pursue these lateral forms? To begin to answer this question, let us first lay out the alternatives, then list the choice determining factors.

The choice, shown in Figure 3, is indicated by the wide range of alternatives between a pure functional organization and a pure product organization with the matrix being half-way between. The Standard Products Co. could have evolved into a matrix from a product organization by adding functional teams and managers. Thus there is a continuum of organization designs between the functional and product forms. The design is specified by the choice among the authority structure; integrating mechanisms such as task forces, teams and so on; and by the formal information system. The way these are combined is illustrated in Figure 3: These design variables help regulate the relative distribution of influence between the product and functional considerations in the firm's operations.

The remaining factors determining influence are such things as roles in budget approvals, design changes, location and size of offices, salary, and so on. Thus there is a choice of integrating devices, authority structure, information system, and influence distribution. The factors that determine choice are diversity of the product line, the rate of change of the product line, interdependencies among subunits, level of technology, presence of economies of scale, and organization size.

Product Lines

The greater the diversity among product lines and the greater the rate of change of products in the line the greater the pressure to move toward product structures.[6] When product lines become diverse, it becomes difficult for general managers and functional managers to maintain knowledge in all areas; the amount of information they must handle exceeds their capacity to absorb it. Similarly, the faster the rate of new product introduction, the more unfamiliar are the tasks being performed.

Managers are, therefore, less able to make precise estimates concerning resource allocations, schedules, and priorities. During the process of new product introduction, these same decisions are made repeatedly. The decisions concern trade-offs among engineering, manufacturing, and marketing. This means there must be greater product influence in the decision process. The effect of diversity and change is to create a force to locate the organization farther to the right in Figure 3.

Interdependence

The functional division of labor in organizations creates interdependencies among the specialized subunits. That is, a problem of action in one unit has a direct impact on the goal accomplishment of the other units. Organizations usually devise mechanisms that uncouple the subunits, such as in-process-inventory and order backlogs. The degree to which inventories and backlogs develop is a

---

[6]For product line diversity, see Alfred Chandler, *Strategy and Structure* (Cambridge, Mass.: The M.I.T. Press, 1962); for product change rate, see Tom Burns and G.M. Stalker, *Management and Innovation* (London: Tavistock Publications, 1958).

function of how tight the schedule is. If there is a little slack in the schedule, then the functional departments can resolve their own problems. However, if rapid response to market changes is a basis of competition, then schedules are squeezed and activities run in parallel rather than series.[7] This means that problems in one unit directly affect another. The effect is a greater number of joint decisions involving engineering, manufacturing, and production. A greater need for product influence in these decisions arises due to the tight schedule. Thus the tighter the schedule, the greater the force to move to the right in Figure 3.

Although the tightness of the schedule is the most obvious source of interdependence, tight couplings can arise from reliability requirements and other design specifications. If the specifications require a more precise fit and operation of parts, then the groups designing and manufacturing the parts must also "fit and operate" more closely. This requires more coordination in the form of communication and decision making.

Level of Technology

If tight schedules and new products were the only forces operating, every organization would be organized around product lines. The level of technology or degree to which new technology is being used is a counteracting force. The use of new technologies requires expertise in the technical specialties in engineering, in production engineering, in manufacturing, and market research in marketing. Some of the expertise may be purchased outside the organization.

However, if the expertise is critical to competitive effectiveness, the organization must acquire it internally. If the organization is to make effective use of the expertise, the functional form of organization is superior, as described earlier in the article. Therefore the greater the need for expertise, the greater the force to move to the left in Figure 3.

Economies of Scale and Size

The other factor favoring a functional form is the degree to which expensive equipment in manufacturing, test facilities in engineering, and warehousing facilities in marketing are used in producing and selling the product. (Warehousing introduces another dimension of organization structure, for example, geographical divisions. For our purposes, we will be concerned only with product and function dimensions.) It is usually more expensive to buy small facilities for product divisions than a few large ones for functional departments. The greater the economies of scale, the greater the force to move to the left in Figure 3. Mixed structures are always possible. That is, the capital intensive fabrication operation can organize along functional process lines, and the labor intensive assembly operation can organize along product lines.

The size of the organization is important in that it modifies the effect of

---

[7]For a case study of this effect, see Jay Galbraith, "Environmental and Technological Determinants of Organization Design" in Jay Lorsch and Paul R. Lawrence, eds., *Studies in Organization Design* (Homewood, Ill.: Richard D. Irwin, Inc., 1970).

expertise and economies of scale. That is, the greater the size of the organization the smaller the costs of lost specialization and lost economies of scale when the product form is adopted. Thus while size by itself has little effect on organization structure, it does moderate the effects of the previously mentioned factors.

The Choice

While research on organizations has not achieved a sophistication that would allow us to compute the results of the above factors and locate a point in Figure 3, we can still make our subjective weightings. In addition, we can locate our present position and make changes in the appropriate directions as product lines, schedules, technologies, and size change during the normal course of business. The framework provides some basis for planning the organization along with planning the strategy and resource allocations.

If the organization's present structure is on the left side of the figure, many of the symptoms occurring in the Standard Products example signal a need for change. To what degree are communication overloads occurring? Are top executives being drawn into day-to-day decisions to the detriment of strategy development? How long does it take to get top level decisions made in order to continue work on new products? If the answers to these questions indicate an overload, then some movement toward a matrix is appropriate. Probably a sequence of moves until the bottlenecks disappear is the best strategy; this will allow for the proper attitudinal and behavioral changes to keep pace.

If the organization is product organized, then movements to the left toward a matrix are more subtle. They must be triggered by monitoring the respective technological environments.

An example from the aerospace industry may help. In the late fifties and early sixties the environment was characterized by the space race and missile gap. In this environment, technical performance and technology development were primary, and most firms adopted organizations characterized by the dotted line at "1" in Figure 3. The functional departments had the greatest influence on the decision-making process. During the McNamara era, they moved to point "2." The environment shifted to incentive contracts, PERT-cost systems, and increased importance of cost and schedule considerations.

Currently, the shift has continued toward point "3." Now the environment is characterized by tight budgets, a cost overrun on the C-5 project, and Proxmire hearings in the Senate. The result is greater influence by the project managers. All these have taken place in response to the changing character of the market. A few firms recently moved back toward point "2" in response to the decreasing size of some firms. The reduction in defense spending has resulted in cutbacks in projects and employment. In order to maintain technical capabilities with reduced size, these firms have formed functional departments under functional managers with line responsibility. These changes show how changes in need for expertise, goals, and size affect the organization design choice.

Many organizations are experiencing pressures that force them to consider various forms of matrix designs. The most common pressure is increased volume of new products. Organizations facing this situation must either adopt some form of matrix organization, change to product forms of organization, or increase the time between start and introduction of the new product process.

For most organizations, the matrix design is the most effective alternative. Managers must be aware of the different kinds of matrix designs and develop some basis for choosing among them.

Job Design

Attention is increasingly being focused on people at work, their jobs, and how they can be more productive. For a considerable period of time, little attention was devoted to defining and understanding job-design factors that affect worker productivity and satisfaction. Traditionally, jobs were designed in the manner prescribed by the scientific management school where work was broken down into its smallest elements and highly specialized and routine tasks were commonly assigned to workers in the belief that this would increase efficiency. People were viewed as extensions of the available technology, and little concern was given to the satisfaction of personal needs on the job.

Current productivity and behavioral problems indicate, however, that the traditional approach was inadequate and that the design of jobs should be approached contingently. A specific job design must be appropriate for the situation if it is to have a high probability of effectiveness in terms of worker productivity, worker satisfaction, and organizational profits.

This section begins with an article by Davis, who traces the evolution of job design and emphasizes the impact that societal factors have on the nature and structure of jobs. He stresses that work is done in a sociotechnical environment and, therefore, social as well as technical considerations must be closely examined when designing specific jobs. He also emphasizes the need to recognize the interaction between society, the organization, the individual, and technology in prescribing job designs. Davis's article provides a meaningful framework at the macro level for understanding those variables that impact on the design of jobs.

The article by Monczka and Reif presents a contingency model of job design. It identifies and operationalizes four sets of interdependent variables that should be assessed in developing task structures: the job itself, the psychosocial environment, technology, and management. Emphasis is placed on diagnosis as the means of determining the potential usefulness of job enrichment in specific organizational settings.

Lawler uses the expectancy theory of motivation to explain why, at the individual level, job enrichment will increase motivation and performance only under certain conditions and not under others. He describes the difference between intrinsic and extrinsic rewards and suggests that these rewards are differentially valued by people. He concludes that jobs can be designed to provide intrinsic rewards to organizational members and to provide for improved motivation and performance in those instances where two prerequisites exist: workers desire to satisfy higher-order needs, and jobs can be changed to utilize abilities valued by the job holder.

Reif and Luthans call for a contingency approach to job enrichment. They are critical of its indiscriminate use and provide strong arguments against such an approach. They also discuss those conditions that, if present, will undermine the potential effectiveness of job enrichment as a strategy to increase worker productivity and satisfaction. Situational variables such as the nature of the job, organizational level, employees' personal characteristics, and the organizational attitude toward innovation and change must be considered before job-enrichment projects can be successfully introduced.

Reading 10

Readying the Unready: Postindustrial Jobs

Louis E. Davis

United States attempts to bring some significant population segments into the economic and social mainstream have so far failed, partly because they were based on a succession of short-lived, inappropriate manpower models. Two factors affecting the texture of societal environment were overlooked: the technology our society uses to provide products and services, and the presence of societal enclaves differing in culture, skills, income, industrial experience, and political status. These factors are related, and manpower policy that ignores them is doomed to fail.

Speeded by changes in social values and developments in technology, the industrial era is showing many signs of coming to a close. The transition into the postindustrial era is discernible in the development of automated technology for goods production, computer technology for provision of services, a tenuous relationship between work and economic production, and the development of new meanings for work and for relationships within and between working organizations.

We should now devote attention to an orderly transition into a postindustrial society. But in the midst of industrial nations there are still preindustrial enclaves of the unemployed, untutored, unskilled, and unsophisticated, and on the international level there are economically underdeveloped nations among highly industrialized ones.

The objective of much government and private effort is to provide the means of introducing members of these enclaves into productive society. Most of the many transition programs assume that entrance into the economic mainstream leads to entrance into the social mainstream. This is more than a simple equating of economic status with social status. It reflects deeply held beliefs that participation in the economic activities of society serves social and psychological needs and provides the basis for political status. Business, industry, and government agencies attempt to induct and train, giving men opportunities to prove themselves on the job. However, government agencies may be overly eager to have the unemployed trained and placed on jobs that may be short-lived. Choosing effective means for merging the unprepared into the economic mainstream presents the problems here discussed.

Many modes of preparing the unskilled for productive activities will be required. The focus here is on those using on-the-job learning and experience

"Readying the Unready: Postindustrial Jobs," Louis E. Davis. © 1971 by The Regents of the University of California. Reprinted from *California Management Review*, vol. XIII, no. 4, pp. 27–36, by permission of The Regents.

(excluding apprenticeship). The on-the-job mode requires that the unprepared be inducted into the work organization in a rapid and orderly fashion, which often means that entry jobs have to be designed *de novo* or by fractionating existing jobs so that they provide progressive learning stages. Job restructuring can provide the means for stepwise learning, but the job segments must be appropriately designed and progression through the segments must be a function of performance rather than of promotion or advancement based on available openings.

A newly developed theoretical framework provides help in understanding the requirements of job restructuring. The concepts were first sketched out nearly twenty years ago in Britain, and Norway has recently employed them as the substructure for a comprehensive program of labor-management relations, but they have yet to come into common practice in the United States. My colleagues and I are employing them as the basis of extensive reorganization of advanced industries. Briefly, one fundamental premise of this school of thought says that in any purposive organization in which men perform the organization's activities, there is a joint system operating—called, in the newly developing language of this theoretical framework, a sociotechnical system. When human beings are required actors in the performance of work, the desired output is achieved through the actions of a social system as well as a technological system. Further, these systems so interlock that achievement of the output becomes a function of the appropriate joint operation of both systems. The operative word is "joint," for it is here that the sociotechnical idea departs from more widely held views—those in which the social system is thought to be dependent on the technical system.

The bearing on the question at hand is this: if the needs of the individual (which underlie the functioning of the social system) are not satisfied, then there will be no effective outcome from any program of job restructuring to provide entry and immediate follow-on jobs.

A second premise supporting the sociotechnical concept is that every system is embedded in an environment and is influenced by a culture and its values, by a set of generally acceptable practices, and by the roles the culture permits for its members. To develop an effective job or organization, one must understand the environmental forces that are operating on it. This emphasis on environmental forces suggests—correctly—that the sociotechnical systems concept falls within the larger body of "open system" theories. These accept that there is a constant interchange between what goes on in a work system or an organization and what goes on in the environment; the boundaries between the environment and the system are permeable. When something occurs in the general society, it will inevitably affect what occurs in organizations. There may be a period of cultural lag, but sooner or later the societal tremor will register on the organizational seismographs.

This, too, bears on the question of job restructuring. It says that programs will fail if they focus on the restructuring of jobs without giving due attention to the societal environment in which the jobs are embedded. Moreover, such programs will fail if they are not addressed to the emergent postindustrial environment whose dimensions are now becoming visible.

Sociotechnical theorists have carried the conceptual development of the discipline beyond these basic premises and are working on a methodology for system analysis that reflects the whole theoretical framework. But the two principles mentioned are sufficient to carry the discussion into the first of the five topics here addressed.

THREE MEANINGS OF JOB RESTRUCTURING

Neither society, the organization, nor the individual is free to ascribe its own meaning to the concept of job restructuring; their differing slants on the concept (like the three sectors themselves) are and must be mutually interdependent. No matter how noble are society's objectives for a program of job restructuring, that program must meet the needs of both an organization and an individual.

Societal goals embedded in the concept of job restructuring are to get unskilled individuals into productive work, to help them acquire skills, and to provide a viable future for them. This listing begins to set some requirements for the outcome of any program of job restructuring.

Society's objectives must also take into account a finding by Clark in his study of the ghetto:

> The roots of the multiple pathology in the dark ghetto are not easy to isolate. They do not lie primarily in unemployment. In fact, if all its residents were employed it would not materially alter the pathology of the community. More relevant is the status of the jobs held . . . more important than merely having a job, is the kind of job it is.[1]

But the organization is also a partner in restructuring; it has a set of needs that it wants to satisfy, and the meaning of restructuring must address itself to these.

1   Management may see job restructuring as a way of coping with a labor shortage. "Demand" or "structural" explanations aside, it is clear that the economy is currently exhibiting both unemployment and labor shortages. To organizations, job restructuring may mean the ability to fulfill production requirements with available workers.
2   The organization has economic objectives and restructuring must contribute to them. On the basis that today's unskilled and untutored do not contribute adequately to an organization's economic goals, the federal government may partially repay the estimated deficit. This is probably a short-run situation—at least for the American economy.
3   The organization wants its members to adapt and cooperate, learning what is necessary and taking appropriate actions to maintain the productive

system in a steady state. The organization will expect this behavior of workers holding restructured jobs. More importantly, it will require that job restructuring for some of the work force not affect adversely the adaptiveness and cooperativeness of other workers whose jobs are not restructured.

Individuals also have requirements and aspirations that affect job restructuring. The first two of these are similar to society's aspirations: entry into gainful occupation and acquisition of skills. Further, the tasks that are performed have to be meaningful to the individual, and the role he performs must be meaningful within the organization. Obviously, the term "meaningful" is conceptual shorthand, glossing over the many questions of satisfaction and status that are examined later.

Finally, the restructured jobs must offer some prospects for a desirable future career. The idea of a career at the working level is novel over most of the industrial world. Accustomed to thinking of jobs as entities in themselves, both managements and unions have lost the sense of the dynamics of working life—the expected progression from stage to stage of development. For many workers there are no dynamics—there is only one job over a lifetime. There is no "career" in the sense of an evolution of the individual matched by an evolution of the work that he does. Job restructuring, particularly if concentrated at the entry level, may be analogous to preparing a man to walk off the edge of a cliff; he is well organized to take the first step, and after that there isn't anything else. The literature— indeed, the whole industrial culture of Western civilization, the United States included—takes the job as a discrete entity, independent of the idea of a career or even of a simple job progression other than promotion.

TRENDS TO STATIC SEPARATION

Specialization of work roles is as old as Western history. Western man specialized his work in relation to a particular product, technology, or material, or because he had to acquire certain skills and wanted to grasp them in a certain way.

Although the jobs created by this trend were, for the most part, highly specialized, they were also highly skilled. But, beginning about 1790, the trend toward specialization took a different turn. New power sources required factories where people could be brought together to do their work. The steam engine determined the placement of machines which, in turn, determined the placement of people.

But there was no body of people conveniently ready to be marshalled together for this purpose; there was no industrial work force. The economy of England was essentially agricultural, and its rural population was untutored and unskilled. Two things changed this. The first was the passage of the Corn Laws, which forced large numbers of people off the farms and into the cities, artificially creating a manpower reservoir. The second was a new kind of specialization of labor in which jobs were deliberately broken down so that unskilled people could do them. In fact, almost anything that can be said about the "modern" industrial practice of breaking down jobs can be found in Babbage's book, *On the Economy of Machinery and Manufactures,* which was written in 1835 and reflected twenty years of experience.

In the United States, around 1890, Frederick W. Taylor rediscovered Babbage and created an approach called "scientific management" which is the basis of industrial practice in the United States today. The environmental field in which Taylor worked was not unlike that of England a century earlier. The United States was in a period of rapid industrial expansion, characterized by a large immigration of unskilled people. Taylor's was the mechanism by which industry could use these people. He specified the means for subdividing jobs so that their skill content was reduced to the minimum. Taylor's approach was widely accepted because American society held certain values and because the technology of the time had certain characteristics. For the good of society, or for the good of an organization, one could use people as "operating units."[2] Within broad limits, and as long as economic goals were being satisfied, the individual and his needs did not matter.

Scientific management, as developed by Taylor, can be called the machine theory of organization, and is characterized by the following elements:

1 The man and his job are the essential building blocks of an organization; if the analyst gets these "right" (in some particular but unspecified way), then the organization will be correctly defined.

2 Man is an extension of the machine, useful only for doing things that the machine cannot.

3 The men and their jobs—the individual building blocks—are to be glued together by supervisors who will absorb the uncertainties of the work situation. Furthermore, these supervisors need supervisors, and so on, *ad infinitum,* until the enterprise is organized in a many-layered hierarchy. In bureaucratic organizations, the latter notion ultimately leads to situations in which a man can be called a "manager" solely because he supervises a certain number of people.

4 The organization is free to use any available social mechanisms to enforce compliance and ensure its own stability.

5 Job fractionation is a way of reducing the costs of carrying on the work by reducing the skill contribution of the individual who performs it. Man is simply an extension of the machine, and the more you simplify the machine (whether its living or nonliving part), the more you lower costs.

To talk of job restructuring now—at the beginning of the 1970s—is to evoke this whole dismal history. People have seen this used to get work done cheaply. They have seen it used to control many kinds of workers, and now a number of kinds of professionals. The success of current programs of job restructuring will depend on overcoming or averting the problems that were created by similar movements in history, and this, in turn, will depend on the correctness with which such programs assess the emerging environment, both changes on the social side and in the technology.

ENVIRONMENTAL NATURE AND EFFECTS

What are some of the forces operating in the social and technological environments? What can be predicted about the short-run future? What effect should these forces have on programs of job restructuring?

Socially, there seems to be a collapse of Western society's basic proposition about the relationship between work and the satisfaction of material needs. The "Protestant ethic" says that man is put into the world to work; to satisfy his basic needs, he has to work hard because the environment is hostile and demands difficult, extended endeavor. This is now being very seriously questioned by American youth, by industrial workers, and (to our great surprise) by the unemployed, although they question it in widely differing ways. People see technology as being capable of providing for material needs without any real effort on anybody's part. Whether this is an accurate or inaccurate perception is, perhaps, irrelevant. It is partly accurate and will grow more accurate over time.

This change implies that the use of individuals to satisfy the economic goals of an organization is no longer a viable social value. People will not let themselves be used. They want other things out of the work situation than the material reward. They want to see some relationship between their own work and the social life that goes on around them and to see some desirable future for themselves in a continuing relationship with the organization.

This change is already explicit in the words of college students about their work expectations. They say, "We want a chance to participate and to control; we want a chance to make a contribution to developing more meaning in what we do." And they carry these words into action, turning down jobs that would put their feet under the corporation board in favor of jobs with the Peace Corps or as members of Nader's Raiders.

That the unemployed may be saying this as well is seen in a study of the Boston area by Doeringer,[3] which indicates that the unemployed seem to be as selective about accepting jobs as the employed are in changing jobs, because there are means—partly provided by society—for the jobless to subsist in the ghetto.

In short, many people in the United States are newly concerned about the quality of working life, about alienation from work, about job satisfaction, about personal freedom and initiative, and about the dignity of the individual in the work place. These questions are now arising because the relationship between work and the satisfaction of material needs is becoming more tenuous.

Another factor is that continuously rising levels of education are changing the attitudes, aspirations, and expectations of many members of our society. Although the focus here is on the United States, I offer an example from Norway because it illustrates so strikingly the connection between education and work expectations.

A few years ago the Norwegian government decided to extend the school-leaving age of children by one year because education was an important requirement for the future society. Very soon, Norway's important maritime industry was seriously threatened by an inability to recruit new workers. Before the school-leaving age was extended, about 80 percent of the boys were willing to go to sea; afterwards, only 15 percent sought seafaring careers. They wanted a different kind of life because the extra schooling had had an impact on them. (A creative solution was found by shifting from a focus on maritime jobs to one on careers.)

Other social forces in the environment might be mentioned. There is the drive toward professionalization; people want to be identified with activities of a professional nature, and we find a movement to provide a dignity for work that is analogous to that exhibited by the professions. The issue of appropriate labor-management relations, as now narrowly defined, has pretty well been settled. Consequently, labor unions are having some difficulty expanding their member-ship, keeping old members loyal, attracting new members, and so on.

What of the technological side? The most significant aspect of technological development is generally (and somewhat vaguely) called "automation." This means that there are devices in productive work systems that can be programmed to do routine tasks, sense outcomes, adjust machines if necessary, and continue the work process.

Man once had three roles to play in the production process, two of which have been preempted by machines. Man's first role was as an energy supplier, but since the advent of steam and electricity this role is now practically nonexistent in the United States. Man's second role was as a guider of tools. This is essentially what is meant by the term "skill"—the trained ability to guide tools or manipulate machines or materials—and this role for man is increasingly being programmed into machines. The third contribution remains: man as regulator of a working situation or system, an adjuster of difficulties. Under automation, man's work in the physical sense has disappeared. The notion of skill in the conventional sense has disappeared. What is left are two kinds of skills related to regulation—skills in monitoring and diagnostics, and skills in the adjustment of processes.

This shift in the role of man unites the forces emergent in the social and technological environments in the following way. In conventional work the transformation system can be described as "deterministic." What is to be done, when it is to be done, and how it is to be done are all specifiable. The whole of Taylor's scientific management movement was based on the fundamental idea that the world was deterministic.

In the presence of sophisticated or automated technology, the deterministic world disappears into the machine. Only two kinds of functions are left for man: deterministic tasks for which machines have not yet been devised, and control of stochastic events—variability and exceptions. For example, in modern banks where third-generation computers are already in use, human functions fall very neatly into these two categories. There are people carrying pieces of paper from one machine to the next (because there is no machine for carrying paper). And there are people handling the indeterminate, randomly occurring situations with which the self-regulating capacities of the computer cannot cope.

In a production system, stochastic events have two characteristics. They are unpredictable as to time and nature. For economic reasons they must be overcome as rapidly as possible. These characteristics impose certain requirements on workers. First, they must have a large repertoire of responses, because the specific thing that will happen is not known. Second, they cannot depend on supervision because they must respond immediately to events that occur irregularly and without warning; they must be *committed* to undertaking the necessary tasks on their own initiative.

This makes a very different world, in which the organization is far more dependent on the individual (although there may be fewer individuals). Let us trace the chain of causation that determines these differences starting from the point of view of the organization.

1 If the production process collapses, the economic goals of the organization will not be met.

2 If appropriate responses are not taken to stochastic events, the production process will collapse.

3 If the individual employees are not committed to their functions, the appropriate responses will not be made.

4 Commitment cannot be forced or bought; it can only arise out of the experiences of the individual with the quality of life in his working situation—i.e., with his job.

5 Therefore, highly automated organizations do their best to build into jobs the characteristics that will develop commitment on the part of the individual.

Comparing two industries—one highly automated and one not—will demonstrate these differences very clearly. In the oil refining industry, residual human tasks are almost entirely control and regulation, and the line between supervisor and worker has almost disappeared. In the construction industry, man still retains prominent roles as a source of energy and guidance, and supervision (often at several levels) mediates all system actions.

Management in the oil industry is proud of "advanced and enlightened" personnel practices. They were not adopted for the sake of their enlightenment but because they are a necessary functional response to the demands of process technology.

Here is the point at which both the social and the technological forces can be seen working toward the same end, because "job characteristics that develop commitment" (participation and control, personal freedom, and initiative) are exactly those characteristics beginning to emerge as demands for "meaningfulness" from the social environment.

Most industries are neither all automated nor all conventional. If an industry has some employees whose jobs are designed to meet the requirements of automated technology, then the characteristics of those jobs are visible to, and desired by, all the employees of the industry, and it becomes very difficult to maintain a distinction in job design solely on the basis of a distinction in technological base.

JOB DESIGN SUGGESTIONS

A considerable amount of formal and informal experimentation with job and organization design has occurred in the past twenty years in business and industry. Most of the experiments have been done in the United States, Norway, and England. They are usually reported in highly specialized publications, and only occasionally in general, widely read journals. So far, researchers are talking to researchers and rarely to managers or union officials.

The research results point to three categories of job requirements, the first of which concerns the matter of "autonomy"—jobs so designed that those performing them can regulate and control their own work worlds. They can decide when they are doing well or poorly, and they can organize themselves to do what is needed. Management's function is to specify the outcomes desired. Autonomy implies the existence of multiple skills, either within a single person (the French call such a person the "polyvalent craftsman") or within the work group. Autonomy also implies self-regulation and self-organization, a radical notion in the industrial world of the United States. Further, it implies that those working will be managed or evaluated on the basis of outcomes rather than on conformity to rules.

Nevertheless, the research shows that when the attributes of jobs are such that autonomy exists in the working situation, the result is high meaning, high satisfaction, and high outcome performance. This has been demonstrated in such widely different settings as coal mining,[4] chemical refinery maintenance,[5] and aircraft instrument manufacture.[6]

The second category, so far mainly the province of psychologists, concerns "adaptation." The elements of the job have to be such that the individual can learn from what is going on around him, can grow, can develop, can adjust. (This, by the way, is pure biology. It ignores, without meaning to slight, the psychological concept of self-actualization or personal growth.) All living organisms adapt or they cease to exist, and man's every act is adaptive. Too often, jobs created under scientific management principles have overlooked that people adapt or learn and, in fact, that the organization needs them to adapt. (In automated technology, the very role of the individual depends on *his adaptability and his commitment,* because nobody is around at the specific instant to tell him what to do.) Unintentionally overlooked is that the job is also a setting in which personal psychic and social growth of the individual takes place. Such growth can be facilitated or blocked, leading to distortions having costs for the individual, the organization, and society.

Where the job and technology are designed so that adaptive behavior is facilitated, positive results occur at all levels in the organization, as demonstrated in studies of oil refineries,[7] automated chemical plants,[8] pulp and paper plants,[9] and aircraft instrument plants.[10]

The third research category concerns "variety." If people are to be alert and responsive to their working environments, they need variety in the work situation.

Science began to get some notion of this after World War II, when research began on radar watchers. Radar watchers sit in a darkened room, eyeing blips on the radar screen that appear in random patterns. Eventually this blurs into a totally uniform background for the individual, and precisely when the important "foreign" signal appears, the watcher has become incapable of attending to it. Psychologists have also studied this phenomenon in various "deprived environments." Monkeys raised in restricted environmental conditions do not develop into normal adult primates. Adult humans confined to "stimulus-free" environments begin to hallucinate. Workers may respond to the deprived work situation in much the same way.

Specifically, what do the experiments say about the restructuring of jobs? All jobs, even fractionated jobs, should contain categories of activity that are important to the individual's development of self-organization and self-control in the work situation. There are preparatory tasks, transformation tasks, control tasks, and auxiliary tasks in a work process. Preparatory tasks, as the name implies, get the worker ready to do the work required. Transformation tasks cover the main productive activity. Control tasks give the individual short-loop feedback about how he is doing. (In many cases, this means that people may have to become their own inspectors, to carry out the requirements of providing themselves with feedback.) Auxiliary tasks include getting supplies, disposing of materials, and so on; they may provide relief from other more stressful tasks. If possible, a job ought to contain at least these components in order to incorporate autonomy.

To promote adaptability, the job—given objectives set by the organization—should permit the individual to set his own standards of quantity and quality of performance and to obtain knowledge of results over time (long-loop feedback). Within the content of the conventional industrial culture, this notion is taken to be either heretical or quaint. But research suggests that if overall goals are specified, people will respond appropriately, will determine what is right and wrong, and will work at meeting the goals.

To incorporate variety, the job should contain a sufficiently large number and kind of tasks. Some companies recognize at least one aspect of this need for variety. For instance, in very flat, unvarying situations, such as assembly lines, companies may rotate people through jobs to provide them with variety. This is an artificial mechanism, but it probably does keep workers from falling asleep at the switch.

Another aspect of the need for variety, less well recognized, will become increasingly important in the emergent technological environment. W. R. Ashby[11] described this aspect of variety as a general criterion for intelligent behavior of any kind; adequate adaptation is only possible if an organism already has a stored set of responses of the requisite variety. In the work situation, this means that since unexpected things will happen, the task content and training for a job should match this variance.

A fourth specification for the design of restructured jobs goes beyond autonomy, adaptation, and variety into the study of the total system of work: the tasks within a job should fall into a meaningful pattern reflecting the interdependence between the individual job and the larger production system. In sociotechnical terms, this interdependence is most closely associated with the points at which variance is introduced from one production process into another. The variance may arise from human action, from defects in the raw materials, or from malfunction of the equipment. A job must contain tasks and incorporate skills that permit the individual to cope with these variances. If the job does not provide this, the worker cannot control his own sphere of action; worse, he is forced to export variance to other interconnecting systems. In deterministic systems, the layers of supervision, buttressed by various inspectors, utility and repair men, and the like, absorb the variances exported from the workplace.

A related specification is that the tasks within the job ought to build and maintain the interdependence between individuals and the organization. This may occur through communication, through informal groups (if these are appropriate), and through cooperation between individuals. The tasks within the job and the jobs themselves ought to be seen as permitting relationships between individuals, permitting rotation, and encouraging the social support of one individual for another, particularly in stressful work situations. Otherwise, one gets isolation of the individual and conflict in the work situation.

Finally, the job should provide the basis on which an individual can relate his work to the community. Ask many American workers what they do and they will say, "Oh, I work for Company X." This is a good signal that the person either does not know or cannot explain the meaning of his work; it is merely some unspecified and unlocated portion of activity in a featureless landscape called "the company." This perception can have very serious consequences for his performance and for the satisfactions he derives.

THE JOB-HOLDER

The general requirements of job design also suggest some new ways of looking at job-holders. First, the job-holder ought to have some minimal area of decision-making that he can call his own. If he is to adapt and to achieve an autonomous working relationship, the content of his tasks ought to be sustained and bounded by recognition of the authority and responsibility required to perform them. However, in tightly interconnected systems and those with high variance, the extension of responsibility and control to encompass the interconnections is a particular requirement of job and organization design.

Second, the content of a job ought to be reasonably demanding of the individual in other than simply physical ways. This is related in part to growth and to learning, to the idea that jobs ought to provide for at least some minimum variety of activity, and to the idea that they should be related to the environment.

One of the problems in modern industrial life is to cope in a meaningful way with individual growth. Promotions are the only mechanism in wide use. Promotion assumes that a man is moved to another and better job. But in fact, the content of a given job held by a given man may be continually changing. That the same job should be different for people who have been working at it for a long time than it is for a beginner is simply not accepted. The whole standardization movement—represented by standardization of occupations and published job descriptions—is antithetical to this possibility and works against it.

To close this topic, a real example is offered in which some of these job specifications were applied. In 1968, the Director of the Institute for Work Research in Norway asked me and a colleague from the Tavistock Institute of Human Relations, London, to aid in an interesting experiment.[12] A company in Norway was in the process of designing an automated chemical fertilizer plant. They asked if jobs could be designed solely on the basis of the blueprints of the factory before it was built or staffed. In that way, as the physical plant was going up, they could begin to prepare the organization and the jobs and skills of the people who would man the plant when it was finished. The plant has now been in operation for over two years, with remarkable success.

The engineers had designed the plant so that the work to be done (monitoring, diagnosing, and adjusting, there being no physical work done in the plant other than maintenance) would be carried out in three monitoring or control rooms, in front of control panels. The equipment was so sophisticated that it required only one man in a control room. For three work shifts, this would have required nine men. (Other miscellaneous functions brought the total work force to sixteen men, excluding maintenance workers.) Based on the theoretical grounds reviewed above, the research team wished to avoid a situation in which people would work in isolation. But to put two men in a control room would have been economically inefficient. Therefore, totally new jobs were created by combining the maintenance and control functions. As the completed plant now operates, at least two men are based in each control room, alternately leaving it to perform maintenance tasks. They support each other, and the new job design also brings feedback from the plant by means other than the instruments on the control panels. For the company, this meant that maintenance men had to learn chemistry, and chemical operators had to learn maintenance skills. But totally different jobs were developed than had ever existed before. Looking at any of the previous job histories would have revealed none of this. It had to come out of the theory rather than out of past practice. And it has been extremely successful.

To adduce another Norwegian example—an American ocean-going tanker has 57 men; new Norwegian tankers have 15 men. The difference is that between conventional and automated technology. The engineers who designed these Norwegian ships and their automated equipment learned that they could construct almost any kind of arrangement if they knew what kind of social system was wanted on board the ship.

UNEXAMINED QUESTIONS OF POLICY

All of the foregoing provides a background against which to examine some questions of policy for job restructuring. The first concerns the existing job definitions and job boundaries that are cast in concrete in agreements between unions and managements, in state and federal civil service commissions, in personnel policies, and in a multitude of other ways. What will be required to break these molds? Simply to go to an employer with a proposal for job restructuring is, in many instances, to go to only half of the essential power. The union is the other half. Federal and state governments have contributed to the rigid stance of both halves by institutionalizing jobs and job descriptions. Jobs can be made infinitely better than they are. Jobs can be restructured for entry purposes and for advancement. But the issue must be made a matter of public and private policy, arrived at by open discussion.

The second policy question concerns the commitment to career development (in the sense it has been used throughout this paper), and not specifically to the individual job or to training for the individual job. A career-development approach was employed when the Norwegian maritime industry, in concert with government and labor, solved its recruitment problem. To get boys to go to sea, the maritime industry built career chains reaching out in both directions beyond the work on shipboard itself. Pretraining equips the boy to work on merchant ships and tankers for a number of years. Then the work and training aboard ship are designed to prepare him for later functions ashore. The man's entire working life is viewed as a continuum, his service at sea is an integral part of this continuum, achieving economic objectives for the maritime industry and preparatory, developmental objectives for the seaman.

American industry has ignored the issue of career development, except for professionals, and its omission is as detrimental to individuals within the mainstream of our productive society as it is to individuals seeking entry to it. Furthermore, planning programs that concentrate on a single entry level do violence to the job-design requirements discussed. The job designer, free to examine an entire logical sequence of activities, might find that some activities in the present entry-level job belonged in a higher stage, and that some in higher stages belonged at the entry level. In short, job restructuring has the potential of improving the whole range of industrial and service jobs[13] but only if commitment to the concept of career progression becomes a matter of public concern.

A third matter of public policy concerns the quality of working life. This matter goes beyond mere satisfaction with working conditions and directly to the essential involvement of individuals in the working world. As noted above, many younger people—who are in the next working generation—quite clearly feel that they need not work to live. But it remains unclear whether this is a response to work itself, or to the negative aspects of work as it is organized in American culture.

The following additional questions also require consideration:

• How flexible must an organization become in permitting individuals to pass through it to some level at which they can stabilize and perform usefully? There is a gain to flexibility, but there is also a cost, and the trade-offs will have to be worked out with the organizations involved.

• What advantages might be gained from an alteration of on- and off-the-job continued learning? America has only begun to scratch the surface with the manpower programs it has developed so far.

• What commitment should organizations make to job changes that facilitate the acquisition of knowledge and skills?

Finally, job restructuring should not be reduced to simplification.

SUMMARY

Many planners behave as if one way of putting a job together were as good as any other. It may be possible to cut a skill in two and give half to man A and half to man B. But if that cut destroys any meaning in the work, the job designer had better spare the surgery.

Taking apart a job is very much analogous to disassembling a clock or dissecting an animal: in a clock or an animal, there is an ordered relationship among parts; in jobs, there is an ordered relationship of the individual tasks to the functioning of the whole sociotechnical system. If the needs of individuals for meaningfulness are at issue, then the results of taking apart a job and reconstructing it become very serious indeed. New job structures that are created must be relevant to the social outcomes that are required.

There should also be an ordered set of relationships through which an individual progresses to arrive at a job that is viable and meaningful, and that has continuity for him and for the organization. This notion of different jobs as stages in a chain has to be made explicit in any program for job restructuring. The employer must develop a chain of jobs from the entry point into the mainstream of his productive system, so that individuals can arrive at some desirable future. Acquiring skills is a transitional act in a person's life. It is unreasonable to expect a person to remain in transition for twenty years, or even two years. He must be able to get to some level, and this level must be specified.

Technology today is so rich in potential variations and arrangements that design decisions can depend almost exclusively on the social side of the situation. Machinery and tools can be organized in a variety of ways that will achieve the same economic objectives. The real question is, what social objectives are to be satisfied? Any program for job restructuring must first define its social objectives with respect to the organization, the individual, and the whole society.

REFERENCES

1 K. B. Clark, "Explosion in the Ghetto," *Psychology Today* (September 1967).
2 R. Boguslaw, *The New Utopians* (New York: Prentice-Hall, 1965), Chapter 5.

3   P. B. Doeringer, "Ghetto Labor Markets and Manpower Problems," *Monthly Labor Review* (March 1969), p. 55.
4   E. L. Trist, *et al., Organizational Choice* (London: Tavistock, 1963).
5   L. E. Davis and R. Werling, "Job Design Factors," *Occupational Psychology,* 28 (1960), 109.
6   L. E. Davis and E. S, Valfer, "Studies in Supervisory Job Design," *Human Relations,* 19:4 (1966), 339.
7   Technical Reports (London: Tavistock Institute of Human Relations).
8   E. Thorsrud and F. Emery, *Moten Ny Bedriftsorganisasjon* (Oslo: Tanum Press, 1969), Chapter 6, "Norsk Hydro Plant."
9   *Ibid.,* Chapter 4, "Hunsfos Paper Plant." Also E. Engelstad, *The Hunsfos Experiment,* in press.
10 L. E. Davis, "The Design of Jobs," *Industrial Relations* (October 1966), 21.
11 W. R. Ashby, *Design for a Brain* (New York: Wiley, 1960).
12 Thorsrud and Emery, *Moten Ny . . . ,* Chapter 5.
13 W. J. Paul, K. B. Robertson, and F. Herzberg, "Job Enrichment Pays Off," *Harvard Business Review* (March 1969), 61.

Reading 11

A Contingency Approach to Job Enrichment Design

Robert M. Monczka
William E. Reif

Job enrichment, based upon the publicity it has received, has to be considered the leading contender for the crown "solution to motivational and productivity problems in industry." The concept is receiving extensive coverage in academic journals, business and professional periodicals, and the press. Job enrichment seminars are being conducted throughout the nation and are attracting high-level managers from leading business and governmental organizations. Two foreign firms, Saab and Volvo, are holding an international symposium to discuss how job enrichment can be used to solve problems associated with that symbol of American know-how, technological and industrial dominance, and production efficiency—the automobile assembly line.

After all is said and done the fact remains that little is really known about the concept and its application in industry. Moreover, there is evidence to suggest that even some firms practicing job enrichment have a rather limited knowledge of the concept, are not sure how, when, and where to apply it, and have only a vague notion of what they hope to receive from it.[1]

"A Contingency Approach to Job Enrichment Design," Robert M. Monczka and William E. Reif, *Human Resource Management* XII, 4 (Winter, 1973), 9–17. Reprinted with permission.

JOB ENRICHMENT: WHAT IS IT?

The first problem encountered in any discussion of job enrichment is reaching agreement on what it is. The concept in a very short time has become all things to all people. During the last three years job enrichment has been associated with the four-day work week, flexible hours, participative decision making and other human relations techniques, work simplification, job rotation, improved fringe benefits, particularly those that relate to working conditions, and numerous other programs designed to increase job satisfaction and productivity. The authors contend that none of the above constitute true job enrichment.

In order to grasp the real meaning of job enrichment one must first familiarize himself with Frederick Herzberg's two-factor theory of motivation.[2] Herzberg contends there are two distinct sets of job-related variables operating within the work environment: job content variables or what he refers to as motivators, and job context or hygiene variables. The motivators include achievement, recognition, advancement (based on merit), and personal (psychological) growth. These need satisfiers are intrinsic to the job. The hygiene factors are extrinsic to the job and include company policy and administration, the worker's relationship with his boss and his peers, working conditions, and salary and fringe benefits.

The key to Herzberg's theory of motivation is his contention that it is the motivators, or job content variables, that are primarily responsible for job satisfaction (and motivation). If the hygiene factors are not present in sufficient quantity to meet workers' expectations, the result will be job dissatisfaction. If they meet or even exceed workers' demands, however, the result is not job satisfaction, at least not for long, but merely no job dissatisfaction.

Herzberg concluded that if management wants to motivate workers it must concentrate on improving their jobs. In applying two-factor theory, job enrichment attempts to make workers more productive by changing job content in such a way that they are able to receive recognition, achievement, and the other intrinsic motivators from performing the work itself.

Another distinction that is carefully drawn by proponents of job enrichment is the difference between vertical and horizontal job loading. Vertical job loading is concerned with increasing the depth of a job by building into it higher level knowledge and skill requirements, greater autonomy, and increased responsibility for planning, directing, and controlling the work performed. An example would be to give a lathe operator the responsibility for scheduling his work and inspecting the finished product.

Horizontal job loading, sometimes referred to as job enlargement or job extension, involves increasing the *number* of operations or tasks performed by the worker. For example, expanding the scope of an assembly line worker's job by having him tighten the lug nuts on the left front wheel *and* the left rear wheel as the automobile passes his work station, or changing the job of a dishwasher so that he washes and dries the dishes. Combining two or more meaningless tasks into one job does not make it more meaningful. An enriched job design may increase the scope as well as the depth of the job. The job is not enriched however, if the new design constitutes an increase in scope only.

To summarize, job enrichment is concerned with designing jobs that include a greater variety of work content, require a higher level of knowledge and skills, give the worker more autonomy and responsibility for planning, directing, and controlling his job, and provide the opportunities for personal growth and meaningful work experience.

THE APPLICATION OF JOB ENRICHMENT

Having defined the concept we can move on to the primary purpose of the article, which is to develop a conceptual model of job enrichment design that can be used to identify, analyze, and evaluate the organizational variables upon which the successful application of job enrichment is contingent.

Management cannot just enrich jobs, concentrating solely on making changes in job content, and hope to achieve the expected results of increased job satisfaction and job performance (productivity). Rather it must view the application of job enrichment within the much broader context of the total work environment. This requires an understanding not only of the job and its requirements but of (a) the psychosocial environment, which shapes the attitudes, values, and beliefs of the workers, (b) technology, which places definite constraints on a jobs' potentiality for enrichment, especially in terms of conversion costs, availability of equipment and systems, and technical expertise, (c) management, which ultimately is responsible for the success, or failure, of any major organizational change, and (d) the complex set of interrelationships between jobs, workers, technology, and management.

Few practitioners who are involved in implementing job enrichment and even fewer writers who, supposedly, are developing guidelines for implementation have attempted to go beyond the boundaries of the job and carefully and systematically analyze the four sets of organizational variables that are included in the authors' contingency model of job design (see Figure 1). This article endeavors to fill the void that exists in our knowledge of when, where, how, and under what conditions job enrichment can be applied successfully. The contingency model provides the necessary framework for analyzing the variables primarily responsible for determining the potentiality of a job for enrichment, and serves as a means of predicting the degree of success that can be expected from a job enrichment project.

THE ORGANIZATION AS A SYSTEM

The contingency model takes a systems approach to job design. A system is a set of units or parts, with relationships among them, forming a complex whole. The systems approach emphasizes the relationships between parts and how these

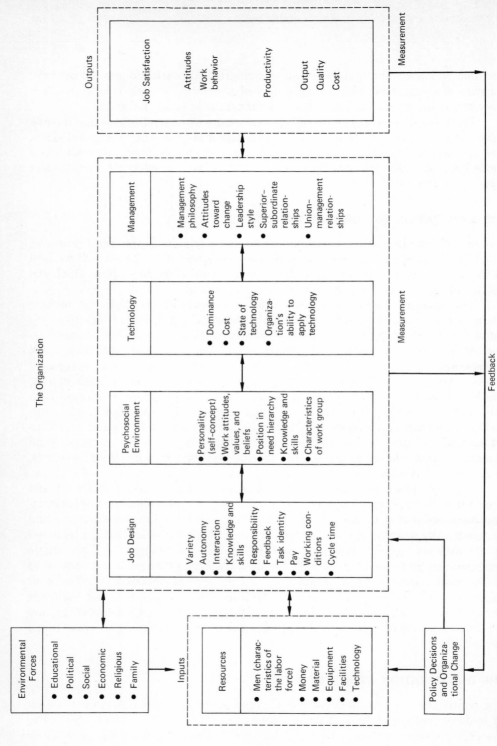

Figure 1 A contingency model of job design.

relationships affect the performance of the whole. Primary concern is given to the overall effectiveness of the system, not the effectiveness of the respective components, and to the interdependence of the elements of the system.

The basic elements of a system are (1) the objectives of the system, (2) the inputs to the system, (3) the transformation process in the system that converts inputs to outputs, (4) the outputs from the system, and (5) the measurement and feedback loop that monitors results and compares them to the expected performance levels of the system.

The principal inputs to the contingency model of job design are the resources available to the organization, which are affected by environmental forces that also influence the character of the organization and its individual members. The transformation process includes the four sets of organizational variables—job design, psychosocial environment (workers), technology, and management—and their interactions. The outputs of the system include job satisfaction and productivity. The feedback loop measures actual performance, compares it to expected performance, and provides information about results to the individual(s) responsible for making decisions to effect changes that are necessary to increase the efficiency and effectiveness of the system. (Efficiency refers to the productive use of resources or inputs available to the organization; effectiveness is a measure of the organization's ability to achieve its objective.)

Consistent with the systems approach, the model stresses the interrelationships among all components. Job enrichment focuses on job characteristics, which make up just one of four sets of variables that are involved in the transformation process. Changes in job design will eventually affect all other model variables and similarly will be affected by them. This means that if an organization wants to maximize its return from job enrichment it must be willing to adopt new policies and make other appropriate changes that will bring the whole system into phase with the newly created job design. Otherwise the system will be out of harmony, and attempts to enrich jobs will probably be defeated by the combined efforts of the other components to bring the system back into a state of equilibrium.

Emphasizing the interrelationships among model variables helps to clarify the role that job enrichment plays in influencing the outputs of the system. It becomes clear that job enrichment is not the cure-all that it sometimes is presented to be, but is a concept uniquely suited to deal with situations where it has been determined that job content is the root cause of the problem. And even if the diagnosis is correct job enrichment may still not be effective. Its effectiveness is dependent upon the support it receives from the psychosocial environment, technology, and management. In other words the concept works best in situations where the workers seek fulfillment in their work and are eager to move to enriched jobs, technological considerations are favorable, and management is committed and capable of developing and implementing job enrichment projects.

If the diagnosis reveals that job content is not the problem, job enrichment is not the answer and management would be wise to choose another alternative. For example, if the results of an attitude survey indicate that morale is low, and the cause can be traced to the job, job enrichment may be the solution. On the other hand, if the workers "don't give a damn" because the company's fringe benefits do not meet their expectations (e.g., "they're not as good as the guy's across the street") management had better first review the compensation package before ever considering job enrichment.

The job designer must be cognizant of the total environment within which he is operating and must be willing to make decisions that are in the best interest of the organization, even though they may not at times be in strict conformance with the principles of job enrichment. For example, if the need to find fulfillment in work is not a dominant characteristic of the work force, enriched jobs will probably result in few changes in attitudes and job performance. Under these conditions an increase in pay or an incentive bonus plan may be what is needed to induce greater output. Or, if the investment in new equipment and training far exceeds the expected benefits from enrichment, management may decide against changes in job design.

Viewing job enrichment within the framework of the contingency model helps to develop the appropriate perspective for the concept's application. The systems approach forces the job designer to think in terms of the system as a whole, and to realize that he is dealing directly with just one part of a highly complex, dynamic organization.

A CONTINGENCY APPROACH TO JOB ENRICHMENT DESIGN

The transformation element of the contingency model will now be broken down into its basic components for detailed analysis. Major emphasis will be placed on how each component affects the results expected from a change in job design and acts as a determinant of the success, or failure, of a job enrichment project.

Job Design

Ten key job characteristics or dimensions have been identified that are manageable, that are capable of being modified or changed, and related to job satisfaction and job performance.[3] They are variety, autonomy, interaction, knowledge and skill, responsibility, task identity, feedback, pay, working conditions, and cycle time.

Variety is broken down into object variety, which refers to the number of parts, tools and controls to be manipulated, and motor variety, which includes variety in work pace, physical location of work, and prescribed physical operations of work.

Autonomy refers to the amount of worker latitude in selecting work methods, work sequence, and work pace, and the amount of worker choice in accepting or rejecting the quality of materials and other inputs, and in securing outside services.

Interaction refers to the amount (number of persons contacted and time spent) of required interaction with others that is part of the job, and optional interaction that is for purposes other than assistance in performing the work.

Knowledge and skill requirements are determined by the amount of time spent in becoming proficient at the job.

Responsibility is defined as the ambiguity of remedial action required to solve routine job problems, the time span of discretion allowed the worker before his performance is reviewed by superiors, and the probability of costly errors in work for which the individual is accountable.

Task identity refers to the ability of the individual to relate to his work. This includes such things as clarity of cycle closure, visibility of transformation (seeing how his job contributes to the total work effort), and the value added to the finished product by his contribution.

Feedback refers to the quantity and quality of information the individual receives about his job performance.

Pay refers to the economic rewards the worker receives for doing his job.

Working conditions refers to the physical aspects of the job and the immediate work environment, such as lighting, temperature, and cleanliness in work area.

Cycle time refers to the length of time required to perform the major unit of work.

These ten dimensions provide the basis for enriching jobs. Although most job designers are quite familiar with the individual dimensions, relatively little is known about their interrelationships with each other and the other sets of organizational variables. This raises some interesting questions: Should one attempt to make changes in the dimensions simultaneously or sequentially? If sequentially, in what order? Which of the job characteristics have the greatest effect on motivation and productivity? Do the same characteristics affect both motivation and productivity, or do some cause changes in job satisfaction and others job performance?

Research and experience have not as yet provided answers to all of these questions. The information that is available suggests that the enriched job designer should concentrate his efforts on variety, autonomy, responsibility, knowledge and skills, feedback, and task identity. This is not meant to imply that the other job characteristics should be ignored. It only proposes that the ones mentioned appear to be most effective in increasing worker satisfaction and productivity.[4]

Perhaps the best piece of advice to those who are interested in designing enriched jobs is to improve your diagnostic skills. Since the ability of any job dimension to effect a change in workers' attitudes or behavior is highly dependent upon the unique characteristics of a given work situation, a correct diagnosis of the problem is crucial to sound job design. Taking a look at it from the other end, the results that can be expected from job enrichment are contingent upon the designer's analytical skills and, based upon his assessment of the work situation, his ability to build enriched jobs.

Psychosocial Environment

The job itself is the focus of job enrichment. The concept cannot be applied successfully however without support from the other organizational variables included in the contingency model. The psychosocial environment is a composite of *(a)* the psychological characteristics (self concept) of the individual workers, *(b)* the perceived status (role concept) of the individual as a member of the formal and the informal organizations, and *(c)* the sentiments, activities, interactions, and norms of the small work group.

People can be characterized along many different dimensions. This discussion will be limited to three that are considered most pertinent to the application of job enrichment: position in the need hierarchy, level of knowledge and skills, and work values, attitudes, and beliefs.

An organization considering job enrichment will want to be able to answer the question: Where are the workers positioned along Maslow's hierarchy of needs? If workers are concerned with fulfilling their physiological, safety and security, and social needs, job enrichment may not hold much promise for them and, if implemented, may not lead to the expected increases in job satisfaction and job performance. The worker who has not fulfilled his lower level needs is likely to be strongly motivated by economic rewards, which can be used to satisfy physiological and safety and security needs. He may not express any interest in having his job changed and, in fact, may react negatively to any change, possibly viewing it as nothing more than another attempt by management to get more out of him without additional pay. On the other hand, individuals who are interested in satisfying higher level needs at work (esteem and self-actualization) are good prospects for job enrichment. They readily identify with the rationale for job enrichment and probably would welcome, and find challenging, the increased variety, autonomy, responsibility, and interaction of the enriched job.

The second question that must be answered is: Are the workers capable of handling the increased requirements of enriched jobs? One must keep in mind that job enrichment by its very nature creates a situation in which the individual is faced with *(a)* greater autonomy, which means less structure, more freedom of action, and opportunity to use discretion, *(b)* more responsibility, which means he will also be held accountable for results, *(c)* more variety, which means a greater number of different tasks to perform, and *(d)* more complex interactions, which increases the need for communications skills and requires a better understanding of human behavior.

Assuming that not all individuals will be qualified initially to operate at the level required by the enriched job, management must be willing to provide the necessary training and development. This question of qualification is similar in many respects to the one where the best salesman is promoted to the position of regional sales manager only to discover that he is not capable of meeting the demands of his new job. If management for any reason is not willing or able to include adequate training in its plan of implementation, it would be wise not to pursue job enrichment. Putting workers on jobs for which they are not qualified and for which they have not received the training that would allow them to operate proficiently is one of the best ways of insuring that no organizational benefits will result from job enrichment efforts.

The third question that must be answered is: Do the workers want job enrichment? Research and experience would indicate that the answer is not always yes. After an exhaustive review of the literature Hulin and Blood concluded that as a means of motivating workers and increasing productivity, job enrichment is valid only when applied to certain segments of the work force, which they identified as white-collar workers, supervisors, and nonalienated blue-collar workers.[5] (They define nonalienated blue-collar workers as those who subscribe to the work values and norms of the middle class.) In their article, "Does Job Enrichment Really Pay Off?", Reif and Luthans discuss several reasons why workers may resist a move to enriched jobs, among them attitudes toward change, fear of inadequacy and fear of failure, previous work experience, and relationship with the informal work group.[6]

Fortunately, answers to the above questions can be obtained through well designed, properly administered questionnaires and employee interviews. The information received will help determine the extent to which job enrichment can be applied. If it is found that workers who are being considered for enriched jobs (a) are concerned with satisfying lower level needs, (b) do not possess the knowledge, skills, and experience necessary for proficiency and do not respond favorably to training efforts, and (c) do not identify with the work values of occupational achievement, belief in the intrinsic value of hard work, and striving for the attainment of responsible positions, the likelihood of success is marginal at best. Viewing the situation positively, if the psychosocial environment is supportive of the job enrichment concept, the probability of success increases significantly.

Technology

The third major factor influencing the success of job enrichment is technology. Technology should be examined along three dimensions. The first dimension is dominance, which refers to the extent technology delimits the human aspects of the job and determines output. Perhaps the best example of technological dominance is the assembly line. Some companies are so committed to the assembly line method of production (e.g., the Lordstown Plant of General Motors) that only small changes in job content are possible in the short run. Under these conditions true job enrichment is very difficult to implement and if it were might not have much of an effect on productivity.

The reason for this is twofold. First, technology decides the role of the worker to the extent that it "tells" the worker what to do, when to do it, and how much time he has to complete his task. Because of the highly structured nature of such jobs, meaningful changes in job content are, economically, nearly impossible, assuming that the state of technology and method of production stay the same.

The second reason for limited success in applying enrichment to jobs dominated by technology concerns the degree to which workers can affect their productivity (as defined by individual output rates). Most jobs are designed so that the worker within prescribed limits is able to determine the rate at which he will produce. Job enrichment assumes that by increasing worker satisfaction the organization benefits by some proportionate increase in job performance. On jobs where the worker has little or no control over productivity the benefits will not be forthcoming. Therefore, the potential payoff is greater from jobs that are not dominated by technology than jobs where the machine, process, or pace of the assembly line is the primary determinant of productivity.

For example, a highly motivated life insurance salesman or research engineer will probably outperform an unmotivated one since he is capable within certain limits of controlling his output. It is unlikely, however, that the performance of a highly motivated production worker on a mechanically paced assembly line will vary significantly from that of an unmotivated one.

The second major technological dimension of concern is cost. How much will it cost to change the characteristics of the job? Again, the automobile assembly plant is a good example with its high fixed investment in tools, equipment, systems, and production methods. In order to produce cars at the rate of 60 to 80 per hour, it is necessary to place a great deal of attention on the technical engineering and design of jobs. If a major technological change were implemented as a means of enriching jobs, it would be very expensive, units of output per hour would probably drop, and the cost of the car to the consumer would probably increase. In this case, cost considerations are overriding, and job enrichment is not a practical, cost/effective solution to the problem of worker dissatisfaction.

Finally, changes in job design can be limited by the state of technology and the organization's ability to apply that which is available. One of the alternatives to enriching dull, repetitive, routine jobs is to automate them, thus relieving the worker from having to perform base, meaningless tasks. Unfortunately, the present state of technology may not permit that alternative to be chosen. Or, technology may be available for totally automating the job or work process but the organization lacks the expertise to apply it.

Management

The application of job enrichment also is contingent on management. The major considerations here are management philosophy, attitude toward change, leadership style, superior-subordinate relationships, and union-management relationships.

Management philosophy is a composite of the attitudes, values, beliefs, and experiences of the management group. It is primarily responsible for molding and rigidly maintaining the character of the organization. Character defines the purpose of the organization, decides the policies by which it will be governed, and determines the means it will employ to achieve its objectives. The philosophy of management is pervasive and represents a very dominant force in the organization.

Management's general reaction to job enrichment will depend on its commitment to improve the quality of life at work and/or its acceptance of the concept as a ready means of increasing productivity. A genuine concern for improving the meaningfulness of work cannot be instilled by company memos, but most be a part of the moral fiber of the organization. An organization that only sees job enrichment as a means of wresting more output from the system will not receive the long run benefits that can be obtained from application of the concept.

Management's attitude toward change is another key factor. As has been mentioned, job enrichment will require major changes in the work situation, not just job content changes. The effect of job content changes cannot be isolated to the job itself, but will eventually be felt throughout the entire transformation process as shown in the contingency model of job design. In other words, job design changes will affect the psychosocial environment, technology utilized, and management. For job enrichment to be successful, management will have to view these encompassing changes realistically and fully support the enrichment effort once it has been decided that the perceived risks are worth taking.

Management's attitudes about workers can also color its reaction to job enrichment. If management has a basic Theory X orientation and assumes that most workers inherently dislike work, will avoid it if they can, are lazy, have little ambition, and must be coerced, controlled, and threatened with punishment to get them to put forth effort, there will be many problems associated with the implementation of enriched jobs. If the opposite view is held (Theory Y), job enrichment will be very compatible with management's assumptions about the qualities, capabilities, and motivation of the work force.

What a manager believes about workers is reflected in his leadership style and his relationship with subordinates. The Theory X assumptions about workers' values and work behavior is frequently found in a highly structured, centralized organization that is characterized by autocratic managers and authoritarian leadership styles. The autocratic manager would find it difficult to more freely delegate responsibility, to give up some of the planning and control aspects of his job to his subordinates, and to give them the opportunity to use their own discretion in matters relating to job performance. At the same time, these are the building blocks of enriched jobs.

Turning the situation around, organizations that are not too highly structured, are decentralized, whose managers are oriented to the needs of the workers, and where participative leadership is the dominant style, are generally highly receptive to job enrichment. In fact, accepting job enrichment as a philosophy of job design may require nothing more than giving formal recognition to a program that has been practiced informally for some time.

Managers must also be ready to accept the fact that job enrichment will require changes in their own jobs as well as those of their subordinates. The enrichment of subordinates' jobs can impoverish the job of the individual to whom the enriched job holders report. This is the main reason some firms have been able to eliminate an entire level of organization. Incorporating into an enriched job the managerial responsibilities that previously had been performed by the boss can eliminate the need for his position.

The fear of seeing one's job erode under the pull of vertical job loading can cause strong negative feelings to develop among those who feel threatened. What those who feel threatened fail to realize is that by giving their subordinates the opportunity for personal growth and a meaningful work experience their own jobs stand to be enriched. Theoretically, enriching the lowest level job starts a chain reaction that if allowed to run its course will eventually result in the enrichment of all jobs. Management should be aware of the magnitude of changes in the organizational structure that can be traced to the design of one enriched job, and begin to plan accordingly.

The final consideration is union-management relationships. The mere existence of a union can make the implementation of job enrichment more difficult. Negotiated job classifications and work rules, for example, place practical limits on the kinds and amount of changes that can be made in job content. As a rule, union support for company sponsored job enrichment projects will depend on the relationship that has been established between the two parties over time. Companies that have had good relations with their unions have experienced little opposition to job enrichment projects.

Many companies that practice job enrichment consider management to be the key to its success, or failure. A management team that is *committed* and, equally important, *capable* of designing and implementing sound projects can lick many of the problems and delays that otherwise can defeat the effort.

Many of these same companies have established "support of management" as the main criterion for selecting jobs for enrichment.[7] They take the position that the line manager must request to have job enrichment applied in his area before any action is taken by the company. They acknowledge that this "wait until called on" approach can slow down the implementation process, but they have found that projects that are undertaken have a very high probability of success.

MEASUREMENT

The measurement, or feedback, loop that is part of the contingency model should be able to answer three basic questions:

What is the present status of the organizational variables that are included in the transformation process, and what is the existing level of outputs from the system?

What are the specific results that management wants to achieve from job enrichment?

What progress is being made toward the achievement of job enrichment project objectives?

The answer to the first question will provide management with good information about the state or condition of key variables, such as job characteristics, workers' attitudes and work behavior, technological dominance and cost, and management receptiveness, prior to implementing job enrichment. The other two questions force management to define "success" for specific job enrichment projects and to establish the system for measuring progress toward the achievement of whatever objectives are set.

Some of the measurements will be objective, and quantifiable, such as a job satisfaction index that is computed from attitudinal test scores, while others will necessarily have to be subjective and rely heavily on experience, judgement, and personal observation. However the measurements are obtained, they cannot be ignored for they are an integral part of the job enrichment process.

Once a job enrichment project is under way a continual monitoring program should be established so that periodic feedback is received about how changes in job design are affecting job satisfaction and productivity. The answers received, presuming they are positive, help to reinforce what has been done and serve to increase acceptance and support for job enrichment throughout the organization.

CONCLUSION

Job enrichment has become recognized in a relatively short time as one of the best solutions to problems associated with the job itself and as an effective means of increasing worker satisfaction and productivity. Unfortunately, the concept is often presented in simple how to do it terms like: select the job, enrich it via a brainstorming session, and then implement it. Implying that this is all there is to implementing job enrichment projects is a disservice to any organization that is interested in the concept. What is lacking in such a simplistic approach is a conceptual framework that can be used to identify the key dimensions of job design and show how they fit into the total work environment. One cannot afford to ignore the other organizational variables upon which the successful application of job enrichment is contingent.

The purpose of this article was to develop a conceptual model of job design that provides the basis for identifying, analyzing, and evaluating the factors that contribute the most to effective job enrichment projects. Definition and discussion of the psychosocial environment, technology, and management, and the interrelationships among them and with job design, establishes an understanding of the conditons that must exist in order for an organization to realize maximum benefits from job enrichment.

The application of job enrichment is a complex undertaking. Management must be fully aware of the factors influencing its success as well as the benefits and the consequences that can be expected from enriched jobs, both in terms of individual workers and the organization. This knowledge further enhances the planning effort and improves the likelihood of an organization seeing a job enrichment program through to fruition.

REFERENCES

1   To receive a copy of the results of a comprehensive study of job enrichment in industry write to Dr. William E. Reif, Associate Professor of Management, College of Business Administration, Arizona State University, Tempe, Ariz. 85281.

2   For a good review of two-factor theory see: Frederick Herzberg, "One More Time: How Do You Motivate Employees?" *Harvard Business Review* (January–February, 1968), pp. 53–67.

3   Arthur N. Turner and Paul R. Lawrence, *Industrial Jobs and the Worker* (Boston: Harvard University, Division of Research, Graduate School of Business Administration, 1965).

4   See, for example: Edward E. Lawler and J. Richard Hackman, "Corporate Profits and Employee Satisfaction: Must They Be In Conflict?" *California Management Review* (Fall, 1971), pp. 46–55; and Robert N. Ford, "Job Enrichment Lessons From AT&T," *Harvard Business Review* (January–February, 1973), pp. 96–106.

5   Charles L. Hulin and Milton R. Blood, "Job Enlargement, Individual Differences, and Workers' Responses," *Psychological Bulletin* (January, 1968), pp. 41–55.

6   William E. Reif and Fred Luthans, "Does Job Enrichment Really Pay Off?" *California Management Review* (Fall, 1972), pp. 30–37.

7   William E. Reif and Robert J. Evans, Jr., "The Current Status of Job Enrichment in Insurance Companies," *Best's Review—Life/Health Insurance Edition*, forthcoming.

Reading 12

Job Design and Employee Motivation

Edward E. Lawler III

The psychological literature on employee motivation contains many claims that changes in job design can be expected to produce better employee job performance. Very few of these claims, however, are supported by an explanation of why changes in job design should be expected to affect performance except to indicate that they can affect employee motivation. Thus, I would like to begin by

"Job Design and Employee Motivation," Edward E. Lawler III, *Personnel Psychology*, Winter 1969, pp. 426–435. Reprinted with permission.

considering the WHY question with respect to job design and employee performance. That is, I want to focus on the reasons for expecting changes in job design to affect employee motivation and performance. Once this question is answered, predictions will be made about the effects on performance of specific changes in job design (e.g., job enlargement and job rotation).

A THEORY OF MOTIVATION

Basic to any explanation of why people behave in a certain manner is a theory of motivation. As Jones (1959) has pointed out, motivation theory attempts to explain "how behavior gets started, is energized, is sustained, is directed, is stopped and what kind of subjective reaction is present in the organism." The theory of motivation that will be used to understand the effects of job design is "expectancy theory." Georgopoulos, Mahoney, and Jones (1957), Vroom (1964) and others have recently·stated expectancy theories of job performance. The particular expectancy theory to be used in this paper is based upon this earlier work and has been more completely described elsewhere (e.g., Lawler & Porter, 1967; Porter & Lawler, 1968). According to this theory, an employee's motivation to perform effectively is determined by two variables. The first of these is contained in the concept of an effort-reward probability. This is the individual's subjective probability that directing a given amount of effort toward performing effectively will result in his obtaining a given reward or positively valued outcome. This effort-reward probability is determined by two subsidary subjective probabilities: the probability that effort will result in performance and the probability that performance will result in the reward. Vroom refers to the first of these subjective probabilities as an expectancy and to the second as an instrumentality.

The second variable that is relevant here is the concept of reward value or valence. This refers to the individual's perception of the value of the reward or outcome that might be obtained by performing effectively. Although most expectancy theories do not specify why certain outcomes have reward value, for the purpose of this paper I would like to argue that the reward value of outcomes stems from their perceived ability to satisfy one or more needs. Specifically relevant here is the list of needs suggested by Maslow that includes security needs, social needs, esteem needs, and self-actualization needs.

The evidence indicates that, for a given reward, reward value and the effort-reward probability combine multiplicatively in order to determine an individual's motivation. This means that if either is low or nonexistent then no motivation will be present. As an illustration of this point, consider the case of a manager who very much values getting promoted but who sees no relationship between working hard and getting promoted. For him, promotion is not serving as a motivator, just as it is not for a manager who sees a close connection between being promoted and working hard but who doesn't want to be promoted. In order for motivation to be present, the manager must both value promotion and see the relationship between his efforts and promotion. Thus, for an individual reward or outcome the argument is that a multiplicative combination of its value and the appropriate effort-reward probability is necessary. However, an individual's motivation is influenced by more than one outcome. Thus, in order to determine an individual's motivation it is necessary to combine data concerned with a number of different outcomes. This can be done for an individual worker by considering all the outcomes he values and then summing the products obtained from multiplying the value of these outcomes to him by their respective effort-reward probabilities.

According to this theory, if changes in job design are going to affect an individual's motivation they must either change the value of the outcomes that are seen to depend upon effort, or positively affect the individual's beliefs about the probability that certain outcomes are dependent upon effort. The argument in this paper is that job design changes can have a positive effect on motivation, because they can change an individual's beliefs about the probability that certain rewards will result from putting forth high levels of effort. They can do this because they have the power to influence the probability that certain rewards will be seen to result from good performance, not because they can influence the perceived probability that effort will result in good performance. Stated in Vroom's language, the argument is that job design changes are more likely to affect the instrumentality of good performance than to affect the expectancy that effort will lead to performance.

Before elaborating on this point, it is important to distinguish between two kinds of rewards. The first type are those that are extrinsic to the individual. These rewards are part of the job situation and are given by others. Hence, they are externally-mediated and are rewards that can best be thought of as satisfying lower order needs. The second type of rewards are intrinsic to the individual and stem directly from the performance itself. These rewards are internally-mediated since the individual rewards himself. These rewards can be thought of as satisfying higher order needs such as self-esteem and self-actualization. They involve such outcomes as feelings of accomplishment, feelings of achievement, and feelings of using and developing one's skills and abilities. The fact that these rewards are internally-mediated sets them apart from the extrinsic rewards in an important way. It means that the connection between their reception and performance is more direct than is the connection between the reception of externally-mediated rewards and performance. Hence, potentially they can be excellent motivators because higher effort-reward probabilities can be established for them than can be established for extrinsic rewards. They also have the advantage that for many people rewards of this nature have a high positive value.

Job content is the critical determinant of whether employees believe that good performance on the job leads to feelings of accomplishment, growth, and self-esteem; that is, whether individuals will find jobs to be intrinsically motivating. Job content is important here because it serves a motive arousal function where higher order needs are concerned and because it influences what rewards will be seen to stem from good performance. Certain tasks are more likely to arouse motives like achievement and self-actualization, and to generate, among individuals who have these motives aroused, the belief that successful perform-ance will result in outcomes that involve feelings of achievement and growth. It is precisely because changes in job content can affect the relationship between performance and the reception of intrinsically-rewarding outcomes that it can have a strong influence on motivation and performance.

There appear to be three characteristics which jobs must possess if they are to arouse higher order needs and to create conditions such that people who perform them will come to expect that good performance will lead to intrinsic rewards. The first is that the individual must receive meaningful feedback about his performance. This may well mean the individual must himself evaluate his own performance and define the kind of feedback that he is to receive. It may also mean that the person may have to work on a whole product or a meaningful part of it. The second is that the job must be perceived by the individual as requiring him to use abilities that he values in order for him to perform the job effectively. Only if an individual feels that his significant abilities are being tested by a job can feelings of accomplishment and growth be expected to result from good perform-ance. Several laboratory studies have in fact shown that, when people are given tasks they see as testing their valued abilities, greater motivation does appear (e.g., Alper, 1946; French, 1955). Finally, the individual must feel he has a high degree of self-control over setting his own goals and over defining the paths to these goals. As Argyris (1964) points out, only if this condition exists will people experience psychological "success" as a result of good performance.

Thus, it appears that the answer to the *why* question can be found in the ability of job design factors to influence employees' perceptions of the probability that good performance will be intrinsically rewarding. Certain job designs apparently encourage the perception that it will, while others do not. Because of this, job design factors can determine how motivating a job will be.

JOB DESIGN CHANGES

Everyone seems to agree that the typical assembly line job is not likely to fit any of the characteristics of the intrinsically-motivating job. That is, it is not likely to provide meaningful knowledge of result, test valued abilities, or allow self-control. Realizing this, much attention has been focused recently on attempts to enlarge assembly line jobs, and there is good reason to believe that enlarging assembly line jobs can lead to a situation where jobs are more intrinsically motivating. However, many proponents of job enlargement have failed to distinguish between two different kinds of job enlargement. Jobs can be enlarged on both the horizontal dimension and the vertical dimension. The horizontal dimension refers to the number and variety of the operations that an individual performs on the job. The vertical dimension refers to the degree to which the job holder controls the planning and execution of his job and participates in the setting of organization policies. The utility man on the assembly line has a job that is horizontally but not vertically enlarged, while the worker who Argyris (1964) suggests can participate in decision making about his job while he continues to work on the assembly line, has a vertically but not a horizontally-enlarged job.

The question that arises is, what kind of job enlargement is necessary if the job is going to provide intrinsic motivation? The answer, that is suggested by the three factors that are necessary for a task to be motivating, is that jobs must be enlarged both vertically and horizontally. It is hard to see, in terms of the theory, why the utility man will see more connection between performing well and intrinsic rewards than will the assembly line worker. The utility man typically has no more self-control, only slightly more knowledge of results, and only a slightly greater chance to test his valued abilities. Hence, for him, good performance should be only slightly more rewarding than it will be for the individual who works in one location on the line. In fact, it would seem that jobs can be over-enlarged on the horizontal dimension so that they will be less motivating than they were originally. Excessive horizontal enlargement may well lead to a situation where meaningful feedback is impossible, and where the job involves using many additional abilities that the worker does not value. The worker who is allowed to participate in some decisions about his work on the assembly line can hardly be expected to perceive that intrinsic rewards will stem from performing well on the line. His work on the line still is not under his control, he is not likely to get very meaningful feedback about it, and his valued abilities still are not being tested by it. Thus, for him it is hard to see why he should feel that intrinsic rewards will result from good performance.

On the other hand, we should expect that a job which is both horizontally and vertically enlarged will be a job that motivates people to perform well. For example, the workers Kuriloff (1966) has described, who make a whole electronic instrument, check and ship it, should be motivated by their jobs. This kind of job does provide meaningful feedback, it does allow for self-control, and there is a good chance that it will be seen as testing valued abilities. It does not, however, guarantee that the person will see it as testing his valued abilities since we don't know what the person's valued abilities are. In summary, then, the argument is that if job enlargement is to be successful in increasing motivation, it must be enlargement that effects both the horizontal and the vertical dimensions of the job. In addition, individual differences must be taken into consideration in two respects. First and most obviously, it must only be tried with people who possess higher order needs that can be aroused by the job design and who, therefore, will value intrinsic rewards. Second, individuals must be placed on jobs that test their valued abilities.

Let me now address myself to the question of how the increased motivation, that can be generated by an enlarged job, will manifest itself in terms of behavior. Obviously, the primary change that can be expected is that the individual will devote more effort to performing well. But will this increased effort result in a higher quality work, higher productivity, or both? I think this question can be answered by looking at the reasons we gave for the job content being able to affect motivation. The argument was that it does this by affecting whether intrinsic rewards will be seen as coming from successful performance. It would seem that high quality work is indispensable if most individuals are to feel they have performed well and are to experience feelings of accomplishment, achievement, and self-actualization. The situation is much less clear with respect to productivity. It does not seem at all certain that an individual must produce great quantities of a product in order to feel that he has performed well. In fact, many individuals probably obtain more satisfaction from producing one very high quality product than they do from producing a number of lower quality products.

There is a second factor which may cause job enlargement to be more likely to lead to higher work quality than to higher productivity. This has to do with the advantages of division of labor and mechanization. Many job enlargement changes create a situation in which, because of the losses in terms of machine assistance and optimal human movements, people actually have to put forth more energy in order to produce at the prejob enlargement rate. Thus, people may be working harder but producing less. It seems less likely that the same dilemma would arise in terms of work quality and job enlargement. That is, if extra effort is devoted to quality after job enlargement takes place, the effort is likely to be translated into improved quality. This would come about because the machine assistance and other features of the assembly line jobs are more of an aid in bringing about high productivity than they are in bringing about high quality.

THE RESEARCH EVIDENCE

There have been a number of studies that have attempted to measure the effects of job enlargement programs. These were examined to determine if the evidence supports the contention stated previously that both horizontal and vertical job enlargement are necessary if intrinsic motivation is to be increased. Also sought was an indication of whether the effects of any increased motivation were more likely to result in higher quality work than in high productivity.

In the literature search, reports of ten studies where jobs had been enlarged on both the horizontal and the vertical dimensions were found. Table 1 presents a brief summary of the results of these studies. As can be seen, every study shows that job enlargement did have some positive effect since every study reports that job enlargement resulted in higher quality work. However, only four out of ten studies report that job enlargement led to higher productivity. This provides support for the view that the motivational effects produced by job enlargement are more likely to result in higher quality work than in higher productivity.

There are relatively few studies of jobs enlarged only on either the horizontal or the vertical dimension so that it is difficult to test the prediction that both kinds of enlargement are necessary if motivation is to be increased. There are a few studies which have been concerned with the effects of horizontal job enlargement (e.g., Walker & Guest, 1952), while others have stressed its advantages. However, most of these studies have been concerned with its effects on

Table 1

Research study	Higher quality	Higher productivity
Biggane and Stewart (1963)	Yes	No
Conant and Kilbridge (1965)	Yes	No
Conant and Kilbridge (1960)		
Davis and Valfer (1965)	Yes	No
Davis and Werling (1960)	Yes	Yes
Elliott (1953)	Yes	Yes
Guest (1957)	Yes	No
Kuriloff (1966)	Yes	Yes
Marks (1954)	Yes	No
Rice (1953)	Yes	Yes
Walker (1950)	Yes	No

job satisfaction rather than its effects on motivation. None of these studies appears to show that horizontal enlargement tends to increase either productivity or work quality. Walker and Guest, for example, talk about the higher satisfaction of the utility men but they do not report that they work harder. Thus, with respect to horizontal job enlargement, the evidence does not lead to rejecting the view that it must be combined with vertical in order to increase production.

The evidence with respect to whether vertical job enlargement alone can increase motivation is less clear. As Argyris (1964) has pointed out, the Scanlon plan has stressed this kind of job enlargement with some success. However, it is hard to tell if this success stems from people actually becoming more motivated to perform their own job better. It is quite possible that improvements under the plan are due to better overall decision making rather than to increased motivation. Vroom (1964) has analyzed the evidence with respect to the degree to which participation in decision making *per se* leads to increased motivation. This evidence suggests that vertical job enlargement can lead to increased motivation when it leads to the employees' committing themselves to higher production goals.

Perhaps the crucial distinction here is whether the participation involves matters of company policy or whether it involves matters directly related to the employees' work process. Participation of the former type would seem much less likely to lead to increased motivation than would participation of the latter type. Thus, it seems to be crucial to distinguish between two quite different types of vertical job enlargement, only one of which leads to increased motivation. Considered together, the evidence suggests that, of the two types of job enlargement, vertical is more important than horizontal. Perhaps this is because it can lead to a situation in which subjects feel their abilities are being tested and where they can exercise self-control even though horizontal enlargement does not take place. Still, the evidence, with respect to situations where both types of enlargement have been jointly installed, shows that much more consistent improvements in motivation can be produced by both than can be produced by vertical alone.

SUMMARY

It has been argued that, when a job is structured in a way that makes intrinsic rewards appear to result from good performance, then the job itself can be a very effective motivator. In addition, the point was made that, if job content is to be a source of motivation, the job must allow for meaningful feedback, test the individual's valued abilities, and allow a great amount of self-control by the job holder. In order for this to happen, jobs must be enlarged on both the vertical and horizontal dimensions. Further, it was predicted that job enlargement is more likely to lead to increased product quality than to increased productivity. A review of the literature on job enlargement generally tended to confirm these predictions.

REFERENCES

Alper, Thelma G. "Task-orientation vs. Ego-orientation in Learning and Retention." *American Journal of Psychology,* XXXVIII (1946), 224–238.

Argyris, C. *Integrating the Individual and the Organization.* New York: John Wiley & Sons, 1964.

Biggane, J.F. and Stewart, P. A. *Job Enlargement: A Case Study.* Research Series No. 25, Bureau of Labor and Management, State University of Iowa, 1963.

Conant, E. H. and Kilbridge, M. D. "An Interdisciplinary Analysis of Job Enlargement: Technology, Costs, and Behavioral Implications." *Industrial and Labor Relations Review,* XVIII (1965), 377–395.

Davis, L. E. and Valfer, E.S. "Intervening Responses to Changes in Supervisor Job Designs." *Occupational Psychology,* XXXIX (1965), 171–189.

Davis, L. E. and Werling, R. "Job Design Factors." *Occupational Psychology,* XXXIV (1960), 109–132.

Elliot, J. D. "Increasing Office Productivity through Job Enlargement," *The Human Side of the Office Manager's Job.* A.M.A. Office Management Series, No. 134, New York, 1953, 5–15.

French, Elizabeth G. "Some Characteristics of Achievement Motivation." *Journal of Experimental Psychology,* L (1955), 232–236.

Georgopoulos, B. S., Mahoney, G. M., and Jones, M. N. "A Path-goal Approach to Productivity." *Journal of Applied Psychology,* XLI (1957), 345–353.

Guest, R. H. "Job Enlargement: A Revolution in Job Design." *Personnel Administration,* XX (1957), 9–16.

Jones, M. R. (Editor), *Nebraska Symposium on Motivation.* Lincoln, Nebr.: Nebraska University Press, 1959.

Kilbridge, M. D. "Reduced Costs through Job Enlargement: A Case." *Journal of Business,* XXXIII (1960), 357–362.

Kuriloff, A. H. *Reality in Management.* New York: McGraw-Hill, 1966.

Lawler, E. E. and Porter, L. W. "Antecedent Attitudes of Effective Managerial Performance." *Organizational Behavior and Human Performance,* II (1967), 122–142.

Marks, A. R. N. "An Investigation of Modifications of Job Design in an Industrial Situation
    and Their Effects on Some Measures of Economic Productivity." Unpublished Ph.D.
    dissertation. University of California, Berkeley, 1954.
Porter, L. W. and Lawler, E. E. *Managerial Attitudes and Performance.* Homewood, Ill.:
    Irwin-Dorsey, 1968.
Rice, A. K. "Productivity and Social Organization in an Indian Weaving Shed." *Human
    Relations,* VI (1953), 297–329.
Vroom, V. H. *Work and Motivation.* New York: John Wiley & Sons, 1964.
Walker, C. R. "The Problem of the Repetitive Job." *Harvard Business Review,* XXVIII
    (1950), 54–59.
Walker, C. R. and Guest, R. H. *The Man on the Assembly Line.* Cambridge, Mass.: Harvard
    University Press, 1952.

Reading 13

Does Job Enrichment Really Pay Off?

William E. Reif
Fred Luthans

During the last few years, behavior-oriented management scholars and practitioners have generally extolled the virtues of Frederick Herzberg's job enrichment
approach to employee motivation. Much of the management literature, especially
journals aimed at the practicing manager, propose that "Job Enrichment Pays
Off,"[1] Lately, it has become commonplace for behavioral scientists to criticize
Herzberg's research methodology but then admit the overall motivational value of
the technique of job enrichment.[2] Only in a few instances have scholars or,
especially, practitioners, seriously questioned the motivating effect of job enrichment. It is widely felt to be an excellent way of motivating employees in today's
organizations.

In the mad dash to modernize and get away from the Theory X (Douglas
McGregor) or Systems I and II (Rensis Likert) or Immaturity (Chris Argyris) or
9,1 (Robert Blake and Jane Mouton) approaches to the management of people,
both professors of management and practicing managers may be guilty of the
same thing: blindly accepting and over-generalizing about the first seemingly
logical, practical and viable alternative to old style management—Herzberg's job
enrichment. It now seems time to take a step back, settle down, and take a hard

Job Variety, Responsibility & Growth

Low   *High*

└───┘

  Rotation   Extension   Enlargement   Enrichment

look at the true value that job enrichment has for motivating employees. Does job enrichment really pay off or is it merely a convenient crutch used by professors and practitioners to be modern in their approach to the management of human resources? This article attempts to provide another point of view and play the devil's advocate in critically analyzing job enrichment.

ENRICHMENT OR ENLARGEMENT?

The logical starting point in the analysis would be to see how, if at all, job enrichment differs from the older job enlargement concept. Although Herzberg, M. Scott Myers, Robert Ford and others portray job enrichment as one step beyond job enlargement, the real difference may lie more in the eyes of the definer than any actual differences in practice. The distinction between the terms becomes even cloudier when concepts such as job extension and job rotation enter the discussion. The differences between these various terms can perhaps best be depicted on a continuum of variety, responsibility, and personal growth on the job. Most job enrichment advocates carefully point out that enrichment advocates carefully point out that enrichment, relative to rotation, extension, and enlargement, infers that there is greater variety, more responsibility, and increased opportunity for personal growth. Yet, for practical purposes, the differences, especially between enlargement and enrichment, may be more semantic than real. Researchers who have studied job enlargement define their term almost exactly the same way that Herzberg defines job enrichment.

CONCLUSIONS FROM RESEARCH

To develop a framework of analysis for job enrichment, conclusions from research must first be summarized. William Reif and Peter Schoderbek's 1965 study revealed that 81 percent of the firms which responded to a mailed questionnaire survey were not using job enlargement. Of the 19 percent (forty-one firms) who were using the concept, only four indicated their experience was "very successful."[3] A more recent National Industrial Conference Board study disclosed that even though 80 percent of the responding companies expressed interest in the behavioral sciences, that even though 90 percent replied that their executives read books and articles about the behavioral sciences, and that more than 75 percent sent their executives to outside courses and seminars dealing with behavioral science concepts, there were very few firms which indicated they had put such concepts into actual practice.[4] Although a number of companies stated they were engaged in some form of job design activity, the N.I.C.B. study revealed that few have made any *sustained* effort in redesigning jobs.

The two companies which are cited most often in discussions of job enrichment are Texas Instruments and American Telephone and Telegraph. The two are given as examples of the outstanding success that can be attained when applying the job enrichment concept. However, one may question what constitutes "success." For example, Mitchell Fein, a long-time industrial engineer, assessed the Texas Instruments' job enrichment program as follows:

> Texas Instruments' management was probably more dedicated to job enrichment than any other company in the world. They earnestly backed their managing philosophies with millions of dollars of efforts. After 15 years of unrelenting diligence, management announced in its 1968 report to the stockholders its program for "increasing human effectiveness," with the objective: "Our goal is to have approximately 10,000 TI men and women involved in team improvement efforts by the end of 1968 or 1969." Since TI employed 60,000, the program envisioned involving only 16 percent of its work force. The total involved was actually closer to 10 percent.[5]

In another instance, Robert Ford, who has been primarily responsible for implementing job enrichment in AT&T, reports, "Of the nineteen studies, nine were rated 'outstandingly successful,' one was a complete 'flop,' and the remaining nine were 'moderately successful.'"[6] Even more noteworthy perhaps is the fact that although Ford does not hesitate to generalize from the nineteen studies, he appears at one point to question his own optimism over the applicability of the benefits derived from job enrichment. He states: "No claim is made that these 19 trials cover a representative sample of jobs and people with the Bell system. For example, there were no trials among the manufacturing or laboratory employees, nor were all operating companies involved. There are more than a thousand different jobs in the Bell system, not just the nine in these studies."[7]

In an early study (1958), James Kennedy and Harry O'Neill published findings on the effects job enlargement had had on the opinions and attitudes of workers in an automobile assembly plant. Attitude surveys were given to both assembly line workers whose jobs were highly routine, unskilled, and paced by the assembly line, and to utility men whose jobs were quite varied. The results showed no statistical difference between the two sets of scores. This finding led Kennedy and O'Neill to conclude:

> If job content is a factor in determining how favorably workers view their supervisors and their work situation, the difference in content apparently must be along more fundamental dimensions than those observed in this study.[8]

In 1968, Charles Hulin and Milton Blood conducted an in-depth study of job enlargement. They concluded that, "The case for job enlargement has been drastically overstated and overgeneralized. . . . Specifically, the argument for larger jobs as a means of motivating workers, decreasing boredom and dissatis-faction, and increasing attendance and productivity is valid only when applied to certain segments of the work force—white-collar and supervisory workers and nonalienated blue-collar workers."[9]

Unfortunately, these studies are not widely cited in the management literature. Instead, a number of widely known and quoted management oriented behavioral scientists, among them Herzberg, McGregor, Likert, Argyris, and Blake and Mouton, are most often interpreted, sometimes wrongly, to advocate the opposite.[10] The popular position is that job enrichment is a key to successful motivation and productivity and many scholars, consultants, and practitioners actively campaign for its widespread use in modern organizations. McGregor summed up the feelings of job enrichment advocates when he said, "Unless there is opportunity at work to satisfy these high level needs (esteem and self-actualization), people will be deprived, and their behavior will reflect this deprivation."[11] In other words, the predominant conclusion is that people have a need to find fulfillment in their work and job enrichment provides them with the opportunity.

Why the wide divergence on the conclusions about job enrichment? Why the differences of opinion not only among scholars but also among practitioners, and between scholars and practitioners, about the efficacy of job enrichment? These are questions that the article tries to answer. The approach taken is to critically analyze the three most important concepts in job enrichment: (1) worker motivation, (2) job design, and (3) resistance to change.

WORKER MOTIVATION: ONE MORE TIME

The stated purpose of early job enlargement programs was to provide job satisfaction for unskilled blue-collar and low level white-collar (clerical) workers whose jobs were highly standardized and repetitive, operated on a short time cycle, required little knowledge and skill, and utilized only a few low-order abilities. Only a cursory review of management literature reveals that the majority of job enlargement programs in existence today are concerned with enriching the jobs of highly skilled workers, technicians, professionals, supervisors and man-agers, not unskilled blue- and white-collar employees. For example, in the William Paul, Keith Robertson, and Frederick Herzberg article on job enrichment in British companies, none of the employees in the studies could be classified as blue-collar workers.[12] Fein reports, "My experience in numerous plants has been that the lower the skills level, the lower the degree to which job enlargement can be established to be meaningful to the employees and management."[13]

The Reif and Schoderbek study discovered that of the firms using job enlargement, 73 percent used it at the supervisory level, 51 percent used it to enlarge clerical jobs, and 49 percent used it in the production area. Of the firms practicing job enlargement in the plant, 35 percent replied that the employees were primarily skilled, while only 15 percent classified the employees on enlarged jobs as unskilled.[14] In follow-up interviews three major reasons clearly emerged why it was more difficult to get unskilled workers to accept job enlargement than skilled or semi-skilled workers: (1) the unskilled prefer the status quo, (2) the unskilled seem to prefer highly specialized work, and (3) the unskilled show a lack of interest in improvements in job design which require learning new skills or assuming greater responsibility. A representative comment was: "Most unskilled workers prefer the routine nature of their jobs, and it has been my experience that they are not eager to accept responsibility or learn new skills."

In a parallel manner, the most frequent response to another question, "What are the major considerations taken into account in determining the particular job(s) to be enlarged?" was "The potential skills of employees." The survey respondents noted that in their experience, the higher the skill level of employees, the greater the probability of success with the enlarged job. Another question was, "What do you consider to be the major disadvantages of job enlargement?" The second most frequent response was that some workers were just not capable of growing with the enlarged job that was designed for them. Follow-up interviews indicated that the workers referred to by the respondents were primarily unskilled and semi-skilled blue-collar workers. Of particular interest was the response from a number of company spokesmen that in their experience many workers seemed capable of growing with the job but simply were not willing to do so. This observation was confirmed in interviews with a number of workers who had declined the opportunity to work on enlarged jobs.

The above results seem to directly contradict the commonly held motivational assumptions made by well-known behavioralists. It has become widely accepted that:

1 *Man seeks and needs meaningful work.* Many behaviorists would contend that man's psychological well-being is dependent upon his ability to find expression and challenge in his work.

2 *Motivation is a function of job satisfaction and personal freedom.* As was noted in a comprehensive N.I.C.B. study on job design: "Satisfaction with job content and the freedom to work on a self-sufficient independent basis are viewed as the crucial variables in the motivation to work."[15]

3 *Job content is related to job satisfaction.* This major assumption is primarily derived from Herzberg's two-factor theory of motivation which provides the foundation for job enrichment. Herzberg implies that people are capable and desirous of greater responsibility and can be positively motivated by work which provides "meaning" to them.

These motivational assumptions do not account for why some workers show little or no interest in job enlargement. Beside the overall social and cultural impact on the values toward work, there are other specific but less widely held assumptions about worker motivation. One possible alternative assumption is that some people actually prefer highly routine, repetitive jobs. Numerous studies have pointed out that repetitive work can have positively motivating characteristics for some workers.[16] For example, Maurice Kilbridge found that assembly line workers in a television factory did not necessarily regard repetitive tasks as dissatisfying or frustrating. Also, the mechanical pacing of the conveyors was not necessarily distasteful to most workers. The Reif and Schoderbek study found that some workers preferred routine tasks because there was little thinking involved, and as a result, they were free to socialize and daydream without impairment to their productivity.[17]

Do these results suggest that workers' attitudes toward work and their ideas of what constitute satisfactory working conditions have gradually conformed to the technical requirements of our modern, industrialized society? For decades scholars and practitioners have been concerned with changing the design of work in order for it to be compatible with the psychological make-up of today's workers. In the meantime, is it possible that scholars and managers alike have failed to observe adaptation of the worker to his environment or, even more important, fundamental changes in the psychological need structure of the individual? Is there any tangible evidence which would give positive support to these intriguing possibilities?

Although not widely known to students of management, there is a small but significant literature which contradicts and is in opposition to the widely held assumptions made by job enrichment advocates. The study by Hulin and Blood is a good example. After closely analyzing practically all relevant research, they conclude that the effects of job enrichment on job satisfaction and worker motivation are generally overstated and in some cases unfounded.[18] Their study raises a number of interesting questions about the popular assumptions of worker motivation and the relationship between job enrichment, job satisfaction, and motivation. They argue that many blue-collar workers are not alienated from the work environment but are alienated from the work norms and values of the middle class. The middle class norms include: *(a)* positive effect for occupational achievement, *(b)* a belief in the intrinsic value of hard work, *(c)* a striving for the attainment of responsible positions, and *(d)* a belief in the work-related aspects of the Protestant ethic. On the other hand, these blue-collar workers do follow the norms of their own subculture. The implications are that workers who are alienated from class values do not actively seek meaning in their work and therefore are not strongly motivated by the job enlargement concept.

Fein's study of blue-collar and white-collar worker motivation came up with essentially the same conclusion. He states:

> Workers do not look upon their work as fulfilling their existence. Their reaction to their work is the opposite of what the behavioralists predict. It is only because *workers choose not to find fulfillment in their work* that they are able to function as healthy human beings. By rejecting involvement in their work which simply cannot be fulfilling, workers save their sanity.[19]

Fein goes on to say:

... the concepts of McGregor and Herzberg regarding workers' needs to find fulfillment through their work are sound *only for those workers who choose to find fulfillment through their work.* In my opinion, this includes about 15–20% of the blue-collar work force. These behavioralists' concepts have little meaning for the others. Contrary to their postulates, the majority of workers seek fulfillment outside their work.[20]

Whether one agrees or disagrees with the above observation, it does raise an interesting point. One could speculate that Fein's 15 to 20 percent is about the proportion of the worker population that David McClelland and David Winter would regard as high achievers.[21] Assuming this percentage were accurate, it would be vitally important to the analysis of job enrichment. It would follow that high achievers are essentially self-motivated and would not require the external stimulus of job enrichment to perform well. By the same token, the low-achievers would not respond to job enrichment because work holds too little meaning for them to be motivated by it. They find satisfaction outside the work place.

Another interesting parallel is provided by Hulin and Blood's analysis of William F. Whyte's study of rate busters.[22] They contend that Whyte's rate busters rejected the norms of their peer group and accepted the norms of management whereas the "quota restricters" retained their peer group norms. One might safely speculate that Whyte's quota restricters belong to the group known as the "alienated from the work norms of the middle class" workers or McClelland's low-achievers or Fein's 80 to 85 percent. Thus, a plausible answer to the question, "Why isn't job enrichment used more extensively on jobs of blue-collar and low-level white-collar workers?" is that a majority of these workers may not be positively motivated by an enriched job content with the accompanying motivators. Instead, they may be willing to exchange their minimum efforts on the job so that they can live satisfactorily outside the job.

A RE-EXAMINATION OF JOB DESIGN

Louis Davis defines job design as the "specification of the contents, methods, and relationships of jobs in order to satisfy technological and organizational requirements as well as the social and personal requirements of the job holder."[23] Traditionally, the technological requirements of work were given primary consideration in designing a job. For example, Frederick W. Taylor's work improvement efforts were directed at the task. Adjustments between technology and human needs were made in terms of the individual's adjustment to the system rather than designing the system to meet human needs. Because of the recent influence of the behavioralists, more emphasis has been devoted to the human aspects of job design. Today, the commonly expressed purpose of job design is to create more meaningful and satisfying work with the assumption being that productivity can be increased not so much by improving the technology as by improving the motivational climate.

Job enrichment is very compatible with "work is a human as well as a technical process" approach to job design. The conceptual similarity between job enrichment and the human approach to job design is very evident in the two factor motivation theory of Frederick Herzberg.[24] According to Herzberg, motivation is intrinsic to the job and the true rewards (achievement, recognition, work itself, responsibiliby, advancement, growth) come from doing the work, from performing effectively on the job. Many other behaviorally oriented theorists are in agreement with Herzberg's emphasis on job content, notably Argyris and McGregor who both express the desire to redesign jobs so they are capable of fulfilling esteem and self-actualization needs.

If Herzberg is correct, why hasn't job enrichment been more readily implemented into modern organizations? Possibly one of the major reasons is the failure to fully understand the significance of that part of job design which is concerned with meeting the social and personal requirements of the job holder. Everyone agrees that work is a social activity and probably most would agree that the framework for social interaction is largely an outgrowth of technology, the specific task, and the authority relationships prescribed by the formal organization. As a result, the social system or informal organization is usually structured along the lines of plant layout, machine processes, job specifications, the physical proximity of workers to each other, and operating policies and procedures. Finally, most would agree that the social system is an important means of fulfilling workers' needs for companionship, affection, reputation, prestige, respect, and status; of providing for interpersonal communication; and of helping protect the integrity and self-concept of the individual. This conclusion is brought out in a classic statement by Chester Barnard:

> The essential need of the individual is association, and that requires local activity or immediate interaction between individuals. Without it the man is lost. The willingness of men to endure onerous routine and dangerous tasks which they could avoid is explained by this necessity for action at all costs in order to maintain the sense of social integration, whether the latter arises from "instinct," or from social conditioning, or from physiological necessity, or all three.[25]

It is entirely possible that for many blue-collar workers, the affiliation motive is much stronger than the Herzberg "motivators" to which job enrichment is aimed. Enriched job designs that reduce the opportunities for social interaction may have a negative rather than positive impact on worker satisfaction and productivity. The Reif and Schoderbek study found a number of workers dissatisfied with the job enrichment program for this reason. A typical response was: "I don't see my old friends anymore except during coffee breaks and at lunch. On the line a bunch of us used to talk and tell jokes all the time."[26] For these workers the only satisfaction they had experienced at work was their interaction and identification with other members of their primary group. It should not be surprising that they expressed an unwillingness to give up their group membership for the promise of more meaningful work through job enrichment. To them, a newly enriched job which threatened to destroy the established social pattern was unacceptable.

RESISTANCE TO CHANGE: THE DILEMMA OF JOB ENRICHMENT

In the Reif and Schoderbek study, the most frequent reply (almost half of firms using job enlargement) to the inquiry "What are the major problems encountered in applying job enlargement?" was "overcoming resistance to change." By far the most frequent response to another question, "What are the major problems experienced by the workers in adjusting to job enlargement?" was "adjustment to increased duties."[27] It became clear during follow-up interviews that the two answers were related. This led to a specific investigation of why workers would resist the opportunity to work on enlarged jobs. Four basic reasons emerged as to why workers resisted job enlargement:

- First, there was anxiety expressed by some workers who felt they would not be able to learn the new and modified skills required by the job enlargement design. Was this lack of confidence in one's ability to perform efficiently on the new job justified? The answer appeared to be yes. Most of the routine jobs did not require a great amount of skill and initiative. The very routine nature of a job reduced the possibility that an employee could ever develop the necessary knowledge and skills required by the enlarged or enriched job design.
- Closely related to the feeling of inadequacy was the fear of failure. Many workers spend years developing the skills which make them highly proficient at their present jobs. Why change now? Why give up a job which affords a relatively high degree of security for one which requires learning new skills, adjusting to unfamiliar methods and operating procedures, and establishing new working relationships? Furthermore, it should be recognized that over time most workers become highly competent in performing specialized, routine tasks. Despite the seemingly unchallenging nature of a job, the worker develops a sense of pride in knowing he can execute his job better than anyone else. This feeling of accomplishment, however limited it may appear to academicians and managers, may give the employee cause to decline an offer, or react negatively, to an enriched job.
- Third, employees' attitudes toward change can be influenced by their relationship with superiors. As workers become highly proficient in their jobs, they require less direct supervision and, as a result, achieve a high degree of freedom and independence. This feeling can be quite satisfying to the worker. Initially, the move to an enriched job would require closer and more frequent supervision, especially if the worker has to rely on his supervisor for the training necessary to master new and often more difficult job skills. Going from a state of independence to even a temporary state of dependence may not be welcomed by the worker.

    • A fourth reason for resisting job enrichment is characteristic of any change, at work or otherwise, and is commonly known as psychological habit.

Originally Chester Barnard, and since, many others, believed that psychological habit is a major cause of resisting change. Barnard noted that "Another incentive . . . is that of customary working conditions and conformity to habitual practices and attitudes. . . . It is taken for granted that men will not or cannot do well by strange methods or under strange conditions. What is not so obvious is that men will frequently not attempt to cooperate if they recognize that such methods or conditions are to be accepted."[28] Barnard's argument seems to directly apply to the modern job enrichment technique.

CONCLUSIONS

The preceding discussion of worker motivation, job design, and resistance to change was geared toward answering the question of whether job enrichment really pays off. Obviously, there is no simple answer. On the other hand, the preceding analysis of job enrichment has raised some very significant but badly neglected points that need emphasis. These include the following:

    1 There seems to be a substantial number of workers who are not necessarily alienated from work but are alienated from the middle class values expressed by the job enrichment concept. For these workers, job content is not automatically related to job satisfaction, and motivation is not necessarily a function of job satisfaction. These alienated workers are capable of finding need satisfaction outside the work environment. If they do experience satisfaction at work, it is not strictly the result of job content or formal job design but instead is largely influenced by social interactions with other primary group members. Job enrichment may not motivate this type of worker.

    2 For some workers, improved job design by job enrichment is not seen as an even trade for the reduced opportunity for social interaction. The present job may be considered unpleasant and boring, but breaking up existing patterns or social isolation is completely unbearable.

    3 The introduction of a job enrichment program may have a negative impact on some workers and result in feelings of inadequacy, fear of failure, and a concern for dependency. For these employees, low level competency, security, and relative independence are more important than the opportunity for greater responsibility and personal growth in enriched jobs.

These three points do not negate nor are they intended to be a total indictment of the job enrichment concept. On the other hand, they are intended to emphasize that job enrichment is not a cure-all for all the human problems presently facing modern management. This word of caution seems very appropriate at the present time. Many management professors and practitioners have jumped on the job enrichment bandwagon without carefully considering the research and analysis that is reported in this article. If nothing else, both professors and practitioners should take another hard look at their position on job enrichment as a method of motivating workers.

Like all sound management programs, job enrichment must be used *selectively* and with due consideration to situational variables such as the characteristics of the job, the organizational level, and the personal characteristics of the employees. Finally, job enrichment probably works best in organizations which have a supportive climate for innovation and change and a management which is genuinely interested in achieving greater job satisfaction for *its own sake.* Under these conditions, job enrichment can be practiced successfully and can offer great potential for the future, not only in terms of enriching the work experience for countless organizational participants, but also for increased productivity and organizational goal accomplishment.

REFERENCES

1   See William J. Paul, Jr., Keith B. Robertson, and Frederick Herzberg, "Job Enrichment Pays Off," *Harvard Business Review,* (March–April, 1969), pp. 61–78.

2   See Valerie M. Bockman, "The Herzberg Controversy," *Personnel Psychology* (Vol. 24, No. 2, 1971), pp. 155–189.

3   See Peter P. Schoderbek and William E. Reif *Job Enlargement* (Ann Arbor, Michigan: Bureau of Industrial Relations, Graduate School of Business Administration, The University of Michigan, 1969).

4   Harold M. F. Rush, "Behavioral Science-Concepts and Management Application," *Studies in Personnel Policy,* No. 216 (New York: National Industrial Conference Board, 1969).

5   Mitchell Fein, *Approaches to Motivation* (Hillside, N.J.: 1970), p. 20.

6   Robert N. Ford, *Motivation Through the Work Itself* (New York: American Management Association, Inc., 1969), p. 188.

7   *Ibid.,* p. 189.

8   James E. Kennedy and Harry E. O'Neill, "Job Content and Workers' Opinions," *Journal of Applied Psychology* (Vol. 42, No. 6, 1958), p. 375.

9   Charles L. Hulin and Milton R. Blood, "Job Enlargement, Individual Differences, and Worker Responses," *Psychological Bulletin* (Vol. 69, No. 1, 1968), p. 50.

10 See Frederick Herzberg, *Work and the Nature of Man* (Cleveland: The World Publishing Company, 1966): also, Douglas McGregor, *Leadership and Motivation* (The MIT Press, 1966); also Rensis Likert, *The Human Organization* (New York: McGraw-Hill Book Company, 1967); also Chris Argyris, *Personality and Organization* (New York: Harper & Row, Publishers, 1957); also Chris Argyris, *Integrating the Individual and the Organization* (New York: John Wiley & Sons, Inc., 1964); and Robert Blake and Jane Mouton, *Corporate Excellence Through Grid Organizational Development* (Houston: Gulf Publishing Company, 1968).

11 Douglas McGregor, *op.cit.,* p. 40.

12 Paul, Robertson, and Herzberg, *op. cit.*

13 Mitchell Fein, *op. cit.,* p. 15.

14 Peter P. Schoderbek and William E. Reif, *op. cit.,* pp 41–72.

15 Harold M. F. Rush, *Job Design for Motivation, Conference Board Report, No. 515* (New York: The Conference Board, Inc., 1971), p. 10.

16 Patricia C. Smith, "The Prediction of Individual Differences in Susceptibility to Industrial Monotony," *Journal of Applied Psychology* (Vol. 39, No. 5, 1955), pp. 322–329; also Patricia C. Smith and Charles Lem, "Positive Aspects of Motivation in Repetitive Work: Effects of Lot Size Upon Spacing of Voluntary Work Stoppages," *Journal of Applied Psychology* (Vol. 39, No. 5, 1955), pp. 330–333; also Maurice D. Kilbridge, "Do Workers Prefer Larger Jobs?" *Personnel* (Sept.–Oct., 1960), pp. 45–48; also Wilheim Baldamus, *Efficiency and Effort: An Analysis of Industrial Administration* (London: Tavistock Publications, 1967); also Victor H. Vroom, *Some Personality Determinants of the Effects of Participation* (Englewood Cliffs: Prentice-Hall, Inc., 1960); also Arthur N. Turner and Amelia L. Miclette, "Sources of Satisfaction in Repetitive Work," *Occupational Psychology* (Vol. 36, No. 4, 1962), pp. 215–231; and Arthur W. Kornhauser, *Mental Health of the Industrial Worker: a Detroit Study* (New York: John Wiley & Sons, Inc., 1965).

17 William E. Reif and Peter P. Schoderbek, "Job Enlargement: Antidote to Apathy," *Management of Personnel Quarterly* (Spring, 1966), pp. 16–23.

18 Hulin and Blood, *op. cit.*

19 Mitchell Fein, *op. cit.,* p. 31.

20 *Ibid,* p. 37.

21 David C. McClelland and David J. Winter, *Motivating Economic Achievement* (New York: The Free Press, 1969).

22 Hulin and Blood, *op. cit.,* p. 49.

23 Louis E. Davis, "The Design of Jobs," *Industrial Relations* (October, 1966), pp. 21–45.

24 Herzberg, *op. cit.*

25 Chester I. Barnard, *The Functions of the Executive* (Cambridge, Mass.: Harvard University Press, 1938), p. 119.

26 Reif and Schoderbek, *op. cit.,* pp. 16–23.

27 *Ibid.,* pp. 64–70.

28 Chester I. Barnard, *op. cit.,* p. 77.

Part Three

Managerial Processes

Planning

The planning process, by its very nature, requires a contingency approach because of the multitude of factors, internal and external to the organization, that affect it. Plans and planning systems should be designed to meet situational requirements and to operate effectively given the resources available to the organization and the conditions in which the firm operates. This section examines considerations affecting the development of strategic plans and planning support systems, including external environmental factors, and also discusses the requirements for strategic planning to make a meaningful contribution to current organizational decisions.

Wheelwright utilizes a contingency approach in discussing the characteristics of strategic plans. Sound strategic plans require commitment by management and are characterized by an appropriate fit with company objectives, external environmental conditions, and company resources. Case studies of three firms are used to demonstrate how the establishment of strategic plans is affected by the following factors: (1) procedures used in the strategic planning process, (2) the background of the strategic planner, (3) the strategic task exemplified by the company situation, and (4) the urgency and motivation for strategic planning necessitated by the general environment in which the firm operates.

The Lorange article discusses how to establish planning support systems contingently. Lorange classifies multinational firms as geographically oriented, product-oriented, or as evolving global companies. The planning requirements for each of these three types of firms are different and therefore the planning systems should be organized differently. Differential organization should occur along three major planning system design components that are identified as (1) the pattern of hierarchical involvement, (2) the pattern of interaction between organizational units, and (3) the approach to environmental scanning. A model is presented which suggests the appropriate characteristics of planning systems that should be developed given the type of multinational firm being considered.

Denning emphasizes those aspects of the firm's external environment that affect strategic planning. He argues that the establishment of sound strategies is a function of strategic environmental appraisal, strategic corporate appraisal, and the formulation, testing, and execution of a strategic plan. A sound strategic environmental appraisal is based on a thorough understanding of the structure of the industry in which the firm operates, demand factors in the industry, technology of the industry, and government legislation. Differential approaches are then presented for determining relevant factors in strategic planning, approaches to gathering information from the external environment, and forecasting methods.

Gerstner identifies and discusses reasons *why* strategic planning has not been effectively used in making current decisions. He suggests that for strategic plans to be effectively used in decision making management must ensure that the planning effort is decision-oriented, it is getting "top-down" leadership, guidelines are provided for capital deployment decisions, and responsibilities are well defined and rewarded.

Reading 14
Strategic Planning in the Small Business
Steven C. Wheelwright

There are few industries in the world today where a company can achieve satisfactory profitability simply by meeting its competition head-on. This is particularly true for small, growth oriented firms; companies of this kind usually achieve success by developing an approach that gives them some competitive advantage in meeting the needs of the market. The development of such an approach, most often referred to as "a strategy," has been the subject of considerable discussion during recent years.

The reason for the tremendous interest in corporate strategy and strategic planning is twofold: first, managers realize that a good strategy greatly enhances the likelihood of a firm's success; second, a body of research results has been developed that can help a company to formulate a strategy and then evaluate it to determine how good it is.

Taking the importance of strategy as given, this article considers some of the important characteristics of strategy, summarizes the findings to three small but growing companies in order to develop strategies for them, and finally summarizes those factors that should be considered as a company develops its own approach to strategic planning.

CHARACTERISTICS OF STRATEGY

The first aspect of corporate strategy that is of major importance is the identification of a set of criteria that can be used to evaluate a strategy. While the most accurate evaluation can be given only after the firm has followed a strategy for some time, this is of only minimal value to the firm planning a new strategy. What is needed is some method for evaluating corporate strategy before it is implemented.

The best approach available today for making such an evaluation is to use a set of questions regarding the strategy. A variety of questions have been suggested;[1] most of these relate to one of four basic areas:

"Strategic Planning in the Small Business," Steven C. Wheelwright, *Business Horizons*, August 1971, pp. 51–58. Reprinted with permission.
[1]See Edmund P. Learned and others, *Business Policy: Text and Cases* (Homewood, Ill.: Richard D. Irwin, Inc., 1965); George W. McKinney III, "An Experimental Study of the Effects of Systematic Approaches on Strategic Planning," unpublished Ph.D. dissertation, Stanford University Graduate School of Business, August, 1969; Seymour Tilles, "How to Evaluate Corporate Strategy," *Harvard Business Review*, XLI (July–August, 1963), pp. 111–21; and S. C. Wheelwright, "An Analysis of Strategic Planning as a Creative Problem Solving Process," unpublished Ph.D. dissertation, Stanford University Graduate School of Business, June, 1970.

How well does the strategy fit with corporate objectives and purposes?
How well does the strategy fit with the company's environment?
How well does the strategy fit with the company's resources?
How committed is the corporate management to the strategy?

Questions along the lines of the first three are based on the notion that a good strategy effectively matches the firm's resources with the opportunities and realities of the market in order to accomplish the goals of the firm. The assumption is that matching or fitting the strategy to the specific situation will result in a unique (differentiated) approach that will lead to the development of some kind of competitive advantage. The fourth question relates to how well (and how rapidly) the firm will be able to adopt the desired strategy, since the greater the commitment to the strategy, the more likely the company will follow it successfully.

A second aspect of strategy and strategic planning that is of major importance is the purpose it is to serve in a company. Since corporate situations vary widely, the role of strategic planning in the success of the firm also varies widely. At least three major purposes can be aided through the development of a strategy: the need for specialized skills and resources within the firm can be identified and defined; corporate activity can be focused and coordinated; and a standard can be established against which future performance can be compared.

RECENT RESEARCH

Identification of the specific purpose of strategy in a given firm is particularly important to the selection and development of an effective procedure for strategic planning. Recent literature on strategic planning has suggested a number of procedures that a firm might follow in preparing a strategy.[2] Since these procedures vary widely, one would expect that the resulting strategies would also vary.

In order to study the effect of various factors, especially the strategic planning procedure, on corporate strategy a program of research was carried out over a two-year period at the Stanford Graduate School of Business.[3] This research consisted of three phases.

[2]See H. Igor Ansoff, *Corporate Strategy* (New York: McGraw-Hill Book Company, 1965); J. Thomas Cannon, *Business Strategy and Policy* (New York: Harcourt, Brace & World, Inc., 1968); Frank F. Gilmore and Richard G. Brandenburg, "Anatomy of Corporate Planning," *Harvard Business Review,* XL (November–December, 1962), pp. 61–69; Robert L. Katz, "Cases and Concepts in Corporate Strategy," Stanford University Graduate School of Business, unpublished, 1967; Robert F. Stewart, *A Framework for Business Planning* (Long-Range Planning Report No. 162; Menlo Park, Calif.: Stanford Research Institute, 1963); George A. Steiner, "Long-Range Planning: Concept and Implementation," *Financial Executive,* XXXIV (July, 1966), pp. 54–61.

[3]Henry B. Eyring, Edwin V. W. Zschau, George W. McKinney, and Steven C. Wheelwright, "Research in Methods for Formulating and Analyzing Changes in a Corporate Strategy: Progress Report No. 1," Stanford University Graduate School of Business, unpublished, 1968; McKinney, "An Experimental Study of the Effects . . ."; and Wheelwright, "An Analysis of Strategic Planning. . . ."

The first phase of the program was strictly exploratory. Using two time-shared computer terminals, a number of business managers enrolled in the nine-week Stanford Executive Program (summer, 1968) were asked to use a computer program to help develop a strategy for a situation described in a business policy case. This interactive computer program acted like a consultant, probing the businessman (student) with questions to help him formulate and improve his strategy. The results of this part of the program showed that those who used the computer program developed much more creative and unusual strategies; in most cases, they felt that their strategies were improved significantly through use of the computer program.

Because the initial research was only exploratory, the second phase aimed at developing a controlled experiment that could effectively test the impact of an interactive computer program on strategies. This work, carried out by McKinney, not only tested a research methodology for examining some of the factors relevant to strategic planning, but also compared two complementary procedures for strategic planning recommended by Cannon.[4]

McKinney's work produced four major findings. *First,* it showed that the experimental methodology he devised was suitable for examining strategic planning. *Second,* by using the two procedures in sequence, as recommended by Cannon, students developed significantly better strategies than when using either of them separately. *Third,* the first procedure recommended by Cannon (referred to as opportunity oriented) led to better strategies than those developed without following one of these set procedures. *Fourth,* the second procedure (referred to as tactically oriented) resulted in strategies that were inferior to those developed without following one of these set procedures.

Because the results of the second phase of the research showed that some procedures for strategic planning can be better than no set procedure and that some can be worse, it was decided that a natural third phase of the research program would be to examine at least two different procedures for strategic planning in more detail.[5] To help in identifying the important factors in this phase of the research, the simple model shown in the figure below was developed. This model indicates that the final strategy depends not only on the procedure that is followed, but also on the strategic planner (his background, bias, and so on), the strategic task (the company's situation), and the general environment (the urgency and motivation for strategic planning, for example). While these factors overlap somewhat, they do present a scheme that is useful in designing research and in determining what type of approach would be best for a specific company to adopt.

The third phase of this research began by identifying two general classes of procedures for strategic planning—the synoptic and incremental. These two were

[4]McKinney, "An Experimental Study of the Effects . . ." Cannon, *Business Strategy and Policy.*
[5]Wheelwright, "An Analysis of Strategic Planning. . . ."

A model of strategic planning

chosen because a number of examples of each can readily be found in the strategic planning literature.

Procedures that are synoptic in nature emphasize setting corporate objectives, generating a range of alternative strategies, and then using the stated objectives to evaluate these alternatives and select the best one. This type of procedure focuses on examining the entire range of possible strategies for the company and selecting the one that will best accomplish a stated set of objectives.[6]

Incremental procedures, on the other hand, generally consist of identifying the firm's existing strategy, examining the strengths and weaknesses of the firm, and the threats and opportunities of the environment (particularly competition), and then improving the existing strategy.[7] Thus the incremental approach does not seek a comprehensive analysis of alternative strategies as does the synoptic approach, nor does it involve explicit specification of corporate objectives at the outset.

The methodology used in testing these two classes of procedures was developed by McKinney.[8] The results of this phase of research were indeed striking. *First,* it was found that even though the strategies developed using the synoptic approach were more creative (distinctive) than those developed using the incremental approach, the incremental prepared strategies were better—overall—than those prepared with the synoptic procedure. *Second,* it was found that the strategic planner, the strategic task, and the environment in which the planning took place each had an impact on the relative effectiveness of the synoptic and incremental procedures of preparing strategy.

[6]Alan R. Eagle, *Analytical Approaches in Planning* (Long-Range Planning Report No. 238; Menlo Park, Calif.: Stanford Research Institute, 1965); Ansoff, *Corporate Strategy;* Cannon, *Business Strategy and Policy,* and Steiner, "Long-Range Planning. . . ."

[7]Robert L. Katz, "Cases and Concepts in Corporate Strategy," Stanford Univeristy Graduate School of Business, unpublished, 1967; Edmund P. Learned and others, *Business Policy: Text and Cases* (Homewood, Ill.: Richard D. Irwin, Inc., 1965); Robert F. Stewart, *A Framework for Business Planning* (Long-Range Planning Report No. 162; Menlo Park, Calif.): "Organized Entrepreneurship: a Network of Tasks That Produce a Coherent Chain of Reasoning," Stanford Research Institute, unpublished, 1969; and Eyring and others, "Research in Methods . . . ."

[8]McKinney, "An Experimental Study . . . ."

Those planners who were "quantitative" in their general problem solving orientation (such as engineers and mathematicians) preferred the synoptic approach and thought it was most effective. Planners who were "nonquantitative" preferred the incremental approach.

Three different strategic planning tasks (three different corporate situations) were assigned. The company that was most successful and could follow a wide range of alternatives was handled best by planners using the synoptic approach; the company with the least amount of flexibility in its options was handled best by planners using the incremental approach.

The two aspects of the general planning environment that were examined were the motivation for planning and possible carry-over effects from the synoptic to the incremental approach. It was found that planning done in a supportive atmosphere, produced a much better strategy than planning in a nonsupportive atmosphere. There was no carry-over effect, indicating that using the synoptic and then the incremental approach is generally no better than using the incremental approach alone.

Since the results of this three-phase research program were very significant, the researchers felt the need to interpret these findings in terms of how they might apply to the practicing manager. This was done by helping three small, growth oriented firms to each develop a procedure for strategic planning and a strategy through application of these experimental results. (This was not a controlled experiment; it was simply an attempt to apply what had been learned.)

STRATEGY IN THREE FIRMS

The three companies in which these results were implemented included a new enterprise in the computer peripheral equipment industry, a prominent firm in the urban planning field, and a well-established firm in the yearbook printing industry. Each of these will be discussed in turn by first describing the firm's situation in terms of the factors identified in the figure, then describing the procedure for strategic planning that was used in each situation, and, finally, reviewing the effectiveness of each of these.

Computer Peripheral Company (Company A)

This company was in its first year of operation at the time the author became involved in the development of a procedure for strategic planning. The company had been started by two "quantitatively" oriented members of a graduate business school faculty who were interested in meeting some of the needs of the unsophisticated users of computers. Thus the orientation of those involved in strategic planning for this firm was quantitative.

In terms of the general environment, the principals in the company were well aware of the need for developing a strategy to guide them in decision making, especially since they did not yet have an established set of operating procedures which could serve as a basis for most of their short-term decisions. The strategic task facing this company was indeed mixed in nature, since its managers could follow a wide range of alternative strategies; the risk of corporate failure, however, was very high because of the competitive nature of the industry.

The first steps taken by Company A in developing a procedure for strategic planning were essentially synoptic in nature. They focused on trying to state a set of objectives for the firm and formulating some alternative strategies that could accomplish these objectives. While several ideas were generated during this phase, it soon became apparent that the range of alternatives had to be narrowed considerably in order to move forward in the strategic planning process.

This narrowing was achieved, first, by using the objectives to determine what alternatives were acceptable. Second, pressing problems were examined to decide what some of the subparts of the strategy would be, for example, what type of production facility to have, what type of marketing sales force to employ, and so on. The approach of making decisions on a subject of a strategy before the composite strategy has been stated would normally be risky, since it could easily lead to suboptimization in one area that would not fit into the over-all strategy at some later point in time. This did not seem to be a major problem in this case, however, because the company had examined a range of alternatives and these were still fresh in their minds as they began to make these decisions.

In the case of Company A, the major focus of the strategic planning process (after the initial search for alternatives) was the development of a strategic plan that could serve as a guide to action. This purpose was effectively accomplished in initiating the subparts of the strategy in such a way that they could be a guide in making the important decisions that the company faced.

Urban Planning Firm (Company B)

Unlike Company A, the urban planning company that was involved in this study had been operating for about eight years and enjoyed a solid reputation in the urban planning market. The firm had been built around the abilities of two men, each recognized in the industry for his skill in architectural design and urban planning. The president of the firm, who was professionally the better known of the two founders, was definitely "qualitative" in his approach, but had been very successful in his handling of the company's financial affairs, as well as in directing several of their consulting projects.

Company B had grown rapidly during the two years preceding this study and was close to doing $1 million in annual sales. The general environment was one in which strategy was little known in the terms generally used in business. The firm chose to focus on strategic planning at this point because their recent growth had fully utilized their existing financial resources, and they recognized that they would either have to severely limit their growth or look for other financing. The second alternative would obviously commit the founders to staying with the company for some years, and they were not certain they wanted to make such a commitment.

The strategic task facing the company provided a wide range of alternatives, each of which appeared likely to be successful, but each of which would leave the founders in a very different position in three to five years. Thus personal objectives were extremely important in the selection of a strategy for the company.

The first step in the strategic planning process was to specify a suitable set of objectives for the firm, which the principals could agree on. The background of the planners seemed to suggest that an incremental approach would be best. However, a synoptic approach (starting with objectives) was used because of the importance of objectives in this situation and because the firm recognized the need for a major decision on strategy rather than a mere modification of existing strategy.

The firm identified a number of important objectives during this first phase; these were grouped into four areas so that the impact of various strategies on them could be more easily evaluated. It was particularly important at this stage of the planning to keep the process moving so that it would not get bogged down in attempts to resolve minor differences in the objectives.

Once the relevant objectives had been identified, it was possible to evaluate and compare a number of alternative strategies in terms of how well they accomplished the four major objectives. After some lengthy discussion and additional investigations, the company was able to agree on a strategy that would meet the majority of the firm's objectives without overly constraining the principals who were involved.

Thus the major focus of strategic planning in Company B was to select a strategy which would ensure the continued success of the firm and be acceptable to the two founders of the company. Finding such a strategy was of critical importance in order to get the commitment of the entire firm to that strategy so that it could be effectively followed, and so that the decisions that were to be made in the next several months would be made in a consistent manner.

Printing Company (Company C)

The third company for which a strategy was developed as a part of this study was a family-owned printing firm. This company had originally been founded by two brothers. For approximately twenty years, the older brother had been president and in charge of sales, and the younger brother had been in charge of production.

About three years before the study was made, the older brother left the firm (selling his half to his brother) to become an administrator in a nearby university. Thus the younger brother suddenly became president and owner of the entire company. This man was knowledgeable in the production aspects of the business and systematic in his analysis of problems, but he felt somewhat unsure of himself in the sales area and as chief executive.

The company was quite aware of technological advancements being made in the industry and anxious to take advantage of them. The firm enjoyed a good reputation for quality in their geographical region, but had recently felt their position slipping somewhat as other firms seemed to be advancing more rapidly than they were. The management team (composed of five people) seemed to be convinced of the need for strategic planning but were uncertain of the procedure they should follow.

In terms of the strategic task involved, the company was anxious to maintain its position of prominence. There appeared to be at least two or three alternative strategies they could follow in order to do that. It was apparent from the start that a major shift in strategy did not seem feasible or attractive; rather, what was needed was a sharpening of strategy and a rounding out of some of the areas overlooked in the past.

An incremental approach to strategic planning appeared to be the most appropriate. Therefore, the first step was to examine what the company's strategy had been in the past. The management team of Company C spent three days (away from the office) examining their strengths and weaknesses, and the opportunities and challenges in the environment. Eventually, the team came up with a revised strategy. This strategy was stated both in simple prose and as a series of actions that were to be taken. Since many of these actions were spread out over time and since it was felt that other actions would have to be added as the strategy was adopted, the management team decided to hold a monthly planning meeting to evaluate their progress in implementing the strategy and to define these additional actions.

Thus in Company C, the major purpose of the strategy was to strengthen the corporation's position by focusing management attention on those actions required to implement the strategy. In addition, management was provided with a broader base on which to relate its many day-to-day decisions.

THE PLANNING PROCEDURE

A general approach for selecting and implementing a strategic planning procedure in a firm can now be suggested. Because of the complexity of most situations, the exact planning procedure that will work best is difficult if not impossible to specify before-hand. Nevertheless, it is possible to suggest some guidelines that will usually lead to the utilization of an effective procedure.

The first step in selecting a strategic planning procedure is to specify and define the three major variables that are relevant: the planners, the environment, and the strategic situation. Some of the factors that are important to each of these variables are listed in the accompanying table.

The second step in selecting a procedure is to identify the major purpose of strategic planning within the firm in question. The most common purposes are to:

Develop a strategy that will lead the firm to a strong competitive position
Focus and coordinate corporate activity on those areas that are most important

Establish criteria that can be used to guide decision making and to evaluate performance.

Important Variables in Strategic Planning

The planners

Their background
Their orientation in problem-solving situations
Their roles in the company (managers, professionals, owners, and so on)

The environment
The factors prompting the development of a strategy
The motivation of the planners
The urgency in completing the task

The strategic situation
The range of alternatives available to the company
The company's current competitive position
The range of alternatives the company might be willing to consider.

Rather than merely saying that all of these purposes are important in a specific situation (which would be of little value in selecting a planning procedure), it is important to state the one main objective of strategic planning in the situation in question.

Once the above two steps have been taken, the strategic planning procedure can be selected. The aim is to select a procedure somewhere between the incremental and the synoptic that will fit the company involved and will best help its managers to achieve their purpose.

Once a procedure has been selected, the major task of implementing it can be undertaken. The first phase of implementation is to assign responsibility for preparing, recording, and communicating the corporate strategy to the appropriate members of the management team. Obviously, the chief executive officer must take over-all responsibility for strategic planning.

The second phase is to start the task of strategic planning and to keep moving. This requires keeping the major purpose in mind so that if things start to slow down on a minor point, the chief executive can get them moving onto a more important part of the task. Staying on the move also requires that the planners be somewhat flexible in the procedure they are following so that, as unforeseen difficulties arise, they can make the necessary adjustments.

The final phase of strategic planning is to get the strategy in written form so that it can be communicated to others and easily be referred to. The plan is not complete until it is in writing.

In order to ensure that the company adopts the strategy which it develops, it is important that the written strategy be translated into a series of specific actions so that the completion of these actions can be measured. This evaluation of adoption of the strategy will be most effective if the firm establishes a series of periodic planning meetings (monthly or quarterly) to review progress in the adoption of the strategy and to solve special problems as they may arise.

The importance and value of strategic planning is often discussed in management seminars and publications. However, few of the details of how a firm might approach the task of strategic planning have been investigated in a research setting. This article describes how the recent program of research on strategic planning conducted at the Stanford Business School has been related to three corporate situations. The procedures used in these three situations and the general approach for selecting and implementing a strategic planning procedure are intended to help the small, growth oriented firm achieve satisfactory profitability.

Reading 15

Formal Planning in Multinational Corporations

Peter Lorange

The difficulties encountered by top management in directing complex organizations necessitate the development of support systems which implement strategy. A formal planning system is typically an important type of support system. This is especially relevant for multinational corporations because they operate in diverse environments.

How should the design process be approached? Since no algorithm exists, each design must be tailored to the specific characteristics and policies of the multinational under consideration. The design should reflect both the strategies that are to be supported and the particular demographic and economic environment of the company.

Company strategies, of course, differ along several dimensions. Thus the planning system of a conglomerate should differ markedly from that of a divisional company. Interacting with this interrelationship between corporate strategy and formal planning is a background of demographic factors such as products, markets, and organizational structure, which characterize the specific setting of a company. The nature of the settings in which the mechanics of a planning system are to be incorporated will, therefore, differ widely between different types of organizations. These background factors will constrain the actual design of the system.

"Formal Planning in Multinational Corporations," Peter Lorange, *Columbia Journal of World Business*, Summer 1973, pp. 83–88. Reprinted with permission.

Once successfully designed the system should force a continual re-evaluation and modification of the original company strategy. Environmental and intercompany pressures must be taken into account, and the design plan must be flexible enough to adapt to these changes. The main problem, then, of an established plan is the implementation of such a dynamic updating process which will be continually effective in supporting company strategy.

A thorough planning system demands a very detailed, microlevel, and tailored approach. The complexity of strategies and environments of a multinational makes the design creation process difficult. However, beyond this increase in complexity, there is no fundamental difference in designing planning systems for multinational or national companies. The planning system must be appropriate to the structure and activities of the firm.

BASIC STRUCTURES

A number of classification schemes for multinational companies exist, reflecting differences in formal organizational structures and in informal communication channels between headquarters and subsidiaries. A useful taxonomy for considering planning requirements of firms follows:

- the geographically oriented company
- the product-oriented company
- the evolving global company

The geographically oriented company is typically characterized by a predominance of national units. However, corporate headquarters usually will be actively involved in overall decision-making. This overall coordination is the result of product similarities among the subsidiaries. Often, corporate headquarters will coordinate each of the major product groups among all national subsidiaries. Nevertheless, in order to deal with local conditions better, the subsidiaries will have considerable autonomy in making local modifications in manufacturing and marketing.

The product-oriented company is typically organized globally along product lines. Normally, a number of product divisions will be fairly autonomous in producing and selling a narrow range of products. Often, divisional headquarters will be located at corporate headquarters. Worldwide production, based mainly on company-wide production cost minimization and not on domestic production considerations alone, is determined by each division. Many divisional activities are performed on a world-wide basis, such as standardization of production technology; the intercompany transference of components, semifinished parts, and finished products; and marketing procedures. The global approach to marketing strategy may result in a worldwide product image. However, sales may be constrained by limited possibilities for product modification in response to local conditions. Subsidiaries will generally play a minimal role in planning and decision-making, in sharp contrast to the dominant role of national subsidiaries of the geographically oriented company.

Decision makers in the evolving global company are structurally, behaviorally, and legally free to allocate resources globally. Such a company may implement an organizational structure incorporating divisional, functional, and geographic considerations. This grid structure has a number of characteristics, the most important of which is the extensive use of team decision-making, joint responsibility, and overlapping areas of work performance. The formal organization chart is complicated; a number of "dotted lines" indicate dual responsibility relationships and stress the enhanced channels of communication. Depending on the type and width of its product lines, the evolving global company can be seen as a modification of one of the previously described multinational companies. For example, in firms where several products are sold through many outlets there may be similarities with the nationally organized multinational and, in firms with fewer products, there may be more similarities with the product-oriented company.

This taxonomy does not include companies engaged in developing export markets, companies with an international division but with functional expertise remaining within the domestic divisions, and multinational holding companies or conglomerates. These have been excluded because their similarity to domestic structures does not pose special planning problems and because, in the case of conglomerates, of their rarity.

This proposed taxonomy has at least two major shortcomings. While in reality companies may evolve through several organizational forms, the taxonomy can offer instances of only certain specific stages of this evolution. The model can not describe the dynamics of multinational evolution. Secondly, the exact categorization of any real-life firm is often quite difficult. Hybrid and variant multinationals abound. However, the benefit of this generalization is that it allows the normalization of the structures of multinationals.

DESIGN ISSUES

Turning to the more general design issues in a formal planning system, the process can be classified as relating to portfolio, business or program planning.

Portfolio planning involves overall company policies such as the allocation of the firm's resources. Business planning is the process of deciding on policies for each major business segment of the company. Finally, programming arrives at specific action schemes within the various functional areas of the business. These three types of planning support corporate, business, and functional strategies, respectively.

Operating with three levels of strategies and with three types of strategic planning entails important consequences for the design of formal planning support systems. Therefore, three major systems design components—the pattern of hierarchical involvement, the pattern of interaction between organizational units, and the urgent need for environmental input—will adapt different designs to different situational settings.

PLANNING IN THE GEOGRAPHICALLY ORIENTED FIRM

The geographically oriented multinational typically will place strong emphasis on production and marketing in response to the particular circumstances in each region of operation. Hierarchical involvement centers in a corporate headquarters which deals with a number of national subsidiary headquarters. These subsidiaries are quite similar to independent national multidivision firms, with separate divisions for major product area and function.

Corporate headquarters will establish objectives for long-term growth, profitability, and risk. The implementation of these overall objectives into corporate strategy will involve substantial input from the national subsidiaries. Corporate headquarters will decide the broad product parameters of the company. Also, it will analyze the overall growth potential and risk factors of each environment in which the firm operates. These considerations, when applied to all geographical units or subsidiaries, will yield an overall picture of the firm's growth potential and risk characteristics. Within this framework, each geographical unit or subsidiary will be expected to meet its target rates of return. Overall resource allocation will be in the form of "adjustments" to the world portfolio.

The national subsidiaries will, in turn, engage in a kind of planning which is similar to the strategic planning of independent companies. Each subsidiary's national objectives must be in line with the overall strategic plan of the firm; within that framework, detailed strategy and goals are developed. At this level, opportunities and threats to the national economic environment are analyzed. Each of the major divisions is asked to formulate a capital expenditure budget and a national strategic plan which allocates resources among the divisions for national diversification, and for research and development efforts. The final goals of the long-rang plan of the national subsidiary, the resources committed to each division, and the performance objectives set for each division will be finalized after negotiations among the planning units involved.

Business planning is developed for each of the major areas in which the national subsidiary is engaged. It is usually carried out at the national division level by the respective division planners. Typically, each division is given a charter and a set of performance constraints by the national headquarters. The potential of the division is assessed and planning gaps are identified These gaps represent differences between potential and extrapolated development. The resulting plan will contain the divisional responses necessary to fill these gaps. The divisional strategy will then be backed up by specific action programs developed by each of the functional areas within the division.

The business and functional plans will be influenced by prevailing factors in each national economy. Environmental scanning will be performed by each of the national subsidiaries. Their familiarity with their local settings will usually ensure an adequate monitoring of local environments. The plans will contain product and marketing modifications in response to local conditions. Although the heavy reliance on national subsidiary units reduces intersubsidiary activity, some transfer of goods will take place. The subsidiaries will be free to set transfer prices by bargaining among themselves. Thus, there is no compelling need for worldwide planning of production and marketing, and corporate headquarters will have few coordinating functions to perform.

What are the main strengths and weaknesses of planning in the geographically oriented company? The major advantage is the tailoring of business and functional plans to specific national settings. The national units continually scan the environment and are able to effectively seize new opportunities in the local markets. Also, threats are more quickly perceived and effective counteractions can be taken. In total, the revenue side of the multinational business will be effectively handled.

On the other hand, however, considerable economies of scale might be lost through failure to coordinate and integrate production, product development, and research and development on a worldwide basis through vertical and horizontal interaction among units. Loss of these costs savings must be weighed against gains from the ability to tailor product lines to specific national market requirements and against additional coordination costs to determine the profitability of this planning system.

However, the most serious objection to geographically oriented companies is that corporate headquarters would have only limited control over the risk profile of the company, i.e., that the overall "mix" of national subsidiaries might not add up to a total company which accords with the stated corporate growth earnings and risk objectives. The reason for this is the strictly hierarchical pattern of involvement and the heavy "bottom-up" flow of interaction. Finally, a global perspective on the highly fractional environmental scanning data becomes difficult to obtain.

PLANNING IN THE PRODUCT-ORIENTED FIRM

The formal planning process in a product-oriented multinational company resembles the planning process of any large national divisional company. The strategic planning process starts with a formulation of overall global corporate objectives. Top executives participate and the process will be rather informal. The multinational product divisions will be integrated into the planning process through a dialogue with corporate headquarters. The objectives thus defined will then be formulated in more precise operational terms by the corporate management. Corporate strategy and goals are analyzed to reveal their impact on each worldwide division.

In contrast to the geographically oriented multinational, where national subsidiaries are to a large extent financially autonomous, the product-oriented corporate headquarters will have substantial influence on the direction of the company through resource allocation. Thus, major investment decisions in physical facilities, as well as allocations to research and development, will be important components of the strategic plans.

The business planning of each product division will proceed from its divisional charter. With the broad overall objectives of the business set through negotiations with headquarters, the division might extensively evaluate its worldwide strengths, weaknesses, and opportunities. Environmental inputs will be needed for the entire firm. The divisional headquarters probably will rely on elaborate reporting systems for each of its functional activities. After weighing the available alternatives within the limitations of the overall divisional objectives, business planning will solidify into a worldwide divisional strategy and specification of goals.

PRODUCTION AND MARKETING

Programming will take place for each of the worldwide functional areas of the division. The worldwide scope of functional activities complicates the programming task. Worldwide production programming, for example, will often be a difficult and highly complex process which requires the active participation of a large number of people from all sectors of this worldwide functional area. Programming, of course, should be closely coordinated with the division's overall business plan. Coordination across functional areas is quite important and will entail the enforcement of worldwide programs. Thus it is essential that the final programs implement business strategy and that they not become counterfunctional.

The strengths and weaknesses of the planning process for this type of company result from the particular systems design options chosen. The chief strength of a properly functioning product-oriented planning system is that central headquarters will have, to a considerable degree, an opportunity to lead the company in a desired direction, either by its own planning actions or by influencing the substance of a division's planning. This is the result of the heavy concentration of top level involvement and the "top-down" dominance of the interaction. A properly functioning planning system will ensure that research and development expenses are minimized, thus benefiting the entire corporation. Also, economies of scale in production will be realized by the worldwide organization.

Planning in this type of company might also entail disadvantages: the problem of integrating timely, reliable, and relevant environmental data from all segments of the worldwide business is formidable; hence, the extensive centralization of worldwide production and marketing activities might result in substantial opportunity losses from ineffective adjustments to local conditions.

PLANNING IN THE EVOLVING GLOBAL FIRM

The strategic planning process in the evolving global corporation differs from the two previous classes of firms. The first reason for this relates to the choice of overall objectives. Because top executives will typically be of different nationalities, and because the ownership of the company will often be largely international, the global company will have little or no national domination at the corporate headquarters. Nor will the subsidiaries be likely to have a geographic-nationalistic mode of operation. Thus it is likely that the organization will define more rational and effective global goals with freedom from structural, psychological, and legal constraints. Strategy will specify considerable geographical build-up programs as well as contractions and will specify shifts in overall product patterns. The strategic plan, then, normally will be a synthesis of inputs from various product areas, geographical areas, and functional areas. Through negotiations between executives representing product, functional, and geographical elements, the process will consolidate and operationalize inputs to fulfill overall corporate objectives.

Business planning described for the two other classes of multinationals probably will not exist in the global multinationals. Instead, the three-dimensional approach, stressing product, functional, and geographical points of view, will also be applied to subplans. The rationale for subglobal planning is a desire to gain efficiency and save time in the planning process. The heavy involvement of many persons, as well as the intricate matrix patterns of hierarchical interaction, necessitate streamlining the planning process to save time. The subglobal "modularization" of planning may serve such a function. Because stress will be on subglobal rather than global points of view, there will be a danger of suboptimal planning. However, heavy interpersonal contact patterns and the availability of good information may help to prevent this. The firm's programming activities will be undertaken in a similar "matrix-type" fashion.

The formal planning process in the global multinational has a number of distinctive characteristics. Accurate environmental inputs from environmental scanning at relevant points in the organization will constantly inform the product, functional, or geographic-type sector of the firm. An effective information and communication system will be needed to monitor these inputs into a reliable and useful environmental data bank. Interactive aspects of the planning process might become more complicated because of the wide use of matrix-type decision-making by committees. This will require more complex behavioral patterns of interaction. Since there often is shared responsibility, and since functional responsibility for different parts of the operations rests at different organizational levels, the interaction between headquarters and subsidiary units, as well as the interaction among subsidiary units at different levels, will be very complex and most aspects of this planning process should approach simultaneity.

What are the potential strengths and weaknesses of planning in an evolving global multinational? The major strength of such a planning system, provided it functions reasonably well, is that it allows the multinational firm to adapt its activities to its situational business settings, so that its resources will be optimally utilized and global objectives attained. Only with this type of planning will there be a reasonable chance to avoid suboptimalities due to fractionalization and overemphasis of geographic or divisional considerations found in the other two types of multinationals.

However, the state of the art in formal planning systems design does not yet provide sufficient operational guidelines to enable the implementation of workable matrix systems. The relatively complicated lines of responsibility, the number of persons involved, and the extensive hierarchical interaction create the danger that the planning structure will be unwieldy. Thus, the complexity of the process in operation might be so imposing that the company would revert to a simplified planning structure.

CONCLUSIONS

Figure 1 shows the distinctively different design choices facing the three types of firms and provides a set of generalized design rules. This underscores the necessity of tailoring the planning system of a firm to its particular setting and operations. The designer will, nevertheless, have a formidable job elaborating the system in the context of the firm's setting. He should, of course, remember the simplifying assumptions on which this discussion rests.

Figure 1   Summary of the Situational Design Structure for Formal Planning Systems in Multinational Corporations

	Design Factor		
Situational setting	Hierarchical involvement	Pattern of interaction	Approach to environmental scanning
Geographically oriented	Several organizational levels. Decentralized.	Strictly hierarchical, and "bottom-up" dominated interaction.	At the national levels. No integrated global scanning.
Product-oriented	Concentrated at top. Centralized.	"Top-down" dominated interaction.	Global level scanning. Few scanning inputs from national level.
Evolving global	Several organizational units in a grid pattern.	Highly interactive and in the several directions of the grid pattern.	Scanning performed and monitored at all levels.

Reading 16
Strategic Environmental Appraisal*
Basil W. Denning

Few business executives today would argue seriously with the proposition that certain events which take place outside the business may have a far more important effect on the year's results than anything which takes place inside the business. For example, British entry into the Common Market involves significant changes in the environment in which firms operate and may well determine growth, survival, adaptation or liquidation almost without regard to the company's short term operating efficiency. Furthermore, for the majority of businesses, the ability to control changes in the environment is vastly less than the ability to control projects or operations within the firm. This combination of characteristics, overwhelming importance and inability to control, raises vital considerations for the executives of any company attempting to take a systematic approach to future strategy.

The evolution of a deliberate strategy essentially involves three different activities which clearly interact but which can be separately examined and described. These three activities are:

- Strategic environmental appraisal;
- Strategic corporate appraisal;
- Formulation, testing and execution of a strategic plan.

Where any of these activities is inadequately performed, the company runs the risk of operating with an ineffective or inappropriate strategy, the penalty for which may well be liquidation or loss of autonomous control, and will certainly be a loss of potential profit.

In considering the first of these tasks, strategic environmental appraisal, the initial problems are to define what is meant by a firm's environment and to generate adequate systematic information about it. More specifically, if it is realised that events in the outside world are important and that some are partially predictable, how can a company so structure its approach to the mass of external events and influences that it can make reasoned assumptions about those external trends and changes which are vital to the future of that business? If a satisfactory and relevant structure can be devised, there then arises a set of problems in the area of information. On what events should information be obtained? How regularly? In what depth? By whom? At what cost? What use will be made of this

"Strategic Environmental Appraisal," Basil W. Denning, *Long Range Planning*, March 1973, pp. 22–27. Reprinted with permission.

*This text is taken from the joint Society for Long Range Planning/Institute of Cost & Works Accountant's book *Corporate Planning and the Role of the Management Accountant*, to be published in the Spring or Summer of 1973.

information when it is gathered? What forecasting techniques can be used? With what probable margins of error?

The resolution of these issues can be approached by answering the question with which managers are now familiar from their experience with internal information systems. For what purpose is this information required? And by whom?

At this point it seems important to stress that there may be significant differences in the type of external information which is required on a day to day basis for efficient operating and the type of information necessary for strategic purposes. In the course of everyday business a great deal of information about short term operating factors is normally obtained and used. However, in this paper we are not considering the question of present operations but the more complex problem of a company's future strategy. There is no necessary reason why the information gathered on a day to day basis in the ordinary course of business should be the same as is required to resolve a company's strategic problems. Indeed, in one useful study of methods used by a group of American companies to gather external information it emerged that only about 47 per cent of the information collected in the ordinary course of operations was of value for strategic purposes.[1] Nor, of course, was there any guarantee that this 47 per cent contained all the information relevant to the strategic problems of the company.

There are a number of interrelated problems in approaching the question of strategic environmental appraisal. These can usefully be set down in the form of questions as follows:

- Within what broad structure can events, trends and factors in the environment be considered?
- How can a particular company determine which of those factors are relevent to its strategic problems?
- What methods should be used for gathering information in the areas which are considered relevant?
- What methods of forecasting from this information are available which would be helpful?
- Is there any way in which the costs of obtaining this information, processing it, and making forecasts from it, can be compared with the benefits obtained from having it?

A STRUCTURE FOR ANALYSIS

There is a variety of possible and relevant structures within which one can assemble information and organize analysis for strategic appraisal. No one structure is ever right or wrong in any absolute sense, and choice of the most suitable structure in a particular company must be determined on grounds of relevance and practicality.

In a situation where a company is starting to develop a more systematic approach to these problems a useful starting point may be the structure shown in

Figure 1. The figure sets out the elements of a structure and illustrates each point from the situation in the packaging industry in the U.K.

The starting points of the analysis in this case are four key factors, the structure of the industry, demand in the industry, the technological position of the industry, and the situation with regard to government legislation. This last includes general legislation in areas such as tax or monopolies, and special legislation in areas such as standards of health and tariffs. Within this framework of key factors, clearly the first task is to obtain an accurate statement of the present position. As shown on the chart, which does not attempt to be comprehensive, there are several factors in each of these areas which need close attention. Some of these can be quantified—for example, the number, size and output of existing companies; others may be more qualitative such as the real nature of competition in the industry and the extent to which the key competitive factors are price, delivery, credit, technical quality or some other factor.

The second stage in the analysis is to use this information about the present position plus other relevant knowledge and opinion to determine likely future trends over which the management of any one company will have very little control. For example, in the packaging industry there has been a close correlation between demand for packages and gross national product. Clearly a forecast of GNP will be highly relevant in this situation. Similarly, in packaging, changes in prices of the major raw materials—wood, paper, glass, tin plate, aluminum and plastic—can shift a substantial volume of demand from one type of packaging to another.

The third stage in the analysis is in some ways the most critical. Once a broad picture of the likely changes in the environment of a particular industry has been developed, these changes should be examined to see how far they represent threats, on the one hand, or opportunities on the other. To pursue our example, all companies in the packaging industry will have to formulate a response at least to six foreseeable environmental trends, each of which involves both threats and opportunities.

1 The tendency for customers to shift their purchasing from one type of product to another in response to changes in relative price, consumer preference and availability of new products. This may be a powerful argument for not specializing in any one product. Alternatively, if specialization in one product type is chosen, it may be wise to develop a broader product base than packaging to allow for the pattern of change, which is predictable, as opposed to the actual amounts and timing of changes which are much more uncertain.

2 The increase in private branding which may displace a substantial volume of nationally branded manufactured goods. There may be a need to shift production from long standard runs for a few large customers to a wider variety of customers who may require smaller quantities. This may affect the whole economics of production and the pattern of selling arrangements.

3 A squeeze on costs and prices. To prepare for this, financial policies may need review, or diversification may be considered as a means of maintaining

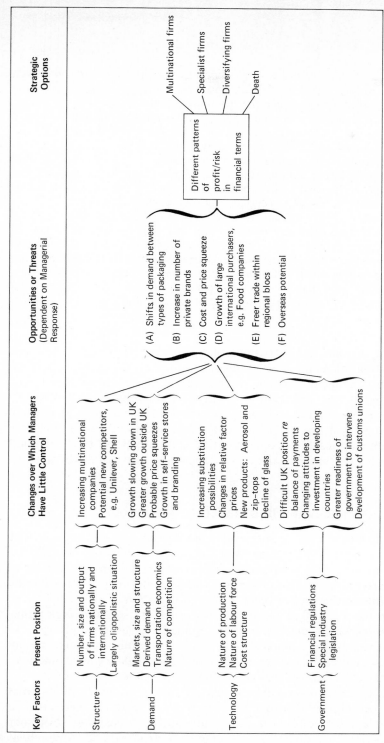

Figure 1 Structuring a strategic environmental analysis for the packaging industry.

profitability. Alternatively, a company may increase its investment in research and development to give greater differentiation, novelty or higher technical characteristics so that higher margins may be maintained.

    4   The increasing power and influence of multi-national companies. Where a substantial volume of packaging is bought by the large multi-national food companies, there is a real possibility that they will use their purchasing power to favour the multi-national packaging company which can meet their global requirements and give larger volume discounts. This would impact upon the geographical spread of factories and could offer scope for a competitive advantage to be gained by a company recognizing this trend and adapting to it.

    5   Freer trade within regional blocks such as the EEC. This clearly increases potential competition and increases the possible market to be served without artificial trade barriers. Thus the geographic scope of competition is changed and the question of transportation economics will need reconsideration.

    6   The industrialization of developing countries. As this takes place new needs, both consumer and industrial, are emerging. This offers a substantial growth potential which is reasonably predictable by area and offers new opportunities.

    Clearly, these are not the only areas of opportunity or threat. There are questions of pollution, of technological advance, possible new entrants into the business from petro-chemical companies and many others. However, the major aim of this paper is to draw attention to the process whereby a series of partly predictable factors can be set out and the opportunities or threats to all companies in the industry can be systematically assessed. When this process is put together with the corporate appraisal the opportunities and threats to the individual company stand out more sharply and allow executives to make deliberate and reasoned choices.

WHICH FACTORS ARE RELEVANT IN STRATEGIC APPRAISAL?

A major difficulty in environmental appraisal is the problem of selecting only that information which is genuinely strategic. With the enormous quantity of statistics, technical reports, market data, political intelligence and so on which is available, the individual company can easily be swamped with data and emerge after months of analysis with little in the way of really useful information.

    Again the problem is to find a systematic approach to selecting data rather than to prescribe rules which can be universally applied. One useful approach is to explore the sensitivity of the company in terms of its future markets, trading operations and financial results to different factors on which data can be obtained, and then to concentrate effort only on those factors which are most sensitive.

    To illustrate this approach Table 1 sets out some examples of external factors with different sensitivity to two companies in different industries, a manufacturer of telephone equipment and an integrated oil company. Consider two different economic parameters, gross national product and government

Table 1 Examples of Comparative Environmental Sensitivities

	A major manufacturer of telephone equipment	An integrated oil company
GNP	Medium	High
Government capital spending	Very high	Low
Technical change	Very high	Medium/Low (except for electric car)
Sociological change	Very high (communication habits)	Very high (private car movements)
Environmental pollution	Low	High
Political risks Middle East	Low	High

capital spending. Demand for oil is acutely sensitive to changes in gross national product whereas in the short run, a telephone equipment manufacturer is not very sensitive to such changes.

In contrast, the level of government authorized capital spending is a critical element in demand for major communications equipment but is not a major determinant of demand for oil. This simple example of exploring external sensitivities, some quantitative, some qualitative, illustrates the use of an important method of choosing factors to which one will choose to devote effort.

METHODS OF GATHERING INFORMATION

The next problem facing the executive in this area centres on the means which he will use and the costs which he will incur in obtaining the relevant information. Mention has already been made of the enormous volume of data, comment, gossip and reports, all of which may have something useful to contribute to an understanding of the environment. Again, one is concerned primarily with the question of developing some systematic approach to allocating effort to different areas.

Little effective research has been done on this problem but one useful book *Scanning the Business Environment* has been written by F. J. Aguilar.[1] The book reports the results of a research effort to examine the ways in which a small group of American companies actually obtained external information, to what use they put the information, how it was disseminated in the company, and what value it had to strategic or operational problems. The book reveals a fairly haphazard state of affairs as being normal. Reviewing the results found in practice, Aguilar suggests that some order can be brought into the situation by broadly classifying means of scanning areas of the environment into four modes. These are set out in Table 2.

Essentially these four classifications represent different levels of effort which may be devoted to different types of environmental information and therefore provide a framework for choosing a level of effort. They range from

Table 2   Modes of Scanning Environmental Factors

Undirected viewing	General exposure with no specific purpose, e.g. newspapers, general journals, magazines.
Conditioned viewing	Directed exposure to a more or less clearly identified area of information plus readiness to assume it may be important, e.g. trade journals, lunching in the City.
Informal search	Limited and unstructured effort to obtain specific information, e.g. telephoning small group of contacts.
Formal search	Deliberate effort to receive particular information, e.g. market survey, economic forecasting model, needs research, acquisition search.

'undirected viewing', i.e. general exposure to newspapers and journals at minimal expense, to the formal search through means such as a specially commissioned piece of market research, normally an expensive undertaking.

In attempting to choose how much effort to put into scanning of different factors, it is helpful to draw together the structure of environmental appraisal and the concept of sensitivity. It can reasonably be argued that some effort should be made to scan all the areas which are seen as being significant in the appraisal of the present position and the ensuing forecasted changes over which the company has no control. But where a choice has to be made about increasing the level of effort above the minimum of undirected viewing, clearly a company should devote a greater degree of effort to those factors to which it is most sensitive. For example, it makes sense for an integrated oil company to build econometric forecasting models in order to provide regular and sophisticated forecasts of the gross national products of the major industrial nations, whereas the telephone equipment manufacturer may well feel that conditioned viewing, in this case a critical review of published economic forecasts, is adequate. Similarly, the telephone equipment manufacturer may well decide to use formal search to examine technical and scientific developments in electronics and spend a substantial amount on this effort, an expenditure which would not be justified in the oil company.

In reaching decisions about the appropriate level of effort and the means of information gathering to employ, it is important to distinguish between the type of information needed for short term operating purposes and the information needed for strategic appraisal. All companies have enormous amounts of information reaching them every day from the outside world. Aguilar demonstrates that a large amount of this information is relevant only to operational decisions. Examples would be the rumour of a new promotion by a competitor, comparisons of wage and salary rates between firms, and competitors' anticipated price changes. Much of the information required for strategic purposes, however, is of a different order—proposals for new legislation, news of a company in one's field looking for a buyer, the report of a new process being introduced by a competitor which will reduce his operating costs. Since any company is likely to receive much of its information from operating personnel one of the important tasks is to help them to develop the necessary perception to identify relevant strategic information and to transmit it to those concerned with strategic problems. In most companies, positive efforts need to be made to explain what is strategic and to encourage reporting of this sort of information across a broad band of executives.

METHODS OF FORECASTING

In certain selected areas, chosen hopefully on reasoned grounds, companies will choose to make individual forecasts. This is not the place to examine critically the many techniques of forecasting but it is appropriate to consider some of the problems of forecasting environmental factors.

The first point which needs to be stressed centres on the importance of defining clearly the purpose of the forecast. Writing in the *Harvard Business Review* in 1967, Professor J. B. Quinn, a pioneer in the field of technological forecasting, wrote:

> To be useful, technological forecasts do not necessarily need to predict the precise form technology will take in a given application at some specific future date. Like any other forecasts, their purpose is simply to help evaluate the probability and significance of various possible future developments so that managers can make better decisions.[2]

Using this thought, it is worth remembering that environmental forecasts are used primarily to provide assumptions on which planning can take place. Forecasting to provide planning assumptions, however, is a different exercise from forecasting to determine production requirements or to inform shareholders. And it is different essentially in the degree of accuracy required. It may be considerably more valuable to forecast that over the next 10 years the structure of an industry, say pump manufacturers, is highly likely to shift from a large number of small companies to an oligopolistic structure with four or five dominant firms and a selection of smaller specialist firms, than to forecast gross national product to plus or minus 2 per cent in 1976. Again, a test of the accuracy necessary in forecasting environmental variables can be assisted by applying the sensitivity approach described earlier.

In many companies this limited requirement of accuracy means that considerable reliance will be placed not on the internal development of sophisti- cated forecasting techniques but on a critical appreciation of published forecasts. Although this will call for a considerable degree of expertise, it is a different task from that of the working forecaster. It lays stress on an ability to question assumptions, to examine for coherence, to compare differences with other forecasts and to apply judgement.

A second point is that many of the key environmental variables are not quantitative in nature. For example, a critical forecasting area for an integrated oil company is the political situation in the Middle East. While the effects of certain actions can be quantified, the forecast of probable developments and of their timing is essentially an exercise in sifting expert opinion and establishing probabilities.

A summarizing chart which tries to draw some of these threads together in terms of the areas where forecasts may be required, the typical information available and the techniques likely to be useful inside a company, is shown on Table 3.

COSTS AND BENEFITS OF SYSTEMATIC ENVIRONMENTAL APPRAISAL

It would be comforting to the writer, if not the reader, if an article such as this could end with convincing quantified evidence that a systematic approach to the strategic analysis of the environment paid direct cash dividends. Alas, I know of no studies of this type and would be hesitant about accepting their conclusions if they exist. One needs only to be reminded of the complete failure of the German general staff in the second world war to use the priceless information obtained by 'Cicero' about future allied intentions to realise the difficulty. Information obtained from any source must be absorbed and believed and acted upon. In the Cicero case, the information was not absorbed because it contradicted other information arising from a separate and 'private' source. Many individuals may absorb information but not really believe that it has value, especially if it conflicts with conventional wisdom or practice. And even if it is believed and acted upon, there is no guarantee that the action will be wise. It would be imprudent therefore to expect too solid a result from any cost benefit research study.

Perhaps one is wiser to return to first principles. The basis of the argument for a more systematic and professional approach to any management problem is not that you will ensure a 'right' answer, but that you increase the probability of success of a series of decisions over time. One can reasonably argue from first principles, observation and experience that knowledge of the environment is necessary to any company in deciding how it will conduct itself in the future. Obtaining knowledge of the environment can be carried out haphazardly or systematically. A systematic approach means that one determines the type of information which one needs from some structured picture of the environment, and makes efforts to obtain information on all the factors within that structure. Since the finding of information takes time and money, one would examine what level of effort and cost was being devoted to what types of information and one would want to be clear about the necessary accuracy of that information for the purpose one had in mind. One could then choose on a reasoned basis against some subjective assessment of the value of the information and its cost, whether the benefit justified the cost. Similarly one can assess the extent to which relevant information is being passed from technical, marketing and financial executives at

Table 3 Environmental Forecasting for Planning Assumptions

	Sources of information	Techniques
Economic forecasts **(a)** National economy **(b)** Sector forecasts	**(i)** Government and private forecasts. **(ii)** Industry association, government, private forecasts. **(iii)** Market research.	**(a)** Critical appreciation of published forecasts. **(b)** Development of models or relationships for sector forecasts. **(c)** Input-output analysis. **(d)** Large number of quantitative techniques.
Technological forecasts	**(i)** Technical intelligence service reports. **(ii)** Technical market research. **(iii)** Research into competitors' developments.	**(a)** Demand and conditional demand analyses. **(b)** Opportunity identification techniques. **(c)** Theoretical limits testing. **(d)** Parameter analysis. **(e)** Various systems analysis methods. **(f)** Discipline reviews. **(g)** Expert opinion.
Sociological forecasts	Wide variety of sources of data, including government reports, educational forecasts, population forecasts, regional forecasts, skilled labour forecasts, institutional changes, etc.	**(a)** National models such as built by Battelle (unlikely to be done in any one corporation). **(b)** Expert opinion.
Political forecasts	Political intelligence services and government reports.	Expert opinion.
Forecasting competitors' actions	Any intelligence about competitors.	Any relevant technique to give information from intelligence.

an operating level in the organization to the areas where it may be needed for strategic decisions.

These would be the essentials of a systematic approach. It would be reasonable to argue that an approach of this type would be more likely to ensure that a company was not missing out on vital knowledge of the environment, was reasonably well informed about the key external factors affecting it, was more likely to have an effective grasp of its opportunities and threats and was thus more likely to take better decisions about the future than a company which relied solely on haphazard methods. In practice, few companies of any size are completely haphazard. They cannot afford to be. Nevertheless, one can safely say that most companies could improve the probability of making wise strategic decisions and using their external information gathering resources more effectively if they examined their approach to the problem in a systematic way along the lines described in this article.

REFERENCES

1 F. J. Aguilar, *Scanning the Business Environment,* Macmillan (1967).
2 J. B. Quinn, Technological Forecasting, *Harvard Business Review* (March/April 1967).

Reading 17

Can Strategic Planning Pay Off?

Louis V. Gerstner, Jr.

One of the most intriguing management phenomena of the late 1960s and 1970s has been the rapid spread of the corporate or strategic planning concept. Except for the so-called computer revolution, few management techniques have swept through corporate and governmental enterprises more rapidly or completely. Writer after writer has hailed this new discipline as the fountainhead of all corporate progress. In 1962, one published report extolled strategic planning as "a systematic means by which a company can become what it wants to be" (Stanford Research Institute). Five years later, it was called "a means to help management gain increasing control over the destiny of a corporation" (R. H. Schaffer). By 1971, praise of strategic planning verged on the poetic; it had become "the manifestation of a company's determination to be the master of its own fate . . . to penetrate the darkness of uncertainty and provide the illumination of probability" (S. R. Goodman).

It is not surprising, therefore, that one company after another raced to embrace this new source of managerial salvation, and, as a result, most major companies today can boast a corporate planning officer, often with full attendant

"Can Strategic Planning Pay Off?" Louis V. Gerstner, Jr., *Business Horizons,* December 1972, pp. 5–16. Reprinted with permission.

staff. It seemed appropriate to ask some CEOs whether strategic planning has lived up to its advanced billings. Three anonymous reactions were as follows:

> Strategic planning is basically just a plaything of staff men.
> It's like a Chinese dinner: I feel full when I get it, but after a little while I wonder whether I've eaten at all!
> Strategic planning? A staggering waste of time and money.

Some CEOs, of course, would disagree with these comments, and certainly few if any would agree publicly. But the fact remains that in the large majority of companies corporate planning tends to be an academic, ill-defined activity with little or no bottomline impact. Observations of many companies wrestling with the strategic planning concept strongly suggest that this lack of real pay-off is almost always the result of one fundamental weakness, namely, the failure to bring strategic planning down to current decisions. Before describing this problem and some possible ways to overcome it, I shall briefly define what I mean by the term strategic planning.

FORECASTS ARE NOT STRATEGIES

Many strategic planning programs begin with the extension of the annual operating budget into a five-year projection. This can be a valuable exercise, particularly for institutions that have operated on a yearly or even monthly planning cycle. Most companies, however, soon discover that five-year operational and financial forecasts, in and of themselves, are ineffective as strategic planning tools for a fundamental reason: they are predicated on the implicit assumption of no significant change in environmental, economic, and competitive conditions.

In other words, they are purely extrapolative projections, and, by practically everyone's standards, fall far short of real strategic planning. They offer no overview, no analyses of external trends, and no perceptive insights into company strengths and weaknesses—elements that both theorists and practitioners would agree are central to real corporate planning.

Forecast planning of the sort I have described can usually be identified by leafing through a company's planning documents. Pages and pages of accounting information, detailing five years of financial forecasts with little or no explanatory material, are one earmark. Graphs of projected future performance also tend to follow a predictable pattern, that is, if recent performance has been good, the forecast calls for more and more of the same—on into eternity.

On the other hand, if performance has been poor, the forecast will allow for a year or two to effect the inevitable turnaround, and then—off to eternity. (The manager doing the forecasting hopes, of course, that he will get promoted before the two-year period is up.) Working with forecasts like this, executives tend to dismiss the second, third, fourth, and fifth years as irrelevant and continue to concentrate solely on the current year, that is, the annual budget. Most companies seem to have passed beyond forecast planning, and its weaknesses are fairly manifest—namely, a preoccupation with accounting data as the principal output of a planning program and the assumption that the future, at least in relation to general economic indexes, will closely resemble the past.

Recognizing these weaknesses, many institutions have introduced a more rigorous planning program aimed at defining or redefining the basic objectives, economics, competitive profile, and outlook of the company. These formal strategic planning processes show a distinct family resemblance. They usually begin with an assessment of environmental trends and an analysis of the company's strengths and weaknesses. A statement of corporate goals is then developed. From these three elements, a juxtaposition between the organization's present position and its desired position is derived; comparison of the two positions defines the well-known strategic gap. Finally, plans are developed to close the gap and bring the two positions together (Figure 1).

Of course, the steps required to arrive at the statements of present and desired position are quite detailed. For example, one large U.S. company requires each of its more than fifty profit centers to include in its annual strategic plans all the information shown in Figure 2. For each profit center, the initial written output may run to a hundred pages. Such an effort is inevitably painful and time-consuming, but it may be necessary in the first planning cycle. Barring major changes inside or outside the company, subsequent plans can be considerably shorter. Since the specific elements of a good strategic plan have been described in many texts, I shall not dwell on them here. Instead, I shall move on to the central question of why strategic planning so often fails to pay off and what can be done about it.

MAKE DECISIONS—NOT PLANS

As mentioned earlier, the most fundamental weakness of most corporate plans today is that they do not lead to the major decisions that must be made currently to ensure the success of the enterprise in the future. All too often, the end product of present-day strategic planning activities is a strategic plan—period. Nothing really new happens as a result of the plan, except that everyone gets a warm glow of security and satisfaction now that the uncertainty of the future has been contained. Unfortunately, warm feelings do not produce earnings or capture market share. Neither do graphs of five-year earnings projections, gap charts, or complex strategy statements.

What does produce earnings are strategic decisions, and strategic decisions should be the ultimate output of a strategic planning program. That is, the strategic plan should clearly set forth the critical issues currently facing a company or division in terms of alternative courses of current action. If there are more than five or six issues, they are probably the wrong ones. If the decisions do not involve major risks or investments and/or changes in competitive posture, they are the

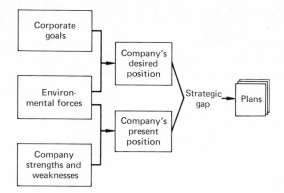

Figure 1 The basic strategic planning concept.

wrong decisions. If the decisions do not have to be made now, they are wrong.

This is the creative leap that too many managements fail to make in strategic planning. They fail to ask, "What do we do now as a result of this plan?" They fail to recognize that the end product of strategic analysis should not be plans but current decisions. Some of the reasons why the leap to decisions is not made are important to understand.

It Is Risky Probably the most significant reason is that stating plans in terms of decisions frequently requires an executive to take a personal stand on an important and controversial issue. In other words, it can often make or break his career. All of us can call to mind men who have staked their careers and reputations on major strategic recommendations, for example, Learson leading IBM into digital computers, and Donaldson opening DLJ to public capital.

Figure 2 Elements of a strategic plan.

But most of us can also call to mind a few corporate casualties of such decisions—men who took a strong position as an adversary on a major strategic move and found themselves on the losing side. So the leap to decisions takes courage, and most executives prefer to play it safe. We can look at the top management teams of too many companies without finding any risk-taking, success-story managers.

It Is Difficult   Strategic planning, almost by definition, deals with the most complex questions facing a company. Just assembling the data to measure the variables is a considerable task. Moreover, once the data are in hand, the real job begins—the job of synthesizing critical issues and strategic options to resolve those issues. This is fundamentally a creative process. It cannot be programmed or systematized. To structure meaningful, practical action programs requires insight, wisdom, and perspective. Many executives find it an elusive, uncomfortable task.

It Requires Leadership   Most strategic decisions are controversial. The underlying issue being addressed is rarely new to the corporate executive team; typically, it has been debated within the company for some time. I use the word "debate" advisedly; these discussions tend to be problem-definition, opinion-swapping sessions. Because the issues they address have vital implications for individual careers, they soon become less than objective, and they almost never lead to action. In some companies propositions such as "We ought to liquidate that business" can bounce about in the executive committee for months or even years without any decisions being made. The missing ingredient is the leadership needed to push through toughminded analysis and action on controversial matters.

I know of one company that has been facing a rather critical strategic problem for fully a year now—namely, survival. The underlying strategic issues were correctly identified and thoroughly analyzed over three years ago. A detailed action program was outlined. It is still valid, still ready for implementation, yet the company is headed for bankruptcy. The reason is simple: the CEO simply cannot bring himself to make some tough decisions. He is waiting and hoping that his key lieutenants will reach a consensus. Given the nature of the decisions, this is impossible. In a situation of this kind only the CEO can exert the needed leadership, and this CEO is not the man to do it.

The Value System Works Against It   Too often a company's executive motivation system flies in the face of strategic decision making. This occurs for two reasons. First, good managers tend to be promoted so fast that they never have to live with the medium- to long-run outcome of their plans. Second, incentive compensation is often tied either to short-term earnings performance or to stockprice movements, neither of which has anything to do with strategic success.

DOWN TO THE "BOTTOM LINE"

As we have seen, the leap from plans to decisions is an entrepreneurial step that cannot be reduced to a routine. Making it happen is an educational, attitudinal task, but some concrete steps can be taken to facilitate the process.

Meet External Risks

To begin with, the formal strategic planning program should be thoroughly reviewed to ensure that it requires a decision-oriented approach. Many planning systems simply are not designed to demand decisions as the end product. Instead, they produce forecasts of financial results or statements of objectives, or future action steps. This type of planning, which is basically "momentum" planning as opposed to dynamic planning that is attuned to the realities of external change, often results from excessive internal focus in the planning process. To overcome this problem, heavy emphasis should be given to three critical aspects of strategic analysis that are particularly important in identifying key issues and decisions: evaluating competitive strategies, developing contingency plans, and assessing environmental forces.

Evaluating Competitive Strategies   Too many corporate plans fail to give even minimal attention to the present and future action of competitive firms. They set out elaborate strategies without any real consideration of competitive reaction. Two examples of a simple analysis that can be extremely helpful in overcoming this weakness are shown in Figure 3 (note that 3b calls for a review of each major competitor's existing strategy). Figure 4 then attempts to evaluate the strength of the company's own strategy against that of each competitor. In most cases, analysis of this kind leads to the identification of opportunities or threats that call for current management decisions.

Contingency Plans   Most companies with active planning programs recognize the value of asking "what if" questions, taking important contingencies into account. Yet few really address this issue in a substantive way. A frequent excuse is that there are so many potential contingencies that it would take years to analyze them all.

The obvious answer to this objection is that one can and should be very selective, and deal only with the one or two possible contingencies that could upset the entire strategy. Here are two examples:

An American packaging company selling a commodity product regularly reviews potential price changes by one of its smaller competitors. This competitor dropped prices sharply several years ago, catching the market leaders by surprise and increasing its own market share significantly.

Last year, in speculating on the major contingencies they might face, the management of the packaging company asked, in effect, "What if they should do it again?" In view of the capacity situation in the industry, it was not an unrealistic question. Accordingly, the company meticulously planned a contingency program to

Figure 3   Analysis for Overcoming Competitive Action
a   Example of Strategic Issues and Decisions

Strategic issues	Current decision alternatives
Should investment be made to strengthen our position in product line X?	Commit to $5 million now, $40-50 million over next five years or Begin to "milk" or divest product line X
Should we pursue direct distribution in product line Y?	Begin to phase out current distributors or Significantly upgrade present distribution program and reduce direct sales
Should we seek offshore sourcing on product line Y?	Begin search for offshore sites or Initiate a major study of cost reduction/productivity in domestic facility
Should we diversify away from our present business base?	Initiate active acquisition program or Launch major internal new product development program

be put into effect if and when its small competitor should move again. Early this year he did. The packaging company was ready and responded immediately and effectively.

An electronic components company depended on a single large customer for 30 percent of its sales. Management simply asked, "What if they should integrate backward?" There was no visible reason to believe that such a move was in the offing, and the question would probably not have surfaced as a serious issue without the forcing device of required contingency planning. But development of the contingency plan led to two real benefits. *First,* it brought out the need for some preventive medicine, and this became a continuing part of the company's relationship with its big customer. *Second,* it led to a detailed economic analysis of the risks and disadvantages to the customer of backward integration. One year later that analysis was instrumental in convincing the customer that a tentative step he had been about to take toward integration would be unwise.

b   Assumed Strategies of Key Competitors

		Competitors A	B	C
Product line	Systems primarily		X	
	Components primarily	X		
	Systems and components			X
Markets	Domestic	X		
	World wide		X	X
	Domestic with foreign licenses			
Technology	Leader	X		X
	Follower		X	
Customers	Government		X	X
	OEM	X		X
	Direct		X	X
Profit economics	Mass production/high volume			X
	Specialized, high price	X	X	

Assessing Environmental Forces   We can all think of companies that have failed to anticipate important changes in their external environments. The U.S. automobile industry, with all its vast managerial and financial resources, was simply unprepared for the explosive issues of automotive safety and air pollutants. And during the late 1960s, stock brokers on Wall Street almost drowned in their own success because they had failed to anticipate the volume growth of the industry and its attendant "back-office" requirements.

Despite the difficulties of forecasting sociopolitical or even marketplace trends, the most aggressive companies are energetically taking steps to raise their present level of competence in this arena. These are some of the approaches they have found productive:

Drawing on the work of the so-called "futurologists," who seek to identify major developments emerging in the world. Their work is rarely directly applicable to a given industrial situation, but it can serve as a starting point for rigorous internal assessment of issues highly relevant to the corporation's future.

Building on broad economic forecasts. Here again it will be necessary to translate general trends into specific issues, but this simply requires thoughtful attention by corporate management and their advisors. A number of large companies annually prepare a general economic forecast to be used by all their operating units. These forecasts cover such subjects as government spending programs, expected major shifts in international trade and monetary policies, and potential new regulatory programs in ecology, safety, hiring, and so on.

Simply requiring a written assessment of critical environmental trends in every strategic planning document.

Figure 4   Assessing Corporate Plans Against Each Competitor's Strategy

| | Key Elements of Our Strategic Program | | | |
Competitor A's basic strategy	Build continental production capacity	Expand continental sales force	"Unbundle" system pricing	Concentrate R&D on applications
Component supplier	Effective	Neutral	Effective	Neutral
Domestic only	Neutral	Strong	Neutral	Neutral
OEM market	Neutral	Neutral	Effective	Effective
Leader in technology	Neutral	Neutral	Neutral	Weak
Specialized/high price	Weak	Neutral	Effective	Weak

The assessment of environmental forces is not easy; nevertheless, the major issues (and therefore the strategic decisions) facing many institutions today are arising more and more in the external sociopolitical milieu. Merely being able to anticipate the issues (even if the "right" response is not clear) is a lot better than being caught completely unaware.

Provide Effective "Top-Down" Leadership

Since the purpose of strategic planning is to make basic decisions on the future course of the company, it is ultimately a responsibility of the CEO and his key lieutenants. In other words, top management cannot confine itself to perusing written plans and giving a perfunctory once-a-year approval. That would be abdication, not responsible delegation. To ensure that the right set of critical issues and decisions is in fact identified, top management must actively involve itself in the planning process. Even before the process of issue identification begins, the CEO should satisfy himself that the company's financial targets are properly integrated.

Most companies today include some statement of financial objectives in their corporate plans. Surprisingly often, however, these objectives fail to take into account the inherent interrelationships among most financial targets. Sales, earnings, and return-on-investment targets, which are of course inextricably interlinked, often are set apart from each other in the manner of a diner ordering a meal at a Chinese restaurant: one from group A, two from Group B. Since the objectives chosen are inherently inconsistent and thus worthless if not actually debilitating, the result is frequently a case of strategic indigestion.

More important, too many companies fail to recognize the potential advantages of making trade-offs among various financial objectives. As Figure 5 shows, a company can choose widely different sets of financial and operating objectives and still achieve an identical over-all earnings per share target. Each set of objectives implies a fundamentally different way of operating the company, and each set is internally consistent.

Again, top management can vitally enhance the effectiveness of the whole strategic planning process by instituting a regular and rigorous process of *strategic review*. Most companies today accept without question the fact that operational planning is inseparable from operating control, that one without the other is meaningless. But too often they ignore the logical corollary in the strategic planning area and omit the vital follow-up linkage between planning and control. To be sure, top management conscientiously reads the strategic plans and sits through strategic planning presentations, but it rarely challenges the validity of the plans or their relevance to current decisions. This situation is dangerous, because a division manager cannot be both advocate and challenger of his strategic plan.

Strategic review should not be a mechanistic process. One of the most successful approaches I have seen is to get a few key members of the top management team out of the office for two or three days of informal but intensive review of the strategic options as set forth in the plan. Superb leadership by the CEO is required to keep the discussion centered on the critical problems and opportunities, keep it on an objective plane so that no one feels threatened, and come out with a set of actionable decisions as the end product. Given such leadership and adequate advance preparation by the participants, valuable results can be achieved.

Strategy review, of course, is not entirely a free-form creative process; it can be supported by an analytical framework. For example, one CEO has his staff subject the plans submitted by division managers to a set of validity tests designed to identify and evaluate the key assumptions underlying performance forecast in the plan (Figure 6). This top-down testing process ensures that issues and

Figure 5 Three Strategies to Achieve 15 Percent EPS

High volume approach		High asset utilization approach		Aggressive financing approach	
	%		%		%
Sales growth	15.0	Sales growth	7.0	Sales growth	10.0
PBIT/sales	4.0	PBIT/sales	4.0	PBIT/sales	4.0
Asset turnover	3.5	Asset turnover	4.0	Asset turnover	3.5
Dividend payout	60.0	Dividend payout	60.0	Dividend payout	40.0
Debt/equity	50.0	Debt/equity	50.0	Debt/equity	60.0

Figure 6   Testing Key Strategy Assumptions

Major assumptions in proposed plan	Validity test
Market growth up 7 percent per annum	Consistent with historical rate
Market share up 10 percent over next five years	Possible, but unlikely; down 5 percent over past five years
Prices will hold firm	Unlikely; 2 percent per annum decline for past two years
Japanese will not move into market	No substantiation

Net assessment:

1. Plan is unrealistically optimistic.
2. Highly unlikely that market share can be increased without substantial price reduction.
3. Competitive threat from Japanese not adequately dealt with.

decisions that the division managers have failed to identify will be brought to the surface for top management consideration.

Provide Guidelines for Capital Deployment

As a company diversifies its activities, the task of capital allocation tends to emerge as the central function of the corporate CEO—the heart of strategic decision making in a multibusiness enterprise. Resource allocation or portfolio decisions arise because of the need to maximize over-all results by managing a collection of relatively independent operating units or product lines as a single portfolio. This means setting earnings targets and making investment decisions for any one division (or product line) within a framework that encompasses the whole enterprise. Of course, it can be argued that portfolio management is not a required function in a multibusiness company, since the pieces can simply be allowed to operate idependently. But by that reasoning, a corporate management team is equally unnecessary, since if all the parts operate, independently, there is no "value added" at the corporate or holding company level.

Too often, companies actually undermine their strategic planning programs by approaching major capital deployment decisions purely on a traditional capital budgeting basis. That is, in principle all requests for capital funds are filled no matter what division or product line they come from, provided only that they clear a single financial hurdle such as a pay-back or discounted cash-flow rate of return. Of course, when the requests exceed the available resources, some ranking system is employed, but, in effect, the hurdle is simply raised and a new single-number decision rule is applied uniformly to all requests.

This approach fails to provide any portfolio assessment of the various parts of the enterprise considered as a group. Therefore, capital can flow to a mediocre division or product line at a rate that is the same as—or even faster than—the rate at which it flows to a high-potential division. This simply perpetuates the status quo, frequently negating the value of the strategic planning at the corporate level. In other words, the CEO's all-important decision of allocating capital is blurred and in fact abdicated.

One simple but powerful approach some multibusiness managers are using today is to sort their individual businesses into three broad portfolio categories: sources of growth (future earnings); sources of current and intermediate earnings; and sources of immediate cash flow. One of my colleagues has suggested that these categories relate directly to the so-called product life-cycle curve which can also, for these purposes, be termed a business life-cycle curve. When a company views its operations in this manner, some interesting implications for the capital allocation process may emerge.

Of course, change in capital allocation decisions is only one of the many management implications of multibusiness strategic planning. The impact of this broad perspective can and should carry over to every facet of management responsibility. For example, Figure 7 illustrates its impact on marketing planning and, more important, on decisions relating to the marketing mix.

The need for such top-down guidelines is perhaps most vividly apparent in the "pruning" or divesting activities of a multibusiness company, aimed at milking declining divisions or products for cash, which will then be redeployed in more attractive opportunities. (Hopefully, opportunities exist for redeployment, but this kind of analysis can bring to light imbalances at either end of this spectrum.)

While such a deinvestment program often makes eminent sense from a corporate point of view, it is a rare division or product manager who willingly plans himself out of business. Most managers will argue that the new growth is just around the corner; all they need to get the pay-off is a little more investment "up front." For this reason, strategic planning efforts rarely bring deinvestment-redeployment decisions to the surface, unless the CEO has provided explicit guidelines. He must find ways to create an environment in which different planning criteria and different performance criteria are not only acceptable but demanded.

This brings us to the human relations dimension of strategic planning, and the final action step needed to make it effective.

Target Responsibility and Reward Results

No strategic planning program will produce bottom-line results without careful attention to human motivations. This is a highly subjective matter, tied inextricably to the leadership style of the CEO, but two general recommendations apply almost universally.

First, involve the decision makers. In a decision-oriented planning environment, developing and implementing strategies can only be the responsibility of line managers. This does not mean that the CEO should do away with his planning staff and planning processes. Rather, it means that the output of such staffs and

Figure 7 Impact of Multibusiness Strategic Planning on Marketing

Marketing decision area	Strategy adopted for division or product line		
	Invest for future growth	Manage for earnings	Manage for immediate cash
Market share	Aggressively build across all segments	Target efforts to high-return/high-growth segments Protect current franchises	Forego share development for improved profits
Pricing	Lower to build share	Stabilize for maximum profit contribution	Raise, even at expense of volume
Promotion	Invest heavily to build share	Invest as market dictates	Avoid
Existing product line	Expand volume Add line extensions to fill out product categories	Shift mix to higher profit product categories	Eliminate low-contribution products/varieties
New products	Expand product line by acquisition, self-manufacture, or joint venture	Add products selectively and in controlled stages of commitment	Add only sure winners

processes should only be an input to top management. It is top management's responsibility to weigh strategic issues, apply judgment, and make the decisions. Strategic planning may be a staff function, but strategic decision making is the responsibility of the CEO and his top management team. Several companies have underscored this point by requiring division managers to present and defend their strategies and plans in the absence of their staff planners. It seems to work.

Second, reward good strategic decision makers. If all promotions, bonuses, and other rewards go to the executives who meet or exceed short-term budget goals, without regard to the way they position their organizations for future success, then strategies and strategic plans will be no more than a charade. I am not suggesting that short-term performance measures should be eliminated; rather, I am saying that long-term performance milestones must be added and built into the annual performance review, particularly in companies where the best line managers get promoted every eighteen to twenty-four months.

An example of the sort of multidimensional performance appraisal system I have in mind is shown in Figure 8. The weighting factors shown are purely illustrative. They should be tailored for each individual operating unit to reflect the importance of short- versus long-term performance. To return to our earlier example, "building" criteria ought to be weighted more heavily in "future growth" units, while short-term goals should have most of the emphasis in "cash" units.

Figure 8   Performance Appraisal: Balancing Current and Future Needs

	Current performance (0-100)			Future building performance (0-100)				
Division manager	Profits % budget	ROI versus budget	Weighting factor	Success of implementing long-term program	Quality of strategy	Quality of man-power	Weighting factor	Over-all rating
A	100	100	1	20	20	50	3	310
B	80	100	3	100	80	80	1	530
C	120	80	2	100	90	90	2	585
D	70	70	1	75	80	100	3	475

Following the widespread introduction of data processing in the 1950s, many companies sooner or later were obliged to recognize that the promise of this great management tool was stubbornly refusing to materialize. Real, tangible return on investment was low or nonexistent. Today, a great many companies have largely overcome this problem. Not without a struggle, they have substantially brought their computer systems under control, and most of these managements are a good deal wiser for the experience. The most successful among them, I believe, would include at least the following among the lessons they have learned:

The effort must be integrated directly into the important decision making activities of the company. Each potential new project must pass the "so what" test.

The chief executive holds the key to success; his commitment and leadership are absolutely necessary.

The pay-off when it works is substantial, and it can be measured in dollars and cents.

All of these lessons apply to strategic planning. When it is focused on current decisions, under the leadership of a committed CEO, it works. And when it works, we may be sure that the pay-off will show on the bottom line.

Decision Making

This section examines contingency approaches to decision making. Primary emphasis is placed on the various considerations that determine the appropriateness of various group decision strategies, committee structures, and utilization of quantitative techniques.

Hall, O'Leary, and Williams utilize a managerial grid approach to identify and define five strategies of group decision making. They are Default Decision Making, Good Neighbor Decision Making, Traditional Decision Making, Self-Sufficient Decision Making, and Eye-to-Eye Decision Making. The two grid dimensions are (1) the concern for decision adequacy and (2) the concern for commitment of others to the decision. Each of the strategies is discussed along the effectiveness dimensions of time-loss, implementation of decision, and ability of the group to profit from its experience in the future. This kind of analysis should enable management to choose the decision-making approach that is most effective in a given situation.

Delbecq's article focuses on three different strategies for utilization of group structure, roles, processes, style, and norms which should be understood and used by managers confronted with different task situations. Routine decision-making, creative decision-making, and negotiated decision-making tasks differ from each other, and managers must utilize the appropriate structure and processes in response to each of these three situations.

Filley analyzes the use of committees for decision making. He contends that effectiveness is contingent upon three major considerations: committee size, role of the chairman, and composition of the membership, and suggests that size should be determined on the basis of the task to be accomplished, the chairman chosen on the basis of the type of role he is expected to play, and the membership selected on the basis of need for cooperation versus competition and homogeneity versus heterogeneity.

Browne argues that the use of operations-research techniques in decision making must be applied contingently for optimum results. Browne suggests that the technique applied to a specific problem should depend on the type of problem, complexity of the problem, type of input available or output required, ability and experience of the users of the technique, and amount of money available to solve the problem. A hierarchical framework of problem types is also presented to help the reader determine when each technique should be used.

Reading 18

The Decision-Making Grid:
A Model of Decision-Making Styles

Jay Hall
Vincent O'Leary
Martha Williams

The success of the group decision-making process depends on the combined capacities of those engaged in decision making to work together with satisfaction and creativity. Too often decisions are made on the basis of fire-fighting methods, "rules of thumb," and gut-level intuition, rather than on the basis of any sound systematic procedures. The fact that decisions reached in the traditional manner frequently fail to accomplish the desired goals is reflected, for example, in continuing conflict between labor and management. Groups of decision makers find themselves making the same "bread and butter" decisions over and over again. Improperly solved dilemmas continue to pop up persistently until appropriate solutions have been found.

The paradox of decision making is that, despite the fact that groups generally tend to produce more adequate decisions than individuals working alone,[1] most executives are at a loss regarding the effective employment of groups in reaching decisions. This occurs even though individuals do most of their living, learning, working, and deciding within a group setting.

The confusion, frustration, and waste of time which may characterize an unsystematic attempt at group problem solving frequently result in the stronger members' adopting a "give me the ball—no strings attached" attitude which foreshadows the disintegration of the group. Rather than reflecting the resources in the group in such a way as to insure successful implementation, decisions are frequently imposed on the responsible groups. Time loss and confusion are avoided. Individual needs for action are met. But the decisions thus made must eventually be made again, resulting in more loss of time, additional confusion, and administrative impotence.

Failure to employ a systematic approach is not necessarily the fault of today's decision makers, however, for little theoretical information concerning decision making has been available to them from researchers in the field. A theory of decision making—individual or group—has proven to be a particularly slippery and elusive item for social scientists, despite forty years of research. By and large, investigators have had to content themselves with discovering and identifying facets of the decision-making process which seem to result in a decision of one quality or another. Consequently, decision makers who must daily confront realistic problems have been left to play business games, construct probability tables, and either "pass the buck" or monopolize the responsibility for decision making in their organizations.

A CONCEPTUAL FRAMEWORK

The purpose of this discussion, therefore, is to provide a conceptual framework from which a theory of decision making might be built. In keeping with the assumption that one must first be able to understand what is happening before one can undertake experimentation, this discussion will attempt to make sense out of the group decision-making dilemma through the use of a conceptual model called *The Decision-Making Grid* so that individual styles of decision-making behavior in a group context may be analyzed, and the consequences associated with particular styles may be explored.

Following are some typical approaches to decision making:

Frankly speaking, too many chefs spoil the broth. If a man wants good decisions and action, then he shouldn't let himself get bogged down by "what the group thinks." All they'll do is run around in circles. Groups waste time looking at every irrelevant issue they think of and wind up with a decision which is a poor compromise. Facts are facts; and no amount of discussion is going to change that. When it comes to making decisions, turn me loose—no strings attached.

Groups make me uncomfortable! I've seen some people get stepped on every time they open their mouths and I've known others who get so carried away with the group that they lose their own identities. I think most decisions have either already been made by the experts or can be made by following precedent. Personally, I can't see going out on a limb in front of a bunch of people and embarrassing myself. It's better to just "mark time" till the furor dies down and then throw in with the fellows who know what they're doing.

Getting along with the people you work with is a lost art. The easiest thing in the world is to be critical of others and disagree with any idea you didn't think of first. It takes work and a certain amount of self-sacrifice to really understand other people, but in the long run things run smoother and everybody is happier if they all try to do this. I don't feel comfortable with decisions which everyone can't be happy with.

No man is an island. Everybody would like to have his own way in making decisions, but the world doesn't work that way. You've got to work with other people and get the best decision you can with as much agreement as you can. You can't ever expect everybody to agree, but as long as enough support a position you're all right. It's a funny thing, but a good majority is just about always right.

It seems to me that the more people share the responsibility for reaching a decision, the better it will be. There are a lot of resources floating around that you never know about unless you can get everybody involved in the decision. Disagreement occurs, sure, but it usually turns out to be valid and everybody wasn't aware of all the issues. I think it's sounder if a decision reflects the best thinking of everybody and not just my own. A decision without support is like a Cadillac without any gas; looks good, but can't go anywhere.

Each of the above statements reflects an individual's feelings about how "good" decisions can best be obtained. Each reflects a fairly common approach to decision making which all of us have encountered or used at one time or another. In practice, each differs from the other; but they all have some basic similarities in that they each represent behavior stemming from some "concerns" individuals have in working on decisions. The concerns people bring with them to the group decision-making situation often determine how well the group will be able to work in reaching decisions.

In an earlier discussion of decision making, it was suggested that one of the main factors contributing to the group decision-making dilemma was the difficulty in deciding how to tackle a given problem. It was further suggested that this difficulty reflected the inability of parties to the decision to arrive at a common understanding of the decision issues; that is, difficulties in group decision making may stem primarily from the failure to find and adopt a shared frame of reference for viewing the group's task.[2]

Assuming that the principal means of attaining a shared frame of reference is the interchange of information and opinions, the quality of the interaction of individuals becomes important. For a group to succeed in finding such a shared viewpoint, the individual members must be able to relate to one another in such a way as to create conditions under which people can be candid and open without fear of reprisal and under which everyone feels equally responsible.

The decision-making styles employed by the group members are important determinants of the extent to which people can relate to one another in this manner. More often than not, however, individuals are unaware of either the style they employ or its consequences for the group process. An instrument designed to delineate types of individual decision-making behavior in the group and the way in which these types affect the group process is the *Decision-Making Grid.*

A TEACHING MODEL

Rationale for the Grid

A grid format as a means of integrating fairly abstract kinds of information into meaningful conceptual tools has proven to be an effective teaching instrument in a number of settings.[3] Blake and Mouton,[4] for example, adapted many of the seemingly disparate theories and practices of management into the *Managerial Grid,* thus providing both a sound model for understanding managerial behavior and a vehicle for communicating otherwise nebulous concepts to managers in the field. The success obtained with the *Managerial Grid* suggests that a conceptual model employing a grid format might also lend a much-needed structure to the area of group decision making.

Basic Grid Dimensions

The *Decision-Making Grid* is constructed in such a way as to reflect the relationships between two basic dimensions. The two dimensions chosen for investigation are:

- The concern for decision adequacy experienced by the individual decision maker.
- The concern for commitment of others to the decision which individuals experience when working on a joint decision-making task.

Research in group decision making,[5] while not focusing directly on these two areas of concern to decision makers, has indicated that the degree of concern for either dimension—as reflected in the way members work on the task—is closely related to the effectiveness of the decision-making group. As stated earlier, the various concerns which individual members bring with them to the group session have been demonstrated to affect significantly the manner in which all parties to the decision are able to work together. Therefore, concerns bearing directly on decision-making behavior per se would seem to provide meaningful material for an investigation of group decision-making effectiveness through an analysis of the individual behavior of members in the group.

Orienting the Grid

The concern for decision-making adequacy and the concern for commitment are conceived in the Grid format as being independent of one another. A concern for one does not necessarily indicate a concern for the other. It is possible, therefore, for an individual to have a concern for adequacy without a concern for commitment, and it is possible for him to experience concern for commitment without having a concern for adequacy.

These two dimensions, because of their assumed independence, might be thought of as being at right angles to one another as shown below. The horizontal axis of the Grid represents the concern for decision adequacy among those engaged in decision making. The vertical axis represents the concern for commitment of others which individuals experience in working toward decisions.

Each axis has been scaled from 1 to 9 in order to reflect the degree of a particular concern which individuals possess. Thus, for purposes of discussing the degree of concern for either dimension which is characteristic of a person, the value 1 denotes minimal "concern for" while the value 9 denotes maximal "concern for." By placing the two concerns at right angles to one another, decision-making styles can be evaluated from the standpoint of the relationship between concern for decision adequacy and concern for commitment which a given style represents.

The Decision–Making Grid

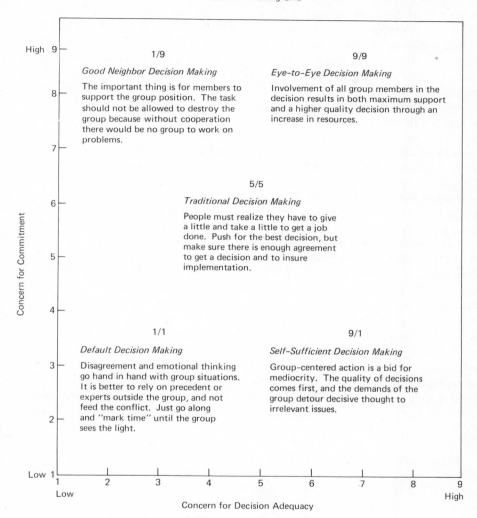

Concern for Commitment (vertical axis)

Concern for Decision Adequacy (horizontal axis)

1/9

Good Neighbor Decision Making

The important thing is for members to support the group position. The task should not be allowed to destroy the group because without cooperation there would be no group to work on problems.

9/9

Eye-to-Eye Decision Making

Involvement of all group members in the decision results in both maximum support and a higher quality decision through an increase in resources.

5/5

Traditional Decision Making

People must realize they have to give a little and take a little to get a job done. Push for the best decision, but make sure there is enough agreement to get a decision and to insure implementation.

1/1

Default Decision Making

Disagreement and emotional thinking go hand in hand with group situations. It is better to rely on precedent or experts outside the group, and not feed the conflict. Just go along and "mark time" until the group sees the light.

9/1

Self-Sufficient Decision Making

Group-centered action is a bid for mediocrity. The quality of decisions comes first, and the demands of the group detour decisive thought to irrelevant issues.

THREE CONFLICT APPROACHES

Conflict "Theories"

Three approaches to decision making rest on the assumption that the concern for decision adequacy and the concern for commitment are mutually exclusive. They are seen as being in conflict. It is not deemed possible to experience concern for both simultaneously. Two of these individual "theories" view the two concerns as being so different that they embrace one to the exclusion of the other entirely. The third approach results in suppressing both concerns in order to make continued membership in the group tolerable.

Self-sufficient Decision Making   The 9/1 position, at the lower right-hand corner of the Grid represents decision making which is characterized by a maximum concern for adequacy of the decision and minimal concern for commitment. This style is based on the assumption that the group is an inappropriate place for decision making and that discussion among several individuals can only result in losing sight of the relevant issues. The 9/1 decision maker feels most confident with his own assessment of a problem. The facts—as he sees them—dictate the solution. He does not allow himself to become involved with others' thoughts or attitudes, but rather pushes for a solution to the problem which seems "best" to him. Whatever the circumstances, he conducts himself as if final responsibility for the decision were his alone and feels it is incumbent upon him either to "lead" the group to the correct solution or to make the decision and impose it on the group.

The success of the person who employs the 9/1 approach to decision making, in terms of getting his decisions incorporated in the group solution, is directly related to the amount of power he possesses. To the extent that the 9/1 individual possesses either formal or informal power over the group, his decisions will tend to be incorporated in the final group product. Thus, a powerful 9/1 may usurp the power of the group and control the quality of its output. The powerless 9/1, however, frequently meets with open opposition from the group—since it is not immobilized by an imbalance of power—and he may be rejected if he persists in selling his point of view. While the powerful 9/1 may also be rejected on a covert level, the powerless 9/1 can easily receive the type of open rebuffs reported in studies of opinion deviates.[6] This may result in the powerless 9/1's withdrawing from active participation in the group and assuming a more passive role, thus, in effect, reducing the size of the group.

Good Neighbor Decision Making   The good neighbor "theory" of decision making, as represented in the 1/9 or upper left-hand corner of the Grid, reflects a preoccupation with maintaining harmony and understanding among group members. The concern for commitment is high and overrides a concern for decision adequacy. The 1/9 decision maker feels that the group must be maintained in the face of task requirements and that the way to accomplish this is to work for agreement among members. Good neighbor decision making proceeds on the basis of an ostensible assumption of mutuality and trust among members, fair play, and peaceful co-existence. In reality, however, it occurs because of an innate feeling of *distrust;* directed primarily at one's self. The 1/9 decision maker trusts neither his own opinions nor his ability to deal effectively with conflict. Therefore, the primary responsibility of the 1/9 decision maker becomes one of minimizing conflict and promoting the general welfare within the group. The 1/9 individual is sensitized to discordant notes in the group's activity and is more concerned with fostering an atmosphere of co-operation than in pursuing conflict-laden issues, however relevant they might be to the decision.

The 1/9 decision-making style may take the form of conformity behavior in the group. The individual may have such an aversion to disagreement and conflict that he tends to discredit his own opinions and, rather than open up touchy areas, may shift his judgments so that his ideas correspond with the rest of the group. Asch[7] has described this type of conformity behavior and attributed it to a "distortment of judgment" resulting from social pressures. Should the 1/9 individual's attempt at smoothing over troubled waters fail, he is likely to adopt a more passive role and go along with the group even though he disagrees.

Default Decision Making Decision making by default, as depicted in the lower left-hand or 1/1 corner of the Grid, is not viewed as a "natural" phenomenon as are 9/1 and 1/9 styles of behavior. Rather, a 1/1 behavior is seen as a reaction to some potential or actual occurrence in the group which forces an individual to assume a passive, non-participating role. People commonly adopt 1/1 behavior because they are not interested in the discussion at hand. Still others become 1/1 in order to protect themselves. The person who feels inadequate or perceives others in the group as threatening frequently will assume the role of a "silent member," for example. Whatever the case, the individual may assume such a role only when he has suppressed his natural concern for either adequacy or commitment and when he sees such suppression as being in his own best interests. Thus, the powerless 9/1 described earlier may well fall back on a protective facade of 1/1 decision making. Similarly, the 1/9 individual may retreat to a less frustrating role of passivity when he is ineffective in his peacemaking attempts. Default decision making, like 1/9, may also take the form of conformity. Unlike the unconscious conformity via distorted judgments which characterizes 1/9 behavior, however, 1/1 conformity falls into a second category, identified by Asch[8]: conformity purposely adopted in order to avoid "seeming different."

Default decision making reflects an abdication of responsibility and concern for either adequacy or commitment. Thus, the 9/1 who assumes the 1/1 style is abdicating his concern for decision adequacy. The 1/9 who moves to the 1/1 position has suppressed his concern for commitment. Each has had to sacrifice but a single concern. While it may be possible to forego a decision-making style based on but one concern in assuming a 1/1 orientation, it seems unlikely that an individual whose decision-making style reflects a concern for both adequacy and commitment could comfortably suppress both concerns in coping with frustration in the group.

THREE MIXED APPROACHES
Mixed "Theories"

While the three "theories" discussed so far represent conflict or suppression orientations to the concerns for adequacy and commitment, there are several mixed approaches which reflect the notion that these concerns, though opposed to each other, may be considered simultaneously. These mixed "theories" employ the 9/1, 1/9, or 1/1 positions in combinations.

Traditional Decision Making   In the center of the *Decision-Making Grid* is found the 5/5 or traditional decision-making style. This approach to decision making proceeds on the assumption that, while concerns for adequacy and commitment are both necessary, they exist in opposition to one another. The 5/5 individual believes that the more one concern is emphasized the less the other can be. Basically, the 5/5 decision/maker is more concerned with the adequacy of a decision; but, in view of his awareness that some commitment is necessary, he is willing to compromise decision-adequacy to a degree in order to insure "enough" commitment. Usually, "enough" commitment is defined as support from a majority of those participating in the decision making. This type of decision making is the more common style currently found at both the cultural and individual levels and reflects an attempt to employ the democratic process.[9]

The 5/5 individual is willing to confer with the group members on decision, share some of his power with them, and modify his position to reflect at least some of their views. He does this, however, more out of a perceived necessity for insuring action than out of an assumption that he or the decision can profit from the exchange of information. Traditional decision making is motivated primarily by the desire for an adequate decision, but it operates on the implicit notion that the majority is usually right. Thus, a great deal of 5/5 energy is expended in mustering a majority block of support, rather than in focusing on the basic issues as in 9/1 decision making.

The Bargaining Pendulum   Bargaining, as a special type of decision-making behavior, may be viewed as an attempt to insure incorporation of those elements of particular importance to the individual in the final decision. The motivation for bargaining behavior is that of a primary concern for decision adequacy, as defined by the individual, coupled with his awareness of resistance on the part of other group members. In order to get his own set of judgments accepted, the bargainer "trades out" with other group members on an "I'll support your two points if you'll support my three" basis. The bargainer is unconcerned with adequacy on the traded points. He is also unconcerned with commitment as such and simply employs a bargaining strategy in an attempt to satisfy his concern for decision adequacy. Thus, the bargaining pendulum may be viewed as swinging from 9/1 (on "own" points) to 1/9 (on "traded" points) and back to 9/1 as long as necessary.

Needless to say, the bargaining pendulum style of decision making is not based on the notion that both commitment and adequacy are necessary, but on the expediency of reducing resistance by pledging support. Bargaining is frequently employed by groups in conflict such as labor and management or UN members and seems to represent a more extreme form of 5/5 traditional decision making.

The 9/1 Boomerang Effect   Another style which seems to represent a combination of concerns is the 9/1 boomerang or the "I told you so" ploy. In this style of decision-making behavior, the individual has withdrawn from a 9/1 position in the face of conflict to a 1/1 "marking time" attitude. The 1/1 phase of boomerang behavior is characterized by passivity and a form of self-contained hostility on the part of the individual. Should events fail to support the position taken by the individual, he might well continue to behave in a passive and hostile way; but should he be proven correct, he bounces back to a 9/1 orientation and reminds the group of its treatment of him—thus completing the boomerang swing.

Thus, groups which mistakenly feel that they have "convinced" a member that his position is wrong may be creating the conditions for 9/1 boomerang effect. The powerless 9/1 described earlier frequently employs this tactic in decision making when rejected by the group.

The Benign 9/1   On the surface benign 9/1 behavior closely resembles 1/1 decision making in appearance. The individual who employs benign 9/1 in working with others to reach decisions actually is primarily concerned with the adequacy of the decision as he sees it. He is unwilling to become involved in the group activity, however, unless he feels the group is prepared to adopt his ideas. His participation is contingent upon invitation from the group since this assures him that the group is aware of his presence and of its own reliance on him.

Once such an invitation is offered, the benign 9/1 individual abandons any semblance of 1/1 behavior and proceeds to "tell" the group of the solution to its problem. By waiting until he is asked, the benign 9/1 musters additional power for his position in that he can then remind the group "You asked me, remember!" In this way, otherwise powerless 9/1 individuals are often able to place the group at a disadvantage and force acceptance of their ideas.

Relevance and the 1/1 Seesaw   Probably the most commonly used mixed "theory" of decision making is the 1/1 seesaw. All of us have employed this style of behavior at one time or another, often unconsciously. Under this style, the individual adopts a polite detachment from group discussion during periods in which he is disinterested in the discussion content. Should the discussion turn in a direction which holds more relevance for his area of interests, however, he enters in vigorously with whichever style is characteristic of him. Thus, relevance is viewed as a weighting factor in this style and acts to counterbalance 1/1 withdrawal. The less relevant the discussion, the more 1/1 the behavior; the more relevant the discussion, the less 1/1 behavior becomes. The individual seesaws up and down in his interaction with the group, with the result that he may unintentionally undermine the group's motivation and contribute to a breakdown of group cohesion.[10]

By orienting the concern for decision adequacy and the concern for commitment dimensions at right angles to one another, it has been possible to delineate several styles of decision making which are commonly encountered when individuals join ranks for the purpose of reaching a group decision. In addition to three "pure" styles represented in the Grid, five "mixed" approaches have also been discussed. The individual theories of decision making which have been touched on thus far reflect a strong orientation toward the incompatibility of *concerns for decision adequacy* and *concerns for commitment*. It may be this orientation which is responsible for the general lack of a systematic approach which currently characterizes group decision-making activity.

Integrating Adequacy and Commitment

Realistically, if a decision-making group is to be effective, its members must have concern for the adequacy of the decision they reach. The notion that such a concern is basically incompatible with a concern for commitment may simply reflect the fact that most individuals do not possess either the theoretical orientation or the skills necessary for creating conditions under which the concerns can be satisfied simultaneously. Traditional 5/5 decision making would seem to represent an intuitive attempt at the integration of adequacy and commitment concerns, but once again it occurs as a result of the assumed incompatibility of the two.

A quite different orientation is represented in the assumption that a *concern for commitment is a concern for adequacy.* This is the assumption underlying the remaining anchor position on the Grid. It is an assumption based on research in decision making which indicates that task groups in which there is a high level of participation and involvement produce better decisions than groups not characterized by both task orientation and shared participation.

THE INTEGRATED APPROACH

Eye-to-eye Decision Making

This style, represented by the 9/9 position, is based on the assumption that better decisions can be reached if all available resources in the group are utilized. The utilization of resources, in turn, is viewed as possible only when all members are involved and contributing to the group task. Thus, eye-to-eye decision making represents a maximum concern for an adequate decision, on the one hand, as it is facilitated by a maximum concern for commitment, on the other.

The individual who employs 9/9 decision-making behavior has a learned tolerance for conflict because he considers conflict as symptomatic of an incomplete understanding of the issues on someone's part. He believes that a frank, yet constructive, facing up to and resolution of conflict is necessary if an understanding of issues—and hence, an adequate decision—is to be obtained. He shares individual power with other members, not in an attempt to win support as under 5/5 decision making, but because he recognizes the fact that to do otherwise tends to stifle creativity and suppress the expression of "different" ideas and opinions. The 9/9 decision maker considers a high degree—if not total—

agreement among group members as definitely possible, in fact as necessary, for obtaining decisions of superior quality. Succinctly, the 9/9 individual views the group as a productive place for decision making.

A disciplined knowledge of human relations and an awareness of the by-products of particular kinds of interpersonal relationships are much greater under 9/9 decision making than under any of the other styles. Thus, the 9/9 decision maker employs an approach to conflicts, to the expression of feelings and opinions of members, to the use of power, and to the utilization of resources in the group which reflects a systematic use of the scientific method. In contrast to other styles of decision making, eye-to-eye decision making reflects a style based on conscious experimentation and study.

By-products of This Style   Probably the three factors which most seriously impair the satisfaction and creativity of members in decision-making groups are:

1   Time-loss resulting from endless discussion of points not germane to the decision.
2   Lack of assurance that a decision once reached will be implemented.
3   Inability of the group to profit by its experience in future work sessions.

Self-sufficient decision making represents a style designed to deal with the first of the factors. Time-loss is generally reduced under 9/1 conditions, but assurance of implementation and a foundation for future decisions are sorely lacking under this style.

1/9 good neighbor decision making, on the other hand, usually results in an increased assurance that the decisions reached will be carried out because of the high commitment level among members. But time is lost in gaining commitment and the constant shifting of ideas which characterizes the 1/9 approach provides a shaky learning foundation at best for decision action in subsequent sessions.

Because of the "manipulative" character of 5/5 traditional decision making in trying to reach majority agreement, time is misused, assurance of implementation is qualified, and the foundations for continued work are too pragmatic under this approach to be of real utility. The 1/1 individual, in reaching decisions by default, neither saves time, insures implementation, nor learns anything from his efforts. In short, none of these styles can be said to deal effectively with all three disruptive factors of the decision-making situation.

9/9 eye-to-eye decision making, if it is actually to reflect that orientation, must necessarily deal with each of the three factors. Time-loss, implementation, and the generalization of learning are all problems for the decision-making group; and 9/9 decision making operates on the premise that problems must be confronted directly and dealt with constructively, rather than left to themselves.

While more time may be spent in working through procedures initially, in the long run time is saved since once the problem of "How do we do this?" is solved, it remains solved for the majority of decisions which will confront the group.

Whereas the 9/1 spends little time in discussion and, consequently, feels that he has saved time, he will continue to spend time on the same problem over and over.[11] He saves time in discussion but loses it in repeated arguments. Rather than accumulating experience he confronts the same experience time and again. In addition to his obvious problems of gaining commitment, the self-sufficient decision maker may generate so much intragroup conflict that an adequate decision is unlikely to be obtained.[12] Conversely, eye-to-eye decision making may be characterized as saving time over the long haul because it avoids the duplication of effort characteristic of the other styles.

Implementation is seldom a problem in the 9/9[13] group, for the high level of commitment which accompanies decisions made on the basis of an integration of adequacy and commitment concerns insures a concomitantly high level of responsibility for success on the part of each member. People tend to support what they help create.

Perhaps in no other area does the 9/9 approach to decision making differ as greatly as it does from other styles as in learning from experience. Since the 9/9 style occurs on the basis of conscious experimentation with an evaluation of techniques for decision making on the parts of group members, individuals are acutely sensitive to what the results of their experimentation have been. Consequently, the group devotes time to criticizing its own performance in an attempt to identify those elements of process which facilitate group performance and those factors which hinder it. On the basis of such an evaluation, plans for continuing group activity can be made which insure utilization of tested procedures and lay the foundation for an improvement of skills.

Choosing a Style[14]   The fact that eye-to-eye decision making is a result of systematic learning on the part of group members may pose a practical barrier to the individual's adopting a 9/9 style of decision making, for opportunities for such learning are limited by the individual's own initiative. Frequently individuals who employ other styles are just not interested in modifying their behavior in the 9/9 direction because of their perception of the 9/9 style.

For example, the 9/1 self-sufficient decision maker tends to view 9/9 as if it were 1/9 behavior because of its strong commitment component. He rejects it as being an unsatisfactory way of meeting his concern for adequacy. Conversely, the 1/9 good neighbor decision maker tends to see the strong adequacy component in 9/9 decision making as representing 9/1 behavior. He resists moving down the 9/1 path, and as a consequence, may also reject the 9/9 position.

Unlike the 9/1 and 1/9 decision makers, the 5/5 traditional decision maker does not view 9/9 as a style which focuses on concerns in which he has no interest, but rather he sees it as the style he is already employing. As far as the traditional decision maker is concerned, 9/9 is 5/5. For this reason—and this is important in terms of inducing change—the 5/5 person does not reject 9/9 but neither does he see any reason to change his present style.

Since the 1/1 default decision maker is concerned for neither adequacy nor commitment, 9/9 decision making represents the embodiment of all he is attempting to escape. For this reason it might be predicted that he may well reject the 9/9 style for himself more violently than either the 9/1 or 1/9 individuals. On the other hand, the heightened involvement and assumption of responsibility which characterize 9/9 behavior might lead him to support such behavior in others so that he might become even less conspicuous in the ongoing activity. Thus, the 1/1 person will remain passive with no desire to adopt 9/9 behavior but will not condemn others' attempts at change.

USES OF COMMUNICATION

Sharing Frames of Reference

In addition to affecting the group in terms of the degree of adequacy or commitment which it facilitates, the choice of a decision-making style may also be evaluated in terms of how well it aids in the creation of conditions for sharing frames of reference. The characteristic use of communications and power and the degree of sensitivity to the feelings of others associated with each style of decision-making behavior outlined in the Grid provide some insight into the efficacy of these styles in creating such conditions.

Communication under the 9/1 self-sufficient style is unilateral; that is, it flows from the 9/1 decision maker to his listeners, with little opportunity for an interchange. The 9/1's frame of reference is not explored but is merely repeated time and again until it is either completely accepted or completely rejected. If the self-sufficient decision maker has power, objections to his point of view are immediately cut off and his frame of reference is imposed on the group. Coerced compliance, of course, does not denote acceptance.

The "something for everybody" flow of communications and use of power which characterize 1/9 good neighbor decision making results in a confused array of issues and feelings which frequently provide little in the way of a useful frame of reference for decisions. While the 1/9 frame of reference may well be "shared," it often cannot be verbalized by the group members and, therefore, has little utility in helping the group move toward a decisive statement of the problem which precedes solution. Members of 1/9 groups have a tremendous sense of sharing, but they share they know not what. The general lack of structure and systematic orientation which results from this approach obscures the group's learning about its decision-making activity and frustrates the attempt to improve as a result of the experience.

The frame of reference which results from an interaction of 5/5 traditional decision makers usually reflects the views of the majority of the group and is shared to that extent. Those members who constitute the minority vote often fail to share the viewpoint, however, and despite the fact that the majority expects support and understanding from them, they are unable and reluctant to conform.

Communication is used to "convince" others of the frame of reference and closely resembles the 9/1 use of communication. Power, on the other hand, is characteristically used in support of the sanctity of the "democratic process" and minority members are made to feel that they are obligated to yield to the majority position.

The frames of reference which result from both 1/1 and 9/9 behavior need little comment. Default 1/1 decision-making behavior minimizes the likelihood of any frame of reference being generated by the total group, and usually results in "borrowing" a viewpoint from someone else without bothering to test its appropriateness. In effect, 1/1 behavior creates conditions in the group for what Durkheim has labeled *Pluralistic Ignorance;* that is, conditions under which the viewpoints of the more articulate members are perceived as representative of the total group opinion cause individuals to adopt a "go along" attitude rather than to risk exposure. Eye-to-eye 9/9 decision makers, on the other hand, seem to represent those individuals who, when working in groups, are most adroit at creating the conditions for sharing frames of reference because of the open flow of communications, the equalization of power, and the assumption of responsibility by the total group.

VALUE OF THE GRID

Summary

An understanding of the *Decision-Making Grid* may be helpful for understanding the current state of group decision making. Through its analysis of the relationships of concerns for decision adequacy and concerns for commitment, it sheds some light on many of the day-to-day behaviors encountered in decision-making groups. In addition, it highlights some of the reasons for the inability of group members to work together with satisfaction and creativity.

While a number of "pure" and "mixed" theories of decision-making behavior have been discussed, the greatest emphasis has been placed on the 9/9 eye-to-eye decision-making style since most individuals are familiar with the other Grid styles. Eye-to-eye decision making represents a style which is based on theories and data from the behavioral sciences and, as such, presents a more novel method of approaching group decision making. It is suggested that, in terms of decision adequacy, commitment, and efficient use of group resources in establishing a common frame of reference, the 9/9 approach is more effective than any of the other styles discussed.

Eye-to-eye decision making is not noted for the ease with which it may be employed. The learning involved is tedious and of a different nature than that usually undertaken by people. But programs are currently in operation in industry and government which facilitate the acquisition of 9/9 skills.[15] For example, training techniques and instruments for improving interpersonal relations and adaptations of group dynamics principles are being employed in a number of training programs across the nation with members of state and federal parole boards. A test[16] designed to afford self-evaluation of individual decision-making styles within a Grid framework is currently being used effectively with this group of decision makers.

Individuals can learn 9/9 decision-making behavior if they are motivated by the desire for a more systematic approach to decision making and wish to increase their own contributions to the groups in which they are members. More fundamental than the learning of behavior, however, is the adoption of a philosophy; for 9/9 is a state of mind. Normally, treatment of 9/9-*ism* has focused on the issue of "what constitutes 9/9 behavior?" But the answer to this question lies in experimentation, and any attempt to spell out the A-B-C's of eye-to-eye decision making seems premature. Therefore, it seems that the first step in obtaining the benefits of a 9/9 approach to decision making is one of discarding old assumptions regarding the relationship of decision adequacy and commitment and personally experimenting with the orientation or philosophy that *concern for commitment is a concern for adequacy.* By and large, one learns by doing and, at the same time, influences others to modify their own behavior. Thus, 9/9 decision making affects not only the individual who practices it, but those with whom he works as well.

REFERENCES

The National Parole Institutes are administered by the National Council on Crime and Delinquency and co-sponsored by its Advisory Council on Parole, the United States Parole Board, the Interstate Compact Administrators Association for the Council of State Governments, and the Association of Paroling Authorities. The program is supported by a grant from the President's Committee on Delinquency and Youth Crime under P.L. 84–274.

1 H. H. Kelley and J. W. Thibaut, "Experimental Studies of Group Problem Solving and Process," in G. Lindzey, ed., *Handbook of Social Psychology,* Vol. I (Cambridge, Mass.: Addison-Wesley, 1954); I. Lorge, D. Fox, J. Davitz, and M. Brenner, "A survey of studies contrasting the quality of group performance and individual performance, 1920–1957," *Psychological Bulletin,* IV (1958), 337–372.

2 J. Hall and V. O'Leary, "Frames of Reference in Decision Making," National Parole Institutes, unpublished paper.

3 A. W. Halpin and D. B. Croft, "The Organizational Climate of Schools," research project under a grant from the United States Office of Education, Department of Health, Education, and Welfare, 1962; G. A. Pownall, "An Analysis of the Role of the Parole Supervision Officer," doctoral dissertation, University of Illinois, 1963.

4 R. R. Blake and Jane S. Mouton, *The Managerial Grid* (Houston, Texas: Gulf Publishing Co., 1964).

5 H. H. Kelley and J. W. Thibaut, *op. cit.;* I. Lorge, *et al., op. cit.;* D. Barnlund, "A Comparative Study of Individual, Majority and Group Judgment," *Journal of Abnormal Social Psychology,* LVIII (1959), 55–60.

6 S. Schachter, "Deviation, Rejection, and Communication," *Journal of Abnormal Social Psychology*, XLVI (1951), 190–207.

7 S. E. Asch, "Effects of Group Pressures upon the Modification and Distortion of Judgments," in G. E. Swanson, T. M. Newcomb, and E. L. Hartley, eds., *Readings in Social Psychology* (2nd ed.; New York: Holt & Co., 1952).

8 S. E. Asch, *ibid.*

9 The majority vote has become a self-reinforcing practice as evidenced by the frequent use and teaching of Robert's Rules of Order and parliamentary procedure. Because of its utility with large assemblages, it has become the required decision-making technique in most formal groups, ranging from the legislature to stockholders' groups to ad hoc committees. One notable exception to the general rule of "majority will" is the requirement of a unanimous decision on the part of jurors for criminal cases. With many civil cases the majority vote is still sufficient. Hall, Mouton, and Blake, in a study now in progress, have found that untrained decision-making groups—as opposed to trained groups—composed of either business executives or neuropsychiatric patients resort to a majority vote technique almost immediately in dealing with the experimental task.

10 D. Rosenthal and C. Coffer, "The Effect on Group Performance of an Indifferent and Neglectful Attitude Shown by one Group Member," *Journal of Experimental Psychology*, XXXVIII (1948), 568–577.

11 A certain amount of psychological rigidity is indicated on the part of the 9/1 decision maker by virtue of the relationship of 9/1-*ism* to certain personality attributes. Robert Shaw, in an unpublished master's thesis at the University of Texas, has obtained significant correlations between 9/1 scores on the Decision-Making Grid Test and (1) dogmatism, (2) anxiety, (3) inflexibility, and (4) intolerance. In addition, negative correlations between 9/1 scores and intellectual efficiency, as measured by the *California Psychological Inventory*, were obtained in the same study.

12 R. Exline and R. Ziller, "Status Congruency and Interpersonal Conflict in Decision-Making Groups," *Human Relations*, XII (1959), 147–162.

13 M. A. Wallach, N. Kogan, and D. J. Bem, "Diffusion of Responsibility and Level of Risk Taking of Groups," *Journal of Abnormal Social Psychology*, LXVII (1964), 263–274.

14 The generalizations contained in the following section stem from research on the "relativity of judgment" phenomenon and the distortion effects of egocentric attitudes on the perception and judgment of attitude statements. Results indicate that individuals tend to displace attitudes and philosophies away from their own as a result of "lowered thresholds of rejection and raised thresholds of acceptance" which come into play during the comparison process. Thus, succinctly, individuals become hypercritical of beliefs and, by inference, of behaviors not in complete agreement with their own. For a further discussion of this phenomenon see: C. I. Hovland and M. Sherif, "Judgmental Phenomena and Scale of Attitude Measurement: Item Displacement in Thurstone Scales," *Journal of Abnormal Social Psychology*, XLVII (1952), 822–832; and M. Sherif and C. I. Hovland, *Social Judgment: Assimilation and Contrast Effects in Communication and Attitude Change* (New Haven and London, Conn.: Yale University Press, 1961).

15 See *Proceedings: Human Relations Training Laboratory*, Laboratory in Management Development Seventh Annual Session, The University of Texas, Austin, Texas, 1961;

Proceedings: Patient's Training Laboratory, VA Hospital, Houston, Texas, 1961–1964; R. Blake and Jane S. Mouton, "Developing Revolution in Management Practice," *American Society of Training Directors Journal*, XVI (1962), 29–50; R. Blake and Jane S. Mouton, *Group Dynamics: Key to Decision Making* (Houston, Texas, Gulf Publishing Co., 1961).

16   J. Hall and Martha Williams, *The Decision-Making Grid: An Analysis of Individual Behavior in the Decision-Making Group*, instrument developed for The National Parole Institutes, 1963.

Reading 19

The Management of Decision Making within the Firm: Three Strategies for Three Types of Decision Making*

Andre L. Delbecq

Recent theory concerned with group problem-solving suggests that different types of decision making require different group structures and processes. The administrator who "manages" the decision-making process must, therefore, organize the executive team in different ways as he deals with the variety of decision-making situations within the firm.

Every practicing administrator is well aware of these qualitative differences in the problem-solving situations which he and his management team face. Further, even without conscious effort on his part, the management group will often change its pattern of communication and individual managers will adjust their roles, as the management team faces different tasks. Research evidence shows that over time, problem-solving groups tend to adjust their behavior in keeping with changes in the nature of group problem-solving.[1]

On the other hand, the process of adjustment to new decision-making situations is often slow, usually incomplete, and occasionally nonexistent. Managers develop expectations about appropriate behavior in decision-making meetings

"The Management of Decision-Making within the Firm: Three Strategies for Three Types of Decision-Making," Andre L. Delbecq, *Academy of Management Journal*, December 1967, pp. 329–339. Reprinted with permission.

*This article is adapted from a chapter in a forthcoming book, *Decision-Making in Organizations: Perspectives and Techniques*, Fremont A. Shull, Andre L. Delbecq, and Larry Cummings (New York: McGraw-Hill).

[1]Harold Guetzkow and Herbert A. Simon, "The Impact of Certain Communication Nets Upon Organization and Performance in Task Oriented Groups," *Management Science*, I (1955), 233–250; Rocco Carzo, Jr., "Organization Structure and Group Effectiveness," *Administrative Science Quarterly* (March, 1963), pp. 393–425.

with their superiors, so that their behavior falls into a pattern with limited variability which may be appropriate for some types of decision making, but highly inappropriate for other decision-making situations.[2] However, if the manager is highly sensitive to differences in the decision-making tasks faced by the management team, and can verbally redefine both his own and his subordinates' roles in a fashion congruent with the new decision-making situation, research indicates that the management group can much more readily change its behavior as the result of such role redefinition in order to adjust to a new decision-making situation.[3]

The purpose of this article is to set forth three decision-making strategies, each of which is tailored to a different type of problem-solving situation encountered within the firm. Further, each strategy will be examined to determine the degree to which it differs from the logic of classical organization models. It is hoped that this examination of the three different strategies will fulfill the following purposes:

1 The administrator will become more sensitive to the kind of group structure and process which each of the three problem-solving tasks demands,

2 The problems of implementing the strategies within a traditional formal organization culture will be clearer, and

3 The implications for the redesign of traditional formal organization models to facilitate greater flexibility for problem-solving can be suggested.

THE RELEVANCE OF "TASK" FOR GROUP STRUCTURE

Since the body of this article proposes that managers should reorganize group structure and process as they face different types of decision tasks, a word about the relevance of task as a variable around which to construct "organization" is appropriate. It is axiomatic to say that individual behavior is goal directed,[4] and that group behavior is purposeful or goal directed as well.[5] The task of a group is normally thought of, however, only in terms of the stated goal of the group's activity. Thus, there are familiar typologies of groups based on stated goals. For example, Wolman classifies groups as being Instrumental Groups (which individu-

[2]Leonard Berkowitz, "Sharing Leadership in Small, Decision-Making Groups," *Journal of Abnormal and Social Psychology* (1953), pp. 231–238; Andre L. Delbecq, "Managerial Leadership Styles in Problem-Solving Conferences," *Academy of Management Journal*, VII, No. 4 (Dec., 1964), 255–268.

[3]Andre L. Delbecq, "Managerial Leadership Styles in Problem-Solving Conferences: Research Findings on Role Flexibility," *Academy of Management Journal*, VIII, No. 1 (March, 1965), 32–43.

[4]Harold J. Leavitt and Ronald A. H. Mueller, *Managerial Psychology* (Chicago: University of Chicago Press, 1964), pp. 8–9.

[5]Robert T. Golembiewski, *The Small Group* (Chicago: University of Chicago Press, 1962), p. 181.

als join for the satisfaction of "to take" needs, e.g., business associations), Mutual Acceptance Groups (in which "give" and "take" motives are important, e.g., friendship relations), and Vectorial Groups (which people join for the purpose of serving a lofty goal).[6]

Another typology dealing with organizations as macro-groups is that of Scott and Blau who speak of Mutual Benefit Associations (where the prime beneficiary is the membership), Business Concerns (where the owner is the prime beneficiary), Service Organizations (where the client group is the prime beneficiary), and Commonweal Organizations (where the prime beneficiary is the public at large.)[7]

What is not immediately apparent in each of these descriptive typologies is that task, as a variable, affects several dimensions of the system (regardless of whether one is referring to a small group or a large organization) including:

1 *Group Structure:* In terms of the relationship between the individual members,

2 *Group Roles:* In terms of the behavior required of individual group members which are necessary to facilitate task accomplishment,

3 *Group Process:* In terms of the manner of proceeding toward goal accomplishment,

4 *Group Style:* In terms of the social-emotional tone of interpersonal relationships (e.g., the amount of stress on individual members, the congeniality of interpersonal relations, the perceived consequences of individual and group success or failure,

5 *Group Norms:* Relative to each of the preceding four dimensions.

Thus, in treating task as merely the end goal, many of the theoretical as well as the practical implications of the group's or organization's tasks are not made explicit. For example, when mutual benefit organizations are compared with business concerns, one would expect the former to be characterized by greater dispersion of power (structure), broader membership participation in goal setting (roles and process), greater emotional support of individual members (style), and stronger egalitarianism (norms).

In a similar fashion, the problem-solving "task" faced by a particular managerial team, within a particular organization, at a particular point of time, likewise must affect the structure, roles, process, style, and norms of the management team if the group is to optimally organize itself to deal with its task.[8]

---

[6]Benjamin Wolman, "Instrumental, Mutual Acceptance and Vectorial Groups," Paper read at the Annual Meeting of the American Sociological Association, August 1953.

[7]Peter M. Blau and W. Richard Scott, *Organizations, A Comparative Approach* (San Francisco: Chandler Publishing Company, 1962).

[8]W. C. Schutz, "Some Theoretical Considerations for Group Behavior," *Symposium on Techniques for the Measurement of Group Performance* (Washington, D.C.: U. S. Government Research and Development Board, 1952), pp. 27–36.

STRATEGIES FOR GROUP PROBLEM SOLVING

Against this background, we can now proceed directly to classify decision situations as found in groups and organizations and to specify group strategies implied in behaviorally oriented group and organization studies appropriate for dealing with each of the situations.[9]

Strategy One: Routine Decision Making

The first decision situation with which we will deal is the routine decision-making situation. In Simon's terminology, this is the "programmed" decision-situation; in Thompson's terminology, the "computational" decision.[10] Here, the organization or group agrees upon the desired goal, and technologies exist to achieve the goal. In such a situation, the following strategy can be specified as consistent with behavioral models:

1   *Group Structure:* The group is composed of specialists, with a coordinator (leader).
2   *Group Roles:* Behavior is characterized by independent effort, with each specialist contributing expertise relative to his own specialty, including the coordinator (leader) who specializes in coordination across task phases.
3   *Group Process:* At the beginning of the planning period, specialists, with the coordinator, specify the productivity objectives. Subsequently, excepting occasional joint meetings to review progress, coordination of specialist endeavors is generally obtained by means of dyadic (two-person) communication between individual specialists and their coordinator, or through horizontal communication between specialists.
4   *Group Style:* Relatively high stress is characteristic. Stress is achieved through quality and quantity commitments and time constraints, agreed upon in joint consultation at the beginning of the planning period. Responsibility is decentralized within areas of specialization, but coordination is centralized in the coordinator.
5   *Group Norms:* Norms are characterized by professionalism (high sense of individual responsibility and craftsmanship); commitment to shared team objectives relative to quantity and quality of output; economy and efficiency.

The above strategy evidences both similarity and dissimilarity when compared with classical organizational models. It is similar in that there is a clear

---

[9]The reader should be clearly forewarned that each of the strategies is the author's own conceptualization. While an extensive review of the literature, both theoretical and empirical, underlies each strategy, it is not meant to be implied that the strategy represents a model about which scholars universally agree. Rather, the strategies represent the theoretical position of the author which is consistent with much of the literature, but is admittedly open to question and refinement.

[10]J. Thompson and Arthur Tuden, "Strategies, Structures and Processes of Organizational Decision," *Comparative Studies in Administration*, ed. Thompson, et al (Pittsburgh, Pa.: University of Pittsburgh Press, 1959), pp. 198–199; H. Simon, *The New Science of Management Decisions* (New York: Harper Brothers, 1960), Chapters 2, 3.

division of labor, functional and structural specialization (specialization in work, and between work and coordination), and centralized coordination.

On the other hand, this "optimal" model is dissimilar in several significant ways. To begin with, responsibility is obtained primarily through team commitments to group objectives, dealing with both the quantity and quality of the output. This commitment, elicited through joint discussion between the specialists and the coordinator at the beginning of the planning period, places responsibility on both the team members and the coordinator, rather than locating responsibility solely in the coordinator.

Control is obtained in two ways. First, the coordinator provides the feedback mechanism for the team by monitoring the progress of individual specialists to assure conformity to shared productivity and time objectives. Situations where actual performance deviated from prior commitments are brought to the shared attention of the team, which institutes appropriate correction measures. Thus, discipline rests upon joint commitments rather than upon superordinate sanctions.[11] Second, because motivation is task-intrinsic, specialists are "normatively" expected to be "self-controlled" through professional, reference-group standards. Authority is likewise decentralized, based upon specialist expertise and shared norms.

Since responsibility, authority, and discipline are shared within the management team, there is less status disparity between the coordinator and the specialist than is the case between supervisor and subordinates in traditional organization models. Indeed, coordination is seen as a type of specialization, rather than as a function of superior personal attributes, or positional status. As a consequence, there is a propensity for fluid changes in group personnel; different task experts bring to bear their differentiated competences at different points of time as the group encounters various phases of decision making in the completion of a project. Further, the role of the coordinator may shift between the specialists on occasions, as the coordination requirements demand different admixtures of skills at various phases of project management.

Admittedly, the strategy assumes high quality personnel in terms of both task skills and interpersonal skills. Further, it requires a degree of autonomy for both individual specialists and each specialist team, an autonomy which must be predicated on personal and organizational maturity. It also assumes that the objectives of the organization and each group can be integrated into a meaningful, internally consistent ends-means chain, where, at each level and between each area, objectives can be translated in terms of appropriate technologies.

Nonetheless, although a "pure" strategy (best approximated in project management, matrix management, or task-force groups), movement towards such

---

[11]For a treatment of the manner in which group norms control individual behavior, see Andre L. Delbecq and Fremont A. Shull, "Norms, A Feature of Symbolic Culture: A Major Linkage Between the Individual, The Small Group and Administrative Organization," *The Making of Decisions*, ed. W. J. Gore and J. W. Dyson (N.Y.: The Free Press of Glencoe, 1964), pp. 213–242.

a model for structuring groups dealing with "routine" tasks appears capable of avoiding many of the dysfunctions of classical organizational models, while captivating the advantages of division of labor, specialization, centralized coordination, and task-intrinsic motivation.

Strategy Two: Creative Decision Making

The second decision situation with which we will deal is the creative decision-making situation. Here we are talking about decision making which in Simon's terminology is "heuristic" and in Thompson's terminology is "judgmental."[12] The central element in the decision making is the lack of an agreed-upon method of dealing with the problem; this lack of certitude may relate to incomplete knowledge of causation, or lack of an appropriate solution strategy. In such a situation, the following strategy can be specified as consistent with behavioral models:[13]

1   *Group Structure:* The group is composed of heterogeneous, generally competent personnel, who bring to bear on the problem diverse frames of reference, representing channels to each relevant body of knowledge (including contact with outside resource personnel who offer expertise not encompassed by the organization), with a leader who facilitates creative (heuristic) processes.

2   *Group Roles:* Behavior is characterized by each individual, exploring with the entire group all ideas (no matter how intuitively and roughly formed) which bear on the problem.

3   *Group Processes:* The problem-solving process is characterized by:
  a   spontaneous communication between members (not focused in the leader)
  b   full participation from each member
  c   separation of idea generation from idea evaluation
  d   separation of problem definition from generation of solution strategies
  e   shifting of roles, so that interaction which mediates problem solving (particularly search activities and clarification by means of constant questioning directed both to individual members and the whole group) is not the sole responsibility of the leader
  f   suspension of judgment and avoidance of early concern with solutions, so that emphasis is on analysis and exploration, rather than on early solution commitment.

4   *Group Style:* The social-emotional tone of the group is characterized by:
  a   a relaxed, nonstressful environment

---

[12]Herbert A. Simon and Allen Newell, "Heuristic Problem Solving: The Next Advance in Operations Research," *Operations Research Journal* (Jan.–Feb., 1958); Thompson and Tuden, *op. cit.*
[13]Particularly useful models dealing with individual and group creativity can be found in William E. Scott, "The Creative Individual," *Journal of Management* (Sept., 1965); Larry Cummings, "Organizational Climates for Creativity," *Journal of the Academy of Management* (Sept., 1965); Victor A. Thompson, "Bureaucracy and Innovation," *Administrative Science Quarterly* (June, 1965); Gary Steiner, The Creative Organization (Chicago: University of Chicago Press, 1965); and Norman R. F. Maier, *Problem-Solving Discussions and Conferences* (New York: McGraw-Hill, 1963).

    b ego-supportive interaction, where open give-and-take between members is at the same time courteous

    c behavior which is motivated by interest in the problem, rather than concern with short-run payoff

    d absence of penalities attached to any espoused idea or position.

5 *Group Norms:*

    a are supportive of originality, and unusual ideas, and allow for eccentricity

    b seek behavior which separates source from content in evaluating information and ideas

    c stress a nonauthoritarian view, with a relativistic view of life and independence of judgment

    d support humor and undisciplined exploration of viewpoints

    e seek openness in communication, where mature, self-confident individuals offer "crude" ideas to the group for mutual exploration without threat to the individual for "exposing" himself

    f deliberately avoid credence to short-run results, or short-run decisiveness

    g seek consensus, but accept majority rule when consensus is unobtainable.[14]

Obviously, the above prescription for a strategy to deal with creativity does not easily complement classical organization theory. Structural differentiation and status inequality (other than achieved status within the group) are deemphasized. The decisive, energetic, action-oriented executive is a normative misfit. Decisions evolve quite outside the expected frame of reference of the "pure" task specialist. Communication is dispersed, rather than focused in a superior or even a coordinator. Motivation is totally task-intrinsic, the pleasure being much more in the exploration than in an immediately useful outcome. Indeed, the very personnel who thrive by excellent application and execution of complex technologies in the first strategy, find the optimal decision rules for the second strategy unnatural, unrealistic, idealistic, and slow.

Nonetheless, although all members of any organization will not find both of the strategies equally comfortable, it can be expected that most organizational

---

[14]In development of the above model, we have consciously avoided the issue of "nominal" groups (where members work without verbal interaction in generating solution strategies) vs. "interacting" groups. While preliminary evidence favors "nominal" groups in generating ideas, the question as to the appropriateness of the nominal group strategy for the total decision process (i.e., evaluation as well as idea generation) remains in question.

Further, the experimental tasks used in the studies may be different in kind from organizational decision making. In any event, the above model seems quite adaptable to separation into nominal and interacting processes at various phases, using modifications which do not vitiate the general tenor of the model. For a discussion of nominal vs. interacting groups, see Alan H. Leader, "Creativity in Management," Paper read at the Midwest Division of the Academy of Management, April 8, 1967; P. W. Taylor, P. C. Berry, and C. H. Block, "Does Group Participation When Using Brainstorming Facilitate or Inhibit Creative Thinking?" *Administrative Science Quarterly, III* (1958), 23–47.

members can approximate the strategy given appropriate role definitions. The point, here, is that the group structure and process which is called for to facilitate creativity is intrinsically different from our first strategy. While the first strategy called for an internally consistent team of complementary specialists who are "action" oriented, the second strategy calls for a heterogeneous collection of generalists (or at least generically wise specialists not restricted to the boundaries of their own specialized frame of reference, and even, not necessarily of the immediate group or organization) who are deliberately and diagnostically patient in remaining problem-centered. The membership, roles, processes, style, and norms of strategy two are more natural to the scientific community (or a small sub-set thereof) than to the practicing executive. The general implications, however, must await the exposition of the third strategy.

Strategy Three: Negotiated Decision Making

The third decision situation with which we will deal is the negotiated decision-making strategy. In this instance, we are concerned with a strategy for dealing with opposing factions which, because of differences in norms, values, or vested interests, stand in opposition to each other, concerning either ends or means, or both.[15] Organization theory has never given much attention to groups in conflict, since several elements of classical models precluded such open conflict. One element was, of course, the existence of monocratic authority. At some level in the hierarchical system, authority to "decide" was to be found. Parties representing various opinions might be given a hearing, but ultimately Manager X was to make the decision. Another element in classical thought which precluded open conflict was the conviction, however utopian, that conflict was merely symptomatic of inadequate analysis. Adequate problem solving would surely show that the conflict was artificial and that an integrative decision could be reached. Thus, the study of mechanisms for negotiation between groups in conflict was left to the student of political science and social conflict and was excluded from organizational models.

　　Nonetheless, the realities of conflict have been ubiquitous. Present models encourage the sublimation of conflict, veiling it in portended rationality. As one wag expressed the matter. "If people don't agree with me, it isn't that I am wrong, or that they are right, but merely that I haven't been clear." In spite of Trojan efforts at "clear communication," the elimination of all conflict through analysis is, indeed, a utopian desire. There have been, and will be, instances where the organization finds itself encompassing two "camps," each supported by acceptable values and logic, and each committed to a different course of action, relative to either means, ends, or both. The question remains, then, as to what would be an appropriate strategy in those cases where "analysis" cannot provide an accept-

[15]In this respect, we assume a position different from that of Thompson and Tuden in their earlier model who posit that "compromise" decision making is predicted on disagreement about ends. Thompson and Tuden, *op. cit.*

able solution to both parties since the disparate opinion or positions are based on assumptions and premises not subject to total decision integration.

The following strategy can be specified:

1 *Group Structure:* The group is composed of proportional representation of each faction (but with the minority never represented by less than two persons), with an impartial formal chairman.[16]

2 *Group Roles:* Each individual sees himself as a representative of his faction, seeking to articulate and protect dominant concerns of the group he represents, while at the same time negotiating for an acceptable compromise solution.

3 *Group Processes:* The problem-solving process is characterized by:

  a orderly communication mediated by the chairman, providing opportunity for each faction to speak, but avoidance of factional domination

  b formalized procedures providing for an orderly handling of disputation

  c formalized voting procedure

  d possession of veto power by each faction

  e analytical approaches to seeking compromise, rather than mere reliance on power attempts.

4 *Group Style:* Group style is characterized by:

  a frankness and candor in presenting opposing viewpoints

  b acceptance of due process in seeking resolution to conflicts

  c openness to rethinking, and to mediation attempts

  d avoidance of emotional hostility and aggression

5 *Group Norms:* Group norms are characterized by:

  a desire on the part of all factions to reach agreement

  b the perception of conflict and disagreement as healthy and natural, rather than pathological

  c acceptance of individual freedom and group freedom to disagree

  d openness to new analytical approaches in seeking acceptable compromise

  e acceptance of the necessity of partial agreement as an acceptable, legitimate, and realistic basis for decision making.

There is, obviously, no parallel in either structure or norms to the above strategy in classical organizational models. The acceptance of open conflict; provision for due process between conflicting groups; openness to compromise; evolution of policy and objectives through negotiation; and "representative groups" while found in the "underworld" in most organizations, are outside the general organizational model. Indeed, managers involved in "negotiations," either in the personnel (labor relations) or marketing (customer relations) areas, find it

---

[16]The justification for the minority never being represented by less than two persons is that it is difficult for one person to represent his group across the boundary and that a minority of one is easy prey for a majority coalition of two members, let alone more than two.

difficult to articulate the legitimacy of many of their decisions except through rationalizations.

CONCLUSIONS AND IMPLICATIONS

Both the propensities for groups to change the nature of their interaction as they change task, and/or task phases, and the prescriptions for group strategies dealing with differentiated decision situations (as set forth above) indicate that the structure and processes of groups must be related to changes in the characteristics of the decision-making tasks. (Whether one agrees with each proposition in each of the decision strategy models set forth in this article or not, the fact that each of the decision-making situations is endemically different is difficult to refute.)

On the other hand, formal organizations as conceived in present organizational models are presumably structured in terms of the predominant type of task encountered by the system. (Thus, the "bureaucratic" model is based on facilitating "routine" decision making; the labor union council is structured to deal with negotiated decision making; etc.) Since task is, in the most pertinent sense, what members of the organization subjectively define it to be as they respond to the situation in which they find themselves, the internal features of a decision group within the organization will generally be conditioned by the predominant structured roles created to deal with the "typical" decisions encountered in day-to-day organizational tasks. As a result, role expectations and behaviors conditioned in the central organizational system (the formal organization) may inhibit the decision task performance in the subsystem (the decision-making committee, conference, or task force).

Since there are several types of decisions to be made within complex organizations, with each general type calling for a different group structure and process, a major role of the manager in such a system is the evoking of appropriate changes in behaviors on the part of the managerial team as it moves across task types by means of role redefinition. This assumes that the manager can classify decision tasks according to the models presented here, or some other conceptual scheme, and that the managerial team can respond with congruent role flexibility. Earlier pilot research by the author indicates that such flexibility seems to be within the capacities of a large portion of the population, given appropriate role redefinition by the superior.[17]

In a real sense, then, management of the decision-making process is management of the structure and functioning of decision groups, so that these decision-making processes become congruent with changes in the nature of the decision-making task being undertaken at a particular point of time within the organization.

[17]Andre L. Delbecq (March, 1965). We agree that some individuals will find it impossible to assume flexible roles due to their particular developmental history which results in a fixated behavior pattern. We also agree that some roles will be more natural than others for individuals due to their developmental history. We disagree, however, with the notion that the normal population cannot assume at least functionally relevant roles in accordance with the various strategies, a point which appears to be the position of some theorists. A more conservative viewpoint than ours is assumed by Abraham Zaleznic in *Human Dilemmas of Leadership* (New York: Harper & Row, 1965).

Finally, we spent considerable time delineating the "task-force," "systems management" or "matrix organizational" approach (strategy one)[18] as the appropriate strategy for routine decision making purposefully, since it seems to provide a mechanism for integrating various types of decision making at various phases of project management within a flexible structure. It is felt that strategy one avoids the structural rigidity of formal organization models such as "bureaucracy." There is no reason, for instance, why "creative" or "negotiated" strategies cannot be incorporated into the objectives and standards-setting decision sessions at the beginning of the planning period. Further, there is no reason why personnel other than the "task specialists" cannot mediate the decision making by participation in these early decision phases. Thus, by dropping the assumption of "agreed upon technologies" and "agreed upon objectives," and incorporating strategies two and three into these early planning sessions, or intermittently juxtaposing these strategies with strategy one, the possibility for incorporating decision-making flexibility into the "project management" context of strategy one seems not only feasible, but a desirable movement in the direction of fluid group structures and processes. Such a movement toward organizational fluidness is more congruent with the need for role flexibility as the management team moves across decision strategies at various phases of project planning and implementation.

Reading 20

Committee Management: Guidelines from Social Science Research

A. C. Filley

The committee is one of the most maligned, yet most frequently employed forms of organization structure. Yet despite the criticisms, committees are a fact of organization life. For example, a recent survey of 1,200 respondents revealed that 94 percent of firms with more than 10,000 employees and 64 percent with less than 250 employees reported having formal committees.[1] And, a survey of organization practices in 620 Ohio manufacturing firms showed a similar positive relationship between committee use and plant size.[2] These studies clearly indicate that committees are one of management's important organizational tools.

[18]For an elaborated treatment of "Matrix Organization" see Fremont A. Shull, *Matrix Structure and Project Authority for Optimizing Organizational Capacity* (Monograph, Business, Research Bureau. Southern Illinois University, Carbondale, Illinois, 1965); Warren Bennis, "Beyond Bureaucracy," *Transactions* (Summer, 1965); John F. Mee, "Ideational Items: Matrix Organization," *Business Horizons* (Summer, 1964), pp. 70–72; and Carl R. Praktish, Evolution of Project Management." Paper read at Midwest Academy of Management, April, 1967.

"Committee Management: Guidelines from Social Science Research," A. C. Filley. © 1970 by The Regents of the University of California. Reprinted from *California Management Review*, vol. XIII, no. 1, pp. 13–21, by permission of The Regents.

My thesis is that committee effectiveness can be increased by applying social science findings to answer such questions as:

- What functions do committees serve?
- What size should committees be?
- What is the appropriate style of leadership for committee chairmen?
- What mix of member characteristics makes for effective committee performance?

COMMITTEE PURPOSES AND FUNCTIONS

Committees are set up to pursue economy and efficiency within the enterprise. They do not create direct salable value, nor do they supervise operative employees who create such value.

The functions of the committee have been described by business executives as the exchange of views and information, recommending action, generating ideas, and making major decisions,[3] of which the first may well be the most common. After observing seventy-five conferences (which were also referred to as "committees"), Kriesberg concluded that most were concerned either with communicating information or with aiding an executive's decision process.[4] Executives said they called conferences to "sell" ideas rather than for group decision-making itself. As long as the executive does not manipulate the group covertly, but benefits by its ideas and screening processes, this activity is probably quite legitimate, for members are allowed to influence and to participate, to some extent, in executive decision-making.

Some committees also make specific operating decisions which commit individuals and organization units to prescribed goals and policies. Such is often the province of the general management committee composed of major executive officers. According to one survey, 30.3 percent of the respondents reported that their firms had such a committee and that the committees averaged 8.6 members and met 27 times per year.[5]

Several of the characteristics of committee organization have been the subject of authoritative opinion, or surveys of current practice, and lend themselves to evaluation through inferences from small-group research. Current practice and authoritative opinion are reviewed here, followed by more rigorous studies in which criteria of effectiveness are present. The specific focus is on committee size, membership, and chairmen.

COMMITTEE SIZE

Current Practice and Opinion

The typical committee should be, and is, relatively small. Recommended sizes range from three to nine members, and surveys of actual practice seldom miss these prescriptions by much. Of the 1,658 committees recorded in the Harvard Business Review survey, the average membership was eight. When asked for their preference, the 79 percent who answered suggested an ideal committee size that averaged 4.6 members. Similarly, Kriesberg reported that, for the 75 conferences analyzed, there were typically five or six confereees in the meetings studied.[6]

Committees in the federal government tend to be larger than those in business. In the House of Representatives, Appropriations is the largest standing committee, with fifty members, and the Committee on Un-American Activities is smallest, with nine. Senate committees average thirteen members; the largest, also Appropriations, has twenty-three.[7] The problem of large committee size is overcome by the use of subcommittees and closed executive committee meetings. The larger committees seem to be more collections of subgroups than truly integrated operating units. In such cases, it would be interesting to know the size of the subcommittees.

Inferences from Small-Group Research

The extent to which a number is "ideal" may be measured in part in terms of the effects that size has on socio-emotional relations among group members and thus the extent to which the group operates as an integrated whole, rather than as fragmented subunits. Another criterion is how size affects the quality of the group's decision and the time required to reach it. Several small experimental group studies have evaluated the effect of size on group process.

Variables related to changes in group size include the individual's capacity to "attend" to differing numbers of objects, the effect of group size on interpersonal relations and communication, its impact on problem-solving functions, and the "feelings" that group members have about proper group size and the nature of group performance. To be sure, the effects of these variables are interrelated.

Attention to the Group Each member in a committee attends both to the group as a whole and to each individual as a member of the group. There seem to be limits on a person's ability to perform both of these processes—limits which vary with the size of the group and the time available. For example, summarizing a study by Taves,[8] Hare[9] reports that "Experiments on estimating the number of dots in a visual field with very short-time exposures indicate individual subjects can report the exact number up to and including seven with great confidence and practically no error, but above that number confidence and accuracy drop."

Perhaps for similar reasons, when two observers assessed leadership characteristics in problem-solving groups of college students, the raters reached maximum agreement in groups of six, rather than in two, four, eight, or twelve.[10]

The apparent limits on one's ability to attend both to the group and the individuals within it led Hare to conclude:

> The coincidence of these findings suggests that the ability of the observing individual to perceive, keep track of, and judge each member separately in a social interaction

situation may not extend much beyond the size of six or seven. If this is true, one would expect members of groups larger than that size to tend to think of other members in terms of subgroups, or "classes" of some kind, and to deal with members of subgroups other than their own by stereotyped methods of response.[11]

Interpersonal Relations and Communication   Given a meeting lasting a fixed length of time, the opportunity for each individual to communicate is reduced, and the type of communication becomes differential among group members. Bales *et al.*[12] have shown that in groups of from three to eight members the proportion of infrequent contributors increases at a greater rate than that theoretically predicted from decreased opportunity to communicate. Similarly, in groups of from four to twelve, as reported by Stephen and Mishler,[13] size was related positively to the difference between participation initiated by the most active and the next most active person.

Increasing the group size seems to limit the extent to which individuals want to communicate, as well. For example, Gibb[14] studied idea productivity in forty-eight groups in eight size categories from 1 to 96. His results indicated that as group size increases a steadily increasing proportion of group members report feelings of threat and less willingness to initiate contributions. Similarly, Slater's[15] study of 24 groups of from two to seven men each working on a human relations problem indicated that members of the larger groups felt them to be disorderly and time-consuming, and complained that other members became too pushy, aggressive, and competitive.

Functions and Conflict   An increase in group size seems to distort the pattern of communication and create stress in some group members, yet a decrease in group size also has dysfunctional effects. In the Slater study check-list responses by members rating smaller groups of 2, 3, or 4 were complimentary, rather than critical, as they had been for larger groups. Yet observer impressions were that small groups engaged in superficial discussion and avoided controversial subjects. Inferences from post hoc analysis suggested that small group members are too tense, passive, tactful, and constrained to work together in a satisfying manner. They are afraid of alienating others. Similar results have been reported in other studies regarding the inhibitions created by small group size, particularly in groups of two.[16]

Groups of three have the problem of an overpowerful majority, since two members can form a coalition against the unsupported third member. Four-member groups provide mutual support when two members oppose the other two, but such groups have higher rates of disagreement and antagonism than odd-numbered groups.[17]

The data reported above are not altogether consistent regarding the reasons for dysfunctional consequences of small groups. The "trying-too-hard-for-agreement" of the Slater study seems at odds with the conflict situations posed in the groups of three and four, yet both agree that for some reason tension is present.

Groups of Five   While it is always dangerous to generalize about "ideal" numbers (or types, for that matter), there does appear to be logical and empirical support for groups of five members as a suitable size, if the necessary skills are possessed by the five members. In the Slater study, for example, none of the subjects felt that a group of five was too small or too large to carry out the assigned task, though they objected to the other sizes (two, three, four, six, and seven). Slater concluded:

> Size five emerged clearly . . . as the size group which from the subjects' viewpoint was most effective in dealing with an intellectual task involving the collection and exchange of information about a situation, the coordination analysis, and evaluation of this information, and a group decision regarding the appropriate administrative action to be taken in the situation . . . .
>   These findings suggest that maximal group satisfaction is achieved when the group is large enough so that the members feel able to express positive and negative feelings freely, and to make aggressive efforts toward problem solving even at the risk of antagonizing each other, yet small enough so that some regard will be shown for the feelings and needs of others; large enough so that the loss of a member could be tolerated, but small enough so that such a loss could not be altogether ignored.[18]

From this and other studies,[19] it appears that, excluding productivity measures, generally the optimum size of problem-solving groups is five. Considering group performance in terms of quality, speed, efficiency and productivity, the effect of size is less clear. Where problems are complex, relatively larger groups have been shown to produce better quality decisions. For example, in one study, groups of 12 or 13 produced higher quality decisions than groups of 6, 7, or 8.[20] Others have shown no differences among groups in the smaller size categories (2 or 7). Relatively smaller groups are often faster and more productive. For example, Hare found that groups of five take less time to make decisions than groups of 12.[21]

Several studies have also shown that larger groups are able to solve a greater variety of problems because of the variety of skills likely to increase with group size.[22] However, there is a point beyond which committee size should not increase because of diminishing returns. As group size increases, coordination of the group tends to become difficult, and thus it becomes harder for members to reach consensus and to develop a spirit of teamwork and cohesiveness.

In general, it would appear that with respect to performance, a task which requires interaction, consensus and modification of opinion requires a relatively small group. On the other hand, where the task is one with clear criteria of correct performance, the addition of more members may increase group performance.

THE CHAIRMAN

Current Practice and Opinion

Most people probably serve on some type of committee in the process of participating in church, school, political, or social organizations and while in that capacity have observed the effect of the chairman on group progress. Where the chairman starts the meeting, for example, by saying, "Well, we all know each other here, so we'll dispense with any formality," the group flounders, until someone else takes a forceful, directive role.

If the committee is to be successful, it must have a chairman who understands group process. He must know the objectives of the committee and understand the problem at hand. He should be able to vary decision strategies according to the nature of the task and the feelings of the group members. He needs the acceptance of the group members and their confidence in his personal integrity. And he needs the skill to resist needless debate and to defer discussion upon issues which are not pertinent or where the committee lacks the facts upon which to act.

Surveys of executive opinion support these impressions of the chairman's role. The Harvard Business Review survey stated that "The great majority [of the suggestions from survey respondents] lead to this conclusion: the problem is not so much committees in management as it is the management of committees." This comment by a partner in a large management consulting firm was cited as typical:

> Properly used, committees can be most helpful to a company. Most of the criticism I have run into, while probably justified, deals with the way in which committees are run (or committee meetings are run) and not with the principle of working with committees.[23]

A chairman too loose in his control of committee processes is by no means the only difficulty encountered. Indeed, the chronic problem in the federal government has been the domination of committee processes by the chairman. This results from the way in which the chairman is typically selected: he is traditionally the member of the majority party having the longest uninterrupted service on the committee. The dangers in such domination have been described as follows:

> If there is a piece of legislation that he does not like, he kills it by declining to schedule a hearing on it. He usually appoints no standing subcommittees and he arranges the special subcommittees in such a way that his personal preferences are taken into account. Often there is no regular agenda at the meetings of his committee—when and if it meets . . . they proceed with an atmosphere of apathy, with junior members, especially, feeling frustrated and left out, like first graders at a seventh grade party.[24]

Inferences from Small Group Research

The exact nature of the chairman's role is further clarified when we turn to more rigorous studies on group leadership.

We shall confine our discussion here to leader roles and functions, using three approaches. First, we shall discuss the nature of task leadership in the group and the apparent reasons for this role. Then we shall view more specifically the different roles which the leader or leaders of the group may play. Finally, we shall consider the extent to which these more specific roles may be combined in a single individual.

Leader Control

Studies of leadership in task-oriented, decision-making groups show a functional need for and, indeed, a member preference for directive influence by the chairman. The nature of this direction is illustrated in a study by Schlesinger, Jackson, and Butman.[25] The problem was to examine the influence process among leaders and members of small problem-solving groups when the designated leaders varied on the rated degree of control exerted. One hundred six members of twenty-three management committees participated in the study. As part of an initial investigation, committee members described in a questionnaire the amount of control and regulation which each member exercised when in the role of chairman. Each committee was then given a simulated but realistic problem for 1.5 hours, under controlled conditions and in the presence of three observers.

The questionnaire data showed that individuals seen as high in control were rated as more skillful chairmen and as more valuable contributors to the committee's work.

The study also demonstrated that leadership derives from group acceptance rather than from the unique acts of the chairman. "When the participants do not perceive the designated leader as satisfactorily performing the controlling functions, the participants increase their own attempts to influence their fellow members."[26] The acceptance of the leader was based upon task (good ideas) and chairmanship skills and had little to do with his personal popularity as a group member.

The importance of chairman control in committee action has been similarly demonstrated in several other studies.[27] In his study of 72 management conferences, for example, Berkowitz[28] found that a high degree of "leadership sharing" was related inversely to participant satisfaction and to a measure of output. The norms of these groups sanctioned a "take-charge" chairman. When the chairman failed to meet these expectations, he was rejected and both group satisfaction and group output suffered. These studies do not necessarily suggest that committees less concerned with task goals also prefer a directive chairman. Where the committees are composed of more socially oriented members, the preference for leader control may be less strong.[29]

Leadership Roles

A second approach to understanding the leadership of committees is to investigate leadership roles in small groups. Pervading the research literature is a basic distinction between group activities directed to one or the other of two types of roles performed by leaders. They are defined by Benne and Sheats[30] as task roles, and as group-building and maintenance roles. Task roles are related to the direct accomplishment of group purpose, such as seeking information, initiating, evaluating, and seeking or giving opinion. The latter roles are concerned with group integration and solidarity through encouraging, harmonizing, compromising, and reducing conflict.

Several empirical investigations of leadership have demonstrated that both roles are usually performed within effective groups.[31] However, these roles are not always performed by the same person. Frequently one member is seen as the "task leader" and another as the "social leader" of the group.

Combined Task and Social Roles

Can or should these roles be combined in a single leader? The prototypes of the formal and the informal leader which we inherit from classical management lore tend to lead to the conclusion that such a combination is somehow impossible or perhaps undesirable. The research literature occasionally supports this point of view as well.

There is much to be said for a combination of roles. Several studies have shown that outstanding leaders are those who possess both task and social orientations.[32] The study by Borgotta, Couch, and Bales illustrates the point. These researchers assigned leaders high on both characteristics to problem-solving groups. The eleven leaders whom they called "great men" were selected from 126 in an experiment on the basis of high task ability, individual assertiveness, and social acceptability. These men also retained their ratings as "great men" throughout a series of different problem-solving sessions. When led by "great men" the groups achieved a higher rate of suggestion and agreement, a lower rate of "showing tension," and higher rates of showing solidarity and tension release than comparable groups without "great men."

When viewed collectively two conclusions emerge from the above studies. Consistent with existing opinion, the leader who is somewhat assertive and who takes charge and controls group proceedings is performing a valid and necessary role. However, such task leadership is a necessary but not a sufficient condition for effective committee performance. Someone in the group must perform the role of group-builder and maintainer of social relations among the members. Ideally both roles should probably be performed by the designated chairman. When he does not have the necessary skills to perform both roles, he should be the task leader and someone else should perform the social leadership role. Effective committee performance requires both roles to be performed, by a single person or by complementary performance of two or more members.

COMMITTEE MEMBERSHIP

The atmosphere of committee operations described in the classic literature is one where all members seem to be cooperating in the achievement of committee purpose. It is unclear, however, if cooperation is necessarily the best method of solving problems, or if competition among members or groups of members might not achieve more satisfactory results. Cooperation also seems to imply a sharing or homogeneity of values. To answer the question we must consider two related problems: the effects of cooperation or competition on committee effectiveness, and the effects of homogeneous or heterogeneous values on committee effectiveness.

Cooperation or Competition

A number of studies have contrasted the impact of competition and cooperation on group satisfaction and productivity. In some cases the group is given a cooperative or competitive "treatment" through direction or incentive when it is established. In others, competition and cooperation are inferred from measures of groups in which members are operating primarily for personal interest, in contrast with groups in which members are more concerned with group needs. These studies show rather consistently that "group members who have been motivated to cooperate show more positive responses to each other, are more favorable in their perceptions, are more involved in the task, and have greater satisfaction with the task."[33]

The best known study regarding the effects of cooperation and competition was conducted by Deutsch[34] in ten experimental groups of college students, each containing five persons. Each group met for one three-hour period a week for six weeks, working on puzzles and human relations problems. Subjects completed a weekly and post-experimental questionnaire. Observers also recorded interactions and completed over-all rating scales at the end of each problem.

In some groups, a cooperative atmosphere was established by instructing members that the group as a whole would be evaluated in comparison with four similar groups, and that each person's course grade would depend upon the performance of the group itself. In others, a competitive relationship was established by telling the members that each would receive a different grade, depending upon his relative contribution to the group's problem solutions.

The results, as summarized by Hare, show that:

Compared with the competively organized groups, the cooperative groups had the following characteristics:

   1   Stronger individual motivation to complete the group task and stronger feelings of obligation toward other members.

   2   Greater division of labor both in content and frequency of interaction among members and greater coordination of effort.

   3   More effective inter-member communication. More ideas were verbalized, members were more attentive to one another, and more accepting of and affected by

each other's ideas. Members also rated themselves as having fewer difficulties in communicating and understanding others.

4 More friendliness was expressed in the discussion and members rated themselves higher on strength of desire to win the respect of one another. Members were also more satisfied with the group and its products.

5 More group productivity. Puzzles were solved faster and the recommendations produced for the human-relations problems were longer and qualitatively better. However, there were no significant differences in the average individual productivity as a result of the two types of group experience nor were there any clear differences in the amounts of individual learning which occurred during the discussions.[35]

Similar evidence was found in the study of 72 decision-making conferences by Fouriezos, Hutt, and Guetzkow.[36] Based on observer ratings of self-oriented need behavior, correlational evidence showed that such self-centered behavior was positively related to participant ratings of high group conflict and negatively related to participant satisfaction, group solidarity, and task productivity.

In general, the findings of these and other studies suggest that groups in which members share in goal attainment, rather than compete privately or otherwise seek personal needs, will be more satisfied and productive.[37]

Homogeneity or Heterogeneity

The effects of member composition in the committee should also be considered from the standpoint of the homogeneity or heterogeneity of its membership. Homogeneous groups are those in which members are similar in personality, value orientation, attitudes to supervision, or predisposition to accept or reject fellow members. Heterogeneity is induced in the group by creating negative expectations regarding potential contributions by fellow members, by introducing differing personality types into the group, or by creating subgroups which differ in their basis of attraction to the group.

Here the evidence is much less clear. Some homogeneous groups become satisfied and quite unproductive, while others become satisfied and quite productive. Similarly, heterogeneity may be shown to lead to both productive and unproductive conditions. While the answer to this paradox may be related to the different definitions of homogeneity or heterogeneity in the studies, it appears to have greater relevance to the task and interpersonal requirements of the group task.

In some studies, homogeneity clearly leads to more effective group performance. The work of Schultz[38] is illustrative. In his earlier writing, Schutz distinguished between two types of interpersonal relationships: power orientation and personal orientation. The first emphasizes authority symbols. The power-oriented person follows rules and adjusts to external systems of authority. People with personal orientations emphasize interpersonal considerations. They assume that the way a person achieves his goal is by working within a framework of close personal relations, that is, by being a "good guy," by liking others, by getting people to like him. In his later work, Schutz[30] distinguished among three types of needs: *inclusion,* or the need to establish and maintain a satisfactory relation with people with respect to interaction and association; *control,* or the need to establish and maintain a satisfactory relation with people with respect to control and power; and *affection,* or the need to establish and maintain a satisfactory relation with others with respect to love and affection.

Using attitude scales, Schutz established four groups in which people were compatible with respect to high needs for personal relations with others, four whose members were compatible with respect to low personal orientation, and four which contained subgroups differing in these needs. Each of the twelve groups met twelve times over a period of six weeks and participated in a series of different tasks.

The results showed that groups which are compatible, either on a basis of personalness or counterpersonalness, were significantly more productive than groups which had incompatible subgroups. There was no significant difference between the productivity of the two types of compatible groups. As might be expected, the difference in productivity between compatible and incompatible groups was greatest for tasks which required the most interaction and agreement under conditions of high-time pressure.

A similar positive relationship between homogeneity and productivity is reported for groups in which compatibility is established on the basis of prejudice or degree of conservatism, managerial personality traits, congeniality induced by directions from the researcher, or status congruence.[40] In Adams' study, technical performance first increased, then decreased, as status congruence became greater. Group social performance increased continuously with greater homogeneity, however.

The relationship posited above does not always hold, however. In some studies, heterogeneous groups were more productive than homogeneous. For example, Hoffman[41] constructed heterogeneous and homogeneous groups, based on personality profiles, and had them work on two different types of problems. On the first, which required consideration of a wide range of alternatives of a rather specific nature, heterogeneous groups produced significantly superior solutions. On the second problem, which required primarily group consensus and had no objectively "good" solution, the difference between group types was not significant. Ziller[42] also found heterogeneity to be associated with the ability of Air Force crews to judge the number of dots on a card.

Collins and Guetzkow[43] explain these contradictory findings by suggesting that increasing heterogeneity has at least two effects on group interaction: it increases the difficulty of building interpersonal relations, and it increases the problem-solving potential of the group, since errors are eliminated, more alternatives are generated, and wider criticism is possible. Thus, heterogeneity would seem to be valuable where the needs for task facilitation are greater than the need for strong interpersonal relations.

Considering our original question, it appears that, from the standpoint of cooperation versus competition in committees, the cooperative committee is to be preferred. If we look at the effects of homogeneous or heterogeneous committee membership, the deciding factor seems to be the nature of the task and the degree of interpersonal conflict which the committee can tolerate.

SUMMARY AND CONCLUSIONS

Research findings regarding committee size, leadership, and membership have been reviewed. Evidence has been cited showing that the ideal size is five, when the five members possess the necessary skills to solve the problems facing the committee. Viewed from the standpoint of the committee members' ability to attend to both the group and its members, or from the standpoint of balanced interpersonal needs, it seems safe to suggest that this number has normative value in planning committee operations. For technical problems additional members may be added to ensure the provision of necessary skills.

A second area of investigation concerned the functional separation of the leadership role and the influence of the role on other members. The research reviewed supports the notion that the committee chairman should be directive in his leadership, but a more specific definition of leadership roles makes questionable whether the chairman can or should perform as both the task and the social leader of the group. The evidence regarding the latter indicates that combined task and social leadership is an ideal which is seldom attained, but should be sought.

The final question concerned whether committee membership would be most effective when cooperative or competitive. When evaluated from the standpoint of research on cooperative versus competitive groups, it is clear that cooperative membership is more desirable. Committee operation can probably be enhanced by selecting members whose self-centered needs are of a less intense variety and by directions to the group which strengthen motivations of a cooperative nature. When the proposition is evaluated from the standpoint of heterogeneity or homogeneity of group membership, the conclusion is less clear. Apparently, heterogeneity in a group can produce both ideas and a screening process for evaluating their quality, but the advantage of this process depends upon the negative effects of heterogeneous attitudes upon interpersonal cooperation.

REFERENCES

Based on A. C. Filley and J. Robert House, *Managerial Process and Organizational Behavior* (Glenview, Ill.: Scott-Foresman, 1969).

1   Rollie Tillman, Jr., "Problems in Review: Committees on Trial," *Harvard Business Review,* 38 (May–June 1960), 6–12; 162–172. Firms with 1,001 to 10,000 reported 93 percent use; 250 to 1,000 reported 82 percent use.

2   J. H. Healey, *Executive Coordination and Control,* Monograph No. 78 (Columbus: Bureau of Business Research, The Ohio State University, 1956), p. 185.

3   "Committees," *Management Review,* 46 (October 1957), 4–10; 75–78.

4   M. Kriesberg, "Executives Evaluate Administrative Conferences," *Advanced Management,* 15 (March 1950), 15–17.

5   Tillman, *op. cit.*, p. 12.

6   Kriesberg, *op. cit.*, p. 15

7   "The Committee System—Congress at Work," *Congressional Digest,* 34 (February 1955), 47–49; 64.

8   E. H. Taves, "Two Mechanisms for the Perception of Visual Numerousness," *Archives of Psychology,* 37 (1941), 265.

9   A. Paul Hare, *Handbook of Small Group Research* (New York: The Free Press of Glencoe, 1962), p. 227.

10 B. M. Bass and F. M. Norton, "Group Size and Leaderless Discussions," *Journal of Applied Psychology,* 35 (1951), 397–400.

11 Hare, *op. cit.*, p. 228.

12 R. F. Bales, F. L. Strodtbeck, T. M. Mills, and M. E. Roseborough, "Channels of Communication in Small Groups," *American Sociological Review,* 16 (1951), 461–468.

13 F. F. Stephen and E. G. Mishler, "The Distribution of Participation in Small Groups: An Exponential Approximation," *American Sociological Review,* 17 (1952), 598–608.

14 J. R. Gibb, "The Effects of Group Size and of Threat Reduction Upon Creativity in a Problem-Solving Situation," *American Psychologist,* 6 (1951), 324. (Abstract)

15 P. Slater, "Contrasting Correlates of Group Size," *Sociometry,* 21 (1958), 129–139.

16 R. F. Bales and E. F. Borgotta, "Size of Group as a Factor in the Interaction Profile," in *Small Groups: Studies in Social Interaction*, A. P. Hare, E. F. Borgotta, and R. F. Bales, eds. (New York: Knopf, 1965, rev. ed.), pp. 495–512.

17 *Ibid.,* p. 512.

18 Slater, *op. cit.*, 137–138.

19 R. F. Bales, "In Conference," *Harvard Business Review,* 32 (March–April 1954), 44–50; also A. P. Hare, "A Study of Interaction and Consensus in Different Sized Groups," *American Sociological Review,* 17 (1952), 261–267.

20 D. Fox, I. Lorge, P. Weltz, and K. Herrold, "Comparison of Decisions Written by Large and Small Groups," *American Psychologist,* 8 (1953), 351. (Abstract)

21 A. Paul Hare, "Interaction and Consensus in Different Sized Groups," *American Sociological Review,* 17 (1952), 261–267.

22 G. B. Watson, "Do Groups Think More Efficiently Than Individuals?" *Journal of Abnormal and Social Psychology,* 23, (1928), 328–336; Also D. J. Taylor and W. L. Faust, "Twenty Questions: Efficiency in Problem Solving as a Function of Size of Group," *Journal of Experimental Psychology,* 44 (1952), 360–368.

23 Tillman, *op. cit.*, p. 168.

24 S. L. Udall, "Defense of the Seniority System," *New York Times Magazine* (January 13, 1957), 17.

25 L. Schlesinger, J. M. Jackson, and J. Butman, "Leader-Member Interaction in Management Committees," *Journal of Abnormal and Social Psychology,* 61, No. 3 (1960) 360–364.

26 *Ibid.,* p. 363.

27 L. Berkowitz, "Sharing Leadership in Small Decision-Making Groups," *Journal of Abnormal and Social Psychology,* 48 (1953), 231–238; Also N. T. Fouriezos, M. L. Hutt, and H. Guetzkow, "Measurement of Self-Oriented Needs in Discussion Groups," *Journal of Abnormal and Social Psychology,* 45 (1950), 682–690; also H. P. Shelley, "Status Consensus, Leadership, and Satisfaction with the Group," *Journal of Social Psychology,* 51 (1960), 157–164.

28 Berkowitz, *Ibid.,* p. 237.

29   R. C. Anderson, "Learning in Discussions: A Resume of the Authoritarian-Democratic Studies," *Harvard Education Review,* 29 (1959), 201–214.

30   K. D. Benne, and P. Sheats, "Functional Roles of Group Members," *Journal of Social Issues,* 4 (Spring 1948), 41–49.

31   R. F. Bales, *Interaction Process Analysis* (Cambridge: Addison-Wesley, 1951); Also R. M. Stogdill and A. E. Coons (eds.), *Leader Behavior: Its Description and Measurement,* Monograph No. 88 (Columbus: Bureau of Business Research, The Ohio State University, 1957); Also A. W. Halpin, "The Leadership Behavior and Combat Performance of Airplane Commanders," *Journal of Abnormal and Social Psychology,* 49 (1954), 19–22.

32   E. G. Borgotta, A. S. Couch, and R. F. Bales, "Some Findings Relevant to the Great Man Theory of Leadership," *American Sociological Review,* 19 (1954), 755–759); Also E. A. Fleishman, and E. G. Harris, "Patterns of Leadership Behavior Related to Employee Grievances and Turnover," *Personnel Psychology,* 15, No. 1 (1962), 43–56; Also Stogdill and Coons, *Ibid.;* Also H. Oaklander and E. A. Fleishman, "Patterns of Leadership Related to Organizational Stress in Hospital Settings," *Administrative Science Quarterly,* 8 (March 1964), 520–532.

33   Hare, *Handbook of Small Group Research, op. cit.,* p. 254.

34   M. Deutsch, "The Effects of Cooperation and Competition Upon Group Process," in *Group Dynamics, Research and Theory,* D. Cartwright and A. Zander, eds., (New York: Harper and Row, 1953).

35   Hare, *Handbook of Small Group Research, op. cit.,* p. 263.

36   Fouriezos, Hutt, and Guetzkow, *op. cit.*

37   C. Stendler, D. Damrin and A. Haines, "Studies in Cooperation and Competition: I. The Effects of Working for Group and Individual Rewards on the Social Climate of Children's Groups," *Journal of Genetic Psychology,* 79 (1951), 173–197; Also A. Mintz. "Nonadaptive Group Behavior," *Journal of Abnormal and Social Psychology,* 46 (1951), 150–159; Also M. M. Grossack, "Some Effects of Cooperation and Competition Upon Small Group Behavior," *Journal of Abnormal and Social Psychology,* 49 (1954), 341–348; Also E. Gottheil, "Changes in Social Perceptions Contingent Upon Competing or Cooperating," *Sociometry,* 18 (1955), 132–137; Also A. Zander and D. Wolfe, "Administrative Rewards and Coordination Among Committee Members," *Administrative Science Quarterly,* 9 (June 1964), 50–69.

38   W. C. Schutz, "What Makes Groups Productive?" *Human Relations,* 8 (1955), 429–465.

39   W. C. Schutz, *FIRO: A Three-Dimensional Theory of Interpersonal Behavior,* (New York: Holt, Rinehart and Winston, 1958).

40   I. Altman and E. McGinnies, "Interpersonal Perception and Communication in Discussion Groups of Varied Attitudinal Composition," *Journal of Abnormal and Social Psychology,* 60 (May 1960), 390–393; Also W. A. Haythorn, E. H. Couch, D. Haefner, P. Langham and L. Carter, "The Behavior of Authoritarian and Equalitarian Personalities in Groups," *Human Relations,* 9 (1956), 57–74; Also W. E. Ghiselli and T. M. Lodahl, "Patterns of Managerial Traits and Group Effectiveness," *Journal of Abnormal and Social Psychology,* 57 (1958), 61–66; Also R. V. Exline, "Group Climate as a Factor in the Relevance and Accuracy of Social Perception," *Journal of Abnormal and Social Psychology,* 55 (1957), 382–388; Also S. Adams, "Status Congruency as a Variable in Small Group Performance," *Social Forces,* 32 (1953), 16–22.

41 L. R. Hoffman, "Homogeneity of Member Personality and Its Effect on Group Problem-Solving, *Journal of Abnormal and Social Psychology,* 58 (1959), 27–32.

42 R. C. Ziller, "Scales of Judgment: A Determinant of Accuracy of Group Decisions," *Human Relations,* 8 (1955), 153–164.

43 B. E. Collins and H. Guetzkow, *A Social Psychology of Group Process for Decision-Making,* (New York: John Wiley and Sons, 1965), p. 101.

Reading 21

Techniques of Operations Research

William G. Browne

Operations research is a scientific approach to management problems that was introduced during and used since World War II. "Its purpose is to provide a basis for directing and controlling operations,"[1] Operations research does not point to any one particular tool for the scientific approach. "Operations research differs from almost anything else industry has done in the past, chiefly in method and approach to a problem. The techniques of operations research require an exacting statement of the problem with all the variables and factors included with their proper relationships."[2]

The management of businesses, institutions, and governments have a number of operations research techniques available for investigation and analysis of their particular problems. The technique that is ultimately used may depend on the type of problem, the complexity of the problem, the types of input available or the type of output desired, the ability and experience of the users of the technique and the amount that is budgeted for the project. Operations research techniques may be used anywhere in the spectrum of day-to-day decisions and problems to once-in-a-lifetime decisions and problems. The number of people involved varies widely.

The model, in most cases, provides a systematic analysis of the problem or problems confronting the user. For example, one authority finds that, "Simulation models of operating systems have been growing rapidly and promise to become a dominant technique for assisting management, in the decision-making process for day-to-day problems, as well as for comparing basic alternatives of operating policies."[3] The model gives the user material and time to explore the environment, solution alternatives, and objectives of the problem in greater depth. Generally, a model will fall into one of the five following areas in regard to its applications:

"Techniques Of Operations Research," William G. Browne, *Journal of Systems Management,* September 1972, pp. 3–13. Reprinted with permission.

1 It may be used to study a system for possible improvement or to look at the present system to compare it with a renovated or suggested system.

2 The model can be utilized to design systems or outputs of systems for optimal returns. It is a tool for the analysis of different possible alternatives so that the one bringing the optimal or near optimal results can be initiated.

3 A model may help in the clarification of the objectives or goals and the tentative plans of the organizers, planners, and decision makers.

4 Models may be used for training personnel to give them experience that may be used to their advantage when placed on the job.

5 Techniques may be used to set up a model for forecasting or showing possible outputs of the system when there are changes in exogenous or endogenous variables.

Modeling Process

Fred Hansman[4] of the University of Munich and formerly of the Caste Institute Operations Research Group relates an ultimate model to the real world in a very fundamental diagram shown in Figure 1. The flowchart, itself a model, is a good framework for studying the process by which the operations research techniques are applied.

The terms in the diagram need some explanation to give the reader further depth on how it can be used. The *Real World* is the environment in which we find ourselves confronted with the problems that may require the application of an operations research technique to efficiently find an optimal or improved solution. Once the problem is established the operations researcher tries to *conceptualize* the problem's complete environment. He looks for the critical variables or limiting constraints that should be incorporated into the model.

At this point it is necessary for him to decide if one of the techniques is applicable. Once this analysis is completed and it is decided to use an operations research technique, a *Model* is developed that can best relate the significant variables, operating constraints and the stated objectives. To do this one or more of the techniques are used. The model should be tested or verified to see if it has captured all of the characteristics that were to be included.

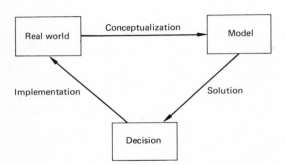

Figure 1

Relevant data is gathered and prepared for the model's format to obtain a *solution* from the model. The solution will be transformed from abstract terms into terms that will be applicable to the users of the system being modeled. The solution(s) may then be evaluated to ascertain its usefulness. If all or parts of the solution are found to be beneficial a *Decision* has to be made by management concerning the *implementation* of the acceptable solution to the problem. If it is decided to implement the solution, plans and controls will have to be established to put the solution into action with a minimum disruption to the system and to gain assurance that the intended results will be obtained.

Emphasis on the different components of the cycle would vary in each type of application. Most of the time the model should not be considered a routine decision maker, but as a tool to explore the different alternatives. In some very routine applications, however, users may justify using the model to select the alternatives to be used.

While Figure 1 is appropriate in relating the modeling process to the real world, Figure 2 presents the more formal steps that take place in the modeling process. These steps are self explanatory. The situation being modeled will determine, to a large extent, the attention and resources placed on any one of these steps. Most individuals or operations research groups usually focus and give adequate consideration to the first six steps in the process, but many of those employed in model construction tend to treat the last three steps of the process too lightly. This results in confusion and distrust of the models being used. Managers should insure that sufficient attention is provided by the model builders in the last three steps.

Most modeling techniques discussed here may be useful in situations unrelated to their original purpose. The theoretical foundations of any one of them may make it feasible to employ it in noncorporate applications or in different situations from its original intent. The format presented in Figure 2 is generally applicable to all model types listed here with changing emphasis on each of the steps. The word "model" is open to many interpretations. The range covered by this term when it is used without regard to any specific application may include[5] (also see Figure 3):

1   Physical models
2   Pictorial models
3   Mathematical programming
    a   Gaming models
    b   Input-output models
    c   Linear programming models
4   Queuing or waiting line models
5   Critical path models (CPM), and
    a   PEP
    b   IMPACT
    c   PERT

6 Simulation models
   a Special purpose
   b General

Although specific types of models can be used in several ways, each type of model has a set of applications for which it is best suited. The classification system presented should give the manager insight into a hierarchical organization and general foundations leading to each of the modeling methods. The practitioner's responsibility is to ascertain and use the modeling method best suited for the particular situation being analyzed and/or researched.

Physical Models

The physical model portrays some aspect of the general problem by physically imitating the problem's pertinent environment. Many companies use physical layout models to study the feasibility of the alternatives available to them for

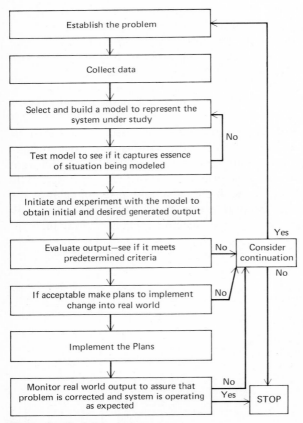

Figure 2 Modeling process.

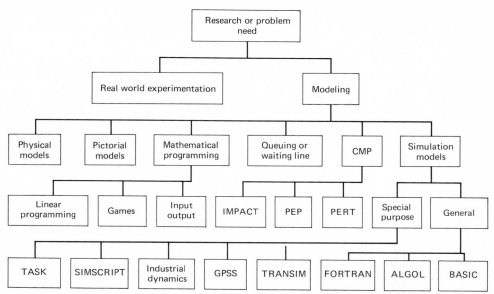

Figure 3   Structure of general types of models.

handling different components of their production function and its related activities so that their goods or services can be produced with improved efficiency. Physical models may be used in direct experimentation to see if there are any possible improvements, such as saving floor space or more direct product movement, that could be made to further economize the process of proceedings within an activity.

Thus, predominant, management use of the physical model is to find more efficient alternatives of equipment arrangement or for pretesting to ascertain the suitability of the various alternatives. This approach may add safety to the final layout or it may save time and cost in the ultimate production line. Physical models consider only physical size and arrangement and not the operating characteristics of the equipment being studied, information flows or decision processes. Because of their limited nature and inflexibility, they are of little use in more complex problems.

Pictorial Models

Pictorial models show a simple relationship between a system's different components or the dimensional characterisitics of one component. For example, they can be used to find the best arrangement of the present components or to fit a new component into the company's production function. Flowcharts or diagrams would be another type of pictorial model representing the various elements of a system.

Since pictorial models are usually the easiest and cheapest to construct and understand, they are widely used. Many times they are used to give managers or researchers background material for construction of more sophisticated models. One advantage of this type is the ease in manipulation once the decision is made to look at something new. This model can be scaled to virtually any size so that components can be easily visualized or handled. The economies of small size have to be played against completeness or coverage of the model. Pictorial models suffer from many of the physical model's disabilities. They may, however, be used as an integral part of other more complex methods. For instance, the flowchart, a part of many of the computer methods, is really a pictorial model of the computer program.

Mathematical Programming

"Mathematics in operations research is the means by which the findings of modern investigations can be expressed, analyzed and computed with the aim of reaching an objective result."[6] The objective result of mathematical programming, which has been defined as a symbolic model, is usually a maximization or minimization of some function. Mathematical programming refers to problem analysis in which some function of one or more variables with non-negative values is to be maximized or minimized when these variables are subject to a number of constraints or conditions, at least one of which is expressed as an inequality.

There are a number of branches of mathematical programming which can be categorized into major headings. Three of the more familiar subdivisions of mathematical programming are input-output analysis, linear programming, and game theory. The common characteristic that permits these three methods to be grouped together is that all require linear restrictions and objective functions. The linear requirement is to keep the problem and analysis in the simplest of all mathematical functions (first degree) so that many functions can be handled with ease. Applications of the mathematical technique are quite general. "Some of the most fertile applications of programming have involved welfare economics and advice to businessmen, both of which aim to tell the relevant persons how they can most efficiently go about working toward their objectives."[7]

Many mathematical programs are either specialized for particular uses or they are of a static nature rendering them useless for broad applications or for dynamic situations. The following quote expresses this problem, "Until recently there has been widespread dependence on the use of 'mathematical models'; these are mathematical relationships describing the operations of the real-life system. However, in a large number of instances, mathematical tools have been inadequate to represent complex system interrelationships and variables with sufficient accuracy."[8]

The linear programming and input-out models are static in nature. Some research is currently underway that has, as a goal, modifications that could make these two methods dynamic. The dynamic developments have not reached a state of maturity that makes it useful for most managers. Generally, mathematical programming models do not have provisions for handling all of the types of input, different kinds of relationships between the phenomenon being analyzed, or the different forms of output required. Mathematical models that do contain sophistication that would be useful in many situations are usually specialized to a point that make them useless. In the future as the state of the art develops, there will probably be deterministic models available to handle many more problem types.

Queuing or Waiting Line Models

The queuing or waiting line model is used in situations in which customers, servers, objects, or products arrive at a service point at irregular intervals. If there is a possibility of a queue being formed, because of faster arrival than departure, a manager may find queuing models useful for identifying more efficient methods of operation. "Waiting-line theory or queuing theory usually provides models which are capable of providing 'solutions' for 'random or nonrandom demands,' in order to predict the behavior of the system."[9] With this model one is able to ascertain if he has enough capacity to serve his customers or products and the general characteristics of the system as it operates under different conditions.

The investigator also may discover some other characteristics about the facility, such as the average length of the waiting line and the average amount of time spent in that line. Costs are estimated to the waiting line periods in terms of lost customers and are derived for providing each of the server configurations under study. These two costs will be compared with one another to discover the optimal point for operating the facility with maximum returns. Except in forced situations (e.g., emergency hospital rooms, landing strips at an airport, or war maneuvers), this optimal point is where marginal costs equal marginal revenues. A study of this information may indicate to the investigator and/or manager that a priority system may be beneficial for optimization or that more alternatives should be available at certain times.

A critical path model is used normally to study an integrated series of activities required for completion of a project. The activities are first placed in a sequential relationship, then the time to complete each activity is estimated. The data are used to construct a network. With this network the required sequencing, interdependencies, and the intradependencies of the different intermediate required steps of a project can be visualized and analyzed. The data in the network are used by a computer program to assign schedules to the different implements and resources being used in the construction of the project. Status information of the various activities is constantly fed into the program so that schedules can be updated. The analysis should help insure that the project is finished in an efficient manner.

The critical path programs most widely used for the network analysis and scheduling are Critical Path Method (CPM), Program Evaluation Procedure (PEP), Program Evaluation and Review Technique (PERT), and Integrated Management Planning and Control Technique (IMPACT). All have the same basic objective—to schedule efficiently all the project's activities in order to complete the project by a particular date or at a minimal cost. The CPM approach is finding wide usage in the construction industry and in many governmental projects. Many requests for proposals now require that a contractor include provisions for monitoring their work through use of CPM.

Simulation Model

"A simulation model is a model of some situation in which the elements of the situation are represented by arithmetic or logical processes that can be executed on a computer to predict the dynamic properties of the situation."[10] Most simulation techniques provide a medium for interconnecting the activities being considered so that cause and effect patterns can be studied in relation to time. The goals of simulation models are spread over a wide spectrum. They may assist an individual or group in formalizing plans, making forecasts, decision making, experimentation, or searching out new problems.

For a more specific area of assistance, dynamic output simulation models may be useful in showing some of the effects of time lags in information systems of a company.[11] They may also provide insight into the complete operation of an enterprise. Useful information, in many forms, can be obtained for advancing a company towards its objectives or subobjectives. The methods of simulation are few and largely untried. Ones given considerable attention in recent literature are TASK, SIMSCRIPT, GPSS, Industrial Dynamics and GASP.

Even though simulation is a non-deterministic type of model in relation to optimal solutions, it does provide a means of studying many different types of phenomenon simultaneously. For instance, normal mathematical techniques have been developed to determine the optimal order quantity, best reorder point and most economic inventory level for one point in a system, but mathematical programming techniques have not been developed to handle simultaneously a system with a growing number of inventory points and a growing activity at each point.

Along with the accommodation of the above phenomenon, a simulation model, for example, could also simultaneously accommodate: a changing failure rate of a system's component parts, changing utilization rate, changing schedule for resource inputs, and/or arbitrary assignments repair capabilities. Simulation provides a means of studying a system, but it does not provide a means of directing one to an optimal solution. In many cases the path to the problem's satisfactory solution is completed through sequential experimentation.

The history of simulation models is not extensive since the field is relatively new in relation to the other modeling techniques. To construct a dynamic model and encompass a wide spectrum of considerations, one needs a systematic and fast medium for handling and processing the necessary material and data. The combination of simulation and the computer partially fills this need. The simulation is needed to organize the input information, and the computer is needed because of its capability to systematically and accurately handle all of the

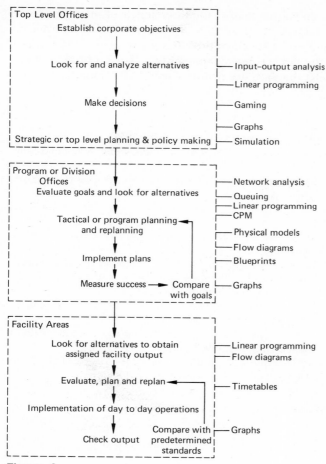

Figure 4

mathematical iterations required by a dynamic simulation model. The computer can quickly process the data, sometimes in minutes, once the model is finished.

Summary

Some of the techniques that have fallen under a heading of their own are used as an agent by other techniques (e.g., linear programming may be, but normally is not, used by a critical path model), so the structures presented here cannot be considered ironclad.

Each potential user of operations research will have to make his framework for evaluating and using the techniques.

Figure 4 shows a structure that imposes the different operations research techniques on the decision making process of the three levels of management. It shows where each technique might be used in an organization. It by no means limits the use of the technique to the specified area, but gives an indication where it may be used most frequently. Since some techniques (e.g., Linear Programming, Graphs) are used by all levels, they are not firmly placed at one point.

REFERENCES

1 Haskins and Sells, *Operations Research* (Haskins and Sells, 1958), p. 8.
2 Robert W. Metzger, *Elementary Mathematical Programming* (John Wiley and Sons, Inc., New York, N. Y., 1958), p. 2.
3 Elwood S. Buffa, *Models for Production and Operations Management* (New York: John Wiley and Sons, Inc., 1964), p. 505.
4 Fred Hansman, *Operations Research in Production and Inventory Control* (John Wiley and Sons, Inc., 1962), p. 8.
5 James R. Emshoff and Roger L. Sisson in *Design and Use of Computer Simulation Models,* (New York: The Macmillan Company, 1970), pages 5–7, classify the modeling field into four major categories: Descriptive, Physical, Symbolic and Procedural. While this breakdown is helpful and covers the same material here, the category titles do not give the reader insights to the possible methodology.
6 Giuseppe M. Ferrero di Roccaferrera, *Operation Research for Business and Industry* (Cincinnati: Southwestern Publishing Comapny, 1964), p. 295
7 William J. Baumol, *Economic Theory and Operations Analysis,* Second Edition (Englewood Cliffs, N. J.: Prentice-Hall, Inc., 1965), p. 71
8 TRANSIM—*General Purpose Transportation System Simulator—User's Manual, No.* 66–6 (Springfield, Va.: U.S. Department of Commerce, May, 1968), p. 3–1.
9 Giuseppe M. Ferrero di Roccaferrera, *Operations Research for Business and Industry* (Cincinnati: Southwestern Publishing Company, 1964), p. 802.
10 James R. Emshoff and Roger L. Sisson, *Design and Use of Computer Simulation Models,* (N. Y.: The Macmillan Company, 1970), p. 8.
11 Adolph F. Moravec, "Using Simulation to Design a Management Information System," *Management Services*, May–June, 1968, pp. 50–58.

Motivation

Undoubtedly the question of greatest concern to managers, whether working for AT&T, General Motors, or the corner gas station is, "How can I motivate my employees?" The problem has plagued organizations throughout recorded history and will do so into the foreseeable future. The answer has begun to emerge: there is no single, simple motivational technique that will work for all persons.

This theme is clearly stated by Morse and Lorsch, who weave together a discussion of the motivational impact of organizational and job-design considerations. They conclude that *any* single set of assumptions about human behavior is inadequate (whether Theory X or Theory Y), and propose instead a contingency view that recognizes the fundamental psychological phenomenon of individual differences in human needs. The article then concludes by describing ways in which competence motivation can best be aroused and utilized by managers.

Greene reviews the controversy over the relationship between satisfaction and performance, and presents a simplified expectancy model of motivation, based on the independent variables of reward value, reward size, and perceived relationships between effort and performance and performance and rewards. He then discusses specific managerial actions that will enhance the likelihood of employee motivation through manipulation of reward types (extrinsic or intrinsic) or reward schedules (fixed or variable interval, fixed or variable ratio).

The concept of behavior modification is a contingency strategy that is easily integrated within the expectancy framework reviewed by Greene. Luthans and Lyman define the steps involved, the results of a training program, and the advantages/disadvantages of "O.B. Mod." The whole point is that you do not make assumptions but rather find out what will motivate each worker, monitor his behavior, and then reinforce desirable behavior appropriately. Lawler proposes the same approach but on a broader scale when considering unique employee groups, such as the new-life-styled worker. Where a group has identifiable and common characteristics, he suggests that compensation policies and programs will have to be adapted to them, including such features as participation in planning, openness, more immediate rewards, and tailoring the plan via "cafeteria-style" benefits.

In the unlikely event that the reader will by now believe the process of motivation to be an easy one, the article by Deci should put the problem back into perspective. Results from laboratory experiments lead Deci to conclude that the basic dilemma in motivation lies in the apparent trade-off in effectiveness between intrinsic and extrinsic forms of rewards.

Reading 22

Beyond Theory Y

John J. Morse
Jay W. Lorsch

During the past 30 years, managers have been bombarded with two competing approaches to the problems of human administration and organization. The first, usually called the classical school of organization, emphasizes the need for well-established lines of authority, clearly defined jobs, and authority equal to responsibility. The second, often called the participative approach, focuses on the desirability of involving organization members in decision making so that they will be more highly motivated.

Douglas McGregor, through his well-known "Theory X and Theory Y," drew a distinction between the assumptions about human motivation which underlie these two approaches, to this effect:

• Theory X assumes that people dislike work and must be coerced, controlled, and directed toward organizational goals. Furthermore, most people prefer to be treated this way, so they can avoid responsibility.
• Theory Y—the integration of goals—emphasizes the average person's intrinsic interest in his work, his desire to be self-directing and to seek responsibility, and his capacity to be creative in solving business problems.

It is McGregor's conclusion, of course, that the latter approach to organization is the more desirable one for managers to follow.[1]

McGregor's position causes confusion for the managers who try to choose between these two conflicting approaches. The classical organizational approach that McGregor associated with Theory X does work well in some situations, although, as McGregor himself pointed out, there are also some situations where it does not work effectively. At the same time, the approach based on Theory Y, while it has produced good results in some situations, does not always do so. That is, each approach is effective in some cases but not in others. Why is this? How can managers resolve the confusion?

A NEW APPROACH

Recent work by a number of students of management and organization may help to answer such questions.[2] These studies indicate that there is not one best

"Beyond Theory Y," John J. Morse and Jay W. Lorsch, *Harvard Business Review*, May–June 1970, pp. 61–68. © 1970 by the President and Fellows of Harvard College; all rights reserved. Reprinted with permission.
[1]Douglas McGregor, *The Human Side of Enterprise* (New York, McGraw-Hill Book Company, Inc., 1960), pp. 34–35 and pp. 47–48.
[2]See for example Paul R. Lawrence and Jay W. Lorsch, *Organization and Environment* (Boston, Harvard Business School, Division of Research, 1967); Joan Woodward, *Industrial Organiza-*

organizational approach; rather, the best approach depends on the nature of the work to be done. Enterprises with highly predictable tasks perform better with organizations characterized by the highly formalized procedures and management hierarchies of the classical approach. With highly uncertain tasks that require more extensive problem solving, on the other hand, organizations that are less formalized and emphasize self-control and member participation in decision making are more effective. In essence, according to these newer studies, managers must design and develop organizations so that the organizational characteristics *fit* the nature of the task to be done.

While the conclusions of this newer approach will make sense to most experienced managers and can alleviate much of the confusion about which approach to choose, there are still two important questions unanswered:

1   How does the more formalized and controlling organization affect the motivation of organization members? (McGregor's most telling criticism of the classical approach was that it did not unleash the potential in an enterprise's human resources.)

2   Equally important, does a less formalized organization always provide a high level of motivation for its members? (This is the implication many managers have drawn from McGregor's work.)

We have recently been involved in a study that provides surprising answers to these questions and, when taken together with other recent work, suggests a new set of basic assumptions which move beyond Theory Y into what we call "Contingency Theory: the fit between task, organization, and people." These theoretical assumptions emphasize that the appropriate pattern of organization is *contingent* on the nature of the work to be done and on the particular needs of the people involved. We should emphasize that we have labeled these assumptions as a step beyond Theory Y because of McGregor's own recognition that the Theory Y assumptions would probably be supplanted by new knowledge within a short time.[3]

THE STUDY DESIGN

Our study was conducted in four organizational units. Two of these performed the relatively certain task of manufacturing standardized containers on high-speed, automated production lines. The other two performed the relatively uncertain work of research and development in communications technology. Each pair of units performing the same kind of task were in the same large company, and each pair had previously been evaluated by that company's management as containing

tion: *Theory and Practice* (New York, Oxford University Press, Inc., 1965); Tom Burns and G. M. Stalker, *The Management of Innovation* (London, Tavistock Publications, 1961); Harold J. Leavitt, "Unhuman Organizations," HBR July–August 1962, p. 90.

   [3]McGregor, *op cit.*, p. 245.

Exhibit I   Study Design in "Fit" of Organizational Characteristics

Characteristics	Company I (predictable manufacturing task)	Company II (unpredictable R&D task)
Effective performer	Akron containers plant	Stockton research lab
Less effective performer	Hartford containers plant	Carmel research lab

one highly effective unit and a less effective one. The study design is summarized in Exhibit 1.

The objective was to explore more fully how the fit between organization and task was related to successful performance. That is, does a good fit between organizational characteristics and task requirements increase the motivation of individuals and hence produce more effective individual and organizational performance?

An especially useful approach to answering this question is to recognize that an individual has a strong need to master the world around him, including the task that he faces as a member of a work organization.[4] The accumulated feelings of satisfaction that come from successfully mastering one's environment can be called a "sense of competence." We saw this sense of competence in performing a particular task as helpful in understanding how a fit between task and organizational characteristics could motivate people toward successful performance.

Organizational Dimensions

Because the four study sites had already been evaluated by the respective corporate managers as high and low performers of tasks, we expected that such differences in performance would be a preliminary clue to differences in the "fit" of the organizational characteristics to the job to be done. But, first, we had to define what kinds organizational characteristics would determine how appropriate the organization was to the particular task.

We grouped these organizational characteristics into two sets of factors:

1   Formal characteristics, which could be used to judge the fit between the kind of task being worked on and the formal practices of the organization.

2   Climate characteristics, or the subjective perceptions and orientations that had developed among the individuals about their organizational setting. (These too must fit the task to be performed if the organization is to be effective.)

We measured these attributes through questionnaires and interviews with about 40 managers in each unit to determine the appropriateness of the organization to the kind of task being performed. We also measured the feelings of competence of

---

[4]See Robert W. White, "Ego and Reality in Psychoanalytic Theory," *Psychological Issues*, Vol. III, No. 3 (New York, International Universities Press, 1963).

the people in the organizations so that we could link the appropriateness of the organizational attributes with a sense of competence.

MAJOR FINDINGS

The principal findings of the survey are best highlighted by contrasting the highly successful Akron plant and the high-performing Stockton laboratory. Because each performed very different tasks (the former a relatively certain manufacturing task and the latter a relatively uncertain research task), we expected, as brought out earlier, that there would have to be major differences between them in organizational characteristics if they were to perform effectively. And this is what we did find. But we also found that each of these effective units had a better fit with its particular task than did its less effective counterpart.

    While our major purpose in this article is to explore how the fit between task and organizational characteristics is related to motivation, we first want to explore more fully the organizational characteristics of these units, so the reader will better understand what we mean by a fit between task and organization and how it can lead to more effective behavior. To do this, we shall place the major emphasis on the contrast between the high-performing units (the Akron plant and Stockton laboratory), but we shall also compare each of these with its less effective mate (the Hartford plant and Carmel laboratory respectively).

Formal Characteristics

Beginning with differences in formal characteristics, we found that both the Akron and Stockton organizations fit their respective tasks much better than did their less successful counterparts. In the predictable manufacturing task environment, Akron had a pattern of formal relationships and duties that was highly structured and precisely defined. Stockton, with its unpredictable research task, had a low degree of structure and much less precision of definition (see Exhibit II).

    Akron's pattern of formal rules, procedures, and control systems was so specific and comprehensive that it prompted one manager to remark: "We've got rules here for everything from how much powder to use in cleaning the toilet bowls to how to cart a dead body out of the plant." In contrast, Stockton's formal rules were so minimal, loose, and flexible that one scientist, when asked whether he felt the rules ought to be tightened, said: "If a man puts a nut on a screw all day long, you may need more rules and a job definition for him. But we're not novices here. We're professionals and not the kind who need close supervision. People around here *do* produce, and produce under relaxed conditions. Why tamper with success?"

    These differences in formal organizational characteristics were well suited to the differences in tasks of the two organizations. Thus:

- Akron's highly structured formal practices fit its predictable task because

Exhibit II Differences in Formal Characteristics in High-performing Organizations

Characteristics	Akron	Stockton
1 Pattern of formal relationships and duties as signified by organization charts and job manuals	Highly structured, precisely defined	Low degree of structure, less well defined
2 Pattern of formal rules, procedures, control, and measurement systems	Pervasive, specific, uniform, comprehensive	Minimal, loose, flexible
3 Time dimensions incorporated in formal practices	Short-term	Long-term
4 Goal dimensions incorporated in formal practices	Manufacturing	Scientific

behavior had to be rigidly defined and controlled around the automated, high-speed production line. There was really only one way to accomplish the plant's very routine and programmable job; managers defined it precisely and insisted (through the plant's formal practices) that each man do what was expected of him.

On the other hand, Stockton's highly unstructured formal practices made just as much sense because the required activities in the laboratory simply could not be rigidly defined in advance. With such an unpredictable, fast-changing task as communications technology research, there were numerous approaches to getting the job done well. As a consequence, Stockton managers used a less structured pattern of formal practices that left the scientists in the lab free to respond to the changing task situation.

• Akron's formal practices were very much geared to *short-term* and *manufacturing* concerns as its task demanded. For example, formal production reports and operating review sessions were daily occurrences, consistent with the fact that the through-put time for their products was typically only a few hours.

By contrast, Stockton's formal practices were geared to *long-term* and *scientific* concerns, as its task demanded. Formal reports and reviews were made only quarterly, reflecting the fact that research often does not come to fruition for three to five years.

At the two less effective sites (i.e., the Hartford plant and the Carmel laboratory), the formal organizational characteristics did not fit their respective tasks nearly as well. For example, Hartford's formal practices were much less structured and controlling than were Akron's, while Carmel's were more restraining and restricting than were Stockton's. A scientist in Carmel commented: "There's something here that keeps you from being scientific. It's hard to put your finger on, but I guess I'd call it 'Mickey Mouse.' There are rules and things here that get in your way regarding doing your job as a researcher."

Climate Characteristics

As with formal practices, the climate in both high-performing Akron and Stockton suited the respective tasks much better than did the climates at the less successful Hartford and Carmel sites.

Perception of Structure   The people in the Akron plant perceived a great deal of structure, with their behavior tightly controlled and defined. One manager in the plant said: "We can't let the lines run unattended. We lose money whenever they do. So we make sure each man knows his job, knows when he can take a break, knows how to handle a change in shifts, etc. It's all spelled out clearly for him the day he comes to work here." In contrast, the scientists in the Stockton laboratory perceived very little structure, with their behavior only minimally controlled. Such perceptions encouraged the individualistic and creative behavior that the uncertain, rapidly changing research task needed. Scientists in the less successful Carmel laboratory perceived much more structure in their organization and voiced the feeling that this was "getting in their way" and making it difficult to do effective research.

Distribution of Influence   The Akron plant and the Stockton laboratory also differed substantially in how influence was distributed and on the character of superior-subordinate and colleague relations. Akron personnel felt that they had much less influence over decisions in their plant than Stockton's scientists did in their laboratory. The task at Akron had already been clearly defined and that definition had, in a sense, been incorporated into the automated production flow itself. Therefore, there was less need for individuals to have a say in decisions concerning the work process.

Moreover, in Akron, influence was perceived to be concentrated in the upper levels of the formal structure (a hierarchical or "top-heavy" distribution), while in Stockton influence was perceived to be more evenly spread out among more levels of the formal structure (an egalitarian distribution).

Akron's members perceived themselves to have a low degree of freedom vis-à-vis superiors both in choosing the jobs they work on and in handling these jobs on their own. They also described the type of supervision in the plant as being relatively directive. Stockton's scientists, on the other hand, felt that they had a great deal of freedom vis-à-vis their superiors both in choosing the tasks and projects, and in handling them in the way that they wanted to. They described supervision in the laboratory as being very participatory.

It is interesting to note that the less successful Carmel laboratory had more of its decisions made at the top. Because of this, there was a definite feeling by the scientists that their particular expertise was not being effectively used in choosing projects.

Relations with Others   The people at Akron preceived a great deal of similarity among themselves in background, prior work experiences, and approaches for tackling job-related problems. They also perceived the degree of coordination of effort among colleagues to be very high. Because Akron's task was so precisely defined and the behavior of its members so rigidly controlled around the automated lines, it is easy to see that this pattern also made sense.

By contrast, Stockton's scientists perceived not only a great many differences among themselves, especially in education and background, but also that the coordination of effort among colleagues was relatively low. This was appropriate for a laboratory in which a great variety of disciplines and skills were present and individual projects were important to solve technological problems.

Time Orientation   As we would expect, Akron's individuals were highly oriented toward a relatively short time span and manufacturing goals. They responded to quick feedback concerning the quality and service that the plant was providing. This was essential, given the nature of their task.

Stockton's researchers were highly oriented toward a longer time span and scientific goals. These orientations meant that they were willing to wait for long-term feedback from a research project that might take years to complete. A scientist in Stockton said: "We're not the kind of people here who need a pat on the back every day. We can wait for months if necessary before we get feedback from colleagues and the profession. I've been working on one project now for three months and I'm still not sure where it's going to take me. I can live with that, though." This is precisely the kind of behavior and attitude that spells success on this kind of task.

Managerial Style   Finally, the individuals in both Akron and Stockton perceived their chief executive to have a "managerial style" that expressed more of a concern for the task than for people or relationships, but this seemed to fit both tasks.

In Akron, the technology of the task was so dominant that top managerial behavior which was not focused primarily on the task might have reduced the effectiveness of performance. On the other hand, although Stockton's research task called for more individualistic problem-solving behavior, that sort of behavior could have become segmented and uncoordinated, unless the top executive in the lab focused the group's attention on the overall research task. Given the individualistic bent of the scientists, this was an important force in achieving unity of effort. All these differences in climate characteristics in the two high performers are summarized in Exhibit III.

As with formal attributes, the less effective Hartford and Carmel sites had organization climates that showed a perceptibly lower degree of fit with their respective tasks. For example, the Hartford plant had an egalitarian distribution of influence, perceptions of a low degree of structure, and a more participatory type of supervision. The Carmel laboratory had a somewhat top-heavy distribution of influence, perceptions of high structure, and a more directive type of supervision.

Exhibit III   Differences in "Climate" Characteristics in High-performing Organizations

Characteristics	Akron	Stockton
1 Structural orientation	Perceptions of tightly controlled behavior and a high degree of structure	Perceptions of a low degree of structure
2 Distribution of influence	Perceptions of low total influence, concentrated at upper levels in the organization	Perceptions of high total influence, more evenly spread out among all levels
3 Character of superior-subordinate relations	Low freedom vis-à-vis superiors to choose and handle jobs, directive type of supervision	High freedom vis-à-vis superiors to choose and handle projects, participatory type of supervision
4 Character of colleague relations	Perceptions of many similarities among colleagues, high degree of coordination of colleague effort	Perceptions of many differences among colleagues, relatively low degree of coordination of colleague effort
5 Time orientation	Short-term	Long-term
6 Goal orientation	Manufacturing	Scientific
7 Top executive's "managerial style"	More concerned with task than people	More concerned with task than people

COMPETENCE MOTIVATION

Because of the difference in organizational characteristics at Akron and Stockton, the two sites were strikingly different places in which to work. But these organizations had two very important things in common. First, each organization fit very well the requirements of its task. Second, although the behavior in the two organizations was different, the result in both cases was effective task performance.

Since, as we indicated earlier, our primary concern in this study was to link the fit between organization and task with individual motivation to perform effectively, we devised a two-part test to measure the sense of competence motivation of the individuals at both sites: Thus:

The *first* part asked a participant to write creative and imagnative stories in response to six ambiguous pictures.

The *second* asked him to write a creative and imaginative story about what he would be doing, thinking, and feeling "tomorrow" on his job. This is called a "projective" test because it is assumed that the respondent projects into his stories his own attitudes, thoughts, feelings, needs, and wants, all of which can be measured from the stories.[5]

The results indicated that the individuals in Akron and Stockton showed significantly more feelings of competence than did their counterparts in the lower-fit Hartford and Carmel organizations.[6] We found that the organization-task fit is simultaneously linked to and interdependent with both individual motivation and effective unit performance. (This interdependency is illustrated in Exhibit IV.)

Putting the conclusions in this form raises the question of cause and effect. Does effective unit performance result from the task-organization fit or from higher motivation, or perhaps from both? Does higher sense of competence motivation result from effective unit performance or from fit?

Our answer to these questions is that we do not think there are any single cause-and-effect relationships, but that these factors are mutually interrelated. This has important implications for management theory and practice.

CONTINGENCY THEORY

Returning to McGregor's Theory X and Theory Y assumptions, we can now question the validity of some of his conclusions. While Theory Y might help to explain the findings in the two laboratories, we clearly need something other than Theory X or Y assumptions to explain the findings in the plants.

For example, the managers at Akron worked in a formalized organization setting with relatively little participation in decision making, and yet they were

[5]For a more detailed description of this survey, see John J. Morse, *Internal Organizational Patterning and Sense of Competence Motivation* (Boston, Harvard Business School, unpublished doctoral dissertation, 1969).

[6]Differences between the two container plants are significant at .001 and between the research laboratories at .01 (one-tailed probability).

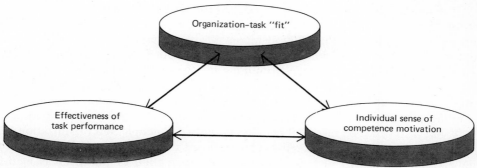

Exhibit IV Basic contingent relationships.

highly motivated. According to Theory X, people would work hard in such a setting only because they were coerced to do so. According to Theory Y, they should have been involved in decision making and been self-directed to feel so motivated. Nothing in our data indicates that either set of assumptions was valid at Akron.

Conversely, the managers at Hartford, the low-performing plant, were in a less formalized organization with more participation in decision making, and yet they were not as highly motivated like the Akron managers. The Theory Y assumptions would suggest that they should have been more motivated.

A way out of such paradoxes is to state a new set of assumptions, the Contingency Theory, that seems to explain the findings at all four sites:

1   Human beings bring varying patterns of needs and motives into the work organization, but one central need is to achieve a sense of competence.
2   The sense of competence motive, while it exists in all human beings, may be fulfilled in different ways by different people depending on how this need interacts with the strengths of the individuals' other needs—such as those for power, independence, structure, achievement, and affiliation.
3   Competence motivation is most likely to be fulfilled when there is a fit between task and organization.
4   Sense of competence continues to motivate even when a competence goal is achieved; once one goal is reached, a new, higher one is set.

While the central thrust of these points is clear from the preceding discussion of the study, some elaboration can be made. First, the idea that different people have different needs is well understood by psychologists. However, all too often, managers assume that all people have similar needs. Lest we be accused of the same error, we are saying only that all people have a need to feel competent; in this *one* way they are similar. But in many other dimensions of personality, individuals differ, and these differences will determine how a particular person achieves a sense of competence.

Thus, for example, the people in the Akron plant seemed to be very different from those in the Stockton laboratory in their underlying attitudes toward uncertainty, authority, and relationships with their peers. And because they had different need patterns along these dimensions, both groups were highly motivated by achieving competence from quite different activities and settings.

While there is a need to further investigate how people who work in different settings differ in their psychological makeup, one important implication of the Contingency Theory is that we must not only seek a fit between organization and task, but also between task and people and between people and organization.

A further point which requires elaboration is that one's sense of competence never really comes to rest. Rather, the real satisfaction of this need is in the successful performance itself, with no diminishing of the motivation as one goal is

reached. Since feelings of competence are thus reinforced by successful performance, they can be a more consistent and reliable motivator than salary and
benefits.

Implications for Managers

The major managerial implication of the Contingency Theory seems to rest in the
task-organization-people fit. Although this interrelationship is complex, the best
possibility for managerial action probably is in tailoring the organization to fit the
task and the people. If such a fit is achieved, both effective unit performance and a
higher sense of competence motivation seem to result.

   Managers can start this process by considering how certain the task is, how
frequently feedback about task performance is available, and what goals are
implicit in the task. The answers to these questions will guide their decisions about
the design of the management hierarchy, the specificity of job assignments, and
the utilization of rewards and control procedures. Selective use of training
programs and a general emphasis on appropriate management styles will move
them toward a task-organization fit.

   The problem of achieving a fit among task, organization, and people is
something we know less about. As we have already suggested, we need further
investigation of what personality characteristics fit various tasks and organizations. Even with our limited knowledge, however, there are indications that
people will gradually gravitate into organizations that fit their particular personalities. Managers can help this process by becoming more aware of what psychological needs seem to best fit the tasks available and the organizational setting, and by
trying to shape personnel selection criteria to take account of these needs.

   In arguing for an approach which emphasizes the fit among task, organization, and people, we are putting to rest the question of which organizational
approach—the classical or the participative—is best. In its place we are raising a
new question: What organizational approach is most appropriate given the task
and the people involved?

   For many enterprises, given the new needs of younger employees for more
autonomy, and the rapid rates of social and technological change, it may well be
that the more participative approach is the most appropriate. But there will still be
many situations in which the more controlled and formalized organization is
desirable. Such an organization need not be coercive or punitive. If it makes sense
to the individuals involved, given their needs and their jobs, they will find it
rewarding and motivating.

CONCLUDING NOTE

The reader will recognize that the complexity we have described is not of our own
making. The basic deficiency with earlier approaches is that they did not recognize

the variability in tasks and people which produces this complexity. The strength of the contingency approach we have outlined is that it begins to provide a way of thinking about this complexity, rather than ignoring it. While our knowledge in this area is still growing, we are certain that any adequate theory of motivation and organization will have to take account of the contingent relationship between task, organization, and people.

Reading 23

The Satisfaction-Performance Controversy: New Developments and Their Implications

Charles N. Greene

As Ben walked by smiling on the way to his office, Ben's boss remarked to a friend: "Ben really enjoys his job and that's why he's the best damn worker I ever had. And that's reason enough for me to keep Ben happy." The friend replied: "No, you're wrong! Ben likes his job because he does it so well. If you want to make Ben happy, you ought to do whatever you can to help him further improve his performance."

Four decades after the initial published investigation on the satisfaction-performance relationship, these two opposing views are still the subject of controversy on the part of both practitioners and researchers. Several researchers have concluded, in fact, that "there is no present technique for determining the cause-and-effect of satisfaction and performance." Current speculations, reviewed by Schwab and Cummings, however, still imply at least in theory that satisfaction and performance are causally related although, in some cases, the assumed cause has become the effect, and, in others, the relationship between these two variables is considered to be a function of a third or even additional variables.[1]

"The Satisfaction-Performance Controversy: New Developments and Their Implications," Charles N. Greene, *Business Horizons,* October 1972, pp. 31–41. Reprinted with permission.
    [1]Initial investigation by A. A. Kornhauser and A. W. Sharp, "Employee Attitudes: Suggestions from a Study in a Factory," *Personnel Journal,* X (May, 1932), pp. 393–401.
    First quotation from Robert A. Sutermeister, "Employee Performance and Employee Need Satisfaction—Which Comes First?" *California Management Review,* XIII (Summer, 1971), p. 43.
    Second quotation from Donald P. Schwab and Larry L. Cummings, "Theories of Performance and Satisfaction: a Review," *Industrial Relations,* IX (October, 1970), pp. 408–30.

THEORY AND EVIDENCE

"Satisfaction Causes Performance"

At least three fundamental theoretical propositions underlie the research and writing in this area. The first and most pervasive stems from the human relations movement with its emphasis on the well-being of the individual at work. In the years following the investigations at Western Electric, a number of studies were conducted to identify correlates of high and low job satisfaction. The interest in satisfaction, however, came about not so much as a result of concern for the individual as concern with the presumed linkage of satisfaction with performance.

According to this proposition (simply stated and still frequently accepted), the degree of job satisfaction felt by an employee determines his performance, that is, satisfaction causes performance. This proposition has theoretical roots, but it also reflects the popular belief that "a happy worker is a productive worker" and the notion that "all good things go together." It is far more pleasant to increase an employee's happiness than to deal directly with his performance whenever a performance problem exists. Therefore, acceptance of the satisfaction-causes-performance proposition as a solution makes good sense, particularly for the manager because it represents the path of least resistance. Furthermore, high job satisfaction and high performance are both good, and, therefore, they ought to be related to one another.

At the theoretical level, Vroom's valence-force model is a prime example of theory-based support of the satisfaction-causes-performance case.[2] In Vroom's model, job satisfaction reflects the valence (attractiveness) of the job. It follows from his theory that the force exerted on an employee to remain on the job is an increasing function of the valence of the job. Thus, satisfaction should be negatively related to absenteeism and turnover, and, at the empirical level, it is.

Whether or not this valence also leads to higher performance, however, is open to considerable doubt. Vroom's review of twenty-three field studies, which investigated the relationship between satisfaction and performance, revealed an insignificant median static correlation of 0.14, that is, satisfaction explained less than 2 percent of the variance in performance. Thus, the insignificant results and absence of tests of the causality question fail to provide support for this proposition.

"Performance Causes Satisfaction"

More recently a second theoretical proposition has been advanced. According to this view, best represented by the work of Porter and Lawler, satisfaction is considered not as a cause but as an effect of performance, that is, performance causes satisfaction.[3] Differential performance determines rewards which, in turn, produce variance in satisfaction. In other words, rewards constitute a necessary

---

[2]Victor H. Vroom, *Work and Motivation* (New York: John Wiley & Sons, Inc., 1964).

[3]Lyman W. Porter and Edward E. Lawler, III, *Managerial Attitudes and Performance* (Homewood, Ill.: Richard D. Irwin, Inc., 1968).

intervening variable and, thus, satisfaction is considered to be a function of performance-related rewards.

At the empirical level, two recent studies, each utilizing time-lag correlations, lend considerable support to elements of this proposition. Bowen and Siegel, and Greene reported finding relatively strong correlations between performance and satisfaction expressed later (the performance-causes-satisfaction condition), which were significantly higher than the low correlations between satisfaction and performance which occurred during the subsequent period (the "satisfaction-causes-performance" condition).[4]

In the Greene study, significant correlations were obtained between performance and rewards granted subsequently and between rewards and subsequent satisfaction. Thus, Porter and Lawler's predictions that differential performance determines rewards and that rewards produce variance in satisfaction were upheld.

"Rewards" as a Causal Factor

Closely related to Porter and Lawler's predictions is a still more recent theoretical position, which considers both satisfaction and performance to be functions of rewards. In this view, rewards cause satisfaction, and rewards that are based on current performance affect subsequent performance.

According to this proposition, formulated by Cherrington, Reitz, and Scott from the contributions of reinforcement theorists, there is no inherent relationship between satisfaction and performance.[5] The results of their experimental investigation strongly support their predictions. The rewarded subjects reported significantly greater satisfaction than did the unrewarded subjects. Furthermore, when rewards (monetary bonuses, in this case) were granted on the basis of performance, the subjects' performance was significantly higher than that of subjects whose rewards were unrelated to their performance. For example, they found that when a low performer was not rewarded, he expressed dissatisfaction but that his later performance improved. On the other hand, when a low performer was in fact rewarded for his low performance, he expressed high satisfaction but continued to perform at a low level.

The same pattern of findings was revealed in the case of the high performing subjects with one exception; the high performer who was not rewarded expressed dissatisfaction, as expected, and his performance on the next trial declined significantly. The correlation between satisfaction and subsequent performance,

[4]Donald Bowen and Jacob P. Siegel, "The Relationship Between Satisfaction and Performance: the Question of Causality," paper presented at the annual meeting of the American Psychological Association, Miami Beach, September, 1970.

Charles N. Greene, "A Causal Interpretation of Relationship Among Pay, Performance, and Satisfaction," paper presented at the annual meeting of the Midwest Psychological Association, Cleveland, Ohio, May, 1972.

[5]David J. Cherrington, H. Joseph Reitz, and William E. Scott, Jr., "Effects of Contingent and Non-contingent Reward on the Relationship Between Satisfaction and Task Performance," *Journal of Applied Psychology,* LV (December, 1971) pp. 531–36.

excluding the effects of rewards, was 0.00, that is, satisfaction does *not* cause improved performance.

A recent field study, which investigated the source and direction of causal influence in satisfaction-performance relationships, supports the Cherrington-Reitz-Scott findings.[6] Merit pay was identified as a cause of satisfaction and, contrary to some current beliefs, was found to be a significantly more frequent source of satisfaction than dissatisfaction. The results of this study further revealed equally significant relationships between (1) merit pay and subsequent performance and (2) current performance and subsequent merit pay. Given the Cherrington-Reitz-Scott findings that rewards based on current performance cause improved subsequent performance, these results do suggest the possibility of reciprocal causation.

In other words, merit pay based on current performance probably caused variations in subsequent performance, and the company in this field study evidently was relatively successful in implementing its policy of granting salary increases to an employee on the basis of his performance (as evidenced by the significant relationship found between current performance and subsequent merit pay). The company's use of a fixed (annual) merit increase schedule probably obscured some of the stronger reinforcing effects of merit pay on performance.

Unlike the Cherrington-Reitz-Scott controlled experiment, the fixed merit increase schedule precluded (as it does in most organizations) giving an employee a monetary reward immediately after he successfully performed a major task. This constraint undoubtedly reduced the magnitude of the relationship between merit pay and subsequent performance.

IMPLICATIONS FOR MANAGEMENT

These findings have several apparent but nonetheless important implications. For the manager who desired to enhance the satisfaction of his subordinates (perhaps for the purpose of reducing turnover), the implication of the finding that "rewards cause satisfaction" is self-evident. If, on the other hand, the manager's interest in his subordinates' satisfaction arises from his desire to increase their performance, the consistent rejection of the satisfaction-causes-performance proposition has an equally clear implication: increasing subordinates' satisfaction will have no effect on their performance.

The finding that rewards based on current performance affect subsequent performance does, however, offer a strategy for increasing subordinates' performance. Unfortunately, it is not the path of least resistance for the manager. Granting differential rewards on the basis of differences in his subordinates' performance will cause his subordinates to express varying degrees of satisfaction

[6]Charles N. Greene, "Source and Direction of Causal Influence in Satisfaction-Performance Relationships," paper presented at the annual meetings of the Eastern Academy of Management, Boston, May, 1972. Also reported in Greene, "Causal Connections Among Managers' Merit Pay, Satisfaction, and Performance," *Journal of Applied Psychology,* 1972 (in press).

or dissatisfaction. The manager, as a result, will soon find himself in the uncomfortable position of having to successfully defend his basis for evaluation or having to put up with dissatified subordinates until their performance improves or they leave the organization.

The benefits of this strategy, however, far outweigh its liabilities. In addition to its positive effects on performance, this strategy provides equity since the most satisfied employees are the rewarded high performers and, for the same reason, it also facilitates the organization's efforts to retain its most productive employees.

If these implications are to be considered as prescriptions for managerial behavior, one is tempted at this point to conclude that all a manager need do in order to increase his subordinates' performance is to accurately appraise their work and then reward them accordingly. However, given limited resources for rewards and knowledge of appraisal techniques, it is all too apparent that the manager's task here is not easy.

Moreover, the relationship between rewards and performance is often not as simple or direct as one would think, for at least two reasons. First, there are other causes of performance that may have a more direct bearing on a particular problem. Second is the question of the appropriateness of the reward itself, that is, what is rewarding for one person may not be for another. In short, a manager also needs to consider other potential causes of performance and a range of rewards in coping with any given performance problem.

Nonmotivational Factors

The element of performance that relates most directly to the discussion thus far is effort, that element which links rewards to performance. The employee who works hard usually does so because of the rewards or avoidance of punishment that he associates with good work. He believes that the magnitude of the reward he will receive is contingent on his performance and, further, that his performance is a function of how hard he works. Thus, effort reflects the motivational aspect of performance. There are, however, other nonmotivational considerations that can best be considered prior to examining ways by which a manager can deal with the motivational problem.

Direction   Suppose, for example, that an employee works hard at his job, yet his performance is inadequate. What can his manager do to alleviate the problem? The manager's first action should be to identify the cause. One likely possibility is what can be referred to as a "direction problem."

Several years ago, the Minnesota Vikings' defensive end, Jim Marshall, very alertly gathered up the opponent's fumble and then, with obvious effort and delight, proceeded to carry the ball some fifty yards into the wrong end zone. This is a direction problem in its purest sense. For the employee working under more usual circumstances, a direction problem generally stems from his lack of understanding of what is expected of him or what a job well done looks like. The action indicated to alleviate this problem is to clarify or define in detail for the employee the requirements of his job. The manager's own leadership style may also be a factor. In dealing with an employee with a direction problem, the manager needs to exercise closer supervision and to initiate structure or focus on the task, as opposed to emphasizing consideration or his relations with the employee.[7]

In cases where this style of behavior is repugnant or inconsistent with the manager's own leadership inclinations, an alternative approach is to engage in mutual goal setting or management-by-objectives techniques with the employee. Here, the necessary structure can be established, but at the subordinate's own initiative, thus creating a more participative atmosphere. This approach, however, is not free of potential problems. The employee is more likely to make additional undetected errors before his performance improves, and the approach is more time consuming than the more direct route.

Ability　What can the manager do if the actions he has taken to resolve the direction problem fail to result in significant improvements in performance? His subordinate still exerts a high level of effort and understands what is expected of him—yet he continues to perform poorly. At this point, the manager may begin, justifiably so, to doubt his subordinate's ability to perform the job. When this doubt does arise, there are three useful questions, suggested by Mager and Pipe, to which the manager should find answers before he treats the problem as an ability deficiency: Could the subordinate do it if he really had to? Could he do it if his life depended on it? Are his present abilities adequate for the desired performance?[8]

If the answers to the first two questions are negative, then the answer to the last question also will be negative, and the obvious conclusion is that an ability deficiency does, in fact, exist. Most managers, upon reaching this conclusion, begin to develop some type of formal training experience for the subordinate. This is unfortunate and frequently wasteful. There is probably a simpler, less expensive solution. Formal training is usually required only when the individual has never done the particular job in question or when there is no way in which the ability requirement in question can be eliminated from his job.

If the individual formerly used the skill but now uses it only rarely, systematic practice will usually overcome the deficiency without formal training. Alternatively, the job can be changed or simplified so that the impaired ability is no longer crucial to successful performance. If, on the other hand, the individual once had the skill and still rather frequently is able to practice it, the manager

---

[7]For example, a recent study reported finding that relationships between the leader's initiating structure and both subordinate satisfaction and performance were moderated by such variables as role ambiguity, job scope, and task autonomy perceived by the subordinate. See Robert J. House, "A Path Goal Theory of Leader Effectiveness," *Administrative Science Quarterly,* XVI (September, 1971), pp. 321–39.

[8]Robert F. Mager and Peter Pipe, *Analyzing Performance Problems* (Belmont, Calif.: Lear Siegler, Inc., 1970), p. 21.

should consider providing him greater feedback concerning the outcome of his efforts. The subordinate may not be aware of the deficiency and its effect on his performance, or he may no longer know how to perform the job. For example, elements of his job or the relationship between his job and other jobs may have changed, and he simply is not aware of the change.

Where formal training efforts are indicated, systematic analysis of the job is useful for identifying the specific behaviors and skills that are closely related with successful task performance and that, therefore, need to be learned. Alternatively, if the time and expense associated with job analysis are considered excessive, the critical incidents approach can be employed toward the same end.[9] Once training needs have been identified and the appropriate training technique employed, the manager can profit by asking himself one last question: "Why did the ability deficiency develop in the first place?"

Ultimately, the answer rests with the selection and placement process. Had a congruent man-job match been attained at the outset, the ability deficiency would have never presented itself as a performance problem.[10]

Performance Obstacles   When inadequate performance is not the result of a lack of effort, direction, or ability, there is still another potential cause that needs attention. There may be obstacles beyond the subordinate's control that interfere with his performance. "I can't do it" is not always an abili; it may be a real description of the problem. Performance obstacles can take many forms to the extent that their number, independent of a given situation, is almost unlimited.

However, the manager might look initially for some of the more common potential obstacles, such as a lack of time or conflicting demands on the subordinate's time, inadequate work facilities, restrictive policies or "right ways of doing it" that inhibit performance, lack of authority, insufficient information about other activities that affect the job, and lack of cooperation from others with whom he must work.

An additional obstacle, often not apparent to the manager from his face-to-face interaction with a subordinate, is the operation of group goals and norms that run counter to organizational objectives. Where the work group adheres to norms of restricting productivity, for example, the subordinate will similarly restrict his own performance to the extent that he identifies more closely with the group than with management.

Most performance obstacles can be overcome either by removing the

---

[9]See, for example, J. D. Folley, Jr., "Determining Training Needs of Department Store Personnel," *Training Development Journal,* XXIII (January, 1969), pp. 24–27, for a discussion of how the critical incidents approach can be employed to identify job skills to be learned in a formal training situation.

[10]For a useful discussion of how ability levels can be upgraded by means of training and selection procedures, the reader can refer to Larry L. Cummings and Donald P. Schwab, *Performance in Organizations: Determinants and Appraisal* (Glenview, Ill.: Scott, Foresman & Co., 1972; in press).

Rewards and effort

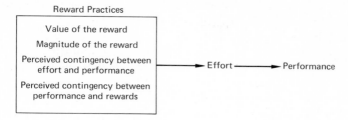

Reward Practices

| Value of the reward |
| Magnitude of the reward |
| Perceived contingency between effort and performance |
| Perceived contingency between performance and rewards |

Effort ⟶ Performance

obstacle or by changing the subordinate's job so that the obstacle no longer impinges on his performance. When the obstacle stems from group norms, however, a very different set of actions is required. Here, the actions that should be taken are the same as those that will be considered shortly in coping with lack of effort on the part of the individual. In other words, the potential causes of the group's lack of effort are identical to those that apply to the individual.

The Motivational Problem

Thus far, performance problems have been considered in which effort was not the source of the performance discrepancy. While reward practices constitute the most frequent and direct cause of effort, there are, however, other less direct causes. Direction, ability, and performance obstacles may indirectly affect effort through their direct effects on performance. For example, an individual may perform poorly because of an ability deficiency and, as a result, exert little effort on the job. Here, the ability deficiency produced low performance, and the lack of effort on the individual's part resulted from his expectations of failure. Thus, actions taken to alleviate the ability deficiency should result in improved performance and, subsequently, in higher effort.

Effort is that element of performance which links rewards to performance. The relationship between rewards and effort is, unfortunately, not a simple one. As indicated in the figure, effort is considered not only as a function of the (1) value and (2) magnitude of reward, but also as a function of the (3) individual's perceptions of the extent to which greater effort on his part will lead to higher performance, and (4) that his high performance, in turn, will lead to rewards. Therefore, a manager who is confronted with a subordinate who exerts little effort must consider these four attributes of reward practices in addition to the more indirect, potential causes of the lack of effort. The key issues in coping with a subordinate's lack of effort—the motivation problem—or in preventing such a problem from arising involve all four of the attributes of rewards just identified.[11]

---

[11]The discussion in this section is based in part on Cummings and Schwab, *Performance in Organizations,* and Lyman W. Porter and Edward E. Lawler, III, "What Job Attitudes Tell About Motivation," *Harvard Business Review,* LXVI (January–February, 1968), pp. 118–26.

Appropriateness of the Reward Regardless of the extent to which the individual believes that hard work determines his performance and subsequent rewards, he will obviously put forth little effort unless he *values* those rewards—that is, the rewards must have value in terms of his own need state. An accountant, for example, may value recognition from his boss, an opportunity to increase the scope of his job, or a salary increase; however, it is unlikely that he will place the same value on a ten-year supply of budget forms.

In other words, there must be consistency between the reward and what the individual needs or wants and recognition that there are often significant differences among individuals in what they consider rewarding. Similarly, individuals differ in terms of the *magnitude* of that valued reward they consider to be positively reinforcing. A 7 or 8 percent salary increase may motivate one person but have little or no positive effect on another person at the same salary level. Furthermore, a sizable reward in one situation might be considered small by the same individual in a different set of circumstances.

These individual differences, particularly those concerning what rewards are valued, raise considerable question about the adequacy of current organization reward systems, virtually none of which make any formal recognition of individual differences. Lawler, for example, has suggested that organizations could profit greatly by introducing "cafeteria-style" wage plans.[12] These plans allow an employee to select any combination of cash and fringe benefits he desires. An employee would be assigned "X" amount in compensation, which he may then divide up among a number of fringe benefits and cash. This practice would ensure that employees receive only those fringe benefits they value; from the organization's point of view, it would reduce the waste in funds allocated by the organization to fringe benefits not valued by its members. As a personal strategy, however, the manager could profit even more by extending Lawler's plan to include the entire range of nonmonetary rewards.

Rewards can be classified into two broad categories, extrinsic and intrinsic. Extrinsic rewards are those external to the job or in the context of the job, such as job security, improved working facilities, praise from one's boss, status symbols, and, of course, pay, including fringe benefits. Intrinsic rewards, on the other hand, are rewards that can be associated directly with the "doing of the job," such as a sense of accomplishment after successful performance, opportunities for advancement, increased responsibility, and work itself.

Thus, intrinsic rewards flow immediately and directly from the individual's performance of the job and, as such, may be considered as a form of self-reward. For example, one essentially must decide for himself whether his level of performance is worthy of a feeling of personal achievement. Extrinsic rewards, to the contrary, are administered by the organization; the organization first must identify good performance and then provide the appropriate reward.

---

[12]Edward E. Lawler, III, *Pay and Organizational Effectiveness: a Psychological View* (New York: McGraw-Hill Book Company, 1971).

Generally speaking, extrinsic rewards have their greatest value when the individual is most strongly motivated to satisfy what Maslow has referred to as lower level needs, basic physiological needs and needs for safety or security, and those higher level ego needs that can be linked directly to status. Pay, for example, may be valued by an individual because he believes it is a determinant of his social position within the community or because it constitutes a means for acquiring status symbols.

Intrinsic rewards are likely to be valued more by the individual after his lower level needs have been largely satisfied. In other words, there must be an adequate level of satisfaction with the extrinsic rewards before intrinsic rewards can be utilized effectively. In order to make the subordinate's job more intrinsically rewarding, the manager may want to consider several actions.

Perhaps most important, the manager needs to provide meaningful work assignments, that is, work with which the subordinate can identify and become personally involved. He should establish challenging yet attainable goals or, in some cases, it may be more advantageous for him to create conditions that greatly enhance the likelihood that his subordinate will succeed, thus increasing the potential for attaining feelings of achievement, advancement, and recognition. The manager may also consider such means as increased delegation and job enlargement for extending the scope and depth of the subordinate's job and thereby increasing the subordinate's sense of responsibility and providing greater opportunity to make the job into something more compatible with his own interests.

In short, the manager should as best he can match the rewards at his disposal, both extrinsic and intrinsic rewards, with what the subordinate indicates he needs or wants. Second, he should, by varying the magnitude and timing of the rewards granted, establish clearly in the subordinate's mind the desired effort-performance-reward contingencies.

Establishing the Contingencies   The contingency between effort and performance (that is, the extent to which the individual believes that by working harder, he will improve his performance) is largely a function of his confidence in his own abilities and his perceptions of the difficulty of the task and absence of obstacles standing in the way of successful task performance. When the effort-performance contingency is not clear for these reasons, the manager should consider several actions. He can reassign work or modify the task to be more consistent with the individual's perceptions of his own abilities; treat the problem as a "real" ability deficiency; remove the apparent performance obstacles; or simply reassure the individual.

The second contingency, the individual's belief that the rewards he receives reflect his accomplishments, is usually more difficult to establish. Here, two rather vexing predicaments are frequently encountered, both of which stem primarily from administration of extrinsic rewards. First, the instrument (usually a merit evaluation or performance appraisal device) may inaccurately measure the individual's contribution and thus his performance is rewarded in error. Reward schedules constitute the source of the second problem. Given fixed reward schedules (that is, the ubiquitous annual salary increase) adopted by the great majority of organizations, there is more frequently than not a considerable delay between task accomplishment and bestowal of the reward. As a result, the individual may not only fail to perceive the intended contingency but may incorrectly associate the reward with his behavior just prior to being rewarded. In other words, he may perceive a nonexistent contingency, and his subsequent behavior will reflect that contingency and, this time, go unrewarded.

Reward Schedules   The manner in which a given reward, or reinforcer, is scheduled is as strong a determinant of the effectiveness of that reward as is the value of the reward itself, or, for that matter, any other attribute of the reward. In organizations, the only plausible forms of reward schedules are intermittent as opposed to the continuous reward schedule in which the reward or punishment is administered after every behavioral sequence to be conditioned. In the case of the intermittent schedules, the behavior to be conditioned is reinforced only occasionally. There are four schedules of interest to the manager, each with varying effects on performance as a number of investigations in the field of experimental psychology have revealed.

1   *Fixed-interval schedule*—Rewards are bestowed after a fixed period, usually since the last reward was granted. This schedule is equivalent to the annual salary increase schedule in organizations, and its effects on performance are well-known. Typically, the individual "saves up," that is, he exerts a high level of effort just prior to the time of the reinforcement, usually his annual performance review. His performance more than likely will then taper off until the time just prior to his next annual review.

2   *Variable-interval schedule*—Rewards are administered at designated time periods, but the intervals between the periods vary. For example, a reward may be given one day after the last rewarded behavior sequence, then three days later, then one week later, and so on, but only if the behavior to be conditioned actually occurs. This schedule results in fairly consistent rates of performance over long periods of time. Praise or other forms of social reinforcement from one's peers and superior, as an example, usually occur according to a variable-interval schedule, not by intention but simply because they are too involved with their own affairs to provide systematic reinforcement.

3   *Fixed-ratio schedule*—Reinforcement is provided after a fixed number of responses or performances by the individual. Incentive wage plans so frequently utilized in organizations constitute the prime example of this type of schedule. It is characterized by higher rates of effort than the interval schedules unless the ratio is large. When significant delays do occur between rewards, performance, much like in the fixed schedule, declines immediately after the reward is bestowed and improves again as the time for the next reward approaches.

4   *Variable-ratio schedule*—The reward is administered after a series of responses or performances, the number of which varies from the granting of one reward to the next.

For example, an individual on a 15:1 variable-interval schedule might be reinforced after ten responses, then fifteen responses, then twenty responses, then ten responses, and so on, an average of one reinforcement for every fifteen responses. This schedule tends to result in performance that is higher than that of a comparable fixed ratio schedule, and the variation in performance both before and after the occurrence of the reward or reinforcement is considerably less.

Virtually all managers must function within the constraints imposed by a fixed-interval schedule (annual salary schedule) or fixed ratio schedule (wage incentives). However, this fact should not preclude consideration of the variable schedules, even within the framework of fixed schedules. Given their more positive effects on performance, such consideration is indeed highly desirable. It is conceivable, at least in a sales organization, for example, that monetary rewards (bonuses in this case) could be administered according to a variable-ratio schedule. From a more practical point of view, the entire range of nonmonetary rewards could be more profitably scheduled on a variable-interval basis, assuming that such scheduling was done in a systematic fashion.

CONCLUSIONS

This article has reviewed recent research concerning the relationship between satisfaction and performance and discussed the implications of the results of this research for the practicing manager. As noted at the outset, current speculation on the part of most practitioners and researchers continues to imply that satisfaction and performance are causally related, although confusion exists concerning the exact nature of the relationship. While the performance-causes-satisfaction proposition is a more recent development, the contention that satisfaction causes performance, nonetheless, remains the more widely held of the two beliefs, particularly among practitioners.

The recent research findings, however, offer only moderate support of the former view and conclusively reject the latter. Instead, the evidence provides rather strong indications that the relationship is more complex: (1) rewards constitute a more direct cause of satisfaction than does performance and (2) rewards based on current performance (and not satisfaction) cause subsequent performance.

For the manager who is concerned about the well-being of his subordinates, the implication of the finding that rewards cause satisfaction is self-evident. In order to achieve this end, the manager must provide rewards that have value or utility in terms of the subordinate's own need state and provide them in sufficient magnitude to be perceived as positively reinforcing. The manager whose goal is to increase a subordinate's performance, on the other hand, is faced with a more difficult task for two reasons. First, the relationship between rewards and performance is not a simple one. Second, there are other causes of perform-ance—direction, the subordinate's ability, and existence of performance obstacles standing in the way of successful task performance—which the manager must also deal with.

The relationship between rewards and performance is complex because in reality there is at least one intervening variable and more than one contingency that needs to be established. An employee exerts high level effort usually because of the valued rewards he associates with high performance. Effort, the intervening variable, may be considered a function of the value and magnitude of the reward and the extent to which the individual believes that high effort on his part will lead to high performance and that his high performance, in turn, will lead to rewards.

Therefore, the manager in addition to providing appropriate rewards, must establish contingencies between effort and performance and between performance and rewards. The first contingency, the extent to which the individual believes that "how hard he works" determines his performance, is perhaps the more readily established. This contingency is a function, at least in part, of the individual's confidence in his own abilities, his perceptions of the difficulty of the task, and the presence of performance obstacles. When a problem does arise here, the manager can take those actions indicated earlier in this article to overcome an apparent ability deficiency or performance obstacle. The performance-reward contingency requires the manager, by means of accurate performance appraisals and appropriate reward practices, to clearly establish in the subordinate's mind the belief that his own performance determines the magnitude of the rewards he will receive.

The establishment of this particular contingency, unfortunately, is becoming increasingly difficult as organizations continue to rely more heavily on fixed salary schedules and nonperformance-related factors (for example, seniority) as determinants of salary progression. However, the manager can, as a supplement to organizationally determined rewards, place more emphasis on nonmonetary rewards and both the cafeteria-style reward plans and variable-interval schedules for their administration.

It is apparent that the manager whose objective is to significantly improve his subordinates' performance has assumed a difficult but by no means impossible task. The path of least resistance—that is, increasing subordinates' satisfaction—simply will not work.

However, the actions suggested concerning reward practices and, particularly, establishment of appropriate performance-reward contingencies will result in improved performance, assuming that such improvement is not restricted by ability or direction problems or by performance obstacles. The use of differential rewards may require courage on the part of the manager, but failure to use them will have far more negative consequences. A subordinate will repeat that behavior which was rewarded, regardless of whether it resulted in high or low performance. A rewarded low performer, for example, will continue to perform poorly. With knowledge of this inequity, the high performer, in turn, will eventually reduce his own level of performance or seek employment elsewhere.

Reading 24

Training Supervisors to Use Organizational Behavior Modification

Fred Luthans
David Lyman

The contingency theory of management as applied to leadership and organizational design has already been well validated, and in mental health and education,
contingency-based behavior modification approaches are also being widely used.
Largely overlooked, however, has been the potential of these concepts and
principles in the overall management of human resources. This article points out
how contingency management in general and behavior modification techniques in
particular can be taught to and successfully employed by supervisors in managing
workers in modern organizations.

  The authors, along with Robert Ottemann, all of the University of Nebraska,
recently completed a training program for a group of supervisors in a medium-size
manufacturing plant. (There were ten foremen in the initial program; subsequently, 17 more first-line supervisors, five general foremen, and two plant managers
went through it.) In ten weekly, 90-minute sessions, the trainers used a process,
rather than a lecture, method to teach the supervisors how to use the principles of
operant psychology/behavior modification in analyzing and solving human performance problems in their departments. This new contingency strategy for managing
human resources is called organizational behavior modification, or O.B. Mod.

The O.B. Mod. Training Program

There are several identifiable steps in training supervisors to utilize O.B. Mod.
effectively. Here we shall briefly summarize some of them and how they were
actually implemented in the training program for the manufacturing plant.

  Identifying Behavioral Events The early sessions in the program were spent
teaching the foremen to pinpoint employee problems in terms of observable,
measurable behavioral events. This meant taking constructs such as attitudes or
values and defining them in a manner that would allow them to be observed and
measured. Initially, this was no small task, because the men spoke only of
problem employees as having "bad attitudes" or being "unmotivated."

  Measuring Frequencies of Behavior After the supervisors were able to
identify an employee's problem behavior, they were taught to keep records of

how often and/or when this behavior occurred. Since it was often impossible to keep track of every instance, time sampling methods were worked out. For example, one foreman observed a particular employee twice an hour on a random basis. By observing their subordinates at random intervals, the foremen were able to get an overall picture, or baseline measure, of the frequency and circumstance of the problem behavior.

Making Functional Analyses of Behavior   In addition to keeping records, the supervisors were shown how to observe the events immediately preceding a pinpointed behavior—its *antecedents*—and the events immediately following the behavior—its *consequences*. By observing these before-and-after circumstances, they were able to make a functional analysis of what cures, or stimuli, elicited the behavior and what kinds of things reinforced or maintained that behavior.

Developing Intervention Strategies   Once the foremen were able to analyze functionally, they were ready to devise strategies to encourage desirable behaviors and discourage undesirable behaviors. These intervention strategies took many forms, but the essential goal was to *reinforce* appropriate behaviors and *extinguish* inappropriate behaviors. Extinguishing meant ignoring or providing no gratifying consequence for an undesirable job behavior. To encourage desired behaviors, the foremen had to determine what sorts of events were reinforcing to their workers, often a trial-and-error process. When a reinforcer was found, the desired behavior often increased dramatically. Reinforcers that were found to be effective included social approval, additional responsibilities, rescheduling of breaks, job rotation, special housekeeping or safety duties, positive feedback, and more enjoyable tasks upon completion of less enjoyable tasks. All the reinforcers used in the program lay within the normal pattern of the organizational environment; no artificial or contrived reinforcers were necessary. (For cost-conscious management, this is one of the most persuasive aspects of the program.)

Converting to Positive Reinforcement   Adopting a positive, rather than punitive, reinforcement strategy at first was not easy for the foremen, because even though they all believed in reinforcement, punishment was a consequence they had traditionally resorted to in order to change behavior. The trainers stressed the point that punishment would, indeed, suppress unwanted behavior, but seldom permanently, and would often create counterproductive hostility and resentment toward the supervisor. Having adopted a positive reinforcement intervention strategy, the foremen implemented it on the job and recorded the results.

Understanding the Importance of Being Contingent   By keeping records the supervisors were able to compare the rate of behavior occurrence prior to the intervention strategy with the later rate. Not all of the foremen met with success in their first attempts, but by analyzing what happened in the training sessions and modifying their behavior or their strategies, all of them were eventually able to effect some change. This was a crucial learning step, for it dramatically showed the power of being contingent, the relationship between the worker's behavior and their own. The supervisors found that by setting up "if-then" contingencies with their people, they could effectively manage behaviors toward improved performance: *If* the worker evidenced certain desirable, productive behaviors, *then,* and only then, was he reinforced by the supervisor.

The Training Experience: Practicing What Was Preached

Some familiar problems were encountered in the training program. At times, attendance was one of them, even though top management "highly recommended" the program. The noncompulsory attendance policy, plus daily "brush fires" to put out, worked against perfect attendance. And some of the supervisors didn't always complete their "homework" assignments (recording behaviors on the job), largely because of the minor crises and poor management of time. This problem lessened, however, when they learned better use of time sampling and were themselves reinforced when they began to see the results of record keeping. The trainers also helped alleviate this situation by paying attention to participants who had their data and, to a degree, ignoring those who had not carried out their assignments. Since the trainer was a source of social reinforcement, his ignoring those not prepared was a negative consequence and his attending to those who were was a positive consequence. In other words, the trainer himself was being contingent with the trainees. As a result, data collection improved.

Again, when the group discussion during a session was moving in a productive direction, the trainer would give his attention to those who were contributing; if they digressed, he would bring the verbal interaction back on track and ignore inappropriate comments. Thus, group participation was encouraged and reinforced during the sessions, while general conversation and banter were held to a minimum, so that each participant had a chance to make suggestions and provide alternatives or interpretations to the problem situations being discussed. Since those who made contributions experienced social reinforcement from the trainer, the foremen came to understand first-hand how O.B. Mod. might have an effect on their subordinates.

All in all, the training experience was very successful. Every supervisor in the program was able to improve the performance of at least one worker in his department, and most were able to effect change on the part of several workers. And these changes were reflected in the supervisors' effectiveness ratings, which were calculated daily. The foremen boosted their individual effectiveness ratings at least 5 percent, an increase that represented a considerable cost saving to the company. In general, the foremen reported that the training they received was very useful and that they would continue using the O.B. Mod. techniques learned in the program.

Evaluation of an O.B. Mod. Approach

A program to train supervisors to be contingency managers offers several advantages. It also has its problems, but let's consider the advantages first.

This approach deals only with behaviors that can be tied to job performance. Unlike training programs that attempt to change vaguely defined internal states of employee attitudes and values, this program precisely measures whether or not an observable job behavior of an employee has been changed. The measures may take the form of units produced, tasks completed, orders filled, or even the number of words typed. When a daily performance record is kept, a change in the rate of behavior change becomes immediately apparent. This feedback is continuous and can be used as a learning device and source of reinforcement. Thus, performance feedback is one of the biggest pluses of O.B. Mod.

A second advantage of O.B. Mod. supervisory training is the assumption that if an employee cannot currently perform a particular task, he can be taught to do it. Of course, this does not imply that employees can perform *all* jobs in the organization; it would be foolish to expect key punchers to solve engineering types of problems or personnel managers to take on maintenance of machines. On the other hand, through the process of shaping behaviors, where successive approximations of desired behaviors are selectively reinforced, new behaviors can be effectively learned and maintained and the job can be enlarged in scope, or the employee can be moved to a more demanding one.

A third advantage is that O.B. Mod. is an effective means of altering organizational environments to prevent or solve employee behavioral problems. This entails altering some behaviors in the environment, including those of supervisors, to maintain others. It is unrealistic to assume that as a result of several traditional human relations training sessions supervisors are going to change their ways; changes in supervisory behavior will come about only when the actual job environment changes, and the O.B. Mod. approach is meant to do just that—alter environmental situations to allow and encourage people to perform in a more productive manner.

Perhaps the most important advantage of O.B. Mod. is that it is based on a rational, scientific methodology. It requires the collection and analysis of data, decision making on the basis of the data, implementation of the decisions on the job, and assessment of results. More specifically, this means pinpointing problem behavioral events, observing and recording the frequency of this behavior, carrying out a functional analysis by examining antecedents and consequences of the behavior, devising an intervention strategy utilizing positive reinforcers, implementing the strategy in practice by being contingent, and observing and measuring the results. These O.B. Mod. techniques for managing human resources lead in no haphazard way to improved performance and greater satisfaction.

Now we come to the problems and criticisms that an O.B. Mod. training program is likely to run into.

Probably the most frequently encountered reason for reluctance to use the approach has to do with manipulation of people. Critics contend that changing behavior in this way is "using" people, making them do things against their will, or perhaps even exploiting them. What the critics overlook is not only that control of behavior is inevitable, but that it can be desirable. When a job requires a person to wear a suit and tie (formally or informally), the job is controlling certain behaviors. Schedules, time clocks, appointments, and even daily memos are only a few of the everyday controls found in all organizations. The O.B. Mod. approach is merely a systematic way of changing behaviors so that desirable, productive behaviors occur more often, as they are systematically reinforced. Indeed, the person whose behavior is being changed is "manipulating" the behavior of the modifier, too. One is reminded of the old cartoon about the rat in the Skinner box, with the caption reading, "I really have the experimenter conditioned. Every time I push the bar he gives me a reward." The accusation of manipulation can be countered by a clear explanation of the content and purpose of O.B. Mod.

Another negative element is the complexity of the modern organizational environment. Unlike a research laboratory, mental hospital, or classroom where behavior modification has been sucessfully carried out with experimental subjects, patients, and children, a manufacturing plant or business office has many distractions that can disrupt the use of any technique. During a typical day in a business organization, there are phone calls, hastily called meetings, special orders, machinery breakdowns, to name but a few of the noncontrollable events that occur. An O.B. Mod. approach must be able to try to deal with these events so that the intervention strategy being employed is not damaged or misleading. To write off the business organization as being too complex an environment does not seem justified.

A third obstacle to overcome is plain, old resistance to change. Managers— and training directors—are naturally hesitant about launching new techniques that they do not completely understand. In this case, they should spend as much time as is needed to find out what O.B. Mod. is based on, what it can and cannot do, how it can and cannot be used, and how long it would take to get it going in a supervisory training program of their own. This and subsequent articles should be useful in this respect and in breaking down resistance to change. The authors and their associates in the department of management at the University of Nebraska are actively involved in expanding the theory, research, and practice of O.B. Mod.

Implications of O.B. Mod. for the Future

As modern organizations become more automated and productivity-conscious, workers seem to become more dissatisfied, and some, apparently, deliberately do not perform anywhere near their potential. The experience of the Vega plant at Lordstown, Ohio is an extreme case in point, but every day newspapers, television specials, and formal and informal discussions focus on the management (or mismanagement) of human resources vis-à-vis the productivity concern. To turn the trend around, or even turn it in another direction, managers of all organizations must look to new approaches. One thing they can do immediately is provide a more reinforcing organizational climate for their employees.

There are many reinforcers readily available to any supervisor. The tried-and-true pat on the back for a job well done is one, but it soon gets to be old-hat to an employee, and other means of reinforcement must be found. Money is definitely a reinforcer, but it is unrealistic to propose that every time a worker does a good job he should get a monetary reward. It is necessary, then, for supervisors to make better use of the reinforcers that are already at hand on the job. Through O.B. Mod. supervisors can be taught how to be contingency managers. If they understand that behavior depends on its consequences and if, on this premise, they utilize the steps of O.B. Mod. to change behaviors, they should be able to manage their human resources more effectively, with lower cost to the company and greater satisfaction to its employees.

There is no reason that O.B. Mod. should not work just as well with personnel in other situations as it did with workers in the plant we have talked about. Actually, applications of O.B. Mod. seem limited only by the creativity and ingenuity of those who study it and recognize the capacity of contingency management to direct human effort toward, instead of away from, organizational objectives.

Reading 25
Compensating the New–Life-Style Worker
Edward E. Lawler III

Never before in the history of American business has there been so much discussion of problems in dealing with younger workers. The problems are, of course, part of a larger societal issue, reflected in much concern with the generation gap, "Consciousness III," new life styles, and young people in general.

There is a good reason for the last few years' focus on the younger generation. All generations are different, but this one is in a sense *more* different. That is, its values, attitudes, and norms depart more radically from those of the immediately preceding generation than did those of earlier generations from their immediate predecessors'. It is precisely because of this leap that so many organizations have found it difficult to deal with the workers who are now joining them in large numbers.

These young people have failed to respond to traditional organizational practices in a number of areas, including selection, leadership, communication, and compensation. In this article the emphasis will be on compensation practices

"Compensating the New–Life-Style Worker," Edward E. Lawler, III, *Personnel*, May–June 1971, pp. 19–25. Reprinted with permission of the publisher. © 1971 by the American Management Association, Inc.

and how they will have to be changed if they are going to be compatible with the values and attitudes of many of the new-life-style workers—with the implication that many of the same kinds of changes are also needed in the other areas.

Just who is this "new" worker, and what is he like?

Many of those who are beginning business careers accept the traditional American values, the Protestant-ethic approach to life; they present no particular problem. Others constitute groups in some ways different, yet similar—the culturally deprived, and the middle- or upper-class workers who reject traditional values and are committed to a self-actualizing approach to life. Although these two groups have disparate backgrounds, they share many attitudes and values that organizations find hard to understand and even harder to adapt to. Therefore, these attitudes and values need to be examined:

Immediacy of Gratification The currently popular term the "now generation" expresses the tendency of this generation to demand immediate action and results. Its members will have none of the view that some things must wait, that you can't change the world overnight. They are impatient and want to make tangible, basic changes this minute. It follows that when they perform in a way that they feel deserves a reward, they are not content to wait; they want the reward now.

Bases of Authority In most business organizations authority historically has been based on position, and in society it has been based on age and position, but today's younger generation does not go along with these criteria of authority. Its criteria are personal integrity, expertise, and accomplishment. Moreover, it wants greater influence in decisions that affect people. For example, a study by D. A. Ondrack has shown that over the last 15 years college students' scores on Rokeach's dogmatism scale have gone down. Low scorers on the scale are likely to prefer participative decision making; to question the basis of authority; to be liberal, experimental, and intolerant of ambiguity; and to evaluate critically the legitimacy of authority and messages that come from authority figures.

Traditional Ways of Doing Things The younger generation is often described as being very skeptical about traditional ways of doing things, unwilling to believe that "the right way" is automatically "the way it's always been done." This attitude ties in with the rejection of traditional authority; in both cases, this generation is saying that it has to be convinced by evidence or logic that a particular action is right. Often, the only means of getting young people's commitment to a particular action is to have them involved in the decision process.

Hypocrisy and Openness Personal integrity, openness, a willingness to confront issues, and letting people know where they stand are all high values of the now generation. Indeed, its members have an exaggerated fear and mistrust of decisions and actions that are taken in secret or behind closed doors and that are not open to close public scrutiny.

Mobility   Change and personal mobility are not feared by the new-life-style worker; rather, he seems to seek them out. Many of these workers are concerned primarily with their own intellectual and emotional growth, and they recognize that to realize these aims they may have to be mobile. Thus, they are willing to change jobs, companies, and geographical locations frequently in the search for personal development.

Where Opinions Differ

Although the culturally deprived worker and the well-educated younger worker share many of the same values and attitudes, they part company when it comes to attitudes about material goods. Today's college graduate often seems to have a very cavalier attitude toward money and at times a contempt for the material goods it can purchase. Some even scorn the materialism of our society to the point of joining communes. More and more college students are turning down high-paying careers for lower-paying, to them more rewarding, ones. The disadvantaged worker, on the other hand, is demanding a greater share of the material goods that we are producing. He wants money and goods that it can buy. These groups thus differ widely in the kinds of rewards they want from work. This is not to say that money isn't important to the college-educated youth; it is important, but not to the same extent that it is to the less well-off, culturally deprived worker.

The two also differ in the kind of financial remuneration they want, because for them it serves different purposes. The culturally deprived worker needs cash to cover his day-to-day expenses, whereas the more affluent college-educated employee, if he is concerned about his pay, often wants special fringe benefits, such as time off to work on community problems. In either case, what the younger workers want in the way of compensation is quite different from the package that suits the older employee.

Adjusting Pay Practices

It is obvious that many established compensation practices do not fit the attitudes and values of the new-life-style worker. In fact, some of the most common practices, such as secrecy and authoritarian decision making, represent the very characteristics of large organizations to which the younger generation objects most strongly. Eventually, compensation practices will have to change to accommodate the preferences of these new workers, because business needs them now and they, of course, represent the "establishment" of tomorrow. The only real question is how rapidly and how willingly companies are going to make these changes. Undoubtedly, some will change only after great pressure, but others will recognize that change is inevitable and will take the initiative.

What are these changes that will make pay practices more compatible with the values and expectations of the new kind of employee? It is impossible to predict all of them, but some can be pinpointed:

Immediacy of Reward   The typical pay plan calls for raises to be given at regularly scheduled and often widely separated intervals. For example, many organizations have annual salary reviews, and raises are given out to all employees once a year. But a year can seem like an eternity to the kind of worker we are concerned with. Telling him that if he works hard now he will earn more money next year probably has no motivational effect on him at all, because he simply doesn't think that far in advance. He lives in the here-and-now and so responds best to short-term rewards and incentives.

Particularly in the case of the ghetto resident holding his first job, it is important that small, frequent raises be given if he is performing well. This recognition is preferable to giving a larger raise at a later time, because it provides more immediate feedback and goals to work toward. It also gives the company a means of building trust: It can promise something (a raise if performance is acceptable) and make good on that promise early in the relationship with an employee. The idea of giving immediate rewards is not new; learning and motivation theorists have for a long time pointed out the obvious advantages. However, the advent of the new-life-style worker now gives them added significance and suggests that the practice be extended beyond piece-rate and other incentive plans.

Elliott Jaques' work on time span of discretion is most relevant to the idea of giving immediate rewards. He points out that jobs differ in terms of the length of time it takes to identify how well employees are performing in them. As a rule, poor performance in lower-level jobs shows up very quickly, whereas poor performance in higher-level jobs may take years to show up. One inference from this fact is that the time between salary reviews may have to vary widely from one level to another. The yearly time interval that is commonly used for all levels may in fact be correct for many upper-level jobs (those the new breed of employee will eventually attain) but not for lower-level jobs (where they are now).

Participation in Pay Decisions   Pay plans have almost always been administered in a very authoritarian manner, even in companies that have moved toward Theory Y decision making. The superior decides who should receive raises, and the personnel or compensation department decides the type of pay plan that is used, the fringe benefits, and the rates that are paid for each nonunion job. The employee has no say at all, and the possibility of his having one never occurs to anyone, the assumption being that the workers' preoccupation with bettering their own pay would make it impossible for them to behave responsibly in these matters.

There is sound evidence, however, that the new-style workers who want to participate in some of the decisions concerning their pay should be allowed to. One study that I made showed that when workers were given the opportunity to participate in the design of an incentive plan they did behave responsibly, designing one that was not only effective but less expensive than the one management had in mind.

Companies that have had employees participate in job evaluation studies and salary surveys have hit on an easy and obvious way to increase employee involvement in pay decisions. In some cases, this involvement may lead to the employees' deciding the same thing that would have been decided if they had not participated. It may also turn out that they decide the traditional way of doing things is best, but this is all to the good. Young people today mistrust tradition; they have to discover things for themselves, even if this may sometimes mean that they in effect end up rediscovering the wheel.

Among compensation managers these days, there is considerable talk about employees' selecting the fringe benefits that they want, so that their benefits package will fit their individual needs. This "smorgasbord" approach has the double advantage of letting workers make important decisions about their pay at a relatively low cost to the organization.

In a few companies employees have been involved in deciding what their raises should be. This kind of participation as a general practice is a long way off, however, because it is so difficult to build the openness and trust that it requires, but as more of the younger generation grow into positions of authority, it, like participation in other areas, will be more common. Without waiting for that day, however, if the pay plans of organizations are to keep pace with the beliefs of this new group of employees they are going to have to make room for greater participation generally in decisions concerning pay.

Openness Secrecy about management salaries is taken for granted in almost all business organizations, but it is a practice very likely to change as a result of the new workers' arrival on the scene. Secrecy is impossible if employees won't cooperate, and everything that is known about the younger generation suggests that it is something that they are not likely to go along with, because they strongly believe in openness and confrontation. In fact, the ones I have interviewed see salary secrecy as absurd and as a sign of how "up tight" most bureaucratic organizations are. At the lower managerial levels of many companies secrecy has already broken down, because the younger managers openly discuss their pay with each other. As these managers are promoted, it can be expected that secrecy will break down at the higher levels, too.

The disappearance of this secrecy may not be a bad thing, provided organizations prepare for it by participatively developing defensible pay systems. At the moment, many companies keep pay secret for the very good reason that they simply cannot justify their current pay systems. Since it is unlikely that they are going to be able to keep pay secret much longer, it behooves them to prepare now for the time when pay will be more open to scrutiny.

There is also evidence that secrecy has a number of dysfunctional consequences that are not generally recognized. It has been shown, for example, that where secrecy exists managers overestimate the pay of other managers at their own levels and at levels below them, so they are more dissatisfied with their pay than they would be if they knew the actual pay received by others. In addition, they tend to underestimate the pay of managers above them, with the result that promotion seems less attractive. Thus, making pay more public might actually be a step forward from the company's point of view.

Individualizing Compensation Plans It has been suggested that organizations use smorgasbord, or cafeteria-style, benefits plans, so that individuals can pick the fringe benefits they want. In addition to the psychological advantage of allowing them to make important decisions about their pay, with the ever-increasing diversity in the working population, such plans seem to be the only way that companies can tailor benefits to the specific needs of their employees. The ghetto resident, the young college graduate, the older manager, and the older blue-collar worker—not to mention top executives—do not want or need the same fringe benefits. This situation is usually handled by giving somewhat different plans to managers and to workers, but it is a solution that really doesn't individualize the plans enough. Often, there is more similarity among certain groups of managers and workers—for example, older managers with families and older workers with families—than there is among all the nonmanagerial or all the managerial employees.

In the case of the now-generation workers we are discussing, there is particular interest in portability of pensions, because these workers are so much more mobile than their older counterparts. But these younger workers are only reinforcing a broader trend, and it looks as if companies must make pensions portable or the federal government will intervene and require that it be done.

Speaking more generally, if the importance of pay fluctuates among various groups, then the importance of flexible pay plans will increase. It doesn't make sense to put a person who doesn't value pay on a pay-for-performance plan. Some other source of motivation must be found—job redesign, leadership, what have you. The point is that as individual differences multiply the organization will have to multiply its efforts to adapt to the individual in setting pay practices. This may mean placing only those people who value compensation on incentive plans; therefore, a concomitant adjustment in placement procedures seems to be in the wind.

If these prognostications about the impact of the new-life-style worker are correct, the next decade will be a difficult one for company managers, and especially for those who administer compensation. What they are doing will be questioned closely, and they will be asked to make major changes in pay practices by some employees at the same time they are told by others that pay is really not very important. Aside from this confusion, some of the changes demanded will require basic shifts in management philosophy. For example, openness about salaries and participation in salary decisions are totally incompatible with an authoritarian management style—and management style is, after all, set by top executives. In the end, of course, many of these changes will come about, because of the pressures exerted by the new generation—but not without perhaps unprecedented stress on the "older generation."

Reading 26

Paying People Doesn't Always Work The Way You Expect It To

Edward L. Deci

For many people, the words money and motivation are nearly synonymous. An abundance of research indicates however, that this is not the case. Paying workers doesn't necessarily motivate them. Furthermore, money is not the only reward which workers seek to achieve. In order to use money as a motivator, it is necessary that pay be contingent on effective performance. That is, the reward system must be structured so that receiving pay depends on good performance. Money will then motivate performance because performance is instrumental to receiving payments. If money and performance are not tied together, money will not serve as an effective motivator.

Two areas of psychological research have provided support for this assumption about motivation. (1) Behaviorists have substantiated and refined the Law of Effect which states simply that when a response is followed by a reinforcement it will have an increased probability of recurrence. Contingent payments presumably reinforce the response of producing output and should, therefore, strengthen that response. (2) The use of contingent payments can also be defended by cognitive theories of motivation. These theories state that man's behavior is goal directed; in other words, man will engage in behavior which he believes will lead him to desired goals. Since money is probably one goal all workers accept, cognitive theories would suggest that a worker would produce efficiently in order to get substantial wages, if that was the easiest way he could get them.

One approach to management which has recognized the importance of tying rewards to performance is Scientific Management which was developed by Frederick Winslow Taylor over half a century ago. He used piece-rate payments (i.e., wage incentives) which involve paying people a set rate for each unit of output. Sales commissions and bonus plans work similarly. The motivational assumption underlying these pay schemes is that a person will perform effectively to the extent that his rewards are made contingent upon effective performance. For this motivational system to work effectively, it is necessary that there be clear standards for performance which the workers understand. Then, performance has

"Paying People Doesn't Always Work the Way You Expect It To," Edward L. Deci, *Human Resource Management*, Summer 1973, pp. 28–32. Reprinted with permission.

to be monitored, and rewards must be administered consistently. Further, the output must be quantifiable so that performance can be measured, and jobs should be relatively independent so that a worker has control of his own production rate.

The rewards in these systems are money, promotions, fringe benefits etc. These rewards are of course extrinsically mediated, that is, they are given to the employee by someone other than himself. Management administers them to try to control (or motivate) the behavior of the employees. Although this system seems to have advantages for motivating employees, there are also many limitations to it. Perhaps the most serious is that there are many rewards which *cannot* be administered by management. Money is *not* the only reward which workers are looking for. People also need what we call *intrinsic rewards;* that is, internal rewards which the person derives from doing what he likes or meeting a challenge. They give him a feeling of satisfaction and accomplishment. Many studies have reported that employees consider these intrinsic rewards to be important. It follows then that there are many important motivators of human behavior which are not under the direct control of managers and, therefore, cannot be contingently administered in a system such as piece-rate payments.

More recent approaches to management—often referred to as participative management, Theory Y Management, Management by Objectives—have assumed that man can be intrinsically motivated to perform effectively. These approaches focus on structuring jobs so that workers will become ego-involved in their work and committed to doing it well.

There are two essential aspects to motivating intrinsically. The first involves designing tasks which are interesting and which necessitate creativity and resourcefulness. The second involves allowing workers to participate in decisions which concern them so they will feel like they have a say about what they do. The newer participative management theories, then, stress the importance of giving employees a voice in decisions which affect them, and giving them greater latitude in the way they do their jobs. There is less reliance on authority as a control mechanism, and employees are judged by their results. These theories suggest that jobs should be enlarged or enriched so as to be more challenging.

These behavioral scientists believe that participative management is the most effective way of achieving high performance and also more conducive to satisfied and mentally healthy employees. There are some experimental results which substantiate that organizations which have implemented these practices are more productive and have higher levels of employee satisfaction.

Theories of work motivation which recognize the importance of intrinsic motivation often suggest that work should be structured to elicit this intrinsic motivation and that workers should be rewarded extrinsically for doing well. This presumably has the advantage of motivating employees both intrinsically and extrinsically at the same time, and it assumes that the effects of intrinsic and extrinsic motivation are additive.

It now seems appropriate to ask whether piece-rate payments or other extrinsic reward systems which tie rewards (especially money) to performance

are compatible with participative management, which focuses on intrinsic motivation? That is, will a person's intrinsic motivation to do a job remain unaffected by
extrinsic rewards?

To investigate this question I have conducted a number of experiments
where subjects worked on an intrinsically interesting activity and were given
extrinsic rewards for doing so.[1] Then I assessed their intrinsic motivation after
their experience with the extrinsic rewards. The hundreds of college students who
served as subjects worked on an intrinsically interesting spatial relations puzzle
which has seven differently shaped, three dimensional pieces, each of which is
made to look like it is composed of 3 or 4 one inch cubes. Subjects used these
puzzle pieces to reproduce various configurations which had been drawn on paper
for them. Pilot testing showed clearly that subjects found the activity of
puzzle-solving highly interesting and enjoyable.

In the experiments to be reported, the experimenter gave each person four
configurations to solve and allowed ten minutes to solve each. If a subject were
unable to solve one of the puzzles within the ten minutes, he was stopped and
shown how to do it. He then proceeded to the next puzzle. At the end of the
session with the four puzzles he was left alone in the room to read magazines,
solve more puzzles, or do whatever he liked, while the experimenter ostensibly
was at a computer terminal.

It was reasoned that subjects were intrinsically motivated if they spent time
working on the puzzles when they were alone and when there were other things
they could do such as reading magazines. Hence, the amount of time they spent
working on the puzzles while they were alone was a measure of their intrinsic
motivation.

Some of the subjects were told at the beginning of the experimental session
that they would receive one dollar for each of the four puzzles which they solved
within the ten minutes; some were not. Earnings for the puzzle-solving (which
took about 20 minutes) ranged from one dollar to four dollars (average was over
2 dollars), and this was paid to subjects in cash at the end of the session. It is
important to note that, for those who were promised pay, these money payments
were contingent upon performance ($1 per puzzle solved).

Those students who had been paid spent significantly less time working on
the puzzles when they were alone in the room than did those who had worked on
the same puzzles for no pay. Once subjects began to receive contingent monetary
payments for doing an interesting activity their intrinsic motivation to perform the
activity decreased. That is, they were less willing to perform the activity in the
absence of the external rewards than were subjects who had not been paid. The
paid subjects had, to some extent, become dependent on the external rewards
(money), and their intrinsic motivation had decreased. Or in other words, the

---

[1]For a fuller presentation of these experiments, see my papers "The Effects of Contingent and
Non-Contingent Rewards and Controls on Intrinsic Motivation" in *Organizational Behavior and
Human Performance*, Vol. 8, 1972, pp. 217–229; and "The Effects of Externally Mediated Rewards on
Intrinsic Motivation" in the *Journal of Personality and Social Psychology*, Vol. 18, 1971, pp. 105–115.

locus of causality of their behavior seems to have shifted from within themselves to the external reward.

In another experiment which Wayne Cascio and I conducted,[2] subjects were told that if they were unable to solve any of the puzzles within the ten minutes, a buzzer would sound indicating that their time on that puzzle had expired. They were then given a short exposure to the buzzer so they would realize that it was truly noxious. Consequently, these subjects were performing the activity because of intrinsic motivation and also because they wanted to avoid a punishment (the buzzer). The results indicate that subjects who had performed under the threat of buzzer condition were also less intrinsically motivated than subjects who had received no threats. Since most subjects were able to solve all or all but one of the puzzles, they received little or no punishment (the buzzer) and they experienced little or no failure in doing the task, so it appears that the threat of punishment was the crucial element in decreasing intrinsic motivation in this experiment.

Their behavior, like the behavior of the paid subjects, had apparently become dependent on the external causes (avoiding punishment), and their intrinsic motivation decreased. In summation, one process by which intrinsic motivation can be affected is to have the intrinsically-motivated behavior become dependent on external causes such as tangible rewards like money or the avoidance of punishment. The perceived locus of causality shifts from within the person to the external reward and causes a decreases in intrinsic motivation.

In the studies involving money payments, the money was made contingent upon performance ($1 per puzzle solved). In another study, subjects were paid $2 for participating in the experiment regardless of their performance, and they showed no change in intrinsic motivation. This seems consistent with the change in perceived locus of causality proposition mentioned above. With the contingent payments, the subject's performance of the activity is instrumental to his receiving the reward, so he is likely to come to perceive the rewards as the *reason* for his performing the activity. With non-contingent payments, however, the payments are not directly tied to performance, so he is less likely to perceive the money as the reason for his performance. Hence, he is less likely to experience a decrease in intrinsic motivation.

We've said that a change in perceived locus of causality is one process by which intrinsic motivation can be affected; the second process involves feedback. Through this process, intrinsic motivation can either be enhanced or decreased. Subjects in one experiment were males who were reinforced with verbal statements such as "Good, that's very fast for that one," each time they solved a puzzle. The intrinsic motivation in these subjects increased due to the experience with positive verbal feedback. They liked the task more and spent more free time working on it than non-rewarded subjects. To understand why verbal reinforcements increase intrinsic motivation, we need to look at what underlies intrinsic

---

[2]Wayne Cascio, now an Assistant Professor of Psychology at Florida International University, assisted me in these experiments while he was my student.

motivation. Being intrinsically motivated involves doing an activity not because it will lead to an extrinsic reward but rather because it will allow a person to have internal feelings of competence and self-determination. Therefore, any feedback which is relevant to the person's feelings of competence and self-determination has potential for affecting his intrinsic motivation. This means, then, that external rewards can have at least two functions. One is a "controlling function" which makes a person dependent on the reward, and the other is a "feedback function" which affects his feelings of competence and self-determination.

Money and threats are commonly perceived as controllers of behavior. As a result, subjects become dependent on these controls and lose intrinsic motivation even though the money or avoided punishment *could* provide them with positive information about their competence and self-determination. On the other hand, a subject is less likely to become dependent on verbal reinforcements because he is less likely to perceive the feedback as the reason for his performance. In fact, the effect of verbal feedback may not be distinguishable from the internal feedback which he gives himself (namely, recognizing that he is competent and self-determining). So, in the experiment described above, the positive feedback would indeed have strengthened the subjects' feelings of competence and self-determination, thereby increasing their intrinsic motivation.

In a replication of the verbal reinforcement experiment we used both male and female subjects and were surprised to find a sex difference. Positive verbal feedback increased the intrinsic motivation of males, but it decreased the intrinsic motivation of females. Apparently, due to socialization processes, females more readily become dependent on verbal praise than males do. For females, we see a change in perceived locus of causality which causes a decrease in intrinsic motivation; however, the same does not happen for males.

Now imagine a situation in which the feedback is negative. It should decrease intrinsic motivation because it decreases the subjects' feelings of competence and self-determination. Wayne Cascio and I did an experiment which utilized a different set of puzzles that were much more difficult. The subjects failed badly in solving these puzzles, and afterwards, they were less intrinsically motivated than subjects who had worked on somewhat easier puzzles with a higher success rate. The negative feelings associated with failure had offset some of the internal rewards associated with the activity causing a decrease in intrinsic motivation. Failing at an activity made the people less motivated to do it.

We have seen that intrinsic motivation appears to be affected by two processes: change in locus of causality, and change in feelings of competence and self-determination. Intrinsic motivation decreases when a person's behavior becomes dependent on an extrinsic reward or threat. It also decreases when a person receives negative feedback about his performance on an intrinsically-motivated activity. But it increases in males as a result of positive feedback.

To understand the importance of these results for organizations, it is necessary to distinguish between keeping a person on the job and motivating him to perform effectively on that job. To attract and keep a person in an organization, it is necessary to satisfy his needs. He will have to be paid a competitive salary and given other comforts. However, satisfying a worker does not guarantee that he will be motivated to perform well on the job. Let us, therefore, consider how payments and intrinsic factors relate to satisfaction on the one hand and effective performance on the other. Paying workers is necessary to attract them to jobs and keep them satisfied with those jobs. However, in order to use money as a motivator of performance, the performance has to be perceived by the worker as being instrumental to his receiving the money. As we've said, this is generally accomplished by making pay contingent upon performance. In other words, it is not the money *per se* which motivates performance but rather the way that it is administered. To use money as an extrinsic motivator (or controller) of behavior, it has to be administered contingently. However, we've seen that not only are there many difficulties in making such a system work effectively, but also such a system decreases intrinsic motivation.

On the other hand, a system for motivating employees such as participative management which—through participation and job enlargement—attempts to arouse intrinsic motivation, appears to motivate effective performance at the same time that it satisfies intrinsic needs. Since advocates of participative management stress the importance of intrinsic motivation, the experimental results which demonstrate that money decreases intrinsic motivation have led some antagonists to the conclusion that workers should not be payed. Clearly, such a prescription is absurd. The importance of the non-contingent payment study is that money does not decrease intrinsic motivation if it is paid non-contingently. It is possible to pay workers and still have them intrinsically motivated. So we are left with a dilemma. To use money and other extrinsic rewards as effective motivators they must be made contingent on performance. However, doing this decreases intrinsic motivation.

This suggests then that we must choose between trying to utilize either intrinsic or extrinsic reward systems. I personally favor the prescription that we concentrate on structuring situations and jobs to arouse intrinsic motivation, rather than trying to structure piece-rate and other contingency payment schemes. This preference is based on the evidence which indicates that intrinsic approaches seem to lead to greater productivity and more satisfied workers.

Leadership

Leadership is the dynamic process of exercising power to influence employees to behave in a manner consistent with the prescriptions of the formal organization. Ability to succeed as a leader is far more than a function of having certain definable personality traits; it is a product of applying appropriate behaviors within the context of a unique environment, group of workers, and task. Therefore it is a difficult and complex process that desperately requires the development of analytical models to aid managers in adapting their behavior to meet situational needs.

The extent of the classical difficulty in prescribing a "one best style" is clearly portrayed in the reading by Lippert, in which he reviews the long-standing debate over the merits of "participative" versus "autocratic" leadership styles. Either extreme conclusion can be supported if research data are selected out of context. The student of management has the responsibility to adapt these behavioral findings to fit his personality, that of his subordinates, and the character of his environment.

The environmental theme is continued by George and Von Der Embse, who developed six general propositions from a combined literature review and survey research of 650 managers. The propositions strongly support the need for a leader to be flexible in choosing his style and delineate some of the determining variables of effectiveness: cultural factors, line versus staff positions, external forces, and others. Although the propositions are not really prescriptive, they do provide an initial framework that can assist managers in the early stages of problem diagnosis and the development of an appropriate pattern of leadership behavior.

Shetty moves us another step closer to a meaningful contingency model as he specifies some of the more critical interacting forces that shape leadership styles and determine their potential effectiveness: those in the manager, his subordinates, the organizational system, and the situation itself (the problem, time availability, financial considerations, etc.). He suggests that a successful manager needs to integrate the forces operating in the situation in question.

One of the significant forces is found in the relationship between organizational characteristics (task structure, performance expectations, reward and control systems) and a manager's felt need to exercise or defer to authority. Higgins found that the more successful firms were characterized by a high degree of congruence between managerial self-perceptions of their leadership approach and that of the organization's philosophy. The data serve to support a contingency approach, focusing on organizational design variables as strong determinants of appropriate leadership style.

Fiedler provides us with an updated review of his classic research that has been single-handedly most responsible for generating constructive thought along situational lines in the past two decades. He answers the vital question, "What kinds of situations are best suited for which type of leader?", by analyzing each situation on the basis of three variables: leader-member relations, task structure, and position power. He then proposes a significant action step—that we train leaders not to change their deeply ingrained behavior but to diagnose their situations and change the key features of the environment in which they work so as to have a better "fit" between leadership style and work environment.

Reading 27

Toward Flexibility in Application of Behavioral Science Research

Frederick G. Lippert

In the practitioner's efforts to apply behavioral science research findings to his own management or leadership style, there is a tendency for him to make an "either/or" evaluation of the findings; i.e., to categorize the substance of what he reads either as "that is the answer, I'll try to do that from now on," or as, "that's a lousy idea—that guy's all wet."

This is far too pat an approach. A device that is a useful starting point for exercising more discrimination in the selection process is Lewin's precept that behavior is a function of both personality and environment, or, in mathematical symbols, $B = f(P,E)$. This model has been elaborated by Sanford to identify separately the personalities of the other parties involved. Thus, for the leader or manager, the concept becomes: $B_L = f(P_L, P_{OP}, E)$.

Given that there exist both a broad range of individual differences and a myriad number of possible states of the environment, it would be foolish to make any simplistic prediction that person "A" will always give the same response, or that in a given environment, say Type "1," all persons will behave in a similar fashion. Rather, the practitioner should be aware that in situations which he personally experiences, the actors, the prospective field of operation, and the outcome will probably not replicate those of the reported studies or experiments. It is up to the practitioner to identify those factors that are significantly different from those reported in the research he is examining and to assess the differences in behavior that may (or may not) be expected as a result of these differences.

It is well documented that there are personality differences which affect a manager's preference for and competence with a certain style and which, in turn, affect the performance of his subordinates. But even though the manager may spontaneously or by deliberate choice decide upon a style which fits comfortably, or which just comes naturally, there still is no firm basis for making a yes/no advance determination of its compatibility with the personalities of his subordinates.

For example, Vroom found a significant difference in the reactions of high and low authoritarian subordinates, when offered the opportunity to participate in decisions affecting their work.[1] (Low authoritarians were more responsive.) But Tosi, in an experiment designed to parallel Vroom's, obtained "results clearly

"Toward Flexibility in Application of Behavioral Science Research," Frederick G. Lippert, *Journal of the Academy of Management*, June 1971, pp. 195–201. Reprinted with permission.
[1] V. H. Vroom, *Some Personality Determinants of the Effects of Participation* (Englewood Cliffs, N. J.: Prentice-Hall, 1960), pp. 9, 10, 15-a.

different from those of Vroom."[2] He found that the subordinate's response was not a function of his level of authoritarianism and suggested that in further studies environmental factors be evaluated with care. In any event, is it practical for the manager to measure the authoritarian attribute of his subordinates as a prelude to his adoption of a certain style? And even if he does so, would his own personality permit him to vary his style to suit the person with whom he is currently interacting?

Here, this writer found that low authoritarian leaders are more prone to employ a participative style, but that their high authoritarian contemporaries can and will essay this style on receipt of a strong cue from their superior.[3] However, only one of every two would-be participative style-users were so perceived by their subordinates. And these leaders came in equal numbers from the high and low authoritarian groups. Thus, it appears that even the well-intentioned leader who deliberately attempts to use a participative style does not necessarily induce psychological participation in his subordinates. (Vroom defines psychological participation as the amount of influence an individual *perceives* that he exerts on decision-making.[4])

But, given that the answers to the two questions posed above could, fortuitously, be "yes," we are brought up short by Hyman who found that authoritarianism varies directly with age in an individual and inversely with his level of education and organizational status.[5] Hence, what might be compatible with a given personality mix in period "t" might become incompatible in period "t +1" for the same group of actors, or might become so at any time as the result of substitutions in the group.

In addition to the personalities of leaders and followers, there is the environment, both physical and organizational, to consider. Most experiments on leadership or management style are conducted within one environment. This may be a "laboratory" (contrived and controlled) environment or a "field" environment where on-going, real-world conditions exist, hopefully unchanged by the fact that an experiment is taking place. But, in either case, the findings will depend in large measure on the peculiarities of that one particular environment. If, as in the cases discussed below, the environment were changed, the findings would also be changed—sometimes becoming diametrically opposite to the original conclusions. And in practice, what manager can duplicate the environment of a researcher's experiment? Physical aspects are difficult to reproduce precisely, and organizational relationships in situation "A," even though formally reproducible, are operationally dependent upon the history of the organization and the

[2]H. Tosi, "A Reexamination of Personality as a Determinant of the Effects of Participation," *Personnel Psychology,* 23–1 (Spring 1970), pp. 91–99.

[3]F. Lippert, "Participative Management," *New Dimensions in Organization* (New York: Industrial Relations Counsellors, 1970).

[4]V. H. Vroom, *Some Personality Determinants.*

[5]I. Hyman, "Authoritarian Personality Revisited" in R. Christy, ed., *Studies in the Scope and Method of the Authoritarian Personality* (Glencoe, Ill.: Free Press of Glencoe 1954).

personalities of the actors. These are not likely to be duplicated in any other group. Some findings which demonstrate the consequences of transferring a certain behavioral approach from one environment to another are discussed below.

The Lewin-Lippitt-White study of the effect of leadership styles on members of boys' clubs indicated that the "autocratic" leader obtained more output from his group, while the work group under a "democratic" leader displayed greater originality and was more strongly motivated.[6] The conclusion might then be: "If I want production, I should be autocratic." Yet, one reads that Katz, Maccoby, and Morse found that clerical workers were more productive under "general supervision," which has a meaning quite similar to "democratic leadership style."[7] A year later, Katz, Maccoby, Gurin, and Floor found that railroad section hands produced more under "close supervision," which is quite akin to "autocratic leadership style."[8] If one reads no further, he might well assume that an autocratic or close supervisory style will get out production in a boys' club or on a railroad right-of-way but not from clerks working in an office. He would then be confounded by reading that Morse and Reimer found that a group of insurance company *clerks* were *not* more productive (in a short run) when allowed to participate in decision-making, under a "democratic" supervisor.[9] (The study was discontinued before long-run performance could be observed). At this point, he might well throw up his hands and say: "I manage an automobile assembly line. What style works best there?"

Similarly, Coch and French report that employees were more productive, following the introduction of changes in methods, when they were permitted to participate in decisions to adopt and implement these changes.[10] But, some years later, French, Israel, and As found no significant difference in the output of participative vs nonparticipative groups![11] Here we find that "black" is "white," and "white" is "black"! Actually, in the later study, the authors found that the reverse effect was caused by changes that occurred in the environmental variables. Specifically, in the latter case, the formalization of the wage structure in a union agreement and the nature of the manufacturing process made it possible to offer "participation" *only on relatively nonoperational matters,* which the participants did not perceive as directly affecting their output and consequent earnings.

French, *et al.,* then concluded that for participation in decisions to serve as

[6]K. Lewin, R. Lippitt, and R. White, "Patterns of Aggressive Behavior in Experimentally Created Social Climates," *Journal of Social Psychology,* 10 (1939), pp. 271–299.

[7]D. Katz, N. Maccoby, and N. Morse, *Productivity, Supervision, and Morale in an Office Situation* (Ann Arbor: Institute for Social Research, University of Michigan, 1950), pp. 62–63.

[8]D. Katz, N. Maccoby, and L. Floor, *Productivity, Supervision, and Morale among RR Workers* (Ann Arbor: Institute for Social Research, University of Michigan, 1951), p. 33.

[9]N. Morse and E. Reimer, "Experimental Change for Major Organization Variable," *Journal of Abnormal Social Psychology,* Vol. 52, No. 1 (January 1956), pp. 120–129.

[10]L. Coch and J. R. P. French, "Overcoming Resistance to Change," *Human Relations* Vol. 1 (1948), pp. 512–532.

[11]J. R. P. French, J. Israel, and D. As, "An Experiment on Participation in a Norwegian Factory," *Human Relations,* Vol. 13 (1960).

an effective motivator, the subject of the decision must be "legitimate, relevant, and involve the participant" and also, as Professor French later concluded, must have consequences in which the subordinates can discern the effects of their participation in the implementing decision. Here is a Pandora's box of grey-colored conditions and limitations! Taking all of them into consideration, can anyone predict with certainty that a participative leadership style will "always work" or "not work"? The answer appears to be: "Only if you can establish a critical mix of environmental factors."

Behavioral scientists do not suggest that their findings are universally applicable; they describe what they find.[12] Rather, it is the practitioner who entraps himself when he distorts the findings to fit his own set of value stereotypes. He may read a portion of a report, perhaps the "summary of the findings," wherein the cautionary qualifying statements are condensed or omitted. Intent on proving some hypothesis of his own, he reads what he wants to read and in so doing reaches a conclusion that provides an easy, structured, "go/no go" rationale for his evaluation.

Also, the dependent-independent variable relationship $(Y = f[X])$, which is often the vehicle for expressing a behavioral precept, sets a different kind of trap. The practitioner tends to make an exclusively one-way interpretation of the findings because "Y" is reported as a function of "X." He assumes it must be ever thus, i.e., "X" is the variable which one manipulates to achieve a change in "Y." He overlooks the possibility that the reverse may be equally feasible; that if one makes a change in "Y," there will be change in "X."

Thus, consider Etzioni's discussion of the organizational control continuum: totalitarian-utilitarian (economic)-normative.[13] He finds that the degree to which informal organization and alienation from the formal power structure are present will vary directly with the extent to which control is totalitarian (autocratic). The hasty assumption might be that informal organization is a *consequence* of an autocratic formal power structure. But is it not possible that the reverse might also be true—that the power of the informal organization might alarm officials into a tightening of the formal autocratic reins? Gouldner describes such a situation in a gypsum board plant, where a new manager attempted to change the "leniency pattern" which had been tolerated by his predecessor.[14]

Consider the findings (discussed earlier) in which high productivity was found to result from a participative leadership style. Could not an employee group, motivated to be high producers for some other reason, by their very behavior induce their leader to be more "participative" in his attitude toward them? Or, consider the Brayfield and Crockett finding that productivity is not

---

[12]L. Baritz, *The Servants of Power* (Middletown, Conn.: Wesleyan University Press, 1960). Although Baritz in his characterization of them as "the servants of power" intimates that they may, on occasion, succumb to implicit pressure to bias their findings to coincide with the a *priori* intuitions of their sponsors.

[13]A. Etzioni, *Modern Organizations* (Englewood Cliffs, N.J.: Prentice-Hall, 1964), pp. 58–61.

[14]A. W. Gouldner, *Wildcat Strike* (Harper, N.Y.: 1953).

correlated with job satisfaction.[15] A hasty conclusion might be that the two conditions cannot co-exist. Actually, it is possible to have both high satisfaction *and* high productivity! Herzberg has shown that the two are resultants of two distinct sets of determinants.[16] Thus, an apparent relationship between "X" and "Y" may be mere coincidence. They may be variables in two entirely separate systems, and as such, would merely be ships that pass in the night.

Finally, we have the book-length narratives which describe the implementation of a certain managerial philosophy in this or that company. Two biases are at work here, pushing the reader toward a "black" or "white" conclusion: (1) the bias of the writers; and (2) the already established values and predispositions of the reader, which lead him to accept or reject absolutely the applicability of the findings.

Glossed over by the reporters and by the reader are the host of conditions which made the philosophy "work" in the described environment. We find that, perhaps fortuitously, "French's variables" were present in just the right quantities or that changes were made so that they became so.[17] Or, there may have been considerable changes in the environmental variables (equipment, processes, products, even a new management team) which might have been principal causes of success, a success that was attributed by the writers, however, to the implementation of the espoused philosophy. We suggest the dubiousness, in general, of crediting organizational success to any one factor, e.g., to a certain managerial philosophy. Furthermore, in claiming "success," to what do we refer; to the achieved implementation of a certain style of managerial behavior, per se, or to the achievement of basic organization goals, such as: "make a profit, grow, and survive"? As to the contribution of any particular "style of managing," cannot the questions be asked, "Is it not possible that we could have done better, overall, with a *different* leadership style," or, "Was it the leadership or managerial style, of and by itself, which put the organization back on its feet"?

For instance, in the Weldon case (Marrow, Bowers, and Seashore), we read on the dust jacket that " . . . Weldon had become a costly, inefficient, and conflict-ridden operation . . . Harwood (the company which had bought Weldon) set out to bring their policies to Weldon, and in 2 years the change had improved the situation considerably.[18] This book is the story of that *success*"—"Aha!" exclaims the "white" reader and proceeds, his bias considerably reinforced.

Conversely, the "black" reader finds this careful qualifier in the "Foreword" (p. x): "This report . . . is fundamentally a *partisan* book." From that point on, he concentrates on determining what the "partisans" *left out* of their success story.

Actually, in this case, the findings are tinged with grey. "One reason for the

[15]A. Brayfield, and W. Crockett, "Employee Attitudes and Employee Performance" *Psychological Bulletin* (52), 5 (1955), pp. 415–422.

[16]F. Herzberg, *Work and the Nature of Man* (New York: World Publishing Co., 1966).

[17]French, Israel, and As, "Overcoming Resistance."

[18]A. Marrow, D. Bowers, and S. Seashore, eds., *Management of Participation* (New York: Harper & Row, 1967).

success of the Weldon program . . . lies in the sheer amount and variety of resources put to work. The direct dollar costs of the change efforts on the human organization side were about of the same magnitude as the direct dollar cost of *physical plant improvement* (italics mine) . . ." (p. 239), "And, in the merchandising function, the change was brought about by . . . *replacing a large proportion of the key people.* (italics mine) . . ." (p. 241). Furthermore, "The Weldon change program had some clear elements of *coercive pressure.* . . . The paradox of using coercion . . . is a common one, and one that forces a concern about the *conditions* (italics mine) under which a manager should use directive, as compared with consultative, strategies" (p. 243–244).

Burns and Stalker find that a consultative-participative approach is suitable in an "organistic" type of organization, and somewhat superfluous in a "mechanistic" type.[19] We suggest that the reader might be hard-put to place his organization at *either end* of a "mechanistic-organistic" continuum. Certainly, he would not attempt to place it there merely to be able to accommodate or exclude a certain management style! Woodward reveals still another qualifying factor in a study of 203 British firms.[20] She reports that participation in decision-making did not overcome resistance to change, as long as the change appeared to carry a threat to the economic and sociopsychological values of the participants.

There is no need to belabor the issue. *Any* black or white conclusion as to the value of participative leadership may be supportable if one selects portions of findings, out of context: the *reality* is that if a whole host of conditions are satisfied, "participation" may be classed as a *contributor* to success.

In summary, we appeal to the practitioner: Give behavioral scientists and other writers in the field of human behavior in organizations a careful, critical reading. In most cases their reports describe what they found (if occasionally tinged with optimism!). Sad to say, the practitioner overlooks this. All too unwittingly he oversimplifies what he reads to make it *prescriptive,* so that he may forthrightly reject it or add it to his stock of stereotypes. We return to Lewin's "Behavior is a function of personality and environment B = f(P,E)."[21] We have tried to show how this precept is a useful model for analyzing all behavioral findings and theories and how each of such studies, implicitly or explicitly, involves only one value for the parameter "P" and one value for the parameter "E." It helps to explain why such findings must be applied to *other* people, under *other* conditions, with caution. There seems to be no enduring "one best fit" anent the personality and environmental considerations affecting the choice of a leadership style.

[19]G. Burns and M. Stalker, *The Management of Innovation* (Chicago, Ill.: Quadrangle Books, 1962), Ch. Vll.

[20]Joan Woodward, *Organization Theory and Practice* (New York: Oxford University Press, 1966), p. 194.

[21]K. Lewin, "Frontiers in Group Dynamics," in D. Cartwright, ed., *Field Theory in Social Science* (New York: Harper, 1951), pp. 188–237.

Reading 28

Six Propositions for Managerial Leadership: Diagnostic Tools for Definition and Focus

Norman George

Thomas J. Von Der Embse

What is the state of the art of managerial leadership research and theory? Progressing quite well, we suggest, and promising to be useful to management— *provided* we are careful and realistic in suggesting how the research results are to be used.

This article will set forth six propositions which, it is hoped, will add to the growing body of leadership research. These propositions have emerged from research, including our own study of attitudinal orientations of over 650 managers and administrators from a variety of organizations, including nonindustrial institutions. The six propositions focus on the relationships between managers' attitudes and behavior and several other dimensions, including organizational structure, operating systems, environmental conditions, and demographic factors. The relationships are selective. They do not purport to deal with all the ramifications of leadership behavior and organizational effectiveness, but they are sufficiently inclusive to be useful in analyzing conditions and forces in effect within an organization.

OVERVIEW OF LEADERSHIP RESEARCH

Three decades ago, management literature abounded with the traitist approach to leadership analysis. The practice was usually to postulate a profile of the effective leader in terms of personality characteristics. But while the emphasis was on personal traits, the profiles usually included some factors that are better classified as skills rather than traits in the psychological sense. Thus the "good leader" was not only "decisive" and possessed "good judgment," but he was also "able to communicate and could project an air of confidence."

This exclusive emphasis on the make-up and abilities of the individual executive was replaced by the situational approach, which viewed leadership as a process that, in turn, was a function of the interactions among the manager, the work group, and the organizational environment. The manager himself was still a central focus of study, but the emphasis was upon observation of more discrete behavior in the context of the organizational setting.

The polarization of the styles-of-leadership concept in recent years seems,

"Six Propositions for Managerial Leadership: Diagnostic Tools for Definition and Focus," Norman George and Thomas J. Von Der Embse, *Business Horizons*, December 1971, pp. 33–43. Reprinted with permission.

oddly enough, a throwback to the traitist approach. It is perhaps fair to say that McGregor's "X" and "Y" theory of management was the stimulus for the spate of "models" of leadership styles.[1] But before accusing McGregor of resurrecting a kind of traitist approach to leadership, it is important to note that McGregor's approach was essentially cultural rather than psychological. He was still "situational" in the sense that emergent leadership styles, according to his theory, resulted from prevalent cultural values and thus took into account more than the behavior of the individual manager. When he talked about the underlying attitudes of the "X" manager and the "Y" manager, he was discussing not any particular manager but the widely prevalent cultural values of managers in general.

The most recent treatments of leadership theory and research still look carefully at the behavior of the manager, but they relate this behavior more directly to other organizational dimensions. The Woodward studies placed great emphasis on the nature of the production technology. Lorsch, Lawrence, and Morse related competitive conditions to the organization's operating system and the interaction of both of these factors to the resultant behavior within the organization. Fiedler's contingency theory attempts to elaborate a model of managerial leadership in which leadership style becomes a function of managerial and work group attitudes and behavior and organizational conditions, such as task structure and modes of interaction.[2]

USES OF LEADERSHIP RESEARCH

Ideally, the end result of research should be to prescribe or suggest to managers what ought to be done in a given situation. But at this point we urge caution. The nature of the management process and the web of interrelating factors in any given situation are complex, much too complex to permit many, if any, prescriptive statements that are generally applicable. Such statements would almost always have to be qualified by such conditions as "all other factors being equal." But all other factors are seldom equal; each organization has its own unique set of conditions and circumstances. Some recent research, for example, suggests a certain fit between leadership behavior patterns and organization structure, calling for adaptation of one or the other. But any number of factors, in a particular situation, could mitigate against the prescribed fit.

It is much more prudent and realistic, therefore, to regard the relationships that emerge from the research as diagnostic tools of organization analysis, rather than precise guidelines as to what ought to be done. Managers are action and

---

[1]Douglas V. McGregor, *The Human Side of Enterprise* (New York: McGraw-Hill Book Company, 1960).

[2]See, for example, Joan Woodward, *Industrial Organization* (New York: Oxford University Press, 1965); John Morse and Jay Lorsch. "Beyond Theory Y," *Harvard Business Review* (May–June, 1970), pp. 61–68; and Fred E. Fiedler, *A Theory of Leadership Effectiveness* (New York: McGraw-Hill Book Company, 1966).

decision oriented. They must decide what needs to be done and act accordingly. But before management can decide where it wants to go and how to get there, it needs to diagnose where it is now. With this knowledge base, it can better determine likely obstacles and conditions that may require change or adaptation. Management-by-objectives programs, for example, require a degree of consultative goal setting. A diagnosis of existing leadership patterns and organizational factors might point to the need for some preconditioning to increase the likelihood of effective implementation.

It seems accurate to say that a dynamic model of leadership is now evolving. Some refer to this as a contingency model or theory. It is in the context of such a model that the six propositions discussed below should be viewed. They should not be regarded as standing alone; rather, they are intended to be used as related units of analysis.

How an effective manager behaves, whether consultatively or directively, depends upon several factors: the kind of production or operating system; whether a company's production, engineering, and marketing are characterized by rapid changes or relative stability; the level and types of skill and education of the work group; and the degree of structure that emerges as a result of these factors. Not only will these factors vary among organizations, but also within the same organization over a span of time.

The promise of this trend of research and theory building is that the kind of studies evolving, because they constitute a departure from traditional static approaches, can provide useful conceptual tools of analysis. With these tools, a manager has available a framework for determining why certain leadership patterns are present in the organization and what to expect from them, and whether a dominant pattern of directive or consultative management for an organization unit is desirable and appropriate to the present set of conditions, including the operating system, production, marketing and engineering system stability, and personnel characteristics. Finally, if change is desirable, the insight from the newer research approach assists the manager in deciding where to begin and what to expect as a result of the change.

The analysis of our study data did not rely solely on "hard criteria," that is, the quantitative measurements of the scales and bio-organizational information. Through group discussion and individual interviews with a sizable portion of our statistical sample, we were able to add considerably to our understanding and interpretation of the results. This kind of information not only added detail, but often provided key factors and insights that explained relationships in some areas and the lack of relationships in others (see figure on p. 326).

THE SIX PROPOSITIONS

Our six propositions are intended as diagnostic tools of analysis, rather than prescriptions for specific action. They are, in a sense, precedents to decision and action. They point to relationships that the manager should use, along with other considerations, in analyzing the situation as it exists now, anticipating possible obstacles to desired end results, and assessing conditions for success.

The propositions are based upon a combination—a synthesis—of reported research and observations, including our own study and observations. The authors' research, which is now progressing into a new phase, deals with attitudinal factors related to leadership behavior and selected organizational and demographic characteristics. It was designed to complement, build upon, and elaborate other research already reported and referred to.

The propositions themselves are stated in rather broad terms. If they appear to be somewhat general or oversimplified, it is merely because we have chosen to limit the number to six, leaving it for later to elaborate points and delve into some of the ramifications in greater detail.

Proposition 1: Flexibility in Leadership Style Is Both Desirable and Feasible

Probably few will disagree that flexibility in style is desirable. More recent research, such as that of Lorsch and Lawrence, Woodward, and others, serves to

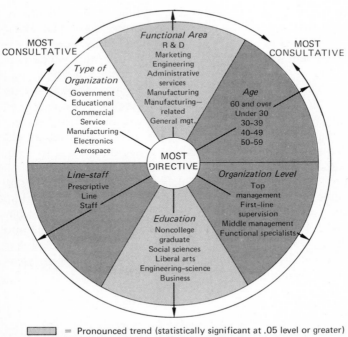

= Pronounced trend (statistically significant at .05 level or greater)
= Moderate trend (statistically significant at .10 level)
= Barely perceptible trend (did not reach at least .10 level)

negate what now certainly appears to have been a tendency of some earlier studies to suggest that consultative management was preferred in nearly all instances. Studies have shown clearly that this is not the case.

Even though some of the research (such as that of Lorsch and Lawrence, and Woodward) approached the problem from the point of view of which styles actually emerge under different organizational and technological settings, there is a strong implication that the desired style differs with the situation. The realities of the situation, including the fact that under certain conditions organizational units that were generally characterized by the directive mode of management were evaluated highly effective, are taken into account. The work structure often simply does not permit much latitude for consultative management, at least not to any great extent.

What may be more controversial is the question of whether or not a manager *can* be flexible. To some behaviorists, this is questionable because, they say, leadership style reflects one's basic personality, which changes little after the early years in life. But this view, it is suggested, has sometimes tended to confuse the issue. The question is not necessarily how much one can change, but how much flexibility in behavior an individual's basic personality permits. This range of behavior is, for the typical manager, not necessarily narrow.

A good deal of the research points out that there is considerable adaptation by managers. When the prevailing organizational structure and management practices influence and even dictate a mode of leadership behavior, many managers obviously have adapted. One facet of our own study throws light on flexibility and adaptation in still another context. Most of the subjects were not extremely oriented in either direction, that is, directive or consultative. A revealing insight emerged from a pursuit of this point with those who were closest to the mid-point of the scale. A large number of these individuals had difficulty classifying their positions as either line or staff. It was not that they had difficulty in distinguishing between line-and-staff responsibilities, but that their jobs had elements of both functions.

Typically, these individuals were in technical or professional positions. For example, a design engineer in charge of a section had line type of responsibility within his department; at the same time, he functioned basically in a staff capacity with other organization units. This type of manager felt it was necessary to be directive on certain aspects of the work and consultative on others. Even within his department, he felt the need for flexibility. At times, he found it clearly necessary to give directives. But at other times, because of the nature of the work project and the fact that a subordinate's expertise was often greater than his own, a collegial relationship naturally evolved, calling for an essentially consultative approach.

The point, then, is that most managers do adapt and are flexible when they need to be. This may seem obvious, but is not always reflected in the behavioral studies.

Proposition 2: The Prime Variables Underlying Organizational Differentiation Are Job Function, Organization Levels, and Operating System Characteristics

An organizational unit can and does tend to develop particular leadership characteristics. But the differentiation is between and among the subunits of a company or a geographical division. That is, within the company or geographic division, different leadership styles can emerge among the subunits, a point emphasized by Leavitt, among others.[3] The obvious question, then, is what are the variables that explain the differences? Our research and that of others points to three as the most significant: job function, organization level, and operating system characteristics.

The term "function" is used here in two contexts. The first involves what some have called organic functionalization, a means of distinguishing between basic business functions. Thus, there is the marketing function, the manufacturing function, the production function, the finance function, and so on. These may be further subdivided. For example, we have found it significant to distinguish between manufacturing and manufacturing-related functions, the former consisting of work activities more directly related to production than the latter. Production planning and control, for example, would usually be defined as manufacturing-related in our context.

The second context in which the term function is used relates to the line-staff concept. Both of these functional differentiations serve to explain differences in leadership modes within a company organization. Marketing managers, as a unit within our total sample, were found to be significantly more consultatively oriented than manufacturing managers, for example. While one must be careful not to generalize too broadly from the functional distinction alone, it is apparent that the greater and more explicit the constraints involved in the function itself, the more likely the manager in that position will be directively, rather than consultatively, oriented. This conclusion is further reinforced by the fact that differences among organizations were not as prominent in our study as were differences among functions. In other words, when comparing manufacturing, aerospace, educational, commercial, service, governmental, and even religious organizations, managers in similar positions do not differ as markedly in leadership orientation as do managers in different positions in a single organization.

The explanation is found by combining with the functional factor the variable often referred to as "operating system characteristics." This factor is similar to the concept used in the Woodward and Lorsch, Lawrence and Morse studies in defining differences in technological systems. The present authors' point of departure from the earlier research, however, lies in the delineation of operating systems within an organization. Thus, it is valid to suggest the existence

---

[3]Harold J. Leavitt, "Management According to Task: Organizational Differentiation" in *Readings in Human Relations* (New York: McGraw-Hill Book Company, 1964), pp. 3–15.

of various operating systems, each relating to particular functional areas but broader in scope than the duties implied and/or described for the function.

The marketing area is a good example. In explaining leadership orientation, it is far more appropriate to examine the technology and operation of the marketing system—in contrast with, for instance, the production system. Marketing systems tend to be more ambient than production systems. Marketing organizational relationships tend toward lower job structure, more positive change orientation, greater diffusion of authority, less fragmentation of work activities, and greater autonomy of individual movement.

The point is that these same considerations carry over into other functional areas. Even more important, these two variables, functional differentiation and operating systems, combine to produce a need for certain leadership orientations. Both are, however, horizontally distinguished from other areas. Organizational differentiation implies both vertical *and* horizontal perspectives.

The vertical factor emerging as most important is organization level. Of the three management groups—supervisory, middle, and top—middle managers tend to be most consultative. The implications of this finding extend beyond internal factors and into certain universal considerations regarding the middle management role.

Greenidge and Steinmetz, in a recent article, reported a management syndrome characterized by a highly consultative and participative orientation.[4] The authors related this, in turn, to the current evangelism of the management and organization development profession. While the authors associated this syndrome with top managers, the point is that the conditioning effect of management training helps also to explain the middle management trend toward high consultation. Middle managers have, in recent years, frequented seminars of all sorts, especially grid training, management by objectives, laboratory "t" group sessions, and similar programs in which the developmental criteria are almost singularly based on democratic, participative management.

Evidence from our research clearly supports this observation. Of all samples in the study, those drawn from practitioners after taking an M.B.A. human relations course were significantly more consultative. While a certain amount of self-selection bias was undoubtedly involved, it is apparent that conditioning through training and education can and does encourage certain leadership models which, in turn, will tend to condition the attitudes of managers on the job.

Another more speculative consideration in the case of middle management relates to the status of the position itself. Various popular conceptions of the middle management position view it as any or all of the following: a paper-shuffling function, a buffer or pressure point between top management and first-line supervision, a proving ground for top management prospects, a repository for "retreads" and organizational deadwood, and/or a junior executive

---

[4]Charles D. Greenidge and Lawrence L. Steinmetz, "Realities That Shape Managerial Style," *Business Horizons* (October, 1970), pp. 23–32.

level with certain important responsibilities but with limited decision authority. Still others view the position as the focal point for decentralized authority.

It is not our purpose to evaluate the merits of these various conceptions of middle management, but rather to underscore the distinctive orientations of middle, first, and top level managers. At the risk of some generalization, the highly consultative attitude of middle managers suggests that, at this organization level, factors such as perceived uncertainty regarding organizational role, limited authority in making decisions, and, more important, getting top management support for those decisions produce the kind of atmosphere in which consultation regarding decision matters will tend to prevail.

Proposition 3: Differences in Leadership Style Orientation Derive from Cultural Factors and Are in a State of Transition

Bennis has postulated that "democracy is inevitable" in organizations.[5] It would not be taking undue liberty to suggest that, in our context, he predicts that the consultative mode of leadership will ultimately prevail. The prediction itself is virtually impossible to dispute, since inevitability suggests no finite time dimension. In a relative sense, however, it seems clear that the over-all trend in leadership attitudes is toward the consultation end of the continuum. However, the matter of emergent leadership behavior is much more complex, as shown in the preceding discussion regarding organizational differentiation. Nevertheless, it is apparent that cultural factors do have an important impact on leadership style orientation.

Two factors stand out: age and education. The findings showed a consistent pattern of leadership orientation based on the age factor. Simply stated, younger managers tend to be more consultatively oriented than older managers. Furthermore, this pattern is fairly consistent as the age brackets are broken out. Age does correlate inversely with the consultative-directive scale, that is (except for the over 60 group), the higher the age, the more directive the manager.

The correlation also holds up with the education factor, although it must be pointed out that the data relative to education are largely confined to formal education. Thus, we found college graduates more consultatively oriented than noncollege managers. The differences are, moreover, quite large from a statistical viewpoint.

Because of the myriad factors that should be considered in assessing the impact of cultural factors, one should not generalize too broadly. On the one hand, as suggested earlier, the quantity and orientation of management training are bound to have some long-range effect on leadership orientation. On the other hand, one might point to competitive conditions and changing technology as among the factors that cannot be overlooked as influences that could shape attitudes in different directions. Nevertheless, we have found considerable

[5]Warren G. Bennis and Philip E. Slater, "Democracy is Inevitable," *Harvard Business Review* (March–April, 1964), pp. 51–59.

evidence in the nature of hard criteria on age and education that do suggest a long-range trend toward more consultative leadership.

Proposition 4: Differences in Leadership Modes Exist between Line-and-staff Managers

The intensive technological base of the newer industries, such as aerospace and electronics, has led several observers to suggest that traditional line-and-staff distinctions will eventually fade and that the deployment of highly trained individuals in project teamwork situations will diffuse decision authority among various organization roles. As indicated earlier, the perceived differences between line and staff are often quite ambiguous. But, considering the difficulties in classification, one cannot dismiss the fact that differences can and do emerge.

The classical line-and-staff distinction focused on different kinds of authority. Thus, staff authority is largely advisory, and line authority is the right to command or issue directives. In the context of leadership styles, staff would find it necessary to rely on its ability to influence line managers, while line could rely to an extent on the weight of its formal authority. Staff, therefore, would be expected to operate in a more consultative mode.

The authors' study lends some support to the classical view, in that staff managers and specialists as a group and across varying types of organizations were more consultative than line managers. It was necessary, however, to include a third category—prescriptive—to distinguish those personnel whose functions may be formally defined as staff, but in practice normally exercise considerable authority regarding organizational decisions related to their specialties, for example, production control, purchasing, quality control, and budget analysis. Separating this group increased the differentiation of the functions. This, in turn, tells the manager that the line-staff distinction is insufficient and that a third group exists, which is neither line nor staff but which tends to be directive in attitude. Awareness of this third dimension could help to prevent line-staff conflict, particularly when viewed as a difference in role behavior and expectations.

Proposition 5: External Forces Can Modify Leadership Modes: Changing Competitive Conditions Are a Prime Example

Leadership patterns are products of a number of interrelating factors. Most of the ones we have discussed so far are internal to the organization in a sense, although new managers in the organization might be viewed as an external influence, at least in the initial phases of their performance. But external factors do have an effect which is sometimes quite discernible. Particularly significant may be the effect of changing competitive conditions.

It should be noted first, as researchers such as Lorsch, Morse, Lawrence, and Woodward have documented in references noted earlier, competitive conditions are significant elements in the system of factors that explain the emergence of differing modes of organizational leadership styles. Although these researchers focused on the internal operating system, it is clear that competitive forces were among the controlling factors. A stable market, for example, will be reflected in the manufacturing technology. The rate of change demanded by the market will also influence directly the general thrust of R&D and design engineering work. And these factors, as has been noted, are related to the kind of leadership that emerges.

But this proposition emphasizes that changes in competitive conditions can and do produce changes in leadership patterns, often with dramatic promptness. While these changes may eventually turn out to be temporary, under certain circumstances, which we will discuss, the change can prove to be relatively permanent.

It is reasonable to expect a general increase in the directive mode of managing internally because of more severe competitive conditions; however, these conditions can produce or influence behavior in the opposite direction for those members of the organization who have regular contact with people outside the organization. The marketing group almost immediately comes to mind. Our study included data on a marketing association group in a specific geographical area. A large percentage of its members represented companies that had been unusually affected by the business downturn in 1970. As a group, this sample was more consultative on the average than the rest of our marketing manager sample and was also less risk oriented.

Even lacking highly rigorous controls in our research design to validate the presumption generated by this finding, it seems reasonable to say that, during times of more intensive competition, marketing personnel in the field are likely to continue their basically more consultative attitude orientation. In view of the likelihood that they must woo the customer even harder, some small shift toward an even greater consultative orientation is at least possible, if not likely.

One might also conjecture that during times of increased competition even the marketing group would generally be subject to directive approaches; marketing managers might begin to breathe more heavily down the necks of their district managers. But the evidence supports the generalization that attitudes of marketing people are strongly influenced by the nature of customer relations. This is not confined to the salesmen themselves, but is also reflected by sales and marketing managers.

A study by Tosi and Carroll, although focusing on objective setting in connection with management by objectives, is consistent in a general way with our results and earlier comments.[6] They found that marketing personnel perceived themselves as having considerably more voice in setting their objectives than did most other classes of managers. Tosi and Carroll explained this by pointing out that salesmen and sales managers almost always have the best and the most information when it comes to the sales outlook in their specific areas.

---

[6]Henry L. Tosi, Jr. and Stephen J. Carroll, "Some Structural Factors Related to Goal Influence in the Management by Objectives Process," *MSU Business Topics* (Spring, 1969).

While Tosi and Carroll were looking at marketing personnel's perceptions of the degree of influence and power they had in setting objectives, we would put it in terms of the degree of consultation in this decision area.

In summary, external forces can modify leadership modes. The external forces operate directly upon some segments of the organization, such as marketing and those groups which regularly meet customers (field services, for example), and less directly for other groups. The impact depends on how sensitive various operations must be to customer or client.

While we have discussed only the force of competition, this is not the only external factor that can change or modify leadership patterns. We might have pointed to such other factors as government regulation, especially in cases when a company might come under investigation with respect to antitrust laws or the Federal Trade Commission, for example. A change in the local union's international affiliation is another example. But most of the evidence so far indicates that competition is the external factor of prime importance affecting leadership patterns.

Proposition 6: Institutional Effects Are Not as Important as the Previously Mentioned Variables as Determinants of Emergent Leadership Patterns

Our study included groups of administrators in secondary education and in religious organizations. These groups, as distinct entities in our study, did not differ greatly from industrial and business groups in attitudinal orientation. Neither the educational nor the religious administrators, as a group, were significantly more consultative, for example, than groups of industrial managers. The differences in orientation within these groups were related basically to the same factors as within manufacturing and industrial groups: the function performed, the nature of the operating system, organizational level, the line-staff differentiation, education, and age.

Perhaps a caveat is in order here. Longitudinal studies may very well show some changes in view of the well-known forces at play in these institutions. These two types of organizations (educational and religious) are experiencing demands for greater participation in decision making, not only by components of the internal system, but external societal elements as well. Perhaps these groups will become more consultative and group oriented on the average. But there is nothing to indicate that differentiation *within* a particular educational or religious organization will decrease. Furthermore, we indicated earlier evidence of long-range trends in average orientations in industrial organizations resulting both from cultural factors and structural considerations (relatively more technical and professional personnel in the firm).

Another way of putting it is this. What is important is that within these types of organizations operating systems may be changing and new functions may be displacing old ones. In addition, a new breed of administrators is coming into the picture. Influence from forces external to the organization unit should also be "plugged in." These are the important units of analysis, the same units applicable to other institutions, including business and industrial.

THE PROPOSITIONS AS TOOLS

We have suggested six propositions for managerial leadership. These propositions, like all the emerging leadership concepts founded on research evidence, should be regarded as diagnostic tools. Their use can be explained by suggesting as strongly as possible how *not* to use these concepts. They should not be used as static descriptions that serve to classify organizations. Instead, the approach here has been to concentrate on relationships.

Furthermore, these relationships can change, and continuous research is necessary to identify the changes. But these relationships, if they are relatively fundamental, should not change too rapidly. If that occurs, we have obviously not yet found the first order or first level of relationships. It is necessary to work from these most basic relationships to use these concepts in a practical sense.

The primary uses of these propositions, then, are as diagnostic tools. Ideally, such tools can be used at any point in time to describe the mix of leadership elements in an organization; predict changes in leadership mode by analyzing and forecasting changes in the mix; and help an individual manager to adapt his behavior or leadership style through analytical assessment of the mix of forces and conditions.

What does it mean—particularly to the manager who looks for something useful? One use is suggested by the postulations of some researchers. They have suggested that, given a certain mix of the elements, certain practices, structures, and policies are predictably dysfunctional. Consequently, they are in conflict with what the mix of elements tends to "force." To this, one should add an elaboration in terms of the time dimension. A manager could make a calculated estimate of the probabilities of correcting the dysfunction within a reasonable and acceptable period of time by viewing the mix as dynamic (that is, subject to change), and by injecting into the system analysis the degree of permanency of certain underlying elements, such as attitude orientation, plus the potency of modifying influences, such as competitive forces and the resultant immediate changes.

Thus, a manager can assess and roughly measure a system's capacity for adaptability. Suppose, for example, that a company or one of its divisions is pondering the advisability and feasibility of going into a line of business that calls for producing a highly standardized product; success will depend upon cost and service efficiency. Described another way, a high technology company seeking to diversify contemplates development of a segment of business that is less technology-intensive and is much more competitive on cost and service efficiency. It proposes to develop this business internally. One question it must ask in determining strategy is whether or not its personnel can adapt to what would essentially be a different operating system. An analytical study of the mix of forces and factors discussed in this article should, it is suggested, enable the company to better assess the chances of successful adaptation.

Obviously, according to recent experiences of some of the defense-related industries, this probability has not always been correctly calculated. We can reasonably surmise that the failures could be explained, partly at least, in terms of the need for quicker decisions, more immediately responsive control, and other factors, all of which point toward a more directive rather than consultative mode of managing.

To have determined accurately the probabilities of successful adaptation to the new leadership mode would have entailed finding out not only the nature of behavior or leadership patterns that had existed, but also the degree and permanency of, for example, a consultative orientation. It may have also entailed pinpointing where and in which particular parts of the organization a rather high degree of directive managing would be required. Conceivably, this could have been a crucial factor in deciding position assignments and over-all criteria for staffing.

It is not suggested that the use of these analytical tools will provide precise or discrete answers. The tools themselves are not that exact, the variables are numerous, and the interrelations highly dynamic. But it is suggested that the analysis can be useful to management in identifying what to look for, what to expect, and what hurdles will need to be overcome, and in developing a framework for applying managerial judgment and knowledge. In short, it could help management focus on the critical problems with which they should be concerned.

This may be all that leadership research and the development of theory and principles can ever do—help managers to define the elements of the problem and focus on the critical issues. But this is no small contribution.

Reading 29
Leadership and Organization Character
Y. K. Shetty

The evidence derived from social science research indicates that leadership does not consist of abstract personal qualities, as was once thought, but is a result of complex interaction between the manager and his employees in dynamic organizational situations. This variable—the organizational system—has a significant influence in shaping individual leadership styles.

Leadership styles can be portrayed on a scale depicting autocratic at the one

"Leadership and Organization Character," Y.K. Shetty, *Personnel Administration*, July–August 1970, pp. 14–20. Reprinted with permission.

end and free-reign on the other. In between these extremes, there is a *range* of leadership behavior which may fall anywhere on the continuum of the scale. At one extreme, the leader uses a high degree of authority and allows little freedom to his subordinates. At the other extreme he gives a high degree of freedom to his subordinates and maintains little control over their daily activities.

Certain leadership styles are more suitable or acceptable in particular organizational settings and for particular organizational structures. Structure, in turn, often depends on whether the organization is engaged in process production, unit production, mass production, or some balance of these activities.

The purpose of this paper is to explore some of the recent research on leadership behavior and organizational systems and point to a scheme for understanding how varying styles of leadership may develop in response to specific combinations of the manager, the employee and the organizational climate.

What Is a Leader?

The concept of leadership has run a varied course. The earliest attempt to explain the phenomenon of leadership was made by writers who have come to be known as "traitists." It was thought that a successful leader was one who had specific leadership traits. These traits were interpreted in terms of qualities such as physical and nervous energy, a sense of purpose and direction, enthusiasm, friendliness, affection, integrity, technical mastery, decisiveness, intelligence, teaching skill, and faith.[1] This approach assumed that leadership could be examined in isolation, without considering other factors. Research in this approach to leadership proved futile, since there was little agreement as to the universal traits required for leadership. Gouldner, after reviewing the empirical and conservatively interpreting evidence relating to "universal traits," concluded, "At this time there is no reliable evidence concerning the existence of universal leadership traits."[2]

The Leader and the Led   The inadequacies of explaining leadership by reference to traits invariably led others to posit that followers are an important variable in effective leadership. This theory emphasized that an effective leader is one who nearly always satisfied the personal needs of his followers. "The follower's persistent motivations, points of view, frames of reference or attitudes will have a hand in determining what he perceives and how he reacts to it. The psychological factors in the individual followers cannot be ignored in our search for a science of leadership."[3]

The follower-theory approach does not emphasize the qualities of the leader as the traitists do, but rather, those of the followers, such as their personal needs, whether present or remote.

The Leadership Situation   The situational approach to leadership is based on the notion that neither leader nor follower traits are the main determinant of who will succeed as a leader; rather the situation or the environment is the relevant variable. Thus, a leader in one situation may not be a leader in another situation. In short, the leader's behavior is always responsive to the situation in which it occurs.

The situational approach is valuable because each organization is unique despite some structural similarities. It focuses attention not on the personality of the leader as such, but on the "personality" or culture of the organization as a whole. It is possible for almost anyone to become a leader, if circumstances allow him to perform functions dictated by the situation. An effective leader, according to situational theory, is one who understands the forces of the situation and effectively uses them.

The situational theorists do not completely abandon the search for significant variables, but they attempt to look for them in situations containing similar elements. "The qualities, characteristics and skills required in a leader are determined to a large extent by the demands of the situation in which he is to function as a leader."[4]

The Emergence of Leadership Styles

In spite of these "Trait," "Follower," and "Situational" theories, each focusing its own aspects, the common attitude, as Sanford points out, is to view leadership behavior as a complex phenomenon determined by all three of these variables. He further comments that to concentrate on any one of these facets represents an oversimplification of an intricate phenomenon.

The Case for Leadership Styles From various definitions of leadership (e.g., Gibb,[5] Bennis,[6] Tannenbaum,[7]) one can delineate several common elements which lead to an understanding of the real *functions* of leadership:

1 *Differentiation of function:* Without group activity the leader is deprived of the opportunity to coordinate the activities of the group, to produce group solidarity in the pursuit of a goal. The leadership function itself is a differentiated activity which arises out of group processes.

2 *The necessity of the group:* Leadership cannot exist without a group to be led.

3 *Objectives:* Leadership is directed toward the attainment of a specified goal or goals.

4 *The leader:* The leader interacts with the group, modifying goals and courses of action so that a unified group opinion results.

From these elements, it becomes clear that leadership is both a process and a function of three variables—the leader, the led, and the situation. Because leadership can be achieved through a variety of behaviors, the concept of types or styles of leadership emerges.

Three of these principal types are the familiar autocratic, democratic, and free-rein leader. Other terms are also used to describe different leadership styles, particularly the autocratic and democratic pattern. The literature on leadership shows that these styles can be characterized in various ways, but essentially they seem to come down to a dichotomy represented by these distinctions:[8]

Even though various concepts are used to characterize the two opposite styles, the characteristics within each style tend to correlate with one another; that is, the participatory leader is also likely to be employee-centered, persuasive, integrative, etc.

The Forces behind Leadership Styles   Tannenbaum and others[9] suggest that there are three types of forces which are significant to the manager in shaping his leadership style: forces in the manager himself; forces in his subordinates; and forces in the general situation.

The forces within the manager involve *(a)* his value system, that is, the extent to which he thinks individuals *should* have a share in the decisions which affect them; *(b)* his confidence in his subordinates; *(c)* his own leadership inclination, that is, under what circumstances he feels most comfortable; and *(d)* his feelings of security in uncertain situations.

The forces within subordinates include (1) their needs for independence; (2) their tolerance for ambiguity; (3) their interest in a problem and its importance; (4) their degree of identification with the goals of the organization; (5) their knowledge and experience; and (6) their expectations that they should share in decision making.

The forces within the situation include (i) the type of organization including its culture, size of working units, geographical distribution and the degrees of inter- and intra-organizational interaction required to attain goals; (ii) group effectiveness; (iii) the nature and complexity of the task; and (iv) the amount of time available to make a decision or take action.

Even though Tannenbaum and others indirectly identify organization as a variable influencing leadership styles in their model, it is absorbed in the situation and given comparatively little analytical attention. This truncated perspective, for the most part, ignores the *crucial* role of technology and organization in shaping the leadership behavior.

In this paper, organizational system (technology and organization structure) is considered as an independent variable, separate from the situation. The situation is considered as a dynamic variable, which is of immediate concern to the leader. The attempt to give an independent status to organizational system or, to put it differently, to pay systematic attention to the role of organizational system in analyzing and studying leadership styles, is believed to be a distinctive feature of this paper.

Organizational Impact on Leadership Styles

It is apparent from some of the recent research findings that both technology and organization structure have a strong influence on leadership patterns. Specifically, methods of production, division of work, work flow, certainty of tasks and

Employee-centered		Production-centered
Considerate		Initiatory
Loose (general)		Close
Integrative	as against	Dominative
Persuasive		Arbitrary
Group-centered		Leader-centered
Participatory		Authoritarian

structural attributes of the organization are inter-related and tend to shape leadership behavior.

Methods of Production   Production technology, as recently suggested by Woodward,[10] seem to limit the amount of discretion which subordinates can be given and the style of supervision used. She found that management structure varied with the type of technology, and that different technologies seem to have varying degrees of "management content."[11]

Some technologies are more management intensive than others.[12] Management content is substantially higher in "continuous-process" technology than in the "unit-production" technology. That is, fewer managers supervise more people in unit production than in mass-production or continuous process technologies. Since technology can dictate the supervisory ratio, it may, therefore, limit the amount of freedom which subordinates can be given.

Also, under unit production technology, relatively higher levels of skills may be necessary at the worker level; in terms of technical knowledge of the job, the methods, the tools, knowledge about operating errors, inspection skills and control. Under these conditions employees are more likely to perform effectively when they are given more freedom on the job. Research suggests that, compared to unskilled workers, skilled workers feel more involved in their jobs and are more eager for an opportunity to participate in making job related decisions.[13] Consequently, under these conditions the leader is *able* to exercise more democratic supervision.

Technology may determine the extent to which the job may be programmed (i.e., employee behaviors may be precisely specified). The kind of leadership required under low task structure is not the same as the kind of behavior required under high task structure.[14] It is meaningless to talk of permitting exercise of discretion to assembly line workers; the very nature of this technology requires that all the essential decisions be centrally programmed. Democratic supervision works best where the *nature of the job* permits the employee to enjoy autonomy.

Division of Work   Ability to delegate is affected by the way in which work is divided among people—the greater the specialization and fragmentation, the less the delegation possible. Functional departmentation based on similarity and relatedness of activities is frequently appropriate for the earlier stages of a company's growth. But as organizations mature, other variations in departmentation may be tried.

The "integrated task team" is a recent form of grouping work, emphasizing a system's approach to work processing. All people who must coordinate their tasks to achieve a common goal are placed together under a common supervisor. This type of departmentation minimizes the problems of coordination and communication that are inevitable in a functionally grouped workforce. Under the integrated task team concept, people handle problems on a face-to-face basis with a minimum of bureaucratic friction among specialized functional areas.

The manner in which the work activities are organized will inevitably influence the style of leadership. People who work near one another and identify with the same group find it much easier to share the information they need to coordinate their jobs than do people who have infrequent contact with one another under a functional arrangement. The task team shares a relatively autonomous task. Each member of the group feels responsible for the entire organization. Under such circumstances competent internal coordination and group responsibility develops. It is far easier to exercise democratic supervision.

Work Flow   The amount of discretion given to subordinates seems to vary according to the work flow and type of specialization within the company. Parallel specialization occurs where work flow is organized so as to minimize the amount of coordination and interaction among individuals and departments. Interdependence specialization occurs where the activities of one individual or department are closely dependent on other individuals or departments.[15] Unit production technology often leads to parallel specialization while mass production technology leads to interdependent specialization.

Under unit-production, employees see themselves as responsible for a total product process and are able to see the total result of their efforts. For these reasons, under parallel specialization, a more democratic style of supervision may be appropriate.

Interdependent specialization is characterized by many more lateral relationships required to obtain effective coordination between specialized groups. Subordinates develop a "vested interest" in their own typical point of view or approach to problems and are unable to see the impact of their actions on others. Since only the personnel at the top (the managers) would be able to see the overall picture and integrate the efforts of different parts in order to achieve the overall organizational goals, they would tend to delegate less authority and rely on more autocratic methods of supervision.

Certainty of Task   Some studies show that leadership style may be related to the degree of certainty about the task in question. Fiedler[16] has assembled data from a variety of situations to relate leadership style to group effectiveness in performing tasks of varying certainty. He has found that where leaders have friendly relations with their groups but relatively few sanctions and rewards to offer, an uncertain task is best handled by a passive, permissive and considerate leadership style. On the other hand, under similar conditions with a highly structured, certain task, a more controlling and active leader is more effective.

These are just two examples of a number of possible situations involving different degrees of positional power and different types of leadership style which have been examined in Fiedler's work. It seems clear that different styles of leadership behavior lead to effective group performance in different conditions. Certainty of the group's task is one of the most important variables related to the effectiveness of a leadership style.

Organization Structure   "Tall" organizations are those that have several pyramidal levels of authority; "flat" structures have few. The tall organizations frequently lead to high supervisory ratios and therefore tend to encourage authoritarian supervision. With a relatively small number of subordinates, the supervisor is in a position to give detailed instructions and to exercise authoritarian control over each one. In a flat organization structure, with a relatively large number of subordinates, this type of supervision is often physically impossible. Since the supervisor frequently cannot make a decision on every problem, he tends to delegate more and appear more democratic.

The Sears, Roebuck Company study of tall vs. flat organizational structures concludes:

> Flatter, less complex structures, with a maximum of administrative decentralization, tend to create a potential for improved attitudes, more effective supervision, and greater individual responsibility and initiative among employees. Moreover, arrangements of this type encourage the development of individual expression and creativity which are so necessary to the personal satisfaction of employees and which are an essential ingredient of the democratic way of life.[17]

A New Leadership Model

The leadership style of a manager is a product of many forces: In the manager himself, in his subordinates, in the organizational system and in the dynamic situation which is of immediate concern. Leadership style seems to evolve through a complex and dynamic interaction between these four "subsystems" which can be depicted graphically as shown in the chart on p. 342.

These forces, acting and interacting simultaneously, shape the pattern of leadership chosen by every manager. Every manager, at every level of the organization, needs to achieve an integration of these varying and complex pressures. Not only must he react to the many pressures and demands of environment, but he needs to understand those forces within himself, the individuals and groups he is dealing with and the forces existing in the organization in order to *adjust* his style of leadership accordingly.

The successful manager is neither an autocrat, nor a complete democrat, rather one who integrates the forces operating in relation to the particular

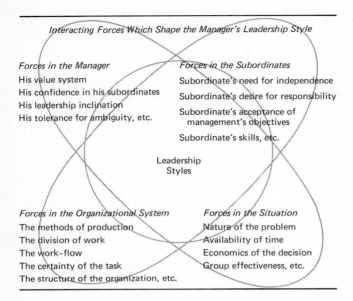

Interacting Forces Which Shape the Manager's Leadership Style

Forces in the Manager
His value system
His confidence in his subordinates
His leadership inclination
His tolerance for ambiguity, etc.

Forces in the Subordinates
Subordinate's need for independence
Subordinate's desire for responsibility
Subordinate's acceptance of
    management's objectives
Subordinate's skills, etc.

Leadership
Styles

Forces in the Organizational System
The methods of production
The division of work
The work–flow
The certainty of the task
The structure of the organization, etc.

Forces in the Situation
Nature of the problem
Availability of time
Economics of the decision
Group effectiveness, etc.

situation in question. The behavior of an effective leader under specific techno-logical considerations may lead to failure under other technological situations. The leadership appropriate in one organizational system may be irrelevant or even dysfunctional in another system.

Questions about leadership style should be answered in terms of what is most consistent with the other elements in the organization. For, in the long run, these system variables may be more useful for identifying and predicting the styles of leadership leading to optimal management in your organization.

References

1   Tead, Ordway, *The Art of Leadership* (New York: McGraw-Hill Book Company, Inc., 1935), p. 83.

2   Goulder, Alvin W. (ed.), *Studies in Leadership* (New York: Harper & Brothers, 1950), pp. 31–35.

3   Sanford, Fillmore H., "Leadership Identification Acceptance," in Harold Guetzkow (ed.), *Groups, Leadership and Men* (Pittsburgh: Carnegie Press, 1951), p. 156.

4   Stogdill, Ralph M., "Personal Factors Associated with Leadership: A Survey of the Literature," *Journal of Psychology,* January 1948, p. 63.

5   Gibb, Cecil A., "The Principles and Traits of Leadership," *Journal of Abnormal and Social Psychology,* July 1947, p. 267.

6   Bennis, Warren G., "Leadership Theory and Administrative Behavior: The Problem of Authority," *Administrative Science Quarterly,* December 1959, p. 261.

7   Tannenbaum, Robert, and Fred Massarik, "Leadership: A Frame of Reference," in *Leadership and Organization* (eds.) Robert Tannenbaum, et. al. (New York, McGraw-Hill Book Company, Inc., 1961), p. 24.

8   Adapted from Berelson, Bernard, and Gary A. Steiner, *Human Behavior: An Inventory of Scientific Findings* (New York: Harcourt, Brace & World, Inc., 1964), p. 347.

9   Tannenbaum, Robert, and Warren H. Schmidt, "How to Choose a Leadership Pattern," in *Leadership and Organization,* op. cit., pp. 67–79.

10   Woodward, Joan, *Management and Technology* (London: Her Majesty's Stationery Office, 1958). Also, Woodward, Joan, *Industrial Organization: Theory and Practice* (New York: Oxford University Press, 1965).

11   The major categories of production methods are: *Unit production*—production of a single non-standardized unit to customer order: one kind of item; *mass production*—standardized parts and products produced in large batches on assembly lines; *process production*—continuous flow of production, largely of liquids, gases and crystalline substances.

12   Management intensity is defined as the ratio of managers and supervisory staff to other personnel in the organization.

13   Vollmer, Howard, *Employment Rights and the Employment Relationship* (Berkeley: University of California Press, 1960), Chapter 4.

14   This important variable is designated by Fiedler. For details see: Fiedler, F. E., *A Contingency Model of Leadership Effectiveness,* Technical Report #10 (Urbana, Ill. Group Effectiveness Research Laboratory, University of Illinois, 1963). (Mimeograph).

15   Sayles, Leonard R., and George Strauss, *Human Behavior in Organizations* (Englewood Cliffs, N.J.: Prentice-Hall, Inc. 1966), p. 177.

16   Fiedler, F. E., "Engineer the Job to Fit the Manager," *Harvard Business Review,* September–October, 1965, pp. 115–122.

17   Worthy, James C., "Factors Influencing Employee Morale," *Harvard Business Review,* January 1950, pp. 169–179.

Reading 30

Managerial Behavior in Upwardly Oriented Organizations

Richard B. Higgins

In the past decade or so, managers have been urged to abandon a "directive" leadership approach to involve subordinates in the decision-making process and be more "democratic" with their subordinates. Such advice seems to conflict with earlier notions of "effective" managerial behavior—that the successful manager is a strong, aggressive leader of men. The net result has been confusion and a growing list of unanswered questions: Is participative management always the

"Managerial Behavior in Upwardly Oriented Organizations," Richard B. Higgins. © 1972 by The Regents of the University of California. Reprinted from *California Management Review,* vol. 14, no. 3, pp. 49–59, by permission of the Regents.

best approach? Under what circumstances is shared decision-making appropriate? When is a more directive approach likely to be successful? The reply, "It all depends on the situation" probably accords with the experience of most managers, but raises the question, "What situational factors influence organizational effectiveness?"

Many researchers have pursued the question of "one best way" of managing and/or organizing people with some interesting results.[1] Effective organizational performance is the result of a "proper fit" among a number of factors: organizational structure and climate (including managerial behavior), the nature of tasks to be performed (including the degree of routinization of tasks) and the people that make up the organization (including their needs and motivations).

While a growing body of research data support the idea that a fit and not a formula may be the key to enhancing organizational effectiveness, some important questions remain unanswered: What kind of managerial behavior represents a "good fit" with routinized tasks in organizations that are highly centralized? Is a directive leadership approach the answer? If so, why? How do well-defined tasks, a centralized structure and a directive leadership approach "fit" with the needs of the human personality? In such an organizational climate, does middle management experience prepare executives for top-level jobs?

We have been involved in a study that provides some interesting insights into these questions. Our research indicated that a good fit among organization, tasks, and people can be achieved by either a democratic or a directive leadership approach. Nothing in our study pointed to the superiority of a single leadership style or approach. Democratic managers and autocratic (directive) managers shared both top and bottom billing and were about evenly divided among effective and less effective operating units.

In certain kinds of organizations, the interface between the manager and his organizational superior (a "followership" relationship) may be more important than the leadership relationship between the manager and his subordinates. In a centralized organization, with routinized tasks, aggressive personality characteristics and behavior (frequently associated with effective top management performance) is apt to be inversely related to middle management effectiveness. Successful middle managers show a high degree of responsiveness to superiors, displaying a fairly high "need to defer to authority." Less effective managers are more aggressive, displaying a lower degree of responsiveness to superiors and showing a greater need for autonomy. The reason for the greater effectiveness of the "upwardly responsive" manager appears to be rooted in the nature of the fit among organization, task, and individual Figures 1 and 2 summarize some of the organizational and managerial characteristics that tend to enhance (or detract from) a good fit (congruence). We have assigned the term "upwardly oriented" to those organizations which are characterized by a high degree of task structure, low levels of employee skills and expectations, traditional reward and incentive systems, and centralized control. As Figure 1 indicates, individual characteristics such as a high need to defer to authority appear to be congruent with the upwardly

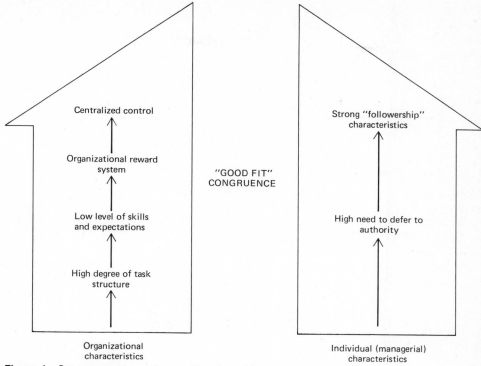

Figure 1   Congruence in an "upwardly oriented" organization.

oriented organization. Conversely, a high need for autonomy, aggressiveness, and a lower need to defer to authority appear to conflict with the major characteristics of the upwardly oriented organization.

THE STUDY DESIGN

Our study was conducted in a large supermarket chain organization and included eighty-eight store managers. The objective was to determine the impact (if any) of the store manager's leadership approach and other individual characteristics on the operating performance of his store. We wanted to know: Does the local manager significantly influence the sales, volume, productivity and profitability performance of his store, and if so, how?[2]

Phase I

Phase I was designed to determine the relationship among a wide array of locational factors—intensity of competition, population of primary trading area (p.t.a.), income of p.t.a., and store performance. The results of computations using

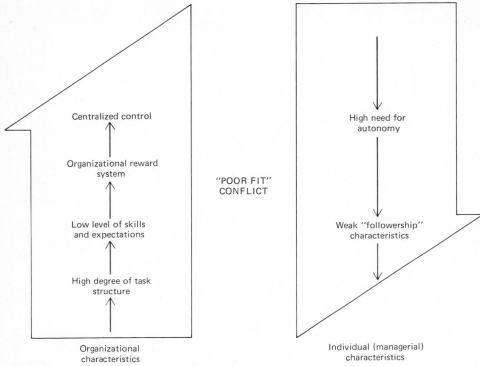

Figure 2 Conflict in an "upwardly oriented" organization.

factor analysis and multiple correlation analysis were interesting. Location factors did tell a very significant story about sales volume, accounting for 85 percent of the fluctuations among stores. However, these market factors told a much less complete story about variations in profitability, accounting for less than 60 percent of the fluctuations among stores. With over 40 percent of the variations in profitability unexplained by location factors, it became apparent that something or somebody was intervening between store sales volume and the bottom line on the monthly operating statement. Evidence seemed to point to the local manager as that somebody.

Phase II

What appeared to be a detour in the original research plans proved to be a vital step. In order to be able to measure the *relative impact* of the local manager on store performance, we needed to isolate the influence of the manager from a wide array of external factors. In Phase I we accomplished the following:

  •   Determined that factors other than store location were "responsible" for store performance—particularly store profitability.

Identified the most significant location factors and developed a method of allowing for the influence of these factors in our study of the store manager.

In Phase II of the study, we related various characteristics of the store manager to fluctuations in store performance—fluctuations unexplained by location factors. One of the managerial characteristics included in the study was leadership approach. We were very interested in determining if there was any relationship between the leadership style of the store managers and store performance. In addition, certain personality characteristics and needs of managers (for instance, the need to defer to authority, the need to achieve and the need to belong to groups) were related to store performance, using multiple correlation analysis. The personality characteristics and needs were measured by the *Perception and Preference Inventory* (PAPI) test, developed by Dr. M. M. Kostick and the Applied Psychology Associates of Brookline, Massachusetts.[3]

MAJOR FINDINGS

1 The "Human Relator" vs. the "Profit Planner"

The results of our study, as presented in Figure 3, tended to reinforce the findings of earlier human relations research when productivity was used as a measure of store performance. Specifically, the high productivity manager (the manager with the more productive store under his supervision) displayed a relatively high social orientation and need to belong to groups. Given the opportunity to satisfy his social needs, this manager was inclined to interact frequently with his subordinates and others. In fact, he was not above helping out on the floor (a relatively low need to assume an active leadership role) in order to solve daily crises. He also had a relatively weak inclination to plan ahead.

Figure 3   Summary of Net Correlation Analysis Results

Independent variables (managerial characteristics)	Dependent variables	
	Productivity[a]	Profitability[b]
Need to assume a strong leadership role	−.28507[c]	+.16840
Need to belong to group	+.26607	−.16639
Planning orientation	−.33271	+.27979
Need to defer to authority	+.05482	+.21648
Years in food industry	−.02154	+.19673

[a]*Productivity* measured by sales per dollar of store wages
[b]*Profitability* measured by store operating gain as a percent of sales volume
[c]Statistical significance, where n = 88, at .10 level = .1904
at .05 level = .2260

Figure 4   Profit Planner vs. Human Relator

High productivity mgr. vs. low productivity mgr.	High profitability mgr. vs. low profitability mgr.	High profitability mgr. vs. the high productivity mgr.
—lower need to assume leadership role.	—stronger planning orientation.	—stronger planning orientation.
—stronger social needs and affiliation needs.	—higher need to defer to authority.	—higher need to assume active leadership role.
—lower inclination to plan ahead.	—more years of experience in the food industry.	—greater need to defer to authority.
	—weaker social orientation and need for affiliation.	

However, when managerial effectiveness and success were measured by store profitability, a considerably different picture emerged. The more successful profitability manager showed a weaker social orientation, a less intense need to interact with people and a stronger need to assume an active leadership role. In addition, he had a far greater inclination to plan activities, to head off trouble on the floor before it occurred. This planning orientation of the successful profitability manager contrasted rather sharply with the high productivity manager.

To summarize, the socially oriented manager was quite successful when success was measured in terms of productivity. However, when profitability was the measure of managerial effectiveness, the high productivity manager was among the less successful in the company. The reverse tended to be true for the successful profitability manager. Figure 4 summarizes these findings.

2   The Democrat vs. the Autocrat

Our study of eighty-eight store managers failed to reveal any significant relationships between leadership approach and organizational effectiveness, whatever measure of effectiveness used. There were approximately as many self-evaluated autocrats among the group of more effective managers as there were among the group of less effective managers. The distribution of democratic or participative managers among the less effective and more effective managerial groups was also about evenly divided.

Of greater significance than the search for a single, most effective leadership approach was the relationship revealed between the leadership style of the manager and what he perceived to be the leadership philosophy of the company as a whole. Approximately three-quarters of the managers of the forty-four most successful stores perceived their attitudes toward leadership to be in line with company philosophy. On the other hand, almost one-half of the managers in the forty-four less successful stores perceived their leadership approach to be in conflict with company philosophy. This strongly suggests that a good fit among individual and organizational chacteristics, rather than any single leadership style, is a key determinant of organizational effectiveness. Figure 5 summarizes our data on the fit between a manager's leadership approach and his perceived company philosophy.

3 The Upwardly Oriented Manager

One of the individual characteristics shared by successful managers in all categories of store performance (sales volume, productivity and profitability) was a relatively high need to defer to authority—a tendency to seek guidance and direction from organization superiors and an inclination to display an upward orientation. Only the relationship between the need to defer to authority and profitability proved to be statistically significant at the .10 level. Further evidence of this upward orientation was the tendency of successful managers to enjoy a close fit between their own leadership approach and what they perceived to be the company leadership philosophy. Close fit could be the result of several processes: an alignment of leadership approaches could be a completely random affair or it could be the result of a selective process of promotion and placement of personnel within the company. Several factors argue that a good fit was due to the adaptive

Figure 5 Congruence and Conflict in Leadership Approaches

Nature of "fit"	44 most suc- cessful stores*	44 less suc- cessful stores*
Good Fit—congruence Percent of managers whose self-evaluated leadership approach was consistent with their perception of company leadership philosophy	72.7%	54.6%
Poor Fit—conflict Percent of managers whose self-evaluated leadership approach differed from their perception of company leadership philosophy	27.3%	45.4%

*Based on a composite measurement combining sales, volume, productivity and profitability performance of stores.

behavior of upwardly oriented managers who took their "cues" from organizational superiors. Those managers who believed that their leadership approach was consistent with company philosophy had a higher need to defer to authority than their counterparts who perceived conflict in leadership approaches.

To summarize, few of the significant managerial characteristics identified in this study support the notion of the successful manager as a bold, innovative, entrepreneurial individual. Contrary to the assumptions of some top executives within the company, the local manager did make a difference, but in an unexpected way. Dynamic aggressive individuals were among the less successful managers in the company. The less aggressive manager, the individual with a greater need to defer to authority, made the positive difference in store performance. On the other hand, our study results failed to support the idea that either a participative or an autocratic approach to managing people is necessarily more effective. Rather, our findings tend to underscore the critical importance of a fit between organization, task and individual. The degree or goodness of fit appears to be a prime determinant of individual and organizational effectiveness.

ORGANIZATIONAL CHARACTERISTICS

Any interpretation of the above findings must attempt to answer at least two questions:

- What is there in this organization that encourages upward orientation—a climate in which, according to one manager, you have to figure out what kind of person your boss is and then play the game his way?
- Why and how does a good fit between individual and organizational orientation enhance organizational effectiveness?

Enabling Factors

Three closely interrelated organizational characteristics combine to allow or permit the local manager to display an upward orientation: the nature of the work load, the degree of employee task structure and the skill levels and expectations of subordinates. Fluctuations in store work load, caused by periods of peak customer demand, encourage the employment of part-time employees to perform tasks that are highly structured. Because of the routinization of these tasks, the local manager is able to staff for fluctuations in work load using unskilled employees who, because of their low skill level, part-time status, and relationship with the company, bring to the job rather modest expectations. With relatively low expectations and without a marketable skill to bolster their bargaining position within the company, the pressures that these subordinates put on the store manager are minimized. Although the above comments apply to part-time employees (who work approximately two-thirds of the store hours worked in a week), many of the same observations apply to full-time employees also.

Routinization of merchandise re-ordering and inventory control procedures have tended to structure the tasks of department heads as well.

The overall impact of this combination of factors—skill level, task structure and employee expectations—tends to insulate the manager from pressures generated from below and provide him with the opportunity to look upward with confidence that he will not have too much trouble with his subordinates. If the store manager is viewed as the man in the middle, he then appears to be spared (or at least partially relieved) from one of the most persistent pressures that confronts the first-line supervisor in industry. The net effect of these organizational factors is to provide the manager with an insulation, an opportunity to maintain a "psychological distance" or certain remoteness from his subordinates. Such a social detachment does not prevent the manager from maintaining contact with subordinates but it does allow him to be far enough away to deal objectively with poor performance.[4]

Reinforcement Factors

If the above organizational factors provide the manager with an opportunity to concentrate much of his attention in an upward direction, other more positive organizational characteristics serve to encourage and reinforce an upward managerial orientation. One such factor is a reward and incentive system which further sensitizes the store manager to signals from above. Not only is the zone manager (the store manager's immediate superior) responsible for the personal development of his managers, but the zone manager is also influential in distributing promotions and raises. Inasmuch as the zone manager's position is typically filled from the ranks of store managers, it is understandable that the store manager views his boss as a vital link in his career progress.

Finally, the opportunities and inducements which encourage an upward managerial orientation appear to coincide with a desire on the part of top management to maintain a close control over store operations. The influence exerted by staff merchandisers in their relationships with local personnel and the impact of a computerized merchandising and inventory control system are just two of the forces operating toward centralized control.

Another, perhaps more subtle, influence appears to be home office control. The more successful store managers were individuals with many years of experience in the industry as well as the company. It is likely that managers with an average of twenty years of experience are programmed with the kinds of operating knowledge of the industry and company which precludes the necessity for close supervision from the home office. Top management is able to predict, with some confidence, that these managers will react to routine problem situations in a manner consistent with sound industry practices, as well as accepted company policies and procedures. To an outsider such an apparent freedom from home office scrutiny may be misinterpreted. With a corps of experienced, programmed managers, a kind of de facto centralization may exist which displays many of the appearances of a decentralized organization.

However, regardless of the methods used to achieve home office control, one of the significant results of centralization is the further stimulation that it provides for an upward managerial orientation. This final factor institutionalizes an upward orientation within the organization.

Upward Orientation and Organizational Effectiveness

Certainly not all store managers included in this study displayed an upward orientation. However, to the extent that a relatively high need to defer to authority reflects upward orientation, then it must be concluded that this orientation is not only widely shared; it is also held by the most effective managers in the company. Enjoying a close fit with the organization, the upwardly oriented manager is able to satisfy his own needs while being exposed to a minimum of conflict between individual needs and organizational pressures.

A manager with a personal orientation that is compatible with that of the organization does more than just "fit into the system," although undoubtedly this is important. In addition, improved performance effectiveness may be the result of opportunities provided to the "congruent" manager. The individual who fulfills the expectations of his superior is rewarded not only in career terms (promotions, raises, and so on), but also in daily operational terms. A compatibility in orientation encourages an interchange between the store manager and his boss which may very well improve the effectiveness of store operations. Whether such an interchange furnishes the local manager with inside tips on future merchandising and promotional schemes or merely provides him with the benefit of his superiors' greater experience is not entirely clear. In either case such interchanges can lead to improvements in store performance.

Conversely, the less successful manager displays a lower need to defer to authority, a less forceful set of followership characteristics and a weaker upward orientation. Why is the more aggressive manager less effective in this company? An answer to this question may be found in the clash between organizational and individual orientations. The amount of damage that is produced in such a conflict situation is difficult to assess. Since the achievement of organizational goals is closely interrelated with the satisfaction of individual needs, such a conflict probably detracts from managerial effectiveness. Also, in such a conflict situation the likelihood of a productive interchange between store manager and his boss is considerably reduced.

IMPLICATIONS FOR MANAGERS

The major focus of our study has been a particular kind of fit—a welding of individual, task and organization into an upward orientation. Although the managerial implications of achieving a good fit go beyond this type of an alignment, there are some special issues raised in the upwardly oriented organization. For example, do certain characteristics of the upwardly oriented organization (centralized control, well-defined tasks, and followership behavior) fit personality needs? Do these characteristics produce a climate that inhibits individual growth and development? Is a good fit and short-run organizational effectiveness purchased at the expense of long-run growth and development?

Some have seized upon the characteristics of the upwardly oriented organization to argue that the needs of the individual are basically incompatible with the requirements of formal organization.[5] Upward orientation is both the cause and effect of dependency relationship (subordinate to boss) which inhibits the growth and development of the mature personality. (In our study, we have no way of determining whether those managers who displayed an upward orientation were made that way by the organization or whether they were guided (or drifted) into their present positions as a part of a matching process. We do know that the strength of people's needs vary and that presumably some have a greater need for autonomy than others. Managers included in our study varied all the way from a very low need to defer to authority to a relatively high need). To address this basic conflict between individual and organization, it is suggested that we alter those organizational characteristics which encourage an upward orientation; tasks must be enlarged, controls should be self-imposed, leadership must become participative, and so forth. In short, we must reverse the organization's directional orientation.

This is sound advice for many firms. Where tasks are ill-defined and loosely formulated, where individuals indicate a strong need for autonomy and good fit among organization, task and people points in the direction of a downward orientation. To predict that such a trend may gather momentum in the future, one has only to look at the challenges to traditional concepts of authority and power in our society today. And yet, there are some indications that the upwardly oriented organization will not disappear completely from the scene. For one thing, some people seem to prefer it.[6] Furthermore, as our study has indicated, under some circumstances, an upwardly oriented organization appears to provide a good fit among structure, task and people. This good fit seems to be related to organizational effectiveness. Finally, the influence of technology must be reckoned with. Because of its present technology, some organizations may be locked into an upward orientation. For example, in an assembly plant where many tasks are predictable and routine (and a considerable investment has been staked in this routinization), it is hard to conceive of job enlargement making serious inroads. Other organizations, enticed by the anticipated benefits of new technology, may discover that one of the unintended consequences of this new computer technology is a thrust toward a greater upward orientation.[7]

But what of the opportunities for individual growth and development in the upwardly oriented organization? Do such organizations undermine the development opportunities for middle management? Is it necessary to search for a different combination of situational factors to achieve a good fit at top management levels? These questions point to what is potentially the greatest hidden cost associated with upward orientation, the problems and difficulties of creating a climate where executive talent can blossom and flourish. Organizations cannot permit their accounting systems to keep these costs out of sight.

An interest in achieving a good fit to do today's job must be matched by a concern for developing human resources to do tomorrow's jobs well. An engineering approach to fitting organization, tasks and people (designing structure and tasks to fit the needs of people and then placing the right people in the right jobs), must be back-stopped by what Douglas McGregor has called an "agricultural" approach. The basis of this agricultural approach lies in providing an organizational climate where individual growth and development can occur. While the developmental climate and the learning process in an upwardly oriented organization will differ considerably from a downwardly oriented organization, we will not deny the possibility of growth and development in the former. Much more study is needed here, both of the environmental requisites for individual growth and development and the learning process itself.

In arguing for both an engineering and an agricultural approach to matching people, tasks and organization, we hope to put to rest the question—Which is more important: selection and placement of personnel or management development; organizational structure or people? Both have their place in the fitting process, although, obviously, the relative emphasis given to one or the other will depend on the nature of the organization, its technology, tasks and people.

Yet, the fitting process will go on, whether by engineering, agriculture, or chance. Some organizations will obtain a better fit than others. Some matches will enhance organizational effectiveness; others will detract from it. After considering the long-term well-being of the organization (the unintended consequences and hidden costs associated with different approaches) some firms will lean in the direction of a downward orientation. Others will favor an upward orientation. The wisdom of these decisions will be reflected in the goodness of fit among the organization, its tasks and its people.

IMPLICATIONS FOR FUTURE RESEARCH

It has become a commonplace observation that every manager assumes at least two roles within his organization: a subordinate in the hierarchy and a leader of his own people. There is a growing body of evidence which indicates that these two roles, while not necessarily incompatible, are quite different.[8]

Much of the behavioral science research undertaken in the past two decades has focused on the second of these two roles—the leadership role and the leader-subordinate relationship. One of the assumptions underlying these studies seems to be the idea that a downward orientation is, or should be, the predominant organizational climate in business firms today. Having accepted this proposition, it follows that the manager-subordinate interaction deserves detailed and extensive study.

And yet surely many organizations share the kinds of bureaucratic characteristics which tend to encourage an upward orientation. True, there are unique situational variables in our study which make generalization hazardous: techno-logical developments of the past several years, the personality and philosophy of certain executives within the company and changing competitive and market environments to name a few. Nevertheless, there are many organizations which have similar reward and control systems, relatively structured tasks and unskilled employees who bring low levels of expectations to their jobs. We would predict that in organizations where such factors do exist, encouraging an upward orientation, managers enjoying a compatibility with this organizational orientation will be among the most effective managers. A prime determinant of the manager's ability to fit in will be followership characteristics such as a high need to defer to authority.

Incidentally, in such organizations, the alignment of leadership philosophies within the hierarchy may be viewed not only as a product of the behavior of an upwardly oriented manager, but also as a tentative *confirmation* of the upward orientation of these managers. The findings of this study suggest that an alignment of leadership philosophies and a congruency in orientation, rather than the

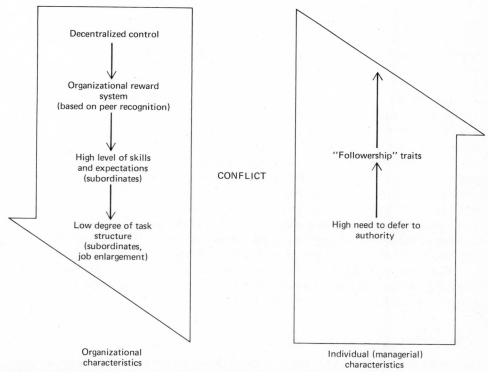

Figure 6 Conflict in a "downwardly (or laterally) oriented" organization.

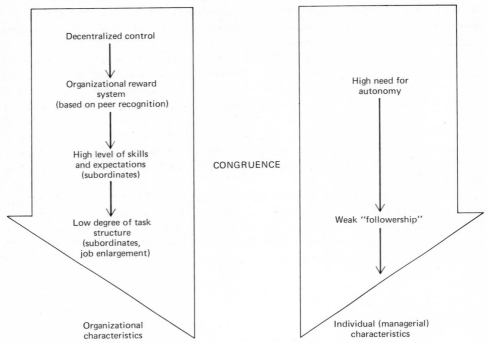

Figure 7   Congruence in a "downwardly (or laterally) oriented" organization.

inherent superiority of any one leadership philosophy, are significant factors influencing managerial effectiveness.

It would also be interesting to observe the managerial characteristics and behavior of successful managers in organizations characterized by a low degree of task structure, higher levels of subordinate skills and expectations and a reward system based on recognition from peers or sources outside of the organizational hierarchy. In this type of an organization (for example, a research laboratory) such factors, if not encouraging a downward orientation, would certainly alleviate the pressures for upward orientation. In this case the individual with a high need to defer to authority will probably find himself in conflict with the organizations orientation and may be hampered in his effectiveness as a manager (see Figure 6).

Conversely, in the downwardly oriented organization, we would predict that a relatively high need for autonomy would be a managerial characteristic directly related to effective performance (see Figure 7).

CONCLUSION

The major thrust of recent findings in the field of leadership research expresses a skepticism of leadership success formulas, whether such formulas are presented in terms of success traits of the leader or effective managerial styles. Rather, the leadership process represents a complex and dynamic interaction among many variables. Viewed in this light, the formula for leadership effectiveness is a product of many situational factors: an interplay among the needs and interests of subordinates, characteristics of the leader and a broad spectrum of organizational factors that range from the degree of task structure to the philosophy of top management.

And yet many of the variables that researchers continue to look at are to be found in the climate of the downwardly oriented organization—leader-membership relations, the power position of the leader, and so on. Without denying the importance of the manager-subordinate relationship, it does seem that future research might profitably explore the interface between managers and their organizational superiors in upwardly oriented firms. Where such an orientation has been institutionalized, the relationship between manager and boss, the followership characteristics of the manager and his behavior as a subordinate may be among the critical determinants of organizational effectiveness.

References

1 See Fred E. Fiedler, *A Contingency Model for the Prediction of Leadership Effectiveness,* Group Effectiveness Research Laboratory, Department of Psychology, University of Illinois, 1963.
   Also, George Strauss and Leonard Sayles, *Human Behavior in Organizations* (New York: Prentice-Hall), pp. 175ff and 226ff.
   Also, John J. Morse and Jay W. Lorsch, "Beyond Theory Y," *Harvard Business Review* (May–June, 1970).
   Also, Robert C. Albrook, "Participative Management: Time for a Second Look," *Fortune* (May, 1967).
2 "Sales" is measured by annual store volume; "productivity" is measured by sales per dollar of wages; "profitability" is measured as store operating gain as % of sales.
3 For a more detailed description of research methodology see *Determinants of Differential Performance: A Study of the Impact of the Local Manager in a Large Supermarket Chain,* unpublished doctoral dissertation, Columbia University, 1968.
4 Francis M. Carp, Bart M. Vitola and Frank L. McLananathan, "Human Relations Knowledge and Social Distance Set in Supervisors" *Journal of Applied Psychology* (XLVII, 1963), p. 80.
5 See Chris Argyris, *Personality and Organization* (New York: Harper Bros., 1957).
6 See Victor H. Vroom, *Some Personality Determinants of the Effect of Participation* (Englewood Cliffs: Prentice-Hall, 1960).
7 See Leavitt and Whistler, "Management in the 1980's," *Harvard Business Review* (Nov.–Dec., 1958).
8 Abraham Zaleznik, "The Dynamics of Subordinacy," *Harvard Business Review* (May–June, 1965).

Reading 31
How Do You Make Leaders
More Effective?
New Answers to an Old Puzzle
Fred E. Fiedler

Let's begin with a basic proposition: The organization that employs the leader is as responsible for his success or failure as the leader himself. Not that this is a new insight—far from it. Terman wrote in 1904 that leadership performance depends on the situation, as well as on the leader. Although this statement would not be questioned by anyone currently working in this area, it also has been widely ignored. Practically all formal training programs attempt to change the individual; many of them assume explicitly or implicitly that there is one style of leadership or one way of acting that will work best under all conditions. Most military academies, for example, attempt to mold the individual into a supposedly ideal leader personality. Others assume that the training should enable the individual to become more flexible or more sensitive to his environment so that he can adapt himself to it.

Before going further let's define a few terms. I will confine my discussion to *task groups* rather than the organization of which the group is a part. Furthermore, we will assume that anyone who is placed in a leadership position will have the requisite technical qualifications for the job. Just as the leader of a surgical team obviously has to have medical training, so a manager must know the essential administrative requirements of his job. We will here talk primarily about training *as a leader* rather than training as a specialist. The effectiveness of the leader will be defined in terms of how well his group or organization performs the primary tasks for which the group exists. We measure the effectiveness of a football coach by how many games his team wins and not by the character he builds, and the excellence of an orchestra conductor by how well his orchestra plays, not by the happiness of his musicians' or his ability as a musicologist. Whether the musicians' job satisfaction or the conductor's musicological expertness do, in fact, contribute to the orchestra's excellence is an interesting question in its own right, but it is not what people pay to hear. Likewise, the performance of a manager is here measured in terms of his department's or group's effectiveness in doing its assigned job. Whether the accomplishment of this job is to be measured after a week or after five years depends, of course, upon the assignment the organization gives the group, and the accomplishments the organization considers important.

When we think of improving leadership, we almost automatically think of training the individual. This training frequently involves giving the man a new perspective on his supervisory responsibilities by means of role playing, discus-

"How Do You Make Leaders More Effective? New Answers to an Old Puzzle," Fred E. Fiedler, *Organizational Dynamics*, Autumn 1972, pp. 3–18. Reprinted with permission.

sions, detailed instructions on how to behave toward subordinates, as well as instruction in the technical and administrative skills he will need in his job. A training program might last a few days, a few months, or as in the case of college programs and military academies, as long as four years. What is the hard evidence that this type of training actually increases organizational performance?

Empirical studies to evaluate the effectiveness of various leadership training programs, executive development, and supervisory workshops have been generally disappointing. Certainly, the two field experiments and two studies of ongoing organizations conducted by my associates and me failed to show that training increases organizational performance.

The first experiment in 1966 was conducted at a Belgian naval training center. We chose 244 Belgian recruits and 48 petty officers from a pool of 546 men. These men were assembled into 96 three-men groups: 48 groups had petty officers and 48 groups had recruits as leaders. The recruits ranged in age from 17 to 24, and none had been in the service longer than six weeks. The petty officers ranged in age from 19 to 45 years, and had an average of ten years' experience. All petty officers had received a two-year technical and leadership training course at petty officer candidate school. Since most successful graduates enlist for a 20-year term, Belgian petty officers are not only well-trained but they are also truly motivated and committed career men.

The petty officers were matched with the recruit leaders on intelligence and other relevant scores. Each group worked on four cooperative tasks which were considered fair samples of the type of work petty officers might perform. One task consisted of writing a recruiting letter urging young men to join the Belgian navy as a career; the second and third tasks required the groups to find the shortest route for a convoy first through ten and then through twelve ports; the fourth task required the leader to train his men without using verbal instructions in the disassembling and reassembling of a .45-caliber automatic pistol.

Despite the fact that the recruits had had no leadership experience or training, their groups performed as well as those led by petty officers.

To test whether these results were not simply due to the chance or to a fault in our experimental design, we conducted a second experiment at a leadership training workshop for officers of Canadian military colleges. This study compared the performance of groups led by captains and majors with groups led by enlisted men who had just finished their eight weeks of basic training. All of the officers were, themselves, graduates of a Canadian military college. In addition, the officers had from 5 to 17 years of leadership experience and training after graduation. The 32 enlisted men were basic trainees between 19 and 22 years of age, and their intelligence scores were substantially below those of the officers'. To reduce the possibility that they might feel anxious or inhibited by working with officers, the officers wore casual clothes and the enlisted men were told that they would work with civilian instructors.

The officers and men worked as three-men groups on three different tasks. They were asked to (a) write a fable, (b) find the shortest route for a truck convoy, and *(c)* draw bar graphs from score distributions that first had to be converted from one scale to another. As in the Belgian study, the tasks were designed so that all three group members had to participate in the work. As in the Belgian study, the groups led by the trained and experienced officers performed no better than the groups led by untrained and inexperienced enlisted men.

It is, of course, possible that experimental tasks do not give realistic results. For this reason we further checked in real-life situations whether the amount of training influenced performance by a study of 171 managers and supervisors in U.S. post offices. The performance of each of these supervisors was rated by two to five of his superiors. Amount of training ranged from zero hours of training to three years, with a median of 45 hours. The number of hours of supervisory training received by these managers was totally unrelated to their rated performance. We also investigated whether the post offices with highly trained supervisors were more effective on such objective post office performance measures as target achievement in number of first-class pieces handled, indirect costs, mail processing, etc. However, 12 of the 15 correlations were slightly *negative;* none was significant. Thus, training apparently did not improve organizational performance.

Another study related the amount of training received by police sergeants with the performance ratings made by their supervisors and other sergeants. Here again, training was unrelated to performance. Thus, neither the two controlled experiments nor the two field studies provide any basis for assuming that leadership training of the type given in these institutions, or in the training programs taken by postal managers or police sergeants, contributed to organizational performance.

I repeat that these findings are by no means unusual. Empirical studies to determine whether or not leadership training improves organizational performance have generally come up with negative findings. Newport, after surveying 121 large companies, concluded that not one of the companies had obtained any scientifically acceptable evidence that the leadership training for their middle management had actually improved performance.

T-group and sensitivity training, which has become fashionable in business and industry, has yielded similarly unsatisfactory results. Reviews of the literature by Campbell and Dunnette and by House found no convincing evidence that this type of training increased organizational effectiveness, and a well-known study at the International Harvester Company by Fleishman, Harris, and Burtt on the effects of supervisory training concluded that the effects of supervisory training in modifying behavior were very short-lived and did not improve performance.

EFFECT OF EXPERIENCE ON LEADERSHIP

Let us now ask whether supervisory experience improves performance. Actually, since leadership experience almost always involves on-the-job training, we are dealing with a closely related phenomenon.

Interestingly enough, the literature actually contains few, if any, studies which attempt to link leadership experience to organizational effectiveness. Yet, there seems to be a firmly held expectation that leadership experience makes a leader more effective. We simply have more trust in experienced leaders. We can infer this, for example, from the many regulations that require time in grade before promotion to the next higher level, as well as the many specifications of prior job in hiring executives for responsible positions.

We have already seen that the experienced petty officers and military academy officers did not perform more effectively than did the inexperienced enlisted men, nor did the more experienced officers or petty officers perform better than the less experienced.

In addition, we also analyzed data from various other groups and organizations. These included directors of research and development teams at a large physical research laboratory, foremen of craftshops, general foremen in a heavy machinery manufacturing company, managers of meat, and of grocery markets in a large supermarket chain as well as post office supervisors and managers, and police sergeants. For all these managers we could obtain reliable performance ratings or objective group effectiveness criteria. None of the correlations was significant in the expected direction. The median correlation relating leadership experience to leadership performance for all groups and organizations was $-.12$—certainly not significant in the positive direction!

To summarize the findings, neither orthodox leadership training nor leadership experience nor sensitivity training appear to contribute across the board to group or organizational effectiveness. It is, therefore, imperative first that we ask why this might be so, and second that we consider alternative methods for improving leadership performance.

THE CONTINGENCY MODEL

The "Contingency Model," a recent theory of leadership, holds that the effectiveness of group performance is contingent upon *(a)* the leader's motivational pattern, and *(b)* the degree to which the situation gives the leader power and influence. We have worked with a leadership motivation measure called the "Esteem for the Least Preferred Coworker," or LPC for short. The subject is first asked to think of all the people with whom he has ever worked, and then given a simple scale on which he describes the one person in his life with whom he has been able to work *least well.* This "least preferred coworker" may be someone he knows at the time, or it may be someone he has known in the past. It does not have to be a member of his present work group.

In grossly oversimplified terms, the person who describes his least preferred coworker in relatively favorable terms is basically motivated to have close interpersonal relations with others. By contrast, the person who rejects someone with whom he cannot work is basically motivated to accomplish or achieve on the task, and he derives satisfaction from being recognized as having performed well

Figure 1   Cells or "Octants"

	Very favorable			Intermediate in favorableness			Unfavorable	
	1	2	3	4	5	6	7	8
Leader-member relations	Good	Good	Good	Good	Poor	Poor	Poor	Poor
Task structure	High	High	Low	Low	High	High	Low	Low
Position power	Strong	Weak	Strong	Weak	Strong	Weak	Strong	Weak

on the task. The task-motivated person thus uses the task to obtain a favorable position and good interpersonal relations.

CLASSIFYING LEADERSHIP SITUATIONS

The statement that some leaders perform better in one kind of situation while some leaders perform better in different situations is begging a question. "What kinds of situations are best suited for which type of leader?" In other words, how can we best classify groups if we wish to predict leadership performance?

We can approach this problem by assuming that leadership is essentially a work relationship involving power and influence. It is easier to be a leader when you have complete control than when your control is weak and dependent on the good will of others. It is easier to be the captain of a ship than the chairman of a volunteer group organized to settle a school bussing dispute. The *job* may be more complex for the navy captain but *being in the leadership role* is easier for him than for the committee chairman. It is, therefore, not unreasonable to classify situations in terms of how much power and influence the situation gives the leader. We call this "situational favorableness." One simple categorization of groups on their situational favorableness classifies leadership situations on the basis of three major dimensions:

1 Leader-member relations. Leaders presumably have more power and influence if they have a good relationship with their members than if they have a poor relationship with them, if they are liked, respected, trusted, than if they are not. Research has shown that this is by far the most important single dimension.

2 Task structure. Tasks or assignments that are highly structured, spelled out, or programmed give the leader more influence than tasks that are vague, nebulous and unstructured. It is easier, for example, to be a leader whose task it is to set up a sales display according to clearly delineated steps than it is to be a chairman of a committee preparing a new sales campaign.

3 Position power. Leaders will have more power and influence if their position is vested with such prerogatives as being able to hire and fire, being able to discipline, to reprimand, and so on. Position power, as it is here used, is determined by how much power the leader has over his subordinates. If the janitor foreman can hire and fire, he has more position power in his own group than the chairman of a board of directors who, frequently, cannot hire or fire—or even reprimand his board members.

Using this classification method we can now roughly order groups as being high or low on each of these three dimensions. This gives us an eight-celled classification (Figure 1). This scheme postulates that it is easier to be a leader in groups that fall into Cell 1 since you are liked, have position power, and have a structured task. It is somewhat more difficult in Cell 2 since you are liked, have a structured task, but little position power, and so on to groups in Cell 8 where the leader is not liked, has a vague, unstructured task, and little position power. A good example of Cell 8 would be the disliked chairman of the volunteer committee we mentioned before.

The critical question is, "What kind of leadership does each of these different group situations call for?" Figure 2 summarizes the results of 63 analyses based on a total of 454 separate groups. These included bomber and tank crews, antiaircraft artillery units, managements of consumer cooperative companies, boards of directors, open-hearth shops, basketball and surveying teams, and various groups involved in creative and problem-solving tasks.

The horizontal axis of the group indicates the "situational favorableness," namely, the leader's control and influence as defined by the eight-fold classification shown in Figure 1. The vertical axis indicates the relationship between the

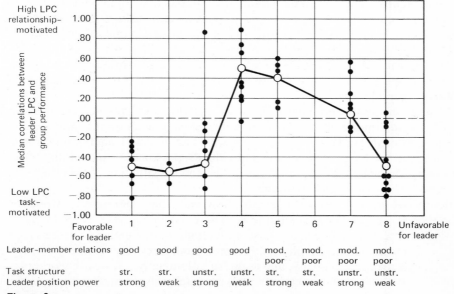

Figure 2

Figure 3   Prediction of the Performance of Relationship- and Task-motivated Leaders

	1	2	3	4	5	6	7	8
High LPC (relationship- motivated)				Good	Good	Some- what better	Some- what better	
LOW LPC (task- motivated)	Good	Good	Good					Good

leader's motivational pattern, as measured by the LPC score, and his group's performance. A median correlation above the midline shows that the relationship-motivated leaders tended to perform better than the task-motivated leaders. A correlation below the midline indicates that the task-motivated leaders performed better than the relationship-motivated leaders. Figure 3 shows the predictions that the model would make in each of the eight cells.

These findings have two important implications for our understanding of what makes leaders effective. First, Figure 2 tells us that the task-motivated leaders tend to perform better than relationship-motivated leaders in situations that are very favorable and in those that are unfavorable. Relationship-motivated leaders tend to perform better than task-motivated leaders in situations that are intermediate in favorableness. Hence, both the relationship-and the task-motivated leaders perform well under some conditions and not under others. It is, therefore, not correct to speak of any person as generally a good leader or generally a poor leader. Rather, a leader may perform well in one situation but not in another. This is also borne out by the repeated findings that we cannot predict a leader's performance on the basis of his personality traits, or even by knowing how well he performed on a previous task unless that task was similar in situational favorableness.

Second, the graph on Figure 2 shows that the performance of a leader depends as much on the situational favorableness as it does on the individual in the leadership position. Hence, the organization can change leadership performance either by trying to change the individual's personality and motivational pattern or by changing the favorableness of the leader's situation. As we shall see, this is really what training is all about.

Before we go further, we must ask how valid the Contingency Model is. How well does it predict in new situations? There have been at least 25 studies to date that have tested the theory. These validation studies included research on grocery and meat markets, a physical science laboratory, a machinery plant, a hospital, an electronics company, and teams of volunteer public health workers in Central America, as well as various experimentally assembled groups in the laboratory. Of particular importance is a large experiment that used cadets at

West Point to test the entire eight cells of the model. This study almost completely reproduced the curve shown on Figure 2. In all studies that were recently reviewed, 35 of the 44 obtained correlations were in the predicted direction—a finding that could have occurred by chance less than one time in 100. An exception is Cell 2, in which laboratory experiments—but not field studies—have yielded correlations showing the relationship-motivated leaders perform better than task-motivated leaders.

EFFECT OF LEADERSHIP TRAINING?

The main question of this paper is, of course, how we can better utilize leadership training and experience to improve leadership performance. While appropriate leadership training and experience apparently do not increase organizational performance, there is considerable evidence that they do affect the manager's attitudes, behavior, and of course, his technical skills and administrative know-how. These programs teach the leader better methods of getting along with his subordinates, more effective handling of administrative routines, as well as technical background required for the job. In other words, the leader who is trained or experienced will have considerably greater control and influence over his job and his subordinates than one who is untrained and inexperienced.

   In contrast, the inexperienced and untrained leader confronts numerous problems that are new to him, and for which he does not have a ready answer. As a result, he cannot give clear and concise instructions to his subordinates. Moreover, since so many situations are novel, he will be more anxious and less sure of himself, which will tend to make him more dependent upon his group and others in the organization. Not even the most detailed manual of operating instructions will enable a new manager to step into his job and behave as if he had been there for years. Thus, situations will be correspondingly less favorable for the untrained and inexperienced leader than for the trained and experienced leader.

   What we are really saying here is that leadership training and experience primarily improve the favorableness of the leadership situation. But, if the Contingency Model is right, a more favorable situation requires a different type of

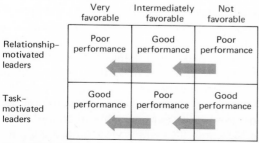

	Very favorable	Intermediately favorable	Not favorable
Relationship-motivated leaders	Poor performance	Good performance	Poor performance
Task-motivated leaders	Good performance	Poor performance	Good performance

Arrows indicate the predicted effect of experience and training

Figure 4   Favorableness of the situation for the trained or experienced leader.

leadership than a less favorable situation. Hence, leadership training and experience that will improve the performance of one type of leader *will decrease the
performance of the other.* On the average, it will have little or no measurable effect
on organizational performance. This is schematically shown by Figure 4. The
arrows indicate that effect of training and experience in improving the favorableness of the leadership situation.

The headings on Figure 4 indicate the situational favorableness for the
already trained or experienced leader. The untrained or inexperienced leader
obviously would face a correspondingly less favorable situation. Thus, while the
situation at the left of the table is very favorable for the trained leader, it is likely
to be intermediate for the leader who lacks training and experience. The training
or experience, as indicated by the arrow, would then change the untrained leader's
situation from one which is intermediate to one which is very favorable. Likewise,
if the trained leader's situation is intermediate in favorableness, the untrained
leader's situation would be unfavorable. Training would, then, improve the
untrained leader's situation from an unfavorable one to a situation which is
intermediate in favorableness.

But why should an inexperienced and untrained leader perform better than
someone with training and experience? Under certain conditions this is not too
difficult to see. An individual who is new on the job is likely to seek good
interpersonal relations with his coworkers so that he can enlist their full
cooperation. He is not likely to throw his weight around and he will, therefore, be
less likely to antagonize his group members. In other words, the proposition is far
from absurd, and it is quite compatible with the behavior of the manager who
learns to rely on his staff of experts in making various decisions.

The proof of this theoretical pudding lies in various studies that bear out our
suppositions.

STUDY OF SCHOOL PRINCIPALS

One study was conducted by McNamara on principals of rural elementary schools
and of urban secondary schools in Canada. The performance of elementary
principals was evaluated by means of ratings obtained from school superintendents and their staffs. The performance of secondary school principals was
measured on the basis of province-wide achievement tests given to all students in
the 11th grade. The average test score was used as the measure of the principal's
effectiveness.

McNamara divided his group into task- and relationship-motivated principals, and again into inexperienced principals who had been on their job less than
two years and those with three or more years of experience.

Let us now consider the favorableness of the leadership situation of
elementary school principals. Their position power is reasonably high, and their
task is fairly structured. The schools in McNamara's sample were quite small, the

curricula of these schools are determined by the authorities of the province and by the school superintendent's office, and the elementary school principal typically is not called upon to make many policy decisions or innovations. His task is, therefore, structured. Hence, the experienced principal will have a very favorable leadership situation, and we would expect the task-motivated principals to perform better than the relationship-motivated principals.

The inexperienced principal faces a considerably less favorable situation. While his position power is high, he does not know his teachers well, and many of the administrative problems that arise will have to be handled in a manner that is new to him. We would predict that his task is unstructured and that the situation is intermediate. Without much experience the relationship-motivated principals will, therefore, perform better than their task-motivated colleagues. That this is the case is shown on Figure 5.

The secondary principal also has high position power. However, his organization is considerably more complex. In McNamara's sample, the schools had from 25 to 40 teachers who, in turn, were supervised by department heads. Thus, the principal's control over the teachers is less direct. In addition, of course, the curriculum of a high school varies from school to school and the high school principal generally has to make a considerable number of policy decisions about the teaching program, his staff, as well as the activities and disciplinary problems of his students. For this reason, the experienced principals of secondary schools were judged to have a situation of intermediate favorableness. Relationship-motivated principals should perform best. The inexperienced high school principal will have to set new precedents and he will have to think through many of the problems for the first time as they arise. Hence, the situation will be relatively unfavorable. We would predict, therefore, that the task-motivated principals with less than two years' experience will perform best in these situations. Here, again, the data follow the prediction. (See Figure 5.)

It is particularly important to note that the relationship-motivated elementary school principal with longer experience actually performed *less well* than the relationship-motivated elementary school principal with less experience. Likewise, the task-motivated secondary school principal with more experience had significantly *poorer* performance than the task-motivated principal with considerably less experience. Thus, for these particular administrators, the more extensive experience not only failed to improve their performance but actually decreased their effectiveness.

STUDY OF CONSUMER COOPERATIVES

Another study that illustrates the effect of training and experience was conducted some years ago on 32 member companies of a large federation of consumer cooperatives. The federation used two indices for measuring company effectiveness and managerial performance. These were *(a)* the operating efficiency of the company, that is, roughly the proportion of overhead to total sales, and *(b)* the proportion of net income to total sales. We used the three-year average of these measures for our study.

In a reanalysis of these data, the managers were divided into those with task-and relationship-motivated leadership patterns, and of these, the ten with the most and then ten with the least years of experience in the organization. Since the federation of the companies maintained a strong management development program, managers with long experience also tended to have the most extensive training.

The leadership situation for the experienced managers was judged to be relatively favorable. They had considerable position power, and their job was

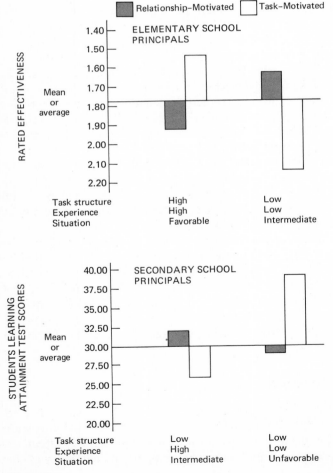

Figure 5

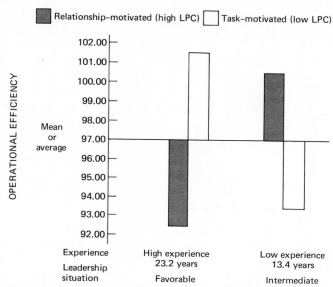

Figure 6 Performance of relationship- and task-motivated managers with relatively high and relatively low levels of experience.

relatively structured. As in the case of school administrators, the inexperienced and less well trained managers would, of course, face a larger number of problems that they had not encountered before, and the task would, therefore, be correspondingly less structured. Hence, for the inexperienced managers the situation would be intermediate in favorableness.

The Contingency Model would then predict that the experienced managers with task-oriented leadership patterns would perform better, as would the inexperienced managers with relationship-motivated leadership patterns. That this was the case is shown on Figure 6 for operating efficiency. Somewhat weaker results were obtained for the net income criterion. It is again apparent that the experienced and trained relationship motivated managers performed less well than did the relatively inexperienced and untrained managers who are relationship-motivated.

We have also studied the effect of training and experience on the performance of the post office managers and supervisors, police sergeants, and formal and informal leaders of company boards. These studies have yielded essentially similar results.

NEW STUDIES OF MILITARY LEADERSHIP

Two studies were recently conducted specifically for the purpose of testing the hypothesis on completely new data. These were of field artillery sections and navy

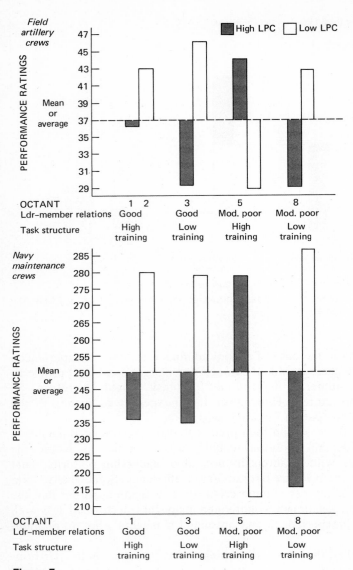

Figure 7

aircraft maintenance shops. Training and experience data were available for the noncommissioned officers in charge of these groups. In these studies, groups were assigned to cells 1, 3, 5, and 8 of the model. (See Figure 7.) Just as predicted, the task-motivated leaders performed best in cells 1, 3, and 8, while the relationship-motivated leaders performed best in cell 5. All findings were statistically significant.

TO TRAIN OR NOT TO TRAIN

What does all this mean for improving managerial performance, and how can we apply the findings that we have described?

In sum, if we want to improve leadership performance, we can either change the leader by training, or we can change his leadership situation. Common sense suggests that it is much easier to change various aspects of a man's job than to change the man. When we talk about leadership behavior, we are talking about fairly deeply ingrained personality factors and habits of interacting with others. These cannot be changed easily, either in a few hours or in a few days. In fact, as we have seen, not even four years of military academy and 5 to 17 years of subsequent experience enable a leader to perform significantly better on different tasks than someone that has had neither training nor experience.

We have seen that a leader's performance depends not only on his personality, but also on the organizational factors that determine the leader's control and influence, that is, the "situational favorableness." As we have shown, appropriate training and experience improve situational favorableness. Whether or not they improve performance depends upon the match between the leader's motivational pattern and the favorableness of the situation. This means that a training program that improves the leader's control and influence may benefit the relationship-motivated managers, but it will be detrimental to the task-motivated managers, or vice versa, depending upon the situation.

The idea that we can improve a leader's performance by increasing the favorableness of his situation is, of course, far from new. A poorly performing manager may be given more authority, more explicit instructions, more congenial coworkers in the hope that it will help him do a better job. Moreover, decreasing the favorableness of the situation in order to improve a manager's performanace is also not quite as unusual as it might appear at first blush. If a man becomes bored, stale, or disinterested in his job, a frequent remedy is to transfer him to a more challenging job. As it turns out, "challenging" is just another way of saying that the job is less structured, has less position power, or requires working with difficult people. It is certainly well known that some men perform best under pressure and that they get into difficulty when life is too calm. These are the trouble shooters who are dispatched to branch offices or departments that need to be bailed out.

What, then, can an organization do to increase managerial performance? As a first step, it is necessary to determine which of the managers are task- and which are relationship-motivated. This can be accomplished by means of a short scale. Second, the organization needs to categorize carefully the situational favorableness of its managerial jobs. (Scales are available in Fiedler, F. E., *A Theory of Leadership Effectiveness*, McGraw-Hill, 1967.) Third, the organization can decide on a number of options in its management of executive personnel.

The least expensive and probably most efficient method is to develop a careful program of managerial rotation that moves some individuals from one job to another at a faster rate than it moves others. For example, it will be recalled that the relationship-motivated elementary school principals on the average became less effective after two years on the job. Moving these men to new jobs probably would have made them more effective than leaving them at the same school for many years. Likewise, moving the task-motivated secondary school principals after two years probably would have increased their performance. In the case of the consumer cooperatives, it took 15 to 20 years in the organization (as employee and assistant manager, as well as manager) before the relationship-motivated managers began to go stale. How long a man should stay on a particular job must, of course, be determined empirically in each organization.

A second major option is management training. The problem here is whether to train only some people or all those who are eligible: training a task-motivated manager who is accepted by his group and has a structured task is likely to improve his performance; training a relationship-motivated manager for the same job is likely to make him less effective. The organization would, therefore, be better off if it simply did not train relationship-motivated managers for these particular jobs. On the other hand, the relationship-motivated but not the task-motivated managers should be trained for jobs in which the situational favorableness is intermediate.

Leadership training should devote more effort to teaching leaders how to modify their environment and their own job so that they fit their style of leadership. We must get rid of the implicit assumption that the environment and the organization, or a particular leadership position, are constant and unchanging. In addition to changes which occur as the leaders gain experience, they also continuously modify their leadership positions. They often speak of showing their men who is boss, presumably to assert their position power or of "being one of the boys" to de-emphasize it; they speak of getting to know their men, presumably to establish better relations with them; they speak of different approaches to their work; they look for certain types of assistants who complement their abilities; they demand more authority, or they play down the authority they already have; they ask for certain types of assignments and try to avoid others. The theory that has here been described merely provides a basis for a more rational modification of the leadership job.

How can we train leaders to determine the conditions under which they are most likely to succeed or fail, and how can they learn to modify their own leadership situation? The frequently negative relationship between leadership experience and leader performance undoubtedly stems in part from the difficulties in obtaining feedback about one's own leadership effectiveness. As research has shown, unless the group fails utterly in its task, most leaders are unable to say with any degree of accuracy how well their group performed in comparison with other groups.

Leadership training away from the organization should provide the prospective leader with a wide range of leadership situations in which he can get immediate feedback on how well he has performed. On the basis of these experiences, he must learn to recognize which situations fit his particular style of leadership and how he can best modify situations so that they will enable him to perform effectively. This may involve the development of six to eight short leadership tasks and situations, or adequately measured organizational tasks, in which each trainee is required to lead. He must then be given an objective appraisal of how well his group's performance compared with the performance of others under the same conditions.

The closest approximation to the all-around good leader is likely to be the individual who intuitively or through training knows how to manage his environment so that the leadership situation best matches his leadership style.

It may be desirable for various reasons to train all managers of a certain level, especially since being sent to executive training programs has in many organizations become a symbol of success. Men are sent to these training programs not because they need to learn, but because they need to be rewarded. If this is the case, the organization might do well to place the manager who completes the training program into a position that matches his leadership motivation pattern. For example, in the consumer cooperative companies, the relationship motivated managers might have been given staff jobs, or jobs with troubled companies at the conclusion of an extensive training program.

CONCLUSION

As a consequence of our research, we have both discredited some old myths and learned some new lessons.

The old myths:

- That there is one best leadership style, or that there are leaders who excel under all circumstances.
- That some men are born leaders, and that neither training, experience, or conditions can materially affect leadership skills.

The lessons, while more pedestrian and less dogmatic, are more useful. We know that people differ in how they respond to management situations. Furthermore, we know that almost every manager in an organization can perform effectively, providing that we place him in a situation that matches his personality, providing we know how to match his training and experience to the available jobs—and providing that we take the trouble.

Communication

Communication is one of the most pervasive of all managerial processes. Managers typically report that they spend between 50 and 80 percent of their time in some form of communication, whether it be in listening, talking, reading, or writing. It is clearly the only means through which managers may accomplish their other tasks such as motivating, leading, resolving conflict, and so forth.

Many years of research have been spent in frustrating attempts to establish answers to questions posed by managers such as, "When should I communicate? To whom? Through what channels? By which methods?" Although no singular answers have emerged, the communications field has provided the clear beginning of some frameworks for the diagnosis of the objectives, resources, and constraints that help to pinpoint the answer for any unique combination of circumstances.

The article by Bavelas and Barrett represents truly a classic introduction to the field of contingency communications. Published a quarter-century ago, it reports the first distinctive attempt to replicate in the laboratory the key characteristics of three different organizational (macro) communication structures, and then identifies the advantages and disadvantages of each along the five dimensions of speed, accuracy, organization, leader emergence, and morale.

Given this data, the manager can proceed in either of two directions. First, he can identify the communication structure within which he must operate in his organization, predict the effects, and take preventive action to diminish its negative features. Alternatively, he can examine his objectives and then choose the communication structure that has the greatest likelihood of accomplishing them. The reader is advised to review the organizational design section to note the close relationship between the need for communication and the type of structure chosen.

The situational approach to communication is further developed by Melcher and Beller, as they recognize the need to differentiate between formal and informal channels (or their sequential use) and written and verbal methods (or their sequential use). The combination of these decisions into a 4 × 4 matrix results in sixteen alternative communication approaches. The authors then complete their presentation of a theory of intraorganizational communication by systematically discussing four major factors that determine which channel to use: the nature of the communication itself, the behavioral characteristics of the relevant persons involved, the degree of integration of the intragroup and intergroup social system, and the six primary attributes of each communication channel. In the process of applying this analytical tool, managers must make several intuitive or explicit judgments about each of the items involved.

The first two articles provide a broad, theoretical, and research-based approach to contingency communication models. The final article, by Level, contains the most explicit data on supervisory ratings of the *effectiveness* of four methods of communication—written, oral, written-then-oral, oral-then-written. He obtained the field evaluations in response to ten different communication tasks, and therefore his data support a situational model that suggests the best, or at least an acceptable, method to use for each of those tasks.

Reading 32

An Experimental Approach to Organizational Communication

Alex Bavelas
Dermot Barrett

Communication as a critical aspect of organization has been attracting more and more attention. If one may judge from articles and speeches, much of the current thinking on communication centers around categories of problems which arise in day-to-day operations—"getting management's point of view to the workers," "stimulating communication up the line as well as down," "obtaining better communication with the union," "establishing more effective communication within management, and especially with the foremen." Knowing how such questions usually arise, it is not surprising that their discussion invariably resolves itself into considerations of *content* and *technique:* on the one hand, analyses of what management ought to be saying to the worker, the union, the foreman; on the other hand, descriptions of devices which can best say it—bulletin boards, letters, films, public address systems, meetings, etc. In its extreme form this approach becomes one of searching for a specific remedy for a specific ill. Helpful and practical as this may be, it is doubtful that such activity can lead to the discovery and understanding of the basic principles of effective organizational communication. Breakdowns and other difficulties at some point of a communication system are often only superficially related to the local conditions which appear to have produced them. They may, rather, be cumulative effects of properties of the entire communication system taken as a whole. But what are these properties, if, indeed, they exist?

Formal and Informal Systems

An organizational system of communication is usually created by the setting up of formal systems of responsibility and by explicit delegations of duties. These categories include statements, often implicitly, of the nature, content, and direction of the communication which is considered necessary for the performance of the group. Students of organization, however, have pointed out repeatedly that groups tend to depart from such formal statements and to create other channels of communication and dependence. In other words, informal organizational systems emerge. One may take the view that these changes are adaptations by the individuals involved in the direction of easier and more effective ways of working, or, perhaps, not working. It is no secret that informal groups are not always viewed by managers as favorable to the goals of the larger body. Also, it is

"An Experimental Approach to Organizational Communication," Alex Bavelas and Dermot Barrett, *Personnel,* March 1951, pp. 366–371. Reprinted with permission of the publisher. © 1951 by the American Management Association, Inc.

by no means obvious that those informal groupings which evolve out of social and personality factors are likely to be more efficient (with respect to organizational tasks) than those set up formally by the managers. Altogether, if one considers how intimate the relations are between communication channels and control, it is not surprising that the managers of organizations would prefer explicit and orderly communication lines.

Is There "One Best Way"?

Unfortunately, there seems to be no organized body of knowledge out of which one can derive, for a given organization, an optimal communication system. Administrative thinking on this point commonly rests upon the assumption that the optimum system *can* be derived from a statement of the task to be performed. It is not difficult to show, however, that from a given set of specifications one may derive not a single communication pattern but a whole set of them, all logically adequate for the successful performance of the task in question. Which pattern from this set should be chosen? The choice, in practice, is usually made either in terms of a group of assumptions (often quite untenable) about human nature, or in terms of a personal bias on the part of the chooser. The seriousness of this situation is illustrated by the following example.

Let us assume that we have a group of five individuals who, in order to solve a problem, must share as quickly as possible the information each person possesses. Let us also assume that there are reasons which prevent them from meeting around a table, and that they must share this information by writing notes. To avoid the confusion and waste of time of each person writing a message to each of the others, a supervisor decides to set up channels in which the notes must go. He strikes upon the pattern shown in Fig. 1.

In this arrangement each individual can send to and receive messages from two others, one on his "left" and one on his "right." Experiments actually performed with this kind of situation show that the number of mistakes made by individuals working in such a "circle" pattern can be reduced by fully 60 percent by the simple measure of *removing one link,* thus making the pattern a "chain" as shown in Fig. 2. The relevance of such a result to organization communication is obvious, simple though the example is. The sad truth, however, is that this phenomenon is not clearly derivable either from traditional "individual psychology" or from commonly held theories of group communication.

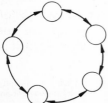

Figure 1

Figure 2

An Integral Process of Organization

Perhaps some headway can be made by approaching the general problem from a somewhat different direction. In the affairs of organizations, as well as in the affairs of men, chance always plays a part. However good a plan may be, however carefully prepared its execution, there is a point beyond which the probability of its success cannot be increased. With the firmest of intentions, agreements and promises may be impossible to carry out because of unforeseen events. Nevertheless, an organization whose functioning is too often interrupted by unforeseen events is looked upon with suspicion. Bad luck is an unhappy plea, and it may well be that the "unlucky" organization is more to be avoided than the simply incompetent one. On the other hand, few things about an organization are more admired and respected than the ability to "deliver" despite widely varying conditions and in the face of unusual difficulties.

In a very broad sense, it may be argued that the principal effort of organizational activities is the making of favorable conditions for the achievement of certain goals. In other words, an effort is made to increase, as much as the economics of the situation will permit, the probabilities of succeeding. This is the essence of the manager's job. The development of training and selection programs, the improvement of methods and the specification of techniques, the organization of research and development activities, the designation of responsibility and the delegation of duties—all these processes have one organizationally legitimate purpose: to increase the chances of organizational success. Upon this point rest almost all of the notions by which we are accustomed to evaluate organizations—in part or as a whole.

An organization is, in short, a social invention—a kind of "machine" for increasing certain sets of probabilities. (Which sets of probabilities are given to it to increase which it chooses, how freely and by what means will not be discussed here. These problems, although they lie well within the scope of this subject, are outside the range of this paper. We will confine ourselves to a consideration of the process by which an accepted set of probabilities is optimized.) Probabilities of success are increased, however, only by taking relevant and appropriate actions. For the manager, these actions reduce in most instances to the gathering and evaluating of information in the form of reports, schedules, estimates, etc. It is entirely possible to view an organization as an elaborate system for gathering, evaluating, recombining, and disseminating information. It is not surprising, in these terms, that the effectiveness of an organization with respect to the achievement of its goals should be so closely related to its effectiveness in handling information. In an enterprise whose success hinges upon the coordination of the efforts of all its members, the managers depend completely upon the quality, the amount, and the rate at which relevant information reaches them. The rest of the organization, in turn, depends upon the efficiency with which the managers can deal with this information and reach conclusions, decisions, etc. This line of reasoning leads us to the belief that communication is not a secondary

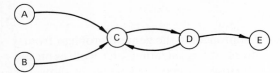

Figure 3

or derived aspect of organization—a "helper" of the other and presumably more basic functions. Rather it is the essence of organized activity and is the basic process out of which all other functions derive. The goals an organization selects, the methods it applies, the effectiveness with which it improves its own procedures—all of these hinge upon the quality and availability of the information in the system.

Patterns of Communication

About two years ago a series of studies was begun whose purpose was to isolate and study certain general properties of information handling systems. The first phase of this research program[1] is directed at a basic property of all communication systems, that of connection or "who can talk to whom."

This property of connection can be conveniently expressed by diagrams. The meaning of the picture in Fig. 3 is obvious. Individuals A and B can send messages to C but they can receive messages from no one; C and D can exchange messages; E can receive messages from D, but he can send messages to no one. The patterns shown in Fig. 3, however, is only one of the many that are possible. A group of others is shown in Fig. 4. An examination of these patterns will show that they fall into two classes, separated by a very important difference. Any pair of individuals in each of the patterns d, e, and f can exchange messages either

[1]These studies are supported jointly by the Rand Corporation and the Research Laboratory of Electronics at M.I.T.

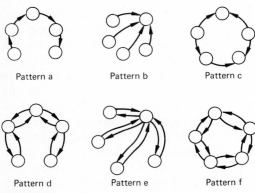

Pattern a   Pattern b   Pattern c

Pattern d   Pattern e   Pattern f

Figure 4

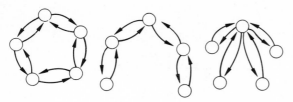

Speed	Slow	Fast	Fast
Accuracy	Poor	Good	Good
Organization	No stable form of organization	Slowly emerging but stable organization	Almost immediate and stable organization
Emergence of leader	None	Marked	Very pronounced
Morale	Very good	Poor	Very poor

Figure 5

directly or indirectly over some route. No pair of individuals in each of the patterns a, b, and c can exchange messages. Patterns like a, b, and c obviously make any coordination of thought or action virtually impossible; we will be concerned from this point on only with patterns like d, e, and f.

Since the individuals in any connected pattern like d, e, and f can share ideas completely, should we expect that the effectiveness of individuals in performing group tasks or solving group problems would be the same in patterns d, e, and f except for differences in ability, knowledge, and personality? Should we expect differences in quality and speed of performance? Is it likely that the individuals working in one pattern would show significantly better morale than the individuals working in a different pattern? Sidney Smith and Harold J. Leavitt conducted a series of experiments[2] which yielded very definite answers to these questions. An experimental design was used which made it possible to equate the difficulty of the tasks which the groups performed, and which permitted the cancelling of individual differences by randomizing the assignment of subjects to patterns. Also, the experiment was repeated with different groups enough times to establish the consistency of the results. A brief summary of the findings is given in Fig. 5. The use of qualitative terms in Fig. 5 in place of the quantitative measurements which were actually made blurs the comparison somewhat, but it gives a fair picture of the way these patterns performed. Since the original experiments were done by Smith and Leavitt, this experiment has been repeated with no change in the findings.

The question very properly arises here as to whether these findings can be "explained" in the sense of being related to the connection properties of the patterns themselves. The answer to this question is a qualified yes. Without

[2]Harold J. Leavitt reports these experiments in detail in the January, 1951, issue of the *Journal of Abnormal and Social Psychology.*

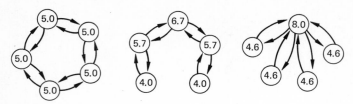

Figure 6

developing the mathematical analysis, which can be found in Leavitt's paper, the following statements can be made:

For any connected pattern, an *index of dispersion* can be calculated. Relative to this index, there can be calculated for *each position in each pattern* an *index of centrality,* and an *index of peripherality.* The data suggest strongly that the rapidity with which organization emerges and the stability it displays are related to the gradient of the indices of centrality in the pattern. In Fig. 6 these indices are given for each position. It should be added at this point that in the patterns in which leadership emerged, the leader was invariably that person who occupied the position of highest centrality.

The index of peripherality appears to be related strongly to morale. In Fig. 7 the indices of peripherality are given by position. Those individuals who occupied positions of low or zero peripherality showed in their actions as well as in self-ratings (made at the end of the experiments) that they were satisfied, in high spirits, and generally pleased with the work they had done. Those individuals who occupied positions of high peripherality invariably displayed either apathetic or destructive and uncooperative behavior during the group effort, and rated themselves as dissatisfied and critical of the group's operation.

A word of caution should be given concerning the slow, inaccurate, but happy "circle" pattern. Subsequent experiments by Sidney Smith indicate that this pattern possesses unusual abilities for adaptation to sudden and confusing changes of task—a quality lacking in the other two patterns.

A Promising Field for Research

Clearly, these experiments are only the beginning of a long story. The findings, although they promise much, settle nothing; but they do suggest that an experimental approach to certain aspects of organizational communication is

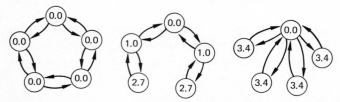

Figure 7

possible and that, in all probability, it would be practically rewarding. As the characteristics of communication nets and their effects upon human performance *as they occur in the laboratory* become better understood, the need will grow for systematic studies of actual operating organizations. The job of mapping an existing net of communications even in a relatively small company is a complicated and difficult one, but it is not impossible. Some work is beginning on the development of field methods of observation. The importance of bridging the gap between the simple, directly controlled experiment and the very complex, indirectly controlled social situation cannot be overestimated.

Reading 33

Toward a Theory of Organization Communication: Consideration in Channel Selection[1]

Arlyn J. Melcher
Ronald Beller

INTRODUCTION

The existence of the formal and informal aspects of organizations is widely known. Even so, there has been little progress in integrating the two in a theory of administration. Others have recognized the problem and called for a solution.

> Where formal organization theory stresses the deliberate planning of structural arrangements and correlation of the work to be done, informal organization takes account of the ways employees actually behave insofar as they deviate from the formal plan. . . . Until it has been corrected by what informal organization theory has to offer, formal organization theory is likely to be inaccurate and incomplete. The obvious challenge to the present generation is to work out a single theory of organization where heretofore there have been two.[2]

In part, the difficulty of working out a single theory of organization is the complexity of the problem. There are a number of dimensions to formal organization. These include formal channels of communication, formal policies,

"Toward a Theory of Organization Communication: Consideration in Channel Selection," Arlyn J. Melcher and Ronald Beller, *Journal of the Academy of Management*, March 1967, pp. 39–52. Reprinted with permission.
[1]The suggestions of Prof. Rance Hill, Department of Sociology, Kent State University, and Dr. James Thompson, Graduate School of Business Administration, Indiana University, on a previous draft are gratefully acknowledged.
[2]Marshall E. Dimock, Gladys O. Dimock, and Lewis W. Koenig, *Public Administration,* rev. ed. (New York: Holt, Rinehart, and Winston, 1961), p. 132.

procedures, and rules, formal authority and duties assigned to each office, and Gesellshcaft norms that the officeholder is expected to observe.[3]

The concept of "informal organization" is used so broadly that it may cover any deviation from the formally prescribed patterns. Progress in developing an understanding of the relationships between formal and informal aspects of organization probably requires that the problem be broken into parts.

This paper focuses upon the communications aspect of organization—a limited but important part of this area. Specifically, the questions posed are where the use of formal or informal communication channels or some combination would contribute to the effectiveness of the administrator and when verbal, written, or some combination of these methods would facilitate an administrator's effectiveness when using the formal or informal networks.

Some suggestions are made in this article for the substantive aspects of a theory of channel selection. The primary purpose of this paper, however, is to present a more systematic approach to the development of theory than presently exists.

THE PROBLEM OF CHANNEL SELECTION

Where there is broad acceptance that unofficial channels are and must be used extensively, there is still the question of *when* it would be more effective to use the formal channels and when the informal channels. Little of the extensive literature on the subject of communication is relevant to the problem of channel selection. A good part of the published material deals with effective speaking and writing, leadership of conferences and committees, and similar personal skills.[4] Most of the other books and articles discuss the design of the formal communication systems. Some authors focus upon special networks such as suggestion plans[5] and grievance procedures;[6] others deal with general problems of information flow associated with utilization of computers,[7] or the specification of hierarchical

---

[3]The Gemeinshaft-Gesellshaft continuum summarized and refined by Loomis clarifies the norms with which an officeholder is expected to conform. See Charles P. Loomis, *Social Systems* (New York: D. Van Nostrand, 1960), pp. 57–128.

[4]Illustrative examples are Charles E. Redfield, *Communication in Management* (Chicago: University of Chicago, 1958; Elizabeth Morting, Robert Finley, and Ann Ward (eds.), *Effective Communication on the Job* (New York: American Management Association, 1963); J. Harold Jones (ed.), *Business Communication Reader* (New York, 1958).

[5]Stanley G. Seimer, *Suggestion Plans in American Industry* (New York: Syracuse University Press, 1959); Herman W. Seinwerth, *Getting Results from Suggested Plans* (New York: McGraw-Hill, 1948); *Suggestions from Employees* (New York: National Industrial Conference Board, 1936).

[6]Neil W. Chamberlain, *Collective Bargaining* (New York: McGraw-Hill, 1951), pp. 96–119. Also Wilson Randle, *Collective Bargaining: Principles and Practices* (New York: Houghton Mifflin Co., 1951), pp. 466–492.

[7]Robert H. Gregory and Richard Van Horn, *Business Data Processing and Programming* (Belmont, California: Wadsworth Publishing Co., 1963); Joseph Becker and Robert M. Hayes, *Information Storage and Retrieval: Tools, Elements, Theories* (New York: John Wiley and Sons, 1963); John Peter McNerney, *Installing and Using an Automatic Data Processing System* (Boston: Graduate School of Business Administration, Harvard University).

relationships that define the route for formal communication. The writers who deal with informal communication networks typically approach the topic on a descriptive level. Attention is primarily directed toward relating the ways in which deviations from the formal structure occur.[8]

A few investigators have offered clues to the functions alternative channels may serve.[9] Still, there is no framework that directs attention to the consequences of using official and unofficial channels. Since there is no systematic way of dealing with the problem, there is a nearly complete absence of theory.

ALTERNATIVE CHANNELS AND METHODS OF USING CHANNELS

The manager has a number of alternatives facing him in communicating. He can follow official channels,[10] proceed in the more nebulous area of using unofficial channels, or combine the two. While using these channels, the manager may

[8]For a summary of some of the literature see Delbert C. Miller and William H. Form, *Industrial Sociology* (New York: Harper and Brothers, 1951), pp. 272–307; Leonard Sayles, *Managerial Behavior* (New York: McGraw-Hill, 1964); Keith Davis, *Human Relations at Work* (New York: McGraw-Hill, 1962), pp. 235–260; Joseph A. Litterer (ed.), *Organizations: Structure and Behavior* (New York: Wiley and Sons, 1961), pp. 138–204; Peter M. Blau and W. Richard Scott, *Formal Organizations; A Comparative Approach* (San Francisco: Chandler Publishing Co., 1962), pp. 87–192 and 222–263; Henry Albers, *Organized Executive Action* (New York: John Wiley and Sons, 1961), pp. 339–342; Keith Davis, "The Organization That's Not on the Chart," *Supervisory Management* (July, 1961), pp. 2–7.

[9]Lyndall Urwick, "The Manager's Span of Control," *Harvard Review*, XXXIV, No. 3 (May–June, 1956), pp. 39–47; also "Fitting in the Specialist Without Anatgonizing the Line," *Advanced Management*, XVII (January, 1952), pp. 13–16; Chester Barnard, *Functions of the Executive* (Boston: Harvard University Press, 1938), pp. 122–123.

[10]A number of terms will be used interchangeably in this paper. Official, organization, and formal are used synonymously. Unofficial, nonorganizational, and informal are also used interchangeably. The official channels are defined as those that coincide with the formal chain of command. Messages follow the hierarchical pattern and cannot bypass any organization member on any level. For example, in the diagram below, a message from 31 to 34 would go to 21, then to 1, on to 22, and finally to 34.

Unofficial channels are all communication routes which do not coincide with the formal structure. A message from 31 to 34 might go directly to 34 or indirectly through any number of intermediaries, some of whom may form a segment of the formal channel—e.g., 31 to 22 to 34; the path is a segment of the formal channel.

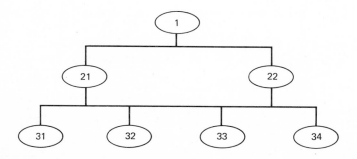

Table 1   Combinations of Channels and Methods of Using Channels in Communicating Channels[11]

Media	Official	Unofficial	Official, then unofficial	Unofficial, then official
Written	1	2	3	4
Verbal	5	6	7	8
Written, then verbal	9	10	11	12
Verbal, then written	13	14	15	16

contact others by written media, by voice (either face-to-face or through other less direct means such as the telephone), or with some combination. There is a fairly complex set of alternatives to choose from in communicating. Table 1 represents 16 combinations of using channels and methods.

Formal communication theory largely deals with combinations 1, 5, 9, and 13, with the emphasis on 1.[12] Writers emphasizing the importance of informal channels largely describe combinations 2, 6, 10, and 14 with emphasis on 6. Lyndall Urwick has stressed the importance of combination 16 where communication occurs verbally on the informal level, then is formalized after consensus is reached or action taken.[13] There are a number of factors that should be considered systematically in deciding which of the combinations to use. These include *(a)* the nature of the communication, *(b)* the personal characteristics of those involved, *(c)* the character of the social system, and *(d)* the communicational attributes of the channels. The elements and their relationships are represented in Figure 1.

Where the nature of the communication is given, factors B, C, and D determine which of the 16 combinations of channels and methods in Table 1 would be most appropriate to use. Each of these factors is discussed in the following sections.

A   Nature of the Communication

Communication can be classified in a number of ways as indicated in Figure 2.

1   Type of Communication   The communication may involve giving or requesting information or striving for consensus on problems or decisions.

---

[11]The administrator operating according to combination 11 would send a written message through the official channel, supplementing this with a verbal contact using an unofficial channel. The remaining combinations of media and channels are similarly interpreted.

[12]For example, see W. V. Merrihue, *Managing by Communication* (New York: McGraw-Hill, 1960), pp. 174–179.

[13]Urwick, *op. cit.*

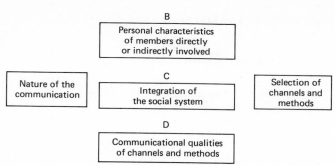

Figure 1 Factors to consider in selecting channels and methods.[14]

Normally, the simplest communication acts are giving or requesting information or giving orders. Even in the case where the message involves detailed logical arguments, charts, tables, mathematical formulae to effectively convey the message, the communication is relatively simple.

A more complex communication problem is achieving consensus on a subject. There may be various combinations of agreement and disagreement in regard to what goals to pursue or the methods to follow in attaining these goals. These variations are partly summarized in Table 2. Situations B, C, and D are increasingly complex communication acts.

The problem facing an administrator is how to operate the most effectively within the given formal structure. He normally cannot modify the structure along more appropriate lines. Where there is disagreement on goals or means of achieving goals, for example, it is desirable to explore areas of possible common interest or conduct informal bargaining on the informal level. Once a consensus is reached at least among key individuals, the formal channels may then be used to legitimize the agreement. Policies such as those of RCA support informal combinations of this nature:

[14]The use of the model should limit the search for a solution, thereby satisfying Deutsch's requirement that a model serve a heuristic function. See Karl W. Deutsch, "On Communication Models in the Social Sciences," *The Public Opinion Quarterly*, XVI (1952), pp. 360–362. The organizing, predictive, heuristic, and measuring capabilities of a model are a function of model content and sequence.

Figure 2   A—Nature of the Communication

1. The type of communication (a) giving an order, (b) giving or requesting information, (c) arriving at a consensus on problems or decisions.

2. The legitimacy / illegitimacy and the public / confidential nature of the message.

3. The extent resources in time, money, or material are involved in implementing the orders, obtaining the information, or achieving consensus.

Table 2   Extent of Consensus on Goals and Means of Attaining Goals[15]

Consensus on the means of attaining the goals	Consensus on goals	
	Agreement	Disagreement
Agreement	A	C
Disagreement	B	D

> The organization structure and the organization chart define the lines of responsibility and authority, but do not indicate channels of contact. The RCA organization permits and requires the exercise of common sense and good judgment, at all organization levels, in determining the best channels of contact necessary for the expeditious handling of the work. Contact between units of the organization should be carried out in the most direct way. In making such contacts, however, it is the duty of each member of the organization to keep his senior informed.[16]

Policies which encourage "oral" processing of grievances would have the same effect.[17] Much of the criticism of participation in decision making, or lack of it, in organizations may be based upon a misunderstanding of the interacting but separate functions that formal and informal action play. Contrary to the critics, low attendance and nominal participation in general meetings or committees where important decisions are made in unions, universities, government, hospitals, and other organizations may reflect a highly viable organization. For instance, when decisions are made with little more than pro forma participation and little discussion, it may indicate an appropriate use of the informal level before the agreement is formalized. Controversial proposals may be screened out or modified in informal negotiations so as to be made generally acceptable.

On the other hand, active participation in meetings may indicate an unstable organization or a misuse of the formal channels. The administrator may be attempting to achieve consensus on the formal level rather than legitimatizing decisions informally achieved. If, for example, the formal channels are initially used when disagreement exists either on goals or methods, it is likely to bring about a formal confrontation between contending groups or individuals. These open conflicts may contribute toward inflexible attitudes and positions that so stymie the administrative process that action cannot ever be taken even on noncontroversial issues. A formal decision under conflict conditions may result in

[15]Adapted from James D. Thompson and Arthur Tuden, "Strategies, Structures, and Processes of Organizational Decision," in James D. Thompson *et. al.* (ed.), *Comparative Studies in Administration* (Pittsburgh: University of Pittsburgh, 1959), pp. 195–216.

[16]*The Four Basic Organizational Concepts of the Radio Corporation of America* (New York: Radio Corporation of America, April, 1954), pp. 4–5.

[17]Robert B. McKersie and W. W. Shropeshire, Jr., "Avoiding Written Grievances: A Successful Program," *The Journal of Business*, XXXV (April, 1962), pp. 135–152.

loss of status and generate ill feelings that might poison relationships for many years. Effective administrators probably carefully choose the occasions when they are willing to have formal confrontations. Many others are probably ineffective largely because these formal conflicts occur often enough to disrupt the social fabric essential to cooperation in an organization.

2 Legitimacy of the Communication A second aspect of the message is its legitimacy. The communication may not be legitimate in the sense of being within the authorized scope of the office or what would normally be approved if brought to the attention of higher level managers or outside auditors. For instance, requests may be made for information that is classified or confidential; informal orders may be given to ignore company policy, or to take some unauthorized shortcut. Arriving at consensus on means or ends may involve accommodations to individuals and groups that would hardly win approval of higher level supervisors or outside auditors. Case studies such as those by Dalton and Kuhn provide extensive examples of the way in which unsanctioned behavior may contribute to the viability of an organization.[18]

3 Resources Used in Communicating Communication of either a legitimate or illegitimate nature may require the use of substantial resources of time, money, or material. The combinations of these two sets of variables are presented in Table 3.

Most writers implicitly assume communications are characterized by the combinations 1 through 6. However, a manager's effectiveness may often rest upon actions that might not be approved by higher management, auditors, or

---

[18]Melville Dalton, *Men Who Manage* (New York: John Wiley and Sons, 1959); James W. Kuhn, *Bargaining in Grievance Settlement* (New York: Columbia University Press, 1961).

Table 3 Characteristics of Information and Resources Required to Obtain It

Resources required to obtain information	Legitimate			Non-legitimate		
	Orders	Requesting or giving information	Arriving at consensus on goals and/or methods	Orders	Requesting or giving information	Arriving at consensus on goals and/or methods
Requires resources of time, money material	1	3	5	7	9	11
Requires little or no resources	2	4	6	8	10	12

outside observers. In some cases, the activities may adversely affect the firm even if they are in the interest of the individual. More characteristically, though, the actions may be a way of adjusting to an obsolete structure, unrealistic rules or policies, incompetent superiors, or problems that are interdepartmental and require continuous contact among individuals in several formal units.

The willingness of a manager to deviate from formal prescriptions is likely to be closely related to the extent to which he can be held accountable for expenditures and the legitimacy of the action he is being asked to take. When organization resources would be utilized in following an order, or honoring a request for information, or if some question exists about the legitimacy, the receiver may ask that the message be transmitted along formal channels and be written so that he is protected if a question ever arises.

This type of request emphasizes a crucial trait of many nonorganizational dealings. There is an element of risk which must be assumed by each participant to permit meaningful cooperation. In these instances, a request for definition of accountability indicates a reluctance to accept this risk and may force adherence to formal channels and written messages. These factors suggest that the receiver, who strives to minimize risks, would require the sender to use the formal channels and written messages (combination 1 or 13 in Table 1). If the receiver is more flexible, he may be willing to use combinations 4 or 16 in Table 1.

B Characteristics of the Channel Members

The characteristics of the message sender, receiver, intermediaries, and higher level supervisors are important variables in channel selection.[19] An outline of the relevant personality variables is given in Figure 3.

It is necessary to evaluate the communication potential of those who might be directly or indirectly involved in communicating. The term "potential" is used to represent their capabilities and restraints on the exercise of their abilities.

1 Goal vs. Means Orientation The degree of commitment of the sending, receiving, and reviewing agents to follow the formal prescriptions of rules, procedure, and authority is a key consideration in selecting methods and channels. As others have observed, some individuals regard the formal prescription as ends.

---

[19]The message sender, receiver, and intermediaries in the respective channels will be referred to as channel members.

Figure 3   Element B: Characteristics of the Channel Members

---

1. The goal vs. means orientation of those who are directly or indirectly involved in communication.

2. The reliability of those involved to interpret and relay the communication.

3. The language capabilities of the recipient and intermediaries.

The policies, rules, and other restrictions are adhered to, even though it is impossible to carry out the assigned responsibilities by doing so.[20] Others are goal-oriented and observe the formal prescriptions when they support their efforts, but freely deviate from them when they impede achievement of goals. The latter attitude is well expressed by a Chinese general, 2000 years ago, who was questioned by his officers about a proposal that would violate government policy, but would counter a threatened annihilation of his unit:

> ... His officers asked how he was to take this initiative without first obtaining permission from the Chinese civil commissioner who was accompanying the army; an objection which exasperated Pan Ch'ao.
> 'Our life and death is to be decided today; what do we care for the opinions of a common civil servant? If we inform him of our plan, he will surely take fright and our projects will be divulged.'[21]

Where those involved are committed to attaining ends rather than following procedures, greater reliance can be placed on nonorganization channels and verbal exchanges.

2 Communication Reinforcement A second determinant of channel selection is the "potential" to contribute to the communication that is to be relayed to others. The recipient and intermediaries can frequently aid the overall effort by adding useful information, by arriving at subsolutions to problems faced by the next member, and by checking the reliability and accuracy of the information transmitted. On the other hand, if the message will be misinterpreted readily or confused by intermediaries, it may be necessary to eliminate some individuals from the channel and require combinations of written and verbal amplification.

Certain individuals may be particularly useful in the communication process. The person could be the "funnel," referred to by Dalton,[22] who is apt to "talk out of turn and carry secrets to the right people," assuring almost predictable communication. The individual might be the leader of one of the informal groups to which the potential receiver belongs. It would also be helpful to identify those who might deal in nonorganizational channels for some personal reward.

3 Language Capabilities The language capabilities of those potentially involved in communication may restrict or eliminate some from the channel. Modification can be made in the way the communication is expressed and supplementary information provided if it is needed for understanding or to establish the pertinence of the communication to the immediate administrative

[20]Robert K. Merton, "Bureaucratic Structure and Personality," *Social Forces*, XVII (1940), pp. 560–568; Dalton, *op. cit.*, pp. 241–261.

[21]Rene Grousset, *The Rise and Splendor of the Chinese Empire* (Berkeley: University of California Press, 1964), p. 72.

[22]Dalton, *op, cit.*, pp. 232–234.

problem.[23] In practice, some individuals would be excluded and revision would be made in the content and method of communicating in order to adjust to the language capabilities of others.

C Integration of the Social System

Critical factors in the selection of channels of communication are the two closely related items of interpersonal relationships and interaction patterns. Figure 4 outlines two sets of polar interaction and relationship characteristics.

These elements may characterize relationships among individuals in a group or express the relationships among groups. The groups may form along organizational or nonorganizational lines. Table 4 indicates the polar combinations of integration and disintegration that may exist in intragroup and intergroup relationships.

The more that intragroup and intergroup relationships develop integrative qualities (combination A), the more it would be possible, and to a large extent necessary, to deal on an informal verbal basis. The use of the formal channels would normally be regarded as aloofness or falling back upon the effective neutral relationships of the formal organization.[24]

Where disintegrative relationships exist both within and among groups (D), communication would probably have to be limited to formal channels. More typical of relationship in organizations is probably the development of integrative elements within groups and disintegrative qualities among groups (C). In this case, the ability to communicate along informal lines among groups may be closely related to membership in various groups or personal contacts with individuals who are members of these various groups. One example of this type of relationship is the "symbolic clique" conceptualized by Dalton.[25] The manager develops contacts with others at various levels in the organization who keep him informed as well as acting as his spokesmen. Without these relationships, one has little choice but to rely on the formal network.

D Channel Characteristics

Each communication channel and method of using the network has specific characteristics which are relevant to communication. Six key elements are speed, feedback, selectivity, acceptance, monetary cost, and establishing accountability.

[23]See Albers, pp. 329–332. Lester Tarnpol, "Attitudes Block Communication," *Personnel Journal*, XXXVII (February, 1959), pp. 325–328.
[24]An alternative to the dichotomy represented in Figure 4 is the Gemeinschaft-Gesellschaft continuum as summarized and refined by Loomis. (See Loomis, *op. cit.*) To the extent that intra- and intergroup relationships are Gesellschaft in character, it probably would require adherence to written communications following formal channels. In terms of the categories developed by another specialist, Jack Gibb, individuals would approach each other with a supportive rather than a defensive orientation where intra- and intergroup integration have developed. See Jack Gigg, "Defensive Communication," *Journal of Communication*, XV, No. 3 (September, 1961), pp. 141–148.
[25]Dalton, *op. cit.*, pp. 57–59.

Table 4   Combinations of Integration and Disintegration Within and Among Groups

Relationships within groups	Relationships among groups	
	Integration	Disintegration
Integration	A	C
Disintegration	B	D

Figure 4   Polar Relationships that May Exist Among Individuals in Groups and Among Groups

"I" Characteristics: Integration	"D" Characteristics: Disintegration

Part I: Action relationships: interaction, communication, & cooperation

High Interaction—Interaction at work and off the job. Members may get together before or after lunch or in various recreational activities during evenings, weekends, and vacations.	*Low Interaction*—Little interaction except as required by patterns defined by formal organization or by instructions from a supervisor. Little or no talking or meeting together off the job.
Intensive and Extensive Communication —Ready flow of communication among members, particularly on informal basis; communication flow is extensive in that it may take place at all times interaction occurs, at work, lunch, before and after work, or at recreation. Little use of formal channels except to record communication when required by others.	*Little Communication*—Restricted flow of communication; careful screening and blockage when feasible; reliance upon formal channels with few informal exchanges.
High Cooperativeness—Spontaneous and ready assistance given without being asked; unhesitant response when requested.	*Low Cooperativeness*—Little assistance given without requests or direction; reluctant or negative responses to requests not formally and regularly part of the position.

Part II: Effective (emotional) relationships

High Cohesiveness—Sense of unity and of being a part of a team; identification with others; "our group" and "we" feeling; sense of belonging; reluctance to leaving group or breaking up existing relationships.	*Low Cohesiveness*—Sense of isolation or in the extreme anomaly; associates regarded as "they" or "the others"; readiness to move into new relationships by leaving or breaking up the group.
High Loyalty and Commitment—Emotional attachment associated with being a group member.	*Low Loyalty and Commitment*—Effective neutral relationship, little emotional commitment to the group.

1   Speed   Where the written or verbal approach is given, unofficial channels generally are more direct and faster than official networks. Where the channel is given, verbal contacts usually are speedier than written. The combination of unofficial channels with verbal communication normally is the fastest. However, any combination of verbal followed up by written forms is as fast when the written message is used for recording rather than immediate communication purposes.

2   Feedback   The more complex the message, the greater the need for two-way interaction between the sender and receiver. This helps the sender to determine the understanding by the receiver and the effectiveness of the channel selected (i.e., whether the channel performed as the sender anticipated in terms of speed, accuracy). Feedback is automatic in face-to-face contact where both can get what Thayer[26] calls "instructions" in interpreting words, gestures, facial expressions, inflection, tone, emphasis, etc. Thus, verbal communication provides greater and quicker feedback compared to written messages since it provides a complete circuit while written media typically provides a one-way transmission.[27] Even when feedback is actively sought by the sender of written messages, the inherent delay in such a process can lead to erroneous actions.

3   Selectivity   Those sending messages frequently wish to exercise control over circulation of the message in the organization. The legitimacy of the communication is an important factor determining the need for control. In other cases, there may be a plan for gradual dissemination of information where only a small group is initially informed of developments. Unofficial channels may permit a greater degree of control than formal channels since the sender can be more selective in determining who will be initially included. Those suspected of leaking secrets to unauthorized personnel would be excluded.

4   Acceptance   One vital skill is the ability to persuade others to take desired actions. Persuasive efforts normally require a large amount of personal interaction between the participants. The channel selected for message transmission is crucial to the effort to enlarge the receiver's "area of acceptance."[28] Where persuasion or arriving at consensus is involved, it is essential to operate on the informal verbal level as positions can be changed without loss of official status. When agreement is achieved, the decision should then be formally processed and written. The latter is necessary since those that were not involved in making the decision are more likely to accept it when the decision is an official act of the authorized office. Barnard observed that the formal organization structure performs a valuable function in defining communication authoritativeness and

[26]Lee Thayer, *Administrative Communication* (Homewood, Illinois: Richard D. Irwin, 1961), p. 70.

[27]Redfield, *op. cit.*, p. 74; Blau and Scott, *op. cit.*, p. 118.

[28]Barnard, *Functions of the Executive*, pp. 167–171.

authenticity.[29] This means that the hierarchical status differentiation is accepted as *prima facie* evidence of these qualities essential to message acceptance. Thus, requests for and giving of information upward in the hierarchy, and communicating decisions or information downward, are likely to receive greater acceptance when official channels are followed.

    5 Cost The monetary cost of using the various channels may be important in selecting a channel. For example, in a geographically dispersed organization, this factor could become important since it is expensive to travel from one location to another in order to meet face-to-face. Long-distance calls, closed circuit television, and other methods that enable verbal person-to-person exchanges may be substituted on economic grounds. Written communication may need to be used where many are competing for the recipient's time. It is considerably cheaper to queue written messages than it is verbal. A great deal of time can be wasted getting in to see the boss.

    6 Accountability Performance measurement and control depend on a clear establishment of accountability in carrying out assigned responsibilities. There must be accountability for (1) making past, present, and future decisions, (2) giving orders and requesting or giving information, (3) initiating communication contacts, and (4) utilizing organization resources in gathering information, or in carrying out orders. Written communications following formal channels are the most effective way of establishing accountability. The communication could initially take place on an informal level to speed up the process, but the communication would have to be officially recorded (written and sent along formal channels) if accountability is to be clearly established.

CONCLUSION

A practicing manager is faced with a choice of methods and channels when he is (1) establishing a program for a previously nonprogrammed activity, (2) reviewing an existing program for possible improvement, (3) working in an organizational context that is changing (new problems, personnel changes, increased cost and time pressures), or (4) orienting himself in a new job. At these times, a judgment must be made on the value of the alternative official or unofficial channels and written or verbal communication. The specification of channels and the methods of using the channels clarify the alternatives available to the manager. Administrative effectiveness probably is critically affected by how quickly a manager familiarizes himself with the orientation of his superiors, subordinates, and members in other departments, the extent to which he integrates himself into the social system, and his awareness of the functional aspects of the alternative channels. He is then in a position to use the channels and media that would best fit

[29]Barnard, "Functions of Status Systems," *loc. cit.*

the nature of the communication. It is unlikely managers have complete information on all these variables to arrive at rational judgments. The important point, though, is that they must make intuitive or explicit judgments about each of these items. Their general effectiveness is likely to turn upon whether they consider all the dimensions of communications that are involved.

While the theory offered in this article is of a tentative nature, it provides some hypotheses that can be further explored. Further, the framework provides a basis for systematically observing in research studies the behavior of effective and ineffective administrators. As projects along these lines are pursued, we will be in a position to take a big step forward in developing a theory of organizational communication and to move toward a single theory of administration.

Reading 34

Communication Effectiveness: Method and Situation

Dale A. Level, Jr.

There has been a long-standing controversy within our ranks over which communication method—oral or written—is the more effective. Most textbooks conclude with a draw, or say, "it depends on the situation." More recently, some studies have included a combination oral and written approach as a method. Few have attempted to relate "method" (written, oral, or combination) to specific situations. This study enlarges on a smaller pilot study in which the participants were asked to indicate the most effective and least effective methods of communication in handling ten varied communication situations. The four methods, evaluated by 72 business supervisors, were: (1) written only, (2) oral only, (3) written methods followed by oral methods, and (4) oral methods followed by written methods.

The most effective ratings made by participants were considered as positive (+) values, and the least effective ratings were treated as negative (−) values. By simple mathematics, a balance is derived and compared to the balances of the other three methods. Thus an additional basis is provided for determining the most effective method of communication besides relying entirely on the incidence of ratings in given categories. The results of the "most effective" and "least effective" methods relative to the ten situations are given in the various tables which follow in the text.

In communicating information requiring immediate employee action (Table

"Communication Effectiveness: Method and Situation," Dale A. Level, Jr.,*The Journal of Business Communication*, Fall 1972, pp. 19–25. Reprinted with permission.

Table 1   To Communicate Information Requiring Immediate Employee Action

N = 72	Written	Oral	Written /oral	Oral /written
Most effective	2	37	2	31
Least effective	55	10	5	2
Balance	−53	+27	−3	+29

1), the participants indicated a preference for using oral methods in handling this situation. Written methods alone were not considered an effective method. The highest positive incidence was received by the oral only method, with 37 most effective ratings. However, oral followed by written had a slightly higher positive balance, 29 to 27. The two individuals who rated oral followed by written as the least effective method selected written only as the most effective.

To communicate information requiring future employee action (Table 2), a combination approach was favored. Written only was rated as most effective by 29 participants; however, 11 also rated this method as least effective. Oral only was also considered the least effective method by a significant margin (−53).

Table 2   To Communicate Information Requiring Future Employee Action

N = 72	Written	Oral	Written /oral	Oral /written
Most effective	29	1	20	22
Least effective	11	54	3	4
Balance	+19	−53	+17	+18

This was the only question of the ten which received a fairly even spread over *three* methods. All others were considered effective by one or two methods. Also, for those questions for which oral only was considered least effective, this question had the highest negative balance.

Table 3   To Communicate Information of a General Nature

N = 72	Written	Oral	Written /oral	Oral /written
Most Effective	44	10	12	6
Least Effective	10	54	2	6
Balance	+34	−44	+10	0

To communicate information of a general nature (Table 3), written only was favored by participants in this situation with 44 choices as most effective and a 34 balance. Oral only was considered least effective by 54 individuals. Of the two combination methods, written followed by oral had the edge +10 to 0. This was the only question which received a "0" balance (oral followed by written).

To communicate a company directive (Table 4), combination methods were

Table 4   To Communicate a Company Directive or Order

N = 72	Written	Oral	Written /oral	Oral /written
Most effective	17	4	22	29
Least effective	11	53	8	0
Balance	+6	−49	+14	+29

considered the most effective. The oral followed by written was the favored method due to a lack of any negative ratings. Written only received 17 most effective ratings but was chosen least effective 11 times. Oral only was considered the least effective method for handling this situation. Ten of 17 persons who selected written only as most effective were over 30 years of age.

To communicate information concerning an important change in company

Table 5   To Communicate Information on an Important Company Policy Change

	Written	Oral	Written /oral	Oral /written
Most effective	10	1	15	46
Least effective	16	45	7	4
Balance	−6	−44	+8	+42

policy (Table 5), combination or oral followed by written methods of communication were favored. Fifteen participants chose the written followed by oral as most effective. The four who rated oral followed by written as the least effective were men with over five years' work experience in their job. Their choice for most effective was written only.

To communicate information to your immediate supervisor concerning your

Table 6   To Communicate with Your Immediate Supervisor about Work Progress

N = 72	Written	Oral	Written /oral	Oral /written
Most effective	11	16	9	36
Least effective	21	40	6	5
Balance	−10	−24	+3	+31

Table 7   To Promote a Safety Campaign

N = 72	Written	Oral	Written /oral	Oral /written
Most effective	4	4	30	34
Least effective	28	36	3	5
Balance	−24	−32	+27	+29

work progress (Table 6), all four methods received a number of most effective ratings but the majority favored the oral followed by written combination. Oral only received 16 most effective ratings but 40 least effective ratings, leaving it with the highest negative balance (−24). All five men rating oral followed by written were over 30 years old and had over five years' experience.

To promote a safety campaign (Table 7), the combination methods far outranked the written only and oral only methods. Oral followed by written and written followed by oral received 29 and 27 balances respectively. The written and oral only methods received negative balances of −24 and −32 respectively. The three men rating written followed by oral as least effective were over 30 and had over five years of experience.

To commend an employee for noteworthy work (Table 8), the oral only method received 35 most effective ratings. Oral followed by written received 32 positive ratings but had a higher balance (31 to 20). Written only had a high negative balance of −50 while written followed by oral appeared rather neutral with two most effective, three least effective, and a balance of −1. All three men rating written only as most effective were over 30 and had over five years of experience.

To reprimand an employee for a work deficiency (Table 9), the oral only method was favored. Written only failed to receive a single rating as most effective (one of two questions for which this was true; see question 10).

Several persons penned written comments to their responses to this question, indicating that they voted for oral only if this was the first time to reprimand the employee, while several indicated they voted for oral followed by written if this was the second (or more) time the employee was reprimanded. All five who responded that oral only was the least effective were over 30 years of age.

Table 8   To Commend an Employee for Noteworthy Work

N = 72	Written	Oral	Written /oral	Oral /written
Most effective	3	35	2	32
Least effective	53	15	3	0
Balance	−50	+20	−1	+32

Table 9 To Reprimand an Employee for Work Deficiency

N = 72	Written	Oral	Written /oral	Oral /written
Most effective	0	47	3	22
Least effective	61	5	6	0
Balance	−61	+42	−3	+22

To settle a dispute among employees concerning a work problem (Table 10), oral methods were favored as an initial approach. Forty-five participants rated oral only as most effective; 11 rated it as least effective, giving a balance of 34. Oral followed by written had a positive balance of 27. All 72 participants rated the most effective methods as *either* oral only or oral followed by written. Written only and written followed by oral did not receive a single most effective rating. This was the only question for which only two methods were chosen (and only one other—question 9—was limited to three methods; all the other eight questions were divided among all four possible responses).

Table 10   To Settle a Dispute Among Employees About a Work Problem

N = 72	Written	Oral	Written /oral	Oral /written
Most effective	0	42	0	30
Least effective	54	11	7	0
Balance	−54	+31	−7	+30

Summary and Conclusions

The highest positive ratings and the greatest negative ratings (first-place votes) for each of the ten situations were distributed in the following manner:

The following conclusions and generalizations would seem to be in order:

	Most effective	Least effective
Written only	2, 3	1, 8, 9, 10
Oral only	9, 10	2, 3, 4, 5, 6, 7
Oral/written	1, 4, 5, 6, 7, 8	
Written/oral		

1 The combination method of oral/written seems to be appropriate most of the time (six vs. two each for written and oral only). This method would never be *in*appropriate, evidenced by its not being chosen as a least effective method for any situation. Communications requiring immediate action (but with follow-up desired), or of a general nature (with documentation available in future), or of an interpersonal nature with positive connotations seem best handled by this method.

2   The written/oral combination method was not chosen as the most effective *or* least effective for any situation. It did, however, receive six plus balances vs. four minus balances but none of these was extreme enough to be considered as most effective or least effective.

3   The written only method was considered the most effective in two situations—where information required future action or where the information was general. The presumed logic here might be that for future action, the oral or combination methods (including oral) are too transitory and may be forgotten, and the information of a general nature may not require the interpersonal contact implied by the oral method.

Written only ranked as least effective in four situations: where (*a*) information required immediate action, and (*b*) some interpersonal contact—to commend, reprimand, or settle a dispute—would presumably be involved.

4   The oral only method was ranked most effective in two situations: for reprimands and settling disputes. Obviously this method has the advantages of immediacy and personal contact (on-the-spot feedback). Further, these two situations may be viewed as ones in which the supervisor's purpose for communicating is to change the worker's behavior. All others can be viewed as information-giving or reinforcement of behavior.

The oral only method was listed as the least effective in the most number of situations—six. Four of the six were included in the most effective list under the combination oral/written method, implying that the oral method is desirable but not by itself.

In summary, it would seem appropriate to use the specific combination method of oral followed by written for most situations—especially those requiring immediate action and also where follow-up and/or documentation is desired, and communicating information of a general nature.

Single methods are most effective for specific situations: written for future action or general information where no personal contact is deemed necessary; and oral where interpersonal contact and immediate feedback are desirable and when the purpose of the communication is behavioral change.

Controlling

The purpose of this section is to demonstrate the need to take a contingency approach to the management process of controlling. The four authors suggest that in order properly to design and operate control systems managers must take into consideration a number of key variables, such as competition, organizational objectives, structure, management and operating systems, and behavioral implications. The articles discuss organizational, functional, financial and budgeting, and human control systems.

The Mockler article encourages managers to rethink the controller's job and take a more situational or diagnostic approach to the design of control systems. He suggests there is a need to look at nonfinancial (operating) as well as the more traditional financial controls and recommends that control-systems designers should be familiar with a wide range of tools—financial and accounting, quantitative, and behavioral. He concludes that by adopting a contingency framework controllers will be in a better position to recognize new control areas and deal with them effectively, whether they involve the control activities of a manager of a typing pool or the overall financial controls of the organization.

Sihler identifies four critical factors that should be considered in designing, operating, and evaluating management control systems. The first factor is that control systems should be congruent with organizational objectives. Second, the system should fit well with organizational structure, especially those aspects related to information flow, reward systems, status congruence, and management control of data. Third, the system must be able to generate information that the manager needs in order to do his job. The fourth factor is the timeliness of information that is provided the manager who is responsible for making control decisions.

Irvine takes a highly integrative approach and relates budgeting as a control technique to the entire management process of planning-executing-controlling. He analyzes the effects of budgeting on people and shows how budgets can lead to positive or negative results depending on how they are applied in various types of organizational settings. A general budgeting model is presented that summarizes the key factors to consider when determining the functional and dysfunctional aspects of introducing and using a budgeting system. Finally, the article cautions the reader that a budgeting process must be applied contingently and that the effectiveness of any system will depend upon a good understanding of key variables, such as corporate strategy, organizational structure, leadership styles, general attitudes of employees toward the organization and control techniques, and methods of achieving organizational objectives.

Oberg takes a look at control systems that evaluate human performance. He contends that since performance-appraisal programs are here to stay, they should be made more effective by first defining their objectives and then selecting the appropriate appraisal techniques to achieve them. He lists the strengths and weaknesses of nine appraisal techniques and shows how they can contribute to the attainment of different performance-appraisal objectives. He maintains that many of the pitfalls frequently encountered in formal performance-appraisal programs can be avoided if management will take a contingency approach.

Reading 35
The Corporate Control Job: Breaking the Mold
Robert J. Mockler

When technicians approach a problem, their first question is often, "How can I use my tools or skills to deal with this situation?" Plumbers and carpenters use this approach; business managers, however, are not supposed to—but they often do, especially in the control area.

Business control is a systematic effort to set performance standards that are consistent with planning objectives; to design information feed-back systems; to compare actual performance with these predetermined standards; to determine whether there are any deviations and to measure their significance; and to take any action required to assure that all corporate resources are being used in the most effective and efficient way to achieve company objectives. This modern concept of business control is a broad one, covering a wide range of management tasks—from the control activities of the manager of a typing pool to the over-all financial control of an entire company. Modern business control also makes use of a wide range of tools—from financial and accounting tools to behavioral science tools.

While this broad view is accepted by business managers, control has continued to have a narrow meaning in many companies, especially where an accounting or finance man is either formally or informally considered to be the control executive. Inevitably, in these organizations financial controls (dollar cost and dollar profit controls) are emphasized.

FINANCIAL AND NONFINANCIAL CONTROLS

While dollar costs and profits are the ultimate focus of business control, financial tools are not necessarily always the best ones for control. If an operating manager is going to control final costs and profits, he must control the many activities that affect costs and profits as they are happening. And these activities can often be monitored by nonfinancial control tools.

For example, a manager in the marketing area needs to control marketing activities, such as use of salesmen's time, inventory levels, customer service, research, new product development, and order backlog, if he is going to effectively control dollar sales, expenses, and profits. In developing his controls, therefore, he first examines the critical activities in his area that affect financial results. Next, depending on the nature of the activity, the marketing manager

"The Corporate Control Job: Breaking the Mold," Robert J. Mockler, *Business Horizons*, December 1970, pp. 73–77. Reprinted with permission.

determines which control standards would be best for each activity. For example, he might use a PERT chart for new product development, historical figures for the acceptable number of customer complaints, planning goals for inventory levels, and the like. Then the marketing manager designates the kind of measurements that will most easily enable him to determine deviations from standard and so control operations in each of these activities. These measurements will range from dollars to units to numbers to days or weeks. Last, he develops a reporting system.

The start of such a reporting system is the development of a list of control reports and standards needed. These would cover such financial areas as sales, profits, and expense, since they are the ultimate focus of all marketing activities. However, the majority of the controls are nonfinancial, and they enable the manager to control those activities that affect financial results. On a day-to-day basis these are the controls most used and of most concern to the marketing manager, for with them he is able to direct the ultimate financial results. The accompanying figure shows how the control checklist might be developed in two important marketing areas.

THE CONTROLLER'S VIEWPOINT

In constructing a chart such as that shown in the figure—that is, in outlining his approach to control or developing his control system—where can a company's operating manager (for example, the marketing manager) turn for help? Presumably, since his problem is a "control" problem, he would turn to the "controller." But who is normally the controller in a large company and how well-equipped is he to give advice on controlling all operating activities?

Many controllers in today's business corporations are financial men, men trained to think in monetary terms and to believe control is ultimately intended to monitor dollar costs and profits. It is only natural, therefore, for them first to study ways to use their "bag of tools," financial controls. If a financially-oriented controller has extra time (which he rarely does) or the inclination (many do not think their job extends very far beyond the financial area), he may try to look at other control aspects of the situation. Generally, however, he will choose to work within the familiar financial channels and concentrate on ways to develop financial controls.

If the controller is a financial executive the marketing manager may encounter a good deal of resistance (and little help) if he wishes to develop an extensive system of activity controls. The marketing manager may even be told in pious tones (this example is drawn from personal experience) that concentrating on financial controls helps him "think profits" and so be a better manager. In reality, such statements are often designed to force the operating manager to do the accounting or financial department's work—to translate his operating standards into their financial standards and to use their financial standards, whether or not these controls are the most effective for him.

Examples of Marketing Management Control Check List

Performance information	Report frequency	Year-to-date	Standard	Method of showing variance	Marketing	Sales	Advertising	Marketing research	Product	Marketing services
Sales										
Total dollars	Daily or wkly.	Yes	Forecast	$ and %	C	C	C	I	C	I
Units and dollars										
By product line	Wkly. or monthly	"	"	Units, $, %	C	C	C	I	C	—
By region	"	"	"	"	C	C	C	I	C	—
By district	"	"	"	"	C	C	C	I	C	—
By territory	"	"	"	"	C	C		I	C	
By major accounts	Monthly	"	"	"	C	C		I	I	
Expenses										
Total marketing	"	"	Budget	$ and %	C					
Each department	"	"	"	"	C					
By region, district, and territory	"	"	"	"		C				
Administrative and rental, each branch office	"	"	"	"	C	C				C
Operating expense, field warehouse	"	"	"	"	C					C
Auto and truck	"	"	"	"	C					C
Product transportation	"	"	"	"	C				I	C

C = For control purposes; I = For information purposes.
Source: Abridged Victor P. Buell, Marketing Management in Action (New York: McGraw-Hill Book Company, 1966), pp. 171–73.

The difference between the viewpoint that supports operating control and the one that favors financial control is revealed in discussing individual reports when the controller says, for example, "You don't really need that report, do you?" His conclusion is that the report should not be instituted because it "isn't worth the expense of preparing it." It probably is not worth the expense to the controller, but it probably is worth a great deal to the operating manager. The difference in viewpoint is also revealed in subtler ways as the discussion covers how to report results, the frequency of reporting, and other details of the control system. Rather than getting help, an operating manager in such a situation is instead busy overcoming resistance and fighting to have the control reports tailored to meet his operating requirements.

FILLING THE VOID: AN EXAMPLE

In one large publishing company, the subscription sales manager recently needed help in developing a reporting system for planning and control. He first turned to the manager with the title "controller," who also handled all the company's financial budgeting functions. At this point he was told, "Here are the best ways we know of measuring costs and profits in the subscription area." In other words, the controller was opening his bag of financial tools. This was interesting, but not the answer needed.

Fifteen years ago, that would have been the end of it. The subscription sales manager would have gone back to his office and developed report formats on his sales activities, hired a girl to keep activity records and establish liaison with the order processing department, and, in essence, developed his own activity control system. In other words, he had no truly broad-based control department that could advise him on control. But the date was not 1955, but 1970, and the company's controller was on the brink of losing part of his job by default.

The company was in the process of changing computer systems, and, a few days later, a systems analyst came around for his first interview with the subscription sales manager. The analyst's first remark was a refreshing change: "I want to chart the flow of your operation to see where the critical decision points are and what information you'll need at these points for planning and control." In other words, the systems analyst was starting with situation or key factor analysis in order to determine the situation's control requirements.

Next, the systems analyst wanted to know what the most convenient report formats and kinds of standards the subscription sales manager needed and preferred—another refreshing change. In other words, the analyst was searching for the control tools that best met the operating manager's needs, unlike many traditional controllers who search for ways to get the operating manager to use a specific set of financial control tools.

As it turned out, the study showed that the subscription sales manager needed information on test results, orders received per thousand mailing, renewal percentages, customer complaints, and the like—all factors which affected the financial results reported on a month or two later. They were not, however, financial controls. They were current activity controls.

The systems analyst then went through the same procedure with the controller in preparation for putting accounting and financial reports on the computer. This process created a significant change in the informal structure of the organization of the control function within the company. As a by-product of the systems development work, the focus of the control function began to shift from the controller to the systems department. The controller's job was narrowed to one area, financial and accounting control, while the systems area's responsibilities had expanded to include major control functions. This shift occurred because there was a control need that was not being filled by the present control executive; it was not a matter of an attempt to take anyone's job.

The shift may not have been a good one. Nor is it certain that the systems department should be made the control department and the systems analyst made controller. The point is that a void existed in the company's control function and that void had to be filled, either by the operating manager himself or by some staff group that could give him the help he needed.

The controller in this case could have filled that gap, but he did not, either because he failed to recognize the need or because he lacked the time or the inclination. And once this part of the control job was lost, it was too difficult to regain.

THE CONTROLLER'S CHANGING JOB

Many controllers have abdicated their titles informally by not taking off the blinders, by not going beyond the financial and accounting mold. And they were all puzzled when their actual functions seemed to narrow slowly over the years, especially as their companies converted to computers. Others, who had been more alert to the changes in control concepts and practices, expanded the range of the control services they offered to operating departments.

The trend towards a broader view of the role of a staff control department will continue. And traditional, financially-oriented controllers will continue to lose part of their job unless steps are taken.

First, they must recognize that control is a broad management function. Over 300,000 C.B.A. and M.B.A. graduates will have been taught a broader concept of control during the next ten years, and top company management seems to be recognizing the wider range of control needs within their companies. For example, Paul Stokes' book *A Total Systems Approach to Management Control* (New York: American Management Association, 1968) lists eight critical control areas of concern to a corporate manager—only one of which is "financial." The expansion of systems development work has contributed greatly to the recognition of the broad range of control needs within a company.

There is thus a movement from many directions to develop control into a staff function providing a wide range of services and drawing upon many areas for its tools, including finance and accounting tools, operating and staff controls (outside the financial area), systems, economic forecasting, operations research, and behavioral science tools. The controller of the future may well be a staff manager who can advise operating and other staff managers (including personnel) on how best to use all these areas in solving a wide variety of control problems. His viewpoint and knowledge bank (or bag of tools) will thus be expanded well beyond the accounting and financial mold.

Second, tomorrow's controllers must use a different approach to control situations, an approach similar to the one described in discussing the development of the figure. The following is an outline of such a situational approach:

> Analyze the situation and review the facts in order to determine the purpose of the controls and the key factors affecting the situation.
> Develop and evaluate alternative control tools or systems which meet these needs, and select the one which best fulfills the situation's requirements.
> Implement the controls.
> Use the controls to monitor operations.

The key difference between this approach and the one used by traditional controllers, such as the one encountered by the subscription sales manager described previously, is that it starts with situation analysis. It does not start with a study of how to apply familiar tools.

What kinds of demands will this approach make on a staff control manager of tomorrow? It may mean taking the time to sit down with operating managers and advising them on how to develop controls appropriate for their operations. In large companies, the control staff might do this in conjunction with the systems analysts. In essence, the control staff would say, "Since we are the control experts, we can best advise operating managers on what balance of financial and nonfinancial controls are the best control measures for their area." Or the staff may have to go further and do the donkey work involved in making the chart and in designing the reporting forms. The control staff may eventually have to advise the operating managers on how best to use the result information generated by the control systems, or even help in the analysis of causes of deviations from standards.

Organizationally, traditional financial controllers are still in the best position to fill the expanding control needs in a company and to exploit the new trends in control—simply because many of them have the title of controller and because business folklore favors thinking of financial executives as controllers. But the nature of the controller's job will change dramatically, and financially-oriented controllers will have to change with it if they are to fill a company's expanding needs.

If existing control executives do not move into the gap and do the work needed, operating managers will not get the staff control assistance they need (and have been taught to expect), and they will look elsewhere for help. It is possible that the control function will thus be dispersed over many departments–accounting, finance, systems, operations research or management sciences, planning, and even the operating departments themselves.

This is already occurring in many companies. This dispersion will continue until company management gradually designates a new focus for the staff control function, either by assigning it to some existing department (such as the systems department) or creating a new organization unit called "control" which could be headed by a management generalist and to which existing financial and budgetary departments would report. Incidentally, I would hate to be the first man to take that job, since his chances of surviving the first round of antagonisms and political maneuvering would be fairly slim. The need is there and the change is coming. One way for controllers to meet the challenges presented by this change is to break the traditional financial mold in control and use the situational approach.

Reading 36

Toward Better Management Control Systems

William H. Sihler

Four central and critical factors should be considered in building, using, and evaluating a management control system:

- Is the system related to and does it reinforce the objectives of the organization? Is there congruence between the system and the goals; or, is there disharmony and friction?
- Is the system well related to the organizational structure? Does information flow in a way which is acceptable to those who generate and use the data? Is coordination and consolidation of information effective and easy?
- Does the manager receive the information he requires to do his job? Does he get too little information? Too much information? Does it tell him something useful about the activities over which he has control and which he can influence? Does it threaten him with punishment on account of activities for which he has neither responsibility nor authority?
- Is the information provided in time to be of use to the manager?

Each of these points is amplified in the pages that follow.

It is not likely that a control system will be perfect along each parameter, but

"Toward Better Management Control Systems," William H. Sihler. © 1971 by The Regents of The University of California. Reprinted from *California Management Review*, vol. 10, no. 3, pp. 33–39, by permission of The Regents.

a serious defect in any one of these four critical areas is sufficient to damage a system that may be well-planned in the other three. For example, enthusiastic and cooperative managers quickly lose interest in a system that does not meet their needs or the needs of others as they see these needs.

The adage is also worth emphasizing that a system is no better than the managers who operate it. No system, however well planned and appropriate, can survive uninformed or intentional misuse, can thrive if it is ignored, or can overcome misapplication by those not trained in its use. An internal combustion engine, no matter how well designed and carefully manufactured, can quickly be immobilized by a few grains of sugar.

The following discussion tends to focus on the design and implementation of an information system for planning and control. The same principles are relevant to the modification of an existing system and, most importantly, to using an imperfect system. A manager himself may not be able to secure modification of a control system to suit his convenience. If he is aware of the basic elements of system design, however, he can often modify the data he receives or interpret them in ways that make his managerial task easier. The topics presented are therefore relevant to the front-line manager as well as to the staff specialist in information systems.

OBJECTIVES

In a full-employment society, where resources are by definition scarce in the sense that it is not possible to have more of one item without sacrificing another, a common criterion for measuring a system's value is whether it helps allocate resources efficiently. This criterion can be applied in two ways. First, for a given level of physical output, is the cost (resources consumed to produce the output) as small as possible? For programs where the output is not measurable in physical terms such as pounds, feet, or dollars, it is possible but difficult to substitute a subjective measure of "psychic-emotional" benefit. Second—the converse of the first criterion—for a given level of cost, is the output as high as possible? Given the time spent generating information, is the most relevant and necessary information being provided? Taken together, these are known as the maximum-output, minimum-cost criteria.

Before the managerial planning and control system can be made to support the organization's specific objectives, it is important that the *substantive objectives* themselves are worked out with some degree of clarity and that they are internally consistent. For example, if an organization's major objective is to minimize reporting errors, the control system will be designed differently than if the objective is to serve the customer in the shortest possible time. In the former circumstance, a report might be double checked in several ways by different men before the transaction is reported. In the latter situation, the system will be designed to keep errors in reporting to a minimum within the constraint of the desired speed of service. As many banks have found, it is necessary to tolerate a painful error level in order to avoid the more painful loss of business to a more responsive competitor. (The contrast between the possible objectives and related systems in the banking industry is particularly striking to those who have dealt with European banks.)

Similarly, there should be a high degree of harmony between short- and long-term objectives. One company found that top management's commitment to a compound long-term growth of 15 percent a year was being achieved at a higher cost than necessary as a result of its short-term policy of rewarding plant managers for minimizing excess capacity in plant operations. Although the growth plans were widely known, plant managers attempted to expand piecemeal, buying the smallest possible piece of equipment to do the job. This conflict in *temporal objectives* resulted in the longer-range managerial planning being subverted by the short-range control systems.

When the objectives of a corporation are reasonably coherent and consistent, it is feasible to develop a control system that will reinforce the objectives by measuring the level of accomplishment and its cost.

It is still necessary to be sure that the control system itself is efficient and measures up to the minimum-cost maximum-output criteria. A control system can develop unmoderated growth, expanding apparently for its own sake alone. In an age when computers can consume in an hour paper costing twice or three times as much as the computer's capital cost per hour, the temptation to report everything to everyone must be avoided. If the purpose of a system is the specific control of a detailed subsection of an operation, it should provide detailed operating information to that subsection's management. The same information usually need not be provided to the senior management level. Similarly, it is not necessary that all shift foremen be provided with monthly consolidated profit and loss statements. They are interesting, and such results may eventually have some impact on the particular shift, but this information is not likely to be of much immediate use to a man with responsibility for first-line management. In other words, the differences in the requirements for specific operating control and general overall evaluation and appraisal must be kept in mind when developing a control system.

ORGANIZATION

The relationships between organizational structure and systems for planning and control are rich and complex. The subject greatly exceeds the space that can be devoted to it here. As a result, just a few of the most significant aspects will be mentioned briefly.

Basic Philosophy

A control system usually reflects the basic attitude toward human nature of those who designed it. In many cases, this attitude has become ingrained in the organization, and the control system then reflects this "organizational consciousness." For instance, one "theory" holds that the individual is basically untrustworthy, must be strictly regulated, and is incapable of taking intelligent initiative. The control systems developed under the influence of this approach tend to be overwhelming in their control of the individual. Action in all possible circumstances is prescribed in advance in minute detail. Massive reports are collected to show just what is done minute-by-minute. In part these systems protect the individual who can demonstrate that his actions at all points were in accord with the regulations.

Other theories tend to emphasize the positive aspects of human behavior. They assume that management and employees are basically motivated toward the good of the organization and that the role of a control system should be to provide information necessary to permit the management to control the operations—not for the operations to control the management. Much less information is passed upward through the administrative structure. Although uniform practices may provide for common occurrences and for those areas in which operational uniformity is critical, the basic purpose of the system is to get information necessary for problem-solving to those with the intelligence and skills to solve the problem in the specific circumstances that may arise.

For example, the two different approaches would result in greatly different designs for an information and management control system in a job-order machine shop. The first approach mentioned, the one emphasizing total organization, might develop a scheduling system that concentrated in the production control department all information on machines, skills, manpower, jobs in process, and backlog. From that department, which might utilize high-speed computational equipment to do the scheduling, would come orders assigning men and machines to jobs and specifying all the details of sequence and working time. Reports would be kept to determine whether the schedules had been met. The foreman's job would be one of insuring that the instructions were followed, reporting results and explaining variances, and checking the standard procedures or the control center if the instructions could not be followed.

An alternative approach could be developed on the assumption that the foremen could do the best job of matching the machine capacity and human skills. A system would be designed which generated information needed by the foreman to manage his subdepartment. Foremen might be provided a current listing of jobs coming into the department including the operations required, the expected time of arrival in the subdepartment, and the maximum completion date feasible. The system could also permit the location and expeditious treatment of jobs whose status had suddenly increased. The emphasis throughout would be on providing information to permit management decision, such as assignment of work to specific men or machines, to be made as close to the point of action as possible.

Organizational Structure

Additional major organizational factors which have a bearing on the nature of a control system are the departmental and shift structure and the line-staff arrangements. To be useful, the control system must be designed so that required information both precedes and follows the flow of work through the organization. This permits anticipatory action and post-action appraisal and evaluation.

It is not necessary that all employees and all management know everything. It is essential, however, that a man has the information he needs to make decisions. Similarly, it is important that the information necessary for evaluation be properly organized so that praise is given where deserved and corrective action taken where required. In the following section, various aspects of these generalities are discussed specifically.

Information Flow

Regarding the flow of information, for example, identification of the causes of defects is critical in maintaining product quality. Rather than have the defects and rejects analyzed by staff quality-control men, some companies have taken a more direct approach. All department heads meet together to review the previous period's defective or problem production. At one iron foundry, senior management from production and production-related staff sections (such as metallurgy) start their day with a conference at the scrap heap. The various rejects are examined, the causes for the defect are jointly determined, and responsibility for correcting the defect is assigned. The face-to-face resolution of the defect issue, usually one of the most acrimonious issues in an organization, eliminates much of the paperwork normally involved in settling this question. It also eliminates a major cause of friction in an operation, friction which can unnecessarily absorb large quantities of management's energy while creating great amounts of ill-feeling between departments and between line and staff management.

An example of information not being provided to the proper sources can be seen in a situation which existed in a ship-repair yard. One set of managers had the responsibility for bidding on jobs, and the bids often had to be made in circumstances that prevented extensive consultation with the yard foremen who would do the work. Further, the items bid on often turned out to be only a portion of the work required. A full assessment could only be made once the ship was in dry dock and the engines had been taken apart. Further work was then negotiated between the contract executives and the shipowners.

Once work had begun, little effort was made to keep track of shop costs on a current basis so that the foremen would have an idea of the costs incurred on a job. Costs were often not even available upon completion of the job when the final negotiation of price took place. It was frequently long after payment had been received that the yard's management learned whether the job had made a contribution to overhead and profit.

A period of profit difficulty inspired the shipyard's president to put more emphasis on cost control. He discovered that more effective information was essential to achieving his objectives. He therefore began to introduce organizational and system changes designed to make it possible for the contract managers to assume overall responsibility for a given job, including negotiation of the price and control of costs. In addition, shop foremen were also to be given information on current job cost more rapidly—perhaps twice weekly. In any event, it was considered essential to have the costs by the time the final price negotiation was undertaken a few days after the job was completed.

Information and Rewards

The impact of the information system and the reward structure on behavior is a familiar subject. Where the reward system conflicts with the corporate goals, the reward system usually has the stronger impact on the actions of managers and employees.

This reaction is reasonable. Corporate goals are rather vague objectives that should find concrete reinforcement in the reward system. Further, the reward system is the source of the dollars-and-cents in the pay envelope, of the promotion, and of other status privileges such as reserved parking spots.

Thus, where the information system and the reward system are in conflict, serious distortions of action are likely to occur. For example, one company's regulations provided that no shift could take any credit for a job not completed by the end of that shift. Work reports were collected thirty minutes before the end of the shift. No doubt these arrangements made sense in departments where the jobs were small, where one transistor more or less did not amount to a great deal. It was probably also thought that the rule would eliminate the difficult task of allocating credit for partly completed jobs.

On the other hand, in departments where jobs were large and frequently required more than one shift to complete, the distortion was substantial and detrimental. Shift foremen hid work that had been partly completed so they could finish it on their shift the next day and obtain some credit for the time and costs charged to them. Also, very little work was done in the last half hour of each shift. Indeed, after the last task was done that could be fully completed before the reports were collected, little was accomplished on the shift. Great distrust was created between shifts, reducing cooperation where cooperation is always difficult to develop.

Another serious type of distortion in the information system can be created, for instance, by a manager who insists that his subordinates meet an unrealistic level of performance. When he backs his demands with threats of major punishment, his men are apt to supplement their ability to produce with "creative" reporting in order to show the required results. Creative reporting can take a variety of forms, from outright fraudulent action to generous estimates of key variables where there is reasonable room for uncertainty.

Creative reporting can create many serious problems. One of the most serious is that it undermines the reliability and effectiveness of the information system by making it a less accurate reflection of reality. A variety of internal audits may help eliminate or reduce the creativity; but, by the time the corrections are made, it may be too late to make effective changes in the operations or to maintain confidence in the general information system.

Status Incongruence

The growth of elaborate information systems has tended to increase the problem of status incongruence—situations in which men of lower status are required to tell executives of higher status what to do. Because of the technical requirements of automated data systems, specialists are required to design, implement, and maintain them. These men may be respected by the organization for their technical skill, but they often are considered to have less status than line operating executives who appear to be inferior in terms of pay and education. There is a danger, therefore, that the ideas of the staff, however valid, may not be well received by the line. The problem is compounded if various analytic, diagnostic, and corrective functions are assigned to these technical departments. When lower status groups not only have responsibility for maintaining the system itself but for analyzing operations and for initiating corrective action or innovation, their suggestions are likely at least to be subverted and perhaps rejected outright by operating managers, to the confusion and consternation of the staff.

It is difficult to lay down general rules for more effective staff-line relationships. The information systems aspect is but a recent development in a history of conflicts between line managers and staff specialists of all sorts, including industrial engineers, controllers, personnel specialists, and others who arrive from central office staff positions claiming to know how to reorganize work and improve efficiency. In the information area, one technique which has often been effective is to pair a technical specialist with an executive from the field, giving them joint responsibility for such tasks as working out a new system and for trouble-shooting when difficulties arise with an existing system.

Wherever possible, appropriate status relationships and information processing should be in harmony with information flowing from lower to higher management while action is initiated in reverse. Yet it is important that innovations and suggestions are not stifled in the junior ranks. A positive response to suggestions is obviously an effective attitude for senior management to have.

Control of Data

The problem of data control is linked to most of the organizational factors that have been discussed. The trend toward electronic data processing has had the tendency to concentrate the collection of data in a few data centers, taking away traditional local control of this function. Whereas local management formerly had some control over what information was generated when and could develop special analyses if necessary from the data at hand, now these functions are performed elsewhere according to schedules that may not be the most convenient or effective for local management. Furthermore, local management has lost control over the nature of information it receives. It is now given data, perhaps by departments of lower status, without being directly involved in the analysis of the data or even its processing.

The control of information thus becomes involved in interdepartmental conflict, status problems, and assumptions about human nature. Interdepartmental rivalry can be particularly serious if one department controls and harbors information that another department must have. For example, if the production scheduling department does not provide sufficiently early warning about impending changes, the production departments themselves may not have sufficient flexibility and time to adjust without waste of resources.

Careful thought must be given, in planning and using control and information systems, to insure that the right information gets to the right place in the organization. It is possible that blocks in the information flow are unintentional—one department may not be aware of another department's needs. The question of what is the "right" information is discussed below.

Excess Information

The preceding comments have suggested some of the dangers of too little information. Although this is perhaps the more common problem, it is also true that too much information can be equally inefficient. Many efforts at "scientific management" have foundered because managers have been unable to make sense of the mass of information that was provided, often in relatively undigested form and in bulky computer printout format. After struggling with the material for a while, field managers conclude that the benefits are not worth the effort. They ignore the elaborate documents and instead concentrate on those few items that are most useful. Their reaction may be one of disillusionment with all data processing.

This reaction is unfortunate and unnecessary. A careful analysis of an executive's needs should also indicate what he does not need. There is a positive benefit in not providing him with relatively useless data, although such data may be kept for background and backup information in the event a special analysis is required.

CRITICAL VARIABLES

An efficient information system generates data relevant to the manager who uses the reports. An important first step in the development of an information system, therefore, is the identification of these critical variables.

The specific nature of the variables changes for different operations. They may be recorded in dollars, hours, weights, in ratio form (such as productivity measure of units per hour or per dollar), or in any of many other ways. The two common characteristics, however, of all relevant control data are:

1 The data must report on a portion of the operation over which management has some actual control, a portion which management can change or influence.

2 The data must relate to the more-significant rather than to the less-significant aspects of the operation.

Although the reasons may be self-evident why these are the two significant common characteristics for effective control and planning systems, it is worthwhile emphasizing a few of the more important factors. First, considering that the manager should be neither over- nor underinformed, it is essential that the information he receives is relevant. This condition requires that the information is focused on what the manager can manage himself, on what he can control. If the labor force is fixed in size and pay, as in many service organizations, the local manager may want information about productivity, about whether he is using his labor force to produce the maximum revenue or accomplish the most work. His superiors, who have responsibility for overall planning, may find total dollars useful in their jobs. Total dollar cost figures might be relatively useless to the local executive, however.

For reasons of relevance, it is often advisable to avoid cluttering reports for operating managers with a myriad of complex accruals and allocations for costs over which they have no control. A plant manager, who has no direct influence whatever over research expenditures, is not aided if his operating budget and reports carry an allocation for corporate research and development. It is confusing enough when these allocations are separately identified on the budget and control reports. It is particularly confusing when they are integrated into standard costs and cannot be separated or segregated when detailed operations analyses are made.

The second point mentioned relates to the importance of concentrating on the significant rather than on the insignificant aspects within the functions over which the manager has control. In the case of a service industry, the most important measures would be those giving an index of productivity. In the space program, quality control might be the most important factor, the one measured first and in several ways. In other situations, the important variable might be production volume, speed, product mix, or almost any combination of these and other elements. But, whatever the critical variables, the information system should generate data of use in their evaluation and management.

The nature of the information required at each level of management may well differ in most cases. The president of a company may be most concerned with the monthly income statements and ultimately with the financial reports for the entire year. Given his responsibility for overall administration and the need to explain the company's policies and prospects to shareholders and public, these aggregate results are necessary for him to exercise his duties. The same reports may be worthless to the manager of one of the company's plants or to a salesman. Likewise, the reports of value to first- or second-line management may not be of use to senior management. A well-designed system allows for these differences in needs, focusing on the relevant variables for each level of administration.

TIMELINESS

From the manager's point of view, the most relevant information on the most critical variables is worth nothing unless it arrives in time for him to take action based on the information it contains. Trends must be discovered in time for corrective action to be taken or, depending on the circumstances, in time for the managers to capitalize on favorable opportunities. It is easy to see the consternation that sets in among stock market traders when the reports of transactions on the security exchanges begin to run late. A few minutes delay can make the difference between affluence and insolvency. Other examples may be less spectacular. For the shipyard cited earlier, the failure to have cost information available at the time final price negotiations were taking place made it very difficult to know where to resist the pressure to make price concessions. In the same company, financial reports were prepared only once a quarter and were not available until four to six weeks after the quarter ended. In these circumstances, management was in the position of a pilot flying in the clouds under instrument control but whose instruments did not work until he had landed.

In many firms, reports for a month are ready by the middle of the following month. Moreover, it is often possible to obtain reports on critical variables weekly or daily or even more often, as is done in the case of electric generating stations in times of peak demand. Occasionally some educated guesses are required for some entries in order to produce reports promptly, but this action may be preferable to delaying until all information can be collected. For example, the Chesapeake and Ohio Railroad releases a preliminary financial report each January 1 for the previous year and has it in the mail that day.

The temptation, given the need for prompt information, is to push for faster and faster reporting. The controller of a large international oil company recently said that when he came with the company thirty years ago, consolidated financial statements were prepared once a year. During the next twenty years, schedules were advanced to permit consolidated reporting on a quarterly basis. The last ten years have seen the development of monthly reporting, and he looks forward to weekly and even daily reporting within the next ten. Given the need to plan transportation and to balance the various sources of production with the demands of the worldwide marketplace, he could use daily information to good advantage.

Faster reporting does have its costs. In the C&O instance cited, it is primarily the preliminary work and the cost of having the financial and accounting staff show up on New Year's Eve. In other cases, faster reporting can be much more expensive, involving massive redesigning of systems, major investments in data processing equipment, and costs of training and supporting the skilled manpower to run the system. It is therefore essential to ask at each step whether the increase in reporting speed is worth the cost of obtaining that speed. The appraisal of the tradeoffs may be (of necessity) intuitive, one in which the figures and facts are not precise, but it is an evaluation worth making.

The same questions need to be asked, the same tradeoffs need to be made, when any change is contemplated in a management information system. Questions should be asked from time to time about existing systems as well. Changes in business practice, in environmental circumstances, in staffing, and in other relevant factors, may change the nature of information needed by an effective manager. As new systems are put in, old systems providing unnecessary information may be phased out. Some companies, such as the large English store chain of Marks & Spencer, have even gone so far as to eliminate almost all central record keeping. The argument they advance is that the cost of maintaining much of the information is far greater than the benefits derived from knowing what it is.

SUMMARY

Time, not dollars, is often the scarcest resource. This is particularly true of skilled managerial time, a scarce commodity indeed. It is essential that managerial time be spent where it can be most productive. One important function of a good management planning and control system is to help managers identify the areas in which their time can be most productively spent. The system should also consume the minimum amount of managerial time in making such an identification. These characteristics have led to emphasis on the development of systems that meet the criteria discussed in this note and to the resulting technique known as "management by exception." Managers concentrate on those areas that are in difficulty and capitalize on those areas that are going unusually well. The information system should assist in bringing these areas to management's attention and should not obscure them amongst massive quantities of useless data.

The key elements required to permit management by exception are:

1   The provision of information on critical and manageable variables;
2   The dissemination of this information to those who can take actions based on it;
3 The generation of the data in time for it to be of use.

Proper organization of the information system, its harmonious support of the corporate goals, and its congruence with the structure of the organization all contribute to its effectiveness.

It is unrealistic to expect perfection in all aspects. Once a satisfactory system is operating, however, it is useful to identify areas of conflict, areas that tend to interfere with the functioning of the system, so that remedial action can be taken should the conflict be sufficiently severe. Otherwise, it may be most efficient to avoid tinkering with the system and to accept the fact that few things are perfect this side of heaven.

Reading 37

Budgeting: Functional Analysis and Behavioral Implications

V. Bruce Irvine

Many of those who have written about budgets have emphasized the problems resulting from typical budgeting systems. Little enthusiasm has been voiced for the practical effectiveness of budgets as a means of obtaining the optimal benefits of which such a device is capable.

A more positive approach might result from a consideration of the control and motivational effects of budgets on the behavior of people. But an analysis of the reactions of these people (supervisors, foremen, laborers) to control devices (such as budgets) has received little attention as a specific subject in the literature of the past decade. The studies reported have usually concentrated attention on improving the usefulness of budgets from a top management viewpoint and have de-emphasized the subordinate positions. Also, many of the studies have been conducted by behavioral scientists and have not been incorporated into accounting and management thought and teaching. Consequently, although accountants and management are aware that their actions have behavioral implications, they have not thoroughly understood what these are. The result is uncertainty, confusion and indecision when human problems do arise.

The purpose of this article will be to make a functional analysis of budgeting towards the goal of maximizing long-run profits (considered to be the present value of the owner's net worth). An analysis of reactions of the employees on whom budgets are primarily exercised, rather than a purely management viewpoint analysis, will be used to develop basic propositions. Human behavioral aspects of budgets, therefore, become a very relevant factor in this approach. After investigation of why employees react as they do, the usefulness of budgets in view of such reactions and the implications of suggestions for making budgets more successful and acceptable can be considered within particular situations facing modern-day business.

DEFINITIONAL AND TECHNICAL CONSIDERATIONS

A functional analysis considers the various consequences of a particular activity and determines whether or not these consequences aid in the achievement of the organization's objective. According to Merton,[1] the consequences of an activity

---

"Budgeting: Functional Analysis and Behavioral Implications," V. Bruce Irvine, *Cost and Management,* March–April, 1970, pp. 6–16. Reprinted with permission.
[1]Merton, R., "A Paradigm for Functional Analysis in Sociology" in *Sociological Theory: A Book of Readings* by L. Coser and B. Rosenberg, New York, MacMillan, 1957, pp. 458–467.

are functional if they increase the ability of a given system to achieve a desired goal. A consequence is dysfunctional if it hinders the achievement of the goal. Consequences of an activity may also be classified as manifest (recognized and intended by the participants in the system) or latent (neither intended nor recognized). Decisions based only on manifest consequences may often be incorrect because of latent consequences.

A budget is a device intended to provide greater effectiveness in achieving organizational efficiency. To be effective, however, the functional aspects must outweigh the dysfunctional aspects. Whether or not this will be true will depend upon many factors which will be discussed and summarized in a model of the elements of budgeting.

First, it is necessary to understand what a budget is. Although formal definitions of a budget exist, a definition is not always the most relevant aspect of understanding a concept.

Amitai Etzioni distinguishes between two types of models in organizational analysis.[2] The survival system consists of activities which, if fulfilled, allow a system to exist. Budgets are not part of such a system. Organizations in the past have functioned and in the future will function without the help of budgets. Budgets can be classified within an effectiveness system. These "define a pattern of interactions among the elements of the system which would make it more effective in the service of a given goal."[3]

A budget, as a formal set of figures written on a piece of paper, is in itself merely a quantified plan for future activities. However, when budgets are used for control, planning and motivation, they become instruments which cause functional and dysfunctional consequences both manifest and latent which determine how successful the tool will be.

Budgets mean different things to different people according to their different points of view. Accountants see them from the preparation aspect, managers from the implementation aspect, and behavioral scientists from the human implication aspect. All of these viewpoints must be melded together if budgets are to obtain the best functional results.

There are many types of budgets. The major purpose for having budgets, the type of organization using a budget, the personalities of people handling the budget, the personal characteristics of people subject to budget direction, the leadership style of the organization, and the method of preparing a budget are all factors accounting for budget type and style.

The technical procedures involved in the preparation and use of budget figures are similar for most organizations. People make estimates (standards) of what they expect should reflect future events. These estimates are then compared to what actually happened and the differences (variances) are studied.

[2]Etzioni, Amitai. "Two Approaches to Organizational Analysis: A Critique and a Suggestion" in Bobbs-Merrill Reprint Series in the Social Sciences 8-80. Reprinted by permission of *Administrative Science Quarterly,* Vol. 5 (Sept. 1960), pp. 257–278.

[3]Ibid., p. 272.

THE FUNCTIONAL ASPECTS OF BUDGET SYSTEMS

In what specific way do budgets make management action more efficient and effective in maximizing the present value of the owners' worth?

Basically, a budget system enables management more effectively to plan, coordinate, control and evaluate the activities of the business. These are functional, manifest consequences in terms of their desirability.

Planning means establishing objectives in advance so that members of the organization will have specific, activity-directed goals to guide their actions. Budgets are quantitative plans for action. As such, they force management to examine the available resources and to determine how these can be used efficiently.

The point that budgets require this clarification and concrete quantification of ideas is not usually recognized directly by budgeting people as a benefit. As such, it could be considered functional and latent.

The planning aspect of budgeting has other latent functions. Planning requires that the plans be communicated to those involved in carrying them out. Communication is enhanced by distributing the budget to those responsible for various parts of it.

A budget makes lower level managers more aware of where they fit into an organization. Their budget indicates what is expected of them and that they have a goal towards which their activities are to be directed.

With a budget, junior (new) members of an organization have a better idea of where the company is going and are made to feel that the business is concerned about their future. This can affect both their own future plans and the company's recruitment policy and turnover problems.

When a person is given an objective, he is more likely to feel that he is part of the organization and that the upper echelons are interested in his work. Conversely, top management is likely to become more interested in, and aware of, the activities of lower level employees.

These latent, functional consequences of budgets create interest and, possibly, enthusiasm which increases morale and could result in greater efficiency and initiative.

Planning of departmental activities must be coordinated so that bottle-necks do not occur and inter-departmental strife can be limited. A budget system can assist in this coordination. By basing organizational activity on the limiting factor (such as sales, production, working capital), a comprehensive budget coordinating all of the firm's activities can be approved by top management and the controller. Such a budget permits these people to bring together their overall knowledge of the firm's abilities and limitations. By using budgets to coordinate activities, the organization is more likely to operate at an optimal level, given the constraints on its resources.

The control consequences are among the more important aspects of budgeting. Because a budget plan exists, decisions are not merely spontaneous reactions to stimuli in an environment of unclarified goals. The budget provides relevant information to a decision maker at the time he must choose between alternatives. Therefore, a budget implicitly incorporates control at the point of the decision. However, provision for taking advantage of unforseen situations should certainly be allowed even though a budget is violated.

A second type of control can be derived from budgets. A comparison of actual with budgeted performance after decisions have been made reveals to management the performance of the organization as a whole and of the individual responsible members.

A comparison merely reveals discrepancies. The action which is taken as a result of variances is in the hands of management. But the investigation of why there are variances, whether or not they are controllable, and the resulting control procedures is stimulated by the budgeting process. The result is the discovery of methods to save costs, improvement in the firm's efficiency, and better future planning.

Control of both types is important to top management because it cannot maintain personal contact with those in the lower management ranks. Devices such as budgets, employment contracts, job descriptions and rules are therefore necessary to direct subordinate behavior. In general, control is based on the assumption that individuals are motivated by their own security needs to fulfil the plans and obey the rules. To the extent that this is true, the benefits to be derived from the control aspects of budgeting can be deemed functional and manifest.

These benefits could be obtained only in the ideal situation where budgets work as they are intended to work. The theoretical benefits make budgets very appealing devices, but the practical problems of implementing and using them greatly affect their usefulness. Most of the problems arise from the difficulty of convincing people to accept and use a budget. Mechanical problems also exist. These difficulties create many possibilities for dysfunctional consequences to occur with the result that some functional consequences become difficult, if not impossible, to attain.

DYSFUNCTIONAL ASPECTS OF BUDGET SYSTEMS

Any system which involves motivation and control of individuals has dysfunctional aspects, simply because human behavior cannot be predicted or controlled with certainty. Frequently, activities by management to obtain desired functional results will actually lead to dysfunctional consequences. Management must understand why such a reversal can occur so that existing problems can be solved or an environment created which prevents problems arising.

This section will indicate how results of a budget system can be dysfunctional in nature. The basic approach will be to analyze the deterrents to achieving particular functional results. Within a particular organization, the dysfunctional aspects must be considered in relation to the functional aspects in order to evaluate the worthiness of a budget system. Obviously, if the dysfunctional consequences of an action outweigh the functional aspects, management should delete the activity. Because each business is unique, no attempt can be made to state that certain activities will be dysfunctional or functional in every situation.

Because factors which can lead to dysfunctional consequences are complex, each will be analyzed separately although it is realized they are usually inter-related.

A The Term "Budget"

The first dysfunctional consequence of a budget system results from the name itself. Traditionally, budgets have carried a negative connotation for many:

> . . . some of the words historically associated with the term budget are: imposed, dictated by the top, authorized. And what are the original purposes of control—to reduce, to eliminate, to increase productivity, to secure conformance, to assure compliance, to inform about deviation. An historical meaning of budget is to husband resources—to be niggardly, tight, Scrooge-like.[4]

If attitudes expressing such beliefs are not eliminated at the start, the budget will never get off the ground. One method of eliminating this problem is to refrain from calling the activity "budgeting."

B Organizational Arrangements of Authority and Responsibility

If a budget system is to be used to control and evaluate personnel, the persons involved must possess responsibility and authority over what is being assigned to them. Consequently a large and/or decentralized organization would probably have a greater potential use for budgeting than would a small, highly centralized business.

Centralized organizations may simply use budgets to plan and coordinate future activities. Because responsibility, control and authority rest with the top executives in such a business, any attempt to reward, punish or hold lower level employees responsible for variances would achieve nothing beneficial and would probably cause resentment. Any negative feelings on the part of those who follow directives in carrying out operations would likely lead to less than optimal achievement of organizational objectives. Therefore, even though budgets can be used to improve planning and coordination, assignment of control responsibilities where there is no power to carry out those responsibilities could easily create dysfunctional, latent consequences.

On the other hand, over-emphasis on departmentalization can also have dysfunctional, latent effects:

---

[4]Green, Jr., David, "Budgeting and Accounting: The Inseparable Siamese Twins," *Budgeting*, Nov. 1965, p. 11.

Budget records, as administered, foster a narrow viewpoint on the part of the user. The budget records serve as a constant reminder that the important aspect to consider is one's own department and not one's own plant.[5]

Over-emphasis on one's own department can lead to considerable cost in man hours, money and interpersonal relations when responsibility for variances, particularly large ones, is being determined. The result is a weakening of cooperation and coordination between departments.

C Role-conflict Aspects of Budgeting

Status differences, or more accurately role-conflict between staff and line personnel, are an important source of dysfunctional consequences. The problems created affect budget usefulness directly and also indirectly through their effect on communication, motivation and participation. The basic difficulties arise because of differences in the way budget staff people and line personnel understand the budgeting system and each other.

From Figure 1,[6] it can be seen how important budgets and the budget staff are in the supervisors' or foremen's working world. Ninety-nine per cent of the supervisors and foremen questioned in four companies stated that the budget department was either first or second in importance of impact on the performance of their activity.

From the supervisors' and foremen's follow-up comments, it was readily apparent that the budget department's influence was not only significant, it was usually considered troublesome as well. Why should this be so? Some suggested reasons are:

1 Line employees see budgets as providing results only and not the reasons for those results. Any explanations of variances by the financial staff, such as failure to meet expected production or inadequate use of materials, prove grossly

[5]Argyris, Chris, *The Impact of Budgets on People,* Ithaca, N.Y. Prepared for the Controllership Foundation, Inc. at Cornell University, 1952, p. 23.

[6]The source of this figure and study is Argyris, C., op. cit., a summary of comments and statements, pp. 10–12.

Figure 1 Responses to the Request "Name the Departments Affecting Your Actions Most" Asked of Supervisors and Foremen Individually in Four Firms.

	Most affect	2nd most affect	Total
Production Control	55%		
Budget Department	45%	54%	99%

insufficient. Causes behind these explanations still have to be determined before the supervisors and foremen could consider budget reports as being useful to them or presenting a fair appraisal of their activities to top management.

2 Budgets are seen as emphasizing past performance and as a device for predicting the future. Supervisors and foremen are basically concerned with the present and with handling immediate problems. Budget figures would often be ignored in order to solve present difficulties.

3 Supervisors and foremen apparently see budgets as being too rigid. In some cases, budget standards have not been changed for two or three years. Even if they now met such a budget, they often would not be performing efficiently. Budget people would then adjust the budget. In such cases, those working under a budget would not really know what was expected of them until after they had submitted their cost reports and had received a control report.

4 Supervisors and foremen would also resent the opposite treatment of constantly changing a budget in the belief that increased efficiency would result. Such a procedure would lead them to believe, and often justly so, that budgets were unrealistically set. Budget men would be seen as individuals who could never be satisfied as they would raise the budget if a person made or came close to his previous budget. This would only result in frustration for the supervisor or foreman. The feeling that the company executives did not believe in the supervisor's own desire to do a good job could easily be implied when budgets are continually changing.

5 Thoughts about budgets are further aggravated when foremen and supervisors receive budget reports on their performance in a complicated format with an analysis that is incomprehensible to them. Supervisors felt that the job of budget people was to be critical and that the use of jargon and specialized formats enabled them to justify their criticism of others without too much debate.

Whether or not these criticisms are logical and rational is not important. The point is that such feelings can and do exist. If the budget is regarded as merely emphasizing history, being too rigid, unrealistic, unattainable and unclear and if budget people are seen as over-concerned with figures, unconcerned with line problems and cut off by a language of their own, there can be no doubt that the effectiveness of a budget system would deteriorate.

The problems are compounded if the budget personnel's attitude is unconducive to overcoming these opinions. Budget people should see their jobs as examining, analyzing and looking for new ways to improve plant efficiency. They should also think of a budget as an objective that should fairly challenge factory personnel. Since it cannot be assumed that line personnel subscribe to or even recognize these ideas, the ideas should be impressed upon them directly through adequate budget introduction and education. Moreover, the effective use of budgets cannot be forced upon supervisors and foremen; it must be accepted by them. This can only be accomplished if budget people try to work constructively with line people as compatriots rather than commanders. This accord is usually very difficult to bring about. Often budget people will not even attempt it or simply give up on it because of lack of success. They conclude, correctly or incorrectly, that the line personnel's unsatisfactory use of budgets is due to their lack of education, understanding and interest.

Given this unwillingness to buck line opposition by the budget personnel and the line's viewpoint of budgeting as a hindrance to their performance, a classic role-conflict is created. The optimal benefits possible from budgeting cannot be obtained in such an environment.

Argyris also determined how foremen and supervisors felt the potential dysfunctional results of budgeting could be overcome. Suggestions dealt mainly with improving the outlook of budget men. According to the line personnel, budgeting people should be taught that budgets are merely opinions, not the "be-all and end-all." They should also be taught, it was felt, that line employees are not inherently lazy, that budget men should learn to look at a problem from another's point of view, and that they are not superior to supervisory people. Also suggested were the use of timely and understandable reports to foremen and supervisors, the practice of conferring with people who have variances so that the budget report indicates the real cause to top management, and the setting of realistic budgets.

The problems arising are not, however, entirely the fault of the budget staff. Supervisors and foremen must put more effort into understanding the budget figures, they must not be continually suspicious of budgets, and they should use budgets in performing their duties. Most important, they should alter their outlook toward budgeting. Budgets must be realistic and fair, but also foremen and supervisors should realize that the budget is designed to help them achieve the standards management expects of them.

How can these requirements be achieved? An educational program involving foremen, supervisors, middle and upper management, and budget personnel could help to clarify the different viewpoints and promote understanding of each other's objectives and difficulties. Such a program should precede the introduction of a budgeting system and continue after the system has been introduced.

D Budgets and Non-Management People

The involvement of laborers (non-management personnel) in the budgeting process presents both functional and dysfunctional possibilities. Often, front-line supervisors who have a budget to meet do not use it as a device to spur their subordinates. According to the comments reported by Argyris, they fear that workers would look upon such action unfavorably and that no benefit would be received.

The proposition that workers would not respond to budgetary pressures is challenged by W. F. Whyte:

> How do workers see budgets? They often recognize that management people are worried about costs, but with the foremen afraid to put the cost situation to them, they remain uninvolved in the struggle.[7]

[7]Whyte, W. F., *Men at Work,* Richard D. Irwin, Inc. and The Dorsey Press, Inc., Homewood, Ill., 1961, p. 495.

Since workers generally have not been directly involved in budgetary systems, the question of whether or not such involvement would be functional is unresolved.

E Motivational Aspects of Budgeting

The most controversial area of budgeting concerns its motivational implications.

The budget makes available information for comparison of expected with actual performance. When such an evaluation of performance is known to result in rewards and punishments, people are expected to be motivated to do their best. Let us examine this assumption and its possible functional or dysfunctional consequences.

Argyris states that budgets are principal instruments for creating pressure which motivates individuals.[8] Budgets can also be seen as creating more pressure than they actually do. This "pressure illusion" is due to the fact that the budget is a concrete, quantitative instrument and managers and supervisors, feeling pressure from more abstract sources, place the blame for it on the concrete budget.

Factors directly related to budget pressures are budget "pep" talks (A), red circles around poor showings (B), production and sales drives using budgets (C), threats of reprimand (D), and feelings of failure if budgets are not met (E). These can all be considered as functional and manifest in terms of their motivational intent.

There are, however, counteracting effects which can be dysfunctional and latent in terms of budget effectiveness. These factors include informal agreements among managers and/or supervisors (V), fear of loss of job if efficiency increases but cannot be maintained (W), union agreements against speedups (X), performance abilities of individual employees (Y), and abilities of work teams as a whole (Z).

Equilibrium is attained when:

$$A + B + C + D + E = V + W + X + Y + Z$$

Management, by increasing one or more of the components on the left hand side of the relationship or by adding additional ones, can increase productivity. This increase is matched by an increase in tension, uneasiness, resentment and suspicion on the part of the employees. This pressure increase is absorbed by joining groups which are strongly cohesive against top management and budget people. Again equilibrium is attained but each time pressures are increased by top management, they must become more intense as resistance is higher.

When and if management feels that the pressures are detrimental to the organization, it may attempt to reduce the causes on the left hand side of the equation. This does not result in decreased anti-management feeling because the groups have developed into relatively permanent social units and the indi-

[8]Op. cit., Argyris.

viduals feel the pressures may occur again. Therefore, in the long run, increasing pressures may be very dysfunctional because of these latent features.

The rational way for management to approach this problem would be to concentrate its activities on reducing the forces that decrease efficiency rather than on increasing the factors that tend to increase efficiency.

Other dysfunctional ways of relieving motivational pressure could easily exist:

1   Interdepartmental strife could occur. A manager, supervisor or foreman could try to blame the variances on someone else. This would result in concentrated effort by individuals to promote only the cause of their own departments. The personal rivalries thus caused and the lack of cooperation among departments could mean decreased efficiency for the company in achieving its overall goals.

2   Another type of strife develops when the line employees blame the staff employees for their predicaments and absolve themselves of the responsibility for the variances. Budget people become scapegoats for problems and salesmen are blamed for incorrect predictions or orders that make the production process unstable.

3   An individual may internalize the personal pressure he feels. By not outwardly showing his problems, he would build up tension within himself. Eventually, frustration would develop and he would perform less efficiently in the long run.

4   If internal means of relieving pressure are used, manipulation of activities may result. Reporting sizable variances when one knows he will be over his budget may allow him to shift his costs so that he will easily make his budget in the next period. Saving easy jobs until just before the end of a budget period may enable a person to achieve the stipulated goal.

The point is that, in the short run, increasing motivational pressure through budgets may be functional but, in the long run, it may also be very dysfunctional.

Andrew C. Stedry postulates additional concepts concerning motivation through budgeting.[9] Through experiment, Stedry developed the findings shown in Figure 2.

The level of costs for which a person will strive (aspired costs) will be conceived by the individual in relation to past experience, confidence in his personal skills, expectation of future difficulties, and his feelings about the budget costs. Aspired and budget costs do not necessarily (or usually) coincide. The aspired costs are what the individual sets for himself. The budget costs are set by top management. When actual costs are compared to these two costs, the reaction of the employees depends on the discrepancies involved:

1   Other things being equal, aspiration levels will move relative to the actual costs depending on the degree of discrepancy.

[9]Stedry, Andrew C., *Budget Control and Cost Behavior*, Englewood Cliffs, N.J., Prentice-Hall, Inc., 1960.

Figure 2 Simplified Model of Stedry's Motivational Relationships Involving Aspirations

Start	Budget Costs	Aspired Costs		Previous Actual Costs	
If Encouragement	Budget Costs ←	New Aspired Costs ←		Start Actual Costs	
If Discouraged	Budget Costs			New Aspired Costs	Start Actual Costs
If Failure		Quit or a change in the system such as a lowering of the budget			

2   A person will be encouraged if the discrepancy between actual costs and aspired costs is not greater than an amount known as the discouragement point. Aspirations would be set higher on the next period of performance measurement.

3   A person will be discouraged if the discrepancy is greater than the discouragement point but less than a failure point. In this case, aspirations would move downward.

4   If the discrepancy is greater than the failure point, the system would cease to exist or a new one would be needed. Otherwise the individual concerned would resign.

Stedry concludes that management should set high, unattainable budgets to motivate individuals to achieve the greatest efficiency. "Unattainable" would have to mean that the discrepancy between aspired costs, formulated after the high budget was presented, and actual costs could not exceed the discouragement point. Such a policy would mean that individuals receiving separate budgets would be manipulated in accordance with the variances in the size of their discouragement points.

This may sound all right in theory but in practice the reactions of employees could make this a dangerous proposition for long-run efficiency. If individuals found out that they were the subjects of outright manipulation, they could become rebellious and ignore future budgets whether they were fair or not. Other management control devices would probably be considered with unwarranted suspicion. Moreover, how is management going to determine the aspiration level and discouragement point of each individual, a necessary requirement for setting "personal" budgets? The use of individual budget standards would also have to be kept confidential. Otherwise, the resentment that employees would feel might lead them to resist all budgeting attempts and even to leave the organization.

Stedry's study suggests that participation in budget preparation is not as beneficial as having management set the budget. He points out, however, that participation may be desirable where low budgets are given as managers, supervisors and foremen would likely feel that they are capable of achieving greater efficiency and would say so.

Stedry's study is limited in that long-run results were not extensively examined. Also, the nature of his "laboratory" data leads to serious questions as to whether "real business world" conditions were reproduced.[10] However, his research on the reactions of lower level management to budgets does help to explain the behavior of these people. The study also indicates how management can improve a budgeting process where budgets are being ignored or causing personnel problems, because it shows why such situations exist.

Another consequence of budgetary motivation which has received little emphasis involves "a fear of failure" on the part of the individual. The failure to meet a budget or at least come close to it when it is accepted and fairly determined and when other members of a person's reference group are successful, represents a potential loss of status both within the group and the organization. A person's self-concept is also deflated in such circumstances.

The fear of such a loss may be a stronger motivating factor for a person to achieve his budget than any of the other pressures mentioned. "Fear of failure" then is a very powerful functional consequence of budgeting systems and, quite likely, is latent.

One of the major benefits of budgeting is motivation, explicitly incorporated in the use of standards. Budgets should reflect a goal which people can strive towards and achieve. To provide maximum motivation for employees, management should judge failure to achieve an objective in the context of the situation causing failure and not merely in terms of a figure circled in red. All members of the organization must be aware of this basic principle.

F Participation in Budgeting

In a participatory system of budgeting, preparation of budget schedules would start at the lower levels of the hierarchy and move upward. As it moved upward, various people would make additional suggestions and some eliminations until the schedules reached the controller and top management. These people would analyze it and see that it was a coordinated plan in accordance with organizational goals before final approval would be given. Movement up and down the hierarchy could be made if drastic changes were necessary. By reciprocal communications, people would know why changes were justified and could constructively criticize them if they desired.

Behavioral scientists and accountants generally believe that such a system would be an improvement on imposed budgets. The functional, manifest results claimed for this system are:

[10]Becker, Selwyn and Green, Jr., David, "Budgeting and Employee Behavior" in *Journal of Business,* Vol. 35 (1962). These are among the authors who debate the practical application of Stedry's conclusions.

1 It would have a healthful effect on interest, initiative, morale and enthusiasm.

2 It would result in a better plan because the knowledge of many individuals is combined.

3 It would make all levels of management more aware of how their particular functions fit into the total operational picture.

4 It would increase interdepartmental cooperation.

5 As a result of their direct involvement in the planning function, it would make junior management more aware of the future with respect to objectives, problems and other considerations.

It is possible to achieve these benefits through successful participation. There are, however, factors that have a significant impact on whether or not participation can lead to successful results.

One essential requirement is that participation be legitimate. If participation is allowed but top management continually changes the budgeted figures resulting from participation, legitimate participation does not exist. This might better be described as a form of "pseudo-participation." The supposed "participants" would likely resent such a policy and the consequences would be dysfunctional. This is borne out by the studies of V. H. Vroom who found that productivity was higher when participation was viewed as legitimate, but lower when it was viewed as not legitimate.[11]

Other factors limiting the usefulness of budget participation are:

1 Personality differences of managers as reflected in their leadership style are important. Aggressive managers can put forth their demands more strongly than meek ones. Subordinates would view the latter as not looking out for their interests and antagonism between subordinates and their superiors, and managers themselves, could easily develop.

2 An autocratic, centralized organization would have little use for a participation policy whereas a democratic, decentralized organization would likely benefit from, and almost require, a participation policy.

3 Those allowed participation rights must be positively oriented towards the objectives of the firm. Only if the group is cohesive in thought and desire toward, and understands, the plan can participation policy be functional.

4 The cultural setting of an organization and the background of employees should be considered. People in rural areas or with a rural background are more inclined to accept assigned tasks. In such an atmosphere, a participation policy would probably meet with little response.

Studies have been carried out showing that participation in any situation is

---

[11]Stedry, Andrew C., "Budgeting and Employee Behavior: A Reply" in *The Journal of Business*, Vol. 37 (April 1964), p. 198.

not necessarily useful for increasing efficiency.[12] Other studies have reported that when a non-participative group became participative and was compared with an existing non-participative or participative group, the former never caught up in terms of performance with the latter two groups. These studies imply that the introduction of a participation policy for a formerly non-participative group would not likely lead to increased efficiency and may even result in decreased efficiency. If this conclusion is accepted, a group should be endowed with the right to participate only when the group is created or the budget system is being implemented and not after either has previously been directed through decisions made by superiors.

The most severe criticism offered against participation is that the increased morale which supposedly results does not necessarily result in increased efficiency. Is high morale a cause of increased efficiency or is greater efficiency a cause of high morale, or is there some intervening variable which must be present if a true causal relationship is to exist? Group cohesiveness seems to be the most significant of possible variables that have been examined although other variables are obviously involved. Figure 3 shows postulated relationships that could develop using group cohesiveness with regard to subordinate thoughts toward management.

As those participating in a budget (foremen and up) would be management-oriented, at least to some extent, they would probably have a positive approach to management activities and objectives. The previous discussion on role-conflict situations shows, however, that negative attitudes towards budgeting are quite possible.

If the group is anti-management or anti-budget, a participation policy would

---

[12]See Stedry, ibid., p. 196; also Morse, Nancy and Reimer, E., "The Experimental Change of a Major Organizational Variable" in *Journal of Abnormal and Social Psychology*,Vol. LII (1956), pp. 120–129; and French, Jr., J. R. P., Kay, E. and Meyer, H. H., *A Study of Threat and Participation in a Performance Appraisal Situation*, New York, General Electric Co., 1962.

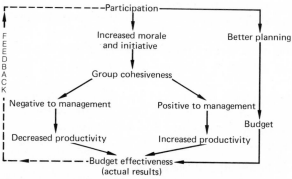

Figure 3 Participation and budgets.

be of little use. Supervisors may even propose ridiculously low standards and upper management would be forced to revise them. Pseudo-participation would exist and likely result in the increase of negative attitudes toward management or budgeting.

If the atmosphere is favorable for allowing participation, group cohesiveness toward management and budgeting should be maintained and enhanced if possible. Group discussions led by an able management man to inform *and* listen to supervisors, foremen and other management people could probably aid in implementing the budget. By listening to and taking action on suggestions made by the group, he would be able to indicate his and top management's sincerity in gaining successful participation in the budgeting system.

Undoubtedly, the evidence on the effectiveness of participation in budgeting is mixed. Supporters of participation readily admit that it is by no means a panacea for achieving the full motivational potential of the budget. The fact is that participation is not a segregated aspect of management but embraces several technical and behavioral concepts which make it more or less useful in different organizations. The organization's particular situation with regard to the development of these concepts must be recognized and thoughtfully considered when contemplating or evaluating a participation policy.

It should be noted that, even if productivity does not increase directly through participation, better planning and increased morale and initiative may, of themselves, justify such a policy.

G Communication Aspects of Budgeting

Researchers on control and motivation generally agree that information on planned and actual results should be communicated to the employee whose performance is being measured.

Nevertheless, many budget departments merely communicate the results to management with the result that the employee does not know how he has done until he is called up to discuss his performance report. Consequently, the individual may ignore the budget and perform without a guide, hoping for the best.

When results are communicated as rapidly as possible, an employee's mistakes can be associated with his recent actions and he is likely to learn more from the experience than if reports are received long after the action has been taken. This learning would likely result in improved performance on future budgets.

When reports given to management employees are timely, reasonably accurate and understandable, functional consequences are more likely to occur than if the opposite exists. Figure 4 summarizes the effect of the communication system on the behavior of line people.

H Employee Group Behavior and its Effects on Budgeting

Peter Blau's study on the use of statistical measures in evaluating employee performance has implications for evaluating and understanding budgeting.[13] The

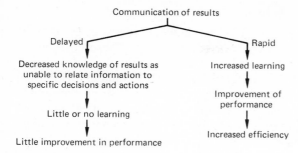

Figure 4 The importance of the communication factor when using budgets to control and motivate employees.

study examined the effect of group cohesiveness, in the sense of willingness to cooperate among members, and the resulting productivity in different situations.

His findings showed that the group which cooperated was more productive than the group which did not cooperate but competed individually among themselves. He also discovered that highly competitive individuals in the latter group were more productive than any individual in the cooperative group. Blau's hypothesis was that a paradox existed:

> . . . The resulting paradox is that competitiveness and productivity are inversely related for groups but directly related for individuals in the competitive group.[14]

In terms of the achievement of organizational objectives, the implication is that cooperative cohesiveness among group members assigned a particular task is most desirable. When this is achieved, cooperation will result in each member helping others in the group even though it may result in a decrease in the performance record of the assisting individual.

Applying this to budgeting, the suggestion is that individual performance should not be the ultimate objective in the eyes of top management or employees. Rewards and punishments should not be based entirely on an individual's performance as compared to the plan. The budget reports should be only one of many factors used for evaluation and superiors should recognize this fact. The result would be a decline in individual competition and greater cooperation towards the achievement of a goal. This environment could eliminate possible dysfunctional consequences. Group cohesiveness will be affected greatly by the leadership style of the group's superior. Whether he believes in rigidity or flexibility, whether he is authoritative or democratic, and the freedom granted him by the organizational structure and policies, will influence the way he controls his subordinates.

---

[13]Blau, Peter M., "Cooperation and Competition in a Bureaucracy" in Bobbs-Merrill Reprint Series in the Social Sciences, S-28. Reprinted by the permission of *The American Journal of Sociology,* Vol. LIX, May 1964.

[14]Ibid., p. 530.

I Mechanical Considerations of Budgeting

Dysfunctional consequences can arise from the mechanical aspects of budgeting.

Budgeting systems cost money to install and continue. These costs must always be considered in evaluating the worthiness of a system.

It must also be remembered that budgets are merely estimates or predictions. As such, they could be incorrect or inappropriate because of economic, technical and environmental changes. The estimating procedure itself may be inappropriate. If budgets are thought of as a goal rather than a means of reaching the goal, the emphasis on budgets cannot help but carry dysfunctional consequences, particularly when the estimates have been incorrectly computed.

A final mechanical problem involves the assignment of costs to the person deemed responsible for them. There is always a strong possibility that costs assigned to one person may have been caused by another. The subsequent bickering and ill-feeling would obviously be dysfunctional.

Budgets must be capable of flexibility. This is fundamentally the result of management attitudes and not inherent in the budget itself. Management must recognize that forced adherence to a plan could cause decisions to be made that are not in the long-run interest of the business. Unforeseen opportunities may arise which were not planned. A decision resulting in a significant, unfavorable variance on the short-range plan may be the best alternative in terms of long-range profitability. Failure to take advantage of such situations may result in adherence to the budget but also in dysfunctional consequences in terms of achieving the objectives of budgeting.

Alternatively, failure to adhere to budget figures when they are correct, merely to protect the individuals involved or their superiors, must also be avoided. Such an attitude would destroy one of the corner-stones of a successful budgeting system.

GENERAL MODEL OF THE CONSEQUENCES OF A BUDGETING SYSTEM

Figure 5 summarizes the factors which must be considered when determining the functional and dysfunctional consequences possible from a budgeting system.

The square immediately outside the BUDGET square indicates the potential benefits to be derived from a successful budgeting system. These benefits are functional to the more efficient achievement of an organization's goal of making profit. The next surrounding square indicates many of the factors which can aid or prevent the achievement of the desired benefits. The descriptive model is arranged so that the effects of various environmental circumstances and managerial policies (participation, motivational intentions, organization structure, etc.) can be immediately related to a particular benefit (planning). The square at the top of the diagram includes factors which are not specifically related to any one

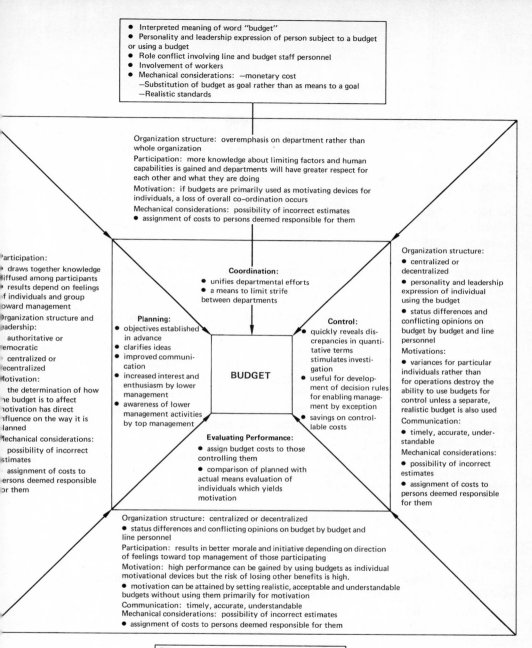

Figure 5 General model of the factors to consider when determining the functional and dysfunctional aspects of introducing and using a budgeting system.

particular benefit but which have an important influence on the success or failure of the overall budget system.

The points mentioned in the peripheral square and the top square cannot be clearly identified as either functional or dysfunctional. The relationship of these points to the benefits of budgeting depends upon the particular circumstances.

CONCLUSION

The model which has been developed to point out the functional possibilities of budgeting and to identify the sources of possible dysfunctional consequences represents a summary of relevant findings and statements by behavioral scientists, accountants and managers.

Budgeting is only one type of control technique used by top management. Many of the propositions developed are equally applicable to other types of quantitatively-oriented control techniques.

The points developed in this paper should be considered by any organization using or contemplating the introduction of a budgeting process. The importance of each point will vary, however, according to the particular organization, its strategy, history, organizational structure, reasons for using the system, the personalities involved, the leadership style of individuals in responsible positions, the general attitudes of employees toward the organization and control devices, the cohesiveness of reference groups working on and with the budget, and the personal attitudes of employees regarding the justification of, and methods of achieving, organizational goals.

The major proposition suggested is that a budgeting system designed to accomplish the designated benefits is something more than a series of figures. Its origination, implementation, and degree of success are significantly related to the behaviorally-oriented problems that can easily arise. Management methods for solving these problems cannot be generalized into a specific set of rules. Definite rules can seldom cover the particular developments of unique situations. There-fore, only general aspects of budgeting systems with emphasis on behavioral topics have been considered.

The only absolute conclusion that can be proposed is that the human factors involved are generally more difficult to identify and deal with and more serious in nature than the development of quantifying and figure determination techniques. Accountants and managers must recognize this fact if they expect to perform their functions adequately.

Reading 38

Make Performance Appraisal Relevant

Winston Oberg

These frequently voiced goals of performance appraisal programs underscore the importance of such programs to any ongoing business organization:

- Help or prod supervisors to observe their subordinates more closely and to do a better coaching job.
- Motivate employees by providing feedback on how they are doing.
- Provide back-up data for management decisions concerning merit increases, transfers, dismissals, and so on.
- Improve organization development by identifying people with promotion potential and pinpointing development needs.
- Establish a research and reference base for personnel decisions.

It has been estimated that over three fourths of U.S. companies now have performance appraisal programs.[1]

In actual practice, however, formal performance appraisal programs have often yielded unsatisfactory and disappointing results, as the growing body of critical literature attests.[2] Some critics even suggest that we abandon performance appraisal as a lost hope, and they point to scores of problems and pitfalls as evidence.

But considering the potential of appraisal programs, the issue should not be whether to scrap them; rather, it should be how to make them better. I have found that one reason for failures is that companies often select indiscriminately from the wide battery of available performance appraisal techniques without really thinking about which particular technique is best suited to a particular appraisal objective.

For example, the most commonly used appraisal techniques include:

1 Essay appraisal.
2 Graphic rating scale.
3 Field review.
4 Forced-choice rating.

"Make Performance Appraisal Relevant," Winston Oberg, *Harvard Business Review,* January–February 1972, pp. 61–67. © 1972 by the President and Fellows of Harvard College; all rights reserved. Reprinted with permission.

[1]See W. R. Spriegel and Edwin W. Mumma, *Merit Rating of Supervisors and Executives* (Austin, Bureau of Business Research, University of Texas, 1961); and Richard V. Miller, "Merit Rating in Industry: A Survey of Current Practices and Problems," ILR Research, Fall 1959.

[2]See, for example, Douglas McGregor, "An Uneasy Look at Performance Appraisal," HBR May–June 1957, p. 89; Paul H. Thompson and Gene W. Dalton, "Performance Appraisals Managers Beware," HBR January–February 1970, p. 149; and Albert W. Schrader, "Let's Abolish the Annual Performance Review," *Management of Personnel Quarterly,* Fall 1969, p. 293.

5   Critical incident appraisal.
6   Management-by-objectives approach.
7   Work-standards approach.
8   Ranking methods.
9   Assessment centers.

Each of these has its own combination of strengths and weaknesses, and none is able to achieve all of the purposes for which management institutes performance appraisal systems. Nor is any one technique able to evade all of the pitfalls. The best anyone can hope to do is to match an appropriate appraisal method to a particular performance appraisal goal.

In this article, I shall attempt to lay the groundwork for such a matching effort. First, I shall review some familiar pitfalls in appraisal programs; then, against this background, I shall assess the strengths and weaknesses of the nine commonly used appraisal techniques. In the last section, I shall match the organizational objectives listed at the outset of this article with the techniques best suited to achieving them.

SOME COMMON PITFALLS

Obstacles to the success of formal performance appraisal programs should be familiar to most managers, either from painful personal experience or from the growing body of critical literature. Here are the most troublesome and frequently cited drawbacks:

• Performance appraisal programs demand too much from supervisors. Formal performance appraisals obviously require at least periodic supervisor observation of subordinates' performance. However, the typical first-line supervisor can hardly know, in a very adequate way, just what each of 20, 30, or more subordinates is doing.
• Standards and ratings tend to vary widely and, often, unfairly. Some raters are tough, others are lenient. Some departments have highly competent people; others have less competent people. Consequently, employees subject to less competition or lenient ratings can receive higher appraisals than equally competent or superior associates.
• Personal values and bias can replace organizational standards. An appraiser may not lack standards, but the standards he uses are sometimes the wrong ones. For example, unfairly low ratings may be given to valued subordinates so they will not be promoted out of the rater's department. More often, however, outright bias dictates favored treatment for some employees.
• Because of lack of communication, employees may not know how they are rated. The standards by which employees think they are being judged are sometimes different from those their superiors actually use. No performance appraisal system can be very effective for management decisions, organization

development, or any other purpose until the people being appraised know what is expected of them and by what criteria they are being judged.

• Appraisal techniques tend to be used as performance panaceas. If a worker lacks the basic ability or has not been given the necessary training for his job, it is neither reasonable to try to stimulate adequate performance through performance appraisals, nor fair to base salary, dismissal, or other negative decisions on such an appraisal. No appraisal program can substitute for sound selection, placement, and training programs. Poor performance represents someone else's failure.

• In many cases, the validity of ratings is reduced by supervisory resistance to making the ratings. Rather than confront their less effective subordinates with negative ratings, negative feedback in appraisal interviews, and below-average salary increases, supervisors often take the more comfortable way out and give average or above-average ratings to inferior performers.

• Performance appraisal ratings can boomerang when communicated to employees. Negative feedback (i.e., criticism) not only fails to motivate the typical employee, but also can cause him to perform worse.[3] Only those employees who have a high degree of self-esteem appear to be stimulated by criticism to improve their performance.

• Performance appraisals interfere with the more constructive coaching relationship that should exist between a superior and his subordinates. Performance appraisal interviews tend to emphasize the superior position of the supervisor by placing him in the role of judge, thus countering his equally important role of teacher and coach. This is particularly damaging in organizations that are attempting to maintain a more participative organizational climate.

A LOOK AT METHODS

The foregoing list of major program pitfalls represents a formidable challenge, even considering the available battery of appraisal techniques. But attempting to avoid these pitfalls by doing away with appraisals themselves is like trying to solve the problems of life by committing suicide. The more logical task is to identify those appraisal practices that are (a) most likely to achieve a particular objective and (b) least vulnerable to the obstacles already discussed.

Before relating the specific techniques to the goals of performance appraisal stated at the outset of the article, I shall briefly review each, taking them more or less in an order of increasing complexity. The best-known techniques will be treated most briefly.

1 Essay Appraisal

In its simplest form, this technique asks the rater to write a paragraph or more covering an individual's strengths, weaknesses, potential, and so on. In most

---

[3]See Herbert H. Meyer, Emanuel Kay, and John R. P. French, Jr., "Split Roles in Performance Appraisal," HBR January–February 1965, p. 123.

selection situations, particularly those involving professional, sales, or managerial positions, essay appraisals from former employers, teachers, or associates carry significant weight. The assumption seems to be that an honest and informed statement—either by word of mouth or in writing—from someone who knows a man well, is fully as valid as more formal and more complicated methods.

The biggest drawback to essay appraisals is their variability in length and content. Moreover, since different essays touch on different aspects of a man's performance or personal qualifications, essay ratings are difficult to combine or compare. For comparability, some type of more formal method, like the graphic rating scale, is desirable.

2 Graphic Rating Scale

This technique may not yield the depth of an essay appraisal, but it is more consistent and reliable. Typically, a graphic scale assesses a person on the quality and quantity of his work (is he outstanding, above average, average, or unsatisfactory?) and on a variety of other factors that vary with the job but usually include personal traits like reliability and cooperation. It may also include specific performance items like oral and written communication.

The graphic scale has come under frequent attack, but remains the most widely used rating method. In a classic comparison between the "old-fashioned" graphic scale and the much more sophisticated force-choice technique, the former proved to be fully as valid as the best of the forced-choice forms, and better than most of them.[4] It is also cheaper to develop and more acceptable to raters than the forced-choice form. For many purposes there is no need to use anything more complicated than a graphic scale supplemented by a few essay questions.

3 Field Review

When there is reason to suspect rater bias, when some raters appear to be using higher standards than others, or when comparability of ratings is essential, essay or graphic ratings are often combined with a systematic review process. The field review is one of several techniques for doing this. A member of the personnel or central administrative staff meets with small groups of raters from each supervisory unit and goes over each employee's rating with them to (a) identify areas of inter-rater disagreement, (b) help the group arrive at a consensus, and (c) determine that each rater conceives the standards similarly.

This group-judgement technique tends to be more fair and more valid than individual ratings and permits the central staff to develop an awareness of the varying degrees of leniency or severity—as well as bias—exhibited by raters in different departments. On the negative side, the process is very time consuming.

[4]James Berkshire and Richard Highland, "Forced-Choice Performance Rating on a Methodological Study," *Personnel Psychology*, Autumn 1953, p. 355.

4 Forced-Choice Rating

Like the field review, this technique was developed to reduce bias and establish objective standards of comparison between individuals, but it does not involve the intervention of a third party. Although there are many variations of this method, the most common one asks raters to choose from among groups of statements those which *best* fit the individual being rated and those which *least* fit him. The statements are then weighted or scored, very much the way a psychological test is scored. People with high scores are, by definition, the better employees; those with low scores are the poorer ones. Since the rater does not know what the scoring weights for each statement are, in theory at least, he cannot play favorites. He simply describes his people, and someone in the personnel department applies the scoring weights to determine who gets the best rating.

The rationale behind this technique is difficult to fault. It is the same rationale used in developing selection test batteries. In practice, however, the forced-choice method tends to irritate raters, who feel they are not being trusted. They want to say openly how they rate someone and not be second-guessed or tricked into making "honest" appraisals.

A few clever raters have even found ways to beat the system. When they want to give average employee Harry Smith a high rating, they simply describe the best employee they know. If the best employee is Elliott Jones, they describe Jones on Smith's forced-choice form. Thus, Smith gets a good rating and hopefully a raise.

An additional drawback is the difficulty and cost of developing forms. Consequently, the technique is usually limited to middle- and lower-management levels where the jobs are sufficiently similar to make standard or common forms feasible.

Finally, forced-choice forms tend to be of little value—and probably have a negative effect—when used in performance appraisal interviews.

5 Critical Incident Appraisal

The discussion of ratings with employees has, in many companies, proved to be a traumatic experience for supervisors. Some have learned from bitter experience what General Electric later documented; people who receive honest but negative feedback are typically not motivated to do better—and often do worse—after the appraisal interview.[5] Consequently, supervisors tend to avoid such interviews, or if forced to hold them, avoid giving negative ratings when the ratings have to be shown to the employee.

One stumbling block has no doubt been the unsatisfactory rating form used. Typically, these are graphic scales that often include rather vague traits like initiative, cooperativeness, reliability, and even personality. Discussing these with an employee can be difficult.

[5]Meyer, Kay, and French, op. cit.

The critical incident technique looks like a natural to some people for performance review interviews, because it gives a supervisor actual, factual incidents to discuss with an employee. Supervisors are asked to keep a record, a "little black book," on each employee and to record actual incidents of positive or negative behavior.

For example: Bob Mitchell, who has been rated as somewhat unreliable, fails to meet several deadlines during the appraisal period. His supervisor makes a note of these incidents and is now prepared with hard, factual data: "Bob, I rated you down on reliability because, on three different occasions over the last two months, you told me you would do something and you didn't do it. You remember six weeks ago when I. . . ."

Instead of arguing over traits, the discussion now deals with actual behavior. Possibly, Bob has misunderstood the supervisor or has good reasons for his apparent "unreliability." If so, he now has an opportunity to respond. His performance, not his personality, is being criticized. He knows specifically how to perform differently if he wants to be rated higher the next time. Of course, Bob might feel the supervisor was using unfairly high standards in evaluating his performance. But at least he would know just what those standards are.

There are, however, several drawbacks to this approach. It requires that supervisors jot down incidents on a daily or, at the very least, a weekly basis. This can become a chore. Furthermore, the critical incident rating technique need not, but may, cause a supervisor to delay feedback to employees. And it is hardly desirable to wait six months or a year to confront an employee with a misdeed or mistake.

Finally, the supervisor sets the standards. If they seem unfair to a subordinate, might he not be more motivated if he at least has some say in setting, or at least agreeing to, the standards against which he is judged?

6 Management by Objectives

To avoid, or to deal with, the feeling that they are being judged by unfairly high standards, employees in some organizations are being asked to set—or help set—their own performance goals. Within the past five or six years, MBO has become something of a fad and is so familiar to most managers that I will not dwell on it here.

It should be noted, however, that when MBO is applied at lower organizational levels, employees do not always want to be involved in their own goal setting. As Arthur N. Turner and Paul R. Lawrence discovered, many do not want self-direction or autonomy.[6] As a result, more coercive variations of MBO are becoming increasingly common, and some critics see MBO drifting into a kind of manipulative form of management in which pseudo-participation substitutes for

[6]*Industrial Jobs and the Worker* (Boston, Division of Research, Harvard Business School, 1965).

the real thing. Employees are consulted, but management ends up imposing its standards and its objectives.[7]

Some organizations, therefore, are introducing a work-standards approach to goal setting in which the goals are openly set by management. In fact, there appears to be something of a vogue in the setting of such work standards in white-collar and service areas.

7 Work-Standards Approach

Instead of asking employees to set their own performance goals, many organizations set measured daily work standards. In short, the work-standards technique establishes work and staffing targets aimed at improving productivity. When realistically used, it can make possible an objective and accurate appraisal of the work of employees and supervisors.

To be effective, the standards must be visible and fair. Hence a good deal of time is spent observing employees on the job, simplifying and improving the job where possible, and attempting to arrive at realistic output standards.

It is not clear, in every case, that work standards have been integrated with an organization's performance appraisal program. However, since the work-standards program provides each employee with a more or less complete set of his job duties, it would seem only natural that supervisors will eventually relate performance appraisal and interview comments to these duties. I would expect this to happen increasingly where work standards exist. The use of work standards should make performance interviews less threatening than the use of personal, more subjective standards alone.

The most serious drawback appears to be the problem of comparability. If people are evaluated on different standards, how can the ratings be brought together for comparison purposes when decisions have to be made on promotions or on salary increases? For these purposes some form of ranking is necessary.

8 Ranking Methods

For comparative purposes, particularly when it is necessary to compare people who work for different supervisors, individual statements, ratings, or appraisal forms are not particularly useful. Instead, it is necessary to recognize that comparisons involve an overall subjective judgment to which a host of additional facts and impressions must somehow be added. There is no single form or way to do this.

Comparing people in different units for the purpose of, say, choosing a service supervisor or determining the relative size of salary increases for different supervisors, requires subjective judgment, not statistics. The best approach

---

[7]See, for example, Harry Levinson, "Management by Whose Objectives?" HBR July–August 1970, p. 125.

appears to be a ranking technique involving pooled judgment. The two most effective methods are alternation ranking and paired comparison ranking.

Alternation Ranking   In this method, the names of employees are listed on the left-hand side of a sheet of paper—preferably in random order. If the rankings are for salary purposes, a supervisor is asked to choose the "most valuable" employee on the list, cross his name off, and put it at the top of the column on the right-hand side of the sheet. Next, he selects the "least valuable" employee on the list, crosses his name off, and puts it at the bottom of the right-hand column. The ranker then selects the "most valuable" person from the remaining list, crosses his name off and enters it below the top name on the right-hand list, and so on.

Paired-comparison Ranking   This technique is probably just as accurate as alternation ranking and might be more so. But with large numbers of employees it becomes extremely time consuming and cumbersome.

To illustrate the method, let us say we have five employees: Mr. Abbott, Mr. Barnes, Mr. Cox, Mr. Drew, and Mr. Eliot. We list their names on the left-hand side of the sheet. We compare Abbott with Barnes on whatever criterion we have chosen, say, present value to the organization. If we feel Abbott is more valuable than Barnes, we put a tally beside Abbott's name. We then compare Abbott with Cox, with Drew, and with Eliot. The process is repeated for each individual. The man with the most tallies is the most valuable person, at least in the eyes of the rater; the man with no tallies at all is regarded as the least valuable person.

Both ranking techniques, particularly when combined with multiple rankings (i.e., when two or more people are asked to make independent rankings of the same work group and their lists are averaged), are among the best available for generating valid order-of-merit rankings for salary administration purposes.

9   Assessment Centers

So far, we have been talking about assessing past performance. What about the assessment of future performance or potential? In any placement decision and even more so in promotion decisions, some prediction of future performance is necessary. How can this kind of prediction be made most validly and most fairly?

One widely used rule of thumb is that "what a man has done is the best predictor of what he will do in the future." But suppose you are picking a man to be a supervisor and this person has never held supervisory responsibility? Or suppose you are selecting a man for a job from among a group of candidates, none of whom has done the job or one like it? In these situations, many organizations use assessment centers to predict future performance more accurately.

Typically, individuals from different departments are brought together to spend two or three days working on individual and group assignments similar to the ones they will be handling if they are promoted. The pooled judgment of observers—sometimes derived by paired comparison or alternation ranking—leads to an order-of-merit ranking for each participant. Less structured, subjective judgments are also made.

There is a good deal of evidence that people chosen by assessment center methods work out better than those not chosen by these methods.[8] The center also makes it possible for people who are working for departments of low status or low visibility in an organization to become visible and, in the competitive situation of an assessment center, show how they stack up against people from more well-known departments. This has the effect of equalizing opportunity, improving morale, and enlarging the pool of possible promotion candidates.

FITTING PRACTICE TO PURPOSE

In the foregoing analysis, I have tried to show that each performance appraisal technique has its own combination of strengths and weaknesses. The success of any program that makes use of these techniques will largely depend on how they are used relative to the goals of that program.

For example, goal-setting and work-standards methods will be most effective for objective coaching, counseling, and motivational purposes, but some form of critical incident appraisal is better when a supervisor's personal judgment and criticism are necessary.

Comparisons of individuals, especially in win-lose situations when only one person can be promoted or only a limited number can be given large salary increases, necessitate a still different approach. Each person should be rated on the same form, which must be as simple as possible, probably involving essay and graphic responses. Then order-of-merit rankings and final averaging should follow. To be more explicit, here are the appraisal goals listed at the outset of this article and the techniques best suited to them.

Help or prod supervisors to observe their subordinates more closely and to do a better coaching job.

The critical incident appraisal appears to be ideal for this purpose, if supervisors can be convinced they should take the time to look for, and record, significant events. Time delays, however, are a major drawback to this technique and should be kept as short as possible. Still, over the longer term, a supervisor will gain a better knowledge of his own performance standards, including his possible biases, as he reviews the incidents he has recorded. He may even decide to change or reweight his own criteria.

Another technique that is useful for coaching purposes is, of course, MBO.

[8]See, for example, Robert C. Albrook, "Spot Executives Early," *Fortune,* July 1968, p. 106; and William C. Byham, "Assessment Centers for Spotting Future Managers," HBR July–August 1970, p. 150.

Like the critical incident method, it focuses on actual behavior and actual results which can be discussed objectively and constructively, with little or no need for a supervisor to "play God."

Motivate employees by providing feedback on how they are doing.

The MBO approach, if it involves real participation, appears to be most likely to lead to an inner commitment to improved performance. However, the work-standards approach can also motivate, although in a more coercive way. If organizations staff to meet their work standards, the work force is reduced and people are compelled to work harder.

The former technique is more "democratic," while the latter technique is more "autocratic." Both can be effective; both make use of specific work goals or targets, and both provide for knowledge of results.

If performance appraisal information is to be communicated to subordinates, either in writing or in an interview, the two most effective techniques are the management-by-objectives approach and the critical incident method. The latter, by communicating not only factual data but also the flavor of a supervisor's own values and biases, can be effective in an area where objective work standards or quantitative goals are not available.

Provide back-up data for management decisions concerning merit increases, promotions, transfers, dismissals, and so on.

Most decisions involving employees require a comparison of people doing very different kinds of work. In this respect, the more specifically job-related techniques like management by objectives or work standards are not appropriate, or, if used, must be supplemented by less restricted methods.

For promotion to supervisory positions, the forced-choice rating form, if carefully developed and validated, could prove best. But the difficulty and cost of developing such a form and the resistance of raters to its use render it impractical except in large organizations.

Companies faced with the problem of selecting promotable men from a number of departments or divisions might consider using an assessment center. This minimizes the bias resulting from differences in departmental "visibility" and enlarges the pool of potential promotables.

The best appraisal method for most other management decisions will probably involve a very simple kind of graphic form or a combined graphic and essay form. If this is supplemented by the use of field reviews, it will be measurably strengthened. Following the individual appraisals, groups of supervisors should then be asked to rank the people they have rated, using a technique like alternation ranking or paired comparison. Pooled or averaged rankings will then tend to cancel out the most extreme forms of bias and should yield fair and valid order-of-merit lists.

Improve organization development by identifying people with promotion potential and pinpointing development needs.

Comparison of people for promotion purposes has already been discussed. However, identification of training and development needs will probably best—and most simply—come from the essay part of the combined graphic/essay rating form recommended for the previous goal.

Establish a reference and research base for personnel decisions.

For this goal, the simplest form is the best form. A graphic/essay combination is adequate for most reference purposes. But order-of-merit salary rankings should be used to develop criterion groups of good and poor performers.

CONCLUSION

Formal systems for appraising performance are neither worthless nor evil, as some critics have implied. Nor are they panaceas, as many managers might wish. A formal appraisal system is, at the very least, a commendable attempt to make visible, and hence improvable, a set of essential organization activities. Personal judgments about employee performance are inescapable, and subjective values and fallible human perception are always involved. Formal appraisal systems, to the degree that they bring these perceptions and values into the open, make it possible for at least some of the inherent bias and error to be recognized and remedied.

By improving the probability that good performance will be recognized and rewarded and poor performance corrected, a sound appraisal system can contribute both to organizational morale and organizational performance. Moreover, the alternative to a bad appraisal program need not be no appraisal program at all, as some critics have suggested. It can and ought to be a better appraisal program. And the first step in that direction is a thoughtful matching of practice to purpose.

Part Four

Organizational Conflict and Change

Conflict Resolution

Each contemporary organization is comprised of a unique combination of capital, technological, and human inputs. Unfortunately, it is the latter one, the human resource, that is ultimately responsible for the seeming inability of many organizations to attain their true potential effectiveness. To be specific, human beings in interaction with each other inevitably seem to encounter (some say strive to achieve) conflict, and much conflict results in detrimental side effects to either the parties involved or the organization as a whole. Whether conflict occurs between societies, organizations, departments, or individuals, managers have a responsibility to diagnose and prevent or resolve instances of dysfunctional conflict.

The diagnostic framework proposed by Blake and Mouton is simple to understand and adaptable to a number of topical areas. They suggest that managers should examine their underlying assumptions regarding not only the inherent desirability of conflict versus conformity, but also the extent to which they emphasize people versus production of results. The dependent variables in the Conflict Grid model are then identified as five "styles" of conflict resolution—suppression, smoothing, withdrawal, compromise, and problem solving. Although it is clear that the extent of use of each of these styles differs widely, the authors suggest there is wide preference for a problem-solving, open-confrontation approach. The contingency implication remains clear: a manager's probable approach to managing conflict will be a direct product of the previous assumptions he makes regarding its functions and dysfunctions for the people and productivity objectives he controls.

The classic problem of interdepartmental conflict is explored in the article by Seiler. Finding three traditional explanations of conflict limited in their explanatory power, he develops a predictive model based on the examination of four conditions: the degree to which departmental energies are productively focused on the unit's own tasks, the extent to which wasteful conflicts over ideas develop, the amount of illegitimate conflicts of authority, and the quantity of clashes over divergent values. Finally, based on those situations where the likelihood of interdepartmental conflict is quite high, two major conflict-management strategies are proposed—one primarily *structural,* to clarify the relationships involved; and the other primarily *behavioral,* to encourage the two factions to integrate their viewpoints.

Applying an approach parallel to that seen in the Communication section, the third reading is highlighted by a micro orientation (at the interpersonal level) and the results of a study indicating the relative effectiveness of several resolution methods. Burke adapted Blake and Mouton's Conflict Grid to the interpersonal level, and determined that, in his sample, the confrontation and problem-solving modes of resolution were most effective. If he were to simply advocate these modes for all situations, we would merely have another limited universal principle. However, Burke then proceeds to delineate thirteen basic conditions required for the confrontation/problem-solving modes to be likely to succeed.

Reading 39

The Fifth Achievement

Robert R. Blake
Jane Srygley Mouton

A great new challenge to the American way of conducting its national life is taking shape. Conformity with older patterns is breaking down. Yet creative definitions of new patterns are not forthcoming, or at best are coming at a snail's pace. Unless the challenge of finding new patterns that can serve to strengthen society is successfully met, some of the nation's most cherished human values may very well be sacrificed. If we can meet it, however, our deeply embedded beliefs as to the role of men in society may not only be reinforced but may find even richer and more extensive applications in the society of tomorrow.

WHAT IS THIS CHALLENGE?

We widely acknowledge the objective of an open and free society based on individual responsibility and self-regulated participation by all in the conduct of national life. That men will differ in the ways they think and act is accepted as both inevitable and desirable. Indeed, this is one hallmark of an open society. Differences are intrinsically valuable. They provide the rich possibility that alternatives and options will be discovered for better and poorer ways of responding to any particular situation. Preserving the privilege of having and expressing differences increases our chances of finding "best" solutions to the many dilemmas that arise in living. They also add the spice of variety and give zest to human pursuits.

When it is possible for a man to make a choice from among several solutions, and when he can make this choice without infringing upon another man's freedom or requiring his cooperation, there is genuine autonomy. This is real freedom.

But in many situations not every man can have his own personal solution. When cooperation and coordination are required in conducting national life—in government, business, the university, agencies of the community, the home, and so on—differences that arise must find reconciliation. A solution must be agreed upon and embraced which can provide a pattern to which those involved are prepared to conform their behavior. Yet efforts to reconcile differences in order to achieve consensus-based patterns of conduct often only serve to promote difficulties. When disagreements as to sound bases for action can be successfully resolved, freedom can be retained and necessary solutions implemented. Dealing with the many and varied misunderstandings that are inevitable in a society dedicated to preserving the privilege of having and expressing differences is the challenge. As individuals, we find this hard to do. As members of organized groups, we appear to find it even more difficult.

FOUR CLASSICAL SOLUTIONS

In the conduct of society there are at least four major and different kinds of formal, structural arrangements which we rely on for resolving differences. They are the scientific method; politics; law, with its associated police powers; and organizational hierarchy.

Of undisputed value in finding the objective solution to which agreement can readily be given are the methods of science. A well-designed experiment confirms which of several alternatives is the most valid basis of explanation while simultaneously demonstrating the unacceptability of the remaining explanations.

Our political mechanisms are based on the one-man-one-vote approach to problem solving. This provides for the resolution of differences according to a weighting approach, and the basis is usually that the majority prevail. By this means, decisions can be made and actions taken even though differences may remain. Simply being outvoted, however, does not aid those on the losing side in changing their intellectual and emotional attitudes. While it ensures that a solution is chosen, the fact that it is often on a win-lose or a compromise basis may pose further problems when those who are outvoted resolve to be the winners of the future. Often the underlying disagreements are deepened.

Legal mechanisms apply only in resolving differences when questions of law are involved and other means of reaching agreement usually have met with failure. With application of associated police powers, the use of force is available to back up legal mechanisms when law is violated. But this constitutes a far more severe solution to the problem. The ultimate failure of law which invites the use of military power is in effect a court of last resort.

Within society's formal institutions such as business, government, education, and the family, organizational hierarchy, or rank, can and does permit the resolution of differences. The premise is that when a disagreement arises between any two persons of differing rank, the one of higher rank can impose a solution unilaterally based on his position. In the exercise of authority, suppression may also sacrifice the validity of a solution, since there is no intrinsic basis of truth in the idea that simply because a man is the boss of other men he is ordained with an inherent wisdom. While this arrangement provides a basis for avoiding indecision and impasse, it may and often does have the undesirable consequence of sacrificing the support of those to whom it is applied for the solution of the problem, to say nothing of its adverse effects on future creativity.

These classical solutions to dealing with differences—science, politics, law, and hierarchy—represent real progress in learning to conduct the national life. Where it can be applied, scientific method provides a close to ideal basis for resolving differences. That politics, courts of justice, and organizational hierarchy, though more limited, are necessary is indisputable. But that they are being questioned and increasingly rejected is also indisputable. Even if they were not, none of these alone nor all of them together provide a sound and sufficient basis for the development of a truly problem-solving society.

WHAT IS THE FIFTH ACHIEVEMENT?

There is another essential ingredient. It is a sharply increased understanding by every man of the roots of conflict and the human skills of gaining the resolution of differences. The acquisition of such insight and skill by every man could provide a social foundation for reaching firm and sound understandings on a direct man-to-man basis of the inevitable disagreements that arise in conducting the national life. This kind of deepened skill in the direct resolution of differences could do much to provide a realistic prospect that the antagonisms, cleavages, or injustices real and imagined in society today can be reduced if not eliminated. It offers the promise that the sicknesses of alienation and apathy, the destructive aggressions, and the organization-man mentality can be healed.

The Fifth Achievement, then, is in the establishment of a problem-solving society where differences among men are subject to resolution through insights that permit protagonists themselves to identify and implement solutions to their differences upon the basis of committed agreement. That men ultimately will be able to work out, face to face, their differences is a hoped-for achievement of the future. Extending their capacity to do so could reduce the number of problems brought before the bench or dealt with through hierarchy. At the same time, scientific and political processes could be strengthened if progress were made in this direction. Even more important, it could perhaps lead to the resolution of many conflicts on a local level that block the development of a creative and committed problem-solving community. Success in meeting this challenge in the period ahead is perhaps the surest way to preserve and strengthen the values of a free society while protecting and even strengthening the privilege of having and expressing differences.

INCREASING SKILL IN MANAGING CONFLICT

Why do men rely on these other four approaches to conflict settlement while placing lower value on the resolution of differences in a direct, man-to-man way? One explanation for this might be that they do not hold in concert a conceptual basis for analyzing situations of disagreement and their causes. It should be said that conceptual understanding, while necessary for strengthening behavior, is clearly not in itself a sufficient basis for learning the skills of sound resolution of conflict. Personal entrapment from self-deception about one's motivations is too great. Insensitivity about one's behavior and the reactions of others to it is too extensive. To connect a conceptual analysis to one's own behavior and conduct in ways that permit insight and change seems to require something more in the way of personal learning.

Classroom learning methodologies that could enable men to gain insights regarding conflict and acquire skills for resolving it seem to be impoverished. To aid men in acquiring both the conceptual understanding for managing conflict and the skills to see their own reactions in situations of conflict, man-to-man feedback seems to be an essential condition. A variety of situations involving laboratory learning that permit this have been designed (Bach & Wyden, 1969; Blake & Mouton, 1968; Bradford, Gibb & Benne, 1964; Schein & Bennis, 1965). They set the stage for men to learn to face their differences and find creative and valid solutions to their problems.

Success in mastering this Fifth Achievement will undoubtedly require reconception of the classroom in ways that permit the study of conflict as a set of concepts and the giving and receiving of feedback in ways that enable men to see how to strengthen their own capacities and skills for coping with it directly.

This paper concentrates upon a first step toward this Fifth Achievement by presenting a conceptual basis for analyzing situations of conflict. The Conflict Grid in Figure 1 is a way of identifying basic assumptions when men act in situations where differences are present, whether disagreement is openly expressed or silently present (Blake & Mouton, 1964; Blake, Shepard, & Mouton, 1964).

Whenever a man meets a situation of conflict, he has at least two basic considerations in mind. One of these is the *people* with whom he is in disagreement. Another is *production of results,* or getting a resolution to the disagreement. It is the amount and kind of emphasis he places on various combinations of each of these elements that determine his thinking in dealing with conflict.

Basic attitudes toward people and toward results are visualized on nine-point scales. These form the Grid in Figure 1. The nine-point scale representing concern for producing a result provides the horizontal axis for the Grid. The phrase "concern for" does not show results produced but rather denotes the degree of emphasis in his thinking that the man places on getting results. The 1 end represents low concern, and the 9 represents the highest possible concern. The same applies on the vertical or concern-for-people axis. Considering the interactions of these two scales, there are 81 possible positions. Each describes an intersection between the two dimensions.

THEORIES OF CONFLICT MANAGEMENT

The following pages discuss strategies of managing conflict according to the five basic theories—those appearing at the four corners and the center of the figure. When these basic styles are understood, one can predict for each how a man operating under that style is likely to handle conflict. There are eight additional important theories composed from various mixtures of these five, but basic issues of conflict resolution can be seen in dealing with these "pure" theories.

No one style is exclusively characteristic of one man in comparison with another, although one style may be dominant in a man's actions. Furthermore,

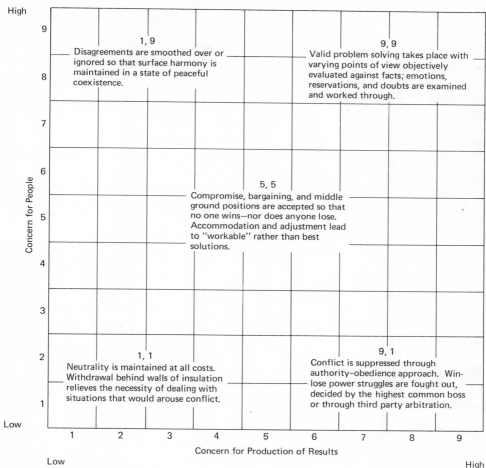

Figure 1 The Conflict Grid.

even though one may be dominant for a time, it may be abandoned and replaced by another when the first has been ineffective in achieving resolution.

What Are Some of the Ways of Dealing with Conflict?

Conflict can be controlled by overpowering it and suppressing one's adversary (9,1 in the lower right corner of the Grid). An ultimate expression of this is in the extremes of police power and military action. Extracting compliance by authority-obedience is possible when rank is present. The conflict can be cut off and suppressed in this way, "Yours is not to question why!" When rank is not available, a win-lose basis expresses the same set of assumptions. Winning for one's own position predominates over seeking a valid solution.

Another strategy is to smooth conflict by cajolery, by letting a man know that with a little patience he will find that all is right (1,9 in the upper left corner). The assumption of sweetness and light often leads to resolution by people's retracting from previously held positions, preferring personal acceptance to solution validity. This can promote accord and harmony, but it sacrifices conviction and insight into differences, while decreasing the likelihood of achieving valid solutions. Staying out of situations that provoke controversy or turning away from topics that promote disagreement represents a set of assumptions about how to live in a conflict-free way (1,1 in the lower left corner). Then one need not be stirred up even though the issue may need resolution. A man can remain composed if he does not let himself be drawn into controversy; he avoids it by remaining neutral. This kind of "see no disagreement, hear no disagreement, and speak no disagreement" represents a withdrawal from social responsibility in a world where the resolution of differences is key to finding sound solutions. It is the ultimate in alienation.

A third set of assumptions leads to a middle-of-the-road solution to differences through accommodation and adjustment. Disagreement is settled through bargaining a compromise solution (5,5). The assumptions underlying compromising of one's convictions are at the root of this approach. It means agreeing so as to be agreeable, even to sacrificing sound action; settling for what you can get rather than working to get what is sound in the light of the best available facts and data.

The mental attitude behind the one-man-one-vote approach often leads to the endorsement of positions calculated to get majority support even though this means giving up a solution of deeper validity. The same assumptions often prevail behind the scenes in out-of-court settlements.

Outside the sphere of industrial management, solutions to major political and international problems of recent years provide classic examples of 5,5 splitting. One is the "separate but equal" approach to solving what is seen as the race problem. The cessation of hostilities in Korea by the establishment of the thirty-eighth parallel as a line of demarcation between North and South in the early Fifties is another. This set a precedent for setting up the "Demilitarized Zone" between North and South Vietnam. The Berlin Wall is probably the most significant symbol of the East-West split. The 5,5 attitude is reflected daily by news reporters and commentators who quote "unidentified but high-level sources" or hide their sources by attributing their facts merely to "usually reliable sources."

Under a 9,9 approach, disagreement is valued as an inevitable result of the fact that strong-minded people have convictions about what is right. A man says, "Nothing is sacrosanct. What are the facts? What are the causes? What are the conclusions?" Reservations and emotions that interrupt agreement based on logic and data are confronted through candid discussion of them directly with the person involved in the disagreement. Insight and resolution are possible but involve maturity and real human skill. This approach may be time-consuming in the short run but time-conserving over the long term. It permits men to disagree, to work out their disagreements in the light of facts, and ultimately to understand one another. Such problem-solving constructiveness in conflict situations is the fundamental basis for realizing the Fifth Achievement.

EFFECTIVE CONFLICT MANAGEMENT

How does effective conflict management interrelate with other social processes of seemingly equal or greater significance in strengthening society? Indeed, it might be maintained that the challenge to society seen today is in nonconformity with its norms, rather than in faulty management of conflict.

In what ways are conflict and conformity interdependent? (Blake & Mouton, 1961) Men in everyday life do conform to the expectations of others and the patterns of their institutions. This readiness to conform reduces conflict and is what permits regularity, order, and predictability. To adhere to common norms provides a basis for organized effort. From conformity with conventionalized social and organizational practices can come a sense of identification, belonging, and *esprit de corps.* On the other hand, failure to conform may stir conflict with one's colleagues and associates so that the nonconformist is rejected. Indeed, anxiety about rejection can be so overwhelming that, for many, conformity becomes an end in itself rather than a means to cooperation through interdependence. Under these circumstances, the capacity to challenge outmoded traditions, precedents, and past practices is lost. With sound ways of approaching and resolving conflict, outmoded patterns can successfully be challenged and upgraded by replacement of them with agreements which themselves can promote problem solving and creativity. In this way, finding new and better ways to accomplish personal, organizational, national, and perhaps even international objectives becomes possible.

Just stimulating people to challenge and contest status quo conformities, however, is likely to do little more than provoke disagreement and controversy, increase polarization, and ultimately end in win-lose, impasse, compromise, or chaos. Yet the status quo requirements must continuously be challenged in a problem-solving and creative way, not in a manner that pits man against man to see who can win or, even worse, in a way that ends in anarchy.

The Conflict Grid is useful in seeing the more subtle connections among conflict and conformity and creative problem solving. Conformity to the 9,1 authority-obedience demands that are involved in hierarchical rank is exemplified by the boss, teacher, or parent who gives the orders to subordinates, students, or children who are expected to obey. The exercise of initiative which produces differences is equivalent to insubordination. Conformity under 9,1 may produce the protocol of surface compliance, but the frustrations of those who are suppressed are often evident. Ways of striking back against the boss, teacher, or parent appear. Such acts may be open ones of resistance and rebellion or disguised ones of sabotage, cheating, or giving agreement without following through. Each of these in a certain sense involves reverse creativity, where ingenuity is exercised in attacking or "beating" the system. It is creativity in resentment of the system, not in support of it.

In another type of conformity, the rules of relationship are, "Don't say anything if you can't say something nice" (1,9). Togetherness, social intimacy, and warmth engendered by yielding one's convictions in the interests of personal acceptance are certainly objectionable solutions in a society where having and expressing differences is relied on as the basis for finding sound courses of action. It can produce a quorum of agreement but smother creative problem solving in sweetness and love. The kind of disagreement that might provoke resentment is avoided. The opportunity for creative problem solving to emerge is absent.

Another kind of conformity relates to adhering to the form and not to the substance of life. Here people conform by going through the motions expected of them, treadmilling through the days, months, and years (1,1). In this way, survival is accomplished by being visible without being seen.

Organization-man conformity (5,5) entails positively embracing the status quo with minimum regard for the soundness of status quo requirements. Yet, even here, as new problems arise, differences appear and disagreements become evident. There are several kinds of 5,5 actions that on shallow examination may give the appearance of approaching problems from an altered, fresh, and original point of view. Pseudo-creativity may be seen when new approaches, even though they constitute only small departures from the outmoded past, are recommended on the basis of their having been tried elsewhere. Under these circumstances a man is forwarding actions taken by others rather than promoting examination of actions on the basis of his own convictions. In this way, he can suggest, while avoiding the challenge or rejection of his own convictions. Deeper examination of 5,5 behavior leads to the conclusion that imitation rather than innovation is the rule.

In other instances, solutions which are proposed as compromise positions can give the impression of "flexibility" in thought. When adjustment and accommodation, backing and filling, twisting and turning, shifting and adapting take place in the spirit of compromise, the motivation behind them is usually to avoid interpersonal emotions resulting from confrontation. Behaving in this manner is a reaction to disagreement, and it means that personal validity is being eroded.

Flexibility is a highly valued component in mature and effective behavior. But is it not contradictory to advocate flexibility on the one hand and to forewarn against compromise on the other? This question is important to clarify.

Flexibility calls for deliberate examination of options and alternatives. It means having back-up tactics that permit swift resolution of unforeseen circumstances, a climate that permits people to move back and forth and in and out from one situation to another, but based on facts, data, and logic of the situation as it unfolds. These are the characteristics of creative problem solving that permit gains to be made as opportunities arrive; that permit opportunities to be created, threats to be anticipated, and risks that result when people fail to react to be reduced.

Thus there are actions to adjust a difference to keep peace and actions to adjust to altered circumstances for better results. It is most important to distinguish between the two kinds. Flexibility for better results is likely to have a stamp of 9,9 on it; "flexibility" to keep peace by avoiding clash of personalities is in the 5,5 area. One is enlivening and promotes creativity. The other leads to the perpetuation of the organization-man mentality of status quo rigidities.

In the final analysis, conformity is to be valued. The problem is to ensure that the thinking of men conforms with sound purposes and premises. Conformity which means adherence to premises of human logic so that decisions reached are furthering growth capacity in sound and fundamental ways is what every individual might be expected to want. It is what man should want in the underpinnings of his daily interactions. It is conformity at this level that promotes the pursuit of creative and innovative solutions. Only when the values of a nation stimulate experimentation and promote a truly constructive attitude toward discovery and innovation is the full potential from creative efforts available as a source of thrust for replacing outmoded status quo conformities with more problem-solving requirements (9,9).

WHAT MEN WANT—TRANSNATIONALLY

Though varying widely in their ways of *actually* dealing with conflict, studies show that leaders in the United States, Great Britain, the Middle and Far East all indicate that they would *prefer* the 9,9 approach of *open confrontation* as the soundest way of managing situations of conflict, particularly under circumstances where outmoded conformities are under examination (Mouton & Blake, 1970). Though extremely difficult, it appears to be the soundest of several possible choices. This is not to imply that every decision should be made by a leader through calling a meeting or obtaining team agreement. Nor for a crisis situation does it imply that a leader should withhold exercising direction. But a 9,9 foundation of interdependence can build a strong basis for an open, problem-solving society in which men can have and express differences and yet be interrelated in ways that promote the mutual respect, common goals, and trust and understanding they must have to achieve results in ways that lead to personal gratification and maturity.

POSSIBILITIES FOR STRENGTHENING SOCIETY

This challenge to America, the need for men to learn to confront outmoded status quo requirements and to manage the resultant conflict in such ways as to promote creative problem solving, promises much for the decades ahead, if we can meet and master it.

Consider for a moment the possibility of success in mastering this Fifth Achievement. What might it mean?

1 Enriched family life rather than the steady rise in the divorce rate.

2 Sounder child rearing, evidenced in teen-age youngsters capable of expression and action in dealing in a problem-solving rather than a protest way with adults and the institutions of society who are capable of interacting in an equally sound way.

3 The conversion of academic environments from subject-oriented learning centers to ones that expand the capacity of individuals for contributing creatively to the evolving character of society.

4 The betterment of communities in ways that more fully serve human wants.

5 The more rapid integration of minorities into a more just society, with the reduction and eventual elimination of disenfranchised, alienated segments.

6 Fuller and more creative use of human energies in conducting the organizations that serve society.

7 A greater readiness to support and utilize science for approaching problems when evidence, facts, and data come to have an ever greater value as the bases for gaining insight.

8 A strengthening of politics by readiness to advocate positions on the basis of statesmanlike convictions rather than to adopt positions for political expediency.

9 Reliance on knowledge rather than rank in the resolution of differences and disagreements in organization situations.

10 A stronger basis for mind-meeting agreements rather than resorting to legal actions to force a resolution of disputes.

If erosion of social institutions has not already become too great, all of these aims can perhaps be forwarded over time by our classical institutions for settling conflicts. But surely men capable of resolving their conflicts directly would forward human progress with a dramatic thrust—and on a far more fundamental and therefore enduring basis.

If this Fifth Achievement is to be realized, it is likely that greater use of the behavioral sciences will be essential. For in the behavioral sciences may well lie the key to a more rewarding and progressive society in which men can share and evaluate their differences, learn from them, and use conflict as a stepping stone to the greater progress that is possible when differences can be resolved in a direct, face-to-face way.

Will this challenge be met, or will the cherished freedom of having and expressing differences be sacrificed?

REFERENCES

Bach, G. R., & Wyden, P. *The Intimate Enemy,* New York: Morrow, 1969
Blake, R. R., & Mouton, Jane S. The experimental investigation of interpersonal influence.

In A. D. Biderman & H. Zimmer (Eds.), *The Manipulation of Human Behavior,* New York: Wiley, 1961.

Blake, R. R., & Mouton, Jane S. *The Managerial Grid.* Houston: Gulf, 1964.

Blake, R. R., & Mouton, Jane S. *Corporate Excellence Through Grid Organization Development: A Systems Approach.* Houston: Gulf, 1968.

Blake, R. R., Shepard, H. A., & Mouton, Jane S. *Managing Intergroup Conflict in Industry.* Houston: Gulf, 1964.

Bradford, L. P., Gibb, J. R., & Benne, K. D. (Eds.) *T-Group Theory and Laboratory Method: Innovation in Re-education.* New York: Wiley, 1964.

Mouton, Jane S., & Blake, R. R. Organization development in a free world, July–August, 1969, Personnel Administration, pp. 12–23.

Mouton, Jane S., & Blake, R. R. Issues in transnational organization development. In B. M. Bass, R. B. Cooper, & J. A. Haas (Eds.), *Managing for Task Accomplishment,* Lexington, Mass.: D. C. Heath, 1970. Pp. 208–224.

Schein, E. H., & Bennis, W. G. (Eds.) *Personal and Organizational Change Through Group Methods: The Laboratory Approach,* New York: Wiley, 1965.

Reading 40

Diagnosing Interdepartmental Conflict

John A. Seiler

- "Purchasing and production are always at each other's throats. I don't know why they can't get along better."
- "If the way research and engineering work together were typical for all departments in our company, our executive vice president would be out of a job. Somehow those guys are able to work out their disagreements."
- "Sales and production just refuse to deal with each other. Every time a decision is needed, someone higher up has to do a lot of handholding or head-knocking. Why won't they bargain?"

If you live in an "interdepartmental world" and particularly if you have some responsibility for what goes on between departments, chances are the phrases, "I don't know why they . . . ," "Somehow those guys . . . ," and "Why won't they . . . ?" in the statements just quoted are not strangers to you. Businessmen are frequently perplexed by the way groups deal with one another. There is certainly cause for wonderment. Interdepartmental problems not only are complicated, but they have received relatively little attention from those not directly engaged in coping with them. Perhaps if we take a look from the firing line at some typical interdepartmental conflicts, we may be able to isolate those aspects which are harmful to productivity and those which represent stimulating and productive competition.

Traditional Explanations

Why are some interdepartmental relationships successful and others not? Managers typically find themselves advancing one or the other of these explanations:

*   One popular opinion is the "personality clash" theory, which holds that stubborn prejudices and differences in ingrained personal styles (none of which are actuated by organizational influences) are behind nonproductive relations. As compelling as this explanation often seems to be, it fails to account for the fact that we seldom, if ever, encounter a group composed of people with identical or even closely similar personalities. Lacking evidence of such group identity, it is difficult to imagine an intergroup conflict between two "group personalities." This reasoning also fails to account for interdepartmental relations which are characterized by high productivity *and* some degree of personal antagonism. While personality differences undoubtedly play a part, they alone comprise an inadequate explanation of productive and nonproductive relations.
*   Another view holds that failure in interdepartmental relations is the result of "conflicting ideas." This theory asserts that nonproductive relations occur between groups whose respective memberships are so different in terms of skills, training, job activities, personal aspirations, and so on that they cannot possibly find a common area in which to communicate. While this explanation seems to apply to some nonproductive relations, it is not unheard of to find an advanced research group which works quite effectively with a nontechnical, highly consumer-oriented sales group. Seemingly, at least, groups can differ on many counts without a breakdown occurring in their relations. Furthermore, it is not unusual to find groups with remarkably similar points of view which seem to go out of their way to make trouble for each other. Something in addition to different points of view must be playing a part in forming the character of these relationships.
*   A third popular explanation for nonproductivity puts the blame on competition between groups for authority, power, and influence. Breakdowns occur because each department operates from an entrenched position which, if compromised, will bring the group nothing but defeat and loss of influence. Many nonproductive relationships seem to display characteristics of this kind. But if this theory is to be sufficient unto itself, the only productive relationship would be one in which either or both of the groups had no desire or opportunity for influence over the other. Under these conditions, passivity would seem to be a requirement for productivity. Yet the most highly productive relations appear to take place between aggressive, confident, and high-achievement departments. Apparently other determinants, in addition to competition for prestige and power, must be operating to make interdepartmental relations successful or unsuccessful.

While no one of these theories is a sufficient explanation of why group relationships turn out the way they do, each has enough sense behind it to make it attractive. Consequently, what is needed is some way of pulling them together into a new and more useful way of thinking about interdepartmental conflicts. This is what I propose to do in this article.

Balance of Energy

Fundamental to understanding why some relationships are productive and others less so is a recognition that people have limited energies. When a multitude of demands are made on us, we naturally assign priorities to them. If the demands for organizationally productive work take second place to other demands, then the organization loses out. Demands on departments can also be viewed in this way. If a department's energies are consumed by plottings of defense and attack, little time will be left for devotion to more fruitful business. Consequently, departments, too, must assign priorities to demands on their energy.

Some demands, of course, are more crucial than others. For example, when a car is heading directly at us, our total mental, physical, and emotional energy is absorbed by the endeavor to escape collision. There is little or no energy left for other pursuits. Similarly, when in business we find ourselves truly challenged by a difficult task, most of our capacity for attention tends to be absorbed in that one endeavor. In most cases, however, we are not so singly motivated but, instead, are caught between complex and conflicting demands on our energies to which we must assign some sort of priority.

Group Control   The setting of priorities by groups is not much different. Groups are, after all, only interdependent individuals who keep their group membership because it is valuable to them. The uniqueness of a group, that which makes it more than the simple addition of its members' wishes and actions, lies in its ability to motivate member behavior toward goals which are attractive to the entire group but which are not attainable by any member alone. Primary among these goals, of course, and basic to group life in general, is the satisfaction of a person's need to belong to something. But groups provide more than simple social satisfaction to their members. They also provide protection from other groups and individuals. They contain power which can be used to gain liberties, self-respect, and prestige for their members. In return for these benefits, the member submits to group discipline.

When a group's existence is threatened by such changes as a formal reorganization which will disperse its members, by rumors of layoff or firing, or by technical change disrupting the relationships among members, the full energy of the group is mobilized. There is a tightening of member discipline, particularly centering on the activities most likely to thwart any alarming changes. On such occasions, the only "work" done is that which protects the group from jeopardy. On the other hand, when groups do not fear for their survival, but see before them a challenging opportunity to work together toward an end of positive value to the group, all their energies become absorbed by the project they are working on.

Energies freed from defense will seek outlets in activities which strengthen the group's ability to survive in the long run and which add zest to the life of its members. If the work formally available to the group is dull and lacking in challenge (or if other obstacles such as restrictive supervisory actions or lack of member skills get in the way), activity is likely to be predominantly social in character. If the work is challenging, and obstacles are not present to hinder its meeting the challenge, the group is likely to find its formal assignment a satisfying outlet for the application of its energy.

With these ideas about available group energy in mind, let us look at four case situations to see how these ideas can be used fruitfully. Each of these real-life examples represents a particular way in which group energies become absorbed as they try to work with another group.[1]

I PRODUCTIVE FOCUS ON TASK

Company A developed and manufactured ethical pharmaceuticals. The activities required to transform a product idea into a marketable item were performed in sequence by subunits of the research, engineering, and production departments. An idea would first take form in a research department test tube. It would then be evaluated by research chemists and chemical engineers in the pilot plant. Next, new process equipment would be designed by mechanical engineers and job designs laid out around the equipment by industrial engineers. Actual plant construction and placement of equipment were accomplished by construction engineers, and, finally, production responsibility was assumed by production chemists. The members of these formal units agreed that research had the highest prestige of all the work groups and that the relative prestige of the other units declined in the order in which each became actively involved in the new product sequence.

The engineering and research departments were housed in their own buildings some distance from each other and from the plant. The chemical engineers worked most closely with the research chemists—sharing many ideas with them because of the similarity in their training, their work, and their aspirations. The chemical engineers also worked closely with the mechanical engineers in the pilot plant and in process equipment design. The chemical and mechanical groups shared a number of ideas, though the mechanical engineers and research chemists thought quite differently about most things. The mechanical engineers worked closely with the industrial and construction engineers, who in turn were in close contact with factory personnel. These four latter groups shared similarities in background and in ideas.

Company A had an outstanding reputation for important production innovations and rapid development of ideas into mass-production items. Nevertheless, there was frequent argument among research, engineering, and production as to who should take responsibility for the product at what point in the development

---

[1]The cases cited in this article have been taken from the case and project research files of the Harvard Business School and are reproduced by permission of the President and Fellows of Harvard College.

sequence. Engineering wanted control at the pilot plant. Production wanted control from the time the product entered its physical domain. Research wanted control, as one of its members put it, "until the actual factory yield reaches the theoretical yield."

The boundaries of control were actually somewhat difficult to pinpoint. Research was in command until factory problems seriously affecting quality were solved, except that research decisions were subject to engineering veto (in turn subject to top-management arbitration) anywhere beyond the pilot plant. In spite of continual argument about control jurisdiction, there were few engineering vetoes that ever reached arbitration.

The physical, mental, and emotional energies of these departments appeared to be devoted to the work at hand to a very high degree. While not absent from their relationships, conflicts took the form of tension between the inherently opposing values of quality and economy. The result was a competitive balance between the extremes of both. Why was conflict not destructive in this situation? There are basically three reasons:

1   Each of the three departments represented a social unit in which members could find not only satisfaction for their needs to belong, but also job interest, promotion opportunity, and so on. No one of these departments suffered from internal fragmentation.

2   At each point of significant interdepartmental contact, the members of the interacting groups agreed on certain important ideas as to how work should be accomplished. Wherever technical interdependence required intergroup contact, the groups tended to view each other and their common work with a markedly similar appreciation.

3   The hierarchy of authority among the departments was identical to the informally agreed-upon prestige hierarchy among these departments. This hierarchy was determined by the technical work limits set by one department for another, and by the initiation of activity by one department for another. The work done by research, for example, limited what the chemical engineers could work on but, at the same time, was the impetus which set the chemical engineers to work on each new product. The same was true of relationships down through the development sequence.

Very simply, then, when a man (or a group) told another what to do and when to do it, he did so as a member of a group of superior prestige, as agreed on by both groups. We might say that the orders which passed from one group to another were "legitimate," since most workers feel that it is legitimate in our society for a person of higher prestige to direct the activities of someone with less prestige, while it is illegitimate for the opposite to occur.

Thus, in the Company A situation, departmental energies were not consumed by internal activities designed to make the department a socially satisfactory place to live nor by struggles to communicate across abysses of viewpoint differences. Because authority was being exerted by socially legitimate persons and groups, little if any energy was wasted in jockeying for prestige positions.

There was an abundance of group energy left for work and for contest over the organizationally desirable balance of quality and economy. Furthermore, since the work itself was intrinsically rewarding and since supervisory practices encouraged work satisfactions, Company A's interdepartmental relations were highly productive, despite continual battles over quality versus economy.

The three elements—*internal social stability, external value sharing,* and *legitimate authority hierarchy*—comprise a triumvirate of measures which indicate the extent to which departmental energy will tend to be freed for productive work. These factors can be thought of as minimum requirements for interdepartmental effectiveness. For, in their absence, it is highly unlikely that either intrinsically interesting work or encouragement from supervision will achieve much in the way of productivity increases.

II WASTEFUL CONFLICTS OF IDEAS

Company B designed, manufactured, and sold precision electronic instruments to scientific laboratories and industrial firms. The sales department was composed primarily of long-service, socially prestigious men (including the president) who had been instrumental in establishing what was referred to as a "family atmosphere" in the company. The sales department was the center of the dominant ideas in the company about how employees should behave.

During the manpower disruptions of World War II, the production department attracted a group of men who had started as workmen and had worked their way up the management ladder, often by transferring from one company to another. These men were perceived by the rest of the company (and even by themselves) as "rough diamonds." Their ideas about personal comportment were very different from those held dear in the sales department.

At the close of the war, certain irregularities in the behavior of top-level, old-line production management were laid bare by the rough diamonds. When the culprits were discharged, they left the rough diamonds in control of production.

At the same time, however, certain checks and balances—in reaction to the ease with which the wartime irregularities were committed—were built into the organization at the expense of production's jurisdiction over such functions as purchasing and stock control. These restrictions were highly resented by the new production regime which felt it was being punished by the "family" school, some of whose members (the discharged old-line production men) were the real culprits. This "injustice" widened an already considerable gap between sales' and production's views of "how things ought to be."

Sales and production came in contact primarily when the quarterly production schedule was being set and whenever sales initiated changes in the schedule within quarters. On these occasions tempers flared, walkouts occurred, and the services of the vice president-controller were required for mediation. Sales' concern for meeting customers' special desires was pitted against production's concern for uninterrupted runs of each instrument in the company's catalog.

Unlike the Company A situation where a balance was struck between quality and economy, in Company B the contest between customer satisfaction and economical production resulted in a breakdown of relations. Furthermore, the production department became an armed camp in which each junior member of the group was strictly warned against dealing with the sales department lest the latter influence production activities at less than the top hierarchical level of the department.

To make sure that sales could not infiltrate production, top production executives allowed the bulk of production's members little influence over internal production affairs. For its part, sales spent a great deal of time devising power plays to force production to deviate from set schedules. Top sales officials wasted hours personally exerting their authority in production offices to obtain schedule deviations. Retributions in the form of ultimatums and unprofitable scheduling "trades" of one instrument for another resulted. Sales' two subsections, scientific and industrial, vied with each other to see who could get the best production deal in the schedule, often at each other's and the company's expense.

In Company B, while the work itself was challenging and although supervision circumscribed that interest only to a modest degree (by removing purchasing and stock control from production's jurisdiction), relationships were relatively nonproductive between sales and production. Minimal standards of performance were met only by the intervention of a vice president in routine sales-production affairs. Energies were not absorbed in an effort to right an illegitimate authority sequence, for sales' commands were legitimated by sales' superior prestige, but in dealing with the breach of communication between two groups whose backgrounds and ideas were diametrically opposed in many important ways.

In turn, each department's internal relations, used as a means of combating the outgroup, absorbed a great deal of effort. Production kept a tight hold on its members, which caused subordinate frustrations, while sales was constantly patching the relations between its own two subgroups. Any work accomplished between the two groups was based on the question, "Will this effort strengthen our position in the battle with the other department?" Almost never could the two groups be said to agree that their combined efforts were satisfying to both, or even to one, of the parties.

The nonproductive conflict between these two departments can be viewed as the result of energies consumed by attempts to right an irreconcilably imbalanced trade.[2] By sales' values, sales' ideas should have dominated, tempered only by "practical" economic considerations. (In other words, production should have provided information on which sales could base its decisions.)

By production's values, however, production ideas received too little weight, if, indeed, they were accorded any weight at all. Production believed that sales' information should be added to production information and the decision should then be a cooperative one. For sales to achieve its idea of balance, production had

[2]For further development of this concept, see Alvin Gouldner, "The Norm of Reciprocity: A Preliminary Statement," *American Sociological Review*, April 1960, pp. 161–178.

to forfeit its idea of balance, and vice versa. So the conflict was irreconcilable. As the mathematicians put it, the two departments were playing a zero-sum game. One's gain was the other's loss, because their different ideas of what was "right" made it so.

III ILLEGITIMATE AUTHORITY CONFLICTS

Company B's production department was engaged in another, but quite different, cross-departmental relationship of nonproductive character. The production engineering department (formally considered a peer of the production department) took research designs and translated them into parts lists, production drawings, and fabrication and assembly specifications, and in addition processed engineering change orders (ECOs). Much of production's work—both its content and its timing—depended on production engineering's efforts, since Company B's product designs were constantly changing.

Thus, production engineering was seen by production as telling production what to do and when to do it. On the other hand, production engineering was composed of men with skills no greater than, in fact, quite similar to, those possessed by production members. Production felt itself capable of performing not only production engineering's tasks but the more important tasks of job design and methods work which were within production's jurisdiction but outside production engineering's.

The two departments had almost no face-to-face contact. Communication between them was conducted through memos carried by lowly messengers. Production managers spent an inordinate amount of time checking for consistency among the various items produced by production engineering. When errors were discovered (as they seldom were), a cry of victory would ring out across the production office. A messenger would quickly be dispatched to carry the offending material back to production engineering, amply armed with a message elaborately outlining the stupidity which had produced such an error. The lack of direct contact between the two departments (other than this agressive kind) made it impossible for technically desirable accommodations between the two departments to be made. The most common topic of production conversation centered about "those goddam ECOs," in spite of the fact that production originated as many ECOs (making changes for its own convenience) as did any other department.

In this case, energies were heavily focused on the impropriety of a low-prestige department like production engineering calling the tune for an equally prestigious or even superior department like production. Production devoted its energies to rebalancing trade between the two departments. In other words, production's prestige could be maintained only by calling more tunes than it danced. This rebalancing process had little to do with accomplishing any work. Yet it consumed vast amounts of production management time (particularly that of the factory superintendent who, of all people, checked every drawing); and, in the last analysis it failed its purpose, since the tide was too great to be stemmed, no matter how much energy was devoted to the effort.

IV VALUE AND AUTHORITY CLASHES

Company C designed, manufactured, and distributed a large variety of electronic tubes of advanced design. One of its most rapidly selling tubes had a poor cost record—primarily, it was finally agreed, because of design inadequacies. In the process of trying to reduce costs through fabrication and assembly changes, the industrial engineering department had generated an idea for basic tube redesign. Several industrial engineers experimented informally with the new idea and achieved favorable results. When the matter was brought to the attention of the research department, it found its full schedule would not permit it to take over and develop the new idea. The industrial engineering inventors were given authority to continue development of the new tube. A development schedule was set and a development budget assigned to the industrial engineers.

For a time, progress was satisfactory. Then, when some metallurgical problems developed, the research department stepped in to make tests in an attempt to solve the problem. Conflict immediately developed. The industrial engineers maintained that the research department was unfair to the new tube because of the unrealistic way it conducted its tests. Research found it could get no cooperation in its desire to use industrial engineering equipment to conduct part of its investigation. Contact between the two groups dropped to zero, and investigations were conducted in parallel, though each group technically required the other's resources. Development schedules became a farce as one date after another passed without expected accomplishment.

The industrial engineers had become engaged in the project in the first place because, as one of its members put it, "I was particularly displeased with our department's general position in the company and felt we didn't really have a chance to show what we could do." One of the members of research mentioned that he thought of the industrial engineers as "just dumb, stupid, and no good." There was no meeting ground on the value which the two groups could bring to a common project. Nevertheless, there was general agreement that the research people possessed considerably greater prestige than did the industrial engineers.

In Company C, interdepartmental conflict became so energy-consuming that relationships were broken off entirely, to the detriment of the project at hand. Normally, research would have held the authority position—and legitimately so, according to its superior prestige. Pressured by scheduling circumstances and by the different points of view concerning what industrial engineering's role should be, the normal authority sequence was turned topsy-turvy. Industrial engineering did the prestige work of invention, directing research to carry out routine tests.

Suddenly, each group attempted to behave in such a way that its own view of a proper relationship would predominate. Research criticized industrial engineering's work and tried to force the industrial engineers back into the subordinate role of helping with tests. Industrial engineering, which always had been eager for a chance to get its "teeth into something," was enjoying the fruits of its initial invention (which, incidentally, later proved to be basically sound). Feeling that its desires were being violated, it tried to keep control of the prestige activities and went out of its way to "prove" that research was barking up the wrong tree.

None of these activities had any necessary relationship to developing a new tube. All energies were devoted to forcing one group's values on the other and maintaining what were believed to be legitimate prestige positions. The two departments were playing another zero-sum game in which what seemed positive trading for one was inevitably interpreted as negative trading by the other.

Varying Viewpoints

In each of these four cases, the forces siphoning energy away from productive work have been of a particular kind. In each instance, relationships within groups were at least socially satisfactory. (In Company B, the production group did enforce limits on member influence, but this discipline, because it was viewed as group defense, did not lessen cohesion within the department.) The work of the various groups was intrinsically interesting to group members. Supervision was relatively permissive in allowing group members to "complicate" their lives about the work itself. Obviously, these elements are not always present in organized situations. Equally obvious from our cases is the fact that these elements, by themselves, do not result in effective interdepartmental relations, though they may be considered to contribute to such relations if other conditions are also met.

Focal Points   What the above cases focus on are the troubles caused by differences in point of view and legitimacy of authority. What these cases teach about group conflicts arising from these two trouble sources is just as true for our understanding of the interrelationships of individuals, for intergroup problems are only special cases of interpersonal issues. The only difference between them is the complexity of dealing with the problem, since the individual persons in our cases are representatives of social groups. Thus, their behavior cannot be modified by actions which are based on the assumption that groups respond exactly as do individuals. In short, the causes of conflict are similar, but the remedies are different.

What happens when groups suffer from authority and viewpoint conflicts is summarized in Exhibit I. Like any diagram dealing with a limited number of factors, Exhibit I runs the danger of implying that these cause-and-effect tendencies represent all that need be known about interdepartmental relations. Such an implication, were it intended, would, of course, be fatuous. Research in the area of interdepartmental problems has scarcely begun. Furthermore, we have already noted that other factors can be expected to intervene and render the exhibit's hypotheses, as they should be called, inoperative. Three of these factors have been emphasized—group cohesion, job interest, and supervisory practices.

Once we allow for these mitigating factors, however, we will find it useful to

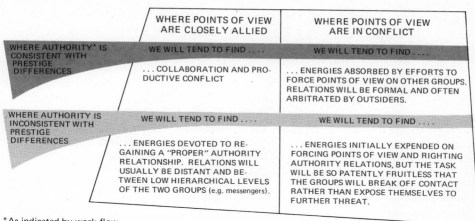

	WHERE POINTS OF VIEW ARE CLOSELY ALLIED	WHERE POINTS OF VIEW ARE IN CONFLICT
WHERE AUTHORITY* IS CONSISTENT WITH PRESTIGE DIFFERENCES	WE WILL TEND TO FIND . . . . COLLABORATION AND PRODUCTIVE CONFLICT	WE WILL TEND TO FIND . . . . ENERGIES ABSORBED BY EFFORTS TO FORCE POINTS OF VIEW ON OTHER GROUPS. RELATIONS WILL BE FORMAL AND OFTEN ARBITRATED BY OUTSIDERS.
WHERE AUTHORITY IS INCONSISTENT WITH PRESTIGE DIFFERENCES	WE WILL TEND TO FIND . . . . ENERGIES DEVOTED TO REGAINING A "PROPER" AUTHORITY RELATIONSHIP. RELATIONS WILL USUALLY BE DISTANT AND BETWEEN LOW HIERARCHICAL LEVELS OF THE TWO GROUPS (e.g. messengers).	WE WILL TEND TO FIND . . . . ENERGIES INITIALLY EXPENDED ON FORCING POINTS OF VIEW AND RIGHTING AUTHORITY RELATIONS, BUT THE TASK WILL BE SO PATENTLY FRUITLESS THAT THE GROUPS WILL BREAK OFF CONTACT RATHER THAN EXPOSE THEMSELVES TO FURTHER THREAT.

*As indicated by work flow.

Exhibit I Dominant influences in interdepartmental relations.

conceive of interdepartmental relations as though they were subject to the dominant influences cited in the diagram. The manager can make this concept more relevant personally if he reviews his own observations of interdepartmental conflict to see how they compare with the kind of analysis described here.

Plan for Action

While the primary purpose of this article has been to explain certain types of interdepartmental problems, the question inevitably arises, "Suppose some sense can be made of interdepartmental difficulties by this kind of thinking; what then do we do with this understanding, even if it does prove to be accurate? How would we go about applying it to lessen interdepartmental conflicts in our company?" Let's look at some action ideas which stem from what has already been said.

Stop, Look, & Listen   As frustrating as it might seem, the first suggestion is to stop to see if action is required and, if it is, whether it is feasible. It often may be wise to heed the admonishment (in reverse of the usual form), "Don't just do something, stand there!" The basis for this wisdom lies in the fact that formal organizations often display some of the characteristics of a biological organism, particularly insofar as the latter has some capacity to heal itself. The administrator, if this contention be true, may find the role of the modern physician attractive. He attempts to control the environment so that natural healing processes can take place unhindered within the human body. Here are some examples of where such inaction might be appropriate:

• Take the case of Company A. Should something be done to alter jurisdictions among Company A's departments? Or are the natural tensions between these departments, the energies to expand jurisdiction, operating in precisely the most beneficial way for the organization? The best advice in this case seems to be to keep an eye on that tension. Watch that it does not degenerate subtly into another Company C situation. If it moves too far in that direction, then action is required.

This example helps clarify an issue which we have been flirting with throughout this article: the problem of distinguishing productive from nonproductive conflicts. It may not suffice to say that conflict is productive if the parties to it end up satisfied and get there under their own steam. In any particular case, in the heat of a tight scheduling situation, many an administrator has interpreted *any* disagreement as nonproductive and has succumbed to the temptation to interfere. If schedules then have to be junked, the blame is thrown on the groups in disagreement. Had the administrator satisfied himself about the basic conditions within which the fighting groups were working, and listened carefully to see if the fights were *working* or *warring* arguments, he might have saved himself and his organization much trouble.

- A case more dramatic than that cited above, and one where action seemed inappropriate, takes us back to the Company B organization. The production department, as might be suspected from what we already know about it, was striving to enlarge its domain to conform to its own ideas about production's importance. This striving provoked a potential clash with the research department when the frequency of special orders began to increase rapidly. Special orders required research design but not production engineering attention, the work of the latter group being devoted to mass-production items. Thus, research would naturally be required to deal directly with production in the case of special orders. Inevitably, production—as isolated historical instances had convinced research—would attempt to dominate these relationships whenever it could.

To avoid this eventuality, research developed a small production unit of its own, though production was fully capable of doing special work. This "organizational invention" of the research department, stepping into work for which it was neither intended nor formally responsible, eliminated the need for contact with production and sidestepped the inevitably nonproductive conflict which would have resulted. The invention was costly in many ways, particularly in terms of valuable research time and space. But on balance it appeared to be the most adequate short-term resolution to a basic interdepartmental problem.

- There are a host of other examples of this kind of self-regulation. Many of these measures are rather simple and expedient, if not conducive to removal of the basic causes of nonproductive conflict. Chief among these is the use of what may be called "expendable linkers" as go-betweens in conflicted interdepartmental relations. For example, a production department was observed to assign to its least important member the task of liaison between itself and other departments, where such expediting connoted the use of illegitimate authority. The expediter himself threatened no one, and adopted a most passive demeanor. Communication then took place not between main contenders who could only lose by such contact but through a neutral intermediary. The cursing went unheard by those for whom a damaging response would have been required.

- Other examples involve the use of formal procedures or instruments such as the production schedule, fought over maybe once a quarter, but exerting independent authority between times and keeping sales and production away from each other's throats. None of these is an ideal solution to interdepartmental problems, but each is likely to emerge as a practical expedient in a difficult situation. The administrator may find his short-run problems solved if he is aware of the importance of these often unnoticed "inventions." Furthermore, if he wants to do away with these sometimes awkward mechanisms, he had better make sure he has something with which to replace them.

Types of Resolution Our cases (and there are unlimited examples like them) have shown that some interdepartmental difficulties go beyond the capacity of the groups to resolve them at anything but a survival level, if that. That level may well be, and often is, intolerable for the organization as a whole. Let us look at the two alternative types of resolution.

First are the resolutions which arise in response to conflicts of authority. In such cases the work flow designed into the organization (e.g., the passage of blueprints from production engineering to production) violates the notions of the organization's members as to who legitimately should, by right of superior prestige, tell whom what to do. Although such problems are not restricted to particular hierarchical levels of the organization, they do tend to become more intense wherever prestige relations are ambiguous or under threat. The higher one goes in many organizations, the more these conditions tend to apply. There are several ways of resolving such problems:

1 An obvious solution is to take whatever steps are available to reduce prestige ambiguity and threat. For example, if Company B's management had realized how pertinent production's resentment at being rated "second class" was to the interdepartmental problems in which it was involved, investigation might have produced ways of clarifying production's status and of enriching its participation in important decisions. Instead, the factory superintendent was the last to be admitted to the executive council and was not accorded vice presidential rank, as were most other department managers. Management failed to take these steps because it feared domination by the superintendent. Yet more careful diagnosis might have revealed that the superintendent's striving for dominance was a result of his impression that management thought him unworthy of participation in decisions for which his expertise was, in fact, badly needed. The circle was vicious.

2 Another step in reducing the amount of nonproductivity in illegitimate authority relations is to reorganize subunits of the organization in such a way that authority and prestige become consistent. In Company B's production engineering and production relationship, such reorganization could have taken the form of incorporating production engineering into production's domain, much as was done in Company A, where the chemical engineers had been removed from research and placed in the engineering department. With production engineering subject to production's control, yet sharing many ideas with both research and production, a mingling of points of view could have been achieved and authority questions dealt with from within.

The very same kind of potential authority difficulty was avoided in Company B because scheduling was incorporated within production's jurisdiction. Another way of justifying such a resolution of conflict is to note that production's technical functions, as well as those of production engineering, were so closely allied and overlapping that to separate them was to form a barrier across which required contact was extremely difficult and at times impossible. Unfortunately, once again Company B's management so feared production dominance that its inclination was much more to reduce production's domain than to enlarge it.

3   Another extremely clear example of how structural reorganization can resolve not only the authority legitimacy problem, but also have side effects in bringing clashing points of view into sufficient harmony for communication to recommence, is contained in the actual resolution of the Company C difficulty reported above. The obvious solution was to take the research initiative away from the industrial engineers and put it back where prestige relations said it belonged, with research. The solution appeared obvious only because the breakdown between the two departments was so catastrophic.

Equally obvious before that breakdown was the apparently logical belief that the people who invent something should continue to develop it, both because the inventors would logically appear to be most expert in understanding the invention and because it is only fair that productive effort should be rewarded by continuing responsibility and credit. In fact, change was not instituted until the industrial engineers became so thoroughly frustrated by their continuing design failures that they could entertain the idea that their "baby" might be reorganized into more "proper" channels. Although costly in some ways and probably unconscious, management's decision to do nothing at first to set the interdepartmental relations back into the normal work pattern allowed industrial engineering to become receptive to such a change when it finally was made.

This crucial aspect of conflict resolution—receptivity to change—brings us to the second major strategy for helping departmental energies engage in constructive action instead of working against members of another department. This strategy involves what might be called intergroup counseling, therapy, or training. Conflicts in points of view are susceptible only to this strategy, short of complete personnel turnover in one or the other of the warring departments. And, because authority illegitimacy must inevitably engender conflict of viewpoint, it too can be mitigated, if only partially, by intergroup training. Several aspects of this strategy are worthy of attention, though the subject is a difficult and complex one.

Some studies show that intergroup conflict resolution hinges on a particular type of training which seeks an integration of viewpoints by making warring groups realize they are dependent on one another.[3] Such a strategy tends to work more readily when both groups fear some external threat to both of them. This idea is not greatly different from the idea contained in the observation that

---

[3]See *Intergroup Relations and Leadership*, edited by Muzafer Sherif (New York, John Wiley & Sons, Inc., 1962).

members of families may fight viciously with one another but when an outsider attacks one of the family, the family abandons its differences to fight together against the intruder. It seems obvious from the analysis presented in this article, however, that this strategy is operable only when prestige-authority issues are not present.

A number of researchers, teachers, and managers have begun to explore more direct methods for reducing point-of-view conflict. Some have pointed out that bringing group representatives together to explore their differences is usually doomed to failure since representatives, if they are to remain such, must be loyal to their respective groups.[4] Simple measures to increase contact also appear fruitless, because negative stereotypes end up simply becoming reinforced by the contact.

Other measures have proved more effective. Although they vary in form, almost all of these contain the following basic element: *the groups in conflict must be brought together as totalities under special conditions.*[5] The goal of all of these conditions is to reduce individual and group anxieties sufficiently so that a point of view can not only be made explicit but can be heard by those who do not share it. This procedure requires not only considerable candor between groups, but also candor within each group and within the individual himself. Naturally, sessions in which such training is supposed to take place can be extremely threatening and should be mediated by an external agent to keep threat within manageable bounds and help guide the groups into explorative rather than recriminative behavior.[6]

Conclusion

Seldom, if ever, do problems of nonproductive conflict exist in isolation. It is extremely likely that wherever such conflict is found it has been engendered by organizational and emotional maladjustments, each of which has fed upon the other. It would make sense, then, to attack interdepartmental problems while fully realizing that they may be spun into the warp and woof of the organization's fabric. Such an attack has far-reaching consequences for the organization. It means, for example, that the goals of the organization must be critically examined, since these tend to influence the way in which the work of the organization has been divided up and division of labor is at the core of interdepartmental problems.

Because goals, in turn, are heavily influenced by the organization's environment and by the way in which that environment is interpreted by executives and directors, the environment and the process by which it is interpreted also must come under scrutiny. Do those in control have a clear idea of their company's relation to its market? If not, why not? Have they made clear to the other

[4]See Robert Blake and Jane S. Mouton, *Group Dynamics—Key to Decision Making* (Houston, Texas, Gulf Publishing Co., 1961).

[5]See Herbert R. Shepard and Robert R. Blake, "Changing Behavior Through Cognitive Change," *Human Organization,* Summer 1962, p. 88.

[6]See Chris Argyris, *Interpersonal Competence and Organizational Effectiveness* (Homewood, Illinois, The Dorsey Press, Inc. and Richard D. Irwin, Inc., 1962).

members of the company the job to be done and what that job requires of each sub-element in the organization?[7]

These questions are fundamental to the building of an organization. Without answers to these questions, any attempt to resolve an illegitimate authority problem usually is a patch-up job, likely to create as many problems as it cures. Furthermore, without these answers, the members of the organization cannot avoid feeling that their relationships to each other are ambiguous—and aimless ambiguity is a breeding ground for insecurity, defensive behavior, and sapped energy.

Involving the members of an organization in the pursuit of clarifying the organization's goals—in establishing a meaningful identity for the firm—is, perhaps, the soundest process for tapping into the wells of productive energy.[8] Such a pursuit, carried on openly and sincerely, cannot help but raise issues of interdepartmental ambiguity, illegitimacy, and conflicting points of view to a level where they can be re-examined and dealt with. An easy process? No. But as "old wives' tales" have told us, no remedy is without pain.

[7]See Wilfred Brown, *Exploration in Management* (London, William Heinemann Ltd., 1960).
[8]Alfred Kenneth Rice, *The Enterprise and Its Environment* (London, Tavistock Publications, 1963).

Reading 41
Methods of Resolving Interpersonal Conflict
Ronald J. Burke

Purpose of This Study

In a previous investigation, Burke (1969a) collected questionnaire data from 74 managers, in which they described the way they and their superiors dealt with conflict between them. It was possible to relate five different methods of conflict resolution originally proposed by Blake and Mouton (1964)—Withdrawing, Smoothing, Compromising, Forcing, and Confrontation or Problem Solving—to two major areas of the superior-subordinate relationship. These were (1) constructive use of differences and disagreements, and (2) several aspects of the superior-subordinate relationship in planning job targets and evaluating accomplishments.

In general, the results showed that Withdrawing and Forcing behaviors were consistently negatively related to these two areas. Compromising was not related to these two areas. Use of Smoothing was inconsistently related, sometimes

"Methods of Resolving Interpersonal Conflict," Ronald J. Burke, *Personnel Administration*, July–August, pp. 48–55. Reprinted with permission.

positive and sometimes negative. Only Confrontation or Problem Solving was always related positively to both. That is, use of Confrontation was associated with constructive use of differences and high scores on various measures of the superior-subordinate relationship.

This study has the dual purpose of attempting to specify more precisely the characteristics of the Confrontation or Problem Solving method of conflict resolution, and replicating the earlier study (Burke, 1969a) using different methodology.

Method

Subjects: The respondents were managers from various organizations who were enrolled in a university course emphasizing behavioral science concepts relevant to the functions of management. Their organizational experience ranged from one year to over thirty years.

Procedure: Each respondent was asked to describe a time when he felt particularly GOOD (or BAD) about the way in which an interpersonal conflict was resolved. The specific instructions stated:

"Think of a time when you felt especially GOOD (or BAD) about the way an interpersonal conflict or disagreement (e.g., boss-subordinate, peer-peer, etc.) in which you were involved was resolved. It may have been on your present job, or any other job, or away from the work situation.

"Now describe it in enough detail so a reader would understand the way the conflict or differences were handled."

This statement appeared at the top of a blank sheet of paper.

Approximately half the respondents were first to describe the instance when they felt particularly good, followed by the instance when they felt particularly bad. The remaining respondents described the instances in the reverse order. No apparent effects were observed from the change in order, so the data from both groups will be considered together in this report.

Results

Fifty-three descriptions of effective resolution of conflict (felt especially GOOD) and 53 descriptions of ineffective resolutions of conflict (felt especially BAD) were obtained. These were provided by 57 different individuals. Some individuals provided only one example. The response rate was about 70 percent of the total available population.

The written descriptions were then coded into one of the five methods of conflict resolution proposed by Blake and Mouton, (1964) (1) *Withdrawing*—easier to refrain than to retreat from an argument; silence is golden. "See no evil, hear no evil, speak no evil." (2) *Smoothing*—play down the differences and emphasize common interests; issues that might cause divisions or hurt feelings are not discussed. (3) *Compromising*—splitting the difference, bargaining, search for an intermediate position. Better half a loaf than none at all; no one loses but no one wins. (4) *Forcing*—a win-lose situation; participants are antagonists, competi-

Table 1   Methods Associated with Effective and Ineffective Conflict Resolution

	Effective resolution (N = 53)		Ineffective resolution (N = 53)	
	N	%	N	%
Withdrawal	0	0.0*	5	9.4*
Smoothing	0	0.0	1	1.9
Compromise	6	11.3	3	5.7
Forcing	13	24.5*	42	79.2*
Confrontation-Problem Solving	31	58.5*	0	0.0*
Other (still unresolved; unable to determine how resolved; irrelevant to assignment; etc.)	3	5.7	2	3.8

*Percentage difference between groups is significant at the 0.5 level of confidence.

tors, not collaborators. Fixed positions, polarization. Creates a victor and a vanquished. (5) *Confrontation or Problem-Solving*—open exchange of information about the conflict or problem as each sees it, and a working through of their differences to reach a solution that is optimal to both. Both can win.

Table 1 presents the method of conflict resolution associated with effective resolution (left half of Table 1) and ineffective resolution (right half of Table 1). Considering the left half of the table, Confrontation or Problem Solving was the most common method for effective resolution (58.5%), followed by Forcing (24.5%), and Compromise (11.3%). The prominence of Confrontation as an effective method is consistent with the earlier study (Burke, 1969a) but the value for Forcing was higher than expected. When these 13 cases are considered as a group, 11 of them are similar in that the party providing the written description benefited as a result of the Forcing. That is, Forcing was perceived as an effective method of resolving conflict by the victor, but not by the vanquished.

Moving to the right half of Table 1, Forcing was the most commonly used method for ineffective resolution, followed in second place by Withdrawal with only 9.4 percent. The vast majority of individuals providing written descriptions of Forcing methods were victims or "losers" as a result of Forcing behavior.

In summary, the major differences in methods of conflict resolution found to distinguish effective versus ineffective examples were: (1) significantly greater use of Confrontation or Problem Solving in the effective examples (58.5% vs. 0.0%); (2) significantly less use of Forcing in the effective examples (24.5% vs. 79.2%); and, (3) significantly less use of Withdrawing in the effective examples (0.0% vs. 9.4%).

When Forcing was seen to be effective, the authors of the examples were "winners" of a win-lose conflict; when Forcing was seen to be ineffective, the authors of the examples were "losers" of a win-lose conflict. Whether the resolution of conflict via Forcing would actually be perceived to be effective by members of the organization outside the conflict (i.e., objectively seen as effective), as it was perceived to be effective by the "winners", remains to be determined by future research.

Effective Conflict Resolution

A few of the examples of effective conflict resolution are provided to highlight specific features of Confrontation or Problem Solving. These were taken verbatim from the written descriptions.

1 *This example highlights the presentation of a problem of mutual interest—meeting deadlines more often at the earliest opportunity (when the problem is observed). Superior is open-minded and asking for help.*

"I once was given the responsibility for managing a small group of technicians engaged in turning out critical path schedules. I spent some time trying to get organized and involved with the group, but I sensed a hostile atmosphere, accompanied by off-hand sarcastic remarks. At the end of the day very little work had been accomplished.

"The next day when I came in, I called the group together and told them that we were falling behind, and asked them to help me find a solution. After the initial distrust had been dissipated, the group produced some good ideas on work re-allocation, office arrangement, priorities and techniques. I told the group that all of their agreed upon suggestions would be implemented at once, and their reply was that backlog would be cleared in three days and would not build up again.

"Within three days the backlog was gone, the group worked together better, and for the six months I was in charge, schedules were always ready before they were required."

2 *This example highlights emphasis on facts in determining the best resolution of conflict. Both had strong convictions but one willingly moved to the other's position when facts indicated that this position was best.*

"The project engineer and I disagreed about the method of estimating the cost of alternative schemes in a highway interchange. Neither of us could agree on the other's method. Eventually I was able to satisfy him using algebra. We were both happy with the result."

3 *Like Example 2, this one highlights an emphasis on facts and the conviction that by digging and digging, the truth will be discovered. Although the superior had a vested interest in the "old" system (a product of his thinking), the discussion was never personalized. That is, it did not involve "me" versus "you," but rather a comparison of two systems, two concepts or two ideas.*

"About a year ago I developed a new system for processing the accounting of the inventory of obsolete material on hand in our plant. It was my estimation that it would prove to be an easier system to operate and control and would also involve a considerable monetary saving for the company.

"When I approached my boss with the system, he immediately turned it down as he had developed the present system and was sure it was the best possible system. As I was sure my new system was superior to the present one. I then convinced him to join me in analyzing a comparison of the two systems, pointing out the strengths and weaknesses of the two. After a period of evaluation involving many differences of opinion, we were able to resolve that my system had definite merit and should be brought into operation."

4   *This example highlights the fact that through problem solving both parties can benefit. Instead of compromising, the issues are discussed until a solution completely satisfactory to both is found. Often this is superior to the ones initially favored by the separate parties.*

"In the _____Board of Education, there were eight inspectors of Public Schools and four superintendents. Last February the inspectors were given the assignment of developing an in-service plan for the training of teachers for the school year 1968–69. The inspectors gave the assignment to a group of three of their number who were to bring a report to the next inspector's meeting. I was not a member of the in-service committee but in conversations with the committee members I discovered that they contemplated having an in-service program for two teachers from each school (there are about 85 schools) once a month for the entire year in mathematics. I felt that this would be a very thin coverage of our 2,000 or so teachers.

"Consequently I worked on a plan whereby utilizing two Thursday mornings a month and the specialized teaching help available in _____, every teacher would have the opportunity to become involved in an in-service training session in a subject of his or her choice once during the year. At the inspector's meeting the sub-committee presented its report and after some procedural wrangling I was permitted to present my plan. The two were diametrically opposed and it looked as if my plan would be voted down except the chairman suggested that both plans be presented to the superintendents.

"At the meeting of the superintendents, the sub-committee made its report and I presented my plan. As the meeting progressed there was some give and take and instead of one or the other being discarded both plans were adopted. For this school year mathematics is stressed for the first eight Thursday mornings (their plan in a rather concentrated form) then for the next eight months on the second and fourth Thursday my plan is used. We came out of this meeting with a combination of the two plans which was better than either one individually."

Ineffective Conflict Resolution

Examples 5, 6 and 7 illustrate Forcing methods of conflict resolution. A win-lose situation is set up, and usually the superior wins. The individual with the greater power triumphs (a personalized disagreement) rather than the one whose position is supported by the most factual evidence.

5 "In a previous job, I worked for a major management consulting group as a consultant. One assignment, lasting four months, was to use a simulation technique to evaluate the most preferable investment decision using defined quantitative criteria. At the end of the job two alternatives were shown to be marginally better than the other. However, later sensitivity tests also showed that the analytical technique could not rate one to be substantially better than the other.

"Therefore, I wrote a 'technically honest' report stating that our analysis could not provide the one best alternative. My manager, feeling that we were hired to recommend a 'one best' alternative, wanted to cover up the limitations of our methodology.

"We disagreed and I was over-ruled. The manager wrote a 'technically dishonest' version of the report and the devised report was sent to the client indicating the 'one best' alternative."

6 "Recently in my firm, management had sprung a secrecy agreement contract upon all of the technical people. No word of introduction or explanation was given. It was simply handed out and we were asked to sign it. Most of us found objection in several clauses in the agreement. However, management officials stated that the agreement would probably not stand up in a court of law. They further stated that it was something that was sent up from the U.S. and was not their idea. The employees continued to show reluctance.

"The vice-president called on everyone individually and stated that there would be no room for advancement for anyone who did not sign the contract. As a result everyone signed."

7 "I was assigned a project by my boss to determine the optimum way, using predetermined times, to lay out an assembly line. It would have to provide optimum efficiency with the following variables: (a) different hourly production rates (e.g. 100/hr. Mon., 200/hr. Tues.) which would mean different numbers of operators on the line; (b) different models of the product (electric motors). The group was on group incentive.

"After much research and discussion, the system was installed utilizing the floating system of assembly (operators could move from station to station in order to keep out of the bottleneck operation). This system was working out well. However, at this time I was informed by my boss that he and the foreman of the area decided that they wished to use the 'paced' system of assembly. This would mean the conveyor belt would be run at set speeds and that the stripes would be printed on the belt indicating that one device would have to be placed on each mark and operators would not float.

"I was dead against this since I had considered it and rejected it in favor of the implemented method. I was, however, given the order to use their proposed system *or else*. There was *no* opportunity for discussion or justification of the method."

8 *This example is a classic description of the Withdrawal as a mode of Conflict resolution. Clearly the problem is not resolved.*

"On the successful completion of a project which involved considerable time and effort, I was praised and thanked for a job well done by my immediate supervisor and his supervisor, the vice president in charge of manufacturing. They promised me that on my next salary review I would receive a substantial increase.

"The next salary review came up and my immediate superior submitted an amount that he and I felt was a good increase. The amount I received was one-third of this figure. I felt insulted, cheated, and hurt that the company considered I was worth this 'token' amount.

"I had a personal interview with the vice president where I argued that I felt I should receive more. He agreed in sort of an off-handed way—he felt the whole salary schedule should be reviewed and that my area of responsibility should be increased. He said the company wants people to 'prove themselves' before they give them increases; and he suggested a salary review. I felt I had just done this in my last project—I felt I was being put off, but agreed to the salary review.

"One month passed and nothing happened. I became frustrated—I purposely slowed down the amount of work I turned out.

"Another month passed and still no action. I became disillusioned with the company and resolved at this point to look for another position. Several months later with still no action, I resigned and accepted another position."

Inability to Resolve Conflict

These descriptions of ineffective resolution of conflict indicate that an impressive number of respondents included termination or change of employment of one member in the situation (19 of 53, 26%). These cases tended to be of two types.

The first is represented by Example 8. Here an employee decides to quit because he felt the problem was not resolved in a satisfactory manner. Forcing is likely to be associated with instances of voluntary termination.

The second centered around an inability to resolve the conflict. Then the "problem employee" (a visible symptom of the conflict) was dismissed.

9   *The following example illustrates this:*

"This concerned a young girl about 18 years old who was a typist in our office. This girl lacked a little maturity, but was not really all that bad. She was tuned to all the latest fashions in both dress and manners.

"I felt and still feel that this girl was a potentially good employee. But it was decided that she should be let go. The argument used was that she was not a good worker and lacked the proper attitude for office work. Rather than spend a little time and effort to understand the girl and perhaps develop her into a good employee, the easy way was taken and the girl was fired."

There were two other clear cases of "effective" conflict resolution resulting in voluntary employee terminations. In both instances a Forcing mode was employed and the "loser" resigned from the organization soon after. Our finding is that these were given as examples of effective conflict resolution by the "winner." In another effective example of Forcing, the "loser" was dismissed.

Conclusions

The results of this investigation are consistent with an earlier study (Burke, 1969a), and the data of Lawrence and Lorsch (1967a, 1967b) in showing the value of Confrontation and Problem Solving as methods of conflict resolution. About 60 percent of the examples of effective conflict resolution involved use of this method, while no examples of ineffective conflict resolution did. The poorest method of conflict resolution was Forcing. This method accounted for 80 percent of the examples of ineffective conflict resolution and only 24 percent of the examples of effective conflict resolution. The latter conclusion is somewhat at odds with Lawrence and Lorsch's findings that Forcing was an effective backup method to Confrontation, from an organizational effectiveness standpoint. In fact, the earlier study (Burke, 1969a) found that the use of these methods tended to be negatively correlated. Managers high in use of one of them tended to be low in use of the other.

Characteristics of Problem Solving

Let us now consider more specific features of Confrontation, the most effective method of resolving interpersonal conflict. Insights from the present investigation and the writings of others (e.g., Blake, Shepard and Mouton, 1964; Maier, 1963; Maier and Hoffman, 1965) becomes relevant. The following then are characteristics of Confrontation or Problem Solving as a method of managing conflict:

    1   Both people have a vested interest in the outcome. (Examples 1, 2, 3 and 4).

    2   There is a belief on the part of the people involved that they have the potential to resolve the conflict and to achieve a better solution through collaboration.

    3   There is a recognition that the conflict or the problem is mainly in the relationship between the individuals and not in each person separately. If the conflict is in the relationship, it must be defined by those who have the relationship. In addition, if solutions are to be developed, the solutions have to be generated by those who share the responsibility for assuring that the solution will work and for making the relationship last.

    4   The goal is to solve the problem, not to accommodate different points of view. This process identifies the causes of reservation, doubt, and misunderstanding between the people confronted with conflict and disagreement. Alternative ways of approaching conflict resolution are explored and tested (Examples 2 and 3).

    5   The people involved are problem-minded instead of solution-minded; "fluid" instead of "fixed" positions. Both parties jointly search out the issues that separate them. Through joint effort, the problems that demand solutions are identified, and later solved.

    6   There is a realization that both aspects of a controversy have potential strengths and potential weaknesses. Rarely is one position completely right and the other completely wrong. (Example 4).

7   There is an effort to understand the conflict or problem from the other person's point of view, and from the standpoint of the "real" or legitimate needs that must be recognized and met before problem solving can occur. Full acceptance of the other is essential.

8   The importance of looking at the conflict objectively rather than in a personalized sort of way is recognized.(Example 3).

9   An examination of one's own attitudes (hostilities, antagonisms) is needed before interpersonal contact on a less effective basis has a chance to occur.

10   An understanding of the less effective methods of conflict resolution (e.g., win-lose, bargaining, etc.) is essential.

11   One needs to prevent "face-saving" situations. Allow people to "give" so that a change in one's viewpoint does not suggest weakness or capitulation.

12   There is need to minimize effects of status differences, defensiveness, and other barriers which prevent people from working together effectively.

13   It is important to be aware of the limitations of arguing or presenting evidence in favor of your own position while downgrading the opponent's position. This behavior often stimulates the opponent to find even greater support for his position (increased polarization). In addition, it leads to selective listening for weakness in opponent's position rather than listening to understand his position.

Attitude, Skill and Creativity

Two related themes run through these characteristics, one dealing with attitudes, and the other with skills (interpersonal, problem solving) of the individuals involved. As the research of Maier and his associates has shown, differences and disagreements need not lead to dissatisfaction and unpleasant experiences but rather can lead to innovation and creativity. One of the critical variables was found to be leader's attitudes toward disagreement. The person with different ideas, especially if he is a subordinate, can be seen as a problem employee and troublemaker or he can be seen as an idea man and innovator, depending on the leader's attitude. There are some people that go through life attempting to sell their ideas, to get others to do things they do not want to do. They set up a series of win-lose situations, and attempt to emerge victorious. Many of these people are able to accomplish their ends. There are others who are more concerned with the quality and effectiveness of their operations, and who, with creative solutions to problems, are genuinely open-minded and able and willing to learn from others (and to teach others), in a collaborative relationship.

The interpersonal skills are related to the development of a "helping relationship" and include among others, mutual trust and respect, candid communication, and awareness of the needs of the others. The problem solving skills center around locating and stating the problem, seeking alternatives, exploring and testing alternatives, and selecting the best alternative. Knowledge and insight gained through experience with the benefits of problem solving and the dysfunctional effects of other strategies would be valuable in developing interpersonal skills.

Further Research Needed

Two additional areas need immediate research consideration. The first needs to explore the notions of conflict resolution from the organizational as well as the individual viewpoint. Lawrence and Lorsch report that Forcing was an effective back-up mode to Confrontation from the organization's standpoint, because at least things were being done. Our data in two separate investigations indicate that this mode of conflict resolution is very unsatisfactory from the standpoint of the one forced, the "loser," and may also have dysfunctional consequences.

The second research area concerns the application of these principles of effective conflict resolution (Confrontation and Problem Solving, with their more specific attitudinal and skill components) in an attempt to arrive at more constructive use of disagreement. Preliminary results from an experiment simulating conflict situations using role playing suggest that knowledge of these principles and some limited practice in their use increase one's ability to use differences constructively in obtaining a quality solution, and decreases the tendency to engage in "limited war" (Burke, 1969b).

REFERENCES

Blake, R. R., and Mouton, J. S., *The Managerial Grid,* Houston: Gulf Publishing Company, 1964.

Blake, R. R., Shepard, H. A., and Mouton, J. S., *Managing Intergroup Conflict in Industry,* Houston: Gulf Publishing Company, 1964.

Boulding, K., A pure theory of conflict applied to organization—In R. L. Kahn and E. Boulding (Eds.), *Power and Conflict in Organization,* New York: Basic Books, Inc., 1964, pp. 136–145.

Burke, R. J., Methods of managing superior-subordinate conflict: Their effectiveness and consequences, Unpublished manuscript, 1969a.

Burke, R. J., Effects of limited training on conflict resolution effectiveness, Unpublished manuscript, 1969b.

Kata, D., Approaches to managing conflict—In R. L. Kahn and E. Boulding (Eds.) *Power and Conflict in Organizations,* New York: Basic Books, Inc., 1964, pp. 105–114.

Lawrence, P. R., and Lorsch, J. W., Differentiation and Integration in Complex Organizations, *Administrative Science Quarterly,* 1967a, 12, 1–47.

Lawrence, P. R., and Lorsch, J. W., *Organization and Environment,* Boston: Division of Research, Harvard Business School, Harvard University, 1967b.

Maier, N. R. F., *Problem-Solving Discussions and Conferences,* New York: McGraw-Hill, 1963.

Maier, N. R. F., and Hoffman, L. R., Acceptance and quality of solutions as related to leaders' attitudes toward disagreement in group problem-solving, *Journal of Applied Behavioral Science,* 1965, 1, 373–386.

McGregor, D., *The Professional Manager,* New York: McGraw-Hill, 1967.

Shepard, H. A., Responses to situations of competition and conflict—In R. L. Kahn and E. Boulding (Eds.), *Power and Conflict in Organizations,* New York: Basic Books, Inc., 1964, pp. 127–135.

Management of Change

The world around and within organizations is changing so fast that "it takes all the running you can do just to stay in the same place." Changes in the competitive, technological, legal, political, and social environments are becoming increasingly commonplace. Internal changes, such as increases in the mobility of managers and a trend toward earlier executive retirement and replacement by younger personnel, are also generating upheavals in organizational systems. What are the appropriate responses to these changes at various stages in a firm's life cycle? What are some strategies for inducing, and responding successfully to, change? And what is the relationship between an organization's environment and its structure and processes? A consistent theme in most of the articles in this section is the organization's *proactive* role, that is, what actions it can take to induce desired changes.

This section begins with an article by Greiner that presents a macro model of organizational growth. The contingency theme emerges clearly from the standpoint that once a manager has identified which of five basic stages of growth his firm is in, he can determine the right combination of five organizational practices (in terms of management forms, organization structure, top management style, control system, and reward emphasis) that would be most effective.

The reading by French and Bell views the environment as the independent variable that not only determines the probable organizational structure that will be most effective (mechanistic or organic), but extends the analysis one step further by predicting in what situations organization development (OD) activities will probably succeed. The reader should note the paradox regarding the dual outcome of OD activities in enhancing both organic and mechanistic characteristics.

Stuart-Kotzé presents a practical analytical model for diagnosing two types of competence within an organization and developing both an organizational and a managerial-style strategy for change that will be consistent with the situation. He argues for no one change strategy as "best," but suggests the importance of congruence between situation and strategy.

Hersey and Blanchard present an integrated set of three readings on the management of change. Part 1 discusses four change levels (knowledge, attitudes, individual behavior, and group behavior) and the differential effectiveness of participative and coerced change approaches for unique situations. Part 2 focuses on change at the level of individual behavior and draws upon the behavior modification principles introduced in the Luthans/Lyman reading in the Motivation section. In Part 3 Hersey and Blanchard adapt Lewin's classic force-field model to intrapersonal change, and discuss the situations in which identification, internalization, or compliance may be most effective as change strategies.

The reading by Sims provides one of the first realizations by students of T-group training that the success of laboratory forms of OD is contingent upon the organization's environment and internal climate. This is consistent with the French and Bell conclusion at the macro level in the earlier reading in this section.

Reading 42

Evolution and Revolution as Organizations Grow

Larry E. Greiner

A small research company chooses too complicated and formalized an organization structure for its young age and limited size. It flounders in rigidity and bureaucracy for several years and is finally acquired by a larger company.

Key executives of a retail store chain hold on to an organization structure long after it has served its purpose, because their power is derived from this structure. The company eventually goes into bankruptcy.

A large bank disciplines a "rebellious" manager who is blamed for current control problems, when the underlying cause is centralized procedures that are holding back expansion into new markets. Many younger managers subsequently leave the bank, competition moves in, and profits are still declining.

The problems of these companies, like those of many others, are rooted more in past decisions than in present events or outside market dynamics. Historical forces do indeed shape the future growth of organizations. Yet management, in its haste to grow, often overlooks such critical developmental questions as: Where has our organization been? Where is it now? And what do the answers to these questions mean for where we are going? Instead, its gaze is fixed outward toward the environment and the future—as if more precise market projections will provide a new organizational identity.

Companies fail to see that many clues to their future success lie within their own organizations and their evolving states of development. Moreover, the inability of management to understand its organization development problems can result in a company becoming "frozen" in its present stage of evolution or, ultimately, in failure, regardless of market opportunities.

My position in this article is that the future of an organization may be less determined by outside forces than it is by the organization's history. In stressing the force of history on an organization, I have drawn from the legacies of European psychologists (their thesis being that individual behavior is determined primarily by previous events and experiences, not by what lies ahead). Extending this analogy of individual development to the problems of organization development, I shall discuss a series of developmental phases through which growing companies tend to pass. But, first, let me provide two definitions:

1 The term *evolution* is used to describe prolonged periods of growth where no major upheaval occurs in organization practices.

"Evolution and Revolution as Organizations Grow," Larry E. Greiner, *Harvard Business Review*, July–August 1972, pp. 37–46. © 1972 by the President and Fellows of Harvard College; all rights reserved. Reprinted with permission.

2 The term *revolution* is used to describe those periods of substantial turmoil in organization life.

As a company progresses through developmental phases, each evolutionary period creates its own revolution. For instance, centralized practices eventually lead to demands for decentralization. Moreover, the nature of management's solution to each revolutionary period determines whether a company will move forward into its next stage of evolutionary growth. As I shall show later, there are at least five phases of organization development, each characterized by both an evolution and a revolution.

KEY FORCES IN DEVELOPMENT

During the past few years a small amount of research knowledge about the phases of organization development has been building. Some of this research is very quantitative, such as time-series analyses that reveal patterns of economic performance over time.[1] The majority of studies, however, are case-oriented and use company records and interviews to reconstruct a rich picture of corporate development.[2] Yet both types of research tend to be heavily empirical without attempting more generalized statements about the overall process of development.

A notable exception is the historical work of Alfred D. Chandler, Jr., in his book *Strategy and Structure.*[3] This study depicts four very broad and general phases in the lives of four large U.S. companies. It proposes that outside market opportunities determine a company's strategy, which in turn determines the company's organization structure. This thesis has a valid ring for the four companies examined by Chandler, largely because they developed in a time of explosive markets and technological advances. But more recent evidence suggests that organization structure may be less malleable than Chandler assumed; in fact, structure can play a critical role in influencing corporate strategy. It is this reverse emphasis on how organization structure affects future growth which is highlighted in the model presented in this article.

From an analysis of recent studies,[4] five key dimensions emerge as essential for building a model of organization development:

[1]See, for example, William H. Starbuck, "Organizational Metamorphosis," in *Promising Research Directions,* edited by R. W. Millman and M. P. Hottenstein (Tempe, Arizona, Academy of Management, 1968), p. 113.

[2]See, for example, the *Grangesberg* case series, prepared by C. Roland Christensen and Bruce R. Scott, Case Clearing House, Harvard Business School.

[3]*Strategy and Structure: Chapters in the History of the American Industrial Enterprise* (Cambridge, Massachusetts, The M.I.T. Press, 1962).

[4]I have drawn on many sources for evidence: (a) numerous cases collected at the Harvard Business School; (b) *Organization Growth and Development,* edited by William H. Starbuck (Middlesex, England, Penguin Books, Ltd., 1971), where several studies are cited; and (c) articles published in journals, such as Lawrence E. Fouraker and John M. Stopford, "Organization Structure and the Multinational Strategy," *Administrative Science Quarterly,* Vol. 13, No. 1, 1968, p. 47; and Malcolm S. Salter, "Management Appraisal and Reward Systems," *Journal of Business Policy,* Vol. 1, No. 4, 1971.

1 Age of the organization.
2 Size of the organization.
3 Stages of evolution.
4 Stages of revolution.
5 Growth rate of the industry.

I shall describe each of these elements separately, but first note their combined effect as illustrated in Exhibit I. Note especially how each dimension influences the other over time; when all five elements begin to interact, a more complete and dynamic picture of organizational growth emerges.

After describing these dimensions and their interconnections, I shall discuss each evolutionary/revolutionary phase of development and show *(a)* how each stage of evolution breeds its own revolution, and *(b)* how management solutions to each revolution determine the next stage of evolution.

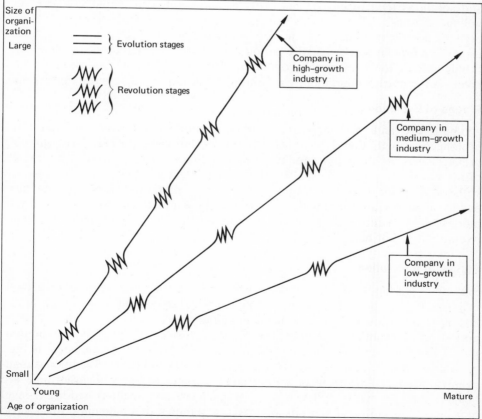

Exhibit I   Model of organization development

Age of the Organization

The most obvious and essential dimension for any model of development is the life span of an organization (represented as the horizontal axis in Exhibit I). All historical studies gather data from various points in time and then make comparisons. From these observations, it is evident that the same organization practices are not maintained throughout a long time span. This makes a most basic point: management problems and principles are rooted in time. The concept of decentralization, for example, can have meaning for describing corporate practices at one time period but loses its descriptive power at another.

The passage of time also contributes to the institutionalization of managerial attitudes. As a result, employee behavior becomes not only more predictable but also more difficult to change when attitudes are outdated.

Size of the Organization

This dimension is depicted as the vertical axis in Exhibit I. A company's problems and solutions tend to change markedly as the number of employees and sales volume increase. Thus, time is not the only determinant of structure; in fact, organizations that do not grow in size can retain many of the same management issues and practices over lengthy periods. In addition to increased size, however, problems of coordination and communication magnify, new functions emerge, levels in the management hierarchy multiply, and jobs become more interrelated.

Stages of Evolution

As both age and size increase, another phenomenon becomes evident: the prolonged growth that I have termed the evolutionary period. Most growing organizations do not expand for two years and then retreat for one year; rather, those that survive a crisis usually enjoy four to eight years of continuous growth without a major economic setback or severe internal disruption. The term evolution seems appropriate for describing these quieter periods because only modest adjustments appear necessary for maintaining growth under the same overall pattern of management.

Stages of Revolution

Smooth evolution is not inevitable; it cannot be assumed that organization growth is linear. *Fortune's* "500" list, for example, has had significant turnover during the last 50 years. Thus we find evidence from numerous case histories which reveals periods of substantial turbulence spaced between smoother periods of evolution.

I have termed these turbulent times the periods of revolution because they typically exhibit a serious upheaval of management practices. Traditional management practices, which were appropriate for a smaller size and earlier time, are brought under scrutiny by frustrated top managers and disillusioned lower-level managers. During such periods of crisis, a number of companies fail—those unable to abandon past practices and effect major organization changes are likely either to fold or to level off in their growth rates.

The critical task for management in each revolutionary period is to find a new set of organization practices that will become the basis for managing the next period of evolutionary growth. Interestingly enough, these new practices eventually sow their own seeds of decay and lead to another period of revolution. Companies therefore experience the irony of seeing a major solution in one time period become a major problem at a latter date.

Growth Rate of the Industry

The speed at which an organization experiences phases of evolution and revolution is closely related to the market environment of its industry. For example, a company in a rapidly expanding market will have to add employees rapidly; hence, the need for new organization structures to accommodate large staff increases is accelerated. While evolutionary periods tend to be relatively short in fast-growing industries, much longer evolutionary periods occur in mature or slowly growing industries.

Evolution can also be prolonged, and revolutions delayed, when profits come easily. For instance, companies that make grievous errors in a rewarding industry can still look good on their profit and loss statements; thus they can avoid a change in management practices for a longer period. The aerospace industry in its infancy is an example. Yet revolutionary periods still occur, as one did in aerospace when profit opportunities began to dry up. Revolutions seem to be much more severe and difficult to resolve when the market environment is poor.

PHASES OF GROWTH

With the foregoing framework in mind, let us now examine in depth the five specific phases of evolution and revolution. As shown in Exhibit II, each evolutionary period is characterized by the dominant *management style* used to achieve growth, while each revolutionary period is characterized by the dominant *management problem* that must be solved before growth can continue. The patterns presented in Exhibit II seem to be typical for companies in industries with moderate growth over a long time period; companies in faster growing industries tend to experience all five phases more rapidly, while those in slower growing industries encounter only two or three phases over many years.

It is important to note that *each phase is both an effect of the previous phase and a cause for the next phase.* For example, the evolutionary management style in Phase 3 of the exhibit is "delegation," which grows out of, and becomes the solution to, demands for greater "autonomy" in the preceding Phase 2 revolution. The style of delegation used in Phase 3, however, eventually provokes a major revolutionary crisis that is characterized by attempts to regain control over the diversity created through increased delegation.

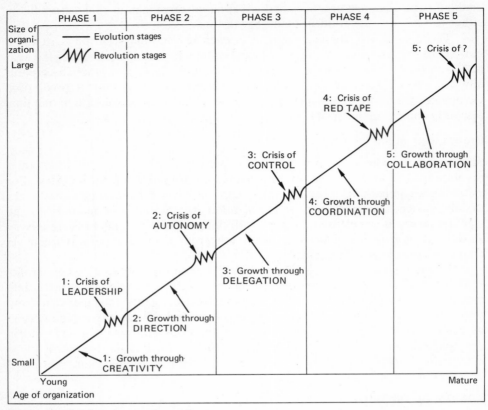

Exhibit II The five phases of growth

The principal implication of each phase is that management actions are narrowly prescribed if growth is to occur. For example, a company experiencing an autonomy crisis in Phase 2 cannot return to directive management for a solution—it must adopt a new style of delegation in order to move ahead.

Phase 1: Creativity . . .

In the birth stage of an organization, the emphasis is on creating both a product and a market. Here are the characteristics of the period of creative evolution:

• The company's founders are usually technically or entrepreneurially oriented, and they disdain management activities; their physical and mental energies are absorbed entirely in making and selling a new product.
• Communication among employees is frequent and informal.
• Long hours of work are rewarded by modest salaries and the promise of ownership benefits.

• Control of activities comes from immediate marketplace feedback; the management acts as the customers react.

. . . and the leadership crisis: All of the foregoing individualistic and creative activities are essential for the company to get off the ground. But therein lies the problem. As the company grows, larger production runs require knowledge about the efficiencies of manufacturing. Increased numbers of employees cannot be managed exclusively through informal communication; new employees are not motivated by an intense dedication to the product or organization. Additional capital must be secured, and new accounting procedures are needed for financial control.

Thus the founders find themselves burdened with unwanted management responsibilities. So they long for the "good old days," still trying to act as they did in the past. And conflicts between the harried leaders grow more intense.

At this point a crisis of leadership occurs, which is the onset of the first revolution. Who is to lead the company out of confusion and solve the managerial problems confronting it? Quite obviously, a strong manager is needed who has the necessary knowledge and skill to introduce new business techniques. But this is easier said than done. The founders often hate to step aside even though they are probably temperamentally unsuited to be managers. So here is the first critical developmental choice—to locate and install a strong business manager who is acceptable to the founders and who can pull the organization together.

Phase 2: Direction . . .

Those companies that survive the first phase by installing a capable business manager usually embark on a period of sustained growth under able and directive leadership. Here are the characteristics of this evolutionary period:

• A functional organization structure is introduced to separate manufacturing from marketing activities, and job assignments become more specialized.
• Accounting systems for inventory and purchasing are introduced.
• Incentives, budgets, and work standards are adopted.
• Communication becomes more formal and impersonal as a hierarchy of titles and positions builds.
• The new manager and his key supervisors take most of the responsibility for instituting direction, while lower-level supervisors are treated more as functional specialists than as autonomous decision-making managers.

. . . and the autonomy crisis: Although the new directive techniques channel employee energy more efficiently into growth, they eventually become inappropriate for controlling a larger, more diverse and complex organization. Lower-level employees find themselves restricted by a cumbersome and centralized hierarchy. They have come to possess more direct knowledge about markets and machinery than do the leaders at the top; consequently, they feel torn between following procedures and taking initiative on their own.

Thus the second revolution is imminent as a crisis develops from demands for greater autonomy on the part of lower-level managers. The solution adopted by most companies is to move toward greater delegation. Yet it is difficult for top managers who were previously successful at being directive to give up responsibility. Moreover, lower-level managers are not accustomed to making decisions for themselves. As a result, numerous companies flounder during this revolutionary period, adhering to centralized methods while lower-level employees grow more disenchanted and leave the organization.

Phase 3: Delegation . . .

The next era of growth evolves from the successful application of a decentralized organization structure. It exhibits these characteristics:

- Much greater responsibility is given to the managers of plants and market territories.
- Profit centers and bonuses are used to stimulate motivation.
- The top executives at headquarters restrain themselves to managing by exception, based on periodic reports from the field.
- Management often concentrates on making new acquisitions which can be lined up beside other decentralized units.
- Communication from the top is infrequent, usually by correspondence, telephone, or brief visits to field locations.

The delegation stage proves useful for gaining expansion through heightened motivation at lower levels. Decentralized managers with greater authority and incentive are able to penetrate larger markets, respond faster to customers, and develop new products.

. . . *and the control crisis:* A serious problem eventually evolves, however, as top executives sense that they are losing control over a highly diversified field operation. Autonomous field managers prefer to run their own shows without coordinating plans, money, technology, and manpower with the rest of the organization. Freedom breeds a parochial attitude.

Hence, the Phase 3 revolution is under way when top management seeks to regain control over the total company. Some top managements attempt a return to centralized management, which usually fails because of the vast scope of operations. Those companies that move ahead find a new solution in the use of special coordination techniques.

Phase 4: Coordination . . .

During this phase, the evolutionary period is characterized by the use of formal systems for achieving greater coordination and by top executives taking responsibility for the initiation and administration of these new systems. For example:

- Decentralized units are merged into product groups.
- Formal planning procedures are established and intensively reviewed.
- Numerous staff personnel are hired and located at headquarters to initiate company-wide programs of control and review for line managers.
- Capital expenditures are carefully weighed and parceled out across the organization.
- Each product group is treated as an investment center where return on invested capital is an important criterion used in allocating funds.
- Certain technical functions, such as data processing, are centralized at headquarters, while daily operating decisions remain decentralized.
- Stock options and companywide profit sharing are used to encourage identity with the firm as a whole.

All of these new coordination systems prove useful for achieving growth through more efficient allocation of a company's limited resources. They prompt field managers to look beyond the needs of their local units. While these managers still have much decision-making responsibility, they learn to justify their actions more carefully to a "watchdog" audience at headquarters.

. . . and the red-tape crisis: But a lack of confidence gradually builds between line and staff, and between headquarters and the field. The proliferation of systems and programs begins to exceed its utility; a red-tape crisis is created. Line managers, for example, increasingly resent heavy staff direction from those who are not familiar with local conditions. Staff people, on the other hand, complain about uncooperative and uninformed line managers. Together both groups criticize the bureaucratic paper system that has evolved. Procedures take precedence over problem solving, and innovation is dampened. In short, the organization has become too large and complex to be managed through formal programs and rigid systems. The Phase 4 revolution is under way.

Phase 5: Collaboration . . .

The last observable phase in previous studies emphasizes strong interpersonal collaboration in an attempt to overcome the red-tape crisis. Where Phase 4 was managed more through formal systems and procedures, Phase 5 emphasizes greater spontaneity in management action through teams and the skillful confrontation of interpersonal differences. Social control and self-discipline take over from formal control. This transition is especially difficult for those experts who created the old systems as well as for those line managers who relied on formal methods for answers.

The Phase 5 evolution, then, builds around a more flexible and behavioral approach to management. Here are its characteristics:

- The focus is on solving problems quickly through team action.
- Teams are combined across functions for task-group activity.

- Headquarters staff experts are reduced in number, reassigned, and combined in interdisciplinary teams to consult with, not to direct, field units.
- A matrix-type structure is frequently used to assemble the right teams for the appropriate problems.
- Previous formal systems are simplified and combined into single multipurpose systems.
- Conferences of key managers are held frequently to focus on major problem issues.
- Educational programs are utilized to train managers in behavioral skills for achieving better teamwork and conflict resolution.
- Real-time information systems are integrated into daily decision making.
- Economic rewards are geared more to team performance than to individual achievement.
- Experiments in new practices are encouraged throughout the organization.

. . . and the crisis: What will be the revolution in response to this stage of evolution? Many large U.S. companies are now in the Phase 5 evolutionary stage, so the answers are critical. While there is little clear evidence, I imagine the revolution will center around the "psychological saturation" of employees who grow emotionally and physically exhausted by the intensity of teamwork and the heavy pressure for innovative solutions.

My hunch is that the Phase 5 revolution will be solved through new structures and programs that allow employees to periodically rest, reflect, and revitalize themselves. We may even see companies with dual organization structures: a "habit" structure for getting the daily work done, and a "reflective" structure for stimulating perspective and personal enrichment. Employees could then move back and forth between the two structures as their energies are dissipated and refueled.

One European organization has implemented just such a structure. Five reflective groups have been established outside the regular structure for the purpose of continuously evaluating five task activities basic to the organization. They report directly to the managing director, although their reports are made public throughout the organization. Membership in each group includes all levels and functions, and employees are rotated through these groups on a six-month basis.

Other concrete examples now in practice include providing sabbaticals for employees, moving managers in and out of "hot spot" jobs, establishing a four-day workweek, assuring job security, building physical facilities for relaxation *during* the working day, making jobs more interchangeable, creating an extra team on the assembly line so that one team is always off for reeducation, and switching to longer vacations and more flexible working hours.

The Chinese practice of requiring executives to spend time periodically on lower-level jobs may also be worth a nonideological evaluation. For too long U.S. management has assumed that career progress should be equated with an upward path toward title, salary, and power. Could it be that some vice presidents of marketing might just long for, and even benefit from, temporary duty in the field sales organizations?

IMPLICATIONS OF HISTORY

Let me now summarize some important implications for practicing managers. First, the main features of this discussion are depicted in Exhibit III, which shows the specific management actions that characterize each growth phase. These actions are also the solutions which ended each preceding revolutionary period.

In one sense, I hope that many readers will react to my model by calling it obvious and natural for depicting the growth of an organization. To me this type of reaction is a useful test of the model's validity.

But at a more reflective level I imagine some of these reactions are more hindsight than foresight. Those experienced managers who have been through a developmental sequence can empathize with it now, but how did they react when in the middle of a stage of evolution or revolution? They can probably recall the limits of their own developmental understanding at that time. Perhaps they resisted desirable changes or were even swept emotionally into a revolution without being able to propose constructive solutions. So let me offer some explicit guidelines for managers of growing organizations to keep in mind.

Know Where You Are in the Developmental Sequence

Every organization and its component parts are at different stages of development. The task of top management is to be aware of these stages, otherwise, it

Exhibit III   Organization Practices during Evolution in the Five Phases of Growth

Category	Phase 1	Phase 2	Phase 3	Phase 4	Phase 5
Management focus	Make & sell	Efficiency of operations	Expansion of market	Consolidation of organization	Problem solving & innovation
Organization structure	Informal	Centralized & functional	Decentralized & geographical	Line-staff & product groups	Matrix of teams
Top management style	Individualistic & entrepreneurial	Directive	Delegative	Watchdog	Participative
Control system	Market results	Standards & cost centers	Reports & profit centers	Plans & investment centers	Mutual goal setting
Management reward emphasis	Ownership	Salary & merit increases	Individual bonus	Profit sharing & stock options	Team bonus

may not recognize when the time for change has come, or it may act to impose the wrong solution.

Top leaders should be ready to work with the flow of the tide rather than against it; yet they should be cautious, since it is tempting to skip phases out of impatience. Each phase results in certain strengths and learning experiences in the organization that will be essential for success in subsequent phases. A child prodigy, for example, may be able to read like a teenager, but he cannot behave like one until he ages through a sequence of experiences.

I also doubt that managers can or should act to avoid revolutions. Rather, these periods of tension provide the pressure, ideas, and awareness that afford a platform for change and the introduction of new practices.

Recognize the Limited Range of Solutions

In each revolutionary stage it becomes evident that this stage can be ended only by certain specific solutions; moreover, these solutions are different from those which were applied to the problems of the preceding revolution. Too often it is tempting to choose solutions that were tried before, which makes it impossible for a new phase of growth to evolve.

Management must be prepared to dismantle current structures before the revolutionary stage becomes too turbulent. Top managers, realizing that their own managerial styles are no longer appropriate, may even have to take themselves out of leadership positions. A good Phase 2 manager facing Phase 3 might be wise to find another Phase 2 organization that better fits his talents, either outside the company or with one of its newer subsidiaries.

Finally, evolution is not an automatic affair; it is a contest for survival. To move ahead, companies must consciously introduce planned structures that not only are solutions to a current crisis but also are fitted to the *next* phase of growth. This requires considerable self-awareness on the part of top management, as well as great interpersonal skill in persuading other managers that change is needed.

Realize That Solutions Breed New Problems

Managers often fail to realize that organizational solutions create problems for the future (i.e., a decision to delegate eventually causes a problem of control). Historical actions are very much determinants of what happens to the company at a much later date.

An awareness of this effect should help managers to evaluate company problems with greater historical understanding instead of "pinning the blame" on a current development. Better yet, managers should be in a position to *predict* future problems, and thereby to prepare solutions and coping strategies before a revolution gets out of hand.

A management that is aware of the problems ahead could well decide *not* to grow. Top managers may, for instance, prefer to retain the informal practices of a small company, knowing that this way of life is inherent in the organization's limited size, not in their congenial personalities. If they choose to grow, they may do themselves out of a job and a way of life they enjoy.

And what about the managements of very large organizations? Can they find new solutions for continued phases of evolution? Or are they reaching a stage where the government will act to break them up because they are too large.

CONCLUDING NOTE

Clearly, there is still much to learn about processes of development in organizations. The phases outlined here are only five in number and are still only approximations. Researchers are just beginning to study the specific developmental problems of structure, control, rewards, and management style in different industries and in a variety of cultures.

One should not, however, wait for conclusive evidence before educating managers to think and act from a developmental perspective. The critical dimension of time has been missing for too long from our management theories and practices. The intriguing paradox is that by learning more about history we may do a better job in the future.

Reading 43

Mechanistic and Organic Systems and the Contingency Approach

Wendell L. French
Cecil H. Bell, Jr.

Two types of organizations, *mechanistic* and *organic,* have been described by Tom Burns and G. M. Stalker; in this chapter we wish to explore the relevance of these concepts to organization development. These terms are being used with increasing frequency, and it is important to understand their meanings and the implications of one system versus the other. These terms can be useful shorthand ways of describing the overall "climate" or mode of operating in an organization or its subunits, but, unfortunately, they can also be used as "bad" or "good" labels. *Mechanistic,* in particular, is frequently used with a "bad" connotation. In general, OD activities tend to result in an organization beginning to take on more *organic* characteristics, but some paradoxes and contingencies need examining.

According to Burns and Stalker, these two types of organizations, mechanis-

"Mechanistic and Organic Systems and the Contingency Approach," Wendell L. French and Cecil H. Bell, Jr., *Organization Development: Behavioral Science Interventions for Organization Improvement,* © 1973, pp. 182–191. Reprinted by permission of Prentice-Hall, Inc., Englewood Cliffs, New Jersey.

tic and organic, in their pure form, are seen as located on opposite ends of a continuum and not as a dichotomy.[1] Various organizations will be found at different points between these polarities and indeed may move back and forth along this continuum, depending upon the degree of stability or change being experienced. In addition, an organization may include both types within its subdivisions.

> Both types represent a "rational" form of organization, in that they may both, in our experience, be explicitly and deliberately created and maintained to exploit the human resources of a concern in the most efficient manner feasible in the circumstances of the concern. Not surprisingly, however, each exhibits characteristics which have been hitherto associated with different kinds of interpretation. For it is our contention that empirical findings have usually been classified according to sociological ideology rather than according to the functional specificity of the working organization to its task and the conditions confronting it.[2]

Thus, implicitly, Burns and Stalker do not see the occurrence of one or the other of these two systems as necessarily accidental, but as frequently stemming from the circumstances being faced by the organization. It would also seem to be implicit that the occurrence of one or the other might also stem from an ideological preference—a phenomenon that could represent a trap for over-zealous adherents to either type of organization.

MECHANISTIC SYSTEMS

To elaborate on the two types, Burns and Stalker see the *mechanistic* form of organization as particularly appropriate to stable conditions and having the following characteristics:

1 A high degree of task differentiation and specialization, precise delineation of rights and responsibilities and methods to be used, and role incumbents tending to pursue technical improvements in means in contrast to focusing on the overall ends of the organization.

2 A high degree of reliance on each hierarchical level for task coordination, control, and communications. That is, each supervisor is responsible for reconciling the activities below him.

3 A tendency for the top of the hierarchy to control incoming and outgoing communications and to be conservative in dispensing information within the system. (Burns and Stalker give an example of a manager who literally controlled *all* correspondence in and out of the firm.)

4 A high degree of emphasis on vertical interactions between superiors and subordinates, with subordinate activities mainly governed by these interactions.

---

[1] Tom Burns and G. M. Stalker, *The Management of Innovation* (London: Tavistock Publications, 1961), pp. 119–25.
[2] *Ibid.*, p. 119

(While Burns and Stalker do not say this, clearly there is an informal social system involving lateral peer interactions which stays mainly "underground" under these circumstances.)

5 Insistence on loyalty to the organization and to superiors.

6 A higher value placed on internal (local) knowledge, skill, and experience, in contrast to more general (cosmopolitan) knowledge, skill, and experience.[3]

Another characteristic, which is not explicit but is perhaps implied in Burns and Stalker's model and which we believe to be one of the key characteristics of a mechanistic system, is:

7 A one-to-one leadership style, that is, with most interactions between superior and subordinate occurring in private discussion, and an absence or minimal attention to group processes and the informal system. As seen in this form of organization, the superior-subordinate relationship tends to be a telling-reporting relationship. (See Figure 1.) To illustrate the existence of such a leadership style, we have had managers tell us that, literally, their superior had never held a meeting involving all his immediate subordinates. They also said that most of the one-to-one conversations centered around assignments initiated by the superior, and in his office, i.e., on his "turf."

ORGANIC SYSTEMS

In contrast, the *organic* system is seen by Burns and Stalker as appropriate to changing conditions and has the following characteristics.[4]

1 A continuous reassessment of tasks and assignments through interaction with others and a high value placed on utilizing special knowledge and experience which can contribute to the "real" problems being faced by the organization.

2 A network of authority, control, and communication, stemming more from expertise and commitment to the total task than from the omniscience of the chief executive or the authority of hierarchical roles. Centers of control and communication are frequently *ad hoc,* that is, are located where the knowledge is. Responsibility is viewed as something to be shared rather than narrowly delimited.

---

[3]*Ibid.,* pp. 119–20. In some respects the mechanistic form of organization is comparable to the "bureaucratic" organization as described by Weber. For example, the features of the bureaucratic form, to Weber, include a "clearly defined hierarchy of offices," emphasis on impersonal rules, and administrators "subject to strict and systematic discipline and control." Max Weber, *The Theory of Social and Economic Organization* (New York: Oxford University Press, Inc., 1957), pp. 333–34. See also William G. Scott, *Organization Theory: A Behavioral Analysis for Management* (Homewood, Ill.: Richard D. Irwin, Inc., 1967), Chap. 12.

[4]Burns and Stalker. *The Management of Innovation,* pp. 119–25. Bennis uses the term *organic-adaptive* in describing a similar type of organization. See Warren Bennis, "Organizations of the Future," *Personnel Administration,* 30 (September–October 1967), 6–19.

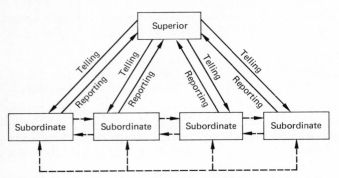

Figure 1   Characteristic pattern of leadership in a mechanistic system.

Although the organic systems "remain stratified," they tend to be stratified more on the basis of expertise:

> The lead in joint decisions is frequently taken by seniors, but it is an essential presumption of the organic system that the lead, i.e., "authority," is taken by whoever shows himself most informed and capable, i.e., the "best authority." The location of authority is settled by consensus.[5]

3   A tendency for communications to be much more extensive and open in contrast to limited and controlled. (This is more implicit in Burns and Stalker's model than explicit.)

4   The encouragement of a communications pattern and style which is lateral and diagonal as well as vertical and which is more of a consultative, information- and advice-giving nature than of a command or decision-relying nature. By *diagonal* we refer to Burns and Stalker's notion about communications between people of different rank and across functional groups.

5   A greater emphasis on commitment to the organization's tasks, progress, and growth than on obedience or loyalty.

6   High value placed on expertise relevant to the technological and commercial milieu of the organization (cosmopolitan skills). One indicator would be "importance and prestige attach[ed] to affiliations. . . ."[6]

And finally, to supplement this model, a characteristic that we believe to be central to a truly organic system:

7   A team leadership style, with an emphasis on consultation and considerable attention to interpersonal and group processes, including methods of decision

[5]*Ibid.*, p. 122.
[6]*Ibid.*, p. 121.

making and more frequent decision by consensus.[7] (See Figure 2.) Perhaps symbolically, meetings are frequently held away from the superior's office, with physical facilities designed to further group dialogue.

THE CONTINGENCY QUESTION

From our experience, organization development activities tend to shift an organization toward the organic mode as described by the above seven characteristics. The reason, of course, is that there is a deliberate emphasis in an OD program toward collaboratively managed group culture and collaboratively managed organizational culture. Whether we call it collaboration, consultation, or open communications, the theme in OD is effective participation. And that theme pervades most of the characteristics of an organic system.

Paradoxically, however, while the thrust of an organization development effort is toward the organic mode, OD activities sometimes increase the mechanistic quality of some organizational dimensions. For example, consensus might develop in a work team so that it would be functional for duties and responsibilities to be more precisely defined or so that there should be more reliance on the superior for coordination and control in the assignment of routine tasks. At the level of examining its methods, the team has organic characteristics; at the level of routine tasks, the team is deciding to become more mechanistic. As another illustration, an organization development effort might strengthen the organic characteristics of the design and engineering departments of an automobile company, while the assembly line departments might remain substantially

---

[7]Likert contrasts *man-man* and *group* patterns of organization which are comparable to the two types of leadership styles we are contrasting. See Rensis Likert, *New Patterns of Leadership* (New York: McGraw-Hill Book Company, 1961), pp. 106–10.

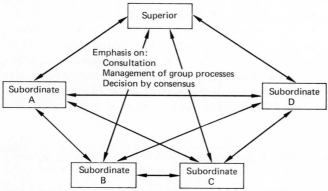

Figure 2   Characteristic patterns of leadership in an organic system.

mechanistic in terms of task delineation although becoming more organic in terms of employee involvement in the control function.

Thus, it will not suffice to have an ideological adherence to one form of organization over the other. There are unquestionably contingencies that affect the appropriateness of one system over the other or the appropriateness of a particular mix of characteristics of the two systems.

We have already noted that Burns and Stalker see the mechanistic form of organization as appropriate to "stable conditions" and the organic form to "changing conditions." Joan Woodward in a study in South Essex, England, found that successful manufacturing firms of the "large-batch production" type (assembly line, or large-batch production) tended to be mechanistic, while successful firms of the unit and "small-batch" (e.g., prototype production) and "process production" (e.g., continuous flow liquids production) tended to be organic.[8] Another study, by Lawrence and Lorsch, found that production units within six firms had a much more formalized structure than the research laboratories in the same firms.[9]

Morse and Lorsch in a study of two research laboratories with unpredictable research and development tasks—one an "effective performer" and one "less effective"—and two container plants involving the manufacture of standarized items with automated, high-speed production lines—again, one plant effective and one less effective—found that the more-effective units had a better "fit" between structure and organizational climate than the less-effective units. The high-performing lab featured scientists' perceptions of minimal and flexible rules, a long-term approach to reviews and reporting, minimal control on their behavior, and high influence on their part. In contrast, the less-effective lab was more restrictive and restraining, more rule oriented, and more structured, with more decisions made at the top.

At the rank-and-file level of the more-effective manufacturing plant, there were comprehensive rules, procedures, and control systems and short-range reporting and review sessions, and there was relatively low rank-and-file influence with a corresponding directive-type supervisor. Thus, influence tended to be concentrated at higher levels. Conversely, in the less-effective container plant, practices were less controlling and structured, with a more participative kind of supervision. In both the effective research lab and the effective plant, employees expressed more feelings of competence than did their counterparts in the less-effective organizations; the researchers concluded that the more effective fit between task, structure, and climate resulted in more feelings of competence, and

---

[8]Joan Woodward, *Industrial Organization: Theory and Practice* (London: Oxford University Press, 1965), p. 71. A rationale that we see for process organizations to be organic is that the equipment does most of the routine work while employees are largely busy with planning, research, and monitoring functions.

[9]Paul R. Lawrence and Jay Lorsch. *Organization and Environment: Managing Differentiation and Integration* (Boston: Graduate School of Business Administration, Harvard University, 1967), p. 32.

implicitly, organizational effectiveness.[10] (For a summary of the study, see Table 1.) While Morse and Lorsch acknowledge the difficulty in imputing cause-and-effect relationships—for example, do feelings of competence stem from unit effectiveness or from the fit between these various dimensions?[11]—the point is that a number of contingencies may determine the "best" structure, "best" design of tasks, or "best" leadership style, and so forth.[12]

In short, the contingency approach suggests that the question is not "Which is better, an organic system or a mechanistic system?" but that the question needs to be posed in terms of contingencies. For example:

1   What is the most effective mix of organic and mechanistic characteristics for a given organization or unit and its current circumstances? Or,

2   Under what conditions is the organic system superior to the mechanistic, and vice versa? Or,

3   Given different technologies, tasks, and human resources, what dimensions do we expect to change with OD-type interventions? Or,

4   Under what circumstances is an organization development effort particularly relevant or most likely to succeed?

While we intend to be somewhat specific in answering the latter question in the final chapter, the following are some of the contingencies that we see as the most relevant in answering question 2—Under what conditions is the organic system superior to the mechanistic, and vice-versa?

Contingency of:

a   Hierarchical level—the more extensive the role requirements in terms of planning, coordination, control, and decision making. The higher the level and thus the more complexity in these functions, the more the need for extensive inputs from diverse specialists and for examining many options; thus the need for acknowledging expertise, for open communications, for clarifying goals, and so forth.

b   Interdependency—the more that role performance is directly associated with the discretionary actions of others. (This contingency is related to the previous one.) The more interdependency, the more that communications need to be open, the more team leadership style is appropriate, and so forth.

c   Skills—the capabilities and talents of the human resources in the system. The greater the cognitive, problem-solving, and interpersonal capabilities of the people in the system, the more the organic style will work. The organic system is

---

[10]John J. Morse and Jay W. Lorsch, 'Beyond Theory Y," *Harvard Business Review,* 48 (May–June 1970), 61–68.

[11]*Ibid.,* p. 66.

[12]Robert Tannenbaum and Warren Schmidt describe a number of contingencies in leadership in their well known essay, "How to Choose a Leadership Pattern, *Harvard Business Review,* 36 (March–April 1958), 95–101. Fred Fiedler has done extensive research relative to what he calls a "Contingency Model of Leadership Effectiveness." See Fred E. Fiedler, *A Theory of Leadership Effectiveness* (New York: McGraw-Hill Book Company, 1967).

Table 1 System Contingencies in Four Organizations

Type of organization	Tasks	Structure	Climate	Feelings of competence	Organizational effectiveness
Manufacturing plant	Predictable manufacturing tasks	Highly structured and defined roles, duties, relationships	Influence concentrated at the top	Higher	Effective
Manufacturing plant		Less structured and defined	Egalitarian distribution of influence	Lower	Less effective
Research laboratory	Uncertain research tasks	Low degree of structure in roles, duties, and relationships	Egalitarian distribution of influence	Higher	Effective
Research laboratory		More structure	Influence tending to concentrate at the top	Lower	Less effective

Based on our interpretation of material in John J. Morse and Jay W. Lorsch, "Beyond Theory Y," *Harvard Business Review*, 48 (May–June 1970), 61–68.

more demanding of people at all levels than is the mechanistic form of organizations.

   d   Group process skills—the more effectively that the leader and the subordinates have basic communications, task, and maintenance skills. In particular, skills in group processes are a necessary prerequisite to a team leadership style; such skills are also important in the effective functioning of taskforces, committees, and so forth.

   e   Rapidity of external change. The more the organization is existing in a rapidly changing environment, the more important the adaptability facilitated by the organic mode. Burns and Stalker see this dimension as particularly important.

   f   Time pressure, danger, or external threat. For example, although the organic system may be better prepared to cope with future uncertainty, at the time of an unanticipated crisis the organization may need to revert to highly mechanistic characteristics to survive.

   g   Technology—the degree to which tasks are predetermined by the machinery or methods of a particular industry. For example, the technology of an assembly line serves to preplan tasks, to narrow interdependency, and so forth.

   h   Attitudes or assumptions about people in organizations—a "Theory X" versus a "Theory Y" set of assumptions. A Theory X set of assumptions will tend to be incompatible with the culture of an organic system. In contrast, if key executives or subordinates are philosophically committed to a participative or democratic leadership style, such values will tend to be more congruent with the organic style than with the mechanistic.

SUMMARY AND CONCLUSION

Mechanistic and *organic* organizations have been contrasted to provide rubrics for thinking about the outcomes of organization development activities. While, in general, OD strategies tend to increase the organic characteristics of a system, paradoxically they can also lead to an increase in mechanistic attributes along certain dimensions, for example, an increase in task differentiation at lower levels of the organization, or more stringent procedures.

   Theory and some research suggest that neither the purely organic form nor the purely mechanistic form may be optimal under all circumstances but that there needs to be a good "fit" between technology, tasks, organization climate, and human resources. Thus, different organization development interventions may have differing degrees of relevance under different circumstances. And those circumstances may vary by hierarchical levels, interdependency, skills and group process skills, time pressure and rapidity of external change, danger or external threat, technology, and values.

   The genius of OD, however, is that the perceptions, feelings, and cognitive inputs of organizational members are tapped to build an optimal, evolving, organizational design for the unique circumstances faced by the organization and its members. Thus the thrust of OD activities is to be responsive to the data—not to impose an organic system. In the process, however, the organization is likely to become more organic.

Reading 44

A Situational Change Typology

Robin Stuart- Kotzé

The trainer or internal change agent in a firm undergoing an organizational development program may be instrumental in designing the implementation of a change strategy. The situational change typology proposed below may be of use as a training instrument to:

1 present a number of different change strategies,
2 examine the situational demands surrounding the change,
3 focus attention on the match of situation to strategy,
4 escape from the concept of the "ideal" organizational change strategy and
5 focus on existing and required management skills.

Two independent determinants of organizational change strategy—managers' interpersonal competence and technical competence—are used to build the situational change typology. This typology is then linked with a recent management style model to demonstrate a tactical approach to implementation.[1]

As Warren Bennis notes, "All change is not 'planned change'."[2] The success with which management is able to implement change depends on a number of factors; and depending on the factor "mix," what is intended as planned change may well turn out to be something quite different.

Findings in a number of studies suggest that the subjects of change must be approached in a consultative manner and be invited to participate in the change decision as equal (no power differential) partners, for change to be implemented most effectively.[3] This underlying idea is supported by research into social or cultural change.[4] It seems that the subjects of change must be sure that their basic value system is not being threatened by the proposed change and that they are afforded a sense of security by being allowed to participate in the change decision, determination of the plan, and introduction or implementation.

Bennis's "Paradigm for Change Processes" (see Figure 1) reflects the general emphasis of the literature on the importance of the informal or social group as the subject of change. He considers (1) the power ratio between the originator and the subject of the change, (2) whether there is mutual or unilateral goal-setting and (3) the deliberateness of goal-setting, as the three independent variables which determine types of change.

While the weight of the evidence seems against him, the average manager might not agree that the participative approach is the best one. As he sees it, there are other variables than those used by Bennis which affect the method of change

"A Situational Change Typology," Robin Stuart-Kotzé, *Training and Development Journal*, January 1972, pp. 56–60. Reprinted with permission.

Figure 1   Bennis's Paradigm for Change Processes

Power ratio	Mutual goal setting		Nonmutual goal setting (or goals set by one side)	
	Deliberate on the part of one or both sides of the relationship	Nondeliberate on the part of both sides	Deliberate on the part of one side of the relationship	Nondeliberate on the part of both sides
.5/.5	Planned change	Interactional change	Technocratic change	"Natural" change
1/0	Indoctrinational change	Socialization change	Coercive change	Emulative change

Taken from Warren G. Bennis, "A Typology of Change Processes," *The planning of Change,* ed. W. G. Bennis, K. D. Benne and R. Chin, Holt, Rinehart and Winston, 1964, p. 154.

he should use. These include such situational demands of his position as the underlying technology, the time horizon, availability and effect of rewards and punishments, competence of organizational members, etc. Therefore, while Bennis is proposing a normative model in which the optimal change strategy is participative in nature, a situational approach to change, which includes the type of factors mentioned above, would offer a more descriptive model.

LEVEL OF COMPETENCE

A powerful variable determining types of organizational change is the level of competence of the organization's members, that is, the degree and type of skill, or competence, possessed by the managers of the organization. Argyris states that, "The administrative competence of an organization is composed of two interrelated but analytically separable components. They are intellective, rational, technical competence and interpersonal competence. The former deals with things and ideas, the latter with people."[5] Thus we could operationally define *technical competence* as referring to the ability of the organization's members to plan, control, design, schedule, produce, etc., and *interpersonal competence* as a function of the degree to which organizational members are aware of their impact upon others, and they upon them.

If these two aspects of competence are independent, that is, a manager can possess varying degrees of technical competence whether he possesses a high degree or a low degree of interpersonal competence, or vice-versa, then the relationship may be represented by Figure 2.

The type of change which will be most effective will depend on the degree of technical and interpersonal competence of the organization's members; i.e., their competence mix in a given situation. A typology of change processes based on the organization members' competence mixes could be represented by Figure 3.

Figure 2 Four Types of Competence Mix; Cutting the Two Scales Into Two Produces Four Types

	Low—Technical competence→High	
Low—Interpersonal competence→High	High interpersonal competence Low technical competence	High interpersonal competence High technical competence
	Low interpersonal competence Low Technical competence	Low interpersonal competence High technical competence

Low—Technical competence→High

TYPES OF CHANGE

Natural change would be most effective where the organization's members have low technical competence and low interpersonal competence. Where management lacks the ability to plan, control, direct and schedule in other than the short run, and at the same time communication skills are minimal, there is a lack of mutual trust, and problem-solving is not attempted in other than a superficial manner, any attempt at implementing a specific organizational change strategy will be ineffective.

    Directed change would be most effective where the organization's members have high technical competence, but low interpersonal competence. Where management is highly skilled in the techniques of planning, scheduling and

Figure 3   A Situational Change Typology; Four Change Strategies Correspond to the Four Types of Competence Mix

	Technical competence	
Interpersonal competence	Cooperative change	Planned change
	Natural change	Directed change

Technical competence

controlling, but trust levels are low and communication tends to be one-way, from the top down, decisions concerning organizational change will tend to be based on technical factors, and implementation will rely on "rational" explanation of the benefits of the change. Rewards and punishments will be closely tied-in to the proposed change for reinforcement, and implementation will be rapid and "all at once." Types of change, other than directed change, will tend to be less effective in this situation because they will either require more time to implement and/or a different set of skills than those possessed by management.

Cooperative change would be most effective where the organization's members have low technical competence, but high interpersonal competence. Management is not highly skilled "technically," but they have developed a high trust level within the organization, and communication flows freely up and down. Management's jobs may entail creativity, or counseling and training. Because of a desire for freedom from direction, they may not indulge in tight, long-term planning and scheduling, or be concerned with formal structural relationships and rapid feedback of end-product measures. Other types of change will be incongruent with the established patterns of communication and the atmosphere of mutual trust within the organization, and hence will tend to be less effective.

Planned change would be most effective where the organization's members have both high technical and interpersonal competence. Stimulated by an image of potential, management will consider a wide range of alternatives for organizational development, requiring a high degree of competence in long range planning, scheduling, organizing, directing and controlling, and a high degree of interpersonal competence to allow for the provision of clear feedback and ideas concerning change. Management is willing to spend a considerable amount of time examining and working through the various alternatives available and ensuring commitment to objectives throughout the organization. Given the mix of both high technical and interpersonal competence, planned change is more effective than any of the other types simply because it employs all the organization's resources to the fullest.

CHANGE AND MANAGEMENT STYLE

This situational change typology is primarily concerned with effective change strategies as determined by the mix of technical and interpersonal competence of the organization's members. But it can also be tied in with a *situational management style typology,* indicating which management styles are optimally employed in the implementation of each type of change. The link with managerial styles is suggested by a finding drawn from Berelson and Steiner that, "Leaders of small groups tend to direct the group's activities along lines at which they themselves are proficient and away from those areas where they are less competent."[6] In other words, managers who possess a high degree of technical competence will tend to use a managerial style which emphasizes this technical competence, while managers who possess a high degree of interpersonal com-

**Figure 4   Reddin's Four Basic
Styles; These Are Four Basic
Styles of Managerial Behavior**

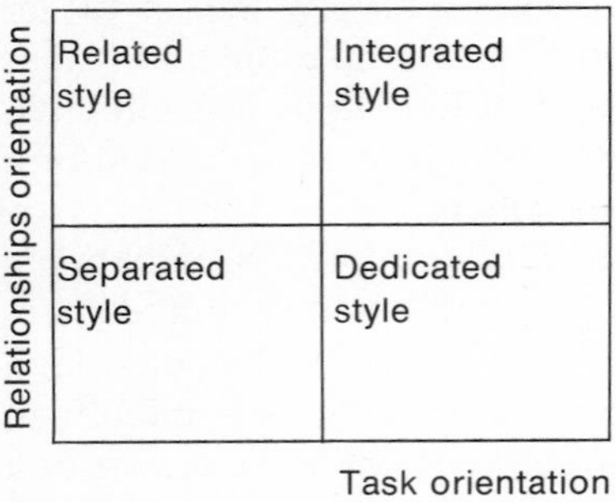

Related style	Integrated style
Separated style	Dedicated style

Relationships orientation

Task orientation

petence will tend to use a managerial style which emphasizes or makes use of this particular skill.

W. J. Reddin's situational management style typology has been chosen here for integration with the situational change typology.[7] As with other situationists, Reddin sees managerial effectiveness as a match of style to situation; to match style and situation, a manager needs situational sensitivity (to size up a situation) and style flexibility (to adapt to it) or situational management (to change it) if necessary.

TACTICS AND STRATEGY

When Reddin's management style typology, as shown in Figure 4, is combined with the situational change typology in Figure 3, both the strategy and tactics of organizational change are shown as being dictated by the situational demand elements of interpersonal and technical competence.

Brief descriptions of Reddin's four basic managerial styles, as shown in Figure 4, may aid in demonstrating the close relationship between management tactics and organizational change strategy.

The *separated* manager is oriented towards procedures, methods and systems, and emphasizes accuracy, conservatism, prudence and non-involvement. He is low in both relationships orientation (extent to which he is likely to have personal job relations characterized by mutual trust, respect for subordinates' ideas, and consideration of their feelings) and task orientation (extent to which he is likely to direct his subordinates' efforts to goal attainment; characterized by planning, organizing and controlling), and therefore, rather than becoming involved with his subordinates in an interpersonal manner, or becoming committed to his job, he takes refuge in rules and procedures, and operates "by the book."

The *related* manager is oriented to other people and produces an atmosphere of security and trust. He stimulates "noise-free" communication and feedback, but is less concerned for the accomplishment of the task at hand than for the well-being of the individuals involved.

The *dedicated* manager directs the work of others and shows little concern for the well-being of his subordinates. He is concerned with conserving time and increasing production, lowering costs, etc., and relies on his own judgment in making decisions. Communication is directed downward toward his subordinates, and feedback is in terms of information which he specifically requests.

The *integrated* manager has both high-task orientation and high-relationships orientation, and tends to indulge in long range planning and motivational techniques. While he is deeply concerned with production in both the short and long-run, he is interested in developing a highly cooperative approach to achieving organizational objectives. He is interested in stimulating commitment, on the part of his subordinates, to the organization's goals, and wants to integrate the needs of the individual to the needs of the organization.[8]

USEFUL APPROACH

This situational approach to organizational change is useful for several reasons. First, it implies that training programs can be designed to increase awareness of the organization's existing competence mix so that commitment to an appropriate change strategy may be obtained. Or it can be used to alter the competence mix of

Figure 5   A Combination of the Situational Change Typology and Reddin's Management Style Typology; Both the Appropriate Strategy and Tactics for Implementing Organizational Change are Determined by the Competence Mix

Cooperative change Related	Planned change Integrated
Natural change Separated	Directed change Dedicated

Interpersonal competence
Relationships orientation

Technical competence
Task orientation

various members of the organization to optimize the effectiveness of a chosen change strategy. Or, finally, it can be used to decide on one organizational change strategy rather than another by fitting the strategy to the organization's competence mix. This is a very different approach to training from the one usually adopted, where a set of values is agreed upon as a normative goal, and training is instituted to implement these values. While there is no doubt that a participative approach to change (e.g., cooperative change) can be effective, this is a far cry from being able to say that it is always optimally effective.

This typology also points out the importance of the congruency of managerial style and organizational change strategy. Neither one determines the other, but rather both managerial style and organizational change strategy are tied to situational requirements. It is interesting to note that a certain management style may be used more effectively in implementing a certain organizational change strategy, but this effectiveness is caused by the independent matching of the managerial style and the change strategy to the *situation*, and not to one another. Given a certain strategy for change then, the question is not "What managerial style would be most effective?" but, "Is this organizational change *strategy* likely to be effective here, and if so, what is the most effective managerial style to adopt in implementing it?"

In addition, the typology has significance for the individual manager since it aids situational sensitivity by serving to point out the variance between his managerial style and that required by the rest of the organization. The alternatives open to the individual manager include developing his style flexibility by adapting his style to that required by the situation, or developing his skill at situational management and changing the situation to adapt to his style.

Finally, the most important and basic contribution of the situational change typology is the idea that there is no best strategy. All arguments for one approach to organizational change versus another are hollow unless they take into account the requirements of the situation. While the typology presented here defines the situation in terms of two variables only, it remains useful as a training tool to focus attention on different approaches to change and the underlying factors determining the effectiveness of the change.

REFERENCES

1   Reddin, W. J., *Managerial Effectiveness,* McGraw-Hill, 1970.
2   Bennis, Warren G., "A Typology of Change Processes," *The Planning of Change,* ed. W. G. Bennis, K. D. Benne and R. Chin, Holt, Rinehart and Winston, 1964, p. 154.
3   This suggestion has been made by F. J. Roethlisberger and W. J. Dickson, *Management and the Worker,* Wiley, 1964; L. Coch and J. R. P. French, "Overcoming Resistance to Change," *Human Relations,* 1, 1948, pp. 512–532; and in a more recent study by J. J. O'Connell, *Managing Organizational Innovation,* Irwin-Dorsey, 1968.
4   Erasmus, C. J., *Man Takes Control,* Bobbs-Merrill, 1961, and W. H. Goodenough, *Cooperation in Change,* Wiley, 1963.

5 Argyris, Chris, *Interpersonal Competence and Organizational Effectiveness,* Irwin-Dorsey, 1962, p. 16.
6 Berelson, Bernard and Steiner, Gary A., *Human Behavior,* Harcourt, Brace and World, 1964, p. 343.
7 Reddin, *op. cit.*
8 Reddin, *op. cit.*

Reading 45

The Management of Change:
Part 1—Change and the Use of Power

Paul Hersey
Kenneth H. Blanchard

In the dynamic society in which today's organizations exist, the question of whether change will occur is no longer relevant. Instead, the issue now is how do managers cope with the inevitable barrage of changes which confront them daily in attempting to keep their organizations viable and current. While change is a fact of life, effective managers (if they are to be effective) can no longer be content to let change occur as it will, they must be able to develop strategies to plan, direct and control change. The purpose of these three articles on "The Management of Change" is to provide practitioners with a general framework of change theory, hopefully with some strategies that can be used in planning and implementing change in their own environments.

In the first article, "Change and the Use of Power," we will discuss two kinds of power, position power and personal power, then examine the use of both in varying situations. We will examine various levels of change from knowledge and attitude to individual behavior and organizational performance. These levels of change will then be analyzed in terms of two change cycles—participative and coerced.

In the second article, "Change Through Behavior Modification," we will look at how managers can create an environment to move people from one level of maturity and responsibility to a higher level. Behavior modification will be examined as a tool for making changes at the operational level for both individuals and groups and we will discuss what implications reinforcement theory can have for the practitioner or change agent.

In the final article, "Planning and Implementing Change," we will attempt to integrate much that we discussed in the first two articles into some theoretical

"The Management of Change: Part 1—Change and the Use of Power," Paul Hersey and Kenneth H. Blanchard, *Training & Development Journal,* January 1972, pp. 6–10. Reprinted with permission.

frameworks that can be used to develop specific change strategies in various situations. In particular, we will examine force field analysis and the process of change and then look at the impact of change on the total system.

CHANGE AND THE USE OF POWER

In developing a change strategy, the practitioner must be conscious of whatever power he has and be able to determine how this power might be appropriately used.

SOURCES OF POWER

Amitai Etzioni discusses the difference between *position power* and *personal power*.[1] His distinction springs from his concept of power as the ability to induce or influence behavior. He claims that power is derived from an organizational office, personal influence or both. An individual who is able to induce another individual to do a certain job because of his position in the organization is considered to have position power, while an individual who derives his power from his followers is considered to have personal power. Some individuals can have both position and personal power.

Etzioni postulates that the best situation for a leader is when he has both personal and position power. But in some cases it is not possible to build a relationship on both. Then the question becomes whether it is more important to have personal power or position power. Happiness and human relations have been culturally reinforced over the past several decades. With this emphasis, most people would pick personal power as being the most important, but there may be another side of the coin.

Machiavelli in the fifteenth century in his treatise *The Prince* presents an interesting viewpoint when he raises the question—whether it is better to have a relationship based upon love (personal power) or fear (position power).[2] Machiavelli, as Etzioni, contends it is best to be both loved and feared. If, however, you cannot have both, he suggest a relationship based on love alone tends to be volatile, short run and easily terminated when there is no fear of retaliation. On the other hand, Machiavelli contends a relationship based upon fear tends to be longer lasting since the individual must be willing to incur the sanction (pay the price) before terminating the relationship. This is a difficult concept for many people to accept; and yet one of the most difficult roles for a leader, whether he be a boss, teacher or parent, to engage in is disciplining someone about whom he cares. Yet to be effective we sometimes have to sacrifice short-term friendship for long-term respect if we are interested in the growth and development of the people with whom we are working. Machiavelli warns, however, that one should be careful that fear does not lead to hatred. For hatred often evokes overt behavior in terms of retaliation, undermining and attempts to overthrow.

SUCCESSFUL LEADERSHIP VS. EFFECTIVE LEADERSHIP

If an individual attempts to have some effect on the behavior of another, we call this stimulus attempted leadership. The response to this leadership attempt can be successful or unsuccessful. Since a manager's basic responsibility in any type of organization is to get work done with and through people, his success is measured by the output or productivity of the group he leads. With this thought in mind, Bernard M. Bass suggests a clear distinction between *successful* and *effective* leadership or management.[3]

Suppose manager A attempts to influence individual B to do a certain job. A's attempt will be considered successful or unsuccessful depending on the extent that B accomplishes the job. It is not really an either/or situation. A's success could be depicted on a continuum (Figure 1) ranging from very successful to very unsuccessful with gray areas in between which would be difficult to ascertain as either.

Let us assume that A's leadership is successful. In other words, B's response to A's leadership stimulus falls on the successful side of the continuum. This still does not tell the whole story of effectiveness.

If A's leadership style is not compatible with the expectations of B and, if B is antagonized and does the job only because of A's position power, then we can say that A has been successful but not effective. B has responded as A intended because A has control of rewards and punishment, and not because B sees his own needs being accomplished by satisfying the goals of the manager or organization.

On the other hand, if A's attempted leadership leads to a successful response, and B does the job because he wants to do it and finds it rewarding, then we consider A as having not only position power but also personal power. B respects A and is willing to cooperate with him realizing that A's request is consistent with his own personal goals. In fact, B sees his own goals as being

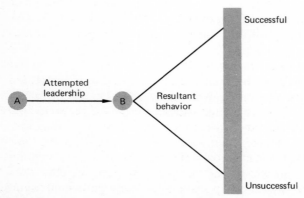

Figure 1   Successful-unsuccessful leadership continuum.

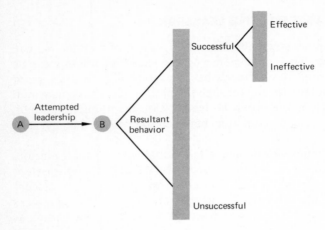

Figure 2   Successful and effective leadership continuums.

accomplished by this activity. This is the meaning of effective leadership, keeping in mind that effectiveness also appears as a continuum which can range from very effective to very ineffective as illustrated in Figure 2.

Success has to do with how the individual or group behaves. On the other hand, effectiveness describes the internal state or predisposition of an individual or group and thus is attitudinal in nature. If an individual is interested only in success, he tends to emphasize his position power and uses close supervision.

However, if he is effective he will depend also on personal power and be characterized by more general supervision. Position power tends to be delegated down from the organization, while personal power is generated from below through follower acceptance.

In the management of organizations, the difference between successful and effective often explains why many supervisors can get a satisfactory level of output only when they are right there, looking over the worker's shoulder. But as soon as they leave output declines and often such things as horseplay and scrap loss increase.

The phenomenon described applies not only to business organizations but also to less formal organizations like the family. If parents are successful and effective, have both position and personal power, their children accept family goals as their own. Consequently, if the husband and wife leave for the weekend, the children behave no differently than if their parents were there. If, on the other hand, the parents continually use close supervision and the children view their own goals as being stifled by their parents' goals, the parents have only position power. They maintain order because of the rewards and punishments they control. If these parents went away on a trip leaving the children behind, upon returning they might be greeted by havoc and chaos.

In summary, a manager could be successful, but ineffective, having only short-run influence over the behavior of others. On the other hand if a manager is both successful and effective, his influence tends to lead to long-run productivity and organizational development.

LEVELS OF CHANGE

We have to look at changes from more than just a behavioral viewpoint because often changes in behavior are a result of changes in knowledge and attitude. In fact, there are four levels of change in people: (1) knowledge changes, (2) attitudinal changes, (3) behavior changes and (4) group or organizational performance changes.[4] The time relationship and relative difficulty involved in making each of these levels of change are illustrated in Figure 3.

Changes in knowledge tend to be easiest to make; all one has to do is give a person a book or article to read, or have someone whom he respects tell him something new. Attitude structures differ from knowledge structures in that they are emotionally charged in a positive or negative way. The addition of emotion often makes attitudes more difficult to change than knowledge.

Changes in individual behavior seem to be significantly more difficult and time consuming than either of the two previous levels. For example, a person may have knowledge about the potential dangers of smoking, even actually feel that smoking is a bad habit he would like to change and still be unable to stop smoking because a habit pattern has been reinforced over a long period of time. It is important to point out that we are talking about change in patterned behavior and not a single event. In our example, anyone can quit smoking for a short period of time; the real test comes months later to see if a new long term pattern has evolved.

While individual behavior is difficult enough to change, when we get to the implementation of group or organizational performance, it is compounded because at this level we are concerned with changing customs, mores and traditions. Being a group, it tends to be a self-reinforcing unit and therefore a person's

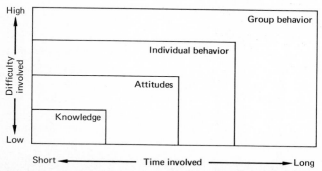

Figure 3 Time and difficulty involved in making various changes.

behavior as a member of a group is more difficult to modify without first changing the group norms.[5]

THE CHANGE CYCLES

The levels of change become very significant when we examine two different change cycles—the participative change cycle and the coerced change cycle.

Participative Change

A participative change cycle is implemented when new knowledge is made available to the individual or group. It is hoped that the group will accept the data and will develop a positive attitude and commitment in the direction of the desired change. At this level the strategy may be direct participation by the individual or group in helping to select or formalize the goals or new methods for obtaining the goals. This is group participation in problem-solving. The next step is to attempt to translate this commitment into actual behavior. This tends to be the real tough barrier to overcome. For example, it is one thing to be concerned (attitude) about a social problem but another thing to be willing to actually get involved in doing someting (behavior) about the problem. One strategy that is often useful is to attempt to identify informal as well as formal leaders within the group and concentrate on gaining their acceptance and behavior. Once this is accomplished you have moved a long way in getting others in the group to begin to pattern their behavior after those persons whom they respect and perceive in leadership roles. This participative change cycle is illustrated in Figure 4.

Coerced Change

We've all probably been faced with a situation similar to one in which there is an announcement on Monday morning that "as of today all members of this organization shall begin to operate in accordance with Form 10125." This is an example of a coerced change cycle. This cycle begins by imposing change on the total organization. This will tend to affect the interaction—influence system at the

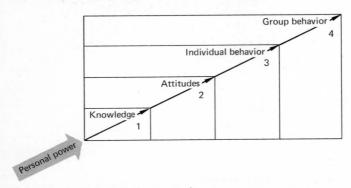

Figure 4   Participative change cycle.

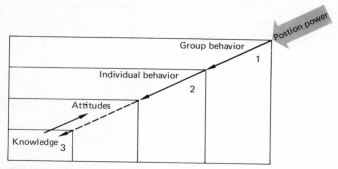

Figure 5 Coerced change cycle.

individual level. The new contacts and modes of behavior create new knowledge which tend to develop predispositions toward or against the change. The coerced change cycle is illustrated in Figure 5.

The intention of this coerced change cycle is that the new behavior creates the kind of knowledge which creates commitment to the change and therefore approximates a participative change cycle as it reinforces the individual and group behavior.

DIFFERENCES BETWEEN CHANGE CYCLES

The participative change cycle tends to be more appropriate for working with mature groups since they tend to be achievement-motivated and have a degree of knowledge and experience that may be useful in developing new strategies for accomplishing goals.[6] Once the change starts, mature people are much more capable of assuming responsibilities for implementation. On the other hand, with immature people the coerced change cycle might be more productive because they are often dependent and not willing to take new responsibilities unless forced to do so. In fact, by their very nature, these people might prefer direction and structure to being faced with decisions that might be frightening to them.

There are some other significant differences between these two change cycles. The participative change cycle tends to be effective when induced by leaders with personal power, while the coerced cycle necessitates significant position power—rewards, punishments and sanctions.

With the participative cycle, the main advantage is that once accepted it tends to be long-lasting, since the people are highly committed to the change. Its disadvantage is that it tends to be slow and evolutionary. On the other hand, the advantage of the coerced cycle is speed. Using his position power, the leader can often impose change immediately. The disadvantage of this cycle is that it tends to be volatile. It can only be maintained as long as the leader has position power to make it stick. It often results in animosity, hostility and in some cases overt and covert behavior to undermine and overthrow.

These cycles have been described as if they were either/or positions. In reality, it is more a question of the proper blend of each, depending upon the situation.

REFERENCES

1 Etzioni, Amitai, *A Comparative Analysis of Complex Organizations*, The Free Press of Glencoe, New York. 1961.
2 Machiavelli, Nicolo, *The Prince and the Discourses*, Chapter XVII, "Of Cruelty and Clemency, Whether It Is Better to be Loved or Feared," Random House, New York, 1950.
3 Suggested by Bernard M. Bass in *Leadership, Psychology, and Organizational Behavior*, Harper & Bros., New York, 1960.
4 R. J. House discusses similar concepts in *Management Development: Design, Imple-
4 mentation and Evaluation*, Bureau of Industrial Relations, University of Michigan, Ann Arbor, Mich., 1967.
5 Brown, J. A. C., *The Social Psychology of Industry*, Penguin Books, Baltimore, Md., 1954, p. 249.
6 For a definition of maturity and a discussion of the relationship between leadership style and the maturity of one's followers see Paul Hersey and Kenneth H. Blanchard, "Life Cycle Theory of Leadership," *Training and Development Journal*. May, 1969.

Reading 46

The Management of Change: Part 2—Change Through Behavior Modification

Paul Hersey
Kenneth H. Blanchard

Rensis Likert found that employee-centered supervisors who use general supervision *tend* to have higher producing sections than job-centered supervisors who use close supervision.[1] We emphasize the word "tend" because this seems to be high probability in our society, yet we also must realize there are exceptions to this tendency which are even evident in Likert's data. What Likert found was that a subordinate generally responds well to a superior's high expectations and genuine confidence in him and tries to justify his boss's expectations of him. His resulting high performance will reinforce his superior's high trust for him, for it is

"The Management of Change: Part 2—Change Through Behavior Modification," Paul Hersey and Kenneth H. Blanchard, *Training and Development Journal*, February 1972, pp. 20–24. Reprinted with permission.

Figure 1   Effective cycle.

easy to trust and respect the man who meets or exceeds your expectations. This occurrence could be called the effective cycle.

Yet, since top management often promotes on the basis of short run output alone, managers tend to overemphasize task accomplishment, placing extreme pressure on everyone to achieve high levels of productivity. This task-oriented leader behavior style, in some cases, does not allow much room for a trusting relationship with employees. Instead, subordinates are told what to do and how to do it. With little consideration, subordinates respond with minimal effort and resentment; low performance results in these instances. Reinforced by low expectations, it becomes a vicious cycle. Many other examples could be given which result in this all too common problem in organizations as shown in Figure 2.

These cycles are depicted as static but in reality they are very dynamic. The situation tends to get better or worse. For example, high expectations result in high performance, which reinforces the high expectations and produces even higher productivity. It almost becomes a spiral effect as illustrated in Figure 3.

In many cases, this spiraling effect is caused by an increase in leverage created through the use of what Frederick Herzberg calls "motivators."[2] In analyzing the data from his research, Herzberg concluded that man has two different categories of needs which are essentially independent of each other and affect behavior in different ways. He found that when people felt dissatisfied about their jobs, they were concerned about the environment in which they were working. On the other hand, when people felt good about their jobs, this had to do with the work itself. Herzberg called the first category of needs *hygiene factors* because they describe man's environment and serve the primary function of preventing job dissatisfaction. He called the second category of needs *motivators* since they seemed to be effective in motivating people to superior performance.

Company policies and administration, supervision, working conditions, interpersonal relations, money, status and security may be thought of as hygiene factors. These are not an intrinsic part of a job, but are related to the conditions

Figure 2   Ineffective cycle.

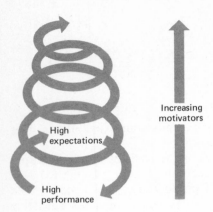

Figure 3 Spiraling effect of effective cycle.

under which a job is performed. Herzberg relates his use of the word "hygiene" to its medical meaning (preventative and environmental). Hygiene factors produce no growth in worker output capacity; they only prevent losses in worker performance due to work restriction.

Satisfying factors that involve feelings of achievement, professional growth and recognition that one can experience in a job which offers challenge and scope are referred to as motivators. Herzberg used this term because these factors seem capable of having a positive effect on job satisfaction often resulting in an increase in one's total output capacity. In terms of the upward spiraling effect, as people perform they are given more responsibility and opportunities for achievement and growth and development, which results in higher productivity and continued high expectations.

INEFFECTIVE CYCLE

This spiraling effect can also occur in a downward direction as shown in Figure 4. Low expectations result in low performance, which reinforces the low expecta-

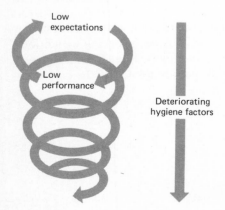

Figure 4 Spiraling effect of ineffective cycle.

tions and produces even lower productivity. It becomes a spiral effect like a whirlpool as shown in Figure 4.

If this downward spiraling continues long enough, the cycle may reach a point where it cannot be turned around in a short period of time because of the large reservoir of negative past experience which has built up in the organization. Much of the focus and energy is directed toward the perceived problems with hygiene factors rather than the work itself. This takes such form as hostility, undermining and slow-down in work performance. When this happens, even if a manager actually changes his behavior, the credibility gap based on long-term experience is such that the response is still distrust and skepticism rather than change.

STYLE CHANGE

One alternative that is sometimes necessary at this juncture is to bring in a new manager from the outside. The reason this has a higher probability of success is that the sum of the past experience of the people involved with the new manager is likened to a "clean slate," and thus different behaviors are on a much more believable basis. This was vividly illustrated by Robert H. Guest in a case analysis of organizational change.[3] He examined a large assembly plant of an automobile company, Plant Y, and contrasts the situation under two different leaders.

Under Mr. Stewart, plant manager, working relationships at Plant Y were dominated by hostility and mistrust. His high task style was characterized by a continual attempt to increase the driving forces pushing for productivity. As a result, the prevailing atmosphere was that of one emergency following on the heels of another, and the governing motivation for employee activity was fear—fear of being "chewed out" right on the assembly line, fear of being held responsible for happenings in which one had no clear authority, fear of losing one's job. Consequently, of the six plants in this division of the corporation, Plant Y had the poorest performance record, and it was getting worse.

Mr. Stewart was replaced by Mr. Cooley, who seemed like a truly effective leader. Three years later, dramatic changes had occurred. In various cost and performance measures used to rate the six plants, Plant Y was now truly the leader; and the atmosphere of interpersonal cooperation and personal satisfaction had improved impressively over the situation under Stewart. These changes, moreover, were effected through an insignificant number of dismissals and reassignments. Using a much higher relationships style Cooley succeeded in "turning Plant Y around."

EXPECTATIONS CHANGE

On the surface, the big difference was style of leadership. Cooley was a good leader. Stewart wasn't. But Guest points out clearly in his analysis that leadership style was only one of two important factors. "The other was that while Stewart received daily orders from division headquarters to correct specific situations, Cooley was left alone. Cooley was allowed to lead; Stewart was told how to lead."[4] In other words, when productivity in Plant Y began to decline during changeover from wartime to peacetime operations, Stewart's superiors expected him to get productivity back on the upswing by taking control of the reins and they put tremendous pressure on him to do just that. Guest suggests that these expectations forced Stewart to operate in a very crisis-oriented, autocratic way. However, when Cooley was given charge as plant manager, a "hands off" policy was initiated by his superiors. The fact that the expectations of top management had changed enough to put a moratorium on random, troublesome outside stimuli from headquarters gave Cooley an opportunity to operate in a completely different style. One could raise the question, what might have happened if instead of hiring Cooley, top management had given Stewart this same kind of support and "free hand"? Could he have turned the plant around like Cooley did? Probably not. The ineffective cycle seemed to have been in a downward spiral far past the point where Stewart would have had a good opportunity to make significant change. But with the introduction of a new manager with whom the employees had no past experience, now-significant changes were possible.

While a new manager may be in a better position to initiate change in a situation which has been spiraling downward, he still does not have an easy task. Essentially, he has to break the ineffective cycle. There are at least two alternatives available to him. He can either fire the low performing personnel and hire people who he expects to perform well or respond to low performance with high expectations and trust.

The latter choice for the manager is difficult. In effect, the attempt is to change the expectations or behavior of his subordinates. It is especially difficult for a manager to have high expectations about people who have shown no indication that they deserve to be trusted. The key, then, is to change appropriately. This is where the concepts of behavior modification might be helpful.

BEHAVIOR MODIFICATION

In the normal work environment, managers feel that either close supervision and pressure (task-oriented behavior) or consideration and trust (relationship-oriented behavior) are the only ways to focus a subordinate on his task or change patterns of behavior. They use these methods even when they prove unsuccessful, because they are often unaware of better techniques. At one time, managers were too structured, rigid and punishing. Now there seems to be a swing to the overly trusting, unstructured manager. Both these strategies when inappropriate have created problems. Another alternative is behavior modification,[5] which can provide a strategy for shifting leadership style appropriately to stimulate changes in maturity. In order to illustrate the differences between these three strategies— task behavior, relationships behavior and behavior modifications—we can compare how a manager using each might handle a potential problem-worker.

Tony, a new employee right out of high school, is a very agressive, competitive individual. During his first day on the job, he argues over tools with another young employee. Table I attempts to illustrate the possible reactions of a high task manager, a high relationships manager and a manager using behavior modification techniques.

Behavior modification (often referred to as operant conditioning or reinforcement theory) is based upon *deserved* behavior and not internal psychological feelings or attitudes.[6] Its basic premise is that *behavior is controlled by its immediate consequences.* Any behavior will be made stronger or weaker by what happens immediately after it occurs. If what happens is positive, it tends to increase the frequency of that behavior occurring again. Positive reinforcement is anything that is rewarding to the individual being reinforced. Reinforcement, therefore, depends on the individual. What is reinforcing to one person may not be reinforcing to another. Money might motivate some people to work harder, but to others money is not a high strength need; the challenge of the job might be the most rewarding incentive. Managers must look for unique differences in their people and recognize the dangers of generalizing.

POSITIVE REINFORCEMENT

In order for a desirable behavior to be obtained, the slightest positive behavior exhibited by the individual in that direction must be rewarded as soon as possible. This is called reinforcing positively successive approximations toward a goal. For example, when an individual's performance is low, one cannot expect drastic changes over night, regardless of changes in expectations or other incentives. Similar to the child learning some new behavior, we do not expect high levels of performance at the outset. So, as a parent or teacher, we would use *positive reinforcement* as the child's behavior approaches the desired level of performance. Therefore, the manager must be aware of any progress of his subordinate, so he is in a position to reinforce appropriately this change.

This is compatible with the concept of setting interim rather than final goals and then reinforcing appropriate progress toward the final goal as interim goals are accomplished. In this process, the role of a manager is not always setting goals for his followers. Instead, effectiveness may be increased by providing an environment where subordinates can play a role in setting their own goals. Research indicates that commitment increases when a person is involved in his own goal setting. If an individual is involved, he will tend to engage in much more goal-directed activity before he becomes frustrated and gives up. On the other hand, if the boss sets the goal for him, he is apt to give up more easily because he perceives these as his boss's goals and not as his own. Goals should be set high enough so a person has to stretch to reach them but low enough so that they can be attained.

So often final goals are set and the person is judged only in terms of success in relation to this terminal goal. Suppose, in our example, the manager had

Table 1 Different Approaches Used in Dealing with a Disruptive Worker

	High task manager	High relationships manager	Behavior modification manager
Manager reaction	"This worker is going to be a trouble-maker. This behavior must be stopped!"	"Oh dear, I hope I can get them interacting and happy."	"Feels Tony needs to learn to cope in positive ways to replace aggressive behavior!" Separates conflicting workers without hostility or comment.
Supervisor subordinate interaction	"Hey, you. Knock it off! We don't allow fighting around here," said with coldness or anger.	"How would you both like to give me a hand on a job over here."	Manager watches for any positive behavior he can immediately reinforce. Supervisor sets limits on some behavior and carefully ignores others.
Worker reaction	Tony builds resentment and hostility. Next few days, behavior becomes more aggressive.	Tony finds he can get attention of supervisor by being disruptive because the supervisor wants to be "understanding." He causes trouble and watches supervisor's reaction. Supervisor pays more and more attention as his behavior gets worse. Disruptive behavior reinforced.	Tony finds the supervisor appreciates good things about him. Wants to gain his respect. Supervisor Strategy: 1 Watches for any occurrences of positive behavior to reinforce. 2 Decides which new behaviors Tony needs to learn first. 3 Plans strategy to get desired behavior. 4 Attempts to better understand Tony in an effort to use incentives appropriate for his need structure. 5 Uses the incentives to reinforce behavior Tony needs to learn. 6 Continues to evaluate to make sure incentives are still appropriate since these tend to change with time.

Outcome   Tony feels disliked by supervisor. Self-image deteriorates as he attempts to defend ego from assaults. Becomes more hostile and aggressive or withdrawn. Avoids supervisor and learning tasks.

Aggressiveness remains. Becomes more obnoxious as other workers withdraw. Creates incidents to get attention and assigned to those jobs he wants. Does not learn. No friends. Low self-image covered by bravado.

Outcome in two or three weeks. Tony's work and acceptance by other members of his work group continue to improve. Builds new self-image on basis of new behavior he has learned. Hostile and aggressive behavior toward other employees stops. Begins to have a sense of accomplishment. Inner needs and feelings start to change. Aggressiveness used in constructive ways. Has friends and becomes a positive rather than a disruptive influence on his work group.

expected Tony to become a "perfect" employee overnight. Suppose after the first week Tony is better but still causes some problems. The result is usually the manager reprimanding him (punishment) even though he has shown improvement. If this reprimanding continues to occur, there is a high probability that Tony may stop trying. His behavior, rather than improving, may become worse. An alternative for the manager is setting interim realistic goals which move in the direction of the final goals as they are attained. Then with a change in the desired direction, even though only moderate, positive reinforcement may be used rather than some form of punishment.

NEGATIVE REINFORCEMENT

While positive reinforcement tends to be more effective in working with people, experiencing some unpleasant consequences or *negative reinforcement* can sometimes strengthen a particular behavior. For example, suppose a manager reprimands Al, one of his subordinates, for sloppy work, rather than giving him his usual "praise." If Al becomes just anxious enough, finds out what he did wrong, then does it right and gets his boss's praise, the unpleasantness of the reprimand becomes a negative "reinforcer." In this case, the manager was not just trying to punish Al because he wanted to make him feel badly but was giving him negative feedback because he wanted him to do better. Al responded as he had hoped he would, giving the manager a chance to use positive reinforcement with him again.

A leader or manager has to be careful in using negative reinforcement or punishment because he does not always know what he is reinforcing in a person when he uses these methods. He might be reinforcing lying, manipulation or all kinds of undesirable behavior because the individuals involved may use these behaviors, rather than improved performance, to eliminate punishment or further negative reinforcement. Another possible reaction to punishment is that the individual may begin to use avoidance behaviors such as attempting to eliminate communications and interactions between himself and the person who makes him feel threatened.

EXTINCTION

Another way to respond to behavior besides positive or negative reinforcement is to not reinforce it at all. This is called *extinction* because it tends to get rid of a behavior. For example, suppose a worker is disruptive to get the attention of his supervisor. What would happen if his supervisor paid no attention to him? After engaging in this behavior on several occasions without accomplishing anything, he soon would be trying other behaviors.

People do not tend to continue doing things that do not provide positive reinforcement. This is even true sometimes when they are behaving well. Parents often get into this situation when they tend to pay attention to their children only when they are behaving poorly. When children are behaving appropriately adults may pay little or no attention to them, which in a sense could put that behavior on extinction. If a child wants attention from his parents (it is rewarding to him), he may be willing to endure what the parent thinks is punishment for that attention. In the long run the parents might be reinforcing the very behavior they don't want and extinguishing more appropriate behavior.

PSYCHOTHERAPY NOT APPROPRIATE

Behavior modification seems like a useful tool for practitioners since it can be applied, to some extent, in most environments. Therefore, it has relevance for most people interested in accomplishing goals through others. This was not the case with psychotherapy. This process was based upon the assumption that to change behavior one had to first start with the feelings and attitudes within an individual.

The problem with psychotherapy from a practitioner's viewpoint is that it is too expensive and is appropriate for use only by trained professionals. This is true because the emphasis in psychotherapy is on analyzing the reasons underlying behavior which often requires extensive probing into the early experiences in the life of an individual. Behavior modification, on the other hand, is not as complex since it concentrates on observed behavior using goals or rewards outside the individual to modify behavior.

REFERENCES

1 Likert, Rensis, *New Patterns of Management* McGraw-Hill, New York, 1961, p. 7.
2 Herzberg, Frederick, Bernard Mausner and Barbara Synderman. *The Motivation to Work,* John Wiley, New York, 1959 and Herzberg, *Work and the Nature of Man,* World Publishing Co., New York, 1966.
3 Guest, Robert H., *Organizational Change: The Effect of Successful Leadership,* Dorsey Press and Irwin Inc., Homewood, Ill., 1964.
4 Perrow, Charles, *Organizational Analysis: A Sociological View,* Wadsworth Publishing Co., Inc., Belmont, Calif., 1970, p. 12.
5 A discussion of behavior modification by Glema G. Holsinger in *Motivating the Reluctant Learner,* Motivity, Inc., Lexington, Mass., 1970, was very helpful in developing this section.
6 The most classic discussions of behavior modification or operant conditioning have been done by B. F. Skinner. See Skinner, *Science and Human Behavior,* Macmillan, New York, 1953, and *Analysis of Behavior,* McGraw-Hill, New York, 1961.

Reading 47

The Management of Change:
Part 3—Planning and Implementing Change

Paul Hersey
Kenneth H. Blanchard

In evaluating effectiveness, perhaps more than 90 percent of managers in organizations look at measures of output alone. Thus, the effectiveness of a business manager is often determined by net profits, the effectiveness of a college professor may be determined by the number of articles and books he has published, and the effectiveness of an athletic coach may be determined by his won-lost record.

Others feel that it is unrealistic to think only in terms of productivity or output in evaluating effectiveness. According to Rensis Likert,[1] another set of variables should be taken into consideration in determining effectiveness. These are *intervening variables* which reflect the current condition of the human resources in an organization and are represented in its skills, loyalty, commitment to objectives, motivations, communications, decision-making and capacity for effective interaction. These intervening variables are concerned with building and developing the organization and tend to be long-term considerations. Managers are often promoted, however, on the basis of short-run output variables such as increased production and earnings, without concern for the long-run and organizational development. This creates a dilemma.

ORGANIZATIONAL DILEMMA

One of the major problems in industry today is that there is a shortage of successful managers. Therefore, it is not uncommon for a manager to be promoted in six months or a year if he is a "producer." Let's look at the example of Mr. X, a manager who realizes that the basis on which top management promotes is often short-run output, and therefore attempts to achieve high levels of productivity by over-emphasizing task accomplishment and placing extreme pressure on everyone, even when it is inappropriate.

The immediate or short-run effect of Mr. X's behavior will probably be increased productivity. Yet if his task-oriented style is inappropriate for those involved, and if it continues over a long period, the morale and climate of the organization will deteriorate. Some indications of deterioration resulting from these intervening variables may be turnover, absenteeism, increased accidents, scrap loss and numerous grievances. Not only the number of grievances, but the nature of grievances is important. Are grievances really significant problems or do

"The Management of Change: Part 3—Planning and Implementing Change," Paul Hersey and Kenneth H. Blanchard, *Training and Development Journal*, March 1972, pp. 28–33. Reprinted with permission.

they reflect pent-up emotions due to anxieties and frustration? Are they settled at the complaint stage between the employee and supervisor or are they pushed up the hierarchy to be settled at higher levels or by arbitration? The organizational dilemma is that in many instances a manager like Mr. X, who places pressure on everyone and produces in the short run, is promoted out of this situation before the disruptive aspects of the intervening variables catch up.

TIME LAG

There tends to be a time lag between declining intervening variables and significant restriction of output by employees under such management climate. Employees tend to feel "things will get better." Thus, when Mr. X is promoted rapidly, he often stays "one step ahead of the wolf."

The real problem is faced by the next manager, Mr. Y. Although productivity records are high, he has inherited many problems. Merely the introduction of a new manager may be enough to collapse the slowly deteriorating intervening variables. A tremendous drop in morale and motivation leading almost immediately to significant decrease in output can occur. Change by its very nature is frightening: to a group whose intervening variables are declining, it can be devastating.

Regardless of Mr. Y's style, the present expectations of the followers may be so distorted, that much time and patience will be needed to close the now apparent "credibility gap" between the goals of the organization and the personal goals of the group. No matter how effective Mr. Y might be in the long run, his superiors, in reviewing a productivity drop, may give him only a few months to improve performance. But as Likert's studies indicate, rebuilding a group's intervening variables in a small organization may take one to three years, and in a large organization, may extend to seven years.

SHORT AND LONG TERM

It should be made clear that the choice for a manager is not whether to concentrate on output or intervening variables but often a matter of how much emphasis to place on each. The decision is between short- and long-range goals. If the accepted goal is building and developing an organization for the future, then the manager should be evaluated on these terms and not entirely on his present productivity.

While intervening variables do not appear on balance sheets, sales reports or accounting ledgers, we feel that these long-term considerations can be just as important to an organization as short-term output variables. Therefore, although difficult to measure, intervening variables should not be overlooked in determining organizational effectiveness.

In summary, we feel that effectiveness is actually determined by whatever the manager and the organization decide are their goals and objectives, but should consider these factors: output variables, intervening variables, short-range goals and long-range goals.

FORCE FIELD ANALYSIS

Force field analysis, a technique for diagnosing situations developed by Kurt Lewin, may be useful in looking at the variables involved in determing effectiveness and in developing strategies for changing in particular the condition of the output or intervening variables.[2]

Lewin assumes that in any situation there are both driving and restraining forces which influence any change which may occur. *Driving forces* are those forces affecting a situation which are "pushing" in a particular direction; they tend to initiate a change and keep it going. In terms of improving productivity in a work group, pressure from a supervisor, incentive earnings and competition may be examples of driving forces. *Restraining forces* are forces acting to restrain or decrease the driving forces. Apathy, hostility and poor maintenance of equipment may be examples of restraining forces against increased production. Equilibrium is reached when the sum of the driving forces equals the sum of the restraining forces. In our example, equilibrium represents the present level of productivity as shown in Figure 1.

This equilibrium or present level of productivity can be raised or lowered by changes in the relationship between the driving and restraining forces. For illustrations, let us look again at the dilemma of Mr. Y, the new manager who takes over a work group where productivity is high but Mr. X, his predecessor, drained the human resources (intervening variables). Mr. X had upset the equilibrium by increasing the driving forces (i.e., being autocratic and keeping continual pressure on his men) and thus achieving increases in output in the short run. By doing this though, new restraining forces developed, such as increased hostility and antagonism, and at the time of his departure the restraining forces were beginning to increase and the results manifested themselves in turnover, absenteeism and other restraining forces which lowered productivity shortly after

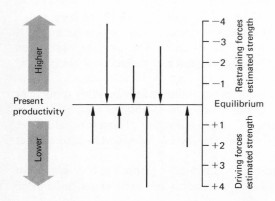

Figure 1 Driving and restraining forces in equilibrium.

Mr. Y arrived. Now a new equilibrium at a significantly lowered productivity is faced by the new manager.

Now just assume that Mr. Y decides not to increase the driving forces, but to reduce the restraining forces. He may do this by taking time away from the usual production operation and engaging in problem-solving and training and development. In the short run, output will tend to be lowered still further. However, if commitment to objectives and technical know-how of his group are increased in the long run, they may become new driving forces, and that, along with the elimination of the hostility and apathy which were restraining forces, will now tend to move the balance to a higher level of output.

A manager, in attempting to implement change, is often in a position where he must consider not only output but also intervening variables, not only short-term but also long-term goals, and a framework which is useful in diagnosing these interrelationships is available through force field analysis.

PROCESS OF CHANGE

In developing a change strategy, another important aspect that must be taken into consideration is the process of change. Kurt Lewin, in his pioneer work in change, identified three phases of the change process.[3] These are unfreezing, changing and refreezing.

UNFREEZING

The aim of unfreezing is to motivate and make the individual or group ready to change. It is a "thawing out" process where the forces acting on an individual are rearranged so now he sees the need for change. According to Edgar H. Schein, some elements that unfreezing situations seem to have in common are: (1) the physical removal of the individual being changed from his accustomed routines, sources of information and social relationships; (2) the undermining and destruction of all social supports; (3) demeaning and humiliating experience to help the individual being changed to see his old self as unworthy and thus to be motivated to change; (4) the consistent linking of reward with willingness to change and of punishment with unwillingness to change.[4]

In brief, unfreezing is the breaking down of the mores, customs, and traditions of an individual—the old ways of doing things—so he is ready to accept new alternatives. In terms of force field analysis, unfreezing may occur when either the driving forces are increased or the restraining forces that are resisting change are reduced.

CHANGING

Once the individual has become motivated to change, he is now ready to be provided with new patterns of behavior. This process is most likely to occur by one of two mechanisms: identification and internalization.[5] *Identification* occurs when one or more models are provided in the environment from whom an individual can learn new behavior patterns by identifying with them and trying to become like them. *Internalization* occurs when an individual is placed in a situation where new behaviors are demanded of him if he is to operate success-fully in that situation. He learns these new behavior patterns not only because they are necessary to survive but as a result of new high strength needs induced by coping behavior.

> Internalization is a more common outcome in those influence settings where the direction of change is left more to the individual. The influence which occurs in programs such as Alcoholics Anonymous, in psychotherapy or counseling for hospitalized or incarcerated populations, in religious retreats, in human relations training of the kind pursued by the National Training Laboratories (1953), and in certain kinds of progressive education programs is more likely to occur through internalization or, at least, to lead ultimately to more internalization.[6]

Identification and internalization are not either/or courses of action and effective change is often the result of combining the two into a strategy for change.

Force or compliance is sometimes discussed as another mechanism for inducing change.[7] It occurs when an individual is forced to change by the direct manipulation of rewards and punishment by someone in a power position. In this case, behavior appears to have changed when the change agent is present, but often is dropped when supervision is removed. Thus rather than discussing force as a mechanism of changing, we would rather think of it as a tool for unfreezing.

REFREEZING

The process by which the newly-acquired behavior comes to be integrated as patterned behavior into the individual's personality and/or ongoing significant emotional relationships is referred to as *refreezing*. As Schein contends, if the new behavior has been internalized while being learned, "this has automatically facilitated refreezing because it has been fitted naturally into the individual's personality. If it has been learned through identification, it will persist only so long as the target's relationship with the original influence model persists unless new surrogate models are found or social support and reinforcement is obtained for expressions of the new attitudes."[8]

This highlights how important it is for an individual engaged in a change process to be in an environment which is continually reinforcing the desired change. The effect of many a training program has been short-lived when the person returns to an environment that does not reinforce the new patterns or, even worse, is hostile toward them.

What we are concerned about in refreezing is that the new behavior does not get extinguished over time. To insure this not happening, reinforcement (rewards and incentives) must be scheduled in an effective way. There seem to be two main reinforcement schedules: continuous and intermittent.[9] Continuous reinforcement means that the individual being changed is rewarded every time he engages in the desired new pattern. With intermittent reinforcement, on the other hand, not every desired response is reinforced. Reinforcement can be either completely random or scheduled according to a prescribed number of responses occurring or a particular interval of time elapsing before reinforcement is given.

With continuous reinforcement, the individual learns the new behavior quickly, but if his environment changes to one of nonreinforcement, extinction (elimination of the behavior) can be expected to take place relatively soon. With intermittent reinforcement, extinction is much slower because the individual has been conditioned to go for periods of time without any reinforcement. Thus for fast learning, a continuous reinforcement schedule should be used. But once the individual has learned the new pattern, a switch to intermittent reinforcement should insure a long lasting change.

CHANGE PROCESS—SOME EXAMPLES

To see the change process in operation, several examples could be cited.

A college basketball coach recruited for his team Bob Anderson, a 6′ 4″ center from a small town in a rural area. In his district, 6′ 4″ was good height for a center. This fact, combined with his deadly turn-around-jump shot, made Anderson the rage of his league and enabled him to average close to 30 points a game.

Recognizing that 6′ 4″ is small for a college center, the coach hoped that he could make Anderson a forward, moving him inside only when they were playing a double pivot. One of the things the coach was concerned about, however, was when Anderson would be used in the pivot, how he could get his jump shot off when he came up against other players ranging in height from 6′ 8″ to 7′. He felt that Anderson would have to learn to shoot a hook shot, which is much harder to block, if he was going to have scoring potential against this kind of competition.

The approach that many coaches use to solve this problem would probably be as follows: The first day of practice when Anderson arrived, the coach would welcome Anderson and then explain the problem to him as he had analyzed it. As a solution he would probably ask Anderson to start to work with the varsity center, Steve Cram, who was 6′ 10″ and had an excellent hook. "Steve can help you start working on that new shot, Bob," the coach would say. Anderson's reaction to this interchange might be one of resentment and he would go over and work with Cram only because of the coach's position power. After all, he might think to himself, "Who does he think he is? I've been averaging close to 30 points a game for three years now and the first day I show up here the coach wants me to learn a new shot." So he may start to work with Cram reluctantly, concentrating on the hook shot only when the coach is looking but taking his favorite jump shot when he wasn't being observed. Anderson is by no means unfrozen or ready to learn to shoot another way.

ANOTHER APPROACH

Let's look at another approach the coach could have used to solve this problem. Suppose on the first day of practice he sets up a scrimmage between the varsity and freshmen. Before he starts the scrimmage he gets big Steve Cram, the varsity center, aside and tells him, "Steve, we have this new freshman named Anderson who has real potential to be a fine ball player. What I'd like you to do today though, is not to worry about scoring or rebounding, just make sure every time Anderson goes up for a shot you make him eat it. I want him to see that he will have to learn to shoot some other shots if he is to survive against guys like you."

So when the scrimmage starts, the first time Anderson gets the ball and turns around to shoot Cram leaps up and "stuffs the ball right down his throat." Time after time this occurs. Soon Anderson starts to engage in some coping behavior, trying to fall away from the basket, shooting from the side of his head rather than the front, in an attempt to get his shot off.

After the scrimmage, Anderson comes off the court dejected. The coach says, "What's wrong Bob?" He replies, "I don't know, Coach, I just can't seem to get my shot off against a man as big as Cram. What do you think I should do, Coach?" he asks. "Well, Bob, why don't you go over and start working with Steve on a hook shot. I think you'll find it much harder to block. And with your shooting eye I don't think it will take long for you to learn." How do you think Anderson feels about working with Cram now? He's enthusiastic and ready to learn. Having been placed in a situation where he learns for himself that he has a problem, Anderson is already in the process of unfreezing his past patterns of behavior. Now he's ready for identification. He has had an opportunity to internalize his problem and is ready to work with Steve Cram.

So often the leader who has knowledge of an existing problem forgets that until the people involved recognize the problem as their own, it is going to be much more difficult to produce change in their behavior. Internalization and identification are not either/or alternatives but can be parts of developing specific change strategies appropriate to the situation.

THE MILITARY EXAMPLE

Another example of the change processes in operation can be seen in the military, particularly in the induction phase. There are probably few organizations that have entering their ranks people who are less motivated and committed to the organization than the recruits the military gets. Yet in a few short months, they are able to mold these men into a relatively effective combat team. This is not an accident. Let's look at some of the processes that help accomplish this.

The most dramatic and harsh aspects of the training are the unfreezing phase. All four of the elements that Schein claims unfreezing situations have in common are present. A specific example follows.

1 The recruits are *physically removed from their accustomed routines, sources of information and social relationships* in the isolation of a place such as Parris Island.

> During this first week of training at Parris Island, the recruit is . . . hermetically sealed in a hostile environment, required to rise at 4:55 a.m., do exhausting exercises, attend classes on strange subjects, drill for hours in the hot sun, eat meals in silence and stand at rigid attention the rest of the time; he has no television, no radio, no candy, no coke, no beer, no telephone—and can write letters only during one hour of free time a day.[10]

2 *The undermining and destruction of social supports* is one of the DI's (Drill Instructor) tasks. "Using their voices and the threat of extra PT (physical training), the DI . . . must shock the recruit out of the emotional stability of home, pool hall, street corner, girl friend or school."[11]

3 *Demeaning and humiliating experiences* are commonplace during the first two weeks of the training as the DI's help the recruits *see themselves as unworthy and thus motivated to change* into what they want a Marine to be. "It's a total shock . . . Carrying full seabags, 80 terrified privates are herded into their "barn," a barracks floor with 40 double-decker bunks. Sixteen hours a day, for two weeks, they will do nothing right.[12]

4 Throughout the training there is *consistent linking of reward with willingness to change and punishment with unwillingness to change.*

> Rebels or laggards are sent to the Motivation Platoon to get "squared away." A day at Motivation combines constant harassment and PT (physical training), ending the day with the infiltration course. This hot, 225-yard ordeal of crawling, jumping and screaming through ditches and obstacles is climaxed by the recruits dragging two 30-pound ammo boxes 60 yards in mud and water. If he falters he starts again. At the end, the privates are lined up and asked if they are ready to go back to their home platoons . . . almost all go back for good.[13]

While the recruits go through a severe unfreezing process, they quickly move to the changing phase, first identifying with the DI and then emulating informal leaders, as they develop. "Toward the end of the third week a break occurs. What one DI calls 'that five per cent—the slow fat, dumb or difficult' have been dropped, the remaining recruits have emerged from their first-week vacuum with one passionate desire—to stay with their platoon at all costs."[14]

Internalization takes place when the recruits through their forced interactions develop different high strength needs. "Fear of the DI gives way to respect, and survival evolves into achievement toward the end of training. "I learned I had more guts than I imagined" is a typical comment.[15]

Since the group tends to stay together throughout the entire program, it serves as a positive reinforcer which can help refreeze the new behavior.

IMPACT OF CHANGE ON TOTAL SYSTEM

The focus in these three articles has been on the management of human resources and as a result we have spent little time on how technical change can have an impact on the total system. And yet, the importance of combining the social and technical into a unified social systems concept is stressed by Robert Guest.

> On his part the social scientist often makes the error of concentrating on human motivation and group behavior without fully accounting for the technical environment which circumscribes, even determines, the roles which the actors play. Motivation, group structure, interaction processes, authority—none of these abstractions of behavior take place in a technological vacuum.[16]

A dramatic example of the consequences of introducing technical change and ignoring its consequences on the social system is the case of the introduction of the steel axe to a group of Australian aborigines.[17]

This tribe remained considerably isolated, both geographically and socially, from the influence of Western cultures. In fact, their only contact was an Anglican mission established in the adjacent territory.

The polished stone axe was a traditionally basic part of the tribe's technology. Used by men, women and children, the stone axe was vital to the subsistence economy. But more than that, it was actually a key to the smooth running of the social system; it defined interpersonal relationships and was a symbol of masculinity and male superiority. "Only an adult male could make and own a stone axe; a woman or a child had to ask his permission to obtain one."[18]

The Anglican mission in an effort to help improve the situation of the aborigines introduced the steel axe, a product of European technology. It was given indiscriminately to men, women and children. Because the tool was more efficient than the stone axe, it was readily accepted but it produced severe repercussions unforeseen by the missionaries or the tribe. As Stephan R. Cain reports:

> The adult male was unable to make the steel axe and no longer had to make the stone axe. Consequently, his exclusive ax-making ability was no longer a necessary or desirable skill, and his status as sole possessor and dispensor of a vital element of technology was lost. The most drastic overall result was that traditional values, beliefs, and attitudes were unintentionally undermined.[19]

This example illustrates that an organization is an "open social system," that is, all aspects of an organization may have an impact on other parts or the organization itself. Thus a proposed change in one part of an organization must be carefully assessed in terms of its likely impact on the rest of the organization.

REFERENCES

1 Likert, Rensis *New Patterns of Management,* McGraw-Hill, New York, 1961, p. 2.
2 Lewin, Kurt, "Frontiers in Group Dynamics: Concept, Method and Reality in Social Science; Social Equilibria and Social Change," *Human Relations,* Vol. 1, No. 1, June, 1947, pp. 5–41.
3 *Ibid.*
4 Schein, Edgar H., "Management Development as a Process of Influence" in David R. Hampton, *Behavioral Concepts in Management,* Dickinson Publishing Co., Belmont, Cal., 1968, p. 110. Reprinted from the *Industrial Management Review,* Vol. II, No. 2, May, 1961, pp. 59–77.
5 The mechanisms are taken from H.C. Kelman "Compliance, Identification and Internalization: Three Processes of Attitude Change," *Conflict Resolution,* 1958, II, pp. 51–60.
6 Schein, *op.cit.,* p. 112.
7 Kelman discussed compliance as a third mechanism for attitude change.
8 Schein, *op. cit.,* p. 112.
9 See C. B. Ferster and B. F. Skinner, *Schedules of Reinforcement,* Appleton-Century Crofts, New York, 1957.
10 "Marine Machine," *Look Magazine,* Aug. 12, 1969.
11 *Ibid.*
12 *Ibid.*
13 *Ibid.*
14 *Ibid.*
15 *Ibid.*
16 Guest, Robert H., *Organizational Change: The Effect of Successful Leadership.* Dorsey Press and Irwin, Inc., Homewood, Ill., 1964, p.4.
17 Sharp, Lauriston, "Steel Axes for Stone Age Australians," in *Human Problems in Technological Change,* ed. Edward H. Spicer, Russell Sage Foundation, New York, 1952, pp. 69–94.
18 Cain, Stephen R., "Anthropology and Change" taken from *Growth and Change,* Vol. 1, No. 3, July, 1970, University of Kentucky.
19 *Ibid.*

Reading 48

The Business Organization, Environment, and T-Group Training: A New Viewpoint

Henry P. Sims, Jr.

There are environmental factors and organizational influences that affect the validity of T-group training as a means of organization development. The primary purpose of this paper is to present a framework to integrate research on T-group training with contingency theory, an important development in organization theory that focuses on the effect of the environment on the organization. A simplified model of the T-group training process is needed first with a brief discussion of the important variables in the process and also a brief discussion of the development and content of contingency theory. Then concepts of contingency theory can be matched against questions of the efficacy of T-group training.

T- GROUP TRAINING

The term T-group training is frequently used interchangeably with sensitivity training and laboratory education, although, technically, they should not be so equated. A "T-group" is only one of many exercises that may be employed in laboratory education.

Shein and Bennis classify laboratory education activities into the following categories:

1 *T-Groups* or small groups (usually 10 to 15 members) that are generally "unstructured" in the sense that the staff provides a minimum of agenda and formal leadership.

2 *Information Sessions* or theory sessions in the format of a lecture or demonstration to impart some concepts relevant to the laboratory goals.

3 *Verbal* (and also non-verbal) *Exercises* designed to deepen or intensify sensory awareness.

4 *Focused Exercises*, that is, specified or structured activities such as role playing or group observation.

5 *Other Activities* such as seminars, dyads, informal "bull sessions," etc.[1]

According to Schein and Bennis, the mix of activities will vary according to

"The Business Organization, Environment, and T-Group Training: A New Viewpoint," Henry Sims, Jr., *Management of Personnel Quarterly*, Winter 1970, pp. 21–27. Reprinted with permission.

[1]E. H. Schein and W. G. Bennis: *Personal and Organization Change Through Group Methods: The Laboratory Approach,* New York, John Wiley, 1967. pp. 14–24.

the goals of the laboratory. A lab that is designed primarily for personal learning will emphasize unstructured face-to-face encounters, supported by theories and focused exercises. Conversely, a laboratory that is intended for role learning and organizational development will de-emphasize (and perhaps eliminate) unstructured exercises and concentrate on focused or "instrumental" exercises. The lab might deal with "live" organizational improvement.

Although goals and conduct of a laboratory can vary widely, each laboratory usually includes most of the following objectives.[2]

1 self-insight, or some variation of learning related to increased self knowledge;
2 understanding the conditions which inhibit or facilitate group functioning;
3 understanding interpersonal operations in groups; and
4 developing skills for diagnosing individual, group, and organizational behavior.

Mangham and Cooper have defined three basic features that distinguish T-group training from conventional group discussions. First, the training is primarily *process-oriented* rather than *content-oriented.*

That is, the primary stress is on the feeling level of communications rather than solely on the informational or conceptual level. This emphasis is accomplished by focusing on the here-and-now behavior and themes in the group.

Second, the training is not structured in a conventional manner. Opportunities are provided for the individuals to decide what they want to talk about, what kinds of problems they desire to deal with, and what means they want to use in reaching their goals. No one tells them what they ought to talk about. As they concern themselves with the problems occasioned by this lack of direction, they begin to act in characteristic ways: some people remain silent, some are aggressive, some tend consistently to initiate discussions, some attempt to structure the proceedings. With the aid of the staff member, these approaches and developments become the focal points for discussion and analysis. The staff member, or trainer, as he is often called, draws attention to events and behavior in the group by occasional interventions in the form of tentative interpretations, which he considers will provide useful data for study.

Third, the heart of a T-group laboratory is found in small groups, allowing a high level of participation, involvement, and free communication. Indeed an intensification of participant involvement is an essential feature of such programs . . . [3]

In essence, T-group training is an educational strategy which is based primarily on the experiences generated in small-group social encounters by the trainees themselves.

[2]Schein and Bennis, p. 35.
[3]I. Mangham and G. L. Cooper: "The Impact of T-Groups On Managerial Behavior" *Journal of Management Studies,* Vol. 6, No. 1, Feb., 1969, pp. 53–54.

Most of the literature on T-group training is devoted to evaluating the effectiveness of the technique, yet there appears to be general agreement that methodological difficulties have substantially interfered with a completely objective evaluation of T-group training. There is significant disagreement regarding interpretation of research data:

Pro "Experience to date suggests that T-group training can help some organizations to overcome some of their problems."[4]
    Con ". . . the assumption that T-group training has positive utility for organizations must necessarily rest on shaky grounds. It has been neither confirmed nor disconfirmed. The . . . utility for the organizations is not necessarily the same as the utility for the individual."[5]

This disagreement is hardly surprising when one considers that the theory underlying T-group training is complex, and the effectiveness of the technique can be significantly influenced by not one, but a myriad of factors.

While the *central* component of the process is the trainee, and the input, or stimulus, is provided to the trainee by the trainer and co-participants, the impact of the training process on the individual will depend partially on the training design and can be significantly influenced by such factors as

1   goals of the training (personal vs. organization development);
2   the dynamics of training exercises (mix of verbal and non-verbal, theory sessions, role playing etc.);
3   the trainee demographic mix *(family vs. stranger; diagonal slice vs. horizontal slice);*
4   the sponsorship of training;
5   the location and duration of training (*cultural island* or once per week, etc.) and the timing and duration of lab exercises within the context of the entire training experience;
6   the personal characteristics and effectiveness of the trainer; and
7   other factors (even such seemingly inconsequentials as food at the lab or, not so inconsequential, the dean and staff of the lab, etc.).

The impact of the training is also obviously dependent on psychological attributes of the individual himself, e.g., his mental health status, or his willingness and ability to learn.[6] The trainee responds to the stimuli of the training process with a change in behavior; that change is, in turn, a stimulus (positive or negative) to the organization. The response of the organization is then dependent on certain

---

[4]C. Agyris, "T-groups for Organizational Effectiveness," *Harvard Business Review,* Vol. 42, No. 2, March–April, 1964, pp. 60–74.
    [5]J. P. Campbell and M. D. Dunnette: "Effectiveness of T-group Experiences in Managerial Training and Development," *Psychological Bulletin,* Vol. 70, No. 2, (1968).
    [6]F. S. Harman, "Effects of Training in Group Process on Open-Mindedness," *Journal of Communication,* Vol. 12, 1963, pp. 236–245. See also, M. Haire, E. E. Ghiselli, and L. W. Porter: *Managerial Thinking,* New York: Wiley, 1966.

external environmental variables (such as demand stability, product or scientific technology, process technology, etc.) and organizational parameters (such as level in the organization, function within the organization, and organizational style—"mechanistic" vs. "organic"). Whether the individual response to the training will be contributory or dysfunctional to the performance of the organization is therefore related to the environment and to the characteristics of the organization itself.

The importance of organizational attributes as a moderator in determining training effectiveness has been well recognized:

1   "If we make a few members of an organization . . . considerate, and they return to an organization which does not reward . . . considerate behavior, what would happen to these people?"[7]

2   ". . . the style of management . . . emerging from the development effort came into conflict with that practiced at higher levels of the company."[8]

3   "More attention must be given to intersections between organizational characteristics, leadership climates, organizational goals, and training outcomes . . ."[9]

However, the influence of environmental variables on the process appears to be universally ignored. Because this paper intends to focus on environmental variables as a moderator of T-group training, a review of the development and content of contingency theory is necessary.

CONTINGENCY THEORY

Practicing managers and academicians have long been interested in organization theory because of their desire to improve the design and efficiency of our society's institutions. Indeed, the major historical trends in the study of organizations have had a profound impact on the practice of management, especially in the business sector.

More recently, a new trend, known as "contingency theory" has emerged, which holds promise of becoming a major advancement in understanding cause-and-effect relationships in organization performance. The chief spokesmen for this new theory are Paul R. Lawrence and Jay W. Lorsch, both Professors at the Graduate School of Business Administration, Harvard University. Their concepts were first published in a research monograph, *Organization and Environment, Managing Differentiation and Integration.*[10]

[7]R. J. House: "T-Group Education and Leadership: A Review of the Empiric Literature and a Critical Evaluation," *Personnel Psychology.* Vol. 20, No. 1, 1967, p. 1.

[8]P. C. Buchanan, "Innovative Organizations—A Study in Organization Development," *Applying Behavioral Science Research in Industry,* New York: Industrial Relations Counselors, 1964.

[9]Campbell and Dunnette.

[10]P. R. Lawrence and J. W. Lorsch, *Organization and Environment, Managing Differentiation and Integration,* Boston, Harvard University, 1967.

Traditional theories of organization have concentrated on discovering *one best way* of organizing under all conditions. Contingency theory, on the other hand, focuses on the organizational characteristics which lead to effective performance given the specific situations which confront an organization, *i.e.* it concentrates on the relationship between organizational variables and the demands imposed upon the organization by external market and technological conditions. Contingency theory attempts to answer the basic question: What kind of organization does it take to deal with various economic, technological, and market conditions?

The theory also provides a basis for resolving the apparent contradictions between the two primary historical trends in organization, classical management theory and human relations theory. To develop this resolution, one must understand the key concepts of differentiation and integration in an organization.

Lawrence and Lorsch[11] define *differentiation* in an organization as, ". . . the differences in cognitive and emotional orientation among managers in different units and the differences in formal structure among units." Specifically, they measured differentiation in terms of (1) the *formality of structure,* e.g. high reliance on formal rules, procedures, and tight spans of control vs. the opposite conditions; (2) *goal orientation* or concern with market goals vs. concern with cost/quality, and efficiency goals vs. concern with scientific goals; and (3) *time orientation,* i.e. long term vs. short term.

Complex organizations must deal with pluralistic environments. Thus, organization subunits are "differentiated" in order to cope with a particular sub-environment. Lawrence and Lorsch, in dealing with differentiation, generally subdivide the environmental variables into three sectors: the market, the technical, and the scientific subsystems, each of which is roughly analogous to, respectively, the sales, production, and research and development sectors in the firm.

Differentiation can therefore be observed as the variation in behavior that stems from the differing orientations and thought patterns that develop among specialists in relation to their respective tasks. Differentiation is a direct result of the need for task specialization in the organization. In general, the greater the need for task specialization, the greater the degree of differentiation.

The converse of differentiation, of course, is integration: the process of bringing together the efforts of the specialists (or sybsystems) in order to effectively achieve the total goals of the organization. Integration is a process of coordination, where the differences brought about by differentiation in the firm are reconciled to the overall objective of the organization.

Lawrence and Lorsch classify types of integration, based on the research of Burns and Stalker, as "mechanistic" and "organic." They explain it this way.

[11]Lawrence and Lorsch, *Studies in Organizational Design,* Homewood, Ill., Richard D. Irwin, 1970.

There seemed to be two divergent systems of management practice. . . . One system, to which we gave the name 'mechanistic,' appeared to be appropriate to an enterprise operating under relatively stable conditions. The other, 'organic,' appeared to be required for conditions of change. In terms of 'ideal types' their principal characteristics are briefly the following.

In mechanistic systems the problems and tasks facing the concern as a whole are broken down into specialists. Each individual pursues his task as something distinct from the real tasks of the concern as a whole, as if it were the subject of a subcontract. "Somebody at the top" is responsible for seeing to its relevance. The technical methods, duties, and powers attached to each functional role are precisely defined. Interaction within management tends to be vertical, i.e., between superior and subordinate. Operations and working behavior are governed by instructions and decisions issued by superiors. This command hierarchy is maintained by the implicit assumption that all knowledge about the situation of the firm and its tasks is, or should be, available only to the head of the firm. Management, often visualized as the complex hierarchy which is familiar in organization charts, operates a simple control system, with information flowing up through a succession of filters, and decisions and instructions flowing downwards through a succession of amplifiers.

Organic systems are adapted to unstable conditions, when problems and requirements for action arise which cannot be broken down and distributed among specialist roles within a clearly defined hierarchy. Individuals have to perform their special tasks in the light of their knowledge of the tasks of the firm as a whole. Jobs lose much of their formal definition in terms of methods, duties, and powers, which have to be redefined continually by action runs laterally as much as vertically. Communication between people of different ranks tends to resemble lateral consultation rather than vertical command. Omniscience can no longer be imputed to the head of the concern.[12]

Thus, in a mechanistic system, integration is accomplished primarily through reliance on the formal authority system as expressed through the chain of command. On the other hand, an organic system relies on a free flow of interpersonal relations for effective integration. The concept of mechanistic and organic systems of integration are considerations that become important when traditional organization theories are re-interpreted.

The roots of classical theory can be traced to the scientific management movement as articulated through the writing of Frederick W. Taylor in the early 1900's. Scientific management concentrated on the coordination and linkage of the *physical* processes in the firm, and then the linking of human beings with these physical processes. The movement attempted to develop efficient methods of organization "from the bottom up," *i.e.* organizing and routinizing the work at the shop floor level through the use of analytical techniques such as time study. It held that tasks can be organized so as to efficiently accomplish the objectives of the organization. The movement utilized techniques that tended to emphasize task

---

[12]T. Burns and G. M. Stalker, *The Management of Innovation*, London, Tavistock, 1959.

specialization and to deepen the degree of differentiation in the firm, and also tended to rely almost wholly on mechanistic systems of integration. An underlying assumption of the movement was the concept of the "rational-economic man" which argued that man calculated the actions that will maximize his self-interest and behaved accordingly. Expressed another way, the movement assumed that man is primarily motivated by economic incentives and will do that which results in the greatest economic gain.

As an extension of the scientific management movement, the "traditional" or "operational-process" school regarded the organization from the viewpoint of top management. Management was regarded as a universal process, independent of its sphere of operation, that concentrates on the processes (or functions) involved in managing, the identification of underlying management principles. The managerial processes include planning, organizing, staffing, and directing. In general, it may be said that the process school was a tight engineering approach to the manager's job of getting work done through others. Like scientific management, the process school tends to emphasize a high degree of differentiation in the firm (e.g. "principles of management") and relies on a formalistic, mechanistic system of integration.

Human relations theory (or the behavioral school) takes as its main topic of interest the behavior of people within the organization. In contrast to the "rational-economic man" model, human relations recognizes that many factors influence the behavior of individuals in groups other than the rules and regulations specified by the formal authorities in an organization. The primary contribution of this movement has been the attempt to identify those behavioral variables which can explain variances in organization performance. A common thread in the behavioral movement has been the criticism of rigorous adherence to "principles of management" as being dysfunctional to the effective motivation of the individual, and destructive to the overall performance of the organization.[13] The movement frequently criticized the classical theory's emphasis on a high degree of differentiation in the organization. In contrast, human relations tended to emphasize organic modes of integration, with high dependence on effective interpersonal relations as a means of achieving organizational objectives.

Thus, human relations focused on the psychological and social aspects of the organization. The organizational hierarchy formed the structure of the system while the informal work relationships were the "variables" of the system which required study. Human relations theory, therefore, regarded the organization as a closed social system where primary variables were the behavioral factors within the system, but tended to ignore the environmental variables of technological and market structures.

A very interesting aspect of contingency theory is the reconciliation of this

[13]Chris Argyris, "Explorations in Interpersonal Competence," *Journal of Applied Behavioral Science*, Vol. 1, No. 1, 1965, pp. 58–84.

disagreement between classical theory and human relations theory. Lawrence and Lorsch essentially state that neither approach is entirely correct, but is partially correct, depending on the specific situation. Different technical systems require different authority relationships. Classical theory, emphasizing high differentiation and "mechanistic" integration, is most appropriate under routine, stable environmental conditions. Human relations theory, emphasizing "organic" integration, is most appropriate under unstable, uncertain environmental conditions. In effect, each theory was correct under a given set of environmental circumstances. Thus, neither theory is completely refuted, but then, neither is accepted as a universal, complete theory. Rather, contingency theory becomes an extension of the primary trends in organization theory that have come before.

Contingency theory may be briefly summarized as shown below. When environmental conditions can be described as stable, routine, and certain, then an organization employing a mechanistic type of integration is more likely to be a superior performer than an organization which emphasizes an organic type of integration. Conversely, when environmental conditions can be described as dynamic, nonroutine, and uncertain, high performance results from an organic, rather than mechanistic type of integration. Stable environments require formal organizations; dynamic environments require adaptive organizations.

Although the thrust of contingency theory is concerned with the organization as a whole, it should not be inferred that a single organizational style should be employed in all sub-sectors of the organization. Contingency theory is clearly concerned with relating the organization to specific situations; the certainty of the situation will be different in different sectors of any organization. Such factors as the level and the functional area within an organization will be important moderators that will determine a range of organizational styles in sub-sectors of the organizations.

Just as Fiedler's theory (1967) attempts to provide a link between the group situation, leadership style, and leadership effectiveness, contingency theory links the organization situation, organizational style, and organizational effectiveness.

Lawrence and Lorsch do not claim that contingency theory is an all-inclusive theory; it is only one step among many steps that ". . . point the way to a more sophisticated model that will not only reduce the confusion in organization

Environmental variables

	Stable, routine certain	Dynamic, non-routine, uncertain
Organic	P = Lo	P = Hi
Mechanistic	P = Hi	P = Lo

P = Performance

theory, but will also have considerable implications for the design and management of complex organizations."[14]

INTEGRATING CONTINGENCY THEORY AND
T-GROUP TRAINING

Why is contingency theory relevant when considering training? According to contingency theory, an adaptive or organic organizational climate is required to meet the demands of a dynamic environment. Any training, therefore, that is undertaken by such an organization, should be evaluated in relation to its potential to direct an organization toward (or away from) a specific mode of organizational style. It can be inferred from contingency theory that any organization that faces a dynamic, unstable, environment should utilize training that propels an organization toward an organic mode or integration. Conversely, an organization that faces an extremely stable environment should utilize training that is consistent with a mechanistic mode of integration.

If the implications of contingency theory are accepted, the next step is to examine the efficacy of T-group training as a means of moving an organization toward an organic mode of integration. Argyris (1965) believes that T-group training improves an individual's interpersonal competence, which he specifically measures in terms of openness, leveling, owning, risk-taking, trust, and interpersonal communication. Miles (1960) reports changes as a result of training as increase in sensitivity to others, equalitarian attitudes, skills in communication and leadership, consideration, and group and maintenance skills. Bunker (1965) reports T-group trained participants as improving in receiving communications, awareness of human behavior, sensitivity to group behavior, sensitivity to other's feelings, acceptance of other people, and tolerance of new information. In summary, most writers would agree with House[15] when he states, "Generally, the T-group experience results in more considerate employee-oriented leader behavior." It is quite apparent that the value and attitudes taught by T-group training coincide significantly with the values attributed by Lawrence and Lorsch to the organic organization. The conclusion, therefore, is that T-group training tends to influence individuals in such a way that results in behavior that is desirable in an organic, rather than mechanistic, type of organization.

This conclusion leads directly to the following hypothesis: T-group training, as a means of organizational development, tends to be more effective in organic organizations facing dynamic environments, rather than in mechanistic organizations facing stable environments.

This hypothesis may help to explain one important reason why T-group training has apparently met with varying degrees of success. For T-group training to be effective for organizational development, the organization must be suppor-

---

[14]Lawrence and Lorsch, *Studies,* 1970, p. 210.
[15]House, 1967, p. 24.

tive of an organic style of management. Certainly the hypothesis lends credence to the contention that T-group training is an effective means of moving an organization toward a higher degree of adaptability; in effect, changing from a mechanistic to an organic style of management.

The fact that most organizations must contend with an ever-increasing rate of environmental change is inescapable. Bennis (1966) has stated that: ". . . stability has vanished . . . One factor accelerating change is the growth of science, research and development activities, and intellectual technology. Another is the increase of transactions with social institutions and the importance of the latter in conducting the enterprise . . . The . . . major shock to bureaucracy has been caused by the scientific and technological revolution. It is the requirement of adaptability to the environment which leads to the predicted demise of bureaucracy and to the collapse of management as we know it now."[16]

Because of this accelerating rate of change, the need for innovative means of organizational development is expanding. The use of T-group training as a means of filling this role can be expected to continue and increase.

CONCLUSION

The influence of the trainee's back-home organization on the effectiveness of T-group training is a problem that is recognized, but has received scant attention in the literature. A relatively new development in organization theory, known as contingency theory, may provide some insight as to why T-group training has met with varying degrees of success in different organizations. Through a research design that recognizes differences in the environment, as well as differences in organizational climate, it may be possible to gain further knowledge about the applicability and effectiveness of T-group training as a means of organizational development. The research may provide the *why and wherefore* to specify why ". . . not all organizations can profit from (T-group training), nor do all organizations need similar amounts of it."[17]

---

[16]Bennis, *Changing Organizations,* New York, McGraw-Hill, 1966.
[17]Argyris, *Interpersonal Competence and Organizational Effectiveness,* Homewood, Ill., Richard D. Irwin, Inc., 1962.

Indexes

Name Index

Subject Index